PRO BASKETBALL FORECAST™
2005–06

John Hollinger

Potomac Books, Inc.

WASHINGTON, D.C.

ISBN 1-57488-962-1

(alk. paper)

Printed in the United States of America on acid-free paper that meets the American National Standards Institute Z39-48 Standard.

Potomac Books, Inc.
22841 Quicksilver Drive
Dulles, Virginia 20166

Designed by Pen & Palette Unlimited

First Edition

10 9 8 7 6 5 4 3 2 1

Contents

Acknowledgments

A small army of people brought this book to fruition, and it couldn't have happened without every one of them. Let's start with my readers, be they fans of this book, my Insider page on ESPN.com, or my column in the *New York Sun*. They constantly pepper me with questions and comments, and much of their feedback seeds the ideas that appear in some form in this book.

On the publishing side, my editors at ESPN.com—Royce Webb, Chris Ramsay, and Patrick Stiegman—as well at the *New York Sun*—Mike Woodsworth and Matt Oshinsky—have been incredibly accommodating throughout the process to allow me to get the book completed. My editor at Potomac Books, Kevin Cuddihy, did yeoman work to get this turned around as fast as possible once I completed the manuscript, as did the designer, Don Rodgers. My agent, Richard Curtis, made this whole thing possible to begin with.

In addition, several scouts and personnel people around the league have taken the time to talk with me, and all of them are greatly appreciated. The small but growing community of statistical analysts also has been a great support network, not to mention an important critical forum. They include Roland Beech, Dean Oliver, Kevin Pelton, Bob Chaikin, and Doug Steele.

The most important thanks go out to my immediate family and friends. Ken Segall and Frank Welles are incredible friends and enthusiastic supporters of my work, and they continue to challenge me every day about the sport. My parents, Walter and Anne, along with the rest of my family—Ellen, Walter, Cathy, Marie, Chris, and Jeff—have provided unwavering love and support, as have Abonim, Amani, Tina, Sun, and Ed. But the biggest thank you of all goes to my wife, Judy, not only for being an unofficial editor and general consultant on all things *Forecast* but also for retaining more basketball knowledge and interest than should be asked of any wife in a marriage.

It's all about the New Guy.

Just look at any NBA team in recent history. If they improved more than 10 games from the previous season, the New Guy got all the credit. If the team dropped 10 or more games, the New Guy took the blame.

The funny thing is, it doesn't matter what the New Guy does—all that counts is how his team performs. Even if the New Guy turns in a carbon copy of his previous season, he's going to be lauded for having a career year if the team wins. Some of them even become MVP candidates.

Yet one can't be the New Guy for very long. Every year there's a fresh crop of New Guys, so one year later the New Guy is just another guy. And even if the team repeats its success of the first season with the New Guy, or repeats its failures, he won't get the same credit or blame.

In 2004–05 the New Guy had a banner year. Two of them, Steve Nash and Shaquille O'Neal, led their teams to the best record in each conference and subsequently finished first and second in the MVP voting. Likewise, new Washington Wizard Antawn Jamison made his first All-Star team, while Chicago rookie Ben Gordon won the Sixth Man award.

Yet amidst all the clamor over the New Guys, we lost track of the other rising stars on their teams. With each of the aforementioned clubs, these players were at least as important to the teams' success as the New Guys. For instance, O'Neal and Nash each had teammates who made huge jumps in productivity, jumps that should have been the focus of our attention considering they catapulted their teams into contention. In Washington, Jamison got the attention even though Gilbert Arenas and Larry Hughes were far more productive. Over in Chicago, Gordon's exploits blinded people to the continued development of Tyson Chandler.

Those improvements became part of the lore of the New Guy. Performance leaps by Dwyane Wade and Amare Stoudemire were written off with the old saw about Shaq and Nash "making their teammates better." While it's been a popular idea for a long time, "making teammates better" is basketball's most famous old wives' tale. For a prominent example, Wade actually played better when Shaq wasn't around to "make him better," shooting 53 percent in games when the big man was sidelined.

As for Stoudemire, all the attention on Nash eclipsed the fairly obvious fact that Stoudemire was the Suns' best player and their true MVP candidate. But even when a player's improvement is as rapid as Stoudemire's and Wade's, it's never as sexy a story as the New Guy. Thus, the papers relegate these players' exploits to the inside pages.

I'll expand more on the infatuation with Nash later in the book, but first let me welcome everyone to this year's edition. I'm John Hollinger, and for those of you who are new to this book, my approach to the game differs from what you'll see in most books or magazines about the NBA. Sure, I watch the games like everybody else, but I watch the story behind the scenes too—a story that is told in numbers. While there is no slide rule attached to my belt and I do not own a pocket protector, the story of the numbers behind the game are as interesting to me as behind-the-back passes and slam dunks. As a result of my analytical (or, um, "stat-geek") approach, my work has challenged much of the conventional wisdom about the game, from popular clichés like "great players make their teammates better" to the myth of "project" centers.

In my previous three books, I've made other important discoveries as well. The Fluke Rule, for instance, states that players who make large improvements after the age of 28 almost always come back to earth the next season. Other key findings include discovering that nearly all players do worse when their minutes come in small doses versus large chunks, and learning that big centers drafted after the first few picks in the lottery are almost always busts—which means L.A. fans shouldn't start making plans for the Andrew Bynum era.

This book is part of something bigger as well. In previous editions I've lamented that basketball is miles behind baseball in its use of statistical analysis, but that's slowly changing. As more people get involved, it becomes easier for us to piggyback on each other's work. For example, Web sites like 82games.com now offer a variety of information that previously was unavailable, including a player's "plus-minus" and breakdowns of shooting and defense that used to require analysts to manually go through play-by-play sheets.

Because more people are taking an interest in basketball analysis, it's been quite an eventful year. As many of you know, I got a much bigger platform for my ideas by joining ESPN.com. In addition, several teams have made concerted efforts to use this information to their advantage. The Sonics became the first team to take the plunge with a full-time analyst, hiring a colleague named Dean Oliver this past season.

Other clubs are incorporating pieces in their draft and free-agent evaluations, and the approach is beginning to move up the food chain to general managers and team presidents.

With this year's edition, I hope to lure more converts out of the basketball dark ages. I have a few new tools in the shed to aid the effort, including a "Brick Index" to identify players who need to stop shooting. I've also considerably expanded the section on European players, revised the section on defense to take advantage of improved data, and refined the Similarity Scores to deliver more accurate statistical projec-tions for the 2005–06 season. And as per usual, this book is loaded with comments on every player and analysis of every team, including a series of statistical markers for each player along with his rank at his position.

In the big picture, the numbers just are there to help us understand what we're seeing—or to explain what we *think* we're seeing. Because often times, when we think the New Guy is making all the difference, the reality is that the big change has come from the players who were there the whole time.

The Methods

Much like basketball teams tend to run a few favorite plays over and over again, my analysis repeatedly draws on a few common tools. Rather than quickly re-explaining them every time they're introduced in the text, this section breaks down my methods in much greater detail and also provides the NBA's best and worst in each of the stats that I've created.

Possessions

Possessions are the base currency of NBA statistics. Nearly every method in this book hinges on the concept of possessions. Only one team can have the ball at any time and when their possession is complete, the other team gets it. In other words, it's impossible to have substantially more possessions than the opponent. Thus, the key to winning basketball

games is to be more effective with those possessions. While that may be master-of-the-obvious stuff, it amazes me how often analysts lose sight of this fact.

On a team level, every possession has three eventual outcomes: a made shot, a turnover, or a rebound by the other team. Thus, we can estimate a team's possessions by adding field goal attempts and turnovers, subtracting offensive rebounds, and adding their number of trips to the line. The last part is the trickiest—if every foul resulted in two free throws, then we could just multiply it by 0.5. But that isn't the case. Because of technical fouls, three-point plays and the like, we need to use a lower number. My research has shown 0.44 is the best estimate, so that's what we'll use:

$$\text{Team Possessions} = \text{Field Goal Attempts} - \text{Offensive Rebounds} + \text{Turnovers} + (\text{Free Throw Attempts} \times 0.44)$$

Pace Factor

Pace Factor is simply a measure of how many possessions a team uses each game. This is important information because it allows us to see the context in which a player operates. For example, scoring five baskets is an impressive accomplishment if your team had only six possessions. If it had 60 possessions, on the other hand, it's not such a big deal. Since some teams play markedly "faster" than others, knowing the Pace Factor for each club is critical for properly evaluating the players.

$$\text{Pace Factor} = \frac{(\text{Team Possessions} + \text{Opponents' Possessions}) \times 48}{\text{Team Minutes} \times 2}$$

Table 1. Top and Bottom Five Teams in Pace Factor 2004–05

Top Five		Bottom Five	
Team	Pace Factor	Team	Pace Factor
Phoenix	98.3	Indiana	89.4
Philadelphia	97.2	Detroit	89.5
Orlando	97.1	New Orleans	90.0
Denver	95.8	Memphis	90.6
Washington	95.8	Utah	90.8

As shown in table 1, Phoenix rocketed to the top of the league charts in Pace Factor, while another rebuilt team, Orlando, came in second. At the other end of the spectrum, Detroit and Indiana lived up to their grind-it-out reputations, playing much slower than the rest of the league.

One way to use Pace Factor is to see where the league is heading over time, and there's some good news to report. Thanks to rules changes that encouraged more open-court play, the league ended a decade of decline in Pace Factor to post the fastest season since 2000–01. Table 2 shows how the pace of the league has changed over the past fifteen years.

Table 2. Pace Factor: League Average by Season

Season	Pace Factor	Season	Pace Factor
1990–91	101.5	1998–99	91.6
1991–92	100.3	1999–00	95.7
1992–93	100.2	2000–01	93.9
1993–94	97.9	2001–02	92.7
1994–95	96.3	2002–03	93.0
1995–96	94.4	2003–04	92.0
1996–97	92.8	2004–05	93.2
1997–98	93.9		

Offensive Efficiency

The NBA ranks teams offensively by how many points per game they score, but that's an incredibly crude measure. Because teams play at different paces, a fast-paced team can have a mediocre offense and still be near the top in scoring average. A better method is to look at how many points a team scores per possession. I call the measure Offensive Efficiency and set it to a team's average per 100 possessions, since that's close to the number teams get in a typical game.

$$\text{Offensive Efficiency} = \frac{\text{Points Scored} \times 100}{\text{Possessions}}$$

Table 3. Top and Bottom Five Teams in Offensive Efficiency, 2004–05

Top Five		Bottom Five	
Team	**Off. Efficiency**	**Team**	**Off. Efficiency**
Phoenix	111.9	New Orleans	96.0
Miami	108.3	Atlanta	97.9
Seattle	108.1	Charlottte	98.0
Sacramento	107.5	New Jersey	98.3
Dallas	107.5	Chicago	98.5

As table 3 shows, Phoenix was easily the best offense in 2004–05, and as I'll discuss in the Suns chapter, it was among the best in history. Additionally, note the huge East-West imbalance in Offensive Efficiency. Seven of the top eight offenses were in the West, while four of the bottom five were in the East. This difference has persisted for years now, although with so much young talent accumulating on Eastern rosters, it could begin reversing soon.

Just as we did with Pace Factor, table 4 looks at the last decade-and-a-half and see whether offense or defense is getting the upper hand. I'm pleased to announce that offense made a strong recovery, thanks mainly to tightened rules against hand-checking on the perimeter. The league average of 103.1 was the best mark in nearly a decade and a massive improvement from the miserable 100.8 of 2003–04.

Table 4. Offensive Efficiency: League Average by Season

Season	Off. Efficiency	Season	Off. Efficiency
1990–91	104.7	1998–99	100.0
1991–92	105.0	1999–00	101.9
1992–93	105.1	2000–01	100.9
1993–94	103.7	2001–02	102.3
1994–95	105.3	2002–03	101.4
1995–96	105.4	2003–04	100.8
1996–97	104.4	2004–05	103.1
1997–98	100.9		

Defensive Efficiency

Defensive Efficiency is the opposite of Offensive Efficiency. Just as teams' offenses should be measured by what they do on a per-possessions basis, so should the defense. As with Offensive Efficiency, I measure it by points allowed per 100 possessions to provide a more digestible barometer.

$$\text{Defensive Efficiency} = \frac{\text{Points Allowed} \times 100}{\text{Opponent Possessions}}$$

Table 5. Top and Bottom Five Teams in Defensive Efficiency, 2004–05

Top Five		Bottom Five	
Team	**Def. Efficiency**	**Team**	**Def. Efficiency**
San Antonio	95.8	Atlanta	108.4
Chicago	97.5	L.A. Lakers	108.0
Detroit	97.9	Utah	107.0
Houston	98.9	Milwaukee	106.7
Memphis	99.9	New York	106.5

Table 5 shows that San Antonio was the NBA's best defensive team for the fourth time in the past five years. It might surprise some to see that Chicago outranked Detroit, but the Pistons' defensive numbers looked better than they really were because of Detroit's anemic pace. On the bottom list, the Hawks fought off the Lakers for the title of the league's worst defensive team.

Expected Wins

Expected Wins estimates the number of games a team will win by how many points it scores and allows. This is important because Expected Wins are a better indicator of future success than real wins. Teams that win more games than their Expected Wins indicate have normally been unusually lucky in close games, while teams that fall short of their Expected Wins have had the opposite happen. Some may think this is the result of "clutch ability" by certain teams and players, but no team has consistently outperformed in this area over a period of years—even championship teams like the recent Bulls, Lakers, and Pistons clubs.

The Expected Wins formula has changed a bit. In the past I suggested taking the team's average victory margin, multiplying by 2.7, and adding 41. This is an easy back-of-the-envelope method but is less accurate than the "Pythagorean 16.5" formula, which involves raising points scored and points allowed to the 16.5 power. I use 82 in the formula below because every NBA team plays 82 games. If you're trying to figure this out during the season rather than at the end, just use the team's actual number of games.

$$\text{Expected Wins} = 82 \times \frac{\text{Points}^{16.5}}{\text{Points}^{16.5} + \text{Points Allowed}^{16.5}}$$

For a second straight season, San Antonio fell a mile short in Expected Wins. Two years ago they won eight games fewer than their record predicted, while they fell seven games short this past season. There is no logical explanation for this (perhaps Mark Cuban bought himself a Tim Duncan voodoo doll?), but looking at Expected Wins makes San Antonio's romp through the postseason much less surprising—they were simply the best team. On the other side of the coin, the most fortunate team was New Jersey. Oddly enough, the Nets were the *least* fortunate team just two years earlier.

Table 6 shows the best and worst from the season. To see an example of how big the swings can be at the extremes, note that Toronto's average victory margin was virtually identical to New Jersey's but the Raptors finished nine games behind in the standings.

Table 6. Wins vs. Expected Wins, 2004–05

Team	Wins	Exp. Wins	Difference
Unlucky			
San Antonio	59	66	−7
Charlotte	18	22	−4
Houston	51	55	−4
Memphis	47	51	−4
Toronto	33	36	−3
Lucky			
New Jersey	42	36	+6
Philadelphia	43	38	+5
Washington	45	40	+5
L.A. Lakers	36	33	+3
Seattle	50	47	+3

40-Minute Averages

While I can use other tools to measure players more accurately, nothing is as quick and easy as 40-minute averages. Just take the player's total in any category (points, rebounds, assists, etc.), divide by minutes played, and multiply by 40. We have better tools for rebounds and assists that I'll describe below, but 40-minute scoring average is an incredibly handy tool. In table 7, Allen Iverson squeaked past Amare Stoudemire for the best scoring rate, while Washington's Michael Ruffin continues to astound observers with his inability to find the net.

Table 7. Top and Bottom Five Players in 40-Minute Scoring Average, 2004–05 (minimum 500 minutes)

Top Five		Bottom Five	
Player/Team	Avg.	Player/Team	Avg.
Allen Iverson, Phi	29.0	Michael Ruffin, Was	3.5
Amare Stoudemire, Phx	28.8	Aaron McKie, Phi	5.4
Jermaine O'Neal, Ind	27.9	Mark Madsen, Min	5.8
Kobe Bryant, LAL	27.1	Greg Ostertag, Sac	6.3
Dirk Nowitzki, Dal	26.9	Eric Snow, Cle	7.0

True Shooting Percentage

True Shooting Percentage (TS%) calculates what a player's shooting percentage would be if we accounted for free throws and three-pointers. Readers of previous editions take note: True Shooting Percentage replaces Points per Shot Attempt. The only difference between this and its predecessor is that True Shooting Percentage is 50 times greater. A player who used to have "1.00 points per shot attempt" now has a "50.0 True Shooting Percentage." I made the switch because TS% is easier for readers to comprehend since shooting percentage is already a common statistic.

However, the standards for TS% are slightly different. The league average in TS% in 2004–05 was 52.9, much higher than the league field-goal percentage average of 44.7. Thus,

our barometer for what is an acceptable TS% needs to be about eight points higher than it is for field-goal percentage.

$$\text{True Shooting Percentage} = \frac{\text{Total Points} \times 50}{\text{Field goal attempts} + (\text{Free throw attempts} \times 0.44)}$$

In table 8, Fred Hoiberg of Minnesota was headed toward a record year in TS% before he cooled off at the end of the season, giving way to Fortson. Most of the top players in PSA are either deadly shooters (Miller, Jones, Hoiberg) or big men who only shoot dunks and lay-ups (Fortson, Rebraca). For the first time in eons, nobody named "Barry" made the top 10.

Most of the guys in the bottom 10 are barely clinging to a spot in the league, although Hunter and Ruffin have secured jobs as defensive specialists.

Table 8. Top and Bottom 10 Players in True Shooting Percentage, 2004–05 (minimum 500 minutes)

Top 10		Bottom 10	
Player/Team	TS%	Player/Team	TS%
Danny Fortson, Sea	68.2	Theron Smith, Char	36.7
Fred Hoiberg, Min	66.4	George Lynch, NO	41.2
Greg Buckner, Den	63.8	Adrian Griffin, Chi	41.9
Damon Jones, Mia	62.5	Kris Humphries, Utah	41.9
Zeljko Rebraca, LAC	62.5	Junior Harrington, NO	42.1
Christian Laettner, Mia	61.9	Darrell Armstrong, NO-Dal	43.0
Amare Stoudemire, Phx	61.7	Greg Ostertag, Sac	43.2
Mike Miller, Mem	61.4	Michael Ruffin, Was	43.2
Yao Ming, Hou	61.4	Ronald Murray, Sea	43.3
Manu Ginobili, SA	60.9	Lindsey Hunter, Det	43.5

Pure Point Rating

Pure Point Rating is something I created to replace the idiotic assist-turnover ratio that everyone insists on using despite its dubious reliability. For example, Brad Miller had a better assist-turnover ratio than Mike Bibby last year, but I don't think Rick Adelman ever entertained the idea of moving Miller to the point.

Pure Point Rating eliminates impostors like Miller by making it an additive rating rather than a ratio. The top-ranked players in this category are all point guards (thus the name), while big men pile up at the bottom. Based on table 9, Charlotte's Brevin Knight was slightly more potent than Phoenix's Steve Nash in this department in 2004–05.

$$\text{Pure Point Rating} = \frac{[(\text{Assists} \times \frac{2}{3}) - \text{Turnovers}] \times 100}{\text{Minutes}}$$

Table 9. Top and Bottom 10 Players in Pure Point Rating, 2004–05 (minimum 500 minutes)

Top 10		Bottom 10	
Player/Team	Pure Pt. Rating	Player/Team	Pure Pt. Rating
Brevin Knight, Char	12.1	Danny Fortson, Sea	−9.0
Steve Nash, Phx	12.0	Eddy Curry, Chi	−8.5
Jason Kidd, NJ	7.4	Alonzo Mourning, NJ-Mia	−7.2
Jason Hart, Char	7.1	Yao Ming, Hou	−7.1
Rick Brunson, LAC	7.1	David Harrison, Ind	−6.5
Anthony Goldwire, Det-Mil	6.7	Jamaal Magloire, NO	−6.5
Speedy Claxton, GS-NO	6.4	Jerome James, Sea	−6.3
Jason Williams, Mem	6.4	Rafael Araujo, Tor	−6.3
Chris Duhon, Chi	6.2	Jackson Vroman, Phx-NO	−6.2
Baron Davis, NO-GS	6.2	Mike Sweetney, NY	−5.9

Assist Ratio

Pure Point Ratio works very well for point guards. For other players, however, I prefer to use something I call Assist Ratio. It provides a more valid evaluation of passing skills for players who aren't their team's primary ballhandler. On the other hand, Assist Ratio tends to favor players who never shoot the ball, which is why Pure Point is better for rating point guards.

$$\text{Assist Ratio} = \frac{\text{Assists} \times 100}{\text{FG Att.} + (\text{FT Att.} \times 0.44) + \text{Assists} + \text{Turnovers}}$$

That being said, table 10 shows the NBA's best and worst in Assist Ratio for last season.

Table 10. Top and Bottom 10 Players in Assist Ratio, 2004–05 (minimum 500 minutes)

Top 10		Bottom 10	
Player/Team	Assist Ratio	Player/Team	Assist Ratio
Brevin Knight, Char	41.9	Danny Fortson, Sea	1.5
Steve Nash, Phx	41.2	Dikembe Mutombo, Hou	1.6
Rick Brunson, LAC	40.2	Steven Hunter, Phx	2.4
Raul Lopez, Min	38.5	Jerome James, Sea	2.7
Anthony Carter, Min	38.1	Dan Gadzuric, Mil	3.2
Chris Duhon, Chi	34.8	Shawn Bradley, Dal	3.2
Marko Jaric, LAC	33.9	David Harrison, Ind	3.3
Luke Ridnour, Sea	33.3	Alan Henderson, Dal	3.3
Milt Palacio, Tor	33.1	Nazr Mohammed, NY-SA	3.4
Jason Kidd, NJ	33.0	Eddy Curry, Chi	3.5

The top performance by a non-point guard was Milwaukee's Toni Kukoc at 27.7, which easily led the field at power forward. Other position leaders were shooting guard Kirk Hinrich (26.2), small forward LeBron James (20.6) and center Brad Miller (20.0). Walton ranked first at his position for a second straight season.

Turnover Ratio

Much as Assist Ratio measures the percentage of a player's possessions he converts into assists, Turnover Ratio measures the percentage that end up in turnovers. The best players almost always lead the league in turnovers because they use so many possessions, so this measure gives a truer picture of which players lose the ball too much.

Turnover Ratio is the one metric where low numbers are better than high ones. As table 11 shows, the top 10 is dominated by stand-still jump shooters who didn't need to risk a turnover on drives to the basket, while the other end consists mostly of big men who rarely shot, but got tagged with turnovers for setting illegal screens.

$$\text{Turnover Ratio} = \frac{\text{Turnovers} \times 100}{\text{FG Att.} + (\text{FT Att.} \times 0.44) + \text{Assists} + \text{Turnovers}}$$

Table 11. Top and Bottom 10 Players in Turnover Ratio, 2004–05 (minimum 500 minutes)

Top 10		Bottom 10	
Player/Team	Turnover Ratio	Player/Team	Turnover Ratio
Fred Hoiberg, Min	4.6	Danny Fortson, Sea	20.8
Ryan Bowen, Hou	4.8	Rafael Araujo, Tor	19.5
Michael Finley, Dal	5.0	Reggie Evans, Sea	19.3
Donyell Marshall, Tor	5.6	Mark Madsen, Min	19.1
Jason Kapono, Char	5.6	Jackson Vroman, Phx-NO	19.0
Brian Cook, LAL	5.8	Michael Ruffin, Was	18.6
Rodney Buford, NJ	5.8	Jerome James, Sea	18.4
Wesley Person, Mia-Den	5.9	David Harrison, Ind	18.3
Anthony Goldwire, Det-Mil	6.2	Curtis Borchardt, Utah	17.1
Antonio Daniels, Sea	6.8	Joel Przybilla, Por	16.9

Brick Index

Brick Index is a fun measure I developed this year to answer the question, "Which player is doing the most to damage his team's offense by shooting too much?" Brick Index figures the difference between the player's True Shooting Percentage and the league average in TS%, and multiplies that by the number of shots a player attempts per 40 minutes. The net result is how many points per 40 minutes a player's shooting costs (or benefits) his team. For further accuracy, I divide the result by Team Pace Factor and multiply by League Pace Factor, which adjusts for pace differences between teams.

$$\text{Brick Index} = \frac{\text{League TS\%} - \text{Player TS\%}}{50} \times 40 \times \frac{\text{League Pace Factor}}{\text{Team Pace Factor}} \times \frac{\text{FGA} + (\text{FTA} \times 0.44)}{\text{Minutes}}$$

Table 12. Top 10 Players in Brick Index, 2004–05 (minimum 500 minutes)

Player/Team	Brick	Player/Team	Brick
Theron Smith, Char	3.59	Tierre Brown, LAL	2.64
Ronald Murray, Sea	3.57	Chris Webber, Sac-Phi	2.57
Kris Humphries, Utah	3.44	Keith McLeod, Utah	2.50
Junior Harrington, NO	3.15	Willie Green, Phi	2.49
Rodney Buford, NJ	2.91	Kirk Snyder, Utah	2.45

Most of the names in table 12 are assorted ne'er-do-wells who came off the bench and immediately started firing, but one name jumps off the page. Chris Webber took 19 field-goal attempts per game despite a horrendous 47.2 TS%, which explains why Sacramento's offense didn't suffer much when he was traded at midseason.

Rebound Rate

Rebound Rate measures the percentage of available rebounds that a player collects while he's on the court. The premise is simple: A player can only get a rebound if somebody misses a shot. Thus, measuring the percentage of those misses a player retrieves is a very precise indicator of rebounding skill.

$$\text{Rebound Rate} = \frac{\text{Rebounds} \times \text{Team Minutes}}{\text{Player Minutes} \times (\text{Team Rebounds} + \text{Opponent Rebounds})}$$

Table 13 shows the NBA's best and worst in Rebound Rate for last season.

Table 13. Top and Bottom 10 Players in Rebound Rate, 2004–05 (minimum 500 minutes)

Top 10		Bottom 10	
Player/Team	Turnover Ratio	Player/Team	Turnover Ratio
Reggie Evans, Sea	23.9	Allan Houston, NY	2.5
Dan Gadzuric, Mil	22.1	Jeff McInnis, Cle	3.3
Kevin Garnett, Min	20.9	Jason Williams, Mem	3.5
Dikembe Mutombo, Hou	20.6	Troy Hudson, Min	3.6
Danny Fortson, Sea	20.3	Howard Eisley, Utah	3.9
Jeff Foster, Ind	20.1	Earl Boykins, Den	3.9
Tyson Chandler, Chi	19.9	Carlos Arroyo, Utah-Det	4.0
Marcus Camby, Den	19.4	Chucky Atkins, LAL	4.1
Tim Duncan, SA	19.4	Sebastian Telfair, Por	4.2
Loren Woods, Tor	18.9	Travis Best, NJ	4.2

Reggie Evans wrested the Rebound Rate title from his Sonics teammates Danny Fortson, who had won it two of the past three seasons. (Incidentally, Fortson is in the top or bottom 10 in virtually every category in this section. He's either great or terrible at everything.) Allan Houston of New York rated the worst because he limped through 532 minutes on one leg. Among healthy players, Jeff McInnis of Cleveland had the worst rate. Despite being nearly a foot shorter, even 5'5" Earl Boykins outrebounded McInnis.

Usage Rate

Usage Rate measures how many possessions a player uses per 40 minutes, which is why it's also been known as "Ball Hog Index." Among other things, Usage Rate allows us to identify who is shooting the ball too much and who needs to get better at creating his own shot.

$$\text{Usage Rate} = \frac{[\text{FG Att.} + (\text{FT Att.} \times 0.44) + (\text{Assists} \times 0.33) + \text{Turnovers}] \times 40 \times \text{League Pace}}{\text{Minutes} \times \text{Team Pace}}$$

Table 14. Top and Bottom 10 Players in Usage Rate, 2004–05 (minimum 500 minutes)

Top 10		Bottom 10	
Player/Team	Usage Rate	Player/Team	Usage Rate
Allen Iverson, Phil	34.7	Michael Ruffin, Was	6.4
Jermaine O'Neal, Ind	31.4	Mark Madsen, Min	7.4
LeBron James, Cle	31.3	Theo Ratliff, Por	8.3
Kobe Bryant, LAL	31.2	Aaron McKie, Phi	9.0
Baron Davis, NO-GS	31.2	Tony Battie, Orl	9.4
Tracy McGrady, Hou	31.2	Ryan Bowen, Hou	9.5
Dwyane Wade, Mia	30.9	Alan Henderson, Dal	9.5
Vince Carter, Tor-NJ	30.7	Adonal Foyle, GS	9.6
Sam Cassell, Min	29.3	John Thomas, Min	10.1
Steve Francis, Orl	29.0	Greg Ostertag, Sac	10.2

The top of the list in table 14 contains the usual assortment of big-name stars, although guards almost always dominate. Allen Iverson has led the league all four years I've done this book, and nobody has come close. Jermaine O'Neal ranked second, and was the only big man to crack the top ten. As for the bottom, it contains the usual assortment of defensive specialists and klutzes, nearly all of whom are centers.

Player Efficiency Rating (PER)

Usage Rate, Rebound Rate, Assist Ratio, Turnover Ratio, Pure Point Ratio and True Shooting Percentage are all pieces of the puzzle. The Player Efficiency Rating, or PER, pulls them all together to generate a single rating for a player. The PER sums up all of a player's positive accomplishments, subtracts the negative accomplishments, and returns a per-minute rating of a player's performance.

Bear in mind that this rating is not the final, once-and-for-all answer for a player's accomplishments during the season. In fact, I think there is one specific area that is still mostly subjective, which I will talk about toward the end of this segment.

What the PER does, however, is summarize a player's *statistical* accomplishments in a single number, which allows us to do a couple of things. First, it unifies the disparate data that we try to track in our heads (e.g., Damon Jones: great three-point shooter, doesn't turn it over, never gets a rebound, etc.) so that we can move on to evaluating what might be missing from the stats.

While I shortened the explanation of the other methods, I've kept the walk-through of the calculations that go into the PER, because it's used so pervasively throughout this book. As always, I must include the usual warning that this is not beach reading. Those who aren't interested in the derivation should feel free to skip ahead. Really, I won't be offended.

I begin by determining a value for each of the statistics on a player's line: field goals, free throws, missed field goals, missed free throws, three-pointers, offensive rebounds, defensive rebounds, assists, steals, turnovers, blocked shots and personal fouls. Let's look at each one.

I will start with **Assists** since this is, in my opinion, the most difficult category. Every other statistic is a record of something that happened, but an assist, at its root level, is an *opinion*. The value of one made basket versus another is easy to quantify: They are both worth two points. The value of one assist versus another, on the other hand, is very hard. A dazzling pass leading to a wide-open lay-up is clearly worth more than a dump-off to a guy who launches a contested 20-footer and drains it—but how much more? What is the best way to deal with these differences?

I have developed a method that I think treats assists fairly given the conundrum that assists present. I count all assists equally in this formula. Every assist is worth one-third of a basket, or 0.67 points. My logic is that a scoring play consists of three actions: the pass, the shot, and the act of getting open. The scorer does two of them so he gets two-thirds of the credit.

The fact this all holds together very well in the final analysis (point guards are not under-represented among the top-rated players, for instance) galvanizes my opinion. In fact, I would argue the actual value is even less, but I keep it at 0.67, because the NBA does not track assists for feeding a player who gets fouled, an oversight in the scoring system.

But are all assists really equal? Isn't a dazzler from Steve Nash worth more than a dump-out pass from Etan Thomas? While there is some merit to that argument, there are still plenty of reasons to rate all assists equally. For instance, a brilliant pass by Nash has a far greater likelihood of becoming an assist than a line-drive pass thrown at the toes of a contested shooter from Thomas. Thomas probably has to throw fifteen passes like that to get an assist; Nash has to throw one. While the two seem unequal once the team makes a basket, that is after the fact. Nash's pass is far more likely to become an assist in the first place.

Therefore, I use 0.67 as the value for every assist. Summing it up, this part of the formula is:

Assist value = Assists × 0.67

Field goals are worth two points; that's simple enough. However, 100 percent of the credit does not always go to the shooter. 59.2 percent of baskets in the NBA last year were assisted, so we have to adjust for this and give some of the credit to the passer. As I stated above, one-third of the value is given to the player who delivered the assist so two-thirds go to the shooter—if the basket is assisted. I currently use a team's percentage of assisted baskets to calculate this, but I hope to have data for individuals at some point.

Next, we have to slightly adjust the formula on the shooter's side. Because scorers award assists for made field goals but not for trips to the free throw line, we have to correct for it so that we don't overrate guys who take a lot of foul shots. That means we need to subtract some of the points awarded on assists from players' free throws rather than made field goals.

As I said above, 59.2 percent of made baskets were assisted last season. I assumed half that number of free throws "would have" been assisted and gave credit to foul shooters accordingly. If we credit a phantom assist for 29.6 percent of made free throws, we have to take it out of the made field goals so everything adds up at the end.

Last year there were 1.82 made field goals for every made free throw, and we are assuming twice as many were assisted as made free throws. If we hand out .296 phantom assists for each made free throw, it means we have to take back (.296/3.64) or about 0.081 assists for each made field goal. As a result, we use 0.586 as our assist factor instead of 0.667. (Note that last year this number was 0.588. This is the one item in the formula that changes slightly from year to year, based on changes in the number of field goals per free throw.)

The field goal value formula is:

$$\text{Field goal value} = \text{Field goals made} \times \left[2 - \left(\frac{\text{team assists}}{\text{team field goals}} \times 0.586 \right) \right]$$

In effect, this produces a value of about 1.65 points for each made field goal.

Three-point field goals are easy. I add one point for every three-pointer since the *extra* point on the basket is all the work of the shooter.

Free throws are worth one point. Remember, however, we need to adjust for the phantom assist on made foul shots so we don't distort the ratings in favor of frequent foul shooters. One point goes to the shooter if it was an unassisted free throw. However, we are assuming that half the free throws have a chance for an assist. Of that half, we use the team's percentage of assisted baskets to deduce the percentage that were assisted. The shooter gets one point if it's unassisted and two-thirds of a point if it isn't.

Thus, this part of the formula is:

$$\text{Free throw value} = \text{free throws made} \times 0.5 \\ \times \left[1 + \left(1 - \frac{\text{team assists}}{\text{team FG}} \right) + \left(\frac{\text{team assists} \times 0.67}{\text{team FG}} \right) \right]$$

This produces a value of about 0.9 points for each made free throw.

Turnovers are worth the value of a possession. Last season NBA teams scored an average of 1.04 points every time

they had the ball so each turnover subtracts this amount from a team's expected total. The turnover value formula is:

$$\text{Turnover value} = -(\text{league value of possession} \times \text{turnovers})$$

This produced a value of −1.04 points for each turnover last season.

Missed field goals are similar to turnovers except there is a chance the offensive team will rebound the ball. Therefore, in addition to multiplying by the value of a possession, we also should multiply missed field goals by the league's defensive rebound percentage (DRB% in the equations that follow). Last year, the defensive team grabbed the ball 71 percent of the time on missed shots so the value of a missed field goal is about negative 0.72 points. The formula is:

$$\text{Missed FG value} = -(\text{Missed field goals} \times \text{league value of possession} \\ \times \text{league DRB\%})$$

Missed free throws are like missed field goals with a few additional complexities. Since each free throw uses only 0.44 possessions, we have to scale the impact of the miss by this amount. Also, only about 56 percent of the free throws can be rebounded; the others are first shot attempts, technical fouls, and the like. Hence, the value of a missed free throw is:

$$\text{Missed FT value} = -\{ \text{Missed FT} \times \text{value of poss.} \times 0.44 \\ \times [0.44 + (0.56 \times \text{league DRB\%})] \}$$

This produces a value of −0.38 for each missed free throw.

Offensive rebounds are the polar opposite of a missed field goal. An offensive rebound completely undoes the damage done by a missed shot. The value then should be exactly opposite. Take away the minus sign from the missed field goal formula and we are done. The formula for offensive rebounds is:

$$\text{Offensive Rebound value} = \text{Offensive rebounds} \times \text{league value of poss.} \\ \times \text{league DRB\%}$$

This produces a value of approximately 0.72 points for every offensive rebound.

Defensive rebounds, on the other hand, complete a defensive stop. A missed shot plus a defensive rebound should add up to the value of one possession. Thus, the value of a defensive rebound should equal the value of a possession minus the value of a missed field goal. Given the formula for missed shots above, the formula for defensive rebounds should then read:

$$\text{Defensive Rebound value} = \text{Defensive rebounds} \times \text{league value of poss.} \\ \times (1 - \text{league DRB\%})$$

This produces a value of nearly 0.3 points for every defensive rebound.

It will no doubt seem odd to some people that offensive rebounds end up being so much more valuable than defensive rebounds. What are defensive rebounds, after all, but the act of *preventing* an offensive rebound?

If you think about it though, offensive rebounds really are more valuable. A player grabbing an offensive board almost always has to rely on a great individual effort, because his teammates are likely to be nowhere in sight. Defensive rebounds do not work that way—if the player had not grabbed the board, there is still a good chance that one of his teammates would have anyway.

Put another way, there are two ways to stop a team on defense: forcing a turnover or forcing a missed shot and grabbing the rebound. If the defense doesn't force a turnover, then they must force a missed shot. However, given that 71.3 percent of the balls will land in the defense's lap once they force the miss, it is creating the miss and not grabbing the board that is the major accomplishment on defense. Fans almost take for granted that a team will grab the board; even as people watch a game they think, "Let's force a miss here," and not, "Let's get this defensive rebound."

For that reason, offensive rebounders have more value in the NBA game. If defensive rebounds were the scarcer commodity, the conclusion would be just the opposite.

That brings us to the defensive categories. **Steals** are easy; we know they produce a turnover so their value is the opposite of a turnover:

$$\text{Steal value} = (\text{steals} \times \text{value of possession})$$

Blocked shots are more complicated. A blocked shot essentially changes a possession into a missed field goal attempt. Therefore, the value of a block should be the same as that of a missed field goal; the team will gain possession if they get the rebound. Otherwise, the opponent will start over. The blocked shot value formula is:

$$\text{Blocked shot value} = (\text{blocks} \times \text{value of possession} \times \text{league DRB\%})$$

Last but not least, there are **personal fouls.** On average, each personal foul resulted in 1.13 opponent free throws last season which, given our value of 0.44 possessions per free throw attempt, resulted in 0.5 possessions used. From those 0.5 possessions, the opposing team scored close to 0.85

points (the league average is 75 percent from the line, times 1.13 free throws).

As a result, the value of a personal foul is the difference between this number and the value of what a team could normally expect from 0.50 possessions. The resulting formula is:

$$\begin{aligned}\text{Personal foul value} = -\{\text{fouls} \times [\text{lg. FT makes per foul}\\ - (\text{lg. FT attempts per foul} \times 0.44\\ \times \text{lg. value of poss.})]\}\end{aligned}$$

The resultant value for a personal foul is approximately −0.35 points.

The PER: Final Adjustments

We're almost there. We just need to make three more adjustments and then we can calculate the final PER. First, we must adjust for minutes. The PER is a per-minute ranking so after adding all the good and subtracting all the bad detailed over the last few pages, we need to divide the total by the number of minutes played. This lets us compare, say, Christian Laettner to Udonis Haslem, even though there is a wide disparity in the minutes they played.

Next, we multiply each player's rating by a multiplier based on his team's Pace Factor. The multiplier is (League Pace/Team's Pace Factor). It will be less than 1.00 for a player on a fast-paced team and greater than 1.00 for those on a slow-paced club. The reason is that there are fewer opportunities to pile up stats on a slower-paced team. That means twenty points in an Indiana Pacers game is worth a lot more than twenty points in a Phoenix Suns game, because there are fewer possessions in the Pacers game. If we do not adjust for this in the PER, it would make all of Indiana's players look much worse than they really are, and all of Phoenix's players much better.

Finally, we **set the ratings to a league average of 15.00.** This does two things. First, it makes comparisons between eras much easier. Regardless of whether offense or defense is dominant at the time, the league average is steady. Second, it provides a known scale we can go by. Fifteen points per game is about what we expect of a pretty decent player if he gets thirty-five minutes or so a night. By using a system that's already hard-wired into the heads of basketball fans, it is easier to show how a player is producing.

The final formula for PER looks like this (I have shortened "league value of possession" to "VOP" for the sake of space):

Player Efficiency Rating (PER) = (**League Pace** / **Team Pace**) × (**15.00** / **League average**) × (**1** / **Minutes played**)

$$\times \big[\text{3-pt. FG}$$
$$+ (\text{Assists} \times 0.67)$$
$$+ \big(\text{FG made} \times \{2 - [(\text{team assists} / \text{team FG}) \times 0.586]\}\big)$$
$$+ \big(\text{FT made} \times 0.5 \times \{1 + [1 - (\text{team assists} / \text{team FG})] + [(\text{team assists} / \text{team FG}) \times 0.67]\}\big)$$
$$- (\text{VOP} \times \text{turnovers})$$
$$- (\text{Missed FG} \times \text{VOP} \times \text{league DRB\%})$$
$$- \{\text{Missed FT} \times \text{VOP} \times 0.44 \times [0.44 + (0.56 \times \text{league DRB\%})]\}$$
$$+ [\text{Def. rebounds} \times \text{VOP} \times (1 - \text{league DRB\%})]$$
$$+ (\text{Off. rebounds} \times \text{VOP} \times \text{league DRB\%})$$
$$+ (\text{steals} \times \text{VOP})$$
$$+ (\text{blocks} \times \text{VOP} \times \text{league DRB\%})$$
$$- \{\text{fouls} \times [\text{lg. FT makes per foul} - (\text{lg. FT attempts per foul} \times 0.44 \times \text{VOP})]\} \big]$$

Now let's delve into how PER works.

The PER: Strengths And Limitations

Readers may notice one thing missing from the PER: position defense. That's because there is nothing in the current statistical line for a player that gives a real strong indication of his on-ball defense. Sure, there are steals and blocks, but most of the time the stealee or blockee is <u>not</u> the man the player is guarding. Even those categories have their flaws: Charges, for instance, are just as valuable as steals but do not appear in a player's stat line.

I have a few ways of dealing with on-ball defense, and I think it's important enough that I have devoted a separate chapter to it. In general, the discussion of defense gets short shrift, because the numbers aren't in front of us and it's a lot less exciting than offense. Therefore, I will be very explicit about this: The PER rates everything *except* position defense. For most players on most teams, the result is still a very accurate representation of their contribution.

However, it underrates a few specialists who do not get a lot of blocks and steals but are nonetheless great defensive players (Bruce Bowen and Rasheed Wallace are the most prominent examples). On the other hand, it overrates a few guys whose *sole* defensive contribution is blocks and steals (Shawn Bradley and, to a lesser extent, Larry Hughes), or who pile up steals despite barely playing any defense at all (Jason Williams).

That doesn't mean the PER can't provide a lot of information. It just means, like any other formula, that we have to combine it with common sense to get the complete picture.

Having said that, table 15 shows the top and bottom 10 in the NBA in PER last season.

Table 15. Top and Bottom 10 Players in PER, 2004–05
(minimum 500 minutes)

Top 10		Bottom 10	
Player/Team	**PER**	**Player/Team**	**PER**
Kevin Garnett, Min	28.35	Theron Smith, Char	5.10
Tim Duncan, SA	27.13	Mark Madsen, Min	6.76
Shaquille O'Neal, Mia	26.95	Rafael Araujo, Tor	6.87
Amare Stoudemire, Phx	26.69	Junior Harrington, NO	7.63
Dirk Nowitzki, Dal	26.18	Ryan Bowen, Hou	7.65
LeBron James, Cle	25.75	Calbert Cheaney, GS	7.76
Andrei Kirilenko, Utah	24.45	George Lynch, NO	7.83
Kobe Bryant, LAL	23.28	Jarron Collins, Utah	7.92
Allen Iverson, Phi	23.23	Walter McCarty, Bos-Phx	7.98
Yao Ming, Hou	23.22	Erick Strickland, Mil	8.01

Kevin Garnett was the top-ranked player for a second straight season. If you're looking for the MVP, Steve Nash finished 18th. Otherwise, all the usual suspects are at the top of the list, with nine of the top 10 making the All-Star Game and Kirilenko only missing it due to injury.

At the bottom, the list mostly consists of grizzled vets trying to hang on in the league for one final season. One exception is Toronto's Rafael Araujo, the biggest bust of the 2004 draft.

Game Scores

Now that we have the formula for the PER, here's an easier system for people to use while looking at the box scores over breakfast. This system is less accurate than the PER, but it's much faster. It's designed to be a convenient way to evaluate single-game performances without insane mathematics and can be done on the back of an envelope.

I call this method Game Scores after the method Bill James developed to rate baseball pitchers' single-game performances. It has the same objective, but for a different sport.

Here's the formula:

- Start with the player's point total for the game.
- Add 0.4 points for each made field goal.
- Subtract 0.7 points for each field goal attempt, made or missed.
- Subtract 0.4 points for each missed free throw.
- Add 0.7 points for each offensive rebound.
- Add 0.3 points for each defensive rebound.
- Add 1 point for each steal.
- Add 0.7 points for each assist.
- Add 0.7 points for each blocked shot.
- Subtract 0.4 points for each personal foul.
- Subtract 1 point for each turnover.

In general, the scale on Game Scores works something like this:

50+	A historic performance.
40–49.9	One of the best games of the entire season.
30–39.9	Probably the best performance in the league that night.
20–29.9	Probable Player of the Game selection.
15–19.9	A very strong effort.
12–14.9	Reasonably solid performance.
8–11.9	Average.
5–7.9	Subpar game or didn't see many minutes.
0–4.9	Poor game or used very sparingly.
<0	Packing his bags for Yakima.

Game scores are not perfect, but I did not intend them to be. They provide a quick, convenient alternative to the PER when time is more important than bulls-eye accuracy.

Methods and Player Comments

The methods introduced in this section are sprinkled liberally throughout the rest of this book. The charts on each player in the team section show each player's PER for the season. I also include each player's 40-minute averages for points, rebounds and assists, field goal and free throw percentages, True Shooting Percentage, Assist Ratio, Turnover Ratio, Usage Rate, and Rebound Rate. Next to each, I list where the player ranked at his position among players who played more than 500 minutes last season (for players who did not meet that threshold, no ranking is given).

By looking at how players rank at their position in each of these categories, we can get a better idea of where their strengths and weaknesses lie. Of course, I also have included all the traditional stats (games, minutes, and field goal and free throw percentages) as a handy reference so readers can see how known markers translate into the stats I have developed in this section. In addition, I've added the most similar player at the top of their stat line, along with their minutes breakdown by position and their defensive PER—which is the next topic.

Measuring defense in pro basketball is much, much trickier than measuring offense. While I have an established system for measuring all of a player's offensive accomplishments, my defensive ratings are still evolving.

In the previous books, I've outlined some of the limitations that stand in the way of detailed defensive analysis, so I won't regurgitate the entire discussion here. But suffice it to say, significant barriers still stand in the way:

- NBA defensive stats provide information only on steals, blocks, and fouls, which are a small percentage of total defensive plays.

- The league doesn't track some important information that would be fairly easy to record, such as charges taken, deflections, and contested shots.

- Consequently, most information regarding an individual's performance has to be gleaned from team data, and translating from the team level to the individual level is perilous.

Fortunately, the data is getting significantly better. Thanks to websites like 82games.com, I can tell at a moment's notice how a player's team performs defensively when he's on the court compared to when he's off it. I also can research how a player defends individually at his position by looking at the PER of his opponent, although a few teams match up in ways that makes this data less meaningful.

Adding this information to what we already know—a player's blocks, steals, and fouls—allows us to analyze a player's defensive impact in a more comprehensive manner than we could before. For instance, by comparing how a team fares defensively when a player is on the court against what a "replacement level" player might do with the same teammates, we can see how much a player's presence improved the overall team defense. Similarly, we can use the same measurement to gauge a player's impact at the individual level. Adding those two data points to our original statistical measures of blocks, steals, and fouls, we're left with a rating of each player's defensive prowess.

To see how I built this rating, let's start with team defense. I used two key pieces of data: how many points a team allowed while a particular player was on the court, and how many points the team allowed overall. Knowing only those two pieces of information and the league average for points allowed per minute, I can figure out whether a player was hurting or helping his club at the defensive end.

I first created a "replacement level" for points allowed per minute that was 10 percent worse than the league average. Then I took one-fifth the difference between the team's points allowed per minute and the replacement level, and added it to the team's points allowed per minute. That would be the amount a team could expect to give up if the other four players remained the same, but the fifth player was of "replacement level" quality.

Then I calculated the difference between the "replacement level" points allowed per minute and the actual number allowed by the team when the player in question was on the court. That was how many points the player theoretically saved his team with his defense, which I call his Team Defense Rating.

I followed the same steps for the player's man-to-man defense, with the player's opponent's PER used in place of the team's points allowed per minute. That gave us the second component of my player's defensive rating, his Man Defense Rating.

Finally, I used the player's statistical accomplishments—his blocks, steals, and personal fouls—and summed how much those factors contributed to the player's PER. I've labeled that his Stats Rating.

To come up with an overall rating, I needed to weigh each of these three factors. Since one aspect deals with team defense while two rate individual defense, it only makes sense to use the Team Defense Rating as one half and the two individual components—Man Defense and Stats—as the other half. Between the two, I weighted the Stats Rating twice as heavily as the Man Defense Rating. This may strike some as odd, but putting a heavier weight on the Man Defense Rating produced some strange results, because some of the players weren't matching up the way their Man Defense Rating suggested. Essentially, I wanted to reduce the effect of the Man Defense Rating to the point that it would only be a tie-breaker between closely ranked players.

So, in total, the Man Defense Rating accounted for ⅙ of a player's overall score—which I call his Defensive PER. The Stats Rating accounted for ⅓, and the Team Defense Rating for ½.

However, we're not done yet, because we have to set some limits. Defensive PER is valid only for players who played a lot of minutes and didn't change teams. This is because the most important element, the Team Defense Rating, was problematic for virtually any player who changed teams or didn't play the entire season.

Take Doug Christie, for instance. His Team Defense Rating with the Kings was unbelievable, but that's partly because he wasn't with Sacramento for the worst part of its season. Around the same time the Magic traded him for Cuttino Mobley, they also traded Chris Webber, lost Bobby Jackson and Brad Miller to injury, and played without Peja Stojakovic for nearly a month. Not surprisingly, the Kings' defensive record post-trade was significantly worse, and that would have been the case even if Christie had been there.

Christie's situation is hardly unique; players who switched teams or played only one portion of the season are significantly over-represented at the top and bottom of the Defensive PER rankings. As a result, I had to eliminate every player who changed teams during the course of the season.

As I mentioned, the ratings also required players to play frequently if they were to have much reliability. I use a fairly low standard for minutes played in the other stats in this book—just 500 for a season. But because Defensive PER isn't directly figuring a player's production but rather inputing it from the team stats, the standard for minutes needs to be much higher. I could only rate players who played a substantial number of minutes and were present for most their team's games. I used 62 games as one standard, since that represents 75 percent of a team's total. For minutes, I used 1,800, which is 24 minutes a game for 75 games—a reasonable amount for a rotation player. Players had to meet *both* standards—62 games and 1,800 minutes—in order to qualify.

With that said, the resultant top 10 (see table 1) is a plausible list of the league's top defenders in 2004–05. Only two players didn't get serious All-Defense consideration—Brendan Haywood and Bobby Simmons. In each case, they're young players, and recognition tends to lag performance by a year or two at the defensive end. Moreover, both players' defensive skills were made fairly obvious in their playoff performances. One other top-10 player, Manu Ginobili, is well regarded as a defender but his Man Defense Rating certainly benefited from the talents of teammate Bruce Bowen. Bowen often cross-matched and took the opposing shooting guard while Ginobili guarded the small forward.

Additionally, every player who received significant All-Defense support—three votes or more—also finished above the league average in Defense Rating. Tim Duncan of San Antonio rated as the best, which is hardly surprising considering he's been first-team All-Defense for eight straight years and was the linchpin of the league's best defensive team.

Similarly, the bottom 10 (table 2) contains nobody generally thought to be a good defender, though Matt Harpring of Utah is a bit of a surprise at the bottom of the list. Two other players, Kurt Thomas and Troy Murphy, are better than they look here. Each spent a lot of time trying to play center and getting beaten up by bigger players.

Table 2. Bottom 10 Players by Defensive PER, 2004–05 (minimum 2,000 minutes)

Player/Team	Def. PER	Player/Team	Def. PER
Matt Harpring, Utah	−1.02	Andres Nocioni, Chi	−0.20
Austin Croshere, Ind	−0.79	Josh Childress, Atl	−0.10
J. R. Smith, NO	−0.77	Chucky Atkins, LAL	−0.07
Tim Thomas, NY	−0.70	Troy Murphy, GS	−0.04
Jalen Rose, Tor	−0.23	Kurt Thomas, NY	0.04

From the top 10 charts, you also can see that the ratings range from a low of about −1 to a high of around 3. Average defenders ended up with a rating near 1.0—the league average is 0.87—making it fairly easy to quickly glance at a player's rating and see if he's pulling his weight or not.

Let's break it down by position.

⸻•⸻

Table 3 shows that the centers suffered from a lack of candidates because I set such stringent requirements for games and minutes. Yao and Stoudemire weren't that bad, but made the bottom five because, well, somebody had to. All the top five are legitimate stoppers, and while some would argue

Table 3. Top and Bottom Five Centers by Defensive PER, 2004–05

Top Five		Bottom Five	
Player/Team	Def. PER	Player/Team	Def. PER
Brendan Haywood, Was	2.76	Primoz Brezec, Char	0.23
Jason Collins, NJ	2.64	Mehmet Okur, Utah	0.38
Ben Wallace, Det	2.40	Marc Jackson, Phil	0.41
Marcus Camby, Den	1.83	Amare Stoudemire, Phx	0.66
Tyson Chandler, Chi	1.74	Yao Ming, Hou	0.67

Ben Wallace should rank first, keep in mind that both he and the Pistons got off to a very slow start in 2004–05. At the bottom, the shortcomings of Brezec, Okur, and Jackson have been well-documented.

⸻•⸻

Table 1. Top 10 Players by Defensive PER, 2004–05 (minimum 1,800 minutes, 62 games)

Player/Team	Def. PER	Player/Team	Def. PER
Tim Duncan, SA	3.08	Ben Wallace, Det	2.40
Brendan Haywood, Was	2.76	Earl Watson, Mem	2.40
Manu Ginobili, SA	2.71	Shane Battier, Mem	2.16
Bobby Simmons, LAC	2.68	Rasheed Wallace, Det	2.08
Jason Collins, NJ	2.64	Tayshaun Prince, Det	1.97

Table 4 has a few surprises. First, Dirk Nowitzki beat out Kevin Garnett for the No. 5 spot, which probably raises a few eyebrows. However, Garnett battled knee problems all last season and frequently had to play center—where his skills were less of an asset and his lack of muscle more of a detriment.

Table 4. Top and Bottom Five Power Forward by Defensive PER, 2004–05

Top Five		Bottom Five	
Player/Team	**Def. PER**	**Player/Team**	**Def. PER**
Tim Duncan, SA	3.08	Austin Croshere, Ind	−0.79
Rasheed Wallace, Det	2.08	Troy Murphy, GS	−0.04
Elton Brand, LAC	1.37	Kurt Thomas, NY	0.04
Antonio Davis, Chi	1.31	Raef LaFrentz, Bos	0.12
Dirk Nowitzki, Dal	1.28	P. J. Brown, NO	0.16

The "forced to play center" story is a common one among the bottom five. Players like Kurt Thomas and P. J. Brown are considered among the better defensive power forwards, but slipped into the bottom five. While both are slowing down a bit due to age, their ranking here also is a result of playing nearly as many minutes as an undersized center as at their natural positions. Murphy and LaFrentz also saw plenty of time in the middle and paid for it. Croshere, however, is just plain bad.

The top players in table 5 are no surprise—all five of those players have outstanding defensive reputations. It's the bottom five, again, that has the surprises. Harpring was coming off a knee injury, so playing on the perimeter may have been a stretch for a guy who wasn't too quick to begin with.

Table 5. Top and Bottom Five Small Forwards by Defensive PER, 2004–05

Top Five		Bottom Five	
Player/Team	**Def. PER**	**Player/Team**	**Def. PER**
Bobby Simmons, LAC	2.68	Matt Harpring, Utah	−1.02
Shane Battier, Mem	2.16	Tim Thomas, NY	−0.70
Tayshaun Prince, Det	1.97	Jalen Rose, Tor	−0.23
Bruce Bowen, SA	1.74	Andres Nocioni, Chi	−0.20
Josh Howard, Dal	1.70	Lee Nailon, NO	0.05

Nocioni's name may also surprise people, but the Bulls played significantly better when he wasn't on the floor, and like Harpring he was stretched at times by having to defend on the perimeter.

The shooting guards (table 6) tend to bunch up around the 1.0 mark, as players like Iguodala and Hughes made the top five at the position despite not being very far above the league average (Hughes fell one game short of the threshold, but since he was voted first-team All-Defense I thought people would be interested to see where he ranked).

Table 6. Top and Bottom Five Shooting Guards by Defensive PER, 2004–05

Top Five		Bottom Five	
Player/Team	**Def. PER**	**Player/Team**	**Def. PER**
Manu Ginobili, SA	2.71	J. R. Smith, NO	−1.77
Ben Gordon, Chi	1.66	Josh Childress, Atl	−0.10
Richard Hamilton, Det	1.62	Jamal Crawford, NY	0.17
Larry Hughes, Was	1.36	Corey Maggette, LAC	0.33
Andre Iguodala, Phi	1.14	Fred Jones, Ind and Michael Redd, Mil	0.34

The one big surprise here is Ben Gordon, whose rating may be in part helped by some cross-matches with Kirk Hinrich. However, the Bulls defended significantly better when Gordon was on the floor, and only his rampant fouling kept the rating from being higher. On the bottom list, Josh Childress and Corey Maggette are natural small forwards who suffered from playing out of position. Indiana's Fred Jones is a more genuine surprise.

As table 7 shows, Earl Watson's absence from the All-Defense voting continues to amaze me. He was clearly the best defender at his position last season and arguably was the

Table 7. Top and Bottom Five Point Guards by Defensive PER, 2004–05

Top Five		Bottom Five	
Player/Team	**Def. PER**	**Player/Team**	**Def. PER**
Earl Watson, Mem	2.40	Chucky Atkins, LAL	−0.07
Chauncey Billups, Det	1.77	Jeff McInnis, Cle	0.04
Tony Parker, SA	1.71	Maurice Williams, Mil	0.04
Eric Snow, Cle	1.58	Damon Stoudamire, Por	0.15
Jason Kidd, NJ	1.49	Damon Jones, Mia	0.19

year before as well. Among the bottom five, poor Damon Stoudamire had to play nearly half his minutes at shooting guard despite standing just 5′10″, which obviously dented his rating. Otherwise it's the usual suspects.

So there you have it. Choosing an All-Defense team from the charts above would arguably have provided better choices than the list the coaches ended up with. Looking at their first and second teams, I don't think too many people would complain if Larry Hughes were replaced by Earl Watson, Dwyane Wade by Manu Ginobili, and Kevin Garnett by either Rasheed Wallace or Bobby Simmons.

For the players who qualified based on my criteria, I included their Defensive PER for the past season. I haven't done so for the players who didn't qualify because in many cases the information is worse than worthless—it's misleading, making us think somebody was great or horrible when in fact they weren't. Tackling how to rate these players is the next step in the quest for defensive statistical evaluations that are as advanced as the ones that have been developed for offense.

Similarity Scores and Player Projections

Throughout this book, I've included stats that demonstrate a player's past performance. But for most teams, the far more relevant question is how a player will perform in the future. For example, if I own the Milwaukee Bucks and I'm debating whether to give Bobby Simmons a $47 million contract, what matters more than his 50 percent shooting last year is whether he'll do it again this year when he's on my team.

While we don't have a crystal ball, it's possible to improve the odds in forecasting how players will perform. One way is to look at past performance—players who shoot a high percentage will continue to do so, other things being equal. An even better tool harnesses the game's statistical history.

For instance, by combing through two decades of player statistics, we can pinpoint the players who were most similar to Bobby Simmons. Then we can take those players and see how they performed in future seasons, which gives us some idea of what to expect from Simmons.

This is the two-part process that I used to create projected stats for every player for the 2005–06 season. First I began with a method I call Similarity Scores. This tool compares two players and scores them from 0 to 100 based on their similarities in statistical production and two physical aspects, age and height.

In last year's book I substantially revised my method for Similarity Scores and was pleased enough with the results that I made only a minor change this year. That change involved evaluating a player's record over three seasons rather than just his most recent season. While I still gave the most emphasis to the most recent season, analyzing the three-year record helped to inoculate the projections against fluke years and injuries. The most recent season was weighted by a factor of three, year two by a factor of two, and year one by a factor of one. I also weighted each season by the player's minutes, so that a 2,000-minute season would get four times the weight of a 500-minute season. Finally, seasons when a player played fewer than 500 minutes didn't count at all because of the statistical anomalies that sometimes arise with small sample sizes.

To review, I compare a player with every player within half a year of his age from the past 20 years (e.g., a 28-year-old would be compared with everyone between 27½ and 28½). In each statistical category, I normalize every player's data relative to that season's standards, allowing us to make better comparisons of data between seasons—an easy example would be how I set the league average PER at 15.00 every year. Then I compare a player's normalized performance for a given season to the normalized stats of nearly 5,000 player-seasons of data and determine which player-seasons were the most similar.

Each attribute doesn't have the same importance. For instance, height is easily the most important determinant of similarity—a 6′6″ guy and a 7-footer with identical stats can't be considered similar players because they're accomplishing their tasks in very different ways. For those who are wondering, weight also is important, but I don't use it in similarity scores because it's too variable (weights fluctuate, heights don't) and often reported incorrectly. Thus, it leads us down stray paths as often as it guides us in the right direction.

On the other hand, fouls per minute is the least important since it's useful only for distinguishing mad-hacking, Danny Fortson types from their peers. Overall, there are 13 categories in which I run similarity comparisons, as shown in table 1.

I also standardize across categories by making comparisons based on the difference between the first and 99th percentile of players in that category. Otherwise, categories with small ranges of performance will be underweighted. For example, virtually every NBA player shoots between 40 and 60 percent from the field, so that category has a very small range of performance. On the other hand, it's not uncommon for one player to have 10 times as many blocked shots

Table 1. Weighting of Attributes in Similarity Scores

Attribute	Weight	Percent of Score
Height	5.5	27.5 %
Usage Rate	2.0	10.0%
3A/FGA	1.5	7.5%
Assist Ratio	1.5	7.5%
Rebound Rate	1.5	7.5%
FG%	1.5	7.5%
PER	1.0	5.0%
PSA	1.0	5.0%
Turnover Ratio	1.0	5.0%
FTA/FGA	1.0	5.0%
Bk/Min	1.0	5.0%
St/Min	1.0	5.0%
PF/Min	0.5	2.5%

as another, so that category has an extremely large range. By setting a range based on the percentiles and then comparing differences between players to that range, I equalize the different categories.

Similarity Scores run from 0 to 100, but in practice two players aren't similar at all until their score gets above 95.

The two most similar seasons in this year's book are Jamaal Magloire in 2004–05 and Rony Seikaly in 1990–91, with a score of 99.9. The two were within percentage points of each other in every statistical category save Rebound Rate, in which Seikaly was superior, and several of the differences were microscopic. For instance, Seikaly had 1.89 times the league average in blocked shots, Magloire 1.88. Seikaly had a True Shooting Percentage 1.04 times the league average, while Magloire's was 1.02. Both were 6'11", and both had a Usage Rate 0.90 times the league average. And it wasn't the only similar season among the two—seven of Seikaly's eight seasons between 1988–89 and 1995–96 rated 99.2 or better.

We also can use similarity scores to see which players were the most "common." Al Harrington had 77 different comparable players with a Similarity Score of 98 or better, which was easily the most of any current player. By contrast, Danny Fortson is the most unusual, with not one comparable player rating above 95.

Alongside each player's statistics, I've shown which comparable player from recent history is most similar at the same age. Keep in mind that a single comparable player may show up as "most similar" for multiple individuals. In this year's book, Derrick Coleman was an especially popular "most similar" player, but others also make multiple appearances in these pages.

But similarity is only half the story. The other half is to use a group of similar players to project future performance. For each player, I selected a block of comparable players based on their Similarity Scores. The idea is to get at least 25 players for comparison, so that one particular player doesn't overly influence the projections. Note that this isn't possible in some cases.

For each player, I started by taking every comparable with a score above 98. If there were at least 25, I stopped there. If not, I lowered the bar by a quarter point (i.e., to 97.75) and kept doing so until I had at least 25 comps. However, I stopped lowering the required score at 95.0 and used however many players qualified, even if it was fewer than 25.

For each of the comps selected, I compared their "year after" statistics to what they did during the season in question. For example, in 1991–92 Seikaly's Rebound Rate increased by nearly three percent, so that increase would go into Jamaal Magloire's projection. I did the same thing for all of Magloire's other comparable players. I created a weighting of each comparable's results by taking their Similarity Score and subtracting 94.0. Thus, a comparable with a score of 98.0 would have twice the weight of a comparable with a score of 96.0, putting greater emphasis on comparables like Seikaly who were the most similar. Then I averaged the results across all the players to obtain the percent increase or decrease Magloire could expect in each of the key statistics.

With that information, I could then project Magloire's stats for the coming season. For instance, his comparable players experience a five percent decline in their Rebound Rate (despite the increase by Seikaly). Therefore, we can conclude that Magloire's rate of rebounds per 40 minutes is expected to drop from 12.0 (his weighted average from the past three seasons) to 11.3.

You'll see these results in the projected stats for each player, which appear at the bottom of his statistics chart. For example, Magloire's projection for 2005–06 is shown in table 2.

The "PRJ" is his projected stats for 2005–06. Note that his scoring and rebounding per minute are projected to drop, but his field-goal and free-throw percentages should increase substantially. As a result, his PER should rise from 2004–05 and more closely resemble his performance from the previous two seasons.

Also, note the "(47.2)" next to the "PRJ." This number stands for the quality of the projection. This can range from 1 to 100, but only rarely gets above 50. For most players this number is somewhere between 20 and 35, so in Magloire's case the projection is better than usual (not surprising considering he has such a good comparable in Seikaly). To calculate this, I slightly modified last year's equation. The new formula is:

$$\text{Projection quality} = 10 \times (\text{Average Sim Score of comps} - 94.9)$$
$$\times (\text{Number of comparables} / 25)$$

Table 2. Jamaal Magloire's 2005–06 Player Statistics

Jamaal Magloire (100% C)				center										Age: 27	Height: 6-11 Weight: 259 Most similar at age: Rony Seikaly	
Year	G	M/G	FG%	FT%	P/40	R/40	A/40	TS%		Ast		TO		Usg	Reb	PER
2002-03 NO	82	29.8	.480	.717	13.8	11.9	1.4	54.1	21	8.6	40	15.4	53	15.2 35	17.2 10	15.41 21
2003-04 NO	82	33.9	.473	.751	16.1	12.2	1.2	55.1	12	6.6	58	15.4	62	17.6 15	18.0 4	17.11 10
2004-05 NO	23	30.6	.432	.602	15.4	11.7	1.7	48.0	57	7.9	23	16.0	55	19.4 8	17.5 13	12.80 38
2005–06 PRJ (47.2)			.459	.689	14.6	11.3	1.3	51.9		7.3		15.1		17.2	16.4	14.74

Similarity Scores and Player Projections

Theoretically, it's possible for a player to score over 100, if his average comparable was in the 99 range and he had at least 60 comparables. In practice only Al Harrington managed this, and nobody else came anywhere close. As with last year's projections, keep in mind that projection quality doesn't mean projection *certainty*—it's just one way to show the value of the information that went into the projection.

In the upcoming chapters, every player who played at least 500 minutes has projected stats for next season. The improvements to the similarity scores—in particular the reliance on three seasons of past data rather than one—should greatly improve the quality of these projections relative to a year ago. Nonetheless, we're hardly at the finish line, and I hope to continue fine-tuning this methodology in coming seasons. In the meantime, fans and fantasy owners alike can develop a reasonable expectation for what their favorite players might produce this season.

The Europeans

Who needs the NBDL when we already have the Euroleague? The NBA set up a new minor league in the latest version of its collective bargaining agreement, but in effect it has already had one for years. The pro basketball teams in Europe provide a perfect, if distant, outlet for players whose games needed some fine-tuning before they were ready for the NBA. It's been a source for the game's burgeoning international talent as well. Thus, even if the NBDL becomes a more realistic minor league in the coming seasons, talent scouts still will be crossing the pond in droves to see the top talent in Europe.

Due to the increasing number of players jumping continents, last year I developed a model for translating performance in Europe's top league, the Euroleague, into an NBA equivalent. For the most part, the model held up. Six players made the transition from the Euroleague to the NBA—Carlos Delfino, Maurice Evans, Viktor Khryapa, Nenad Krstic, Andres Nocioni, and Anderson Varejao—and the predictions were right on target for four of them.

The 2004–05 *Forecast* said Krstic would score but would struggle on the boards, and he did, although he scored slightly more than projected. It said both Khryapa and Delfino would struggle to score, and that proved to be the case. And it nailed Maurice Evans: The formula predicted he would shoot 43.9 percent and have a PER of 12.72, and he shot 44.2 percent with a PER of 12.12.

However, the method missed the mark on two players—one in each direction. For Andres Nocioni, it badly overestimated his performance. Nocioni's per-40-minute stats projected to 14.8 points, 10.2 rebounds, and a 14.16 PER; he ended up at 14.1 points, 8.3 rebounds, and a 9.96 PER. A position switch may have been the culprit—Nocioni saw a lot of time at power forward in Europe but had to play the perimeter in the NBA.

Most mystifying was the case of Anderson Varejao, who became the first European import to play *better* in the NBA than he had in Europe. Varejao's numbers were well ahead of my projections in every category, which will make it interesting to see if they hold up this season. However, he and the other player who outperformed his projection, Krstic, had one thing in common: youth. Varejao was 22 last year, while Krstic was 21, so they may have just raised their games to a new level.

Those six players aren't the only subjects of interest from 2004–05. The road between Europe and the NBA isn't one-way—we also had two Americans, Dion Glover and Travis Hansen, make the jump to the Euroleague last season. Glover joined a team in Turkey and matched Varejao's first—he became the first player to do worse in the Euroleague than he had in the NBA. Hansen, on the other hand, played significantly better than he had here.

I added those eight players to my model and used them to slightly revise how I interpret the Euroleague stats. Two salient factors are at work: First, despite the huddled masses leaving every year for the NBA, the league as a whole is improving. The players making the transition this past season lost less of their productivity than those from previous years, while the NBA players jumping back across had it less easy than in the past.

Second, I decided on a wording change to more accurately represent what we're viewing. I'm calling these "translated stats" for 2004–05, rather than "projected" stats for 2005–06. It's an important distinction because players as young as Varejao and Krstic were a year ago are highly likely to outperform their translated stats from the previous season.

Overall, players still lose quite a bit from their statistical output when switching from the Euroleague to the NBA. On average, scoring drops by 25 percent, field goal percentage sinks by 12 percent and PER by 30 percent, so a player needs to be putting up some impressive stats in Europe to be much of a force at the NBA level. On the other hand, due to differences in pace a player's rebounds increase by 18 percent while assists rise by 31 percent because the statisticians are so stingy with those numbers.

The pool of players for my study still is very small, so in future years we are sure to learn more about the changes in player's productivity when switching continents. In the meantime, let's take a look at the European players who are either on the tips of scouts' tongues or rated highly in my system (note that comments on Europeans who were drafted this year, such as Yaroslav Korolev or Johan Petro, will be found in their team section).

Nemanja Aleksandrov   small forward   Age: 18   Height: 6-1
A young, talented Serbian whose team didn't compete in the Euroleague, Aleksandrov has been one of Europe's most highly touted players and could enter the draft in 2006. He played sparingly for a team in Croatia this past season and tore his ACL late in the season, so his recovery and future development are the keys to how highly he'll eventually be drafted.

David Andersen   power forward   Age: 25 Height: 6-11
Translated 40-minute stats: 14.6 pts, 12.5 reb, 1.8 ast, .485 FG%, 15.93 PER

The Hawks own the rights to this versatile Danish-Australian big man, who hadn't done much to impress the scouts before having a breakout year with CSKA Moscow this past season. Andersen loves to shoot a turnaround from the blocks and is extremely accurate with it. He also showed a lot more muscle on the glass than he had in past seasons. Andersen has already agreed to return to Moscow for another season, so the Hawks will have to wait until at least 2006–07 before he comes to the U.S. With another year like this one, Atlanta could be in position to trade Andersen's rights for some backcourt help.

Robert Archibald   power forward   Age: 25 Height: 6-11
Translated 40-minute stats: 15.5 pts, 14.4 reb, 1.8 ast, .540 FG%, 16.50 PER

Archibald's projections based on last season are impressive, but they come with a major asterisk because they're based on only one season. Most of the other players in this list have three seasons of Euroleague play for us to examine, which is vastly more telling because the Euroleague season is so short (between 14 and 24 games, depending on how long a team stays alive in the postseason).

In Archibald's case, the Scottish forward didn't show nearly this kind of ability in his two seasons with the Memphis Grizzlies, nor during his college years at Illinois, so he'll have to repeat the effort before NBA teams start getting too excited about his prospects.

Malick Badiane   power forward   Age: 21 Height: 6-10
Translated 40-minute stats: 6.7 pts, 13.4 reb, 0.0 ast, .408 FG%, 10.00 PER

A second-round pick by the Rockets two years ago, Badiane only played 66 minutes for one of the Euroleague's worst teams and didn't show much offensive game when he was out there. However, he rebounded like a beast and he's still only 21. Badiane definitely needs more work but could be a decent backup a few years down the road.

Andrea Bargnani   power forward   Age: 20 Height: 6-10
Translated 40-minute stats: 11.5 pts, 10.6 reb, 1.2 ast, .453 FG%, 10.16 PER

Bargnani has played sparingly for European power Benetton Treviso the past two seasons but is considered one of the best prospects in Europe and a possible lottery pick in the 2006 draft. Despite his size the Italian prefers playing on the perimeter, so if he's quick enough he could move to small forward and end up as a Hedo Turkoglu-type of player in the NBA.

Maceo Baston   power forward   Age: 30 Height: 6-10
Translated 40-minute stats: 16.7 pts, 7.6 reb, 2.8 ast, .580 FG%, 19.18 PER

This guy belongs in the NBA. Period. The former Michigan star has turned into a big-time player in Europe and had the highest projected PER of any player studied. Baston shot 68.2 percent from the floor for Maccabi Tel Aviv this past season in helping them to a second straight Euroleague title.

If you think these projections for Baston are too optimistic, check out what he did in 106 minutes for the Raptors in 2002–03. Baston averaged 15.1 points and 8.7 rebounds per 40 minutes, shot 60 percent from the field, and had a PER of 18.06—completely in line with his translated stats above. Basically, every shred of available evidence suggests that if he played in the NBA, Baston would be an extremely high-percentage scorer.

Tanoka Beard   power forward   Age: 34 Height: 6-9
Translated 40-minute stats: 16.3 pts, 14.5 reb, 1.7 ast, .506 FG%, 15.48 PER

Considering his age, I don't think we'll be seeing Beard in the NBA regardless of what he accomplishes in Europe. It's not worth the risk for an NBA team to bring a player in at this age if he is going to be effective for only a year or two. It's a shame for Beard because he projects as a bigger version of Malik Rose, inhaling rebounds, and getting his share of garbage points around the basket.

Marco Belinelli   shooting guard   Age: 19 Height: 6-6
Translated 40-minute stats: 8.0 pts, 3.2 reb, 2.9 ast, .407 FG%, 7.06 PER

Belinelli has attracted scouts' interest because he's been good enough to see minutes in the Euroleague since he was 17. Obviously, if he jumped to the NBA right now he'd be a disaster, but his youth and height have teams intrigued. If he continues improving he could be a lottery pick in another year or two.

Luka Bogdanovic   small forward   Age: 20 Height: 6-9
Translated 40-minute stats: 11.0 pts, 7.8 reb, 1.8 ast, .373 FG%, 7.34 PER

Bogdanovic's Euroleague team, Partizan Belgrade, has four young players who could end up in the 2006 draft: Bogdanovic, Kosta Perovic, Peja Samdardziski, and Uros Tripkovic. None of the four played very well in 2004–05, but Bogdanovic was the best of the bunch. A stereotypical skinny 6'9" European who likes to hang out at the 3-point line, Bogdanovic also can mix it up on the glass despite a slight build. And no, he does not live on the second floor.

Marcus Brown   point guard   Age: 31 Height: 6-3
Translated 40-minute stats: 15.2 pts, 3.7 reb, 5.4 ast, .413 FG%, 11.89 PER

I've been a big fan of Brown's in the past, but his 2004–05 season wasn't as good as some of his previous campaigns and he's starting to get long in the tooth for a point guard. He also has a rich contract by European standards that NBA teams would be reluctant to buy out just to get a backup point guard. Put it all together and he's probably not coming over any time soon.

Jose Manuel Calderon   point guard   Age: 24 Height: 6-3
Translated 40-minute stats: 11.6 pts, 5.1 reb, 4.7 ast, .429 FG%, 12.95 PER

Calderon is both young and skilled, so it's not surprising that the Raptors offered him a contract over the summer. The Spanish guard played off the ball quite a bit for his European teams, raising questions about how he'd adjust to full-time point guard duty in the NBA. Nonetheless, he figures to be Rafer Alston's primary backup in Toronto this season.

Dimos Dikoudis　　　small forward　　Age: 28　Height: 6-9
Translated 40-minute stats: 14.0 pts, 10.8 reb, 2.2 ast, .475 FG%, 13.39 PER

A native of Greece, Dikoudis is a classic example of a player who might be more valuable in the European game than in the U.S. He's a thin 6′9″ forward without a three-point shot. In Europe, you can play a guy like that at power forward and get away with it, but in the NBA, he's likely to get killed in the post. Dikoudis is fairly athletic and would get his share of points and rebounds, but the question is whether he could match up physically as a frontcourt player.

Rudy Fernandez　　　shooting guard　　Age: 20　Height: 6-5

Even though Fernandez's team played in the ULEB Cup, which is one step below the Euroleague, his numbers were fairly poor. Fernandez shot 41.2 percent overall and just 30.6 percent on 3-pointers, which isn't going to cut it as an NBA shooting guard. However, considering his youth and athleticism, the Spaniard is still very high on most scouts' radars. If he shows more consistency as a shooter and adds some strength he'll be a first-round draft pick in the next year or two.

Antonis Fotsis　　　small forward　　Age: 24　Height: 6-10
Translated 40-minute stats: 12.8 pts, 9.3 reb, 0.9 ast, .430 FG%, 9.38 PER

Fotsis already has had one failed stint in the NBA, in 2002 with the Memphis Grizzlies, so he's probably reluctant to try it again. That may be a good thing, as his numbers from the past season were unimpressive. Like his fellow Greek Dikoudis, Fotsis is a tweener at the NBA level but a solid power forward in the Euroleague, so staying may be the best career move for him.

Jorge Garbajosa　　　power forward　　Age: 28　Height: 6-9
Translated 40-minute stats: 13.4 pts, 10.9 reb, 2.6 ast, .400 FG%, 13.49 PER

Garbajosa is an intriguing player because he can bang inside and hold his own, but then will step outside and hit three-pointers. He showed in the 2004 Olympics that he can hang with higher-quality athletes as well. However, Garbajosa is 28 and doesn't project to be anything more than a decent backup in the NBA, which might not be much of an inducement for him to give up a cushy gig in his native Spain.

Andreas Glyniadakis　　power forward　　Age: 24　Height: 7-1
Translated 40-minute stats: 13.6 pts, 6.1 reb, 1.8 ast, .541 FG%, 8.08 PER

Detroit's second-round draft pick in 2003, Glyniadakis fits the classic stereotype of a European 7-footer with a severe rebound allergy. His pathetic average of 6.1 rebounds per 40 minutes belies what otherwise would be fairly encouraging numbers from a young 7-footer. Note that those stats are based on a fairly small sample of minutes, but it still doesn't provide much encouragement for the Pistons.

Paulius Jankunas　　　power forward　　Age: 21　Height: 6-8
Translated 40-minute stats: 9.7 pts, 10.1 reb, 1.8 ast, .476 FG%, 9.87 PER

The young Lithuanian forward hasn't shown up on any list of hot prospects in Europe, but he rates higher than several players who have. The misgivings scouts have about Jankunas probably stem from his short stature for a power forward, but if his game continues to develop he should eventually begin to attract notice.

Sarunas Jasikevicius　　point forward　　Age: 30　Height: 6-4
Translated 40-minute stats: 14.5 pts, 3.3 reb, 7.3 ast, .393 FG%, 12.34 PER

A forgettable player while at Maryland, Jasikevicius has blossomed in Europe. He's been the starting point guard for the Euroleague champion for three straight seasons and earned further notoriety when he led Lithuania to a win over the U.S. in the 2004 Olympics. At this point, however, he might be overrated. Three other players on his Maccabi Tel Aviv team rated higher (Maceo Baston, Anthony Parker, and Nikola Vujcic), and of his past three seasons, only one has been statistically impressive. The Pacers signed him to a three-year deal in the offseason, and though they may have overpaid he'll be an upgrade on Anthony Johnson.

Arvydas Macijauskas　　shooting guard　　Age: 25　Height: 6-4
Translated 40-minute stats: 17.8 pts, 3.6 reb, 4.2 ast, .428 FG%, 14.96 PER

Macijauskas is another sweet-shooting Lithuanian guard who is now the property of the New Orleans Hornets. He hit 40 percent of his three-pointers and shot 90 percent from the line to help his Vitoria, Spain, team to the Euroleague title game. He shapes up as a solid scoring guard off the bench, but teams are concerned about his ability to defend because he's short for an off guard, lacks muscle, and isn't terribly athletic. His hobbit resemblance probably doesn't help either.

Denis Marconato　　　center　　Age: 30　Height: 6-11
Translated 40-minute stats: 11.4 pts, 14.5 reb, 2.1 ast, .532 FG%, 11.93 PER

The Italian veteran is one of the best rebounders anywhere in basketball and gets most of his offense from easy put-backs. However, he's slightly built for an NBA center and offers little upside considering he's already 30. As a result, he'll probably stay in Italy.

Sergei Monia　　　power forward　　Age: 22　Height: 6-7
Translated 40-minute stats: 10.5 pts, 9.4 reb, 2.0 ast, .392 FG%, 12.73 PER

A first-round pick by the Blazers in 2003, Monia had trouble getting minutes on a loaded CSKA Moscow team that lost only twice all season. However, when he did play his offensive numbers were much improved from the previous year. Monia still has work to do to become a competent scorer at the NBA level, but because he defends and can rebound (he might be the best leaper in Europe), he would still be a decent reserve. And at 22, one would think his offense still has room to grow.

The Europeans

Juan Carlos Navarro point guard Age: 25 Height: 6-3
Translated 40-minute stats: 15.1 pts, 3.2 reb, 3.4 ast, .396 FG%, 13.18 PER

The Wizards drafted Navarro in the second round in 2002 and still hold his rights. They might not have much use for him, however. Navarro is basically a poor man's Juan Dixon—a shooting guard in a point guard's body, and one who shoots a low percentage. The Wizards have enough guards who dominate the ball as it is.

Fabrio Oberto power forward Age: 30 Height: 6-10

Oberto has no translated stats because his team didn't compete in the Euroleague in 2004–05. However, in the previous two seasons his numbers translated to a decent pro power forward who could make shots around the basket and provide some toughness. The Spurs signed Oberto over the summer, where he'll join his fellow Argentinean Manu Ginobili. Unfortunately, Oberto will fit in with the Spurs in one other way. He has become a horrendously bad free-throw shooter, making just 20 of 57 this past season. He also may be a bit undersized for an NBA frontcourt.

Theodoros Papaloukas point guard Age: 28 Height: 6-6
Translated 40-minute stats: 11.1 pts, 5.4 reb, 8.4 ast, .477 FG%, 15.03 PER

Papaloukas came off the bench for CSKA Moscow last season, which was odd since he might have been their best player. Despite his size, the Greek import is a pure point guard who projects to average better than an assist every five minutes in the NBA. He's in his late 20s and last season was easily the best of his career, so teams might want to see him do it again before they'll pay to bring him across. But as a third guard who can play either spot, he would fill a need for a lot of teams.

Anthony Parker small forward Age: 30 Height: 6-6
Translated 40-minute stats: 14.3 pts, 7.1 reb, 5.1 ast, .480 FG%, 15.96 PER

With the possible exception of his teammate Baston, Parker is the best American playing in Europe right now. He's a former first-round draft pick who flopped in his first try in the NBA but has thrived the past two seasons for Euroleague champion Maccabi Tel Aviv. As an NBA player, he wouldn't excel in any one area, but he's a jack-of-all-trades who also defends fairly well.

Kosta Perovic center Age: 20 Height: 7-2
Translated 40-minute stats: 10.1 pts, 8.5 reb, 2.0 ast, .397 FG%, 8.85 PER

Perovic is 7'2", so at some point somebody probably will gamble a draft pick on him, but he's a major project. His rebounding numbers are terribly disappointing for a player of his height, and a big center like this should also be able to shoot a much higher percentage. He's in a good position to improve because he plays regularly for his European team, so perhaps in a year or two he'll be more NBA-ready.

Marko Popovic point guard Age: 23 Height: 6-1
Translated 40-minute stats: 14.6 pts, 3.2 reb, 6.6 ast, .397 FG%, 13.15 PER

I haven't seen Popovic on any lists of European prospects, but he's quietly become one of the continent's best point guards at age 23. His porous defense is a turn-off for pro teams and as a shooter he's more "decent" than "great," but stay tuned. If he continues improving, it will be difficult for NBA teams to ignore his production.

Efthimios Rentzias center Age: 29 Height: 6-11
Translated 40-minute stats: 13.5 pts, 9.6 reb, 1.7 ast, .423 FG%, 14.75 PER

A former first-round draft pick, the Greek big man had a shot with the 76ers several years ago. Larry Brown hardly played him though (sound familiar, Darko?), so he went back to Europe. Rentzias is slightly undersized for an NBA center but his stats suggest he'd still be fairly productive. Plus, he's a good deal better than the Calvin Booths and Jason Colliers whom a lot of teams pass off as backup centers.

Sergio Rodriguez point guard Age: 19 Height: 6-3
Translated 40-minute stats: 10.7 pts, 5.2 reb, 7.9 ast, .370 FG%, 8.33 PER

One of the most highly regarded young point guards in basketball, Rodriguez is comparable to Sebastian Telfair in that he already has a high assist rate and only needs to round out as a shooter and cut his turnovers to become a quality player. His size is another asset, as he's big for the position, but he's only 170 pounds and needs to get stronger. He seems likely to be a high first-round draft pick in either 2006 or 2007.

Peja Samardziski center Age: 19 Height: 7-0
Translated 40-minute stats: 5.5 pts, 10.2 reb, 1.8 ast, .389 FG%, 3.22 PER

The Macedonian big man has been drummed up as a prospect, but I have my doubts. Supposedly he is a good shooter, but his offensive numbers last season were absolutely terrible and would equate to microscopic production at the NBA level. He's also regarded as slow and immobile, so he'll need to score in order to have an NBA role. Right now he's Michael Ruffin minus the rebounding and defense.

Luis Scola power forward Age: 25 Height: 6-9
Translated 40-minute stats: 16.0 pts, 10.2 reb, 3.5 ast, .505 FG%, 14.20 PER

San Antonio drafted Scola late in the second round in 2002 and it would have been a great pick if not for Scola's problematic contract. He has a huge buyout in his deal with Spanish club Tau Ceramica that has prevented the Spurs from bringing him over. There's no doubt that Scola can play at the NBA level; the only question is how high his ceiling is. That may not seem obvious from the translated stats above, but his stats last season were his worst in four years, so consider it a bare minimum.

Unlike a lot of foreign imports, Scola also is strong and tough and should be an above-average NBA defender. He's perhaps best known for being the second option behind

Manu Ginobili on Argentina's 2004 gold medal team, and he'll be reunited with Ginobili if he ever joins the Spurs.

Charles Smith shooting guard Age: 30 Height: 6-4
Translated 40-minute stats: 17.9 pts, 4.2 reb, 3.4 ast, .385 FG%, 14.88 PER

Smith's translated stats are consistent with the numbers he produced in his one NBA chance with San Antonio in 2001–02: 15.5 points and 4.7 rebounds per 40 minutes, with a .425 shooting mark and a PER of 13.18. His points were a little higher and his shooting percentage a little lower in Europe last season because he was playing for a bad team and had to become their go-to guy, but the overall effectiveness was about the same. At age 30, he probably has a year or two left of being a solid contributor at the NBA level, especially since he has extremely long arms that help him at the defensive end. Smith has a deal in place to join the Blazers, where he could help fill out their weak bench.

Matjaz Smodis power forward Age: 26 Height: 6-9
Translated 40-minute stats: 13.5 pts, 8.6 reb, 1.7 ast, .481 FG%, 13.87 PER

A Slovenian forward who has stayed under scouts' radars, Smodis nonetheless has put together two solid seasons and at 26 could still take a small step forward from here. He wouldn't be anything more than a solid bench player in the NBA, however, so it may not be worth his while to make the trip.

Vasilis Spanoulis point guard Age: 23 Height: 6-4

A second-round draft pick by the Rockets in 2004, Spanoulis's numbers for Greek club Maroussi were very solid and may earn him a trip across the ocean this year. No translations are possible because his team played in the ULEB Cup and not the Euroleague, but his scoring and assist rates suggest he should stay afloat offensively in the NBA.

Tiago Splitter power forward Age: 20 Height: 6-11
Translated 40-minute stats: 11.3 pts, 11.4 reb, 2.4 ast, .489 FG%, 11.94 PER

A likely lottery pick either this year or next, the Brazilian big man is one of the few young prospects in Europe who could help a team right now. He has good size and athleticism that allow him to rebound and block shots well, but he has a skinny build so he can't play center. Overall his numbers compare very well to countryman Anderson Varejao's last

season in Europe, except that Splitter had his season when he was two years younger.

Marko Tomas small forward Age: 20 Height: 6-8

Tomas certainly can shoot the rock. However, nearly half his shot attempts in the Adriatic League (he has no Euroleague numbers) came from beyond the three-point line, which cements questions about his ability to get to the basket. Although he's big and skilled, that lack of athleticism is why the Croatian sharpshooter didn't stay in the draft in 2005.

Uros Tripkovic shooting guard Age: 19 Height: 6-5
Translated 40-minute stats: 12.1 pts, 2.3 reb, 2.7 ast, .320 FG%, 6.33 PER

Tripkovic appears to be the next Serbian shooting sensation, as he hit 36 percent on 3-pointers and 33-of-34 from the line this past season. It's the rest of his game that still has holes. He hit only 37 percent on two-pointers and had more three-point attempts than twos last season, plus his rebounding numbers are pathetic. If he can add more skills to the outstanding shooting, he'll be a first-round pick in two years or so.

Milos Vujanic point guard Age: 25 Height: 6-3
Translated 40-minute stats: 17.1 pts, 3.7 reb, 3.3 ast, .395 FG%, 13.89 PER

Vujanic appears to be an NBA player statistically, but the one fly in the ointment is that he'll have to switch positions because he's only 6'3". Vujanic plays shooting guard in Europe and is more comfortable as a score-first guard than he is setting up teammates, plus his quickness might be an issue if he has to guard smaller players. However, he might fit in better with an up-and-down team like Phoenix, who as luck would have it currently own his rights.

Nikola Vujcic power forward Age: 27 Height: 6-11
Translated 40-minute stats: 15.2 pts, 9.8 reb, 4.4 ast, .497 FG%, 16.20 PER

The veteran Croatian forward has failed to interest pro teams because he's so soft, and he'll certainly get pushed around on defense. But he's a very efficient offensive player who also is a good passer and can rebound despite his softness. Basically, he'd be the second coming of Dino Radja, and there are teams who could use somebody like that. He's played for back-to-back champions in Europe and still is pretty young, but no NBA team has taken the bait yet.

Key to Player Statistics

The **position** listed for each player is, with a few exceptions, the spot where he played the majority of his minutes in 2004–05.

Age is the player's age as of December 31, 2005.

Height and **weight** are the player's listed height and weight as of June 2005.

Defensive PER is the player's rating for his defensive performance. It's only available for players who played at least 1,800 minutes and didn't change teams.

The **percentages for each position** are how the player's minutes were divvied up in 2004–05. So if it says (67% SF, 33% SG), it means the player spent 67 percent of his minutes at small forward and the other 33 percent at shooting guard.

Most similar at age is the player who was the most similar to this one at the same age.

In the chart itself, the abbreviations are as follows:

G   Games played
M/G   Minutes per game
FG%   Field-goal percentage
FT%   Free-throw percentage
P/40 Points per 40 minutes
R/40 Rebounds per 40 minutes
A/40 Assists per 40 minutes
TS%   True Shooting Percentage
Ast   Assist Ratio
TO   Turnover Ratio
Usg   Usage Rate
Reb   Rebound Rate
PER   Player Efficiency Rating

Next to **TS%, Ast, TO, Usg, Reb,** and **PER** in the chart are the player's **ranking at his position** in each category. This will be blank for players who saw fewer than 500 minutes.

Atlanta Hawks

In January 2004, the Atlanta Hawks decided they would have to get worse before they could get better. On the first part, they've been wildly successful.

With the trades of Shareef Abdur-Rahim, Nazr Mohammed, and Theo Ratliff that January, the Hawks essentially gave up on being competitive for the foreseeable future. As a result of those deals and the subsequent completion of the fire sale over the next six months, Atlanta stumbled through a miserable 13–69 season during which the team never even put up a fight. If rookie forward Josh Smith hadn't been such a surprise the Hawks might have broken the 1972–73 Sixers' record for futility at 9–73. As it was the Hawks still managed to be significantly worse than a first-year expansion team in their own division.

The Hawks kicked things off with a 30-point loss in their first game followed by four double-digit defeats. In fact, they failed to win consecutive games the entire season. Most teams that suffer through such a terrible year do so because of injuries and/or misfortune, but in the Hawks' case the damage was entirely self-inflicted: This team was just plain bad.

In fact, only a slew of injuries to the Hornets prevented the Hawks from achieving a unique double: They were very nearly the worst offensive team *and* the worst defensive team. But because of New Orleans' misfortune, Atlanta ranked 29th in Offensive Efficiency, making offense the Hawks' "good" part.

Atlanta's primary hope for optimism last season wasn't on the court, but rather all the room the team had to spend on free agents in the offseason. Perhaps that's why Atlantans thought that the Hawks' best player last season was named "Cap Space"—as in, "Hey, we're the worst team in the league, but at least we've got Cap Space." Unfortunately, the Hawks have had trouble getting good players to take their money, so the benefit of the cap space has been wasted for two straight summers.

At least Atlanta has procured some young talent. High-flying Josh Smith was only the 17th pick in the 2004 draft, but he had the fourth-best PER among rookies despite turning pro straight out of high school. A stealth secret among the

Hawks at a Glance

Record: 13–69, 5th place in Southeast Division
Offensive Efficiency: 97.9 (29th)
Defensive Efficiency: 108.4 (30th)
Pace Factor: 93.6 (13th)
Top-Rated Player: Josh Smith (PER 15.43, 116th overall)
Head Coach: Mike Woodson. Didn't have much to work with but needs to improve the defense.

small band of Hawks fans, Smith hit the spotlight when he won the dunk contest at midseason. He still has a poor jump shot and several other weaknesses, but his ridiculous leaping ability and shot-blocking mark him as a rising star.

Atlanta's other first-rounder was Josh Childress, and he wasn't too shabby either. He's joined by this year's second overall pick, Marvin Williams, who gives the Hawks some real depth at the forward positions. The same age as Smith, Williams may need some time to live up to his billing as the No. 2 pick, but he gives the Hawks an enviable forward combo to build around.

Atlanta also made a series of trades that resulted in owning a future first-round pick from the Lakers. The Hawks sent Jason Terry and Alan Henderson to Dallas for Antoine Walker before the 2004–05 season started, and then funneled Walker to Boston at midseason in return for two ending contracts (Tom Gugliotta and Michael Stewart) and the draft choice. Additionally, the Hawks own the rights to Australian seven-footer David Andersen, who had a big year in Moscow and could join the club in 2006.

For now, however, the Hawks must deal with a major logjam at forward and a complete lack of talent at the other three spots. In addition to Smith, Williams, and Childress, the Hawks have holdover Al Harrington and 2004 second-round pick Donta Smith. The backup forced Childress to play the entire year at shooting guard and he may have to do so again, even though he's a poor outside shooter and is much more comfortable at small forward.

Playing Childress in the backcourt, along with Smith at small forward instead of at his natural power forward spot, did produce one positive. The Hawks couldn't shoot and they couldn't defend, but they could rebound a little. Atlanta rebounded 50.4 percent of missed shots overall, which was about the only category in which the Hawks scored above the league average. This is fairly amazing considering they were playing Jason Collier and Peja Drobnjak at center, and it's entirely the result of the forward contingent's work on the glass. Atlanta was above average in both offensive and defensive rebounding too.

It was all for naught, of course, since this team was unrelentingly awful in almost every other respect. Kenny Anderson and Jason Collier were the opening-day starters, for crying out loud. The point guard problem was at least half-solved with the trade for Tyronn Lue, but center continued to maim the team all season. Drobnjak was easily the team's best big man, which is depressing enough, but for some reason he only played 20 minutes a game.

Overseeing the mess is general manager Billy Knight and coach Mike Woodson. In their defense, most of the groundwork was laid long before they arrived by predecessor Pete Babcock, who put together one of the most disastrous five-year runs of drafts and trades in NBA history from 1998 to 2003. As a result, the Hawks were both well over the cap and well under .500 when Knight arrived, so he decided to bust out the dynamite and start over.

In his tenure, Knight has at least managed a couple of small steps in the right direction. Last season's draft produced two quality players in Childress and Smith, while Williams figures to be another. However, beyond those three and Harrington, the cupboard is completely bare. Tony Delk is the only other 2004–05 Hawk under contract for this season who even makes a passable backup.

Fortunately, the Hawks fared a bit better in free agency than their colossal whiff in 2004. Not that they were completely on the ball. The team's strategy in the first days of free agency was shocking. Instead of focusing on the Stromile Swifts and Samuel Dalemberts of the world—up-and-coming players the team could build around—the Hawks courted Ray Allen and Zydrunas Ilgauskas.

Granted, it's nice to swing for the fences, but consider the logic here. First, what are the odds that a player approaching his 30s would sign with a lousy team? If anybody offered even remotely the same amount of money, the Hawks were going to lose. Second, what difference would it have made? So the Hawks get Ray Allen . . . by the time the rest of the team is competitive, chances are Allen will already have gone downhill. Moreover, the Hawks missed a chance to sneak in on the competition and grab a younger, less heralded player who really might have taken the money.

The Hawks at least recovered in time to make a maximum offer to Suns' guard Joe Johnson, but this takes the concept of overpaying to get a free agent to some serious extremes. While Johnson is a fine player, almost nobody really thinks he's worth this kind of money. Additionally, the Hawks couldn't consummate the deal until they threw in some incentives for Phoenix not to match the offer—two first-round picks and guard Boris Diaw. Essentially, Atlanta had to bribe Phoenix for the right to pay Johnson double what he's worth.

Johnson's addition worsens another problem—seemingly every decent player on the team is a 6'8" shooting guard/small forward, while point guards and centers are scarce. Those two positions killed the Hawks last season and figure to do so again unless management can come up with some solutions before opening day. Thus far Knight has been obsessed with wiry, long-armed guys and blind to everyone else. At least he managed to procure Bucks big man Zaza Pachulia, and unlike Johnson his was a very reasonable contract at four years, $16 million. Pachulia is young and skilled so he should be a major improvement on the Drobnjak/Ekezie/Collier crew.

Running things on the sidelines is Woodson, Knight's former teammate in Kansas City whom he appointed for 2004–05. Woodson put in some backdoor alleyoop plays to take advantage of the athleticism of the two Joshes, but otherwise he looked the part of a rookie coach. There seemed to be no rhyme or reason to his substitution pattern the entire season, and the team's defensive effort was uniformly poor. Atlanta had the worst field-goal percentage defense in the league (47.6 percent) and the worst three-point defense (37.9 percent). Overall they finished last in the NBA in Defensive Efficiency. This was a surprise considering Woodson came from Detroit and was heralded for his ability to improve the defense when Atlanta hired him. While it's tough to be too critical of his performance considering he had such a pittance of talent to guide, it was not an auspicious debut.

Of course, Woodson has time to figure things out because this isn't going to be a speedy turnaround. While the additions of Johnson and Pachulia will prevent the team from being a complete embarrassment, Atlanta needs to build a more impressive foundation before playoff contention becomes a realistic possibility. In the meantime, Atlanta's two teenage forwards should at least provide some entertainment—just not many wins.

Josh Childress			small forward							Age: 22		Height: 6-8		Weight: 210	
Defensive PER: -0.10 (59% SG, 37% SF, 3% PF, 1% PG)												Most similar at age: Sean Elliott			
Year	G	M/G	FG%	FT%	P/40	R/40	A/40	TS%		Ast		TO	Usg	Reb	PER
2004-05 Atl	80	29.7	.470	.823	13.6	8.1	2.5	54.3	22	12.1	50	10.6 37	15.6 55	11.3 1	15.20 16
2005-06 PRJ (36.6)			.469	.825	14.6	8.1	2.9	54.4		12.6		10.4	16.9	11.5	15.91

Splitting his year between playing for the Hawks and portraying LeBron's little friend Thirst in the Sprite commercials, Childress's rookie year was substantially better than most people realize. Critics panned him when he struggled early on and observers quickly forgot about the Hawks altogether, but Childress's final numbers were extremely solid for a rookie. His Rebound Rate led all shooting guards, and would have ranked highly even if he moved to his natural small forward position. At any position, his quick hops and long arms make him a serious threat on the offensive glass.

First he'll have to improve his jump shot though. Childress has a weird jump shot that he pushes from under his chin with his elbow flying out to the side, which sends the ball on a low trajectory. Basically, it's like Shawn Marion's but without the arc or accuracy, and makes it tough for him to play in the backcourt. However, he still managed to shoot a high percentage because he got so many dunks and lay-ups, and his free-throw percentage is outstanding. He likes to come off curls on the left side and go straight to the rim, which also gets him to the line a fair amount.

Childress came into the league with a rep as a good ballhandler, but he failed to live up to that in his rookie season. He wasn't terribly creative off the dribble and his Assist Ratio was surprisingly poor. Since the Hawks have so few players who can create their own shot, it would be hugely beneficial if he could improve that number this season. He also needs to get better at the defensive end. Childress's Defensive PER was among the worst in the league, and while some of that was a result of playing out of position, he has a ways to go in terms of effort and toughness as well.

Jason Collier			center							Age: 28		Height: 7-0		Weight: 260	
(98% C, 2% PF)												Most similar at age: Kevin Duckworth			
Year	G	M/G	FG%	FT%	P/40	R/40	A/40	TS%		Ast		TO	Usg	Reb	PER
2002-03 Hou	13	8.0	.472	1.000	13.8	11.2	0.4	48.8		2.5		5.0	15.2	16.1	15.07
2003-04 Atl	20	27.2	.479	.788	16.6	8.2	1.3	55.8	11	6.8	57	12.4 29	16.8 18	11.5 69	14.60 28
2004-05 Atl	70	13.5	.463	.676	17.1	7.8	0.8	49.4	53	3.6	60	12.9 32	18.9 10	10.9 62	10.88 49
2005-06 PRJ (57.4)			.460	.712	16.5	8.0	0.9	50.6		4.6		13.2	17.9	11.2	12.11

A year ago, Collier seemed like he might be carving out an NBA future for himself, but last season brought more questions than answers. Collier served as the starting center for most of the season but usually got a quick hook from Woodson due to his amazingly slow feet and inability to rebound. The Hawks used Collier in pick-and-pop plays much as they did with Peja Drobnjak, and Collier was actually the more accurate of the two.

The problem was everything else. Collier couldn't handle the ball at the top of the key, so if he wasn't open for the initial jump shot, the offense would grind to a halt. Defensively he was worse. Opponents murdered him on the boards and he wasn't able to use his size to keep opponents out of prime post position. In addition, he was too slow to be of much use in pick-and-roll defense, often leaving Tyronn Lue out to dry while he hung back in the lane.

If Collier can shoot like he did in 2003–04, the Hawks can live with those weaknesses and use him as their backup center. However, he is so weak in the other facets of the game that he needs to shoot in the high 40s to have much value.

Chris Crawford			power forward							Age: 30		Height: 6-9		Weight: 235	
Year	G	M/G	FG%	FT%	P/40	R/40	A/40	PSA		Ast		TO	Usg	Reb	PER
2002-03 Atl	5	7.6	.615	.875	25.3	7.4	1.1	1.45		5.1		10.2	19.2	10.5	28.98
2003-04 Atl	56	21.6	.448	.866	18.9	5.8	1.5	1.09	15	7.2	62	8.8 5	19.3 24	8.2 64	15.82 26
2004-05 Atl		Out for the season													

Crawford's interminable contract finally expired after the season, but unfortunately his contract year didn't go as planned. Crawford tore up his knee in a preseason game—the second time he's done it in three years—and faces an uncertain future heading into free agency. When he's on the court, Crawford is a strong outside shooter and a good leaper but overmatched physically at the power forward spot. Considering power forward may be the league's most overcrowded position at the moment, he'll have a tough time regaining an NBA spot.

Tony Delk   point guard
(62% PG, 38% SG)

Age: 31   Height: 6-2   Weight: 189
Most similar at age: Voshon Lenard

Year		G	M/G	FG%	FT%	P/40	R/40	A/40	TS%		Ast		TO		Usg		Reb		PER	
2002-03	Phx-Bos	67	28.0	.416	.782	14.0	5.0	3.1	54.7	13	18.0	59	8.5	9	16.6	58	7.0	13	13.70	30
2003-04	Dal	33	15.5	.380	.841	15.5	4.6	2.2	48.4	43	11.3	63	6.8	1	18.0	57	6.3	16	13.15	33
2004-05	Atl	56	23.9	.416	.757	19.9	3.9	3.1	51.2	36	12.9	67	6.7	2	23.0	27	5.4	36	15.07	30
2005-06	*PRJ (39.4)*			*.405*	*.764*	*16.7*	*4.2*	*3.0*	*51.0*		*14.5*		*7.6*		*19.9*		*5.8*		*13.67*	

Delk quietly had one of his best seasons while splitting time between the two guard spots, taking advantage of his skill at creating shots while avoiding turnovers. Delk hadn't seen much of the ball in his past two stops, as his Usage Rates were well below average, but in Atlanta he got plenty of chances to let his jumper rip. Surprisingly, he was able to do it while keeping his shooting percentage and Turnover Ratio steady, resulting in a surprising 19.9 points per 40 minutes.

On the downside, Delk has a number of deficiencies—he's basically a shooting guard in a point guard's body, and he doesn't defend either position very well. If he can keep creating shots and shooting a decent percentage, he's a perfect weapon as a third guard. It's just a shame to see such a productive season by a 30-something player wasted in basketball's Siberia. Delk is a free agent after the season, so look for him to swap uniforms at the trade deadline in February.

Boris Diaw   shooting guard
(65% SG, 20% PG, 14% SF, 1% PF)

Age: 23   Height: 6-8   Weight: 215
Most similar at age: John Salmons

Year		G	M/G	FG%	FT%	P/40	R/40	A/40	TS%		Ast		TO		Usg		Reb		PER	
2003-04	Atl	76	25.3	.447	.602	7.1	7.1	3.8	48.3	47	27.5	4	19.0	63	11.9	60	10.1	6	8.82	58
2004-05	Atl	66	18.2	.422	.740	10.5	5.7	5.0	47.9	53	23.6	3	15.4	65	16.8	48	7.9	17	9.97	50
2005-06	*PRJ (34.3)*			*.434*	*.676*	*9.0*	*6.4*	*4.2*	*48.3*		*24.6*		*16.3*		*14.3*		*9.0*		*10.46*	

Diaw gradually fell out of the rotation as the year wore on since it has become increasingly apparent that the Hawks' first-round pick in 2003 isn't going to pay much of a dividend. Diaw does two things well. First, he's a solid defender who has size and quickness and will work the defensive boards. Second, he can handle the ball and create plays off the dribble, resulting in extremely high Assist Ratios each of the past two seasons.

Unfortunately, those skills are being undermined by his inability to score. Diaw was almost comically unselfish as a rookie but found it in him to take a few more shots last season. However, his accuracy still needs a lot of work, and because he's so reluctant to pull the trigger, teams play for the pass and force him into frequent turnovers. If he can develop a steadier jump shot and overcome his reluctance to shoot he could still be a decent player, but I can say the same thing about dozens of other players. He was traded to Phoenix as part of the Johnson deal but will struggle to find minutes on a talented Suns team.

Predrag Drobnjak   center
(100% C)

Age: 30   Height: 6-11   Weight: 270
Most similar at age: Kevin Duckworth

Year		G	M/G	FG%	FT%	P/40	R/40	A/40	TS%		Ast		TO		Usg		Reb		PER	
2002-03	Sea	82	24.2	.412	.791	15.5	6.4	1.7	45.9	60	8.7	39	6.6	1	19.7	9	9.5	70	12.51	42
2003-04	LAC	61	15.6	.393	.849	16.1	8.3	1.6	45.8	66	7.7	49	9.5	9	19.6	10	12.2	62	12.62	44
2004-05	Atl	71	20.2	.438	.800	16.6	6.6	1.4	50.1	46	6.5	36	10.8	8	18.6	11	9.3	69	12.66	41
2005-06	*PRJ (40.9)*			*.420*	*.782*	*15.3*	*7.1*	*1.5*	*47.5*		*7.7*		*10.1*		*18.3*		*10.3*		*12.00*	

Well at least he's consistent. Drobnjak's PER has hardly wavered in his three pro seasons despite changing teams every season. In Atlanta Drobnjak continued to rely on the pick-and-pop game that has made him an effective offensive force in other stops. Because he shoots almost entirely jumpers, his Turnover Ratio is always very low, helping to make up for a poor shooting percentage. Plus, he annually has one of the highest Usage Rates at his position because opposing centers are reluctant to chase him around the perimeter.

All of that makes him a decent backup center, but his abominable rebounding and inability to block shots prevent him from getting serious consideration as a starter. The Hawks didn't pick up his option for this season because they wanted to maximize their cap space, so Drobnjak left the NBA and signed with Spanish power Tau Ceramica.

Obinna Ekezie   center   **Age: 30**   **Height: 6-9**   **Weight: 270**
(96% C, 4% PF)   Most similar at age: Jason Caffey

Year		G	M/G	FG%	FT%	P/40	R/40	A/40	TS%		Ast		TO		Usg		Reb		PER	
2004-05	Atl	42	17.4	.434	.774	12.6	9.8	0.6	51.6	38	2.9	66	16.1	56	13.5	39	13.7	42	10.34	54
2005-06	PRJ (38.5)			.427	.767	12.5	9.4	0.7	50.5		3.0		16.9		13.5		13.2		10.35	

Ekezie finally got a chance to play for the Hawks after his 2003–04 season was ruined by a preseason knee injury. He was forced into action at the center spot even though his natural position is power forward because Atlanta was running short on bodies, but he managed to do a decent job on the glass, especially offensively.

Ekezie's problems are in the ballhandling and shooting departments. A 43.4 field-goal percentage is poor for an NBA big man, especially one who is giving up inches at the other end of the court. Also, both his assist and turnover numbers were terrible. One would like to give Ekezie the benefit of the doubt since he was coming back from a knee injury, but he's also 30 so the clock is ticking. This upcoming season might be his last good chance to earn a role in the NBA.

Tom Gugliotta   power forward   **Age: 36**   **Height: 6-10**   **Weight: 250**
(74% PF, 26% C)   Most similar at age: Tyrone Hill

Year		G	M/G	FG%	FT%	P/40	R/40	A/40	TS%		Ast		TO		Usg		Reb		PER	
2002-03	Phx	27	16.6	.455	1.000	11.5	8.9	2.8	47.4		15.7		15.7		15.7		12.6		10.87	
2003-04	Phx-Uta	55	14.9	.345	.714	7.9	9.1	3.1	37.4	65	19.9	7	12.3	42	14.4	52	14.2	28	9.02	61
2004-05	Bos-Atl	47	20.6	.411	.767	9.9	7.9	2.8	46.0	68	13.4	10	14.8	61	14.2	54	11.1	57	9.81	62
2005-06	PRJ (21.5)			.384	.712	8.7	7.8	2.9	42.1		15.4		15.6		13.5		11.3		9.00	

The Hawks picked up Gugliotta in the midseason Antoine Walker trade, and Woodson immediately pressed him into service. While Googs doesn't have much left in the tank after a series of knee injuries, Woodson loved him because he was one of the few guys on the team who knew how to play. It was particularly evident at the defensive end, where Gugliotta usually was in the right spot to help teammates and was surprisingly deft at covering his own liabilities.

On the right team, those skills still might be valuable for short stretches, but playing so often for the Hawks exposed Gugliotta's rusting offensive game. His TS% the past three seasons has been horrendous because he can't get to the rim, so nearly all his shots are contested jumpers. Additionally, his Rebound Rate suffered last season and doesn't look to improve with age.

Al Harrington   small forward   **Age: 25**   **Height: 6-9**   **Weight: 250**
Defensive PER: 0.79 (61% SF, 39% PF)   Most similar at age: Juwan Howard

Year		G	M/G	FG%	FT%	P/40	R/40	A/40	TS%		Ast		TO		Usg		Reb		PER	
2002-03	Ind*	82	30.1	.434	.770	16.2	8.3	2.0	49.3	43	9.6	42	12.5	44	19.3	23	11.6	44	12.41	42
2003-04	Ind*	79	30.9	.463	.734	17.2	8.3	2.1	51.4	35	10.0	46	12.4	44	20.4	20	12.3	44	14.92	33
2004-05	Atl	66	38.6	.459	.672	18.2	7.2	3.3	50.8	45	13.4	20	13.1	52	22.1	13	10.1	15	14.32	28
2005-06	PRJ (100)			.454	.709	16.7	7.7	2.7	50.5		12.1		12.6		20.5		10.9		13.89	

* Season rankings are as power forward

As I mentioned in the section on similarity scores, Al Harrington was the most "common" player in this season's book. Over the past 20 years 75 different players had a Similarity Score of 98 or greater when compared with Harrington, the most of any pro player. This fact should permanently end the "Harrington as rising star" discussion. He is what he is: a generic NBA forward who is decent at everything but truly good at nothing. His per-40-minute stats have never hinted at the star potential that his "tools" supposedly indicated he had, and in truth his physical skills hardly seem phenomenal either.

Harrington certainly has some positives, however. He can punish small forwards in the low post from the left block and is an above-average defensive player at either spot. He also has range out to the three-point line and is capable of taking bigger players off the dribble when he plays the power forward spot. However, he lacks the go-to move of most top scorers and isn't athletic enough to leap over defenders in traffic to get himself easy shots. As a result, his PER hasn't climbed above the mid-teens.

(continued next page)

Al Harrington *(continued)*

Harrington is a free agent after the season and could be traded by Atlanta by the time this book is published. With Smith, Williams, and Childress making up the team's forward rotation for the foreseeable future, Harrington isn't filling a need anyway. The Hawks would be better off if they parlay him into a decent center or point guard.

Royal Ivey (66% PG, 33% SG, 1% SF)		point guard								Age: 24	Height: 6-3	Weight: 200 Most similar at age: LaBradford Smith						
Year		G	M/G	FG%	FT%	P/40	R/40	A/40	TS%		Ast		TO		Usg		Reb		PER
2004-05	Atl	62	13.0	.429	.701	10.9	4.2	5.1	48.4	54	24.3	50	14.9	66	17.2	63	5.8	29	8.75 66
2005-06	PRJ (31.0)			.414	.707	11.4	4.0	5.2	47.3		23.8		14.0		17.6		5.6		9.27

The Hawks' second-round pick in 2004, Ivey might have been the best defensive player on the team. Admittedly, that's not saying much, but he has good size for a point guard and does a great job of sliding his feet and taking charges.

All of that won't matter, however, unless he makes some tremendous strides at the offensive end. Ivey didn't play point guard in college and it showed—his Turnover Ratio was horrendous and his Assist Ratio wasn't much better. Ivey also doesn't have much of a burst off the dribble, making it difficult for him to drive by defenders. For the same reason, he had trouble getting open on inbounds passes. Even worse, he can't shoot, making 42.9 percent from the floor and hitting only three three-pointers all season. He won't stick in the NBA much longer with offensive numbers like those, regardless of how well he defends.

Tyronn Lue (100% PG)		point guard								Age: 28	Height: 6-0	Weight: 178 Most similar at age: Chucky Atkins						
Year		G	M/G	FG%	FT%	P/40	R/40	A/40	TS%		Ast		TO		Usg		Reb		PER
2002-03	Was	75	26.5	.433	.875	13.0	3.0	5.3	52.3	22	27.4	26	8.0	6	18.9	48	4.4	56	12.94 34
2003-04	Orl	76	30.7	.433	.771	13.7	3.2	5.4	51.8	18	26.1	42	10.2	21	19.2	46	4.5	55	12.60 40
2004-05	Hou-Atl	70	28.7	.451	.861	15.7	3.0	6.4	54.2	13	27.9	28	9.1	12	21.7	38	4.2	60	14.13 38
2005-06	PRJ (40.7)			.428	.834	13.4	3.1	6.1	51.0		29.1		9.1		19.8		4.3		12.21

The Hawks picked up Lue from Houston when they traded Jon Barry, and it worked out well for Atlanta. Lue filled a gaping hole at the point and had his best season as a pro, setting career bests in field-goal percentage, free-throw percentage, points, and assists. He did most of his damage on the screen-and-roll, especially going to his right. Lue turns the corner very well in that direction and often freed himself for jumpers or a drive-and-dish—although he could look for the dish more often.

Lue got a reputation for defense when he guarded Allen Iverson in the 2001 Finals, but that overstates his case considerably. He's a shaky perimeter defender and opponents can shoot over him with ease. In fact, on the rare occasions when the Hawks played a close game, Woodson would take Lue out in key defensive situations.

Despite those shortcomings, Lue has evolved into a decent point guard who doesn't turn the ball over and creates a healthy volume of shots. He's a free agent and is unlikely to return, but he will make a fine backup at the point wherever he ends up.

Donta Smith (64% SG, 27% SF, 9% PG)		shooting guard							Age: 22	Height: 6-7	Weight: 215 Most similar at age: N/A					
Year		G	M/G	FG%	FT%	P/40	R/40	A/40	TS%	Ast	TO	Usg	Reb	PER
2004-05	Atl	38	11.4	.389	.688	11.7	4.8	3.6	47.3	17.2	12.6	16.7	6.7	10.54

The Hawks' second-round pick saw relatively little action in his rookie season. When he played, he was vaguely reminiscent of DeShawn Stevenson—an above-average athlete with an NBA body but lacking a go-to skill and mysteriously ineffective on the glass. Smith also needs to refine his shooting considerably, as his 39 percent mark from the floor detracted from numbers that otherwise were passable.

Smith was forced to play off guard last season but probably would be better off at small forward. Unfortunately, Atlanta's crowded forward lineup and paucity of decent guards mean that most of Smith's chances for minutes will again come in the backcourt.

Josh Smith — small forward
Defensive PER: 1.08 (60% SF, 25% SG, 15% PF)

Age: 20 Height: 6-9 Weight: 225
Most similar at age: Darius Miles

Year		G	M/G	FG%	FT%	P/40	R/40	A/40	TS%		Ast		TO		Usg		Reb		PER	
2004-05	Atl	74	27.7	.455	.688	14.0	8.9	2.5	50.6	46	11.8	34	13.9	57	17.1	39	12.5	3	15.43	22
2005-06	PRJ (5.8)			.467	.746	14.7	9.0	3.2	52.9		14.5		14.5		18.1		12.5		17.06	

Perhaps the best leaper to enter the league since Jason Richardson, Smith burst on to the national scene in February when he won the Slam Dunk Contest with a series of high-flying maneuvers. He was a brilliant dunker in games as well, especially on alleyoops, and nearly half his field-goals on the season came on dunks.

However, he put his hops to use more at the defensive end. Smith averaged two blocks per game—an extraordinary total for a perimeter player—thanks to his jumping ability and exquisite timing. One effort in particular stood out—a 10-block effort against Dallas in which he thwarted three Dirk Nowitzki dunk attempts and didn't commit a single foul. Smith also keeps his blocked shots in play, which is rare for a young player. As one might expect from a great leaper, he is an outstanding rebounder who had the league's third-best Rebound Rate among small forwards.

Despite those strengths, Smith still has a long way to go in the other aspects of defense. He often lost his man away from the ball and relied too much on his shot-blocking to bail him out rather than moving his feet and beating his man to the spot. Plus, he rarely blocked his man out, which allowed opponents tons of offensive rebounds.

Offensively, Smith's main weapon right now is the dunk. He has no post game to speak of and is skinny enough that he may never be able to do much damage on the blocks. His mid-range jumper improved over the course of the season and served as his other source of points. He has a good release, if a bit low, and has a nice arc and rotation, so with time it should become more of a weapon. However, he has almost no game off the dribble. His moves are slow and mechanical and need much refinement if he's going to become an offensive force.

In terms of projecting his future, Smith's youth means that only five players were valid comps for him. While the example of the most similar player (Darius Miles) is discouraging, Tracy McGrady ranked very highly as well, and one can see similarities in their rookie performance. It's so rare for a player to play this well as a teenager that it's hard to know what Smith's ceiling is, but between the dunks and the blocks it's possible the Hawks have found their first marketable star since Dominique Wilkins.

Michael Stewart — center
(70% PF, 30% C)

Age: 30 Height: 6-10 Weight: 230
Most similar at age: N/A

Year		G	M/G	FG%	FT%	P/40	R/40	A/40	TS%	Ast	TO	Usg	Reb	PER
2002-03	Cle	47	5.3	.378	.667	5.7	8.8	1.0	42.6	10.3	17.2	8.0	12.3	5.85
2003-04	Cle-Bos	25	5.9	.417	.750	3.5	7.9	0.0	47.2	0.0	17.9	3.9	11.2	4.23
2004-05	Atl	12	12.1	.524	.429	6.9	11.0	1.4	51.9	6.6	17.1	8.5	15.4	10.52

A 12th man who almost certainly won't be back in the league next season, Stewart has managed to hang on several years past his shelf life. He actually started a game this past year, believe it or not. Late in the season the Hawks had some frontcourt injuries and started him against the Raptors. Toronto had some maladies of its own and had to play Pape Sow in the middle. Now there's a battle royale, huh? I suppose it's possible there has been a worse center match-up in the past 20 years than Stewart vs. Sow, but I can't imagine how.

James Thomas — power forward
(83% PF, 17% C)

Age: 25 Height: 6-8 Weight: 235
Most similar at age: N/A

Year		G	M/G	FG%	FT%	P/40	R/40	A/40	TS%	Ast	TO	Usg	Reb	PER
2004-05	Por-Atl	11	10.6	.600	.333	8.9	12.6	1.4	57.4	6.5	20.8	10.0	17.7	13.99

Thomas was a solid rebounder at Texas and proved to be one at the NBA level as well. He posted a stellar 17.7 Rebound Rate in his limited minutes and shot 60 percent thanks to the numerous easy putbacks he got for himself. Thomas's skills in other areas are very limited and his size makes him a liability at the defensive end, but if he keeps pulling down so many rebounds, he may be able to carve a niche for himself as a Reggie Evans type.

Kevin Willis				center						Age: 43		Height: 7-0	Weight: 245
(87% C, 13% PF)													Most similar at age: N/A

Year		G	M/G	FG%	FT%	P/40	R/40	A/40	TS%		Ast		TO		Usg		Reb		PER	
2002-03	SA	49	14.5	.479	.614	14.1	10.7	1.1	50.6	42	6.4	59	15.9	56	16.2	24	15.6	20	12.43	43
2003-04	SA	48	7.8	.467	.615	17.6	10.5	1.2	49.1		5.2		15.2		20.5		14.9		14.88	
2004-05	Atl	29	11.9	.389	.739	10.1	8.8	1.0	43.4		5.0		12.1		13.2		12.4		7.88	

Willis's endless career looks like it's finally winding down, but he could have another year or three left in him. After two very solid seasons in San Antonio, Willis's production declined considerably last season, with his numbers taking a swan dive in virtually every category. If he elects to play another season, one would expect him to vigorously shop his services to contenders before he settles on a return to the Hawks.

Marvin Williams	**small forward**	**Age: 19**	**Height: 6-9**	**Weight: 230**

Folks who only saw Williams in the NCAA final are probably wondering how he became the second overall pick, but the jittery hands he showed that night weren't a problem the rest of the year. Williams can step out and hit the three (43.2 percent at North Carolina) or bang inside for put-backs (he averaged nearly a rebound every three minutes). An added plus is that he shot 85 percent from the line. It still remains to be seen how he'll be used in his rookie season because he needs to fill out a bit before he can handle the rigors of power forward, but his collegiate numbers were outstanding for his age group and he should combine with Smith to form a devastating forward combo.

Salim Stoudamire	**shooting guard**	**Age: 23**	**Height: 6-1**	**Weight: 190**

I saw Stoudamire in person when he was still in high school, and even then he was as good a shooter as I've ever seen. Stoudamire shot 50 percent *on three-pointers* in his senior year at Arizona and 91 percent from the line. The two huge knocks against him are that he's a 6′1″ shooting guard, and his athleticism is subpar. With that sweet jumper he should be able to carve out a niche, but it's unclear whether his future is at the point or at shooting guard. At either position, however, he should have plenty of opportunity in Atlanta this season.

Cenk Akyol	**point guard**	**Age: 18**	**Height: 6-4**	**Weight: 195**

The later of Atlanta's two second-round picks, Akyol barely played for Turkish club Efes Pilsen this year and nobody knows why he kept his name in the draft. He's tall for a point guard and is regarded as a good passer, but he's not terribly athletic so he probably won't appear in the Peach State for several more years, if ever.

Boston Celtics

I'll say this for Danny Ainge: He's not afraid to upset the apple cart. When Ainge took over as Celtics team president in 2003, the Celtics were less than two years removed from a trip to the Eastern Conference finals and still viewed themselves as a contender. Ainge looked at his roster and knew better though. The Celtics were staying above .500 thanks to the smarts and intensity of their veterans, but they were an old, capped-out team that was going to decline steadily unless drastic changes were made.

NBA front office people usually handle these types of situations by riding the team into the ground before finally giving up and rebuilding. Ainge could have done the same by importing a few more veterans with unfriendly contracts, trading draft picks, and keeping the Celtics around the 40-win mark for another year or two. But that would have made the fall much steeper and the rebuilding task much longer.

Consequently, he started wheeling and dealing. Antoine Walker went to Dallas for Raef LaFrentz and Jiri Welsch. Tony Battie and Eric Williams went to Cleveland for Ricky Davis and Chris Mihm. Mike James went to Detroit for a first-round pick. Mihm went to the Lakers for Gary Payton. Walker later ended up back in Boston via a trade with Atlanta.

With every deal, Ainge was making the team younger, improving the cap situation, and accumulating draft picks. The picks have paid off too, as the early returns on his drafts are outstanding. Ainge's crop in 2004 included three first-rounders—Tony Allen, Delonte West, and Al Jefferson—all of who contributed immediately. His two picks from 2003, Marcus Banks and Kendrick Perkins, haven't developed quite as quickly, but as a group the five players provided the Celtics with one of the league's best second units, not to mention a young, inexpensive nucleus to rebuild around. None of them were top-10 picks either, showing Ainge's scouting acumen. His first-round 2005 pick, high school phenom Gerald Green, also looks like a steal.

The combination of youth and depth produced one of the league's more interesting stats: The Celtics were much better on the second night of back-to-backs than they were on the first. Boston was only 6–14 on the first night, but the

Celtics at a Glance

Record: 45–37, 1st place in Atlantic Division
Offensive Efficiency: 104.8 (9th)
Defensive Efficiency: 103.3 (13th)
Pace Factor: 95.5 (6th)
Top-Rated Player: Paul Pierce (PER 21.82, 20th overall)
Head Coach: Doc Rivers. A better motivator than a strategist.

young legs helped them go 12–8 in the second, which is when most teams hit the proverbial wall.

Another part of Ainge's vision was to create a fast-paced, offensive-minded team, and he's making progress in that department too. Boston played the NBA's sixth-fastest pace in 2004–05 and had the league's ninth-best offense. The Celtics were third in the NBA in field-goal percentage and fourth in free-throw attempts, with only a high turnover rate holding them back.

Much work is left to be done though. While Ainge's drafts have been brilliant, the free-agent market has proved trickier. Ainge gave center Mark Blount a six-year, $42 million deal in 2004, only to watch him slumber through 2004–05. Ainge followed it up this offseason with a highly questionable deal for Brian Scalabrine. The only free agent to pay dividends has been Payton, and he was a short-term rental who won't be back.

In fact, Blount's languor set the stage for the most interesting and misunderstood development of the season: the reacquisition of Walker. Walker's reputation as a star has remained surprisingly hardy in light of the overwhelming evidence that he's a pretty average player. Unfortunately, the Walker acquisition added fuel to the fire, because Boston went 18–7 in the 25 games after he was acquired. Many assumed this was because Walker's star power had energized the Celtics, but he only improved the Celtics in one way: by not being Mark Blount.

Adding Walker allowed the Celtics to move Blount to the bench, with Raef LaFrentz moving to center. As a secondary effect it allowed Blount to replace Kendrick Perkins as the backup center. If we do a before-and-after analysis of the Walker trade and make the assumption that the starter plays $3/4$ of the game and the backup plays $1/4$, we get the results shown in table 1.

All told, the Celtics gained about 2.5 points in PER at Blount's position. To measure the impact in wins and losses, I have a rule of thumb that for every 2,000 minutes a player plays, each additional point in PER is worth an additional win. Over a full season then, the 2.5 points in PER that Walker's addition provided were worth about five wins. Over

Table 1. Celtics Centers, Before and After Walker Trade

Before		After		Diff.	% of Game	Total Change
Player	PER	Player	PER			
Blount	12.52	Walker	15.41	2.89	75	2.17
Perkins	11.11	Blount	12.52	1.41	25	0.35
Total						2.52

Table 2. Celtics Before and After Antoine Walker

	W–L	Avg. Margin	Expected Win%
Before	27–28	+0.7	.522
After	18–9	+1.3	.543
Change			+.021

the fraction of the season that he was with the team, it was worth closer to two.

So how did a team that began the year 27–28 finish it 18–9? Well, much of it was pure luck. The Celtics outscored their opponents by only 35 points in those 27 games, which normally gives a team a record of 15–12 or 14–13, not 18–9. And while the Celtics were under .500 at the time of the trade, that was more due to bad luck than to poor skill. They had outscored their opponents by nearly a point a game, as table 2 shows.

If we look at victory margin instead of win-loss record, the Celtics barely changed after the Walker trade. Over the course of an 82-game season, the small difference in Expected Winning Percentage would add only two wins to the Celtics' total—even less than what would be expected from the "not being Blount" effect above.

In other words, the Celtics' brief "Walker rebirth" was a case of folks getting fooled by an odd statistical pattern in a small data sample. The Celtics weren't really playing much better. They just went from being comparatively unlucky in close games to relatively lucky, so an effect that was minor was made to seem enormous. Considering that information, Boston's first-round defeat to Indiana was much less surprising.

That also makes it less surprising that the Celtics didn't seem interested in keeping Walker after the season—he was essentially a low-cost, short-term rental much like Payton. Plus, Ainge more than recouped his initial investment. Walker's inflated reputation allowed Ainge to send him to Miami in a complicated, five-team sign-and-trade deal. The upshot was that it brought Boston some minor considerations (forward Qyntel Woods, center Curtis Borchardt, the rights to Spanish forward Albert Miralles, and two second-round picks) and a trade exception. The exception is the big prize, as it can be used any time in the next year to bring in another player more to Boston's liking.

That's a good thing because Ainge will need to keep dealing. While he's established a nice core group, the Celtics are over the cap and won't get under it until at least 2007, when the deals of Raef LaFrentz and Paul Pierce expire. The Scalabrine signing also left him little wiggle room to acquire a point guard to replace Payton, so the Celtics may open the season with Banks and West at the point.

Overall, it may be difficult for the Celtics to repeat as division champions, especially with New Jersey looking like a powerhouse once again. A better goal might be to return to the playoffs, as the inexperience in the backcourt and the softness along the front line could prevent Boston from climbing above .500. Plus, the Celtics were unusually fortunate in the injury department a year ago, with West being the only player to miss any significant time. While the bench is deep enough to soften the blow, it's unlikely the Celtics can be so remarkably healthy for a second straight season.

The iffy short-term outlook shouldn't dampen the enthusiasm for Ainge's project, however. He has built an impressive young core that figures to improve sharply in coming seasons, and Jefferson in particular looks to be an All-Star talent. While the win-loss column may not show it in 2005–06, Ainge's daring rebuilding plan is coming together one step at a time.

Tony Allen — shooting guard — Age: 23 Height: 6-4 Weight: 213
(92% SG, 4% PG, 4% SF) — Most similar at age: Mitchell Butler

Year		G	M/G	FG%	FT%	P/40	R/40	A/40	TS%		Ast		TO		Usg		Reb		PER	
2004-05	Bos	77	16.4	.475	.737	15.6	7.0	2.0	54.2	23	9.7	59	12.9	61	16.8	47	9.8	2	14.68	22
2005-06	PRJ (29.4)			.453	.753	15.3	6.6	2.2	52.4		10.4		12.8		17.0		9.4		14.54	

Athletically, Allen is the most exciting Celtic since Dee Brown. He has a particular penchant for flying in from the weak side and slamming home rebounds, allowing him to post the second-best Rebound Rate among off guards despite standing just 6′ 4″.

Allen's athleticism should allow him to become a suffocating defender. He's pretty good already, as he combines his quickness and leaping with a stopper's mentality. He also has fast hands, averaging a steal every 16.6 minutes—a rate that would put him in the league leaders if he played 35–40 minutes a night. The defensive skill helped earn him a spot in the starting lineup in the second half of the season, although he fell out of favor in the playoffs.

The Celtics knew Allen could defend when they drafted him, but his offense was a pleasant surprise. Allen is great in transition, which he didn't get to show much in college, and playing on a fast-paced team like this one helped him to many easy baskets. His offense is very rough around the edges though. Allen is a mediocre jump shooter and has absolutely no in-between game. His forays to the basket produced far too many turnovers, and he doesn't see the court well.

The Celtics will live with those shortcomings if Allen lives up to his defensive potential. On a team with few defensive stoppers, Allen could become a very important piece of the rebuilt Celtics.

Marcus Banks (100% PG)				point guard							Age: 24		Height: 6-2	Weight: 200 Most similar at age: Randy Brown		
Year		G	M/G	FG%	FT%	P/40	R/40	A/40	TS%		Ast		TO	Usg	Reb	PER
2003-04	Bos	81	17.1	.400	.756	13.9	3.8	5.1	48.0	45	21.9 55		15.6 60	20.0 42	5.4 33	10.99 55
2004-05	Bos	81	14.1	.402	.742	13.0	4.4	5.4	52.0	31	25.8 41		13.4 56	18.4 59	6.2 20	12.27 48
2005-06	PRJ (32.7)			.401	.745	13.7	4.0	5.4	50.2		24.2		13.5	19.6	5.5	12.36

Banks and Allen were the Celtics' two best defenders last season. Banks is amazing at pressuring the ball upcourt. He has quick feet and good hands and often forces turnovers in the opposing backcourt.

However, Banks's offensive development is stuck in neutral, and that's why he hasn't been able to crack the starting lineup. He has good quickness and is strong around the basket, but his penchant for turnovers often put him Doc Rivers's doghouse. Banks has to make better decisions when he takes the ball into the paint, and it would help if he looked to pass more when he drove.

Unlike Allen, Banks can't subsist solely on his defense because offense is too central to his role as a point guard. The point guard job looks wide open with Payton's apparent departure, but Banks won't be able to seize it unless he cuts down the turnovers. He also may not be able to stay on the court long enough to keep it—Banks led all point guards in personal fouls per minute and will need to cut his rate considerably.

Mark Blount Defensive PER: 0.76 (100% C)				center							Age: 30		Height: 7-0	Weight: 250 Most similar at age: Melvin Turpin		
Year		G	M/G	FG%	FT%	P/40	R/40	A/40	TS%		Ast		TO	Usg	Reb	PER
2002-03	Den-Bos	81	17.3	.432	.727	11.4	8.8	1.6	49.1	51	9.9 30		18.2 67	14.2 42	12.5 52	10.67 56
2003-04	Bos	82	29.3	.566	.719	14.0	9.8	1.2	60.1	2	8.1 46		16.2 65	13.3 46	13.9 41	16.00 18
2004-05	Bos	82	26.0	.529	.713	14.5	7.5	2.4	55.9	19	11.5 8		16.2 57	16.0 27	10.4 65	12.52 42
2005-06	PRJ (29.8)			.507	.708	12.8	8.2	1.7	53.9		9.0		16.7	13.8	11.5	12.44

Which year is not like the others? Blount had a career year just in time for his contract to expire in 2003–04, and unfortunately the Celtics decided to pay for it. As the Fluke Rule predicted (see Brevin Knight comment in the Charlotte chapter), Blount came crashing back to earth in 2004–05 and now the Celtics are feeling they wasted their money.

The most disturbing aspect of Blount's season was the degree to which his energy level diminished. Blount looked especially sluggish at the defensive end, and his "effort" stats confirm that impression. His Rebound Rate suddenly declined to one of the worst at his position, while his rate of blocked shots fell by a third. Blount's Defensive PER remained respectable, but it was a much less impressive performance than he submitted a year earlier.

Blount's 56.6 field-goal percentage in 2003–04 was an obvious fluke, but the decline in 2004–05 wasn't as severe as one might have expected. Blount has developed a reliable jump shot from the key that he used for most of his scoring, and he's also become an adept passer from the high post. Because of those skills, he'll have some value to the Celtics as a backup center, but it's doubtful he'll regain a spot in the starting lineup.

Ricky Davis — shooting guard

Ricky Davis   shooting guard   **Age: 26**   **Height: 6-7**   **Weight: 195**
Defensive PER: 0.63 (60% SG, 35% SF, 5% PF)   Most similar at age: Jalen Rose

Year		G	M/G	FG%	FT%	P/40	R/40	A/40	TS%		Ast		TO		Usg		Reb		PER	
2002-03	Cle	79	39.6	.410	.748	20.8	5.0	5.6	48.5	43	18.3	19	11.6	41	27.2	6	7.0	28	16.06	16
2003-04	Cle-Bos	79	31.3	.469	.718	18.4	5.8	4.2	53.3	17	17.1	27	12.4	52	21.9	22	8.2	14	16.08	15
2004-05	Bos	82	32.9	.462	.815	19.4	3.7	3.6	54.7	20	14.9	31	12.5	56	21.9	17	5.2	59	14.97	20
2005-06	PRJ (84.0)			.449	.773	18.5	4.7	4.2	52.9		16.9		12.2		22.4		6.5		15.02	

Davis was a contender for the Sixth Man Award, but it was more a question of quantity than quality. Several other contenders for the award had better PERs and were more defensively active. But Davis averaged nearly 33 minutes per game, an enormous total for a reserve. That helped him earn the best scoring average among bench players, duping several voters into selecting him.

Davis certainly is a capable scorer, averaging in the high teens per 40 minutes and doing it with solid shooting percentages. While he isn't much of a three-point shooter (34.9 percent for his career), he's very good from the middle distances and has a great first step that he uses to get to the basket. He's also an outstanding finisher in transition. His greatest weakness offensively is a propensity for turnovers. Davis isn't a great ballhandler and often loses the ball en route to the basket. Even worse, his turnover rate has only gone up the past few seasons.

Defensively, Davis is quick and very good when motivated, but that spirit isn't there every night. That makes it tougher to pair him with Pierce, because one of them has to be the stopper on the wings and neither seems terribly interested in the job. With Tony Allen emerging, Davis may have a hard time playing so many minutes again unless his defensive effort becomes more consistent.

Al Jefferson   power forward   **Age: 20**   **Height: 6-10**   **Weight: 265**
(60% PF, 40% C)   Most similar at age: Shawn Kemp

Year		G	M/G	FG%	FT%	P/40	R/40	A/40	TS%		Ast		TO		Usg		Reb		PER	
2004-05	Bos	71	14.8	.528	.630	18.1	11.9	0.9	55.4	20	4.4	68	12.7	51	17.6	33	16.6	12	16.59	24
2005-06	PRJ (7.8)			.508	.662	18.8	11.5	1.3	54.5		5.8		12.4		18.9		16.6		16.58	

Other than Dwight Howard, if I had one player to choose from the 2004 draft it would be Jefferson. The 15th overall pick, Jefferson made it obvious in his first season that the Celtics got a steal. Despite coming to the NBA straight from a small high school in Mississippi, Jefferson was a dominant inside force. He has a great post game and already is strong enough to establish deep position. Jefferson loves to work from the left block and turn toward the baseline for his shot, where he shot a sizzling 52.8 percent as a rookie. He also has good hands and catches everything that comes his way.

Jefferson's biggest weakness right now is defense. Although his size should allow him to become a good post defender in time, he's still figuring things out. Help defense particularly befuddled him, as he was slow on defensive rotations and wasn't always in the right place. On a positive note, his Rebound Rate was outstanding, and he blocked a shot every 19 minutes.

Jefferson also has some areas to work on offensively. He was a terrible passer and needs to figure out how to pass out of double teams, since he should plan on seeing plenty of them in coming seasons. He'll also need to improve at the line, because overwhelmed defenders will frequently hack him around the basket.

Those weaknesses don't alter the big picture: Jefferson looks like he'll be a top-notch post player for years to come. He should move into the starting lineup this season now that Walker's gone. If it happens, Jefferson's 40-minute averages indicate that he'll be the Celtics' second-leading scorer after Pierce.

Raef LaFrentz   power forward   **Age: 29**   **Height: 6-11**   **Weight: 245**
Defensive PER: 0.12 (60% PF, 40% C)   Most similar at age: Rasheed Wallace

Year		G	M/G	FG%	FT%	P/40	R/40	A/40	TS%		Ast		TO		Usg		Reb		PER	
2002-03	Dal*	69	23.3	.518	.682	15.9	8.2	1.3	57.8	8	8.3	43	7.0	2	15.2	37	11.3	65	16.53	13
2003-04	Bos	17	19.3	.460	.769	16.1	9.6	2.9	50.9		14.6		6.7		18.6		13.6		16.78	
2004-05	Bos	80	27.4	.496	.811	16.1	10.1	1.8	58.7	6	8.5	39	7.6	7	15.6	47	14.1	25	17.34	16
2005-06	PRJ (24.9)			.485	.801	14.9	9.4	1.6	57.3		8.5		7.9		14.6		12.9		15.64	

* Season rankings are as center

LaFrentz quietly put together a very solid season for Boston, shooting nearly 50 percent from the floor, stretching defenses with the occasional three-pointer, and rarely committing turnovers. Despite his size LaFrentz is a deadly jump shooter, but he's also athletic enough to finish shots around the basket. The one quibble for Boston fans is that he should take a more active role—a player this skilled shouldn't be averaging just eight field-goal attempts per game.

Defensively, LaFrentz has added more muscle in recent years and his Rebound Rate has improved substantially in his time in Boston. However, the rest of his defensive game needs work. LaFrentz's Defensive PER was among the worst at his position, mainly because he shies away from physical play, and yet he has a knack for picking up touch fouls. His shot-blocking rate was outstanding when he was younger, but that also has fallen off—perhaps as a result of the knee problems that knocked him out for most of 2003–04.

One other thing that hurts LaFrentz's Defensive PER is playing the center spot, where he's a bit undersized and his lack of brawn becomes more glaring. He split his time between center and power forward a year ago and looks like he'll be doing so again. LaFrentz probably will man the middle when paired with Jefferson, but then return to power forward when Blount comes in off the bench. It's not ideal, but LaFrentz has never played for a team with enough size to allow him to play his natural position full-time.

Gary Payton					point guard										Age: 37		Height: 6-4	Weight: 180	
Defensive PER: 0.35 (99% PG, 1% SG)																Most similar at age: Rod Strickland			
Year		G	M/G	FG%	FT%	P/40	R/40	A/40	TS%		Ast		TO		Usg		Reb		PER	
2002-03	Sea-Mil	80	40.1	.454	.710	20.4	4.2	8.3	50.4	33	26.8	28	7.6	2	30.0	2	6.1	22	21.16	4
2003-04	LAL	82	34.5	.471	.714	17.0	4.8	6.4	52.8	12	25.9	44	8.7	6	22.6	24	6.9	9	17.29	13
2004-05	Bos	77	33.0	.468	.761	13.7	3.7	7.4	53.7	16	32.8	12	10.3	27	20.5	46	5.2	42	15.18	28
2005-06	PRJ (13.6)			.453	.725	14.8	4.1	6.6	51.1		27.9		10.0		21.6		5.8		15.92	

Despite his advanced age, Payton was a good fit in Boston because he likes to push the ball upcourt. He showed he still had some gas in the tank too, shooting 46.8 percent on his usual variety of short runners and the occasional jumper. Payton also was a very effective distributor, improving his Assist Ratio sharply from his previous two campaigns.

Payton's main problem is that he can't stay in front of people anymore. Fast point guards zoom past him like he's a billboard on the highway to the basket, putting lots of pressure on the Celtics' interior defense. Boston sometimes had Ricky Davis or Tony Allen defend the point guard and put Payton on the opponents' shooting guard, which is a better match-up for him. Payton is extremely effective at guarding bigger players, as he's surprisingly strong and his loss of quickness isn't as easily exposed.

Payton is a free agent and doesn't seem to figure in the Celtics' plans. He is hoping to sign on with a contending team as the starting point guard, but his defense has slipped to the point that a contender probably wouldn't want him in that role. He can be extremely useful off the bench, however, if he's willing to accept that situation.

Kendrick Perkins					center										Age: 20		Height: 6-10	Weight: 280	
(77% C, 23% PF)																Most similar at age: Shawn Kemp			
Year		G	M/G	FG%	FT%	P/40	R/40	A/40	TS%		Ast		TO		Usg		Reb		PER	
2003-04	Bos	10	3.5	.533	.667	25.1	16.0	3.4	58.0		11.1		18.5		26.1		22.6		22.69	
2004-05	Bos	60	9.1	.471	.638	10.9	12.8	1.5	51.5	39	7.3	28	20.6	69	12.8	46	18.0	11	11.11	47
2005-06	PRJ (1.9)			.458	.642	11.3	12.6	2.5	51.1		11.6		17.7		13.5		18.7		11.52	

Two years ago Perkins played very well in limited minutes, which had me wondering why he wasn't being used more. Last year I stopped wondering. Perkins has the basic elements of a promising player—his shooting percentage is decent and he rebounds very well—but he falls short in every other area.

Offensively, Perkins made a turnover for every five possessions he used, a horrendous ratio that more than offset his shooting percentage. Defensively, he accumulated touch fouls by the bushel, getting whistled more than once every six minutes. Occasionally he decided to get his money's worth, though, and that got him ejected twice. He's also quite slow and that makes him vulnerable to screen-and-roll plays.

Perkins' potential is real. He is only 20 years old and has a nice feel for scoring around the basket. Plus, his size makes him a load to deal with on the glass. But until he can iron out the numerous wrinkles in his game, he won't be able to make a push for more minutes. He may even see less action than he did a year ago, as Scalabrine and Blount figure to get most of the frontcourt minutes off the bench for Boston.

Paul Pierce   **small forward**   **Age: 28**   **Height: 6-6**   **Weight: 230**
Defensive PER: 0.77 (91% SF, 7% PF, 1% SG, 1% C)   Most similar at age: Clyde Drexler

Year		G	M/G	FG%	FT%	P/40	R/40	A/40	TS%		Ast		TO		Usg		Reb		PER	
2002-03	Bos*	79	39.2	.416	.802	26.5	7.5	4.5	53.2	20	13.6	41	11.2	37	31.0	3	10.6	4	22.60	2
2003-04	Bos	80	38.7	.402	.819	23.7	6.7	5.3	51.7	28	16.5	16	12.2	44	28.5	3	9.5	18	19.31	7
2004-05	Bos	82	36.1	.455	.822	23.9	7.3	4.7	58.3	4	16.6	6	11.0	39	25.6	6	10.2	12	21.82	4
2005-06	PRJ (29.2)			.431	.821	23.5	7.0	4.9	55.8		16.7		11.4		26.8		9.8		20.44	

* Season rankings are as shooting guard

Pierce played far better last season than he had in his disappointing 2003–04 season, and the key was his shooting. Pierce posted career highs in field-goal and free-throw percentages, averaging more points per 40 minutes despite taking fewer shots. He also shot 37 percent on three-pointers after being mired at 30 percent for two straight seasons, largely because he stopped forcing so many off the dribble.

Pierce is one of the premier foul-drawers in the NBA and kept it up last season, earning over eight free-throws a game from his spinning forays to the basket. He is very strong for a perimeter player and protects the ball well. Plus, he's a master at creating contact while going up for the shot. Combining the free throws with his improved shooting, Pierce's TS% ranked fourth among small forwards, which is an impressive accomplishment considering how often Pierce shot the ball.

In addition, he continues to be among the best at his position in both passing and rebounding, enabling him to fill the stat sheet. His defense is solid too. While Pierce has too much offensive responsibility to play the role of a stopper, his Defensive PER was solid and his anticipation netted him 1.6 steals per game.

Despite his accomplishments, the Celtics were pondering trading Pierce in the offseason. While he's unselfish and plays hard, he's become increasingly grumpy over the past few seasons and might benefit from a change of scenery. His gaffe at the end of Game 6 against Indiana, when he nearly cost the Celtics the game by committing a technical foul after the Pacers intentionally fouled him, also lost him some fans in the organization.

The Celtics need to be careful though. They can't let Pierce's gloominess blind them to the fact that he's the only reason they won the division last year, and that they won't be going back to the playoffs unless they can get a star of equal caliber in return. Considering the low likelihood of doing so, they're probably best off living with his foibles.

Justin Reed   **small forward**   **Age: 23**   **Height: 6-8**   **Weight: 240**
(61% SF, 25% PF, 14% C)   Most similar at age: N/A

Year		G	M/G	FG%	FT%	P/40	R/40	A/40	TS%	Ast	TO	Usg	Reb	PER
2004-05	Bos	23	5.3	.517	.733	13.6	5.3	3.3	57.6	15.7	9.9	15.2	7.4	13.73

The Celtics' second-round pick in 2004 saw limited action, as he was completely overshadowed by Boston's three first-round picks. However, he played fairly well in his rare opportunities and appears to be an NBA-quality defensive player. If Reed can keep shooting over 50 percent he may able to carve out a niche, but Boston's depth makes it tough to prove himself.

Antoine Walker   **power forward**   **Age: 29**   **Height: 6-9**   **Weight: 245**
(95% PF, 3% C, 2% SF)   Most similar at age: Jamal Mashburn

Year		G	M/G	FG%	FT%	P/40	R/40	A/40	TS%		Ast		TO		Usg		Reb		PER	
2002-03	Bos	78	41.5	.388	.615	19.4	7.0	4.6	46.7	53	16.1	12	11.2	34	26.8	3	9.9	57	14.50	31
2003-04	Dal	82	34.6	.428	.554	16.2	9.6	5.2	47.5	54	20.7	6	11.3	29	22.4	9	13.3	38	15.75	27
2004-05	Atl-Bos	77	38.4	.422	.539	19.9	9.4	3.6	47.8	61	12.9	14	12.3	44	25.3	6	13.2	36	15.41	32
2005-06	PRJ (35.3)			.414	.560	17.4	8.7	4.0	47.5		15.9		11.4		23.2		12.0		14.44	

Walker is one of the game's most overrated players and the key to understanding why is his TS%. Walker's overall TS% was awful, partly because of a low field-goal percentage but also because he's become a terrible foul shooter. Walker hit just 53.9 percent last season, and some have speculated that his hot-potato shooting motion was a response to his fear of getting fouled.

From the field, Walker appears to have two different shot releases. Sometimes he catches the ball and flips up almost immediately like the ball is on fire, especially when he drives to the basket. These shots usually miss and account for his poor field-goal percentage. On the other hand, he's a lot more successful when he slows things down and actually shoots the ball instead of throwing it.

Walker's low TS% is the prime proof he isn't nearly the player that some people imagine. He's been considered a star during his entire career, but his numbers the past few seasons are pretty ordinary and even in his prime he was never an All-Star caliber player (despite being named to the team three times).

That's not to say Walker doesn't have some value. He's a decent defensive player despite being a bit short for a power forward, and he's an excellent passer. He also handles the ball very well and is particularly dangerous in the open court. Those skills should help him in Miami if he doesn't get too trigger-happy, because the Heat could use some more offensively skilled players to complement Shaq and Dwyane Wade.

Delonte West			shooting guard							Age: 22		Height: 6-4	Weight: 180			
(56% SG, 43% PG, 1% SF)												Most similar at age: Ray Allen				
Year		G	M/G	FG%	FT%	P/40	R/40	A/40	TS%		Ast		TO		Usg	Reb	PER
2004-05 Bos		39	13.0	.426	.704	13.8	5.1	4.2	52.4	33	19.9	13	9.8	26	17.5 43	7.2 23	12.27 39
2005-06 PRJ (24.7)				.422	.703	14.1	5.6	4.5	51.8		20.4		10.2		18.0	7.8	12.96

West showed some positive signs in his rookie season. He has good quickness, can hit the outside shot, doesn't turn the ball over, and can play either guard spot. He also proved surprisingly potent on the boards, especially at the offensive end.

The Celtics couldn't get a more complete picture though, because West had trouble staying healthy. He missed time with both a broken thumb and a broken finger, so he'll have to prove that he's durable enough to take the pounding over a full season. One thing that would help him would be to pump some iron. West has very little muscle, which impacts his durability and hurts him in strength match-ups against opposing shooting guards.

With the arrival of Gerald Green and the departure of Payton, West is likely to see much more action at the point this coming season and may even start. Boston would probably prefer to see him come off the bench because he needs more game experience before he's ready for such an important role. In any event, he's guaranteed to be part of the backcourt rotation and should be able to build on his promising rookie season.

Gerald Green	shooting guard	Age: 19	Height: 6-7	Weight: 200

Green is a bit older than most preps-to-pros types because he spent five years in high school, but he was regarded as the best prospect in the country in his graduating class. His shooting range, speed, and athleticism all seem to be star caliber, but somehow he fell to 17th in the draft to the Celtics. He still has plenty of youthful kinks to work out and may only see token minutes this season, but in time he could be a star.

Ryan Gomes	small forward	Age: 23	Height: 6-7	Weight: 245

Boston's second-round pick put up big numbers in college but has a difficult transition to make in the pros. Gomes played power forward at Providence but will have to play on the perimeter in the NBA because of his size. While he has the range on his shot to play there offensively, he probably lacks the foot speed to handle the switch on defense and may need to spend a year in the D-League making the adjustment.

Orien Greene	point guard	Age: 22	Height: 6-4	Weight: 208

One of the most obscure picks of the draft, Boston took the guard from Louisiana-Lafayette in the second round even though he shot 39 percent as a senior and had nearly as many turnovers as assists. Obviously, Danny Ainge saw something, but this one looks like a reach.

Charlotte Bobcats

And so it began.

Season 1 of the Charlotte Bobcats was your typical expansion affair, with a couple of high draft picks surrounding a motley crew of veterans and castoffs. As with most expansion teams they played hard and got a lot of help from supportive home crowds, which helped them avoid the cellar. In fact, the Bobcats were better than their record indicated. Charlotte won only 18 games but had 22 Expected Wins, which isn't bad considering some observers thought they would struggle to win half as many. Plus, five of their losses came on the game's final shot.

Of course, the Bobcats still have a ton of work to do. In the team's inaugural season, a few players revealed themselves to be building blocks for the future. Leading the way was Emeka Okafor, the second overall pick in the draft who mostly lived up to expectations and ended up winning the Rookie of the Year award. Okafor wasn't the defensive force that had been advertised, but his ability to score in the post provided one of the few reliable weapons in the Charlotte attack.

Actually, the Bobcats had quite an impressive frontcourt for an expansion team. Most first-year clubs are able to do OK in the backcourt but struggle to come up with competent big men. That wasn't the case in Charlotte because they drafted Okafor and stole Primoz Brezec in the expansion draft. Stuck on the bench in Indiana for three years, Brezec was a revelation in Charlotte, shooting 51 percent and averaging over 16 points per 40 minutes. Better yet, the 'Cats deftly signed Brezec to a bargain contract extension—$8 million over three years—before the season started. Between him and Okafor, the Bobcats' front line should be set for the next several years.

Charlotte also got a nice surprise at point guard, where free-agent afterthoughts Brevin Knight and Jason Hart provided a surprisingly potent combination. Knight led the league in Assist Ratio and Pure Point Ratio while his ability to create shots for others was of huge benefit on a team so lacking in offensive talent. Unfortunately, his was a Fluke Rule season that looks unrepeatable. Hart, meanwhile, has inked for two more seasons and was nearly as productive as Knight, but was inexplicably traded to Sacramento after the season for a second-round pick.

The point guard spot won't be bare, however, as the Bobcats used the 2005 draft to acquire point guard Raymond Fel-

ton. Cynics wonder if the draft wasn't as much about marketing as basketball—Felton and the Bobcat's other first-round pick, Sean May, both attended North Carolina—but Felton's skills suggest he could become a bigger, better-shooting version of Knight. As for May, he had one of the best rebound rates in college basketball and should provide a nice complement to Okafor and Brezec up front.

So some of the pieces already are in place. The Bobcats now have several holes to fill on the wings. Charlotte spent most of the season with a platoon of Keith Bogans and Kareem Rush at shooting guard, and the two were monstrously ineffective. To add insult to injury, Rush was a midyear acquisition whom the Bobcats foolishly traded two second-round picks to acquire, one of the few missteps in what has been a well-organized entry to the NBA. Late-season NBDL call-up Matt Carroll showed slightly more promise and could be a keeper, but his future holds more of an off-the-bench scoring role than a full-time starting one. Until the Bobcats get this glaring weakness filled, they'll have difficulty reaching respectability.

The small forward spot wasn't much better, although Gerald Wallace shows promise as a poor man's James Posey. Wallace can finish in transition and is an excellent defensive player, but his jumper was erratic and his inability to score contributed to Charlotte's offensive woes. Behind him was little of note, as Jason Kapono, Theron Smith, and Tamar Slay all proved to be expansion-caliber players.

Don't expect the Bobcats to address those weaknesses on the wings right away. Charlotte's salary cap increases incrementally until the summer of 2006, when the team has the full cap to spend. As a result, the Bobcats wisely have been watching their pennies in anticipation of playing the market next summer.

In fact, general manager and coach Bernie Bickerstaff made several positive moves in his first season. He was forward thinking enough to use his whole bench most of the season, reasoning that his job this season wasn't to win games but to figure out who among his 15 new players were the keepers.

Additionally, his expansion draft was much more productive than most recent ones. Brezec is a bona fide NBA

Bobcats at a Glance

Record: 18–64, 4th place in Southeast Division
Offensive Efficiency: 98.0 (28th)
Defensive Efficiency: 104.8 (21st)
Pace Factor: 94.7 (11th)
Top-Rated Player: Brevin Knight (PER 18.06, 51st overall)
Head Coach: Bernie Bickerstaff. Not much he could do with first-year expansion team.

center, although he might be better off as a reserve in the long term. Wallace, whom he plucked from the Kings, is another player who figures to be in a Charlotte uniform for a while. He's a restricted free agent this summer, but Charlotte is in a position to match any offer and few teams seem willing to break the bank for his services.

Bickerstaff also traded himself into position to land two others players. He made a draft-day trade with the Clippers to move from No. 4 to No. 2, allowing him to select Okafor. Later, he made another deal with the Clippers that essentially gave him reserve big man Melvin Ely for free. While Ely is no great shakes, he gives the Bobcats a competent fourth big man heading into their second season, which is a luxury few expansion teams have. Finally, he spent wisely in his first free agent market, paying just $1.6 million per season to get Hart and pulling Carroll from the D-League at midyear.

Overall, Bickerstaff could end up with four players from his first season who are long-term Bobcats: Carroll, Wallace, Okafor, and Brezec. Go back and look at some other expansion teams and you'll see the numbers are more like one or two. It didn't show up in the standings, but the Bobcats did an outstanding job of setting the table in their first season.

What may become a fly in the ointment, however, is Bickerstaff coaching the team while operating as the general manager. For the moment, this doesn't seem to be a problem, because he has to get familiar with all the new faces on his team and there is relatively little for the front office to do until they have their full complement of salary cap space. But it might be wise for Bickerstaff to consider handing over the reigns to a seasoned pro after the second or third season. The track record of coaches who take on both roles is extremely poor (although Gregg Popovich is a notable counter-example), so the Bobcats' ownership should encourage him to give way when the time is right.

One thing Charlotte's ownership also should be aware of is the potential for nepotism. Bickerstaff has kept his son J.B. on the coaching staff and some have speculated that he would like his offspring to take over as head coach when Bernie kicks himself upstairs. Considering the younger Bickerstaff's lack of qualifications—he's never been a head coach at any level—this would be a tremendous mistake, and the higher-ups should put their foot down before it comes to fruition.

But if the worst thing I can say about the Bobcats is speculating about their coach's future, then they're doing a heck of a job. With newcomers like Felton and May and perhaps an inexpensive free agent or two, the Bobcats should continue quietly building and end up somewhere in the mid-to-high 20s in wins this season. While the club is still at least a year away from serious playoff contention and is short on star talent, it's been fun to watch the Bobcats' plan take hold. Finally, the people of Charlotte have a basketball team worthy of its fans.

Cory Alexander (95% PG, 5% SG)					shooting guard						Age: 32		Height: 6-1	Weight: 190 Most similar at age: N/A
Year	G	M/G	FG%	FT%	P/40	R/40	A/40	TS%	Ast	TO	Usg	Reb	PER	
2004-05 Cha	16	12.6	.327	.750	9.8	5.8	7.4	45.1	33.6	17.2	19.1	8.1	8.71	

Surprise, surprise. Alexander hadn't been in the NBA in several years but made an out-of-the-blue cameo late in the season when Charlotte needed some guard help. He didn't perform well and is a long shot to return to the pros this year.

Malik Allen (84% PF, 16% C)					power forward							Age: 27		Height: 6-10	Weight: 250 Most similar at age: Peja Drobnjak
Year	G	M/G	FG%	FT%	P/40	R/40	A/40	TS%		Ast	TO	Usg	Reb	PER	
2002-03 Mia	80	29.0	.424	.802	13.2	7.3	0.9	45.5	60	5.3 58	12.5 43	16.8 35	10.6 53	9.89 58	
2003-04 Mia	45	13.7	.419	.758	12.4	7.7	1.0	44.9	60	6.3 65	10.6 18	15.8 44	10.9 54	10.49 57	
2004-05 Mia-Cha	36	14.4	.475	.929	15.0	7.6	1.4	51.2	42	6.6 54	8.0 9	16.4 43	10.7 61	14.23 40	
2005-06 PRJ (38.1)			.436	.840	13.1	7.8	1.1	47.5		6.0	10.7	15.9	10.9	11.48	

Allen went from the penthouse to the outhouse at midseason when he was traded from Miami for Steve Smith. Fortunately for him it won't be a long stay, as he's a free agent and the Bobcats already are stocked in the frontcourt.

Allen has good size for a power forward and can hit a mid-range jumper, qualities which should make him desirable to a team seeking inexpensive frontcourt help. Unfortunately, his lack of athleticism precludes him from taking on a larger role. Allen is annually among the worst rebounders at his position, doesn't block shots, and has no post game to speak of. He does avoid turnovers, however, because he rarely has to dribble—he just waits for a return pass on pick-and-pop plays.

Keith Bogans — shooting guard

Keith Bogans (89% SG, 7% PG, 4% PF) **shooting guard** **Age: 25** **Height: 6-5** **Weight: 215**
Most similar at age: Dion Glover

Year		G	M/G	FG%	FT%	P/40	R/40	A/40	TS%		Ast		TO		Usg		Reb		PER	
2003-04	Orl	73	24.5	.403	.631	11.2	7.1	2.2	49.9	35	14.6	42	11.2	37	13.8	58	10.2	5	10.96	46
2004-05	Cha	74	24.2	.381	.727	15.9	5.0	3.0	46.5	59	13.2	43	11.9	52	20.8	22	7.1	25	10.31	46
2005-06	PRJ (73.7)			.383	.676	13.7	6.0	2.8	47.0		14.2		11.6		17.6		8.4		10.73	

Bogans has managed to hang on to a starting job for the better part of two seasons, which is mystifying considering his pedestrian talent. Bogans's stats resemble those of a 12th man more than they do a starter. He was a subpar shooter in his rookie season in Orlando and when he tried to create more shots this past season, his percentages nosedived further.

Bogans is barely passable as a three-point shooter (34.4 percent career), but his real problems surface when he tries to go inside the line—he hit only 39.8 percent on 2-pointers. He loves to come off a curl on the left side and go to the rim with his right hand, but he has trouble finishing around the basket because he has short arms and isn't terribly athletic. He's also a poor ballhandler who has a high Turnover Ratio and doesn't set up teammates well. Plus, he needs to improve his foul shooting.

He does have some positive markers in his favor. He's an above-average rebounder, although his rate declined from the heights he hit in Orlando. He's also a competent defensive player whose strength and decent quickness make up for a lack of reach. As a free agent, his offensive shortcomings should prevent him from earning much above the minimum contract. In short, he belongs in the NBA, but only in a very limited role.

Primoz Brezec — center

Primoz Brezec Defensive PER: 0.23 (100% C) **center** **Age: 26** **Height: 7-1** **Weight: 255**
Most similar at age: Bryant Reeves

Year		G	M/G	FG%	FT%	P/40	R/40	A/40	TS%		Ast		TO		Usg		Reb		PER	
2002-03	Ind	21	5.2	.395	.600	15.3	8.4	1.5	44.9		6.9		12.1		19.2		11.7		10.89	
2003-04	Ind	18	4.0	.462	.667	15.6	8.3	1.7	48.9		8.0		15.9		19.3		11.7		9.64	
2004-05	Cha	72	31.6	.512	.745	16.5	9.3	1.5	55.0	24	7.2	31	10.1	6	16.8	18	13.0	50	16.17	19
2005-06	PRJ (34.5)			.501	.742	15.6	9.2	1.7	54.1		8.1		10.4		16.3		12.9		15.67	

After three years of sitting on the end of the Pacers' bench, Brezec appeared in Charlotte and immediately demonstrated why the Pacers had made him a first-round pick. Despite his size Brezec has range out to 17 feet, making him an outstanding high-low partner with Okafor in the frontcourt. Additionally, he's a good passer from the high post and protects the ball well—hence his low Turnover Ratio.

While Brezec also has some post moves, that's not his preferred operating area. However, at 7' 1", 255 he's capable of taking advantage of mismatches and punishing opponents who go to smaller lineups. He also uses head fakes well and is adept at getting to the foul line, where he shot 74.5 percent.

Brezec's two failings are defense and rebounding. He is neither quick nor a good leaper, and as a result blocked less than a shot per game despite his imposing size. His work on the boards was also disappointing, as his Rebound Rate was subpar for a center. Finally, he was easily exposed in pick-and-roll situations because he was too slow to provide adequate help to his guards.

Nevertheless, he was a heck of a find by Bickerstaff and should be a solid center for several more seasons. His three-year, $8 million extension signed before the 2004–05 season now looks like one of the best bargains in basketball.

Matt Carroll — shooting guard

Matt Carroll (75% SG, 24% SF, 1% PF) **shooting guard** **Age: 25** **Height: 6-6** **Weight: 220**
Most similar at age: N/A

Year		G	M/G	FG%	FT%	P/40	R/40	A/40	TS%	Ast	TO	Usg	Reb	PER
2003-04	NY-SA	16	4.3	.438	.667	11.0	3.5	1.2	51.0	7.5	22.5	13.6	4.9	3.73
2004-05	Cha	25	17.2	.389	.855	20.8	5.6	1.6	51.7	6.6	9.7	22.1	7.8	14.66

The NBDL MVP came up to Charlotte late in the season and immediately showed why he had played so well in the D-League. Carroll is a jump shooter, but one with a twist—he has a scorer's instincts and doesn't mind taking the ball to the basket. As a result, he gets far more free throws than do most shooting specialists. Carroll averaged .46 free throws per field-goal attempt, an outstanding ratio for a perimeter player, and nailed 85.5 percent of his tries.

Defensively, Carroll has good anticipation and is tall enough for the job, but he seemed overmatched physically against bigger guards. Additionally, he's a step slow, so he's best when in zone defenses or concealed by guarding a low-scoring player. Those weaknesses should keep him from becoming a starter, but he makes a productive bench player because of his ability to get to the line.

Melvin Ely — center — Age: 27 — Height: 6-10 — Weight: 255
(71% PF, 29% C)

Most similar at age: Stacey King

Year		G	M/G	FG%	FT%	P/40	R/40	A/40	TS%		Ast		TO		Usg		Reb		PER	
2002-03	LAC	52	15.4	.495	.703	11.8	8.7	0.7	54.0	22	5.3	66	17.6	64	12.4	52	12.0	60	10.83	55
2003-04	LAC	42	12.1	.431	.595	12.3	7.9	1.7	45.8	67	10.3	26	9.4	7	15.5	27	11.7	68	11.13	61
2004-05	Cha	79	20.9	.432	.575	14.0	7.9	1.8	46.5	62	8.8	16	14.2	41	17.5	16	11.1	58	10.45	51
2005-06	PRJ (63.1)			.449	.616	13.0	8.3	1.6	48.3		8.7		14.1		15.4		11.7		11.01	

It's hard to believe that Ely was a lottery pick because he's displayed so little skill in his three NBA seasons. He's essentially a marginal backup center whom the Bobcats picked up more or less for free in the summer of 2004 when the Clippers were trying to create cap space.

Ely does offer two important assets—decent defense and a post game. He shoots a hook shot with either hand and while his accuracy comes and goes, he can get into position and get the shot off more often than not. Plus, he has the bulk to be a reasonably effective defensive center, although he's not a shot-blocker.

However, the negatives outweigh the positives. Like teammate Malik Allen, Ely is an extremely poor rebounder for a big man. Even worse, his low-percentage shooting isn't just limited to the hook shots. Ely isn't much of a jump shooter nor is he athletic enough to finish well around the basket. He's a terrible foul shooter to boot. As a result, his True Shooting Percentage is annually among the worst at his position.

He's under contract for one more season, so the Bobcats will take advantage of his limited skills to serve as an inexpensive fourth big man. Charlotte can shop for an upgrade when its cap room expands next summer.

Jason Hart — point guard — Age: 27 — Height: 6-3 — Weight: 185
Defensive PER: 1.17 (81% PG, 19% SG)

Most similar at age: Rod Strickland

Year		G	M/G	FG%	FT%	P/40	R/40	A/40	TS%		Ast		TO		Usg		Reb		PER	
2003-04	SA	53	12.5	.447	.767	10.7	4.8	4.9	49.7	35	28.1	29	10.1	19	16.5	61	6.8	12	12.25	44
2004-05	Cha	74	25.5	.449	.785	15.0	4.3	7.8	53.4	19	32.5	16	9.0	11	22.2	33	6.0	23	16.87	18
2005-06	PRJ (41.4)			.448	.781	14.4	4.4	6.6	53.2		29.6		9.3		20.8		6.1		15.74	

One of Charlotte's few free-agent pickups in its first season, Hart exceeded expectations. His only NBA experience prior to the Bobcats came in a brief stint with San Antonio the year before, and it was there that he proved he was a good enough defender to play at the NBA level.

As a matter of fact, his offense proved to be a pleasant surprise. Hart improved on his rookie season in every important category, and several of the jumps were enormous. For example, he suddenly developed a three-point shot, hitting 36.8 percent after making just two the entire season in San Antonio. He also was much more productive running the point, as he sliced his turnover Ratio while improving his assist output. The only area where he declined was rebounding, and he still was above average in that department.

Hart does have room for improvement. He has trouble with traps and should learn to be more elusive with his dribble, but for a cheap free agent pick-up, he was quite a find. That makes it doubly vexing that the Bobcats gave him away so cheaply after the season. Hart will back up Mike Bibby in Sacramento and should be among the league's better No. 2 point guards.

Jason Kapono small forward **Age: 24 Height: 6-8 Weight: 220**
(72% SF, 18% SG, 9% PF, 1% C) Most similar at age: Brian Evans

Year		G	M/G	FG%	FT%	P/40	R/40	A/40	TS%		Ast		TO		Usg		Reb		PER	
2003-04	Cle	41	10.4	.403	.833	13.6	5.2	1.3	51.9		8.0		12.0		14.9		7.3		10.14	
2004-05	Cha	81	18.4	.401	.824	18.5	4.4	1.6	48.6	53	7.5	62	5.6	1	20.7	19	6.2	62	11.80	43
2005-06	PRJ (41.2)			.398	.831	17.9	4.3	1.6	48.7		7.7		5.8		20.0		6.1		12.09	

The Bobcats plucked Kapono from Cleveland in the expansion draft and he provided exactly what was expected of him: lots of outside shooting and precious little else. Kapono is a career 42.4 percent shooter from three-point range and sported the lowest Turnover Ratio among small forwards last season.

For a great shooter, however, Kapono's TS% is awful. The reason is that he's trying too hard to score in other ways instead of sticking with what he does best. Kapono took less than a third of his shots from three-point range, opting to venture inside the arc for most of his attempts. Unfortunately, he's a terrible two-point shooter because he doesn't have the hops to finish in traffic nor the quickness to get separation from his man. Thus, he hit just 39.6 percent on two-pointers.

In addition, he needs to add a shot-fake move that will get him to the line. Kapono had only 85 free-throw tries last season, or about one for every eight field-goal attempts. That's a horrendous ratio and wastes one of Kapono's best skills—his ability to hit free throws.

Kapono has to produce at a high level offensively, because he provides nothing else. His rebound and assist rates are among the worst at his position, and he's a step slow at the defensive end. As a free agent, he'll get another chance from a team that's looking for outside shooting help, but he'll have to get a higher proportion of his shots on three-pointers if he's going to challenge for regular playing time.

Brevin Knight point guard **Age: 30 Height: 5-10 Weight: 170**
Defensive PER: 0.45 (100% PG) Most similar at age: Travis Best

Year		G	M/G	FG%	FT%	P/40	R/40	A/40	TS%		Ast		TO		Usg		Reb		PER	
2002-03	Mem	55	16.9	.425	.541	9.3	3.5	10.0	44.2	58	40.8	1	16.5	62	21.5	33	4.9	46	11.17	49
2003-04	Phx-Wa-Mil	56	18.5	.427	.754	10.1	4.3	7.9	47.5	47	37.1	7	13.1	46	19.0	49	6.3	18	13.63	31
2004-05	Cha	66	29.5	.422	.852	13.7	3.5	12.2	49.5	49	41.9	1	10.4	28	26.6	10	4.9	48	18.06	14
2005-06	PRJ (8.2)			.424	.785	12.5	3.7	10.5	49.1		39.7		11.8		24.6		5.2		16.58	

Knight's season was one of the great surprises of the 2004–05 campaign. He had the league's top Assist Ratio, scored more than he had in years, and used his fast hands to finish among the league leaders in steals.

Unfortunately, Knight is also this year's star candidate for what I call the Fluke Rule. The Fluke Rule identifies players who played beyond their capabilities in a given season, allowing us to determine which players will bounce back sharply the following year. To qualify for the Fluke Rule, a player has to meet three criteria:

- At least 28 years of age
- With a PER above 14.00
- And at least 3.00 higher than the previous year's PER

As a group, Fluke Rule players tend to decline sharply the following season, losing nearly all the gains from their "fluke" season. Last year, seven players qualified for the Fluke Rule: Mark Blount, Vin Baker, Antonio Daniels, Erick Dampier, Jeff McInnis, Dikembe Mutombo, and Scott Williams. Baker and Williams barely played, while of the remaining five players, only Mutombo was better in 2004–05:

Fluke Rule Players, 2003–04

Player	2003–04 PER	2004–05 PER	Difference
Mark Blount	16.01	12.52	−3.49
Vin Baker	14.79	1.20	−13.59
Antonio Daniels	19.67	18.08	−1.59
Erick Dampier	20.17	15.21	−4.96
Jeff McInnis	15.14	12.36	−2.78
Dikembe Mutombo	14.36	16.51	+2.15
Scott Williams	14.30	6.66	−7.64
Average	**16.35**	**11.79**	**-4.56**

Over the past two decades, only one player in 10 has been able to defy the odds and play better than his Fluke Rule season; the other 90 percent fare worse. Thus, there's some real value in identifying Fluke Rule seasons. Certainly, the Celtics and Mavs would have been interested in knowing this information before they paid Blount and Dampier so much money.

Now let's take a look at this year's Fluke Rule candidates. In addition to Knight, we have Othella Harrington, Fred Hoiberg, Allen Iverson, Antonio McDyess, and Jalen Rose. One can argue that there were extenuating circumstances in McDyess's case since the Fluke Rule doesn't adjust for the fact that he was returning from a knee injury. Nonetheless, as a group these players will see their PER drop by nearly three points from 2004–05 (note that the estimated 2005–06 PER in the chart will differ from the players' projected stats).

Fluke Rule Players, 2004–05

Player	2003–04 PER	2004–05 PER	Estimated 2005–06 PER
Othella Harrington	8.98	14.46	11.52
Fred Hoiberg	13.61	16.77	13.83
Allen Iverson	19.22	23.23	20.29
Brevin Knight	13.63	18.06	15.12
Antonio McDyess	12.61	17.20	14.26
Jalen Rose	12.57	16.56	13.62
Average	**13.44**	**17.71**	**14.77**

Knight is a perfect example of a Fluke Rule candidate. Completely without warning, the 29-year-old journeyman set career highs in points, assists, and free-throw percentage; averaged double figures for the first time in his career; and shot above his career percentage. The odds are overwhelmingly strong that he'll revert to the trend of his previous seven NBA seasons, when his weak jumper was too much of a liability to overcome his skills at penetrating and distributing the ball.

It's also important information for the Bobcats, or any other team interested in bidding for Knight's services as a free agent. Yes, he was excellent in 2004–05, but the odds of him repeating the performance are slim. Clubs should adjust their contract offers accordingly.

Emeka Okafor				power forward								Age: 23		Height: 6-10	Weight: 252	

Emeka Okafor — power forward — **Age: 23** **Height: 6-10 Weight: 252**
Defensive PER: 0.53 (63% PF, 37% C) — Most similar at age: Drew Gooden

Year		G	M/G	FG%	FT%	P/40	R/40	A/40	TS%		Ast		TO		Usg		Reb		PER	
2004-05	Cha	73	35.6	.447	.609	17.0	12.2	1.0	47.9	60	4.7	66	9.3	22	19.1	23	17.1	7	16.35	26
2005-06	PRJ (31.4)			.457	.624	17.3	12.1	1.1	49.3		5.3		9.0		19.3		17.0		17.06	

Okafor's rookie season was something of a mixed bag. On one hand, it's hard to argue with 17 points and 12 boards per 40 minutes, especially since the Bobcats weren't sure how far along he was offensively. On the other hand, he was significantly less athletic than he appeared at Connecticut, particularly in shot-blocking. Okafor seemed to be a Mourning-esque dominator in college, but he barely blocked more shots per minute as a rookie than Gerald Wallace.

Offensively, Okafor shot a low percentage because he was forced to be the Bobcats' primary option and faced frequent double-teaming. He has a nice jump hook in the post and also has a reliable turnaround jumper. However, he took too many mid-range jumpers that seemed to be a step beyond his range, and he doesn't have the explosion of some other high draft picks when he finishes around the basket. He's also a poor free-throw shooter.

On a team like this, however, Okafor's biggest weakness was his inability to find the open man. Considering all the attention he received from opposing defenses, Okafor should have had ample opportunity to locate open teammates, but he averaged a measly one assist per 40 minutes. Okafor's Assist Ratio was the fourth-worst among power forwards, a situation that must improve in coming seasons.

The big question for Charlotte fans is how much better Okafor can get. The Bobcats' big weakness right now is a lack of star talent, and Okafor is the one player on the roster who potentially could become a star. He'll need to further refine his post game and develop as a passer in order to get there.

Bernard Robinson — shooting guard

Age: 25 Height: 6-6 Weight: 210
(54% SF, 43% SG, 2% PF, 1% PG)
Most similar at age: N/A

Year		G	M/G	FG%	FT%	P/40	R/40	A/40	TS%	Ast	TO	Usg	Reb	PER
2004-05	Cha	31	10.6	.444	.692	11.3	5.9	3.7	50.3	17.4	14.0	15.5	8.2	9.69

A second-round draft choice in 2004, Robinson has decent athleticism but his offensive game needs a lot of work. For instance, Robinson has a good first step, but he needs to improve his jumper and moves off the dribble to become more of a credible offensive threat. He's also very old for a rookie at 24, so he doesn't have nearly the upside of some other first-year players. He'll be battling just to hang on to his roster spot this season.

Kareem Rush — shooting guard

Age: 25 Height: 6-6 Weight: 215
(86% SG, 10% SF, 4% PG)
Most similar at age: Jimmy Oliver

Year		G	M/G	FG%	FT%	P/40	R/40	A/40	TS%		Ast		TO		Usg		Reb		PER	
2002-03	LAL	76	11.5	.393	.696	10.4	4.3	3.1	44.7	52	17.7	20	16.4	57	15.5	46	6.1	43	5.70	57
2003-04	LAL	72	17.3	.440	.596	14.8	3.1	1.9	50.5	30	10.5	56	8.5	13	16.6	44	4.4	60	10.32	50
2004-05	LAL-Cha	48	20.2	.387	.771	16.6	3.7	2.8	47.1	58	12.5	46	8.7	14	20.8	21	5.1	60	10.02	49
2005-06 PRJ (45.3)				*.398*	*.668*	*14.1*	*3.6*	*2.4*	*46.9*		*12.2*		*10.5*		*17.7*		*5.1*		*9.01*	

They traded two No. 2s for him? Rush proved essentially worthless after the Bobcats traded for him, which shouldn't have surprised anyone who watched him struggle in L.A. His stock-in-trade is three-point shooting, but he's hitting only 34 percent for his career, which isn't nearly high enough for an alleged specialist.

On top of that, Rush brings few other positives to the table. He's a poor rebounder and ballhandler who struggles to create his own shot. In addition, he rarely got to the free-throw line because of his weak off-the-dribble game. Rush averaged only a free throw for every eight field-goal attempts, which is an extremely poor ratio. He did manage to improve his dreadful free-throw percentage to a more respectable 77 percent last season.

Rush is a free agent because the Lakers had opted not to pick up his fourth-year option, which makes the Bobcats' trade doubly puzzling. Even if Rush had played well, he would have been an unrestricted free agent entering the offseason, meaning Charlotte would have had to make a strong bid just to keep him. Considering how Rush played, at least they didn't have that to worry about. Rush re-signed for low dollars and will get more chances to prove he doesn't belong.

Jamal Sampson — center

Age: 22 Height: 6-11 Weight: 258
(95% PF, 5% C)
Most similar at age: N/A

Year		G	M/G	FG%	FT%	P/40	R/40	A/40	TS%	Ast	TO	Usg	Reb	PER
2002-03	Mil	5	1.6	.000	—	0.0	10.0	5.0	0.0	33.3	0.0	15.1	14.6	8.52
2003-04	LAL	10	13.0	.478	.583	8.9	16.0	2.2	51.3	17.0	14.5	11.2	23.6	15.03
2004-05	Cha	23	14.3	.452	.590	9.6	14.8	1.0	49.9	4.6	16.3	11.1	20.7	11.55

Sampson is young and statistically has shown tremendous potential, especially as a rebounder. But his attitude and effort have been found wanting by three teams in three years, and he may be running out of chances. The Bobcats cut him halfway through the season because Bickerstaff felt he was malingering and no other takers emerged. Size-challenged Sacramento decided to take a chance on him, giving him perhaps a final shot at sticking.

Tamar Slay — small forward

Age: 25 Height: 6-8 Weight: 220
(51% SF, 35% SG, 10% PF, 4% PG)
Most similar at age: N/A

Year		G	M/G	FG%	FT%	P/40	R/40	A/40	TS%	Ast	TO	Usg	Reb	PER
2002-03	NJ	36	7.6	.379	.700	13.4	4.5	2.0	42.8	9.9	14.1	18.5	6.5	7.00
2003-04	NJ	22	7.5	.350	.500	12.8	6.1	3.4	40.1	15.4	12.1	20.5	8.7	7.79
2004-05	Cha	8	9.8	.333	.000	14.4	7.2	1.5	35.1	5.9	15.7	23.0	10.0	1.17

The Bobcats seemed giddy that they grabbed Slay in the expansion draft, but he hasn't performed anywhere near an NBA level in his three pro seasons. His one season in Charlotte was marred by injury, resulting in his playing just 78 minutes. For that reason, the Bobcats may bring him back for one more year before they pull the plug on this experiment.

| Theron Smith | | | small forward | | | | | | | | Age: 25 | Height: 6-8 | Weight: 230 |
| (47% SF, 47% PF, 6% C) | | | | | | | | | | | | | Most similar at age: Anthony Avent |

Year		G	M/G	FG%	FT%	P/40	R/40	A/40	TS%		Ast		TO		Usg		Reb		PER	
2003-04	Mem	20	8.9	.372	.750	9.9	9.2	1.6	47.3		10.4		20.7		12.9		13.1		8.36	
2004-05	Cha	33	15.5	.324	.875	8.2	9.1	2.2	36.7	64	10.5	45	13.6	54	13.9	56	12.7	2	5.10	64
2005-06	PRJ (8.3)			.337	.882	8.1	8.7	2.0	37.6		10.4		13.1		12.7		12.2		5.75	

The Bobcats grabbed Smith from Memphis in the expansion draft, and he showed flashes of potential at the defensive end. He's quick enough to defend small forwards and strong enough to muscle power forwards in the post, although he's a little short to play that position permanently. In addition, he's a good athlete, an excellent rebounder, and has three-point range on his jumper.

All of that would make him a player if he wasn't so awful offensively. Despite his shooting range, Smith is a pretty terrible shooter overall. His 32.4 percent shooting speaks for itself, and he did nothing in any other category to remotely make up for it. Smith has no off-the-dribble or post game and despite his athleticism is a poor finisher around the basket. He's also a poor ballhandler who has been excessively turnover-prone in his two pro seasons. Worst of all, he wouldn't stop shooting. Smith led the NBA in Brick Index because he often tried to create shots for himself instead of letting more talented players handle the scoring.

The Bobcats have Smith under contract for one more season so he'll get a chance to redeem himself this season, but it would require substantial improvement for him to remain in the NBA beyond 2006.

| Gerald Wallace | | | small forward | | | | | | | | Age: 23 | Height: 6-7 | Weight: 220 |
| Defensive PER: 1.37 (90% SF, 9% PF, 1% C) | | | | | | | | | | | | | Most similar at age: Derrick Chievous |

Year		G	M/G	FG%	FT%	P/40	R/40	A/40	TS%		Ast		TO		Usg		Reb		PER	
2002-03	Sac*	64	9.4	.492	.527	15.4	9.0	1.6	51.0	37	8.1	52	15.6	55	16.9	34	12.0	43	12.34	45
2003-04	Sac	37	9.1	.360	.458	8.9	8.8	2.3	37.7		15.0		6.3		14.0		13.0		10.60	
2004-05	Cha	70	30.7	.449	.661	14.5	7.2	2.6	51.0	43	12.2	29	15.0	62	17.5	36	10.1	18	14.07	32
2005-06	PRJ (29.7)			.440	.647	14.4	7.5	2.6	49.5		12.3		14.8		16.7		10.1		13.71	

* Season rankings are as power forward

One of two starters the Bobcats found in the expansion draft, Wallace's Defensive PER is no joke. He's a stopper in the making who had one of the defensive highlights of the year with a spectacular spike of a Wally Szczerbiak dunk attempt.

Wallace is athletic and has good anticipation at the defensive end, but he still has some rough edges to iron out since this was his first year playing regularly. Wallace goes for too many steals, leaving gaping holes when he misses, and picks up lots of blocking fouls trying to draw charges. In a year or two he'll figure out how to position himself to get those calls. He also could stand to add some strength so he can fight harder against post-ups.

Offensively, Wallace may never be more than a third or fourth option. He can get easy baskets with his ability to run the floor and finish in transition, but the halfcourt is a different matter. Wallace shoots the ball on the left side of his head even though he's right-handed, a difficult cross-handed delivery that makes it tough to shoot the ball consistently. As a result he's an iffy jump shooter and struggles from the free-throw line.

Wallace also needs to be more careful with the ball, as his Turnover Ratio was among the worst at his position. Because he doesn't have a jump shot he was forced to drive a lot, which precipitated most of his miscues. He'll have to choose his spots more carefully in the future. Nonetheless, he's an attractive commodity as a restricted free agent because he's still very young and already a good defender. He should elicit an offer around the midlevel exception.

Jahidi White — center
(82% C, 18% PF)

Age: 29 Height: 6-9 Weight: 290
Most similar in '04-05: N/A

Year		G	M/G	FG%	FT%	P/40	R/40	A/40	TS%		Ast		TO		Usg		Reb		PER	
2002-03	Was	16	14.4	.472	.680	11.7	12.7	0.3	52.3		2.7		12.0		12.4		18.8		14.84	
2003-04	Was-Phx	62	14.0	.521	.500	12.1	12.1	0.3	53.2	26	2.2	74	20.7	73	12.3	53	17.8	6	11.73	52
2004-05	Cha	17	7.9	.452	.350	12.4	10.1	0.3	43.2		1.4		18.2		15.5		14.1		6.42	

A muscle-bound behemoth with hands of stone, White has been increasingly injury prone the past few seasons and looks to be nearing the end of the line. Charlotte agreed to take his contract in return for a draft pick from the Suns, but they had no plans for White and played him sparingly. He underwent shoulder surgery last February and missed the rest of the season, so it's unclear whether he'll have a place in the league in 2005–06.

Raymond Felton — point guard
Age: 21 Height: 6-1 Weight: 180

Charlotte probably reached a bit in taking Felton with the fifth overall pick, but he's certainly a gifted playmaker. He excels at pushing the ball upcourt and throwing it ahead to start the break, and his defense is top-notch as well. Felton's shooting stroke is still a question mark, however, so he might be a taller version of Brevin Knight. Even last year when he hit 44 percent on three-pointers, he shot only 70 percent from the line.

Sean May — power forward
Age: 21 Height: 6-9 Weight: 260

May reminds me of the late Bison Dele (the artist formerly known as Brian Williams) in many ways. Not completely, of course—May is right-handed, not quite as explosive, and much less of a flake—but the similarities are there. Like Dele, Williams is 6'9" with soft hands, an instinctive understanding of how to score in the post, and a knack for the glass. May's rebound rate was off the charts, averaging a rebound every 2.5 minutes in leading North Carolina to the national title. The only questions are whether he can defend at the NBA level and keep his weight under control.

Chicago Bulls

Finally the Bulls are back. After six years of wallowing in the muck at the bottom of the Eastern Conference, Chicago's young nucleus unexpectedly came together last season and propelled the Bulls to their first playoff appearance since Michael Jordan retired.

At first their season seemed like all the others. Chicago lost its first nine games and at one point was 2–13. Rookie guard Ben Gordon was firing up bricks, Eddy Curry's lethargy was infuriating the coaches, and the Bulls were threatening to be the worst offensive team in history.

Then suddenly Chicago started winning. Few took notice at first figuring even a blind squirrel finds a nut once in a while. Gradually the Bulls battled their way into the play-off chase and, to the shock of even their most ardent supporters, into home court for the first round of the playoffs. Although a series of late-season injuries led to the Bulls' first-round defeat against the Wizards, it still was an immensely successful season. Chicago finished the year on a 45–22 tear to wash away the stigma of the Jerry Krause years and to herald that the rebuilding was over at last.

What changed between that 2–13 start and the 45–22 finish? Basically, everything. First, the Bulls improved dramatically at the defensive end. They weren't bad even at the start, giving up 103.1 points per 100 possessions, but they were considerably better over the final 67 games.

A lineup change helped fuel the turnaround. At the start of the season, Skiles was stretching his defense to the limits by playing Andres Nocioni at small forward and rookie Luol Deng at shooting guard, putting both in compromising positions in terms of quickness. The Bulls won their first game of the year when Skiles inserted Antonio Davis and Chris Duhon into the starting lineup, vastly improving Chicago's defense, and they stayed there all season.

The bigger shift, as shown in table 1, came on offense. The Bulls' overall offensive numbers were quite poor, as they finished 26th in the NBA in Offensive Efficiency. But over the first 15 games, they were on pace to be the worst offensive team in history. Chicago was creating only 91.7 points per 100 possessions, making it virtually impossible for the team to win. Over the final 67 games, the Bulls improved to a more respectable 100.0—which still would have been 26th in the league—but it at least gave them a chance.

The key was Gordon. He was unbelievably awful in the opening games of his rookie season but then he quickly improved. Gordon averaged a whopping 24.7 points per 40 minutes, giving the Bulls the go-to scorer they had been lacking in previous seasons. Chicago also got better post play from center Eddy Curry. He got off to his usual sluggish start but rebounded in time to shoot 53.8 percent while averaging nearly as many points per minute as Gordon. In fact, Curry's absence due to a heart problem torpedoed Chicago in the playoffs.

Let's get back to the defense, however. Chicago doesn't exactly overflow with athleticism the way the Pistons or Spurs do, so it's tough to fathom how the Bulls led the NBA in field-goal percentage defense.

That's because the man most responsible for the defensive dominance was on the sidelines, not in a uniform. Head coach Scott Skiles turned the team into a reflection of his scrappy, determined style and demanded a full effort. It would have been easy for him to throw up his hands after the 2–13 start and say, "I don't have the players." It would have been even easier for the players to quit on Skiles. The fact that neither happened says a lot about Skiles's determination, and if not for the stunning turnaround in Phoenix, it would have earned him the Coach of the Year award.

One could see that toughness in the Bulls' foul count. Chicago ranked second in the NBA with 2,028 personal fouls and was also second in opponents' free-throw attempts per field-goal attempt. The trade-off in forcing such a low field-goal percentage was that the Bulls consistently sent opponents

Bulls at a Glance

Record: 47–35, 2nd place in Central Division
Offensive Efficiency: 98.5 (26th)
Defensive Efficiency: 97.5 (2nd)
Pace Factor: 94.8 (10th)
Top-Rated Player: Tyson Chandler (PER 16.50, 83rd overall)
Head Coach: Scott Skiles. Did amazing work to transform Bulls at the defensive end.

Table 1. 2004–05 Bulls: Start and finish

	First 15 Games	Last 67 Games	Change
Winning Pct.	.133	.672	+.538
Off. Efficiency	91.7	100.0	+8.3
Def. Efficiency	103.1	96.2	−6.9

to the line rather than conceding an easy basket, but they came out ahead in the bargain.

One could see the beginnings of Chicago's defensive turnaround in 2003–04, as the Bulls were more effective defensively after Skiles took over for Bill Cartwright. But with an offseason to change the personnel, Skiles's impact resonated more strongly. Slackers like Eddie Robinson and Jamal Crawford were shown the door in favor of tougher nuts like Nocioni, Duhon, and Deng. The Bulls also benefited from the pain of the previous seasons, as players like Tyson Chandler and Kirk Hinrich gained valuable experience while taking their lumps and turned into accomplished defenders.

Finally, Skiles was very effective in changing defenses, and the Bulls had to be the best zone-defense team in the league. This was particularly true when Chandler was in the game, as he could roam the middle and alter shots with his length and timing.

Now that they're a playoff team, the next step for the Bulls is to continue pushing toward the top of the Eastern Conference. They can't afford to be complacent about it either. When a team has a surprise season, management often views the players who took part in the success as necessary ingredients, even if some need to be replaced.

Duhon is a good example. The team improved when he joined the starting lineup mostly because he was the least-bad alternative. Chicago had almost no backcourt depth and was attempting to get by with Nocioni and Deng on the wings, which was never going to work. Duhon is a rather bad offensive player, and they're never going to get near the league average in Offensive Efficiency with him in the lineup. And picking up the offense is a must if they Bulls are to move forward, because the defense is pretty close to maxed out already.

Chicago also faces two important free-agent decisions, because both Chandler and Curry are restricted free agents. Keeping Chandler appears to be a no-brainer. He's already among the best defensive players and rebounders in basketball, so while his offense is a bit disappointing, his overall value remains quite high. Curry is a trickier case because of his heart problems, poor conditioning, and defensive inat-

tention. If another team makes an outsized bid, the Bulls may have to be content to let him go.

Although the Bulls are young overall, they do have some age concerns. Othella Harrington played out of his mind off the bench, but there's no way he'll shoot 51 percent again. Plus, Davis is now 37 and it's unclear how much longer he can continue to contribute defensively.

Additionally, the Bulls will be reluctant to add much in free agency beyond keeping Chandler and possibly Curry. Chicago is looking at a cap-space bonanza in 2006 when Davis's contract comes off the books and won't do anything to mess it up between now and then, even if it means sacrificing some wins in 2005–06.

Whatever the outcome, there's no denying that the offense must improve. Chicago was the most turnover-prone team in the league, making miscues on 17.5 percent of its possessions. The reason wasn't because players were particularly sloppy with the ball—it was because so many non-scorers were thrust into roles where they had to score more than they were used to. With two zeroes in the starting lineup in Davis and Duhon, the other three Bulls had to take on a huge chunk of scoring responsibility.

One obvious solution would be to put Gordon in the starting lineup, but both he and Hinrich are better suited to playing shooting guard so it creates some odd match-ups. Nonetheless, it seems almost masochistic for a team with Chicago's offensive troubles to limit Gordon's minutes any more than they have to. Besides, Duhon's meager contribution might not be so glaring in a bench role.

Overall, Chicago is running into a familiar adversary for teams that sharply improve: the Plexiglass Principle. This rule states that teams that improve sharply in one season often regress a bit the next. In Chicago's case, it's easy to see why. They had no draft picks, lack free-agent funds, and might be losing Curry. Thus, the Bulls may have to take a step back before they can take another one forward. Just making the playoffs may be the team's most realistic goal. Fortunately, the long-term future remains incredibly bright. With a young nucleus of players like Chandler, Hinrich, Deng, and Gordon, the days of the Abomina-Bulls are officially over.

Tyson Chandler — center

Defensive PER: 1.74 (64% C, 36% PF)

Age: 23   Height: 7-1   Weight: 235

Most similar at age: Brendan Haywood

Year		G	M/G	FG%	FT%	P/40	R/40	A/40	TS%		Ast		TO		Usg		Reb		PER	
2002-03	Chi	75	24.3	.531	.608	15.1	11.3	1.7	56.5	10	9.2	37	16.4	60	15.6	31	15.6	22	15.81	16
2003-04	Chi	35	22.4	.424	.669	10.9	13.8	1.2	50.7	43	8.5	41	14.0	48	12.3	56	19.7	3	14.21	34
2004-05	Chi	80	27.3	.494	.673	11.7	14.2	1.2	56.5	18	5.7	43	15.7	54	12.1	52	19.9	5	16.50	15
2005-06	PRJ (13.1)			.497	.674	12.3	12.9	1.4	56.5		7.4		16.1		12.9		17.9		15.87	

The irony of Ben Gordon winning the Sixth Man award was that he wasn't even the best Sixth Man on his own team—that man was Chandler. Coming off the bench for Chicago, Chandler changed games with his shot-blocking, rebounding, and defensive intensity. It wasn't as spectacular as Gordon's scoring exploits but Chandler was better, with a higher PER and a much better Defensive PER. Despite his accomplishments, all he mustered was three third-place votes.

What made it especially odd was that Chandler didn't just play better than Gordon—he also played more. Chandler averaged 27 minutes per game to Gordon's 24. So he was playing more frequently and at a higher quality, yet got virtually no attention for the honor. What am I missing here?

Obviously it hurt Chandler that the Bulls promoted Gordon for the award instead of him, but the voters should have been more aware of Chandler's talents. Decidedly inferior players like Vladimir Radmanovic, Jerry Stackhouse, and Ricky Davis all got more votes than Chandler did. Oddly, the Bulls also played much better with Chandler as a reserve than as a starter. He played just as well when he started, but the Bulls inexplicably went 0–10 in those games.

Offensively, Chandler remains mistake-prone, but his field-goal percentage recovered from the 2003–04 disaster and he's a major force on the offensive glass. However, Chandler has no post game and needs work on finishing plays around the rim. He struggles to catch the ball and often has to gather himself before he can go up.

His primary value is at the defensive end. He's at his best defending lanky post players like Pau Gasol and Tim Duncan because his height makes it difficult for them to shoot over him. Strength match-ups can give him problems, but he's been improving in that area. Chandler also has to do a better job of keeping his feet. In one game, he fell for three shot fakes by Cleveland's Anderson Varejao in a span of five minutes, and Varejao isn't even a good shooter.

Chandler is only 23 though and already one of the best defenders in the game. Presuming he stays, the Bulls will move him into the starting lineup either this year or next, and barring injury he'll be an All-Defense candidate for the next decade.

Eddy Curry — center

(100% C)

Age: 23   Height: 6-11   Weight: 285

Most similar at age: Rasheed Wallace

Year		G	M/G	FG%	FT%	P/40	R/40	A/40	TS%		Ast		TO		Usg		Reb		PER	
2002-03	Chi	81	19.4	.585	.624	21.6	9.0	0.9	60.7	1	4.2	70	15.7	55	19.4	10	12.4	54	17.48	10
2003-04	Chi	73	29.5	.496	.671	19.9	8.4	1.3	53.8	20	5.5	66	14.3	54	20.4	8	12.0	65	14.78	26
2004-05	Chi	63	28.8	.538	.720	22.3	7.4	0.8	58.3	13	3.5	61	15.3	49	20.8	5	10.4	66	16.22	18
2005-06	PRJ (26.0)			.518	.696	21.4	7.9	1.2	56.1		5.1		15.0		21.3		10.8		15.37	

Curry is a devastating low-post scorer whose per-game numbers don't do justice to his scoring skill. Curry averaged 22.3 points per 40 minutes, and posted one of the best True Shooting Percentages at his position. He has a soft touch around the basket and is so big that it's easy for him to establish position and receive the ball. Curry also is a decent shooter from 12-to-15 feet, although he could use a little more arc on his shot.

Conditioning has been a major problem for Curry, but he improved in that area this past season. He's no Jack LaLane but he was able to get some baskets in transition and got a lot of quick post-ups on the secondary break. If he keeps getting in better shape, he may be able to stay on the floor longer.

The other limitation on Curry's playing time was his defense and effort level, both of which may be related to his conditioning. Curry improved at the defensive end this past season but still has nights where his lethargy is palpable from the upper deck. He's also a mysteriously bad rebounder and actually got worse this past season. Curry's 10.4 Rebound Rate was in the bottom five among centers, which is shameful for a player with his size and skill.

Curry is a restricted free agent, but a heart problem diagnosed late in the season may limit the market for his services. If the doctors give him a clean bill of health he should provide a steady source of post offense, either in Chicago or somewhere else. There are obvious concerns, however, about how hard he'll work on conditioning once he has a big contract in hand.

Antonio Davis — power forward — Age: 37 Height: 6-9 Weight: 245
Defensive PER: 1.31 (75% PF, 25% C) — Most similar at age: Derrick Coleman

Year		G	M/G	FG%	FT%	P/40	R/40	A/40	TS%		Ast		TO		Usg		Reb		PER	
2002-03	Tor*	53	35.7	.407	.771	15.6	9.2	2.8	48.3	56	12.9	17	11.6	18	20.0	5	13.1	48	14.46	31
2003-04	Tor-Chi	80	32.1	.403	.765	11.0	10.4	2.1	46.5	57	13.5	23	11.3	26	14.4	51	14.9	22	11.82	53
2004-05	Chi	72	25.6	.461	.757	10.9	9.3	1.7	51.6	40	8.3	41	14.5	59	12.8	63	13.0	37	11.12	58
2005-06	PRJ (20.8)			.402	.726	10.7	9.2	1.8	45.9		9.7		13.7		13.6		13.0		10.54	

* Season rankings are as center

Davis is nearing the end of his shelf life offensively. He can no longer finish around the rim and his only other weapon, a line-drive push shot from about 15 feet, was never that accurate even in his prime.

His saving grace is that he can defend and rebound, two skills the Bulls prized last season. Davis's muscle and toughness helped to compensate for Eddy Curry's lapses, and his strength made him a good partner for Tyson Chandler. Davis's Defensive PER was among the best at the power forward spot, and that performance may allow him to keep his starting job for another season despite his lack of offense.

Moreover, Davis is on the last year of a huge contract extension signed when he was still a Raptor, and his expiring contract is likely to be a valuable commodity at the trade deadline. Chances are the Bulls will hang on to him and use the cap savings to play the market in 2006. Of course, if an attractive offer comes along Davis could be changing uniforms at midseason.

Luol Deng — small forward — Age: 20 Height: 6-8 Weight: 220
(93% SF, 5% SG, 2% PF) — Most similar at age: Carmelo Anthony

Year		G	M/G	FG%	FT%	P/40	R/40	A/40	TS%		Ast		TO		Usg		Reb		PER	
2004-05	Chi	61	27.3	.434	.741	17.1	7.7	3.2	49.6	50	13.9	16	12.2	48	21.1	17	10.8	9	14.16	30
2005-06	PRJ (14.8)			.456	.757	18.3	7.3	3.8	51.5		15.5		12.4		21.7		10.3		15.15	

For a teenage rookie, Deng put together a very impressive rookie campaign but Gordonmania prevented most people from noticing. Deng is a good, though not great, athlete who already has an NBA body and showed a better-than-expected mid-range jumper as a rookie. Although he has to adapt to the NBA three-point line—he hit just 26.5 percent—he handles the ball well for his size and is a good scorer in transition. It would help if Deng developed a post game to complement his size and went to the basket more, but one can hardly complain with the results of his first season.

Defensively, Deng performed better than expected. Most rookies struggle at that end, but Deng seemed to catch on unusually quickly and has the size and quickness to be a very good defender in short order. He also was among the best rebounders at the small forward spot, helping make up for Curry's deficiencies on the boards.

The downside is that despite Deng's youth, injuries are becoming a concern. Deng missed time with an ankle problem and then hurt his wrist late in the season. The wrist injury is bad enough that he could miss time at the start of this season, and he certainly missed out on a summer of practicing jump shots. That might lead to a slow start this year, but in the long term he should have the Bulls' small forward needs solved for a long time.

Chris Duhon — point guard — Age: 23 Height: 6-1 Weight: 185
Defensive PER: 1.33 (94% PG, 6% SG) — Most similar at age: Lee Mayberry

Year		G	M/G	FG%	FT%	P/40	R/40	A/40	TS%		Ast		TO		Usg		Reb		PER	
2004-05	Chi	82	26.5	.352	.731	8.9	3.9	7.3	47.1	56	34.8	6	11.5	40	17.3	62	5.5	33	9.80	59
2005-06	PRJ (13.9)			.361	.757	10.0	3.8	7.3	48.2		33.7		11.2		18.0		5.3		11.13	

Duhon's defensive PER is well above average for a point guard, and that alone will keep him in the league since his offense certainly won't. Duhon shot a ghastly 35 percent on *two-point* shots and rarely penetrated the lane, putting huge amounts of pressure on the other four Bulls to create shots. Mostly, he hung out at the top of the key and waited for a pass for a three-pointer. He shot respectably on threes (35 percent) but that was his sole offensive contribution.

Defensively, he moves his feet well, willingly takes charges, and was the only Bull with enough foot speed to deal with the quicker point guards. That skill helped him get a three-year, $9 million offer sheet from the Raptors, which the Bulls quickly matched. If he improves his offensive game he'll be a useful backup point guard, but putting him in the starting lineup places an incredible offensive burden on his teammates.

Lawrence Funderburke — power forward
(81% PF, 19% C)

Age: 35 Height: 6-9 Weight: 230
Most similar at age: N/A

Year		G	M/G	FG%	FT%	P/40	R/40	A/40	TS%		Ast		TO		Usg		Reb		PER	
2002-03	Sac	12	3.8	.444	.588	12.9	9.6	1.4	46.6		8.6		6.4		14.9		12.9		11.77	
2003-04	Sac		Did not play																	
2004-05	Chi	2	10.5	.500	.600	17.1	5.7	0.0	54.9		0.0		0.0		15.4		8.0		12.97	

The Bulls were desperate for frontcourt help after Deng and Curry went down and signed Funderburke late in the season. The former Sacramento King had missed the previous season with an injury and was a good find by Chicago. He retains some of his knack for scoring and the southpaw could end up back on the roster this season.

Ben Gordon — shooting guard
Defensive PER: 1.66 (88% SG, 10% SF, 2% PG)

Age: 22 Height: 6-3 Weight: 200
Most similar at age: Gilbert Arenas

Year		G	M/G	FG%	FT%	P/40	R/40	A/40	TS%		Ast		TO		Usg		Reb		PER	
2004-05	Chi	82	24.4	.411	.863	24.7	4.3	3.3	52.6	31	10.8	57	12.2	54	27.5	3	6.0	46	14.80	21
2005-06	*PRJ (26.5)*			*.421*	*.882*	*25.1*	*4.4*	*3.5*	*53.9*		*11.6*		*12.1*		*27.9*		*6.3*		*16.17*	

Gordon won the Sixth Man award with his spectacular scoring exploits, especially in fourth quarters. He led the NBA in double-digit fourth quarters and had one of the highest 40-minute scoring averages in the league. After a slow start, Gordon also defended well due to his speed and surprising upper-body strength. His Defensive PER probably overstates his case because it doesn't account for the cross-matching with Kirk Hinrich. Gordon was foul-prone, however, and struggled with matchups against bigger guards who would post him up.

Offensively, Gordon thrived because he's a great shooter who can also get to the basket. He hit 40.5 percent of his high-arcing three-pointers and has a very quick release on his shot. He also has explosive quickness going to his right and is among the league's best at shooting runners from five to 10 feet. Gordon throws up a one-handed shot with his right-hand that borders on being a hook shot and shoots it halfway to the roof before it drops down through the net. Though hardly textbook, it's incredibly effective.

Nonetheless, Gordon's PER wasn't as high as some might expect because of the other holes in his offensive game. He only shot 41 percent overall because he forced a lot of long jumpers, so his TS% was unimpressive. He also needs to work on his passing and ballhandling. Gordon's Assist Ratio was very poor and is disappointing considering all the attention he receives from opposing defenses. He also needs to keep better control of the ball, as his Turnover Ratio was well below average. While Gordon is extremely quick, he has a relatively high dribble and sometimes seems to struggle to control the ball. He also goes right every time and needs to add more variety to his game.

Despite those weaknesses, Chicago cannot afford to keep him out of the starting lineup. Gordon already is the team's best scoring threat and his continued improvement could be the Bulls' best defense against the Plexiglass Principle.

Adrian Griffin — small forward
(61% SF, 36% PF, 3% C)

Age: 31 Height: 6-5 Weight: 230
Most similar at age: Ron Harper

Year		G	M/G	FG%	FT%	P/40	R/40	A/40	TS%		Ast		TO		Usg		Reb		PER	
2002-03	Dal	74	18.6	.433	.844	9.5	7.7	3.1	46.3	55	20.9	5	9.3	14	13.5	48	10.6	11	11.51	46
2003-04	Hou	19	7.0	.278	.000	3.3	5.7	3.0	27.8		30.5		9.2		9.5		8.3		4.47	
2004-05	Chi	69	9.7	.360	.750	9.1	8.8	3.2	41.9	62	15.1	9	11.4	41	14.3	52	12.2	4	10.68	48
2005-06	*PRJ (21.0)*			*.403*	*.773*	*9.1*	*7.9*	*3.0*	*45.1*		*17.4*		*10.7*		*13.4*		*11.1*		*10.93*	

Signed as an afterthought, the veteran forward contributed to the team's trademark defensive intensity but provided little at the offensive end. Griffin has no jump shot and hit just 36 percent of his shots for Chicago, although he fills the box score in other areas. Griffin has excellent court vision and handles the ball well, so he will penetrate to set up shots for others. He's also among the best rebounding small forwards in the game despite his small stature. Because of those strengths, he's likely to earn another contract for this season, but he won't play unless Deng or Nocioni is hurt.

Othella Harrington   power forward   **Age: 31**   **Height: 6-9**   **Weight: 235**
(89% PF, 11% C)   Most similar at age: Mark Bryant

Year		G	M/G	FG%	FT%	P/40	R/40	A/40	TS%		Ast		TO		Usg		Reb		PER	
2002-03	NY	74	25.0	.508	.820	12.4	10.3	1.3	56.3	9	9.4	43	13.6	50	13.0	51	15.1	19	12.28	46
2003-04	NY	56	15.6	.495	.744	11.8	8.1	1.3	54.6	14	8.8	53	19.7	65	13.2	59	11.6	51	8.98	62
2004-05	Chi	70	18.2	.512	.718	17.7	9.2	1.8	55.9	18	8.4	40	13.1	55	18.1	28	12.8	39	14.46	40
2005-06	PRJ (35.1)			.486	.746	14.4	8.6	1.5	53.7		8.5		13.9		15.5		12.2		12.01	

The projections foresee a dramatic decline in Harrington's output, and so does the Fluke Rule. Players past the age of 30 who improve as sharply as Harrington did nearly always regress the next season (see the Brevin Knight comment in the Charlotte section for more on this). Therefore, the Bulls should treat Harrington's season as a one-time windfall. It's important information because Harrington is a free agent and just using last year's performance might encourage Chicago to overpay.

Harrington can provide occasional post scoring with his left-handed jump hooks, but defensively he's short for a center and not athletic enough to play power forward. Quicker power forwards like Shareef Abdur-Rahim or Drew Gooden blow right by him, and that fraternity of players is growing. Look for him to play a reduced role this season if he stays in Chicago.

Kirk Hinrich   point guard   **Age: 24**   **Height: 6-3**   **Weight: 190**
Defensive PER: 0.87 (53% PG, 46% SG, 1% SF)   Most similar at age: Sam Cassell

Year		G	M/G	FG%	FT%	P/40	R/40	A/40	TS%		Ast		TO		Usg		Reb		PER	
2003-04	Chi	76	35.6	.386	.804	13.5	3.8	7.6	51.0	26	32.0	17	12.6	42	21.4	32	5.5	31	13.07	36
2004-05	Chi	77	36.4	.397	.792	17.2	4.3	7.1	49.5	47	26.2	37	9.3	14	24.8	16	6.1	21	15.23	27
2005-06	PRJ (53.2)			.387	.807	15.6	4.2	6.9	50.4		27.9		10.0		23.0		5.9		14.75	

Hinrich's Defensive PER is above average, but it probably sells short his defensive skills. He's a very good help defender and moves his feet extremely well on the ball, allowing him to guard a variety of players. Even at 6'3", he's able to move to shooting guard without great difficulty, providing Skiles great flexibility in the backcourt. He never goes for fakes and keeps his body very low, but his one weakness is a propensity for fouling. Hinrich reaches in too often, and the resultant foul trouble is the one thing preventing him from averaging over 40 minutes a game.

Hinrich has some useful offensive skills too. He excels at running the screen-and-roll and coming around the screen for a jump shot. In addition, he rarely turns the ball over, helps out on the glass, and hits his foul shots.

Hinrich has one offensive weakness though and it's a fairly major one—he can't get to the basket. His shooting percentage has yet to clear 40 percent because he rarely gets a lay-up. With no easy baskets on his ledger, he has to earn all his points from outside. In his defense, Hinrich often gets stuck with the ball at the end of the shot clock so his percentage would probably improve on a better offensive team.

While stardom isn't in his future, Hinrich's solid defense and shooting make him a valuable player. Since he's on his rookie contract for two more years, he's an inexpensive one too.

Andres Nocioni   small forward   **Age: 26**   **Height: 6-7**   **Weight: 225**
Defensive PER: -0.20 (82% SF, 17% PF, 1% SG)   Most similar at age: Tom Tolbert

Year		G	M/G	FG%	FT%	P/40	R/40	A/40	TS%		Ast		TO		Usg		Reb		PER	
2004-05	Chi	81	23.4	.401	.766	14.3	8.1	2.6	48.4	54	12.3	28	14.1	58	18.0	32	11.4	6	9.96	54
2005-06	PRJ (42.7)			.406	.749	13.6	8.0	2.7	48.7		13.4		14.2		17.0		11.2		10.07	

If there's anyone who needs a nickname, it's this guy. Nocioni is constantly flailing his arms, runs around with a crazy wide-eyed look, and fouls anything that moves. You know the type—he's the manic, annoying guy at a pick-up game who tries way too hard. Adding to the effect, Nocioni wore a Lincoln-esque goatee-minus-the-mustache thing for much of the season. I propose dubbing him "The Wild Bull of the Pampas" in light of his Argentine heritage, but I'm accepting other nominations.

As for his abilities, Nocioni projected to be an adequate NBA player, but his numbers were pretty awful. He continually lost the ball on drives to the basket, struggled to hit outside shots, and got lit up on defense. The only aspect that held up was his rebounding, which was among the best at his position.

I suspect the reason is that Nocioni needs to play power forward, which was his position in Europe. It's a risk to put a player of his size at that position, but Nocioni is so unrelentingly physical that he probably could hold his own defensively. He also might get called for fewer fouls, as officials tend to look the other way more often in the post. Offensively, a switch might help get his game in gear. He would have a quickness edge on opposing power forwards and have an easier time getting to the basket.

Nocioni's physical play fit in perfectly with Chicago's style and endeared him to the locals, but the Bulls have to figure out how to put him in a better position to succeed at both ends of the court. Considering the frontcourt will be shorthanded if Curry leaves, shifting positions might be the perfect solution.

Jannero Pargo   point guard   Age: 26   Height: 6-1   Weight: 175
(100% PG)   Most similar at age: N/A

Year		G	M/G	FG%	FT%	P/40	R/40	A/40	TS%	Ast	TO	Usg	Reb	PER
2002-03	LAL	33	10.3	.398	1.000	10.0	4.3	4.6	44.9	24.9	14.7	16.3	6.1	7.26
2003-04	LAL-To-Chi	31	15.3	.407	.852	17.4	3.1	5.9	49.1	21.3	14.3	24.6	4.5	11.57
2004-05	Chi	32	14.2	.385	.739	18.0	4.2	6.7	45.7	22.1	13.1	27.3	5.8	10.94

A lightning quick guard who played very well in the playoffs against Washington, Pargo hasn't been able to establish a niche in the NBA because he's a shoot-first point guard who doesn't shoot well. He followed that trend last season, hitting only 38.5 percent and posting a miserable TS%.

In order to become a useful player, Pargo needs to use his quickness to penetrate and set up others rather than set up opponents for long jump shots. Luckily for him, NBA general managers are easily duped by playoff performances (see *James, Jerome* and *Dooling, Keyon*), so he'll end up with a richer contract than he deserves.

Eric Piatkowski   shooting guard   Age: 35   Height: 6-7   Weight: 215
(69% SG, 29% SF, 2% PF)   Most similar at age: Dale Ellis

Year		G	M/G	FG%	FT%	P/40	R/40	A/40	TS%		Ast		TO		Usg		Reb		PER	
2002-03	LAC	62	21.9	.471	.828	17.7	4.6	2.1	60.1	1	11.2	49	9.0	15	17.2	42	6.3	39	16.03	17
2003-04	Hou*	49	14.3	.377	.875	11.4	4.2	1.5	50.7	35	10.3	47	11.5	35	13.7	53	6.0	54	8.65	55
2004-05	Chi	68	12.3	.430	.804	15.5	3.8	2.4	57.3	10	11.6	53	10.0	28	16.3	51	5.3	57	12.43	37
2005-06	*PRJ (29.7)*			*.410*	*.811*	*14.3*	*4.1*	*2.2*	*54.5*		*11.6*		*9.7*		*15.6*		*5.7*		*12.02*	

* Season rankings are as small forward

A one-dimensional shooting specialist who is rapidly losing what little athleticism he possessed, Piatkowski nonetheless had some value for the Bulls because of his three-point prowess. He took more than half his tries from beyond the arc and hit 42.5 percent, rebounding strongly from an off year in Houston the previous season.

Piatkowski has one year left on his contract and is likely to be mothballed until the Bulls face a zone defense and need him to loosen things up. His greatest value may be his expiring contract, which could enable the Bulls to swap him for a more current model at the trading deadline.

Jared Reiner   center   Age: 23   Height: 6-11   Weight: 255
(100% C)   Most similar at age: N/A

Year		G	M/G	FG%	FT%	P/40	R/40	A/40	TS%	Ast	TO	Usg	Reb	PER
2004-05	Chi	19	6.9	.333	.250	6.4	11.5	0.3	33.1	1.4	21.6	10.6	16.1	2.08

A burly center who surprisingly stayed on Chicago's roster the entire season, Reiner showed little in his limited minutes and will be challenged to reclaim his roster spot this year. He's willing to be physical though, and that certainly will score him points with Skiles.

Frank Williams	point guard									Age: 25	Height: 6-3	Weight: 210
(90% PG, 10% SF)												Most similar at age: N/A

Year		G	M/G	FG%	FT%	P/40	R/40	A/40	TS%		Ast		TO		Usg		Reb		PER	
2002-03	NY	21	8.0	.273	.667	6.7	4.3	8.1	39.3		39.2		19.6		18.1		6.3		6.37	
2003-04	NY	56	12.8	.385	.854	12.3	3.0	6.8	47.8	46	29.3	24	15.2	58	20.9	35	4.2	58	10.66	58
2004-05	Chi	9	7.9	.150	—	3.4	3.4	6.2	15.0		29.5		8.8		17.7		4.7		0.18	

Williams looked like he would finally get a chance to earn some minutes because of the Bulls' thin backcourt last season, but he quickly fell out of favor and his career is now on life support. Williams is a capable defender but has never proven himself offensively and was passed in the rotation by Chris Duhon. The Bulls didn't pick up Williams's option for this season, and he might have to go overseas to prove himself before he can get back into the NBA.

Chicago Bulls

Cleveland Cavaliers

The Cavaliers had their first winning season since 1997–98, but you'd hardly know it from their reaction. The Cavs cleaned house from the roster all the way up to the owner, and the rebuilt unit now seems like a legitimate Eastern Conference contender.

The ball started rolling relatively late in the season when owner Gordon Gund sold the team to Dan Gilbert. Gilbert immediately set about reshaping the team with a single goal in mind—re-signing LeBron James in two years when the basketball prodigy is eligible for free agency. While salary rules favor Cleveland, keeping James isn't the home run that it would seem. Although James can get more money from the Cavs than from other teams, he could make substantially more in endorsements if he signed with New York, Chicago, or the Lakers, so Cleveland needs to make sure it has the edge in non-monetary factors.

To accomplish that, Gilbert started cleaning house almost immediately. His first move was rash and impulsive and probably did more to repel James than retain him: firing coach Paul Silas with less than a month to go in the season and the Cavs in a playoff race. Out of the blue, Cleveland was playing for an interim coach down the stretch. They went 8–10 under interim coach Brendan Malone to fall from the fifth seed in the East to out of the playoffs entirely.

After the season, Gilbert quickly axed Cavs general manager Jim Paxson, which wasn't entirely unwarranted. Other than the no-brainer of drafting James, Paxson had one big feather in his cap—he traded Tony Battie to the Magic for Drew Gooden, Anderson Varejao, and Steven Hunter before the season, covering a glaring hole left at power forward when Carlos Boozer knifed the Cavs in the back.

However, Paxson's mistakes outnumbered his positives. He mistakenly cut Steven Hunter shortly after acquiring him in the Gooden trade, made a midseason panic trade for Jiri Welsch that cost the Cavs a lottery pick, and none of his free agent signings (Lucious Harris, Ira Newble, and Kevin Ollie) panned out. Longer-term, he had a very poor draft record, with James being the lone bright spot.

To fill Paxson's role, Gilbert briefly courted Pistons coach Larry Brown—which would have been an enormous mistake—before settling on Danny Ferry. Ferry had been with the Spurs' organization since retiring as a player two years ago, but he's more versed in the role of a general manager than most because his father filled that job for several years with the Washington Bullets. Ferry's experience with the league's best-run organization in San Antonio shouldn't hurt either.

Ferry will oversee new head coach Mike Brown, a highly regarded Pacers assistant who is familiar with his new boss from his three-season stint as an assistant with the Spurs. Unusually for a pro coach, he never played in the NBA, but the ones who haven't have tended to have success (Jeff and Stan Van Gundy and Chuck Daly come to mind).

The front office wasn't the only department that got a makeover. When LeBron returns from his summer, he will find many of the nameplates in the locker room are different too. The one legacy Paxson left Cleveland was a treasure trove of cap space, which was greatly abetted by the increase in the salary cap permitted in the new collective bargaining agreement.

Thus, the Cavs set about reshaping their roster to better fit around James. They declined options on Robert Traylor, Lucious Harris, and Dajuan Wagner and then traded Welsch for a second-round pick. These moves opened up even more cap space, which enabled Cleveland to commence shopping.

Cleveland's primary target was an outside shooter to pair with James, but that option wasn't available once Michael Redd rebuffed their advances. They subsequently settled on Washington's Larry Hughes for a five-year, $60 million deal. Hughes is an open-court terror who should thrive with James on the break and can also be paired with him in a huge backcourt. Plus, he's a good defender who should be able to guard the opponents' top perimeter threat and allow James to focus on offense.

Did the Cavs overpay? Probably. Hughes is a poor outside shooter and he'll miss 15 games with injuries. Will it help them keep James in Cleveland in two years? Absolutely.

Cavaliers at a Glance

Record: 42–40, 4th place in Central Division

Offensive Efficiency: 103.2 (14th)

Defensive Efficiency: 102.5 (12th)

Pace Factor: 92.3 (18th)

Top-Rated Player: LeBron James (PER 25.75, 6th overall)

Head Coach: Mike Brown. The Gregg Popovich disciple gets his first shot at the big chair.

Hughes was the best player left on the market and Cleveland had to use its cap space to maintain its credibility.

For its next step, Cleveland stayed at home and re-signed center Zydrunas Ilgauskas to a five-year deal worth close to $60 million. This was a pretty good deal considering the circumstances—the fifth year is only partially guaranteed and the Cavs didn't have to max out Ilgauskas to keep him. Additionally, because they could offer more than the mid-level exception, Ferry wisely calibrated Ilgauskas's deal so they would be able to outbid teams for a third free agent. Considering the paucity of available centers capable of filling his shoes, keeping Ilgauskas was the right move at almost any price.

Cleveland then went to the free-agent market and signed Donyell Marshall, which was an astute maneuver by the Cavs. Marshall might be the single most underrated player in the league right now, an ace three-point shooter who contributes on the boards and can score in the post if needed. His presence should immediately deepen a frontcourt that already boasts Drew Gooden and Varejao. Moreover, his outside shooting should improve Cleveland's greatness weakness.

In fact, Marshall's signing may presage the trade of Gooden for a point guard. Hughes can be used as a stopgap for 10 minutes a night and Eric Snow can come off the bench for another 10, but neither of these players are reliable full-time options. It's the one shortcoming the Cavs need to address before they can do battle with the big boys in the East. Ferry still had over $3 million in cap room left to play the market at publication time, so a free agent addition as a possibility as well.

In addition to Marshall, Cleveland needs another shooter. The Cavs ranked 28th in the NBA in three-pointers, and nearly a third of them came from the now-departed Jeff McInnis. Cleveland let McInnis walk because of his deficient defense and frequent run-ins with coaches and teammates.

Another one-third of the three-pointers came from James, but the idea is to surround him with the shooters, since James can't pass the ball to himself. Besides James, the only returning Cav to make more than 20 three-point shots on the season was reserve forward Sasha Pavlovic. The absence of three-pointers meant the Cavs were well below the league average in True Shooting Percentage despite a field-goal percentage that mirrored the league norm.

Remarkably, the Cavs' offense was respectable due to second shots. With Gooden and Ilgauskas up front and Varejao and Traylor coming off the bench, Cleveland led the NBA in offensive rebounding. The Cavs grabbed 32.5 percent of their misses, compared to the league rate of 28.7 percent,

Table 1. Offensive Rebounding Leaders, 2004–05

Team	Pct. of Misses
Cleveland	32.5%
Seattle	32.4%
Utah	31.9%
Detroit	31.2%
Washington	31.1%
League Average	**28.7%**

and that earned them nearly two extra two points a game (see table 1). Though one doesn't think of Ilgauskas as a Rodman-esque board warrior, he led the NBA in offensive rebounds with 299.

Defensively, the three-point line also proved to be Cleveland's nemesis. The Cavs didn't give up huge quantities of threes, but the shots they allowed were usually wide open. Cleveland opponents hit 37.6 percent from downtown, putting the Cavs ahead of only lowly Atlanta in the league tables. Partly this stems from Cleveland's poor defense against the pick-and-roll. McInnis was eaten alive by this play and Ilgauskas wasn't mobile enough to provide much help, so the Cavs' defense frequently was in a scramble mode that left players open on the perimeter.

The desire to improve defensively is another motivation for the potential trade of Gooden. He's a great rebounder, but his frequent mental lapses have soured the team on his stock. Additionally, Varejao looks like he could become the energetic defensive force that's needed next to the lumbering Ilgauskas.

In any case, Cleveland should be much better on the wings with the addition of Hughes. Last year the Cavs played a grab-bag combo at shooting guard that included Ira Newble, Lucious Harris, and Sasha Pavlovic. Harris is gone and the others will be deep reserves this year. Also stepping into the fray is Luke Jackson, the Cavs' first-round pick in 2004 who spent nearly all of last season on the injured list with a back injury. Jackson could provide another source of perimeter shooting as well.

Because of those upgrades and the retention of Ilgauskas, the Cavs look set to go as far as LeBron can carry them. Amidst the turmoil of last season it's hard to remember that the Cavs have made immense progress from where they were two years ago, and that momentum continued over the summer. With another year of development from James and some new free agents to keep him company, a 50-win season looks well within reach.

DeSagana Diop								center				Age: 23			Height: 7-0		Weight: 280	
(100% C)																Most similar at age: N/A		

Year		G	M/G	FG%	FT%	P/40	R/40	A/40	TS%		Ast		TO		Usg		Reb		PER	
2002-03	Cle	80	11.8	.351	.367	5.0	9.1	1.8	35.6	72	16.2	7	21.0	71	9.4	70	12.8	50	6.66	71
2003-04	Cle	56	13.0	.388	.600	6.9	10.9	1.9	40.4	74	15.5	7	13.3	39	10.8	66	15.5	19	10.49	66
2004-05	Cle	39	7.8	.290	.000	5.2	9.2	2.0	28.1		9.3		12.2		11.9		12.8		6.17	

A complete and utter bust with the eighth overall pick in the 2001 draft, the Cavs severed ties with Diop. He was a classic case of a "project center" who never stopped being a project, but teams continue to draft guys like him every year. But amazingly the Mavs gave him a three-year, $6 million deal despite his steadfastly anemic production.

Drew Gooden								power forward				Age: 24			Height: 6-10		Weight: 242	
Defensive PER: 0.76 (98% PF, 1% SF, 1% C)																Most similar at age: Derrick Coleman		

Year		G	M/G	FG%	FT%	P/40	R/40	A/40	TS%		Ast		TO		Usg		Reb		PER	
2002-03	Mem-Orl	70	26.8	.457	.712	18.7	9.7	1.8	50.3	40	7.5	53	13.6	49	21.0	14	13.7	28	14.97	27
2003-04	Orl	79	27.0	.445	.637	17.1	9.7	1.7	48.4	49	7.7	60	10.9	24	20.0	21	14.0	30	15.55	30
2004-05	Cle	82	30.8	.492	.810	18.8	11.9	2.1	54.8	24	9.7	30	9.9	27	20.1	18	16.7	10	19.77	10
2005-06	PRJ (69.5)			.470	.743	18.4	10.4	2.0	52.3		9.1		10.7		20.8		14.7		17.63	

An NBA talent evaluator who happens to be one of the best in the game introduced me to the concept of "the second draft." He said that smart teams could use first-round picks who had failed at their first stop but were young enough to improve significantly as a cheap source of talent.

Think about it. One of the biggest changes in pro basketball the past few seasons has been the growing pool of young entrants in the draft. In 2004, for instance, eight of the first 19 picks came directly from high school. Many NBA general managers see this as a problem because the players' lack of development means the draft comes with far more uncertainty. The new age limit will only marginally improve the situation, as the draft will continue to be littered with teenage players.

However, a few forward-thinking execs recognize a tremendous opportunity in the new status quo. In the past, a player would leave school at age 21 or 22, sign a three-year rookie contract with an option for a fourth year, and not hit free agency until about age 25. By then, his development as a player was nearly complete, so a team playing the free-agent market couldn't find many bargains.

The current environment has made bargain hunting much easier. If a player joins a team at age 19, he's a free agent by the time he's 22 or 23. In many cases, the players haven't received much playing time and are still making all kinds of mental and physical adjustments to their game. Hence, teams can snap up a player like this in free agency, or even in a trade before he becomes a free agent, and with patience and a little luck they'll have a quality player at a bargain price.

The opportunity is abundant because people aren't used to the new reality of the younger players. In the past, if a player didn't establish himself in his first three seasons, we labeled him a bust and moved on. With a four-year college player, that's an appropriate course of action since he'd be 25 after the third season.

But if it's a player out of high school, our time frame for his expected development not only increases, *it doubles*. It's only in the sixth year when the player is 24, that teams have a good picture about what the player can become. Yes, they get some clues along the way, but examples abound of players blooming late despite turning pro early. Unfortunately, it's very hard for teams (let alone fans) to show that much patience with a player, especially when they've used a high draft pick on him.

In fact, just from last season, we have several instances where players from the "second draft" bloomed with their new team. Gooden is a prominent example. He was labeled a bust in Orlando but was only 23 when Orlando dealt him away. The player Cleveland got was young enough to improve significantly, and he certainly did last season. Now one year later, the Cavs may be able to trade him for a starting point guard, when all it cost to acquire him was an aging backup center.

Along with Gooden, other examples include:

- **Larry Hughes**—Hughes was one of the first "second draftees." The Sixers drafted him when he was 19 but traded him to Golden State halfway through his second season. The Warriors kept him for two-and-a-half years, but Hughes was only 23 and still inconsistent so they let him go. Washington signed him to an inexpensive free-agent contract (perhaps the only smart move of Michael Jordan's tenure) and reaped huge rewards the past two seasons, topped by an All Star–caliber performance last year.

(continued next page)

Drew Gooden *(continued)*

- **Joel Pryzbilla**—Drafted at age 20 out of Minnesota, Pryzbilla was a total flop in nearly four seasons in Milwaukee. Portland signed him for peanuts before last season and, at age 25, he suddenly exploded.
- **Steven Hunter**—Hunter turned pro too early, leaving DePaul at age 19, and struggled in three seasons with the Magic. But Orlando's pain was Phoenix's gain, as the Suns signed him for a minimum contract at age 23 and he proceeded to become one of the league's top backup centers.
- **Bobby Simmons**—Simmons turned pro after his sophomore year at DePaul and bounced around for a couple of seasons. He finally found a home when the Clippers snapped him up and gave them a bargain starter on the perimeter.
- **Zarko Cabarkapa**—The Suns' first-round pick a year ago, Phoenix traded him to Golden State for a draft choice they later used to obtain Walter McCarty. Turns out that Cabarkapa was twice as good as McCarty, had they only played him.

I could cite plenty of other examples, but the point is that there are countless players like this out there, and they're usually available very cheap because the market is undervaluing their future improvement. Keep an eye out for teams that are acquiring these kinds of players, because they're the ones that are going to be steadily improving.

As for Gooden, he improved sharply thanks to major increases in shooting percentage and Rebound Rate. Allowed to play his natural power forward spot full time, he was much more aggressive on the glass and cashed in on the opportunities he got around the basket. He improved his mid-range jump shot while at the same time taking fewer ill-advised three-pointers. Gooden also must have put in some work at the line over the summer, because his free-throw percentage improved nearly 20 points. In fact, he had a better case for the Most Improved Player trophy than most of the players who figured prominently in the voting.

So why do the Cavs seem down on him? In a word—defense. Gooden makes mental mistakes at the defensive end that infuriate the coaches, and he's not strong enough to handle the more physical power forwards. He has long arms and is great at getting his hands on crossover dribbles, even against guards, but he doesn't always bring a tremendous intensity to the proceedings. While his Defensive PER was decent, the Cavs would like more of a tough guy in his spot.

They should be careful not to make the same mistake Orlando did, however. Whoever acquires Gooden is getting an excellent rebounder whose offensive game is rapidly improving. They also may be able to get a bargain locked in by signing him to an extension before the season begins. Anyone up for the "third draft"?

Lucious Harris			shooting guard														**Age: 35**	**Height: 6-5**	**Weight: 205**
(89% SG, 11% SF)																			Most similar at age: Tyrone Corbin
Year		G	M/G	FG%	FT%	P/40	R/40	A/40	TS%		Ast		TO		Usg		Reb		PER
2002-03	NJ	77	25.6	.413	.804	16.1	4.7	3.1	49.4	40	15.0	32	6.9	5	19.8	29	6.7	34	13.52	32
2003-04	NJ	69	21.8	.404	.846	12.7	3.7	3.6	48.1	48	19.7	18	7.7	7	17.4	41	5.3	53	11.06	45
2004-05	Cle	73	15.5	.395	.812	11.1	4.3	1.7	47.5	55	8.3	64	7.1	7	13.9	60	6.0	47	9.00	60
2005-06	PRJ (29.6)			.376	.792	12.3	4.1	2.7	45.5		13.8		7.7		16.3		5.7		9.87	

Harris declined rapidly in his final two seasons in New Jersey, but the Cavs pretended not to notice and signed him in the off-season anyway. Predictably, his decline continued, as Harris seemed noticeably slower at age 35 and struggled to get shots off. In spite of this, he played 1,128 minutes last year, which should tell you how important Larry Hughes's signing was for this team. Harris was released and will have to battle for a spot on the end of a roster somewhere this year.

Zydrunas Ilgauskas			center														**Age: 30**	**Height: 7-3**	**Weight: 260**
Defensive PER: 1.20 (99% C, 1% PF)																			Most similar at age: Elden Campbell
Year		G	M/G	FG%	FT%	P/40	R/40	A/40	TS%		Ast		TO		Usg		Reb		PER
2002-03	Cle	81	30.0	.441	.781	22.8	10.0	2.1	51.6	33	7.5	47	12.5	26	24.5	2	14.1	42	19.39	4
2003-04	Cle	81	31.3	.483	.746	19.5	10.3	1.7	54.1	19	7.7	50	11.5	23	20.4	7	14.1	39	20.20	5
2004-05	Cle	78	33.5	.468	.799	20.2	10.3	1.5	55.0	25	6.7	34	12.8	30	21.1	4	14.4	36	19.55	5
2005-06	PRJ (17.5)			.463	.754	19.6	10.6	1.6	53.0		7.0		13.1		21.0		14.4		18.69	

Ilgauskas had severe foot problems early in his career and even now you'll hear people mention them as a concern. At this point though, what other player would be a better bet to play a full season? Ilgauskas has only missed six games in three years, making him the most durable of the 24 players invited to last season's All-Star game (see how many friends get that trivia question right). After all, it's not like he was constantly hurting different parts of his body—the only thing wrong was his foot, and it looks to be healed now. From that perspective, his new contract wasn't nearly as big a risk as some imagine.

The bigger threat for the Cavs is that similar big centers—Vlade Divac, Patrick Ewing, Elden Campbell, Luc Longley—have cruised along for years with amazing consistency, and then suddenly lost it out of the blue, like when a computer crashes for no apparent reason. At some point in the next two to six years, it will happen to Ilgauskas. The Cavs just need to hope the timing is closer to "six" than to "two."

On the court, Ilgauskas played much harder on defense than he had the previous two seasons, making more of an effort to help against screen-and-rolls and to chase loose balls. Combined with his shot-blocking ability, he put up a solid Defensive PER. He needs to be much more of a force on the defensive boards though. Ilgauskas led the NBA in offensive rebounds yet his overall Rebound Rate was quite ordinary because he did so little at the defensive end.

If he delivers defensively the Cavs will have few complaints, because Ilgauskas remains one of the game's best post players and is a surprisingly accurate shooter. He could stand to get a little better at passing out of double-teams, but that shouldn't be too great a worry as long as LeBron James is around—most of the double-teaming will be directed at him.

Luke Jackson — small forward — Age: 24 — Height: 6-7 — Weight: 215
(62% SF, 38% SG) — Most similar at age: N/A

Year		G	M/G	FG%	FT%	P/40	R/40	A/40	TS%	Ast	TO	Usg	Reb	PER
2004-05	Cle	10	4.3	.370	.833	27.0	5.6	2.8	48.9	8.7	5.8	31.3	7.8	16.26

The Cavs' first-round pick in 2004, Jackson missed nearly all of last season with a back injury but could play an important role this season. When he played Jackson certainly wasn't bashful, averaging a shot every 90 seconds, but he'll need to improve the accuracy if he's going to be the Cavs' sixth man this year.

LeBron James — small forward — Age: 21 — Height: 6-8 — Weight: 240
Defensive PER: 1.13 (95% SF, 5% PF) — Most similar at age: Kobe Bryant

Year		G	M/G	FG%	FT%	P/40	R/40	A/40	TS%		Ast		TO		Usg		Reb		PER	
2003-04	Cle*	79	39.5	.417	.754	21.2	5.5	6.0	48.8	40	19.1	20	11.2	39	28.5	3	7.6	22	18.25	7
2004-05	Cle	80	42.4	.472	.750	25.7	6.9	6.8	55.4	14	20.6	1	9.3	20	31.3	1	9.7	25	25.75	1
2005-06	PRJ (5.6)			.461	.763	26.7	6.2	7.1	53.9		20.0		9.5		32.6		8.6		24.09	

* Season rankings are as shooting guard

James has been compared to Michael Jordan ever since he was in high school, but a more appropriate comparison might be Oscar Robertson. Like Robertson, James is a powerful perimeter player from an Ohio school who is a nightly triple-double threat. James became the fifth player in history to average 25 points, seven rebounds, and seven assists in a season, which Jordan did only once but Robertson accomplished six times. Considering James's youth, he has a good chance of surpassing the Big O in that department.

The incredible thing about James is that he has almost no weaknesses, and he's still just scratching the surface. James's jump shot was a question when he turned pro, but last season he hit 35 percent on three-pointers. He created more plays than any other small forward and easily had the best Assist Ratio at his position, while managing to keep his Turnover Ratio below the league average. As the jumper continues developing, he'll become a devastating inside-outside threat. However, he needs a bit of work at the charity stripe, where he shot 75 percent. He also needs to work on his post game and figure out how to come to a jump stop without traveling, but that will come in time.

James's defense isn't yet to the level of his offense, but he's still quite good. His size and strength make him very difficult to post up against, while his quickness and anticipation in the passing lanes netted him over two steals per game. As explosive as he is, he doesn't seem to move as well laterally, so quicker players can give him some trouble. In addition, he needs to get better from the help side and give a more consistent effort from night to night.

Overall, predicting improvement in a young player is always an inexact science, but compared to others at his age James is miles ahead of every other player in history. If he continues to improve the jumper and develop his many other skills, the comparisons to Robertson and Jordan might not do him justice.

Jeff McInnis   **point guard**   **Age: 31   Height: 6-4   Weight: 179**
Defensive PER: 0.04 (100% PG)   Most similar at age: Vinnie Del Negro

Year		G	M/G	FG%	FT%	P/40	R/40	A/40	TS%		Ast		TO		Usg		Reb		PER	
2002-03	Por	75	17.5	.444	.746	13.2	3.0	5.2	47.7	43	24.4	43	10.8	26	20.1	45	4.5	55	10.00	54
2003-04	Por-Cle	70	33.8	.447	.797	14.0	3.0	7.3	51.1	24	31.6	19	8.8	7	22.1	28	4.1	59	15.13	24
2004-05	Cle	76	34.9	.412	.813	14.7	2.4	5.9	49.5	48	26.2	36	7.8	6	21.6	36	3.3	67	12.36	47
2005-06	*PRJ (42.4)*			*.418*	*.796*	*13.6*	*2.6*	*6.2*	*49.2*		*28.3*		*8.8*		*21.0*		*3.5*		*12.30*	

McInnis has the talent to help a team in need of point guard help, but his attitude continues to be problematic. In the Cavs' final two games when they were battling for a playoff spot, McInnis essentially quit on the team. He sat out most of the penultimate game because he was angry at being pulled in the first quarter, and he didn't even bother making the trip for the finale, citing a vague illness.

On the court, McInnis struggled mightily at the defensive end. He was never terribly quick to begin with but now he's lost a step. Even worse, it led to opponents beating him on pick-and-roll plays. His Rebound Rate reflected his declining athleticism and ranked among the worst in basketball.

McInnis has his positives. He was one of the few Cavs who could hit a three-point shot and he's excellent at getting shots off at the end of quarters. Plus, he doesn't turn the ball over. But for a contender looking for a backup point man, the overall package isn't appealing unless the attitude improves. New Jersey took a chance on McInnis with a two-year, $7 million package to back up Jason Kidd, and McInnis's offense may prove helpful there.

Jerome Moiso   **power forward**   **Age: 27   Height: 6-10   Weight: 260**
(79% PF, 21% SF)   Most similar at age: N/A

Year		G	M/G	FG%	FT%	P/40	R/40	A/40	TS%		Ast		TO		Usg		Reb		PER	
2002-03	NO	51	12.6	.520	.659	12.7	11.1	1.4	54.2	19	8.6	47	17.9	61	14.3	44	16.1	10	14.55	30
2003-04	Tor	35	11.9	.476	.579	9.8	10.8	0.8	50.6		6.0		18.7		11.7		15.9		12.27	
2004-05	Tor-NJ-Cle	20	6.0	.500	.769	9.3	12.3	0.3	59.0		1.6		22.1		9.0		17.2		12.24	

Based on Moiso's numbers from the past three seasons, it's hard to believe he's played as little as he has. Moiso is a good leaper who blocks shots and rebounds, and that gives him value as a reserve big man. While he doesn't contribute much at the offensive end and makes far too many turnovers, he has a decent touch around the basket and will convert most of his chances. The fact that nobody can find room for such a package in their frontcourt rotation, even as a fifth big man, is puzzling. He's better than a lot of players who are getting more consistent minutes, and perhaps somebody will realize that this summer.

Ira Newble   **shooting guard**   **Age: 30   Height: 6-7   Weight: 220**
Defensive PER: 0.80 (88% SG, 11% SF, 1% PF)   Most similar at age: Mike Sanders

Year		G	M/G	FG%	FT%	P/40	R/40	A/40	TS%		Ast		TO		Usg		Reb		PER	
2002-03	Atl	73	26.5	.495	.778	11.7	5.6	2.0	55.7	15	14.7	33	10.2	28	13.0	52	8.0	13	11.78	38
2003-04	Cle*	64	19.5	.391	.783	8.2	5.0	2.3	42.9	58	17.1	13	12.6	47	12.3	58	7.1	51	6.75	58
2004-05	Cle	74	24.8	.429	.797	9.6	4.8	2.0	48.2	51	9.5	60	10.1	29	12.5	66	6.7	35	8.56	64
2005-06	*PRJ (35.0)*			*.426*	*.774*	*9.4*	*5.1*	*2.2*	*47.6*		*12.9*		*10.8*		*12.4*		*7.1*		*8.72*	

*Season rankings are as small forward

A heinously bad free agent signing, Newble provides decent defense but his offense is so poor that the Cavs lose big on the trade-off. Newble has only one offensive skill—a decent outside shot—and other than an over-his-head year shooting the ball in Atlanta, he hasn't made that shot consistently enough to make up for his myriad weaknesses. He can't handle the ball at all, which is a major liability for a shooting guard, and he has no post game despite his size.

While Newble gives a strong defensive effort, he's not particularly quick and doesn't make enough of an impact to justify his lame offense. He'll play a greatly reduced role now that Hughes has been added and Jackson is back, and it's not a moment too soon.

Aleksandar Pavlovic			shooting guard														**Age: 22**	**Height: 6-7**	**Weight: 210**
(58% SG, 39% SF, 2% PG, 1% PF)																		Most similar at age: Derrick Chievous	

Year		G	M/G	FG%	FT%	P/40	R/40	A/40	TS%		Ast		TO		Usg		Reb		PER	
2003-04	Uta*	79	14.4	.396	.774	13.4	5.6	2.1	46.3	51	11.1	38	12.4	46	18.1	29	8.7	32	8.78	54
2004-05	Cle	65	13.3	.435	.688	14.6	3.3	2.3	51.6	41	10.8	56	11.7	49	17.3	45	4.6	62	8.93	61
2005-06	PRJ (22.8)			.435	.754	15.5	4.5	2.2	51.3		10.6		11.5		18.5		6.5		10.28	

*Season rankings are as small forward

What do you think he named his dog?

People consistently presume Pavlovic is a jump shooter because he's a perimeter player from Europe, but he's not. He's a quick slasher who likes to go to the basket but desperately needs to improve his mid-range game.

Pavlovic did manage to boost his three-point percentage to 38 percent, but he did so in just 78 attempts. For a player who likes to go to the basket, he has to get much better at locating teammates. Pavlovic's Assist Ratios have been very poor, and as with most players who drive a lot, he turns the ball over more than average. The biggest mystery though is the state of his rebounding. Pavlovic's Rebound Rate nearly halved in Cleveland, which is why his PER didn't improve despite a major uptick in shooting percentage.

Overall, it's hard to imagine what Paxson saw in this guy that made him give Charlotte a first-round draft pick for his rights. Yes, Pavlovic is quick, but he hasn't managed to use his quickness in a way that's very productive on the basketball court. Until he does, he'll have trouble keeping his spot in the league.

Eric Snow			point guard														**Age: 32**	**Height: 6-3**	**Weight: 205**
Defensive PER: 1.58 (66% PG, 30% SG, 4% SF)																		Most similar at age: Darnell Valentine	

Year		G	M/G	FG%	FT%	P/40	R/40	A/40	TS%		Ast		TO		Usg		Reb		PER	
2002-03	Phi	82	37.9	.452	.858	13.6	3.9	7.0	54.6	10	31.9	11	11.4	35	20.2	44	5.7	29	15.64	19
2003-04	Phi	82	36.2	.413	.797	11.4	3.8	7.6	49.4	39	35.1	12	11.7	36	20.4	39	5.6	27	13.46	32
2004-05	Cle	81	22.8	.382	.738	7.0	3.4	6.9	44.5	64	32.8	14	11.6	41	15.5	66	4.7	51	8.95	64
2005-06	PRJ (30.8)			.392	.763	9.6	3.4	7.0	47.0		32.8		12.3		17.8		4.9		11.47	

Snow had been declining in Philadelphia, but those slight year-to-year drops in Philly turned into a barrel over Niagara Falls once he got to Cleveland. Snow's performance declined sharply in every measurable attribute, as he lost the burst in his step required to get to the basket and had to rely on his marginal outside shot for points.

Thankfully, he can still defend, which is what is keeping him in the league. Snow's Defensive PER was among the best at his position, and at his age it's as much because of attitude and smarts as it is ability. His size and strength haven't withered, however, which gives him an advantage and allows him to defend shooting guards on occasion.

Snow almost certainly will be a reserve this season, but he should be able to bounce back a bit from last season's disaster. If he can just get his PER into double digits, his strong defense should assure that the Cavs aren't losing much ground at the backup point guard spot.

Robert Traylor			center														**Age: 28**	**Height: 6-8**	**Weight: 284**
(59% C, 41% PF)																		Most similar at age: Eduardo Najera	

Year		G	M/G	FG%	FT%	P/40	R/40	A/40	TS%		Ast		TO		Usg		Reb		PER	
2002-03	NO	69	12.3	.443	.648	12.6	12.3	2.4	48.6	54	13.2	15	14.0	43	16.4	22	17.9	7	15.29	25
2003-04	NO	71	13.3	.505	.547	15.4	11.1	1.8	52.7	30	9.6	29	13.8	45	18.1	14	16.4	13	16.80	1
2004-05	Cle	74	17.9	.444	.539	12.3	10.0	1.8	46.1	65	8.8	18	12.6	26	16.1	24	14.0	39	11.96	44
2005-06	PRJ (34.8)			.465	.536	12.9	10.4	2.1	48.2		10.6		12.7		16.5		14.8		13.68	

Traylor has never been in the greatest of shape, and sometimes that hits players in their late 20s as the metabolism slows down. It certainly hit Traylor like a ton of bricks this past season, as both his shot-making and rebounding skills suffered greatly. Traylor's shooting mark dropped by 61 percentage points, but even worse was the attrition in his free-throw attempts. On a per-field-goal-attempt basis, they fell by nearly half, resulting in his TS% dropping to near the bottom at his position.

(continued next page)

Robert Traylor *(continued)*

It's pretty clear what happened—with Traylor losing some zip in his step, he was forced to shoot more mid-range jumpers and got fewer tries around the basket. Those were lower-percentage shots, and also harder attempts on which to draw fouls. Taken all together, the result was a very sharp decline for a man who had been among the league's best backup centers.

Cleveland chose not to pick up Traylor's option so they could have more cap space, a decision no doubt made easier by Traylor's off year. He should latch on somewhere based on his previous track record, but he may have to get more serious about his conditioning to return to his previous glory.

Anderson Varejao — power forward — Age: 23 Height: 6-10 Weight: 230
(83% PF, 17% C) — Most similar at age: N/A

Year		G	M/G	FG%	FT%	P/40	R/40	A/40	TS%		Ast		TO		Usg		Reb		PER	
2004-05	Cle	54	16.0	.513	.535	12.3	11.9	1.3	53.4	30	6.0	60	8.6	15	13.3	61	16.7	11	16.95	20
2005-06	PRJ (17.2)			.513	.526	12.5	11.1	1.7	53.2		7.5		8.9		14.0		15.7		16.65	

Basketball's answer to Sideshow Bob, Varejao was a huge surprise in his first NBA season—and not just with his hair. He was among the best rebounders at his position and a hustling, active defender, but that part was expected. What surprised people was how much he contributed on offense. Varejao's European numbers suggested he would struggle to score, but his numbers were relatively solid as a rookie.

The key for Varejao is his activity. He gets himself easy baskets by going to the offensive boards and moves very well without the ball. While the lack of a post game and a weak jump shot make it all but impossible to run set plays for him, Varejao made the most of the opportunities he had. The one worry for Cleveland is that he was playing over his head, which is a possibility based on his European stats. If that wasn't the case, the Cavs have themselves an outstanding frontcourt reserve who could push for a starting job in another year or two.

Dajuan Wagner — shooting guard — Age: 22 Height: 6-2 Weight: 200
(99% SG, 1% PG) — Most similar at age: N/A

Year		G	M/G	FG%	FT%	P/40	R/40	A/40	TS%		Ast		TO		Usg		Reb		PER	
2002-03	Cle	47	29.5	.369	.800	18.2	2.4	3.8	46.6	46	14.6	34	9.5	22	23.3	11	3.3	57	10.85	41
2003-04	Cle	44	16.1	.366	.681	16.2	3.3	2.9	43.9	58	12.2	48	9.8	22	21.9	24	4.7	59	8.54	59
2004-05	Cle	11	9.3	.327	.750	17.3	0.8	5.1	38.8		16.5		11.4		28.8		1.1		4.74	

Another Paxson-era draft bust, Wagner was laid low by a series of physical problems that put his career on hold. The Cavs declined to pick up his option for 2005–06 after he missed most of the year with colitis, an inflammation of the intestine. His previous maladies included a bladder infection and inflamed liver.

Even if Wagner can overcome his string of internal injuries, he's not likely to earn a roster spot. He showed flashes of potential as a scorer in his rookie season, but he's a shooting guard in a point guard's body who needs to significantly improve the "shooting." With better health he can make it back to the NBA, but he faces a long road.

Jiri Welsch — shooting guard — Age: 25 Height: 6-7 Weight: 208
(62% SG, 23% PG, 15% SF) — Most similar at age: Eric Piatkowksi

Year		G	M/G	FG%	FT%	P/40	R/40	A/40	TS%		Ast		TO		Usg		Reb		PER	
2002-03	GS	37	6.3	.253	.759	10.4	4.8	4.6	34.8		20.2		14.2		19.9		6.4		4.36	
2003-04	Bos	81	26.9	.428	.743	13.7	5.4	3.4	53.1	19	18.0	22	12.7	53	16.5	45	7.7	20	12.61	35
2004-05	Bos-Cle	71	18.6	.402	.763	14.0	5.1	3.1	51.8	39	14.9	33	11.7	50	17.0	42	7.1	24	10.90	44
2005-06	PRJ (57.2)			.424	.749	13.9	5.4	3.3	53.3		17.0		11.9		16.8		7.5		12.30	

In one of the more bizarre deals of the season, the Cavs decided they needed outside shooting and traded a No. 1 pick to Boston for... Jiri Welsch? In a classic example of how every white European is automatically considered a shooting specialist, the Cavs picked up Welsch even though he was shooting 32 percent on three-pointers for Boston.

Predictably, Welsch struggled from outside with the Cavs. What was surprising was that he struggled in other respects too. Cleveland tried using him at point guard and he failed miserably, being far too slow for the position. He looked terrified in his few chances on the court, and overall didn't play nearly as well as he had in Boston.

Cleveland Cavaliers

After the season, the Cavs turned around and traded Welsch to Milwaukee for a second-round pick. He'll get to play his natural wing spot there and should be helpful off the bench. Welsch isn't a great shooter, but he can handle the ball, defends well, and sees the court. He should be able to recover from last year's disappointment, and he'll need to, because he's a restricted free agent at the end of the season.

Scott Williams (90% C, 10% PF)			**power forward**							**Age: 37**		**Height: 6-10 Weight: 260** Most similar at age: N/A		
Year	G	M/G	FG%	FT%	P/40	R/40	A/40	TS%		Ast	TO	Usg	Reb	PER
2002-03 Phx	69	12.6	.411	.786	12.5	8.9	1.0	44.0	68	6.0 62	8.8 4	15.6 32	12.5 53	9.67 63
2003-04 Dal	43	12.3	.484	.593	15.0	10.0	1.3	50.0	52	7.4 53	6.9 2	16.2 19	13.7 46	14.30 33
2004-05 Cle	19	8.0	.293	.818	8.7	7.9	2.1	36.0		10.0	8.5	14.8	11.0	6.66

Williams barely saws any minutes in what apparently will be his final NBA season. The Cavs picked him up to be a positive locker-room influence, but the only thing he influenced on the court was his opponent's scoring average.

Martynas Andriuskevicius center	**Age: 19 Height: 7-3 Weight: 230**
Translated 40-minute stats: 4.9 pts, 5.9 reb, 1.5 ast, .305 FG%, 2.15 PER	

Cleveland traded for a second-round pick to nab this Lithuanian, who will have a welcoming tutor in Zydrunas Ilgauskas. Despite his height, Andriuskevicius is more comfortable playing on the perimeter because of his thin frame and would probably have to play power forward in the NBA. Andriuskevicius's translated stats from the Euroleague were absolutely awful, but take them with a grain of salt as they came in limited minutes. Scouting reports say he's a good shooter and passer with an excellent feel for the game but he needs much more seasoning. Translation: Cleveland should keep him in Lithuania for another year or two.

Detroit Pistons

As Maxwell Smart would say, "Missed it by that much." Considering all that went right for them in winning the championship in 2004, the Detroit Pistons weren't given great odds of repeating last season. But despite multiple distractions and a paper-thin bench, the Pistons were one quarter away from making it back-to-back championships. Only a late rally by San Antonio in the deciding seventh game prevented Detroit from repeating.

The Pistons had plenty of reasons to pack it in. An early season riot in a game against Indiana set an ugly tone for the season (more on that in the Pacers chapter), and then Larry Brown had hip surgery that sidelined him for several games. The team gave an indifferent performance while assistant Gar Heard ran the show and was unable to take control of a mediocre Central Division until well after midseason. Brown subsequently experienced bladder complications from his surgery that caused him to miss more games later in the season. He was out for 17 games total, with the team posting a 9–8 record in his absence.

The biggest distraction for the team was Brown himself as he became a one-man sideshow for most of the season. A notorious nomad throughout his three-decade coaching career, Brown infuriated management by seemingly being linked to every job opening in the league and doing little to quell the speculation. He said coaching the Knicks would be his "dream job," (dude, you were coaching the *world champions*), wouldn't refute rumors linking him to the Lakers' opening, and strongly hinted that he knew Sixers' coach Jim O'Brien would be fired long before O'Brien did. (The Sixers were Brown's former team and several confidants work in their front office.)

That was bad enough, but then there was the whole Cleveland mess. Despite the fact that he was still coaching the Pistons and was under contract for three more years, Brown began talking to the Cavs about a front-office position even while the Pistons were mired in a tooth-and-nail battle with Miami in the Eastern Conference finals. All the while he said he wanted to return to the Pistons, but his actions belied his words.

Thus, it was hardly shocking when the two sides agreed to part ways after the season. For Detroit's management, putting up with Brown's flirtatious nature was the price they had to pay for gaining his expertise two years ago, and it resulted in a championship. But it was going to be much harder for Brown to command respect this season after he had one foot out the door throughout 2004–05. Brown's health was a further concern. While he was able to coach through the bladder complications during the playoffs, doing it throughout a hundred-game season was likely to be a different matter.

In his place comes Flip Saunders, the former Minnesota coach who already has a working relationship with point guard Chauncey Billups from his time in the Twin Cities. Saunders understands zone defenses as well as any coach in the game and should be more open to using the bench, particularly Darko Milicic. The former second-overall pick wasted away in two years under Brown, but Saunders doesn't carry the animus toward rookies that Brown did. Saunders also has a reputation as a players' coach, which might be a nice change of pace after two years of Brown's kvetching.

Yet the Brown saga did little to slow down the Pistons, thanks mostly to a brilliant starting five. Detroit doesn't have a superstar player, but they are above average at every position, and the sum of those advantages allows them to beat teams with brand-name players. After the bumpy start, the Pistons went 31–10 in the second half of the season thanks to their talented quintet.

Fortunately for the Pistons, that starting five also was extremely durable. Other than Ben Wallace's early-season six-game suspension, the starters missed a total of 14 games. It was a good thing, because Detroit's bench was basically a one-man band. Reserve big man Antonio McDyess was the Pistons' lone productive reserve, playing so well that he essentially gave Detroit a "sixth starter" and justifying general manager Joe Dumars's gamble on him last season.

After that it got ugly. No other Piston had a PER above 12, and most were in single digits. Detroit especially had a problem with the backcourt subs early in the season, as Lindsey

Pistons at a Glance

Record: 54–28, 1st place in Central Division

Offensive Efficiency: 102.8 (17th)

Defensive Efficiency: 97.9 (3rd)

Pace Factor: 89.5 (29th)

Top-Rated Player: Chauncey Billups (PER 19.05, 36th overall)

Head Coach: Flip Saunders. Former T'wolves coach has tough act to follow in Larry Brown.

Hunter couldn't score and Smush Parker and Horace Jenkins failed brief trials. Ultimately, Dumars traded a first-round draft pick for Utah's Carlos Arroyo, which at least gave them a competent reserve at the position.

Nonetheless, the bench hurt Detroit all season, and that was the biggest difference between the 2003–04 champions and the 2004–05 runners-up. The previous season, Detroit was able to bring productive players like Mike James, Mehmet Okur, and Corliss Williamson off the pine. But James and Okur signed expensive free-agent contracts and Dumars traded Williamson for Derrick Coleman to try to lessen his future salary obligations.

Unfortunately, two of the replacement players didn't pan out. Milicic spent a second season in Brown's doghouse and played only at the end of blowouts, while rookie Carlos Delfino hurt his knee and couldn't get back into the rotation. Additionally, Father Time slapped around backup center Elden Campbell. The net result was the bench turned from a big strength into a major weakness. As illustrated in table 1, Detroit's average bench PER fell by nearly three points.

In the end, Detroit nearly won it all even with a bench that failed to deliver. Once again, the defense was the key. Detroit was the league's third-best defensive team during the regular season and kicked it up another notch during the playoffs. In the Finals in particular, it was Detroit's defensive pressure than unnerved their opponents and allowed them to stay in the series. Detroit also was third in the NBA in blocked shots, with Ben and Rasheed Wallace combining for nearly four a game.

Detroit's defense was successful because they forced missed shots without fouling. The Pistons were tough and physical, yet they committed the second-fewest personal fouls in basketball and were third in opponent free-throw attempts per field-goal attempt. So while Detroit was only fifth in field-goal percentage allowed, it nearly led the league

Table 2. Opponent TS% Leaders, 2004–05

Team	Opp. TS%
San Antonio	50.2
Detroit	50.4
Chicago	50.7
Houston	50.8
Miami	51.0

in opponent TS%. Only San Antonio was better, and the difference was minimal (see table 2).

Better yet, the lack of fouls masked the Pistons' greatest weakness. By not fouling, they were able to minimize the number of minutes they needed from their weak bench. Only Phoenix had its starters play a higher proportion of the team's minutes than the Pistons, and as a result only three Pistons reserves played more than 500 minutes.

One has to think Brown knew this, and designed his defensive scheme to minimize gambling and fouling that would expose his weak bench. It was even more effective in the postseason, because teams can play their starters for much longer stretches in the playoffs than during the long grind of the regular season. Four of the Detroit starters averaged over 39 minutes a game in the playoffs, and Brown was able to ratchet down to a seven-man rotation. That left the backup guard, Hunter, as the lone weak link in what was suddenly a strong rotation.

For that system to work, however, the Pistons need all six key players to remain healthy the entire season, and the odds of that don't stack up in their favor. While all six are in their prime and, other than McDyess, have no injury history, it behooves the Pistons to develop a more failsafe backup plan. Detroit was still shopping for free agents at publication time, but several internal candidates may secure more prominent roles. Milicic will almost certainly play regularly now that Brown is gone, and Delfino should see minutes behind Prince if his knee is OK. First-round draft choice Jason Maxiell may figure into the picture as well.

However, the fact Detroit's most pressing concern is its seventh man shows what a great job general manager Joe Dumars has done of building a winner in Detroit. All of the key players are signed for the foreseeable future, none has an obscene contract, and the Pistons haven't had to pay a cent of luxury tax. And other than Rasheed Wallace, there isn't a knucklehead among them. Saunders will face high expectations in taking over such a well-oiled machine, but he could hardly ask for better material with which to work.

Table 1. Pistons Bench, 2003–04 vs. 2004–05

2003–04 Player	PER	2004–05 Player	PER	Change
Okur	18.34	McDyess	17.20	−1.12
James	14.40	Arroyo	11.22	−3.18
Williamson	14.38	Dupree	11.72	−2.66
Campbell	13.87	Campbell	6.99	−6.88
Hunter	9.00	Hunter	9.52	+0.52
Ham	8.29	Ham	5.48	−2.81
Average	**13.05**		**10.36**	**−2.69**

Carlos Arroyo				point guard								Age: 26	Height: 6-2	Weight: 202
(93% PG, 7% SG)														Most similar at age: Rumeal Robinson

Year		G	M/G	FG%	FT%	P/40	R/40	A/40	TS%		Ast		TO		Usg		Reb		PER	
2002-03	Uta	44	6.5	.459	.818	16.9	3.6	7.4	51.0		26.3		14.9		25.8		5.5		14.12	
2003-04	Uta	71	28.3	.441	.804	17.9	3.7	7.1	51.7	19	25.8	45	11.3	33	26.4	6	5.7	26	16.79	16
2004-05	Uta-Det	70	20.7	.389	.799	12.7	2.9	7.7	46.6	60	31.8	19	12.1	46	23.1	26	4.0	62	11.22	52
2005-06	PRJ (51.2)			.417	.791	14.5	3.3	7.2	49.0		28.9		11.6		23.7		4.8		13.62	

Arroyo got off to a slow start in Utah and quickly found himself in Jerry Sloan's doghouse. He was sitting at the end of the Jazz bench by the time Detroit liberated him. He struggled with his shot as a Piston, but his ability to run the point was a welcome upgrade from what Detroit had before.

It's ironic that Arroyo got more attention for what he did in the Olympics than what he accomplished in Utah the year before. As the most recognizable player on a Puerto Rico team that blew out the U.S. in Athens, Arroyo was routinely credited with having played great in the Olympics. That actually isn't true. He played well against the U.S. but struggled for most of the tournament and may have picked up some bad habits that spilled over into his NBA season.

Arroyo's numbers dropped sharply in almost every area, but he was only 25 so one suspects his numbers should be able to bounce back. While his jumper is shaky and needs more arc, he's one of the best penetrators in the game and even in a bad year had an excellent Assist Ratio. He's signed for three more years to a very reasonable contract and should provide a solid backup to Billups.

Chauncey Billups				point guard								Age: 29	Height: 6-3	Weight: 202
Defensive PER: 1.77 (92% PG, 8% SG)														Most similar at age: B. J. Armstrong

Year		G	M/G	FG%	FT%	P/40	R/40	A/40	TS%		Ast		TO		Usg		Reb		PER	
2002-03	Det	74	31.4	.421	.878	20.6	4.7	4.9	58.2	1	19.8	57	9.2	12	24.6	13	7.0	15	20.42	7
2003-04	Det	78	35.4	.394	.878	19.1	4.0	6.5	55.0	7	24.3	49	10.3	24	25.4	7	5.4	32	18.59	10
2004-05	Det	80	35.8	.442	.898	18.4	3.8	6.5	60.9	2	26.9	32	10.4	29	23.3	25	5.3	40	19.05	8
2005-06	PRJ (34.4)			.418	.870	17.8	3.9	6.0	57.0		24.6		10.4		23.7		5.5		17.54	

Billups was nearly the MVP of the Finals for a second straight season, yet he's never been to an All-Star game. He's rapidly closing in on Byron Scott and Derek Harper for the title of best player never to make the midseason classic, but that may all change this year because his notoriety has grown considerably.

Billups took a less active role in the offense this season, but made up for it by shooting the ball more effectively. He improved his field goal percentage by nearly 50 points, and his TS% continues to be among the best at his position. That's a result of his ability to both hit lots of three-pointers and earn lots of free-throws. Many players do one or the other, but only a few do both. Billups took nearly half his shots from beyond the three-point line and hit 42.6 percent. In fact, one of Brown's favorite plays late in games was to take Billups off the ball so he could run off a screen and shoot a three from the left corner. Billups also is a strong, physical guard who forced contact on his drives and earned nearly five free throws a game. Better yet, he's a great foul shooter, clicking at nearly 90 percent last season.

Defensively, Billups was a star performer. He had one of the best Defensive PERs at his position and was named second-team All-Defense. Because of his size, he can handle shooting guards and often switched with the more wiry Hamilton when the Pistons faced a physical opponent at that position.

Overall, he's in a position nobody imagined he would be in three years ago when he was a backup point guard for the T'wolves: the best player on a championship-caliber team.

Elden Campbell				center								Age: 37	Height: 7-0	Weight: 279
(100% C)														Most similar at age: N/A

Year		G	M/G	FG%	FT%	P/40	R/40	A/40	TS%		Ast		TO		Usg		Reb		PER	
2002-03	NO-Sea	56	15.5	.397	.801	15.8	8.3	2.3	48.3	55	11.2	26	11.0	15	19.8	8	12.1	59	14.08	33
2003-04	Det	65	13.7	.439	.685	16.2	9.4	2.0	49.0	56	9.4	30	13.2	38	20.0	9	12.8	55	13.87	36
2004-05	NJ-Det	40	9.8	.317	.764	12.3	9.5	1.9	40.8		9.3		14.9		18.8		13.3		6.99	

The Nets and Pistons have a budding rivalry in the Eastern Conference, and Campbell provided a good example of their mutual distaste. As part of the Arroyo trade, Detroit sent Campbell to Utah to even out the salaries, with the understanding that Utah would waive him and Detroit could sign him back. The Nets knew this too, however, and when the Jazz cut Campbell the Nets claimed him off waivers. They had no use for Campbell themselves; few teams do the way he played last year. They just wanted to spite the Pistons and make life more difficult for their nemesis in the East. Unfortunately, Campbell proved so bad that the Nets gave up their ruse and waived him a month later, allowing Detroit to get him back.

In his heyday Campbell was a versatile big man who thrived on driving to his left from the high post, but he's not nearly as nimble these days and his scoring numbers have suffered. Campbell has one skill remaining: He can push Shaquille O'Neal two feet farther from the basket than almost anyone else in basketball. That has come in awfully handy for the Pistons since they've had to get past Shaq each of the past two seasons, and right now it's the only thing keeping Campbell employed.

Derrick Coleman — center — Age: 38 — Height: 6-8 — Weight: 270
(59% C, 41% PF)

Most similar at age: N/A

Year		G	M/G	FG%	FT%	P/40	R/40	A/40	TS%		Ast		TO		Usg		Reb		PER	
2002-03	Phi	64	27.2	.448	.784	13.8	10.3	2.0	52.5	31	11.5	20	12.7	29	15.8	29	15.2	26	15.39	22
2003-04	Phi	34	24.8	.413	.754	12.9	9.1	2.2	47.1	63	11.8	17	14.6	59	17.1	17	12.9	51	11.67	53
2004-05	Det	5	10.0	.214	1.000	7.2	12.0	0.0	29.4		0.0		11.5		13.3		17.7		1.08	

The Pistons traded Corliss Williamson for Coleman knowing full well his knees probably wouldn't allow him to play anymore. They were far more interested in his expiring contract. Coleman tried to give it a go early in the season but the wheels wouldn't allow him to, and he quickly retired.

Carlos Delfino — shooting guard — Age: 23 — Height: 6-6 — Weight: 230
(85% SG, 15% SF)

Most similar at age: N/A

Year		G	M/G	FG%	FT%	P/40	R/40	A/40	TS%	Ast	TO	Usg	Reb	PER
2004-05	Det	30	15.3	.359	.575	10.1	4.8	3.3	43.1	15.8	11.8	16.4	6.7	8.54

A first-round pick by the Pistons in 2003, Delfino came over from Europe in 2004. As his European translations predicted he struggled to make shots from the field, hitting just 35.9 percent. Although Delfino showed tremendous skill as a passer, he took too many risky chances. He also hurt his knee at midseason, so his numbers don't reflect the second-half improvement that most players show in their rookie season.

Delfino is an NBA-caliber defender and his European stats suggest he'll be among the best rebounders at his position, although that didn't hold up last year. The big question is whether the offense will ever come around. Delfino's shooting numbers were abysmal, and unless he greatly improves them it will be tough for him to earn many minutes on a contending team.

Ronald Dupree — small forward — Age: 24 — Height: 6-7 — Weight: 209
(92% SF, 6% SG, 2% PF)

Most similar at age: N/A

Year		G	M/G	FG%	FT%	P/40	R/40	A/40	TS%		Ast		TO		Usg		Reb		PER	
2003-04	Chi	47	19.0	.394	.629	13.1	7.5	2.5	44.5	56	12.7	36	11.7	39	17.5	34	10.7	12	9.67	50
2004-05	Det	47	10.0	.480	.617	12.9	8.1	2.0	51.5		9.7		11.4		15.8		11.3		11.72	

The Pistons had Dupree in camp in 2003 but had to cut him because they didn't have roster space. With the bench blown up in the offseason, there was no such problem last year and Dupree established a niche as Prince's backup on the rare occasions the Pistons went deep on their bench.

Dupree is a strong right-handed driver and can really finish around the basket, but his lack of a jumper leaves him a bit lost offensively. He'd be better on a running team where he could get a couple of easy baskets a game on the break, but the Pistons' snail-like pace isn't doing him any favors. Where he really earns his paychecks is with rebounding and defense, areas where his athleticism can take hold. Dupree is signed for one more year, but Delfino does many of the same things and plays the same position, creating an interesting battle for bench minutes heading into this season.

Darvin Ham			small forward						Age: 32		Height: 6-7		Weight: 240
(49% SF, 47% PF, 4% C)												Most similar at age: N/A	
Year		G	M/G	FG%	FT%	P/40	R/40	A/40	TS%	Ast	TO	Usg	Reb	PER
2002-03	Atl	75	12.3	.447	.481	7.8	6.6	1.6	46.4 52	12.8 39	21.9 59	11.0 56	9.4 27	5.42 57
2003-04	Det	54	8.9	.493	.600	8.0	7.7	1.3	53.1	11.6	22.6	9.9	10.5	8.29
2004-05	Det	47	5.9	.459	.387	6.7	5.1	0.7	45.4	3.5	12.6	8.8	7.1	5.48

Brown created a very interesting job for Ham: end-of-quarter defensive specialist. Ham hardly played in meaningful games, but when he did the scenario was always the same. The Pistons would have a player in foul trouble, it would be the end of a quarter, and the other team would have the ball for the last shot. In those situations, Brown would insert Ham to do the one thing he does reasonably well: defend. Ham played three minutes or less in 21 of his 47 appearances because of that usage.

As for his skills at the other end of the court, there aren't any. Ham might be the worst offensive player this side of Michael Ruffin. He is an amazingly bad shooter, has poor hands, and sets his teammates up for turnovers because he doesn't come back to the ball when it's passed to him. One thing he can do, however, is dunk. Even at 32, Ham has explosive hops and is among the best power dunkers in basketball. Keep an eye on him in garbage time.

Richard Hamilton			shooting guard						Age: 27		Height: 6-7		Weight: 193
Defensive PER: 1.62 (89% SG, 11% SF)												Most similar at age: Allan Houston	
Year		G	M/G	FG%	FT%	P/40	R/40	A/40	TS%	Ast	TO	Usg	Reb	PER
2002-03	Det	82	32.2	.443	.833	24.4	4.8	3.2	53.1 21	10.8 52	10.4 31	28.6 4	7.1 24	18.71 8
2003-04	Det	78	35.6	.455	.868	19.8	4.0	4.5	52.2 24	16.9 30	11.4 42	25.1 8	5.7 48	16.79 10
2004-05	Det	76	38.5	.440	.858	19.5	4.0	5.1	52.8 29	19.2 15	11.2 44	25.5 9	5.6 52	15.96 12
2005-06	PRJ (41.8)			.441	.849	19.0	4.0	4.6	52.4	18.2	11.1	24.8	5.7	16.02

With Reggie Miller retired from the game, Hamilton is now the NBA's best at moving without the ball. The key to his game is his stamina, which allows him to run back and forth through countless screens without tiring. All that motion draws numerous fouls away from the ball, which is how Hamilton averaged nearly six free throws a game despite essentially being a mid-range jump shooter. Unusually for a high-scoring guard, Hamilton has no three-point shot. He hit only 30.5 percent last season and attempted fewer than two per game. Due to all the foul shots, he posted a solid TS% anyway. Hamilton also showed great improvement as a passer last season, often coming off curls and dumping the ball down to the screener for an easy basket when defenses overreacted.

While Hamilton is the Pistons' leading per-minute scorer, he's not the all-around talent that some of his teammates are. Hamilton contributes almost nothing on the boards and can be exposed by bigger guards defensively because he lacks strength. Fortunately, he has the two Wallaces behind him as deterrents. However, he fares much better defensively in quickness match-ups, frequently defending speedy point guards while Billups switches onto a bulkier shooting guard, and his overall Defensive PER was very solid.

Because of his prominent role on a championship team, Hamilton has become mildly overrated in recent years. He's not the star that some imagine, but he's a productive player who generates shots and, thanks to the free throws, gets a decent number of points from them.

Lindsey Hunter			shooting guard						Age: 35		Height: 6-2		Weight: 195
(60% SG, 38% PG, 2% SF)												Most similar at age: Doc Rivers	
Year		G	M/G	FG%	FT%	P/40	R/40	A/40	TS%	Ast	TO	Usg	Reb	PER
2002-03	Tor	29	23.2	.351	.723	16.7	3.5	4.2	43.4 60	15.8 63	12.6 46	24.9 12	5.0 42	10.60 50
2003-04	Det	33	20.0	.343	.625	7.1	4.1	5.2	39.9 63	32.0 1	12.8 55	15.1 53	5.5 50	9.00 57
2004-05	Det	76	15.1	.358	.793	10.0	4.3	4.5	43.5 64	21.7 6	12.9 60	17.5 44	6.0 45	9.52 56
2005-06	PRJ (12.3)			.332	.708	9.5	3.8	4.3	40.4	21.9	13.6	16.9	5.3	8.72

Hunter has enjoyed a renaissance as a suffocating defensive player after overcoming foot injuries that slowed him in L.A. and Toronto. He has long arms and fast hands, enabling him to average nearly a steal a game in just over 15 minutes a night—one of the best rates in basketball. Hunter doesn't need to gamble excessively to get those steals either. He's able to hound his man up the court and stick a hand on the ball while keeping in front, skills that make him exceedingly effective in full-court pressure situations.

Hunter needs to contribute mightily on defense because his offense has become so bad. He's shot 35, 34, and 36 percent the past three seasons. As a result, his TS% is annually among the worst at his position. He's kept shooting three-pointers even though he really ought to stop, hitting only 28 and 27 percent the past two seasons. Finally, he commits at least as many turnovers as he forces. Hunter has never been comfortable at the point and is vulnerable to pressure, plus he often forces passes in traffic. Not surprisingly then, his Turnover Ratio has been abnormally high as a Piston.

Considering those offensive limitations, the Pistons may have to reduce Hunter's role this season. Arroyo is a much better fit as the backup point guard, and Delfino will be challenging for minutes behind Hamilton at shooting guard. Hunter's defensive skills still come in handy against the right opponent, as he showed against Dwyane Wade in the conference finals, but those opportunities may be fewer and farther between this season.

| **Horace Jenkins** | | point guard | | | | | | | **Age: 31** | **Height: 6-1** | **Weight: 180** |
| (100% PG) | | | | | | | | | | | Most similar at age: N/A |

Year		G	M/G	FG%	FT%	P/40	R/40	A/40	TS%	Ast	TO	Usg	Reb	PER
2004-05	Det	15	6.9	.333	.923	16.2	3.5	3.5	41.4	13.5	10.5	24.9	4.8	10.19

A journeyman guard, Jenkins has decent quickness and managed to hang on to a spot on the Pistons' roster last season. Like almost all the Pistons' reserves he struggled to make shots when he got chances to play, and at 31 he faces an uncertain future.

| **Antonio McDyess** | | power forward | | | | | | | **Age: 31** | **Height: 6-9** | **Weight: 245** |
| (98% PF, 2% C) | | | | | | | | | | | Most similar at age: LaPhonso Ellis |

Year		G	M/G	FG%	FT%	P/40	R/40	A/40	TS%		Ast		TO		Usg		Reb		PER	
2002-03	NY		Did not play																	
2003-04	NY-Phx	42	22.1	.470	.551	12.5	11.1	1.6	48.6	58	9.2	33	14.6	58	15.0	32	16.3	14	12.61	45
2004-05	Det	77	23.3	.513	.656	16.5	10.7	1.6	54.2	26	7.5	49	11.0	34	18.2	27	15.0	20	17.20	19
2005-06	PRJ (53.9)			.492	.617	14.1	10.4	1.6	51.7		8.5		12.0		16.4		14.8		14.78	

McDyess's performance was one of the biggest surprises of the season and the catalyst for Detroit's return to the Finals. After his uninspiring performance with New York and Phoenix at the end of the 2003–04 season, Detroit's four-year, $22 million offer raised many eyebrows. But as usual, Joe Dumars knew what he was doing. McDyess stayed healthy all season and was the Pistons' only reliable bench player.

Because of his knee problems, McDyess isn't nearly as explosive as he used to be, but he has plenty of athleticism left. He also has a turnaround jumper from the left block that is nearly unstoppable, and that move provided most of his points. Plus, McDyess was active on the glass and finished well around the basket.

His defense was an unexpected bonus. McDyess looked a step slow early in the season but picked things up as the year wore on. In the Finals, he frequently guarded Tim Duncan and arguably was Detroit's most effective defender against him. While he's not the force that the two Wallaces are at that end, the drop-off was much less severe than one might have imagined for a 30-year-old player with a history of knee problems.

Additionally, McDyess looked like he was still getting warmed up. After nearly three years off, he seemed to be improving and could kick things up another notch this season. The one thing Detroit should be wary of is overuse. McDyess's history says the knee problems could come back at any time, and that could be a deadly blow to the Pistons' title hopes.

| **Darko Milicic** | | center | | | | | | | **Age: 20** | **Height: 7-0** | **Weight: 250** |
| (81% C, 19% PF) | | | | | | | | | | | Most similar at age: N/A |

Year		G	M/G	FG%	FT%	P/40	R/40	A/40	TS%	Ast	TO	Usg	Reb	PER
2003-04	Det	34	4.7	.262	.583	12.1	10.8	1.8	31.8	7.3	13.6	22.4	14.7	6.03
2004-05	Det	37	6.9	.329	.708	10.5	6.7	1.1	38.7	5.2	14.6	16.2	9.4	4.57

Milicic is on pace to be the biggest draft bust in NBA history. Nobody else is even close. But I'm not quite ready to pass judgment yet.

(continued next page)

Darko Milicic *(continued)*

Yes, the early returns are awful, but consider a few things. First, Milicic is extremely young at age 20. Second, one positive marker sticks out in his record—he's blocked nearly a shot every 10 minutes in his NBA career, which tells me he could be an outstanding defensive player in time. And third, I find it hard to believe that he would continue to shoot this badly if he played regular minutes. I mean, 40 percent I could believe, but Darko's career mark is 29.8. *Nobody* shoots that badly over a long period of time. I'm pretty sure that's a function of a small data sample and not his real skill level, and that's the major reason his PER is so poor.

That said, Milicic has plenty of work to do. He seems lethargic when he plays and takes a long time getting up and down the court. He also needs to get much more aggressive, as he has seemed unwilling to mix it up inside the few times he's played. Saunders will be strongly encouraged to give Milicic more burn this year, because the Pistons need to figure out what they have before it's time to offer (or not offer) an extension to him next fall. As a result, the ball is in Milicic's court, and it might be his last chance to shed the bust label.

Tayshaun Prince			small forward									Age: 24	Height: 6-9	Weight: 215
Defensive PER: 1.97 (98% SF, 1% PF, 1% SG)													Most similar at age: Matt Harpring	

Year		G	M/G	FG%	FT%	P/40	R/40	A/40	TS%	Ast	TO	Usg	Reb	PER
2002-03	Det	42	10.4	.449	.647	12.6	4.1	2.2	54.6	14.1	12.3	15.1	6.1	11.68
2003-04	Det	82	32.9	.467	.766	12.5	5.8	2.8	53.6 17	17.4 10	10.9 30	15.5 44	7.9 41	13.37 33
2004-05	Det	82	37.1	.487	.807	15.9	5.7	3.3	55.6 10	15.5 7	9.2 19	18.9 28	8.2 38	16.23 12
2005-06	PRJ (50.5)			.475	.796	14.5	5.8	3.0	54.4	15.8	9.4	17.8	8.2	15.07

Used mostly as a defensive stopper in 2003–04, Prince showed solid improvement at the offensive end last season thanks to an improved jumper. Prince's form is hideous with his elbow flying out to the side, but he nonetheless is accurate from the middle ranges and respectable even at the three-point line.

Prince also can be effective in the post from the left block and earned a lot more free throws last season because Detroit called his number on the blocks more often. However, his success usually requires a smaller opponent. Prince is rail thin and can be pushed off the blocks easily by stronger players, plus he has trouble making his lefty jump hook when the shot is challenged.

Prince is overwhelmingly left-handed but has started turning back to his right more because opponents are overplaying him so extremely. He rarely makes a convincing move with his right hand, but he'll at least spin back to his right once in a while after starting left. Despite that limitation, he's a very effective distributor and rarely turns the ball over—in fact, he's capable of playing shooting guard.

Defensively, Prince remains among the best in the business. He has extremely long arms that allow him to play off his man and still alter the shot. In addition, he's able to get blocks off the ball by coming from behind players who don't see him. Because his quickness is underrated he usually can keep smaller players in front of him too. His one shortcoming is on the glass, where his lack of muscle prevents him from being much of a factor despite his length and leaping ability.

Overall, he's blossomed into one of the league's better small forwards and continues to improve, which will cost the Pistons as they try to negotiate an extension this fall. Prince isn't worth max-level money, but if Detroit can work out a long-term deal that pays him in the range of $7–$9 million annually, they'd be well advised to do so.

Ben Wallace			center									Age: 31	Height: 6-9	Weight: 240
Defensive PER: 2.40 (94% C, 6% PF)													Most similar at age: Dale Davis	

Year		G	M/G	FG%	FT%	P/40	R/40	A/40	TS%	Ast	TO	Usg	Reb	PER
2002-03	Det	73	39.3	.481	.450	7.0	15.7	1.7	48.6 53	16.5 6	12.1 24	9.8 68	23.2 1	17.30 11
2003-04	Det*	81	37.6	.421	.490	10.1	13.2	1.8	44.1 62	12.1 30	10.8 22	14.2 54	18.6 4	17.39 18
2004-05	Det	74	36.1	.453	.428	10.8	13.5	1.8	45.9 67	8.8 17	8.3 2	14.6 32	18.9 8	17.52 11
2005-06	PRJ (10.9)			.443	.454	9.2	12.8	1.9	45.4	12.3	10.2	13.1	17.8	15.99

* Season rankings are as power forward

Since Larry Brown took over in Detroit, we've often heard about the effectiveness of his strategy in making Ben Wallace a bigger part of the offense and what a shame it was that Rick Carlisle wouldn't let Wallace shoot.

Perhaps Larry should get his eyes checked. Wallace is a terrible offensive player and having him take more shots has not been beneficial. Wallace is a poor shooter and even worse from the free-throw line. Just look at his unbelievably bad TS%. Why Detroit would want a player like him using 50 percent more possessions—the change between 2002–03 and 2004–05—is beyond me.

Additionally, some people make the casual inference that because the Pistons nearly won two championships, they must have a great offense, which also means having Wallace shoot more must be working. This is just wrong. Detroit had the league's 15th-best offense last season and was 18th the year before. A lot of the reason is the extra touches they're getting for an abominable offensive player. Moreover, Flip Saunders now faces the challenge of taking away the green light given to Wallace under Brown.

The points Wallace does get usually come on offensive rebounds and alleyoop passes for dunks. He's one of the best offensive rebounders in basketball, averaging four per game for three straight seasons. He also slashed his Turnover Ratio dramatically last season.

Of course, Wallace's real value is at the defensive end. He became only the fifth player in NBA history to record 100 blocks and 100 steals in five consecutive seasons on his way to a third Defensive Player of the Year trophy. While a few players finished the year with a higher Defensive PER than Wallace, including Tim Duncan, it's hard to argue with the vote. Wallace played more minutes than all of them and had added value not shown in the ranking because of his rebounding.

He also has one of the best contracts in basketball, but his deal expires at the end of the season. It behooves the Pistons to get him signed to an extension so he can't test unrestricted free agency. With the possible exception of Billups, he's Detroit's most irreplaceable player.

Rasheed Wallace			power forward												Age: 31		Height: 6-11 Weight: 230	
Defensive PER: 2.08 (69% PF, 31% C)																Most similar at age: Donyell Marshall		
Year	G	M/G	FG%	FT%	P/40	R/40	A/40	TS%		Ast		TO		Usg		Reb		PER
2002-03 Por	74	36.3	.471	.735	20.0	8.2	2.3	55.2	14	10.2	38	9.3	11	21.5	13	12.3	41	18.50 10
2003-04 Por-Atl-Det	68	35.1	.436	.736	18.2	7.7	2.6	51.0	41	11.6	34	8.9	6	22.0	13	10.4	57	17.86 15
2004-05 Det	79	34.0	.440	.697	17.0	9.6	2.1	49.9	50	10.0	29	9.0	18	20.7	15	13.4	32	16.39 25
2005-06 PRJ (45.7)			*.435*	*.707*	*15.9*	*8.5*	*2.3*	*50.6*		*11.3*		*9.9*		*19.6*		*12.0*		*15.30*

Wallace remains an enigma, but he's behaved better in Detroit than he did in Portland. He is a prime example for proponents of the one-bad-apple theory, which holds that a team can have one whack job like Wallace on the roster as long as there isn't a partner in crime (as Bonzi Wells was in Portland). Stephen Jackson would be another example. Paired with the choir boys in San Antonio, he had no problems; paired with Ron Artest in Indiana, mayhem ensued. I'm not sure I'm completely on board with this theory yet, but the anecdotal evidence is building.

Wallace got off to a very poor start last season, and while his numbers recovered somewhat in the second half, it was among his worst seasons overall. He took too many long jump shots and continued to baffle observers by straying from the low left block, where he can dominate with an unblockable turnaround jumper. Wallace is only a 33-percent career three-point shooter but prefers hanging out at the top of the circle and launching away to the more physical play in the post.

Defensively, Wallace has never been better. His long arms are an incredible deterrent and while he sometimes sleepwalks on offense, he almost always goes hard on defense. Overall, Wallace's Defensive PER was among the best in basketball, and he tied his career-high in rebounds. Ironically, it was a defensive gaffe by Wallace that probably cost Detroit the title. He ad-libbed a double-team on Manu Ginobili at the end of Game 5, leaving Robert Horry wide open for a game-winning three-pointer. It's just another example of what a puzzle Wallace is to outside observers, and Saunders's biggest challenge this year will be solving it.

Jason Maxiell   power forward   Age: 22   Height: 6-7   Weight: 250

Maxiell will give up at least two inches every night as an NBA power forward, but it may not matter. He was the toughest SOB in college basketball last season and will fit in perfectly with Detroit's blue-collar mentality. Maxiell has very long arms and is a good leaper, allowing him to block nearly three shots a game for Cincinnati. The big question is whether he can score and rebound enough to stay on the court, since he did neither much in college.

Amir Johnson   power forward   Age: 18   Height: 6-10   Weight: 220

A second-round draft pick, Johnson turned pro out of high school because he didn't qualify academically for college and will probably spend at least a year in the D-League. He's long and athletic and can block shots, but the rest of his game is a blank slate right now.

Alex Acker   shooting guard   Age: 22   Height: 6-5   Weight: 185

The final pick of the draft, Acker is an above-average shooter but mediocre at best in other areas. He can handle the ball and might be able to move to the point, but I greatly doubt he'd be quick enough. Detroit probably will put him in the D-League and see if he does anything noteworthy, but his chances of making the active roster are slim.

Indiana Pacers

I t just wasn't meant to be.

The Pacers entered 2004–05 with dreams of sending Reggie Miller into retirement with a championship ring, but those hopes quickly faded into a lost year awash in injuries and suspensions.

Miller began the string of setbacks with a broken wrist in the preseason that kept him out for 16 games. It turned out he would be one of the healthier Pacers in 2004–05, the year of the incredible shrinking lineup. Jamaal Tinsley missed the second half of the season with foot problems after keeping the team afloat up until mid-season. Jonathan Bender lasted only seven games before knee trouble sent him to the sidelines. At center, Scot Pollard had repeated back problems, while Jeff Foster missed 21 games battling a hip injury and David Harrison missed the final 49 games with knee trouble.

And then there was the fight.

By now everyone knows the details of The Malice at Auburn Hills. The hairy brawl between several Pacers and the patrons of Detroit's arena resulted in a season-long suspension for Ron Artest, a 35-game ban for forward Stephen Jackson, and a 15-game absence for O'Neal, effectively destroying the Pacers' chances at a championship.

Unfortunately, the Pacers were victims of the NBA's need to sweep this ugly incident under the rug as fast as possible. While Artest and Jackson were wrong to go into the crowd and start beating on spectators, it seemed unfair to punish them so severely when the response of the Pistons' security and fans was equally appalling and they received only the lightest slaps on their wrists.

The answer is obvious as to why the league came down so hard on the players and so lightly on the fans—the first rule of business is that the customer is always right. However, by setting a tone of virtual impunity for fans who choose to behave so boorishly and teams whose security staffs are asleep at the wheel, the league places itself at much greater risk of it happening again—which would be a far greater P.R. disaster than handing out a more even-handed punishment.

In fact, they may have provided an even greater incentive for fans to do this. Want Tim Duncan out of your team's way in the postseason? Throw a beer at him and see what happens. It ended up working out that way for Detroit. The Pistons benefited more than any other team from the melee, because the suspensions effectively neutralized their greatest rival in the Eastern Conference.

Once Artest was suspended for the year, Indiana's title hopes were essentially over. Losing him was just the tip of the iceberg. Indiana lost three starters to suspension, lost O'Neal again later in the season to a separated shoulder, and led the league in games lost to injuries and suspension. Overall, the Pacers ended up using 20 players—17 of whom started at least once—and Miller was the only Pacer to start more than 50 games.

Imagine everyone's shock then when the playoffs started and Indiana took the court. This was only possible because the Pacers' enviable depth allowed them to keep their heads above water despite all the injuries. Several players who were expected to play limited roles instead started for much of the season, including Austin Croshere, Fred Jones, and Anthony Johnson. Deep reserves like James Jones, Harrison, and Pollard also saw much more action, and each was able to stop the bleeding.

A few subs failed to close the wound, however, and that's where Indiana experienced much of its slippage from the 61-win season in 2003–04. Backup point guard was a sore point all year, as Eddie Gill played 1,021 minutes despite shooting 33 percent and averaging just 3.3 assists per 40 minutes. Small forward also was a problem spot until Jackson returned. Indiana even experimented for a while with long-time Carlisle fave Michael Curry, who was finished three years ago and proved it emphatically with 40-minute averages of 4.8 points and 4.3 rebounds.

Indiana never got whole again, even minus Artest, as O'Neal battled a sore shoulder in the postseason and Tinsley was limping when he returned. Nonetheless, they knocked out Boston in the first round and took Detroit to six tough games in the second before bowing out. It was perhaps the

---

Pacers at a Glance

Record: 44–38, 3rd place in Midwest Division

Offensive Efficiency: 102.4 (19th)

Defensive Efficiency: 101.9 (11th)

Pace Factor: 89.4 (30th)

Top-Rated Player: Jermaine O'Neal (PER 22.85, 14th overall)

Head Coach: Rick Carlisle. Did miraculous work to get this team to second round of playoffs.

best coaching job of Carlisle's short but distinguished career, as he slowed the pace to a crawl, preached defense, and rode what was left of Reggie Miller to win 44 games.

Miller rode off into the sunset after the season, but with all the other talent around, the Pacers should be able to challenge for a championship this year. O'Neal has been hurt in two straight postseasons but he's one of the game's 10 best players when healthy. Artest was having a monster year before his suspension, and his combination of scoring skill and defensive relentlessness are unmatched at the small forward spot. Jackson will move to shooting guard, where his average of 21.1 points per 40 minutes should more than fill the void left by Miller. And Tinsley, if he can stay on the court all year, is an All-Star caliber point guard who defends as well as he distributes.

Surrounding that group again will be a deep and talented bench. The underrated Foster is one of the game's best rebounders, while Harrison, Croshere, and Pollard give Indiana the NBA's deepest frontcourt—even if they can't re-sign free agent Dale Davis. First-round draft pick Danny Granger was one of the most polished players in the draft and should contribute right away, while Bender could be a scoring machine if his knees can hold up to the pounding. Even the weakest link is deep, as the backcourt of Johnson and Fred Jones form a sold tandem behind Tinsley and Jackson. Plus, the Pacers scored another shooting ace in the offseason when they signed Lithuanian guard Sarunas Jasikevicius.

Jasikevicius will struggle defensively, but his ability to hit from outside at either guard spot should help open things up for Artest and O'Neal in the paint. Indiana also hoped to keep restricted free agent James Jones, though they hardly seem to need him.

With so much talent on hand, one thing Carlisle might consider is quickening the team's pace. The Pacers were fairly ironically named in 2004–05, as they had the league's slowest Pace Factor and were last in the NBA in fast-break points. It's a long-held Carlisle trademark. Indiana was 26th in Pace Factor even during 2003–04, when they had as much talent as any team in the league, and one wonders if Carlisle is unnecessarily putting a chokehold on the offense. The Pacers seem to have the talent to do more in the open court. Tinsley is outstanding in transition, as is Artest, and Jackson, Fred Jones, O'Neal, and Foster also do well in the running game As an added plus, running would also be a way to take advantage of Indiana's superior depth. It's hard to quibble with much Carlisle has done in Indiana, but this is one area where a change of strategy might be in order.

But at any pace, Indiana can hang with anyone. The Pacers have superior depth at every position and two big-time stars as centerpieces in O'Neal and Artest. The Malice at The Palace might have deferred Indiana's title hopes for a year, but in 2005–06, they have as good a chance as anyone of taking the Larry O'Brien Trophy.

Ron Artest — small forward — Age: 26 Height: 6-7 Weight: 252
(92% SF, 8% PF) — Most similar at age: N/A

Year		G	M/G	FG%	FT%	P/40	R/40	A/40	TS%		Ast		TO		Usg		Reb		PER	
2002-03	Ind	69	33.6	.428	.736	18.4	6.3	3.4	52.9	19	14.6	29	10.7	29	21.5	16	8.8	34	17.56	11
2003-04	Ind	73	37.2	.421	.733	19.6	5.7	4.0	51.1	33	15.3	24	11.4	33	25.0	7	8.4	37	18.14	9
2004-05	Ind	7	41.6	.496	.922	23.6	6.2	3.0	60.8		12.2		9.4		24.2		8.4		23.52	

Nobody doubts Artest's talent. The only question is if he can keep his head screwed on straight for an entire season. A forgotten footnote to his season-long suspension for the brawl in Detroit is that the Pacers had already suspended Artest because he told the team he wanted to take time off to promote a hip-hop album. Seriously.

In the seven games he played, Artest was a terror, with a top-10 PER and his usual manic defense. The Pacers can only hope that the year off mellowed him enough that his distracting antics come to an end and he focuses on being an All-Star basketball player.

Jonathan Bender   small forward   Age: 24   Height: 7-0   Weight: 235
(62% PF, 37% SF, 1% C)   Most similar at age: N/A

Year		G	M/G	FG%	FT%	P/40	R/40	A/40	TS%		Ast		TO		Usg		Reb		PER	
2002-03	Ind	46	17.8	.441	.714	14.8	6.5	2.1	52.1	25	11.2	46	11.2	33	16.8	37	9.1	30	13.24	31
2003-04	Ind	21	12.9	.472	.830	21.8	5.9	1.3	58.4		5.3		19.6		22.3		8.3		15.64	
2004-05	Ind	7	13.3	.400	.500	15.5	6.0	1.7	42.2		7.1		17.7		22.4		8.2		5.62	

Bender looked like he was ready to break out in 2004–05, but knee problems kept him on the shelf virtually the entire season. The knee injuries have been persistent enough that one wonders if he'll ever stay healthy for a full season, but Bender has considerable potential as a scorer if he can get on the court. The 7-footer has a nice mid-range jump shot that he can shoot over anybody and handles the ball well for his size. His length also is a major asset on defense, allowing him to play several feet off his man and still contest shots. He needs to add more strength, however, and will have to battle his way back into a crowded forward rotation.

Austin Croshere   power forward   Age: 30   Height: 6-10   Weight: 240
Defensive PER: -0.79 (94% PF, 3% C, 3% SF)   Most similar at age: Sam Perkins

Year		G	M/G	FG%	FT%	P/40	R/40	A/40	TS%		Ast		TO		Usg		Reb		PER	
2002-03	Ind	49	12.9	.411	.815	15.9	9.8	3.5	53.0	25	17.4	10	8.7	7	19.0	26	13.7	26	16.08	20
2003-04	Ind	77	13.6	.388	.894	14.7	9.2	2.0	54.9	11	11.3	38	12.0	39	16.6	38	13.0	40	14.43	41
2004-05	Ind	73	25.0	.378	.883	14.2	8.2	2.1	53.1	33	10.2	28	12.8	53	16.9	37	12.0	46	13.52	45
2005-06	*PRJ (27.1)*			*.381*	*.882*	*13.9*	*9.1*	*2.0*	*53.6*		*10.8*		*11.7*		*16.3*		*13.1*		*13.93*	

Croshere became the starting power forward after O'Neal's suspension but gradually faded from the rotation as the year wore on. Despite his horrible shooting percentages, Croshere is a decent offensive player who has three-point range and uses the threat of his outside shot to set up his drives to the basket. That's actually the most potent part of his game—Croshere averaged better than a free-throw attempt per two field-goal attempts and shot 88.3 percent from the line. He struggled in his supposed specialty though, by hitting only 25.9 percent from downtown. In addition, the penalty for his aggression in going to the basket was a high Turnover Ratio.

Croshere's offense is getting tough to live with, however, because his defense is so bad. A competent defender in his younger days, Croshere's blocked shot rate is but a fraction of what it was in his mid-20s, and his Rebound Rate has declined too. Plus, he has slow feet and isn't strong enough to push opposing players out of the post. Overall, his Defensive PER was among the worst in basketball.

Croshere won't be going anywhere since he's signed for two more years at over $7 million per, but in order to justify even a portion of that income, he needs to either improve his shooting percentage or ramp up the defense. Due to the crowded frontcourt, he'll need to do that just to get onto the court.

Michael Curry   small forward   Age: 37   Height: 6-5   Weight: 235
(79% SF, 15% PF, 5% SG, 1% C)   Most similar at age: N/A

Year		G	M/G	FG%	FT%	P/40	R/40	A/40	TS%		Ast		TO		Usg		Reb		PER	
2002-03	Det	78	19.9	.402	.800	6.1	3.3	2.7	47.4	50	26.3	1	10.9	30	9.9	59	4.8	59	5.72	56
2003-04	Tor	70	17.6	.388	.845	6.6	2.8	1.7	46.0	52	16.4	17	14.9	57	9.8	59	4.1	59	3.61	59
2004-05	Ind	18	13.8	.448	.500	4.8	4.3	2.4	46.1		11.5		9.5		8.2		5.9		4.96	

Curry had a connection to Carlisle from his days in Detroit, and that apparently helped him hook on with Indiana. The Pacers should have known better. Curry has put up embarrassingly poor numbers for three straight seasons and this probably was his last stop as a player. Don't forget about him though. He was head of the players' union and will probably end up as a general manager at some point down the road.

Dale Davis (77% C, 23% PF)				center											**Age: 36**		**Height: 6-11**	**Weight: 250** Most similar at age: Hot Rod Williams
Year	G	M/G	FG%	FT%	P/40	R/40	A/40	TS%		Ast		TO		Usg		Reb		PER
2002-03 Por	78	29.3	.541	.633	10.1	9.9	1.6	56.6	11	13.9	12	10.5	10	11.2	62	14.9	29	14.59 30
2003-04 Por	76	22.1	.473	.613	7.9	9.5	1.7	50.5	46	16.4	6	9.1	5	10.3	69	14.1	38	12.97 42
2004-05 GS-Ind	61	21.4	.479	.606	8.7	11.5	1.4	51.2	42	6.9	33	11.7	15	10.5	58	15.6	27	13.32 35
2005-06 PRJ (25.6)			*.462*	*.591*	*8.0*	*9.6*	*1.5*	*49.1*		*11.7*		*11.3*		*9.9*		*13.6*		*12.08*

Davis was a salary throw-in to the Baron Davis trade between New Orleans and Golden State, but the rebuilding Hornets had no need for this Davis either and waived him. That allowed the Pacers to pick him up for the stretch run, and the grizzled vet proved surprisingly lively. Davis took over the starting center spot and contributed solid defense and rebounding to the Pacers' injury-plagued front line.

Davis's scoring rate has diminished markedly the past few seasons as he has lost athleticism. It's increasingly hard for him to finish around the basket, especially since he always stops to gather himself and never goes up off one foot. Davis also has limited range on his jumper and struggles from the line. His value lies in his size, strength, and toughness, factors that allowed him to make a late-in-life switch from power forward to center. Moreover, he's a surprisingly adept passer for a big man and rarely turns the ball over.

Carlisle stayed with Davis in the starting lineup longer than he should have, however. Once Jeff Foster returned, Carlisle should have sent Davis to the pine. Now that Davis is a free agent, the Pacers are hoping to bring him back, but it's hardly a need. His value a year ago was mainly as a Band-Aid because of the injuries, but he's not a championship-caliber player at this point in his career.

John Edwards (74% C, 26% PF)				center										**Age: 24**	**Height: 7-0**	**Weight: 275** Most similar at age: N/A
Year	G	M/G	FG%	FT%	P/40	R/40	A/40	TS%	Ast	TO	Usg	Reb	PER			
2004-05 Ind	25	5.6	.367	.500	8.3	5.5	0.9	40.1	4.1	17.0	12.5	7.4	4.98			

Only a few people know about this, but the Pacers were so desperate for help that they briefly signed the former vice-presidential candidate from North Carolina, who had little to do after the election since he had given up his Senate seat.

As far as the basketball goes, Edwards doesn't figure in the Pacers' plans for the coming season and will probably have to put in a stint in the D-League before he can get back to the NBA.

Jeff Foster (71% C, 29% PF)				center												**Age: 28**		**Height: 6-11**	**Weight: 242** Most similar at age: Dale Davis
Year	G	M/G	FG%	FT%	P/40	R/40	A/40	TS%		Ast		TO		Usg		Reb		PER	
2002-03 Ind	77	10.6	.360	.540	8.0	13.7	2.5	39.4	71	17.5	4	11.7	20	13.1	47	19.3	5	11.82	47
2003-04 Ind*	82	23.9	.544	.669	10.1	12.4	1.3	57.8	3	11.6	36	10.8	23	10.8	64	18.4	6	16.31	23
2004-05 Ind	61	26.1	.519	.634	10.7	13.8	1.1	55.1	21	5.1	46	11.4	13	11.7	54	20.1	4	15.38	24
2005-06 PRJ (31.6)			*.515*	*.630*	*9.9*	*13.1*	*1.6*	*54.9*		*10.6*		*10.9*		*11.5*		*19.0*		*15.54*	

* Season rankings are as power forward

Foster is one of the best rebounders in all of basketball, especially at the offensive end, because he is unusually quick for a man of his size and aggressively chases caroms. He had the fourth-best Rebound Rate among centers, and those rebounds provided most of his offense in the form of easy put-backs. Foster is a good leaper who can finish dunks, but he's usually looking for rebounding position rather than getting himself open for a shot. He also will shoot an 18-foot jumper on occasion, but he should probably stop. Foster shot 20.7 percent on jump shots but they accounted for nearly a third of his attempts last season. If he deleted that from his arsenal, he would shoot over 60 percent from the field.

Because of his quickness, Foster is a fine defensive player who is at his best when matched up against quick forwards. In strength match-ups, he doesn't fare quite as well, but his rebounding is an asset and he's quick enough to step out on guards against the pick-and-roll. Despite Foster's quickness and leaping ability, however, he's a terrible shot-blocker who had only 12 all season—three fewer than Anthony Johnson.

Foster should retake his spot in the starting lineup this year after hip problems slowed him down in 2004–05. His ability to create havoc on the glass should be an upgrade from Davis. Ironically, as the Similarity Scores show, Foster plays as a younger version of the man he's replacing.

Eddie Gill	point guard								Age: 27	Height: 6-0	Weight: 186
(92% PG, 8% SG)									Most similar at age: Greg Anthony		

Year		G	M/G	FG%	FT%	P/40	R/40	A/40	TS%		Ast		TO		Usg		Reb		PER	
2003-04	Por	22	7.1	.417	.850	12.7	4.3	4.1	55.8		22.0		16.5		17.2		6.2		13.20	
2004-05	Ind	73	14.0	.335	.877	10.5	4.4	3.3	48.4	53	15.5	66	14.3	60	15.5	65	6.0	26	9.41	62
2005-06	*PRJ (4.3)*			*.336*	*.865*	*11.1*	*3.9*	*3.6*	*48.5*		*16.4*		*14.1*		*16.2*		*5.3*		*9.93*	

The Pacers signed Gill when the injuries hit and he ended up being their backup point guard for most of the season. He was a pretty bad one too. Gill shot incredibly poorly, hitting 33.5 percent, but his stewardship of the offense was even worse. Gill was near the bottom of his position in both Assist Ratio and Turnover Ratio, and he nearly accomplished a difficult feat for a point guard by having more turnovers than assists. He was adequate defensively and on the boards, but unless his offense shows major improvement, he won't be able to hang on to a job.

Marcus Haislip	power forward								Age: 25	Height: 6-10	Weight: 230
(71% PF, 29% C)									Most similar at age: N/A		

Year		G	M/G	FG%	FT%	P/40	R/40	A/40	TS%	Ast	TO	Usg	Reb	PER
2002-03	Mil	39	11.3	.431	.684	14.6	4.8	0.8	47.4	4.5	10.5	17.0	7.0	9.57
2003-04	Mil	31	8.5	.486	.714	14.1	8.1	0.6	53.9	4.0	9.1	13.9	11.4	14.60
2004-05	Ind	9	11.8	.342	.545	12.1	5.7	1.1	37.3	5.4	11.6	18.8	7.7	3.78

A lottery pick by the Bucks in 2002, Haislip has been a complete bust. The Bucks cut him before the season and the Pacers signed him briefly, but he couldn't get the job done in Indiana and was waived. Haislip showed some promise in his second season in Milwaukee but badly needs to add muscle and improve his intensity. A stint in Europe might be his best option at this point.

David Harrison	center								Age: 23	Height: 7-0	Weight: 280
(100% C)									Most similar at age: Jelani McCoy		

Year		G	M/G	FG%	FT%	P/40	R/40	A/40	TS%		Ast		TO		Usg		Reb		PER	
2004-05	Ind	43	17.7	.576	.571	13.9	7.1	0.7	58.9	10	3.3	63	18.3	63	14.0	36	9.6	68	12.77	39
2005-06	*PRJ (10.3)*			*.571*	*.585*	*13.8*	*6.9*	*0.9*	*58.6*		*4.1*		*18.1*		*14.2*		*9.3*		*12.78*	

Indiana's first-round draft pick in 2004 put up a reasonably solid performance at the offensive end where he shot 57.6 percent and showed some flashes of having a decent post game. His TS% was among the best at his position and he scored at a decent rate for a big man. He needs to be more careful with the ball and set fewer illegal screens though, because his Turnover Ratio was way too high.

The bigger disappointment was Harrison's mysterious lack of aggression on the glass. Only Peja Drobnjak and Clifford Robinson were worse among centers, and neither of them are seven feet tall and weigh 280 pounds. Harrison also struggled at the defensive end, although that's hardly unusual for a rookie, and his size and strength should allow him to be a good post defender in time.

Harrison had minor knee surgery and missed the second half of the season, but he should return healthy for his sophomore campaign. If he can improve his work on the glass, his offensive skills may allow him to elbow aside Pollard and Croshere for minutes off the Pacers bench.

Stephen Jackson — small forward
(84% SF, 15% SG, 1% PF)

Age: 27 Height: 6-8 Weight: 218
Most similar at age: Walt Williams

Year		G	M/G	FG%	FT%	P/40	R/40	A/40	TS%		Ast		TO		Usg		Reb		PER	
2002-03	SA	80	29.8	.435	.760	16.8	5.1	3.3	52.6	22	14.6	30	14.0	51	20.5	20	7.4	49	14.49	25
2003-04	Atl	80	36.8	.425	.785	19.7	5.0	3.3	52.1	25	13.1	29	12.0	42	23.1	11	7.1	49	16.10	16
2004-05	Ind	51	35.4	.403	.830	21.1	5.5	2.6	51.8	39	10.2	47	10.6	35	24.9	7	8.1	44	15.87	15
2005-06	PRJ (70.0)			.416	.791	18.5	5.2	3.2	52.1		15.0		12.0		22.2		8.2		15.28	

Other than that little incident in Detroit, Jackson had a very solid first season as a Pacer. He stepped up his offensive contribution when O'Neal went out late in the season and ended up averaging a career-best 21.1 points per 40 minutes. While his field-goal percentage dipped, his overall numbers didn't suffer too much because he got to the line more and hit a career-high 83 percent.

Jackson has steadily cut down his Turnover Ratio during his pro career, and last year's drop was noteworthy because he went to the basket as often as ever. Jackson dribbles the ball extremely high, which makes him vulnerable to deflections, but he has become better at protecting the ball and avoiding high-traffic areas. He's also a good scorer in transition, which is amazing for a guy who appears to run without bending his knees.

Jackson had to be the Pacers' defensive stopper last season, which was perhaps a bit beyond his skills. While he's a good athlete and has the size to alter shots, he's not particularly nimble and his instincts are more as a scorer than as a stopper. He'll gladly relinquish that duty to Ron Artest this season.

Anthony Johnson — point guard
(91% PG, 9% SG)

Age: 31 Height: 6-3 Weight: 195
Most similar at age: Chris Childs

Year		G	M/G	FG%	FT%	P/40	R/40	A/40	TS%		Ast		TO		Usg		Reb		PER	
2002-03	NJ	66	12.8	.446	.689	12.8	3.7	4.1	51.2	29	22.0	55	10.5	22	17.1	53	5.3	35	11.21	47
2003-04	Ind	73	21.9	.406	.798	11.3	3.3	5.1	49.7	36	27.7	33	10.3	22	17.5	58	4.8	50	11.61	51
2004-05	Ind	63	27.7	.445	.752	12.2	4.1	6.9	52.6	26	32.9	11	10.6	31	20.0	51	6.0	25	14.25	36
2005-06	PRJ (51.9)			.425	.753	11.3	3.8	5.8	50.5		29.9		10.6		18.4		5.4		12.27	

Johnson chose a good time to have his best pro season, because he was able to help the Pacers weather the loss of Tinsley and subsequently squeak into the playoffs. Johnson was particularly solid as a distributor, as he got into the paint on pick-and-roll plays and repeatedly found the open man. He ended up with the 11th-best Assist Ratio in the league. Offensively, Johnson has the size to post up and is a decent three-point shooter. However, his scoring rates have never been impressive because he's slow and can't jump.

Defensively, Johnson's lack of speed was a bit of a problem, and he tended to foul jump shooters a lot. He mostly made up for it because he's bigger and stronger than most guards, helped out on the boards, and didn't make mistakes. Johnson is extremely unlikely to repeat last season's performance, so the Pacers will welcome Tinsley back to the lineup with open arms. The bigger question is whether he'll even be the second string, as Sarunas Jasikevicius may steal most of Johnson's minutes.

Fred Jones — shooting guard
Defensive PER: 0.34 (87% SG, 7% PG, 6% SF)

Age: 26 Height: 6-4 Weight: 220
Most similar at age: Khalid Reeves

Year		G	M/G	FG%	FT%	P/40	R/40	A/40	TS%		Ast		TO		Usg		Reb		PER	
2002-03	Ind	19	6.1	.375	.750	8.0	3.1	1.7	44.6		13.6		16.3		11.3		4.4		5.49	
2003-04	Ind	81	18.6	.395	.832	10.5	3.3	4.6	52.7	22	27.8	3	11.7	46	15.7	51	4.7	58	11.81	40
2004-05	Ind	77	29.5	.425	.850	14.3	4.3	3.5	55.1	19	16.5	27	10.9	40	17.9	41	6.2	41	13.28	33
2005-06	PRJ (64.1)			.402	.837	12.9	4.0	3.7	52.8		19.4		11.2		17.3		5.7		12.56	

Jones was supposed to come off the bench for 15–20 minutes a night but instead led the team in minutes due to all the injuries. He improved his offense somewhat from his second season, particularly his jump shot. Jones hit 38 percent on three-pointers, making him less dependent on drives to the basket for his points. He can be a spectacular dunker when he goes to the basket, but he isn't very elusive as a dribbler and so he doesn't get to the rim as often as one might expect. Consequently, his scoring rate is low. He is a good passer though.

Jones's defensive stats were much worse than they were in 2003–04, because he didn't have Ron Artest to bail him out. Jones is small for a shooting guard so bigger, more physical guards gave him problems. Despite his leaping ability, he's also a poor rebounder who should get more aggressive on the boards.

Barring injury, Jones will move back to his bench role this season and is a perfectly adequate player in that setting. But 2004–05 exposed why he's not quite ready for duty as a full-time starter.

James Jones (83% SF, 15% PF, 2% SG)		small forward							Age: 25	Height: 6-8	Weight: 220 Most similar at age: Jumaine Jones		
Year	G	M/G	FG%	FT%	P/40	R/40	A/40	TS%	Ast	TO	Usg	Reb	PER
2003-04 Ind	6	4.3	.222	1.000	10.8	3.1	0.0	35.4	0.0	0.0	15.7	4.3	4.89
2004-05 Ind	75	17.7	.396	.855	11.2	5.2	1.7	53.7 22	8.2 60	9.7 25	13.1 61	7.6 47	10.43 51
2005-06 PRJ (37.1)			.376	.838	10.4	5.2	1.7	51.6	8.3	10.3	12.6	7.7	9.95

The fact Jones's most similar player is Jumaine Jones is perhaps fitting in light of the confusion over his name sown in last year's playoffs.

Both Jumaine Jones and James Jones are 6'8", solidly built, and do almost nothing but shoot long jump shots. Jumaine plays for the Lakers and James plays for the Pacers, and they're not related. But in the postseason, multiple announcers kept calling the Pacers' Jones "Jumaine Jones." Worse yet, to differentiate him from Fred Jones, they would occasionally refer to him just as "Jumaine," like he was Prince or Madonna.

Jones can defend, and that might enable him to establish a career as a reserve forward. He also has a decent jumper, hitting 39.8 percent on threes, but he has no handle or first step so his usefulness as a scorer is limited. He's a restricted free agent whom the Pacers claim they want to bring back, but with the addition of Danny Granger and the return of Jonathan Bender, this Jones doesn't appear to have a role by any name.

Reggie Miller Defensive PER: 0.95 (69% SG, 31% SF)		shooting guard							Age: 40	Height: 6-7	Weight: 195 Most similar at age: Dale Ellis		
Year	G	M/G	FG%	FT%	P/40	R/40	A/40	TS%	Ast	TO	Usg	Reb	PER
2002-03 Ind	70	30.3	.441	.900	16.6	3.2	3.2	59.7 2	17.5 21	6.8 4	17.4 41	4.6 53	15.86 18
2003-04 Ind	80	28.2	.438	.885	14.2	3.3	4.4	60.0 1	25.3 6	6.9 3	17.2 43	4.9 56	16.08 14
2004-05 Ind	66	31.9	.437	.933	18.5	3.0	2.8	58.2 6	13.2 42	7.3 8	20.0 28	4.3 65	16.59 11
2005-06 PRJ (0.5)			.387	.842	14.6	2.7	3.0	52.1	15.8	7.8	16.3	3.9	14.26

What a way to go out. No, he didn't get a championship, but when the Pacers' injuries were at their absolute worst, it was the 39-year-old Miller who put the team on his back and dragged it in the playoffs. In the month of March, Miller averaged 19.1 points per game—a figure he hadn't hit since 1997–98—and the Pacers went 9–7 with O'Neal, Artest, and Tinsley on the shelf.

Miller's season was unusual in a less-discussed respect as well: He couldn't buy a three-pointer. One of the greatest shooters of all time, Miller hit only 32.2 percent in his final season, which was easily the worst mark of his career. He made up for it by hitting a career-best 93.3 percent from the line and using his usual assortment of tricks to earn four trips a game to the charity stripe.

Remarkably, Miller remained a competent defender even in his final season. Although Jackson and Fred Jones usually guarded the opposing team's top wing scorer, Miller was never enough of a liability that he had to be substituted and his Defensive PER was very solid. The Pacers spent the summer trying to convince Miller to return before giving up, but his contract still became an asset. Indiana "waived" Miler under the luxury-tax amnesty rule, saving the club millions in luxury tax.

Jermaine O'Neal (70% PF, 30% C)	power forward														Age: 27	Height: 6-11	Weight: 260 Most similar at age: Derrick Coleman

Year		G	M/G	FG%	FT%	P/40	R/40	A/40	TS%		Ast		TO		Usg		Reb		PER	
2002-03	Ind	77	37.2	.484	.731	22.4	11.1	2.2	53.9	20	8.5	48	9.9	15	23.6	8	15.6	16	21.39	5
2003-04	Ind*	78	35.7	.434	.757	22.5	11.2	2.4	48.9	57	8.4	43	9.3	6	27.1	1	16.5	12	21.12	4
2004-05	Ind	44	34.8	.452	.754	27.9	10.1	2.1	52.0	38	6.6	53	10.6	31	31.4	1	14.8	21	22.85	5
2005-06	PRJ (27.4)			.450	.765	22.6	10.3	2.2	50.9		8.1		10.1		26.5		14.8		20.32	

* Season rankings are as center

O'Neal was a more potent offensive force last season because he settled for fewer jumpers and drove to the rim, especially with his improved left hand. As a result he averaged about one free-throw attempt for every two field-goal attempts, compared to his prior-year ratio of 1 to 3. This accounts for the improvement in his TS%.

Plus, O'Neal was more aggressive about going for his shots, leading to another big spike in his Usage Rate. As a result, he scored 27.9 points per 40 minutes, but he might want to tone it down a bit. While O'Neal can create shots from the post at will, his TS% shows he's not a high-percentage player. He's also a poor passer, leaving him vulnerable to double-teams. Indiana averaged a tenth of a point more when O'Neal was off the court than when he was on it, supporting the view that he should focus more on quality than quantity.

With the return of Artest and the rest of Indiana's walking wounded, reducing O'Neal's shot attempts shouldn't be a problem. Last year the Pacers didn't have as much of a choice—pounding it into O'Neal was one of their few consistent offensive weapons. With more options this season, force-feeding O'Neal should become a lower priority.

Despite my misgivings about his shot frequency, O'Neal's defense, rebounding, and post game make him one of the best big men in basketball. Having him for 82 games instead of the 44 he played a year ago improves the Pacers' outlook considerably.

Scot Pollard (98% C, 2% PF)	center														Age: 30	Height: 6-11	Weight: 265 Most similar at age: Amal McCaskill

Year		G	M/G	FG%	FT%	P/40	R/40	A/40	TS%		Ast		TO		Usg		Reb		PER	
2002-03	Sac	30	15.7	.460	.605	12.7	13.0	0.7	49.7		4.8		12.0		13.5		17.5		14.60	
2003-04	Ind	61	11.1	.412	.571	6.3	9.7	0.6	43.0	72	6.4	59	14.2	52	8.6	73	13.6	48	8.32	72
2004-05	Ind	49	17.7	.473	.673	8.8	9.5	0.8	50.6	44	4.0	55	13.0	33	10.5	61	12.9	52	11.12	46
2005-06	PRJ (29.0)			.447	.618	7.6	9.4	0.7	47.7		4.8		13.2		9.3		12.9		10.32	

Pollard is a very solid defensive center when his back allows, as he is physical enough to bang with opposing centers and versatile enough to help guards against the screen-and-roll. However, the bad back limited him to 49 games last season and he rarely had his usual verve when he played. His Rebound Rate is a good example, as it has declined sharply from his days in Sacramento.

Pollard is a good finisher around the basket with an above-average left hand, but he contributes little else. He has trouble with illegal screen calls, which is where he accumulates most of his turnovers, and has no post game to speak of. But if he can overcome the back trouble, he's still good enough to be a productive frontcourt sub for 15 minutes a night. However, Pollard might want to keep his bags packed until February. His contract expires after the season, which means he's the likely bait if the Pacers go shopping for additional help at the trade deadline.

Jamaal Tinsley (100% PG)		point guard									Age: 27	Height: 6-3	Weight: 183 Most similar at age: Doc Rivers
Year	**G**	**M/G**	**FG%**	**FT%**	**P/40**	**R/40**	**A/40**	**TS%**	**Ast**	**TO**	**Usg**	**Reb**	**PER**
2002-03 Ind	73	30.6	.396	.714	10.1	4.6	9.8	46.8 51	40.7 2	14.3 56	21.6 32	6.5 19	13.39 33
2003-04 Ind	52	26.5	.414	.731	12.5	3.9	8.8	54.1 9	37.3 5	13.5 48	22.1 27	5.6 28	16.45 17
2004-05 Ind	40	32.5	.418	.744	18.9	4.9	7.9	51.8 33	26.1 38	13.6 57	28.7 5	6.7 8	18.57 11
2005-06 PRJ (32.7)			*.418*	*.731*	*15.1*	*4.5*	*8.2*	*52.5*	*31.9*	*13.6*	*24.9*	*6.2*	*16.89*

With Indiana's three best scorers suspended, Tinsley shifted his energies from setting up others to scoring himself. He raised his 40-minute scoring average by six points and more than tripled his rate of free-throw attempts. Tinsley was especially effective going left. He would come down the left-side of the court, fake a crossover and continue hard to the basket. The move was so convincing that defenders bit nearly every time. Also, Tinsley has improved as a shooter, making 37 percent on three-pointers for the second straight season after struggling with the jumper early in his career.

The Pacers needed the scoring, but Tinsley should return to his more natural role as a distributor this season. A point of emphasis should be reducing turnovers, which have plagued him his entire career. However, one good sign is that Tinsley managed to hold his Turnover Ratio steady last year despite the drastic increase in shots. It also might help him if Indiana ran more, as Tinsley is at his best in transition.

Defensively, Tinsley is one of the best guards in basketball. He has good quickness and fast hands that plucked two steals a game. Moreover, he's a good rebounder for a guard and is big enough to defend shooting guards if the situation requires.

Overall, he's on the cusp of becoming an All-Star point guard if he can ever stay healthy. Tinsley has played only 92 games the past two seasons and has limped through Indiana's playoff defeats in two straight postseasons. While much of the attention will be on Ron Artest, Tinsley is arguably a bigger key to Indiana's championship hopes. If he's in one piece in June, the Pacers will be tough to beat.

Danny Granger	small forward	Age: 22	Height: 6-8	Weight: 235

At 22, Granger is old for an NBA rookie these days, but his collegiate numbers suggest he'll contribute immediately and be among the best rebounding small forwards in basketball. Granger averaged nearly a rebound every three minutes, and his averages of over two steals and two blocks are further indicators of how active he was at New Mexico. Offensively, he shapes up even better. Granger averaged 25 points per 40 minutes as a senior while shooting 52 percent from the field and 43 percent on threes. How he fell to the Pacers with the 17th pick is a mystery, but he'll be a big improvement on James Jones.

Erazem Lorbek	power forward	Age: 21	Height: 6-10	Weight: 240

Translated 40-minute stats: 11.6 pts, 10.1 reb, 2.0 ast, .495 FG%, 13.10 PER

Lorbek has the requisite size and skill for the NBA, but average athleticism and poor defense have hurt his stock. He played for Michigan State for a year before signing with a pro team in Italy, and his numbers from both places suggest a high-percentage, low-volume scorer who does a decent job on the boards. If that's true and the defense improves, he'll make a decent backup. The Pacers don't have any room for him this year so he'll probably stay in Italy for a while.

Miami Heat

That was fast.

In just two short years, the Miami Heat improved by 34 games, acquired the game's best center, and went from being cellar-dwellers to, very nearly, world champions. But it all came to a familiar end, with the Heat losing a deciding game on its home court for the fourth time in the Riley era. This time it was the Pistons who were the culprits, knocking Miami out in the seventh game of the Eastern Conference finals after Miami held a lead late in the fourth quarter.

Heat fans spent the summer wondering if health was the only thing keeping the team from its first NBA title. Miami suffered two key injuries—a thigh bruise to Shaquille O'Neal late in the season and a rib strain to Dwyane Wade in Game 5 of the Detroit series—that were crucial factors in the Heat's loss to Detroit. Additionally, Damon Jones sprained his ankle early in the deciding seventh game and was virtually useless for the rest of the contest. At full strength, any of those three might have made the difference.

The key to Miami's resurgence, obviously, was the off-season trade for Shaquille O'Neal. When the Lakers suddenly made the dominant big man available, Miami immediately plunged in with its offer of Lamar Odom, Brian Grant, and Caron Butler to nab its cornerstone. O'Neal didn't disappoint either, improving his conditioning and playing harder than he had in his final season in L.A.

However, Shaq-mania has resulted in misleading evaluations of the Heat's season. The story has circulated that Shaq was the entire difference for the Heat's competitiveness and the rest of the players were just window dressing. Nothing could be further from the truth. Even with O'Neal, Miami would have barely cleared .500 if not for a series of significant improvements up and down the roster.

The most important was Dwyane Wade's breakout in his sophomore season. Observers casually linked Shaq's arrival with Wade's breakthrough, but in fact Wade played better when Shaq was off the court. With rules changes making it harder for defenders to hold him up on the perimeter, Wade repeatedly blazed to the basket or pulled up for an improved mid-range jumper when defenders backed off. The Shaq-Wade combo put Miami on top of the league in field-goal percentage with a .486 mark.

In addition to Wade's emergence, some excellent moves by management paid off for Miami. In his second pro season, Udonis Haslem blossomed as the starting power forward and combined with Shaq to form one of the league's top rebounding duos. Damon Jones was signed as an inexpensive free agent and exceeded all expectations, taking over the starting point guard job and leading the NBA in three-pointers. And Christian Laettner was an astute acquisition just before training camp opened, earning a minimum salary but deepening the bench with his mid-range jump shooting.

Two other pick-ups from the scrap heap, Keyon Dooling and Shandon Anderson, also provided help. While neither did much at the offensive end they helped Miami greatly overachieve on defense. Finally, Miami was able to add Alonzo Mourning to the roster late in the year to spark its playoff run. Overall, team president Pat Riley did an amazing job securing cheap help during the course of the season, and as a result the Heat were much deeper than anyone expected.

All that cheap help also made Miami a force from the three-point line. Because Shaq and Wade drew so much attention around the basket, they had ample opportunity to kick the ball out to one of the Joneses for an open three-pointer. Between them, Damon and Eddie nailed 367 trifectas, or close to five a game. Moreover, they did it while taking quality shots, allowing Miami to finish second in the league in three-point percentage.

The combination of Shaq's inside dominance and Wade's drives to the rim set up those three-pointers, but it also forced opponents to foul when those two had them out of position. As a result of opponents hacking Shaq and whacking Wade, the Heat were a free-throw drawing machine. Miami was second in the NBA in overall free-throw attempts but led the NBA in the more vital category of free-throws per field-goal attempt, in table 1.

Heat at a Glance

Record: 59–23, 1st place in Southeast Division

Offensive Efficiency: 108.3 (2nd)

Defensive Efficiency: 99.8 (5th)

Pace Factor: 92.7 (17th)

Top-Rated Player: Shaquille O'Neal (PER 26.95, 3rd overall)

Head Coach: Stan Van Gundy. Did amazing job papering over the team's shortcomings.

Table 1. Free-Throw Attempts per Field-Goal Attempt Leaders, Team

Team	FTA/FGA
Miami	.387
Washington	.364
Utah	.361
Indiana	.358
Boston	.357
League Average	**.324**

Table 2. Free-Throw Attempts per Field-Goal Attempt Leaders, Player (Minimum 500 FGA)

Player	FTA/FGA
Shaquille O'Neal, Miami	.699
Corey Maggette, L.A. Clippers	.666
Dwight Howard, Orlando	.610
Amare Stoudemire, Phoenix	.595
Dwyane Wade, Miami	.578
League Average	**.324**

It's easy to see how the Heat ranked so high when we look at Shaq's and Wade's numbers. Among top-drawer scorers (those with at least 500 field-goal attempts on the season), Shaq led the league in this category (see table 2) and Wade led all backcourt players. Only one other Heat player (Haslem) was above the league average, yet Miami led the league overall by a wide margin because Shaq and Wade were so effective at getting to the line.

Offense was expected to be a Miami strength, but the defense was a pleasant surprise. While Riley gets credit for building up the bench, Stan Van Gundy should get heaps of praise for Miami's defensive performance. At first glance, this team does not appear to be a daunting unit to score against. Damon Jones is slow and lacks muscle, Shaq is immobile, and Eddie Jones and Haslem are undersized. Only Wade appears athletic enough to make a real impact. Moreover, Miami was 29th in steals and well below average in forcing turnovers. Yet the Heat was one of the best defensive teams overall, finishing fifth in Defensive Efficiency.

How did Miami accomplish this? Well, the Heat didn't gamble much, but they forced misses and always got the rebound. Miami ranked fourth in the NBA in opponent field-goal percentage at 42.7 percent, and second in defensive rebound percentage at 74.1 percent. One of the keys was Shaq. Despite his much-criticized pick-and-roll defense, O'Neal was a major deterrent to opponents going to the basket, and it's still virtually impossible to post up against him. Eddie Jones was a significant factor as well, despite his advancing age, as Van Gundy was able to squeeze the maximum from his diminishing talents.

All of those accomplishments should keep Miami in contention this season. But best of all, the Heat didn't stand pat in their quest for a title, as Riley continue a strong record of deal-making in the two years since he gave up coaching. He started by renegotiating Shaquille O'Neal's contract into a five-year, $100 million deal. Shaq was due to make $30 million in 2005–06, the final year of his previous deal, but Miami needed to lower that number to get him some help in coming seasons without paying luxury tax. The two sides reached an agreement that would take his pay to "only" the $20 million range, but pay the big fella until he's 38. That could produce some painful cap situations at the end of the decade, but for now it will be much easier for the Heat to extend Dwyane Wade's contract a year from now and make the other moves necessary to stay in contention. That arrangement provided Miami more spending room to avoid the luxury tax, and the Heat used it well. They started in house by keeping forward Haslem with a five-year, $30 million deal.

Then came Riley's master stroke—a five-team, 13-player trade that was the biggest in NBA history. From Miami's end, the Heat gave up forwards Eddie Jones, Rasual Butler, Qyntel Woods, the rights to Spanish forward Albert Miralles, two second-round draft picks, three French hens, and a partridge in a pear tree. In return, they landed Boston's Antoine Walker and Memphis's James Posey, Jason Williams, and Andre Emmett. It's a home run of a trade for the Heat, who got the three best players in the exchange and simultaneously rid themselves of Jones's onerous contract. The only drawback was that Walker joined Miami on a six-year, $54 million deal that seriously overpays him.

Not that Miami is free of concerns. Shaq is 33, has an arthritic toe, and isn't guaranteed to be as motivated or well-conditioned this season now that he's getting paid until age 38. While he may have been motivated by the Lakers' trade to prove he was still the game's most dominant big man last season, he missed several games due to injury and has appeared increasingly brittle in recent seasons. One wonders if he'll show the same dedication this offseason or revert to his L.A. habit of adding pounds over the summer.

Also, Miami still has some free agent holes to fill. Dooling left as a free agent and Laettner and Damon Jones remained unsigned at publication time. They'll have a hole at center, too, if Mourning isn't healthy enough to rejoin them this season.

Finally, Riley spent the offseason seemingly going out of his way to undermine Van Gundy, issuing halfhearted denials about his desire to return to coaching and leaving Van Gundy twisting in the wind for much of the summer. Considering Van Gundy got the Heat closer to a title than Riley ever did when he was the Heat's coach, it would be an odd and selfish maneuver to say the least. One gets the impression that even if Van Gundy is retained, Riley's shadow will lurk heavily over the team, and that can't be a positive.

Overall, Miami is in a much better place than it was just two years ago, when it seemed the Heat's problems were intractable. Drafting one superstar and trading for another quickly erased those problems, and the blockbuster deal for Walker, Williams and Posey further expands Miami's talent base. In a watered-down Eastern Conference where the Heat probably will be able to breeze to the conference finals, they have as good a chance as anyone of winning a ring this season.

Shandon Anderson				small forward								Age: 32		Height: 6-6		Weight: 210	
(77% SF, 12% PF, 11% SG)														Most similar at age: Johnny Newman			
Year		G	M/G	FG%	FT%	P/40	R/40	A/40	TS%		Ast		TO		Usg		Reb	PER
2002-03	NY	82	21.1	.462	.732	15.9	5.9	2.0	55.3	10	10.6	49	13.9	49	17.3	35	8.6 39	13.33 30
2003-04	NY*	80	24.7	.422	.764	12.9	4.5	2.5	50.0	33	13.9	43	13.5	60	16.2	48	6.4 38	10.04 51
2004-05	NY-Mia	66	17.7	.452	.818	8.7	6.5	2.4	51.8	38	11.4	36	13.7	55	11.4	63	9.8 23	8.93 57
2005-06	*PRJ (39.4)*			*.434*	*.758*	*11.1*	*5.5*	*2.3*	*51.5*		*12.5*		*12.9*		*13.9*		*8.0*	*10.16*

* Season rankings are as shooting guard

The Knicks released Anderson early in the season, and the Heat were waiting with a contract in hand once he cleared waivers. Anderson is a spent force offensively, but defensively he still has the strength and lateral movement to be a nuisance. As a result, Van Gundy was able to use him for short bursts as a defensive stopper off the bench.

Anderson moves very well without the ball and was able to get himself some lay-ups on cuts away from the ball when Shaq was double-teamed. That's about his only offensive skill though, because his jumper is spotty, he's not a threat off the dribble, and he makes far too many turnovers. On the positive side, he's a good offensive rebounder.

Realistically, this role is the absolute limit of Anderson's skills and the Heat are likely to search for somebody more talented to fill it. He's a free agent and should manage to hang on somewhere, but he may have to be content to wave a towel at the end of the bench.

Rasual Butler				small forward								Age: 26		Height: 6-7		Weight: 205	
(84% SF, 14% SG, 2% PF)														Most similar at age: Morris Peterson			
Year		G	M/G	FG%	FT%	P/40	R/40	A/40	TS%		Ast		TO		Usg		Reb	PER
2002-03	Mia*	72	21.0	.362	.731	14.3	4.9	2.5	43.7	54	11.8	47	9.8	25	20.2	24	7.1 26	9.48 46
2003-04	Mia	45	15.0	.476	.762	18.0	3.6	1.4	58.6	5	7.4	56	9.0	12	17.7	31	5.1 58	13.93 31
2004-05	Mia	65	18.5	.399	.771	14.0	5.0	2.1	48.8	52	9.8	51	7.0	4	16.9	41	7.5 51	10.31 52
2005-06	*PRJ (45.3)*			*.401*	*.754*	*14.5*	*4.5*	*2.0*	*49.5*		*9.9*		*8.4*		*17.4*		*6.6*	*11.28*

* Season rankings are as shooting guard

Butler began the year in the starting lineup but quickly fell out of favor when he failed to impress and Damon Jones burst onto the scene. Butler later resurfaced in the playoffs and provided some solid minutes off the bench.

Butler is an adequate defender with fairly long arms, but his main weapon is his jump shot. He has a slow release combined with a high arc that's hard to block and can hit the shot with a hand in his face. As a result, he's effective shooting mid-range jumpers over smaller players in the post. He's also a three-point weapon who hit 37 percent last year and 46 percent the year before.

Unfortunately, that torrid 2003–04 campaign is beginning to look like a fluke year. His other two pro seasons are extremely similar, with the middle year being the outlier. If that's the case his value is limited to occasional use off the bench, but he'll have plenty of chances to prove us wrong. Butler was traded to the Hornets after the season, where he could end up as the starting small forward in a depleted New Orleans lineup.

Michael Doleac   center   **Age: 28**   **Height: 6-11**   **Weight: 262**
(86% C, 14% PF)   Most similar at age: Bill Wennington

Year		G	M/G	FG%	FT%	P/40	R/40	A/40	TS%		Ast		TO		Usg		Reb		PER	
2002-03	NY	75	13.9	.426	.783	12.6	8.4	1.6	45.1	63	9.2	36	10.8	13	16.2	25	12.3	56	8.86	67
2003-04	NY-Den	71	14.5	.435	.865	12.6	10.3	1.7	47.1	62	10.1	28	11.0	16	15.6	26	14.2	35	12.35	48
2004-05	Mia	80	14.7	.447	.610	10.9	8.8	1.6	46.0	66	7.6	24	8.3	3	14.0	35	13.2	48	9.68	59
2005-06	PRJ (36.2)			.439	.717	11.4	9.5	1.6	46.0		8.0		10.0		14.4		13.8		10.67	

I have no clue why the Heat gave Doleac a four-year deal, which was the one misstep in Miami's offseason strategy last summer. Just look at his meager offensive output. For someone his size, his offense is mostly limited to mid-range jump shots, and he's not even that good at it. Doleac's TS% is annually among the lowest at his position because he shoots in the low 40s, and his rate of 0.12 free throw attempts per field-goal attempt is embarrassing for a center.

Sure, Doleac has some value as a backup center because he can use his muscle to knock opposing centers out of the post. However, he has limited mobility and doesn't block shots. Also, he's a below-average rebounder because he isn't quick to the ball. Fortunately for him, he still has three years left on his contract, so he should be secure as Shaq's caddy for a while.

Keyon Dooling   point guard   **Age: 25**   **Height: 6-3**   **Weight: 195**
(100% PG)   Most similar at age: LaBradford Smith

Year		G	M/G	FG%	FT%	P/40	R/40	A/40	TS%		Ast		TO		Usg		Reb		PER	
2002-03	LAC	55	17.6	.389	.772	14.4	3.0	3.7	49.4	42	17.7	60	11.9	41	19.0	47	4.1	58	9.54	57
2003-04	LAC*	58	19.6	.389	.830	12.7	2.8	4.6	45.8	55	22.1	12	11.0	34	18.9	38	4.1	61	9.92	52
2004-05	Mia	74	16.0	.403	.780	12.9	3.0	4.5	48.6	52	21.2	57	11.0	36	18.6	57	4.6	52	10.04	57
2005-06	PRJ (58.8)			.394	.800	13.6	3.1	4.5	47.7		20.6		10.5		19.1		4.5		10.69	

* Season rankings are as shooting guard

The media aren't the only ones who overrate what they see in the playoffs—NBA teams do it too. Take Dooling, for example. During the regular season he was the same erratic jump shooter he's always been, drifting to the left or right as he went up and frequently missing to either side. In the playoffs, however, he enjoyed an unprecedented spurt of accuracy, shooting 49 percent overall and 37 percent on three-pointers. For some reason, teams took that performance at face value instead of viewing it as a short-term fluke. As a result, Dooling got a three-year, $10 million deal from Orlando in free agency despite a shaky season-long performance that mirrored his previous three campaigns with the Clippers.

So which is his real level of performance—the four years when he didn't shoot well or the 15 games that he did? It doesn't take a rocket scientist to figure it out. Dooling probably will shoot around 40 percent next year, just as he did in the previous seasons, and Orlando will end up burned.

Dooling does bring one other positive to the table—he's a good defender who pressures the ball upcourt and has the size to bother shots. But add in his inability to run the point—his Assist Ratios are consistently terrible—and it's questionable whether he's worth more than the minimum. Unfortunately, it's too late for Orlando to get its money back.

Udonis Haslem   power forward   **Age: 25**   **Height: 6-8**   **Weight: 232**
Defensive PER: 0.33 (98% PF, 2% C)   Most similar at age: Jamie Feick

Year		G	M/G	FG%	FT%	P/40	R/40	A/40	TS%		Ast		TO		Usg		Reb		PER	
2003-04	Mia	75	24.0	.459	.765	12.2	10.5	1.1	52.1	36	7.8	48	11.3	20	13.7	40	14.9	30	13.65	37
2004-05	Mia	80	33.4	.540	.791	13.0	10.9	1.6	58.8	5	7.7	46	11.8	39	13.3	62	16.3	14	15.55	30
2005-06	PRJ (35.3)			.491	.778	11.9	9.9	1.6	54.2		8.7		11.9		13.5		14.8		14.20	

Both Haslem and Christian Laettner benefited greatly from the extra attention opponents lavished on Shaq, because each can hit a jump shot from the free-throw line. Miami often would run plays that started with Shaq in the post and Haslem or Laettner on the weak side. Their man would be the primary help defender on Shaq, and when that defender committed too early, Haslem/Laettner could cut to the free-throw line for an easy jumper. As a result, Haslem shot 54 percent and Laettner 58 percent. It was a good example of how Van Gundy made the Heat more than the sum of their parts.

(continued next page)

Udonis Haslem *(continued)*

Haslem also surprised people with his tenacity on the glass. His Rebound Rate was a big improvement on his rookie season and it's where he generated the rest of his offense. Haslem wasn't asked to score in the post or handle the ball much, but between the open jumpers and put-backs, he averaged in the double figures and shot a very high percentage.

Defensively, Haslem gives a great effort but suffers from being short for his position at 6′8″. He's also not particularly explosive and blocked only half a shot per game, an extremely low total for a starting power forward. Nonetheless, his shot-making skill was in demand in the free-agent market and the Heat gave him a five-year deal for the full mid-level exception. Based on how he played in 2004–05, that's probably fair market value.

Damon Jones					point guard											Age: 29	Height: 6-3	Weight: 190
Defensive PER: 0.19 (97% PG, 3% SG)																	Most similar at age: Kenny Smith	
Year		G	M/G	FG%	FT%	P/40	R/40	A/40	TS%		Ast		TO		Usg		Reb	PER
2002-03	Sac	71	11.8	.381	.741	12.6	3.9	4.5	50.5	34	24.6	40	7.1	1	16.7	57	5.3 37	11.44 44
2003-04	Mil	82	24.6	.401	.764	11.4	3.4	9.5	51.6	22	42.1	1	9.1	9	20.8	37	4.9 44	14.18 29
2004-05	Mia	82	31.4	.456	.791	14.8	3.6	5.4	62.5	1	25.9	39	8.1	7	17.9	60	5.4 38	15.57 25
2005-06	*PRJ (29.8)*			*.427*	*.768*	*13.2*	*3.5*	*6.3*	*57.1*		*28.5*		*9.4*		*18.6*		*5.8*	*14.39*

Jones's most similar player at the same age is TNT's Kenny Smith, which is ironic considering their exchanges about "Alfred the Butler" during the playoffs. A career journeyman, Jones showed some signs that he had taken a step forward during his 2003–04 campaign with Milwaukee and took things up another notch in Miami.

The amazing thing about Jones is how he completely changed his game between the two stops. In Milwaukee he led the league in Assist Ratio, but in Miami his role changed from distributor to shooting specialist and he made the transition seamlessly. Jones led all point guards in True Shooting Percentage by standing behind the three-point line and waiting for Shaq to get double-teamed. Fully 72 percent of Jones's shot attempts were from beyond the arc, and he was extremely accurate, finishing fifth in the league at 43.2 percent. In doing so, Jones became the first player since Larry Bird in 1985–86 to lead the league in three-pointers while also finishing in the top five in percentage.

Jones wisely opted out of his contract after the season, because his market value will never be higher. Having displayed a chameleon-like tendency to adapt his skills to whatever his team needs, Jones is in high demand in a thin free-agent market for point guards. The question is whether the purchaser is buying at the peak of the market. In 2005–06, Jones will have to prove his hot shooting wasn't a fluke.

Eddie Jones					small forward											Age: 34	Height: 6-6	Weight: 200
Defensive PER: 1.21 (64% SF, 36% SG)																	Most similar at age: Rod Higgins	
Year		G	M/G	FG%	FT%	P/40	R/40	A/40	TS%		Ast		TO		Usg		Reb	PER
2002-03	Mia*	47	38.1	.423	.822	19.4	5.1	3.9	55.1	16	16.5	25	8.1	9	23.0	12	7.3 21	18.91 7
2003-04	Mia*	81	37.0	.409	.835	18.7	4.1	3.4	53.8	12	15.3	34	7.6	6	21.9	23	5.8 45	16.69 12
2004-05	Mia	80	35.5	.428	.806	14.3	5.7	3.0	55.6	11	14.2	14	8.1	11	16.4	45	8.6 35	13.59 34
2005-06	*PRJ (40.7)*			*.406*	*.805*	*15.4*	*4.9*	*3.2*	*53.1*		*14.8*		*8.3*		*18.2*		*7.1*	*13.88*

* Season rankings are as shooting guard

With Wade's emergence as a scorer, Jones became the Heat's primary wing defender and he handled the role surprisingly well. Although he's getting up in years and is a bit short for a small forward, Jones was athletic enough to grab over a steal a game and adapted to his new position by setting a career high in rebounding.

Where Jones suffered was at the offensive end. His scoring rate dropped precipitously as Shaq and Wade took over the bulk of the offensive load, but his percentages hardly increased. Normally players whose shot totals go down see their percentages go way up because the shots they get are of a much higher quality—which is exactly what happened with Haslem, Damon Jones, and Laettner. The fact it didn't for Jones is a telling sign that Father Time has taken a bite out of his offensive arsenal.

Jones has two years left on a contract that pays him the maximum, which makes it amazing that the Heat were able to trade him. Jones was shipped to Memphis and may not play as much as he did in Miami. Mike Miller and Shane Battier are entrenched as the Grizzlies' starters on the wings and both are better players, so Jones will have to be content with a sixth man role.

| Christian Laettner (83% PF, 17% C) | | power forward | | | | | | | | Age: 36 Height: 6-11 Weight: 240 Most similar at age: Bill Laimbeer | | | |

Year		G	M/G	FG%	FT%	P/40	R/40	A/40	TS%		Ast		TO		Usg		Reb		PER	
2002-03	Was	76	29.2	.494	.833	11.4	9.0	4.2	54.5	17	26.1	4	9.7	13	15.7	40	13.4	32	16.11	19
2003-04	Was	48	20.5	.465	.800	11.5	9.4	3.6	51.1	39	21.8	4	10.3	16	15.1	46	13.2	39	14.52	38
2004-05	Mia	49	15.1	.582	.763	14.1	7.1	2.2	61.9	1	10.6	26	10.4	30	14.2	56	10.6	62	16.30	27
2005-06	PRJ (24.7)			.491	.768	11.2	7.7	3.1	53.7		18.5		10.7		14.0		11.2		14.23	

Van Gundy's substitution pattern with Haslem and Laettner was very odd. Haslem would play virtually the entire first half, and then with about six to eight minutes left in the second quarter, Laettner would come in and finish up. Normally coaches substitute late in the first quarter or early in the second and have the starters back in to end the half, but Van Gundy didn't do that with his power forwards. The reason, I suspect, is that he wanted Laettner on the court with Shaq to take advantage of Laettner's sweet mid-range jump shot.

If so, it worked, as Laettner hit 58 percent from the floor and led all power forwards in True Shooting Percentage. Unfortunately, he's really dropped off in other areas. Laettner's Rebound Rate sank like a stone this past season and defensively he can't be trusted to stop anyone who is remotely skilled. Due to those shortcomings, not to mention a comatose showing in the playoffs, he probably won't be asked back. But because he shot the ball so well, he should find a buyer somewhere.

| Alonzo Mourning (74% C, 26% PF) | | center | | | | | | | | Age: 35 Height: 6-10 Weight: 261 Most similar at age: Dikembe Mutombo | | | |

Year		G	M/G	FG%	FT%	P/40	R/40	A/40	TS%		Ast		TO		Usg		Reb		PER	
2002-03	Mia	Out for the season																		
2003-04	NJ	12	17.9	.465	.882	17.9	5.0	1.5	55.8		7.7		9.6		18.3		7.2		13.25	
2004-05	NJ-Mia	37	19.0	.472	.582	16.1	11.3	1.0	51.5	40	4.9	49	16.3	58	18.0	14	16.9	19	15.33	25
2005-06	PRJ (0.6)			.476	.615	15.6	10.7	0.9	53.1		4.6		16.5		16.7		15.8		14.56	

Mourning simultaneously has become one of the most admired and most detested players in the league. On one hand, his determination in returning to the game after a kidney transplant and his setback in 2003–04 is an inspiration, and few players play harder when they're on the court. On the other hand, he whined his way out of New Jersey even though his contract was the main thing holding the Nets back from contending and the celebratory fist-pumping every time he makes a positive play has become a tired act.

Regardless of one's opinion of his antics, Mourning was a huge help to Miami when he joined them late in the season. He was a major upgrade over Doleac as the Heat's backup center and his presence allowed Miami to rest Shaq more liberally in the opening rounds of the playoffs. Mourning also returned to his shot-blocking self in Miami, rejecting nearly a shot every eight minutes in his regular season and playoff games with the Heat.

To understand how impressive that is, consider that it's a rate of 5.2 blocks per 40 minutes, and that the league's leading shot-blocker, Utah's Andrei Kirilenko, averaged only 4.0. It was the highest shot-blocking rate of Mourning's career, by far, and if he keeps it up, he'd be able to lead the league in blocks while playing 25 minutes a game.

Offensively, however, Mourning is a shadow of his former self. He still can finish around the basket and is a threat on the offensive glass, but he gets called for traveling once a game and a flat jump hook shot is his main offensive weapon.

But as long as his health allows, Mourning should be one of the league's best backup centers. He's already signed for next season at a bargain rate, so it's just a question of getting cleared by his doctor to play. Now, if they can just talk to him about that fist-pumping...

Shaquille O'Neal					center								Age: 33	Height: 7-1	Weight: 325
Defensive PER: 1.28 (100% C)														Most similar at age: David Robinson	

Year		G	M/G	FG%	FT%	P/40	R/40	A/40	TS%		Ast		TO		Usg		Reb		PER	
2002-03	LAL	67	37.8	.574	.622	29.0	11.7	3.3	60.2	3	10.7	28	10.1	8	27.9	1	16.5	15	29.46	1
2003-04	LAL	67	36.8	.584	.490	23.4	12.5	3.2	57.8	6	12.0	16	11.9	26	23.9	2	17.8	5	24.31	1
2004-05	Mia	73	34.1	.601	.461	26.8	12.2	3.2	58.3	12	10.9	10	11.1	10	27.4	1	18.3	9	26.95	1
2005-06	PRJ (1.9)			.584	.477	22.1	11.9	2.7	57.8		11.1		11.1		23.4		16.9		24.24	

Here's the problem I have with Shaq's MVP candidacy: He wasn't on the floor enough to be the most valuable player. O'Neal played only 62 percent of the Heat's minutes last season, an extremely low number for an MVP candidate. By contrast, Dirk Nowitzki played 77 percent of Dallas's minutes, Kevin Garnett played 79 percent of Minnesota's, and LeBron James played 85 percent of Cleveland's.

In fact, it raises the question of whether Shaq was the most valuable player on his own team. Dwyane Wade played 74 percent of the Heat's minutes compared to Shaq's 62 percent. Shaq had a higher PER, but which number is more valuable? Suppose that the replacements for both Shaq and Wade have a PER around 10—a fair assumption looking at the numbers for Michael Doleac and Rasual Butler. We can see what Shaq and Wade were worth to the Heat by taking the difference in PER between them and their replacements and multiplying by the minutes they played.

The difference in PER between Shaq and his replacement is (26.95 – 10) or 16.95, while the difference for Wade is (23.17 – 10) or 13.17. But Wade played 2,974 minutes to Shaq's 2,492. The total for Shaq comes to 42,239, and for Wade it comes to 39,167—still an advantage for Shaq, but a much closer race than some would suspect.

If we run that calculation for the whole league, which I call "Value over Replacement," we can see that Shaq trailed some of his MVP candidate peers by a substantial margin:

Value over Replacement, 2004–05 [(PER – 10) × Minutes]

Player	PER	VOR
Kevin Garnett, Minnesota	28.35	57248
LeBron James, Cleveland	25.75	53367
Dirk Nowitzki, Dallas	26.18	48878
Amare Stoudemire, Phoenix	26.69	48210
Shaquille O'Neal, Miami	26.95	42237
Allen Iverson, Philadelphia	23.23	41985
Tracy McGrady, Houston	22.95	41213
Dwyane Wade, Miami	23.17	39153
Stephon Marbury, New York	21.93	39138
Tim Duncan, San Antonio	27.13	37746

While Shaq still rates substantially higher than Steve Nash, who finished first in the MVP voting (Nash was 19th in VOR), it's hard to summon up much outrage over O'Neal's failure to win the trophy. In truth he should have been fourth or fifth on most ballots. Unfortunately, the media took the story of Shaq turning around the Heat and ran with it, treating Wade's rise in value as part of the Shaq story rather than a legitimate development in its own right. The result was that Shaq got 58 MVP votes and Wade got zero, even though the two were fairly similar in value.

On the court, O'Neal showed more vigor at both ends than he had in his final season with the Lakers. The difference was particularly noticeable on defense. While O'Neal remained vulnerable to pick-and-roll plays, he made far more of an effort to hinder the progress of the ballhandler than he had in L.A. His defensive PER was one of the better ones at the center spot and he improved his Rebound Rate significantly.

Offensively, Shaq is no longer the indomitable force he was five years ago, but he's replaced quantity with quality. He has become much more accurate on the short hook shots and banked turnarounds that now constitute the majority of his shot attempts. The bad news is that he's become a complete disaster at the foul line, hitting below 50 percent for the second season in a row. Since Shaq has one of the highest rates of free-throw attempts to field-goal attempts in basketball, this is incredibly costly. Even if he made only 65 percent from the line, it would add two points a game to Miami's bottom line and earn the Heat nearly five extra wins over the course of a season.

O'Neal opted out of the final year of his contract and then immediately signed a long-term deal with the Heat for less money. The signing helps Miami in the short term because they can add additional players without having to pay luxury tax. Of course, it's a risky proposition because O'Neal will be pulling down $20 million a year at age 38. Fortunately for Miami, big men have tended to keep their value for much longer than guards, so as long as Shaq's questionable commitment to fitness doesn't slacken any further, the final years of the deal shouldn't be too onerous.

Steve Smith			shooting guard											Age: 36	Height: 6-8	Weight: 220
(49% SF, 42% SG, 7% PF, 2% PG)															Most similar at age: Tyrone Corbin	
Year		G	M/G	FG%	FT%	P/40	R/40	A/40	TS%		Ast		TO		Usg		Reb		PER	
2002-03	SA*	63	20.8	.388	.833	14.0	3.8	2.7	52.8	21	15.4	24	9.5	17	16.7	38	5.6	58	11.95	37
2003-04	NO*	71	13.1	.406	.928	15.4	3.5	2.4	54.3	14	13.1	30	9.8	19	18.0	30	5.1	57	12.23	40
2004-05	Cha-Mia	50	15.0	.411	.863	16.7	3.5	3.8	55.4	18	18.0	19	7.1	6	19.2	33	5.2	58	13.62	30
2005-06	PRJ (26.7)			.390	.898	13.8	3.5	3.2	51.9		17.7		10.1		17.1		6.2		11.21	

* Season rankings are as small forward

Smitty returned to where he started his career after a midseason trade for Malik Allen. Incidentally, the Heat also picked up a $1.9 million trade exception in that deal and have a year to use it, which could become important at some point during the coming season.

As for Smith, his jump shot remains a weapon and he continues to handle the ball well, which gives him some value as a shooter coming off the bench. He saw few opportunities once he joined the Heat though because he duplicates many of Butler's skills, but his stay in Miami should be brief. He'll again be looking for a one-year deal to provide occasional bursts of shooting off the bench, and he shouldn't lack for offers considering his play the past two seasons.

Dwyane Wade			shooting guard											Age: 23	Height: 6-4	Weight: 212
Defensive PER: 0.80 (89% SG, 10% PG, 1% SF)															Most similar at age: Kobe Bryant	
Year		G	M/G	FG%	FT%	P/40	R/40	A/40	TS%		Ast		TO		Usg		Reb		PER	
2003-04	Mia*	61	34.9	.465	.747	18.6	4.6	5.2	53.0	11	19.6	60	13.9	50	24.5	10	6.6	14	17.53	12
2004-05	Mia	77	38.6	.478	.762	24.9	5.3	7.0	56.1	13	20.8	10	12.9	58	30.8	2	8.0	16	23.17	2
2005-06	PRJ (22.3)			.477	.748	23.9	5.2	6.2	56.1		19.9		12.3		29.4		7.6		22.39	

* Season rankings are as point guard

It's ironic that Bryant is Wade's most similar player at the same age considering all the comparisons between Wade and Bryant as understudies to Shaq. It also might give some the impression that Shaq was the key to each player's offensive exploits, but don't be fooled. Two factors were the catalysts in Wade's sharp improvement in 2004–05, and neither of them were Shaq "making him better."

First and foremost were the rules changes that restricted hand-checking on the perimeter. Wade benefited as much as any player in the league because he's extremely difficult to contain off the dribble, with an incredible burst going to his left that he complements with a great crossover move. The new rules helped players like Wade get to the basket at will and allowed Wade to more than double his free-throw attempts from his rookie season.

Second, he refined his mid-range jumper. Wade still lacks three-point range—he made only 13 all season—but he's become a reliable shooter from the 17-foot range. Wade shot 36.5 percent on two-point jump shots as a rookie, but he increased that to 39 percent in his second season. He's also added a step-back jumper that's become one of his go-to moves and is virtually impossible to block.

Because Wade drives so much, he's prone to turnovers, and that's the one area besides outside shooting that he needs to improve. Wade's Turnover Ratio was near the bottom among guards, and the miscues were a big reason Miami didn't have the league's best offense despite leading the league in field-goal percentage and free-throws per field-goal attempt.

Wade wasn't asked to do as much at the defensive end because he had so much offensive responsibility, but his quickness and anticipation make him a strong performer at that end of the court too. Additionally, he's a strong rebounder and can play point guard in a pinch. Add it all up and he's become one of the most valuable players in basketball, with or without Shaq.

Qyntel Woods   shooting guard   Age: 23   Height: 6-8   Weight: 221
(82% SF, 18% PF)   Most similar at age: N/A

Year		G	M/G	FG%	FT%	P/40	R/40	A/40	TS%		Ast		TO		Usg		Reb		PER	
2002-03	Por	53	6.3	.500	.350	15.3	6.3	1.4	50.5		7.4		14.2		17.9		9.6		11.17	
2003-04	Por	62	10.8	.371	.633	13.4	8.1	2.7	42.5	62	12.7	47	14.4	61	20.3	32	11.6	1	9.40	54
2004-05	Mia	3	13.3	.417	—	10.0	6.0	0.0	41.7		0.0		14.3		12.7		8.5		7.61	

Waived by Portland after a series of scrapes with the law, Woods got a second chance from the Heat. He hardly played in 2004–05 and doesn't figure to see much action this year, either. Woods was traded to Boston in the Eddie Jones blockbuster, and the Celtics are already overstaffed at the wing positions. Woods has shown some capabilities at the defensive end, but his offensive game has a ways to go. The best thing for him would be to get into a situation where he could play regularly and develop his skills, but that's unlikely to happen unless he goes down to the D-League.

Dorell Wright   small forward   Age: 20   Height: 6-7   Weight: 200
(100% SF)   Most similar at age: N/A

Year		G	M/G	FG%	FT%	P/40	R/40	A/40	TS%	Ast	TO	Usg	Reb	PER
2004-05	Mia	3	9.0	.273	1.000	10.4	1.5	4.4	30.6	17.2	17.2	23.0	2.1	5.10

The jury is still out on the Heat's 2004 first-round pick, because Wright barely played. He's a perfect example of a player who would have benefited from the NBDL becoming a true minor league. Instead of wasting his year on the Heat bench with an "abdominal strain," he would have had chances to play regularly and improve. Scouts regarded him as a potentially deadly scorer entering the 2004 daft, and I don't have much to add from the 27 minutes Wright played in 2004–05.

Wang Zhizhi   center   Age: 28   Height: 7-1   Weight: 240
(96% C, 4% PF)   Most similar at age: N/A

Year		G	M/G	FG%	FT%	P/40	R/40	A/40	TS%	Ast	TO	Usg	Reb	PER
2002-03	LAC	41	10.0	.383	.724	17.7	7.5	1.0	48.5	4.4	13.6	20.1	10.3	11.85
2003-04	LAC-Mia	16	7.1	.370	.900	16.5	6.3	0.7	46.6	3.4	10.3	19.5	8.9	11.55
2004-05	Mia	20	4.6	.472	.583	18.7	7.8	2.2	52.1	9.8	9.8	21.0	11.0	16.28

I still maintain that Wang can play and remain perplexed that he has yet to get the opportunity. His career slowly is wasting away while lesser players—like, say, Michael Doleac—get regular minutes as backup centers. I just don't get it.

Wang is an outstanding outside shooter for a big man, with a 38.5 percent career mark from downtown, and he also can put the ball on the floor after a shot fake and step inside the line. As a result, his scoring rates have always been very high for a center—for his career he averages 19.1 points per 40 minutes. While it's true that he provides nothing on the boards and can be overmatched physically on post-ups, the same can be said for many centers who don't pack nearly the offensive wallop that Wang does. Plus, he has good footwork and is very good at helping guards in pick-and-roll situations.

Hopefully, there's a smart team somewhere scanning the free-agent wire for a backup center, because Wang can be had cheaply and would be vastly more productive than the usual slop on whom teams desperately fling contracts late in summer. To give one prominent example, the Knicks gave Jerome James nearly $30 million, and Wang could be had for $1 million even though Wang is twice the player that James is.

Wayne Simien   power forward   Age: 22   Height: 6-9   Weight: 255

This could be the new Gary Trent. Simien certainly can score, but the rest of his record sends up red flags. His rates of blocks and steals are shockingly low, suggesting he might be in over his head athletically at the defensive end. Also, he was constantly injured while at Kansas, so his ability to stay on the floor is a concern. However, his rebound rate is impressive and he has a well-developed post game, so he may fill up the box score enough that Miami can live with his defense.

Milwaukee Bucks

It's been an interesting year in Milwaukee. Between a disappointing regular season and a very productive offseason, 2005 could go down as a turning point for the franchise.

On the court, it was a wash. Fresh off a surprising playoff appearance under rookie coach Terry Porter, the Bucks hoped to return to the postseason with most of the same crew. Instead, the Bucks were beset by injuries and quickly sunk to the bottom of the Central Division. Point guard T. J. Ford missed the entire season with a bruised spinal cord, high-scoring forward Keith Van Horn kept spraining his ankle, and aging relic Toni Kukoc's balky back prevented him from relocating the fountain of youth he had found a year earlier.

As a result, the team couldn't generate the offensive attack that had propelled it to the postseason the year before. In making the playoffs in 2003–04, Milwaukee had posted the league's fourth-best mark in Offensive Efficiency. It seemed they could match the effort since the Bucks had little turnover in the offseason, but the injuries put the Bucks in a tight spot because they lacked depth, especially at the forward spots vacated by Van Horn and Kukoc. This was important because the Bucks didn't have the A-list talent of some other teams—they relied on having eight or nine players capable of scoring in double figures. As a result of the prolonged absence of three of them, Milwaukee dipped from 4th in Offensive Efficiency to 12th.

The offensive decline subsequently exposed Milwaukee's poor defense. The Bucks dipped from 24th in the league to 27th, and this more than anything may have been what cost Porter his job. The Bucks certainly missed having an enforcer in the middle, as Brian Skinner departed for Philadelphia in free agency and left Milwaukee with the rail-thin frontcourt combo of Joe Smith and Dan Gadzuric. Each is a fine player by himself, but together they were easily out-muscled by bigger frontcourts. While the two held their own on the boards—the Bucks were above the league average in defensive rebounding—Milwaukee finished 28th in field-goal percentage defense because opponents found it so easy to post up.

Additionally, the Bucks lacked athleticism along the front line. Gadzuric was the lone shot-blocker, and Milwau-

kee finished second to last in the league in blocks. Smith and backup center Zaza Pachulia averaged less than a block per game combined, while the other frontcourt players—Kukoc and Marcus Fizer—were even less athletic. Meanwhile, 6'5" Desmond Mason had to start at small forward for most of the season because Van Horn wasn't healthy, and that produced some terrible size mismatches.

Nonetheless, such a poor defensive showing in consecutive seasons normally reflects a poor effort level as well. That in turn becomes a commentary on the coach. Porter did a great job in his first season in Milwaukee to nab an unexpected playoff berth, but he never got his troops committed at the defensive end. That said, the timing of his departure was extremely surprising. Immediately after the season the Bucks had announced Porter would return, only to suddenly fire him two months later. In his stead the Bucks went with former assistant Terry Stotts. It's a well-deserved second chance—Stotts had just begun turning the corner in Atlanta when management blew up the team on him, but he'll have much better odds of success in Brewtown.

The reason Stotts's roster is improved is because general manager Larry Harris quickly realized he would have to shift gears when the Bucks were mired at the bottom of the division at midseason. Milwaukee faced an offseason where its best player, Michael Redd, would become a free agent, and the team looked to have little cap space to sign him if he departed.

Fortunately, Harris made some shrewd moves before the trade deadline. He unloaded forward Keith Van Horn and guard Mike James, who both were productive but each had large contracts. Those deals that netted Milwaukee $12 million in cap savings, allowing the team enough leeway to keep both Redd and underrated center Gadzuric while avoiding the luxury tax. The deal that sent James to Houston also netted Milwaukee two second-round draft choices, although the trades did bring back two dead-weight contracts in the form of Reece Gaines and Calvin Booth.

The Bucks got an added surprise when the new collective bargaining agreement raised the salary cap by several

---

Bucks at a Glance

Record: 30–52, 5th place in Midwest Division

Offensive Efficiency: 103.5 (12th)

Defensive Efficiency: 106.7 (27th)

Pace Factor: 93.3 (15th)

Top-Rated Player: Michael Redd (PER 18.30, 47th overall)

Head Coach: Terry Stotts. Former Hawks boss gets well-deserved second chance.

---

million dollars. Milwaukee suddenly found itself with nearly $9 million in unexpected cap room and used its windfall to sign Clippers forward Bobby Simmons. Simmons doesn't answer the team's need for frontcourt muscle, but he'll be a helpful addition. He was the second-ranked player in the league in my Defensive PER ratings, and should provide the size and strength at small forward that Mason couldn't. His addition also allows Mason to move back to his natural sixth man role.

The question is whether the Bucks overpaid for the three players. Redd, Simmons, and Gadzuric represent a commitment of over $150 million, and their additions will limit Milwaukee's cap flexibility for the next several years. Unfortunately, I'm not sure how the Bucks could have fared better. Let's break down the three deals:

- Gadzuric got $36 million over six years. That might have been overly generous considering Gadzuric was a restricted free agent and the Bucks could have waited to match offers from other teams. However, it's hard to argue with the valuation. Gadzuric may be the game's most underrated center right now and could potentially play alongside Andrew Bogut at power forward. Alternatively, he is now easily tradable.

- Simmons got $47 million over five years, a substantial amount for a player who had only one good year. On the other hand, consider the market. Milwaukee first offered its cap space to power forward Shareef Abdur-Rahim, who turned them down. Then they turned to the next player on their list. Although Memphis's Stromile Swift might have made a better target, Simmons was certainly near the top of the list of available unrestricted free agents, and Milwaukee needed to make an offer of this size to outmaneuver his other suitors.

- Finally, there's Redd. Re-signing Redd at almost any price made all kinds of sense due to an obscure provision of the collective bargaining agreement called a "cap hold." Let me explain. Because Redd made only $3 million last year, his "cap hold" was only $6 million, even though his market value was roughly dou-

ble that. Because of this difference, Milwaukee could sign Simmons first while technically being under the salary cap, and then sign Redd for his mammoth contract afterward. But Redd was the only player they could do this with—if he left Milwaukee was up the creek. Thus, it made perfect sense for the Bucks to max him out, even though the contract seems insane. It's very rare for a player of his caliber to have such a small contract heading into his free-agent year, so it was a major windfall for Milwaukee.

Milwaukee's best stroke of luck, however, came in the draft lottery. The Bucks drew the winning ticket and selected Utah center Andrew Bogut with the first overall pick in the draft. Bogut has been compared to Brad Miller and Vlade Divac because of his talents as a passer, but he also put up big rebounding numbers and is able to score around the basket. The Australian big man fits the Bucks' need for some beef along the front line, although it remains to be seen how he and Gadzuric can coexist and whether he'll be able to command double-teams offensively.

A few other moves have the Bucks feeling optimistic. Ford has been cleared to play and should be able to energize the Bucks' offense with his ability to push the ball up the court. Backup Mo Williams proved himself worthy in Ford's absence last year, giving the Bucks plenty of depth at the point. Milwaukee also picked up Jiri Welsch from Cleveland for a second-round pick to improve its depth on the wings, and he should be another addition that helps to improve the defense. The only key loss was the departure of Pachulia to Atlanta, as the Bucks opted not to match an offer that would have put them into luxury tax territory.

Overall, it's been quite a year in a place that's traditionally been one of the NBA's quieter corners. It should end with the Bucks returning to the postseason. Milwaukee was better than its record a year ago—the Bucks had 33 Expected Wins—and the club added Ford, Welsch, Simmons, and Bogut while losing only Pachulia. If Stotts can ramp up the defensive intensity, the Bucks really could make some noise. It's still unclear how well all these pieces will mesh, but the Bucks are a much more interesting team than they were 12 months ago.

| Calvin Booth | | | | center | | | | | | | Age: 29 | | Height: 6-11 | Weight: 231 |
| (100% C) | | | | | | | | | | | | | | Most similar at age: N/A |

Year		G	M/G	FG%	FT%	P/40	R/40	A/40	TS%		Ast		TO		Usg		Reb		PER	
2002-03	Sea	47	12.2	.437	.723	9.6	7.6	0.8	49.4	49	6.9	57	12.7	28	11.5	60	11.2	66	9.97	61
2003-04	Sea	71	17.0	.466	.798	11.5	9.3	0.9	52.1	37	6.9	56	11.1	18	12.4	52	13.0	49	13.63	38
2004-05	Dal-Mil	51	8.8	.454	.813	11.0	9.5	0.7	50.8		3.4		11.0		11.9		13.9		11.80	

The lanky shot-blocker was shipped to Milwaukee as salary ballast in the Van Horn trade and was waived after the season as the Bucks' luxury-tax amnesty cut. Booth didn't figure to be a major part of the Bucks' plans with Bogut and Gadzuric ahead of him on the depth chart anyway.

However, he's not a bad option as an end-of-the-bench guy. While he doesn't have enough muscle to handle strong post players, can't hold his own on the glass, and has no post game, he can make an open 12-footer and has one of the best shot-blocking rates in the league. For a third-string center, that's acceptable.

Marcus Fizer					power forward							Age: 27		Height: 6-8	Weight: 260	
(80% PF, 20% C)														Most similar at age: Billy Owens		
Year		G	M/G	FG%	FT%	P/40	R/40	A/40	TS%		Ast		TO	Usg	Reb	PER
2002-03	Chi	38	21.3	.465	.657	22.0	10.7	2.4	50.3	39	8.8	45	10.4	23	24.5	7	14.8	21	17.87	14
2003-04	Chi	46	16.0	.383	.750	19.5	10.9	2.3	44.7	61	8.7	55	10.3	15	24.5	5	15.7	17	13.34	46
2004-05	Mil	54	16.7	.455	.680	14.9	7.8	2.8	49.8	51	13.5	9	13.6	56	18.7	25	11.3	53	11.54	55
2005-06	PRJ (60.9)			.441	.704	16.8	9.0	2.6	49.2		11.6		12.1		20.4	12.8	13.15

Keep an eye on Fizer this season. He underwent knee surgery in May 2004 and spent all of last season playing his way back into shape. While his value is limited if he plays the way he did last season, his track record is much stronger. Fizer couldn't leap the way he used to and had no explosion around the basket, facts made obvious by his diminished Rebound Rate and sudden decline in shot attempts.

With a summer to recuperate, he could be much closer to the Fizer of old this season. That player is undersized for the power forward spot and a defensive liability, but he's also a major threat as a low-post scorer coming off the bench. Fizer is very strong and can hit a mid-range jumper, which is why his scoring rates the previous two seasons were around 20 points per 40 minutes. As a result, he could provide an inexpensive source of bench points for somebody.

T. J. Ford					point guard							Age: 22		Height: 6-0	Weight: 165
Year		G	M/G	FG%	FT%	P/40	R/40	A/40	TS%		Ast		TO	Usg	Reb	PER
2003-04	Mil	55	26.8	.384	.816	10.6	4.8	9.7	44.3	57	38.0	3	14.8	57	22.5	25	7.0	7	12.00	49
2004-05	Mil		Did not play

Ford missed all of last season with a bruised spinal cord he suffered in a game midway through his rookie season. Fortunately, he was cleared to return over the summer and figures to be the Bucks' starting point guard. Though listed at six feet tall, Ford is probably closer to 5′10″, so his size can be a liability at the defensive end. However, he makes up for it by pressuring the ball and is a surprisingly adept rebounder.

Offensively, Ford excels at leading the break and should have the Bucks playing at a much faster pace. With two sharp-shooters on the outside in Redd and Simmons, Ford will have plenty of chances to rack up assists. However, his jump shot was a major weakness in his rookie season and he made too many turnovers. He'll have to remedy those problems this season if he's going to keep Mo Williams from taking his job.

Dan Gadzuric					center							Age: 27		Height: 6-11	Weight: 240	
(100% C)														Most similar at age: Marcus Camby		
Year		G	M/G	FG%	FT%	P/40	R/40	A/40	TS%		Ast		TO	Usg	Reb	PER
2002-03	Mil	49	15.5	.483	.518	8.9	10.4	0.5	49.8	47	4.4	69	13.1	36	10.0	66	15.2	25	11.25	53
2003-04	Mil	75	16.8	.524	.492	13.5	11.0	0.9	52.9	29	5.9	64	9.5	8	13.8	39	16.0	17	17.03	11
2004-05	Mil	81	22.0	.539	.538	13.3	15.1	0.7	55.1	23	3.2	65	12.5	22	13.3	41	22.1	1	18.11	8
2005-06	PRJ (28.3)			.501	.505	13.0	13.6	0.8	51.1		4.3		12.0		14.0	19.5	16.52

Gadzuric didn't get the attention of some of the other free agents this past summer because he played so few minutes the last two seasons, but his 40-minute averages make his value clear. Because Gadzuric is extremely quick for his size and an explosive leaper, he had the best Rebound Rate among centers this past season and the second-best in the NBA. Additionally, he's the Bucks' lone shot-blocker, although his rate declined sharply from the year before.

(continued next page)

Dan Gadzuric *(continued)*

There's no evidence his performance will diminish with more minutes either. In the 10 games Gadzuric played at least 30 minutes, he had double-doubles in seven. In those ten contests, he averaged 14.1 points and 12.8 rebounds per game, including posting the Bucks' first 20-20 game in seven years during the season's final week.

Given those numbers, one of the great mysteries of the Porter era is why this guy saw such little playing time, and it's an oversight Stotts needs to correct. But to do so may require moving Gadzuric to the power forward spot, since Andrew Bogut is the Bucks' center of the future. It would probably help Gadzuric at the defensive end, since he gets pushed around too easily when he plays the pivot, but the question is whether he can handle it offensively.

Reece Gaines				shooting guard						Age: 23	Height: 6-6	Weight: 205
(50% SG, 36% SF, 11% PG, 3% PF)												Most similar at age: N/A
Year	G	M/G	FG%	FT%	P/40	R/40	A/40	TS%	Ast	TO	Usg	Reb	PER
2003-04 Orl	38	9.6	.291	.640	7.6	4.3	4.4	35.6	25.8	11.6	15.6	6.2	6.04
2004-05 Hou-Mil	21	8.9	.340	.750	8.8	3.0	1.5	39.6	7.1	10.6	12.8	4.4	3.39

An orca-sized bust after Orlando selected him in the first round in 2003, Gaines is on his third team and has yet to provide any evidence that he belongs in the league. He has one year left on his contract to prove otherwise but will get few opportunities in a deep Milwaukee backcourt. He can take slight comfort in the NBA's doing away with the injured list this season and calling it an inactive list, meaning we won't have to read about his "tendinitis" this season.

Kendall Gill				small forward						Age: 37	Height: 6-5	Weight: 216
(72% SF, 24% SG, 4% PF)												Most similar at age: N/A
Year	G	M/G	FG%	FT%	P/40	R/40	A/40	TS%		Ast		TO		Usg		Reb		PER	
2002-03 Min	82	25.2	.422	.764	13.8	4.8	3.0	47.7	49	15.5	21	10.7	27	18.0	30	6.8	53	10.57	49
2003-04 Chi*	56	25.2	.392	.735	15.3	5.4	2.5	44.3	57	11.4	52	10.6	32	20.1	33	7.7	19	11.10	44
2004-05 Mil	14	20.3	.400	.900	12.0	5.2	3.8	47.9		18.1		7.2		16.7		7.6		12.09	

* Season rankings are as shooting guard

Picked up when the Bucks were short of bodies in the backcourt but released in January, Gill has aged well and remains a competent end-of-the-bench guy. He handles the ball fairly well for a player of his size and can get to the basket, although a shaky jumper limits his value.

Gill also has an interesting offseason hobby—boxing. He fought in two bouts in the offseason and plans to continue doing so once his playing days are over. For now, the putative pugilist will put those plans on hold to seek a one-year contract as a reserve.

Anthony Goldwire				point guard						Age: 34	Height: 6-2	Weight: 182
(100% PG)												Most similar at age: Joe Dumars
Year	G	M/G	FG%	FT%	P/40	R/40	A/40	TS%		Ast		TO		Usg		Reb		PER	
2002-03 SA-Was	15	5.7	.360	.571	11.6	2.8	1.9	44.5		10.5		15.8		16.4		4.1		5.24	
2003-04 Min-NJ	11	7.7	.318	1.000	8.0	3.3	5.2	37.9		30.2		8.2		16.4		4.7		8.85	
2004-05 Det-Mil	33	16.3	.419	.839	12.8	4.4	5.8	57.5	6	27.7	29	6.2	1	17.4	61	6.4	15	15.11	29
2005-06 PRJ (25.1)			*.405*	*.831*	*12.4*	*4.2*	*5.8*	*55.2*		*27.0*		*6.4*		*17.2*		*6.1*		*14.30*	

A career journeyman signed when the Bucks traded Mike James and needed another point guard, Goldwire suddenly and inexplicably had the best season of his career. He had the best Turnover Ratio among point guards and although his field-goal percentage was low, he spiked it by shooting a career-best 41 percent on three-pointers as a Buck.

Absolutely nobody expects Goldwire to do this again—he's 34 and last season was the most minutes he had played since 1997–98. At the very least, his year-end exploits with the Bucks will earn him a contract somewhere as a backup point guard.

Zendon Hamilton — center

(88% C, 12% PF)

Age: 30 Height: 6-11 Weight: 240
Most similar at age: N/A

Year		G	M/G	FG%	FT%	P/40	R/40	A/40	TS%	Ast	TO	Usg	Reb	PER
2002-03	Tor	3	4.0	.400	1.000	20.0	13.3	0.0	51.0	0.0	14.5	21.0	19.0	17.73
2003-04	Phi	45	10.5	.537	.698	14.3	12.3	1.1	61.6	7.3	15.2	13.8	17.5	15.93
2004-05	Mil	16	9.9	.344	.604	12.8	10.6	1.5	48.0	7.2	16.9	15.9	15.8	10.21

A frontcourt journeyman who nonetheless has put up some decent numbers the past few seasons, Hamilton was included in the James trade and waived almost immediately by the Rockets. Throughout his career he's been a very solid rebounder and a good finisher around the basket, but his slender build has hurt him at the defensive end. He's good enough to fill a role as a fifth man in the frontcourt, so hopefully he'll find a willing team this offseason.

Toni Kukoc — power forward

(55% SF, 44% PF, 1% C)

Age: 37 Height: 6-11 Weight: 235
Most similar at age: Clifford Robinson

Year		G	M/G	FG%	FT%	P/40	R/40	A/40	TS%		Ast		TO		Usg		Reb		PER	
2002-03	Mil	63	27.0	.432	.706	17.1	6.2	5.4	55.1	13	22.7	5	12.0	42	22.1	12	9.1	59	17.97	12
2003-04	Mil	73	20.8	.417	.729	16.2	7.1	5.3	51.9	30	22.1	3	12.2	40	21.4	15	10.4	59	16.08	24
2004-05	Mil	53	20.7	.410	.721	10.8	5.8	5.8	52.3	35	27.7	1	12.6	50	16.9	38	8.5	67	12.76	50
2005-06	*PRJ (8.7)*			*.410*	*.712*	*13.2*	*6.3*	*4.9*	*51.7*		*22.9*		*12.3*		*18.1*		*9.1*		*14.00*	

Kukoc found the fountain of youth in his first two seasons with the Bucks, but the tap abruptly ran dry last season. He spent the first two months of the season on the injured list and never seemed to catch up once he returned. Kukoc had a much harder time getting involved in the offense, as the sharp dip in his Usage Rate shows, partly because the Bucks called his number less often on post-ups from the left block.

However, players who see a drop in Usage Rate normally experience an increase in field-goal percentage and a drop in Turnover Ratio, because they're taking fewer contested shots. The fact Kukoc didn't is a worrying sign, especially given his advanced age.

Defensively, Kukoc is a mere speed bump for post players, although he does have fast hands and is very good at tapping the ball away from a dribbler on the blocks. He's also a very poor rebounder for his position and a non-factor as a help defender. Milwaukee re-signed him to a one-year deal, gambling that his offense recovers enough to make up for his defense.

Desmond Mason — small forward

Defensive PER: 0.11 (84% SF, 11% SG, 5% PF)

Age: 28 Height: 6-5 Weight: 222
Most similar at age: Jeff Grayer

Year		G	M/G	FG%	FT%	P/40	R/40	A/40	TS%		Ast		TO		Usg		Reb		PER	
2002-03	Sea-Mil	80	34.5	.449	.749	16.6	7.6	2.4	50.2	40	11.5	45	8.1	6	19.9	22	11.1	9	15.22	18
2003-04	Mil	82	30.9	.472	.769	18.7	5.7	2.4	55.2	9	11.1	40	10.8	28	19.7	23	8.3	38	15.60	19
2004-05	Mil	80	36.2	.443	.802	19.0	4.3	3.0	52.6	33	12.8	26	9.7	26	21.8	14	6.3	60	14.72	24
2005-06	*PRJ (34.1)*			*.458*	*.785*	*18.0*	*5.0*	*2.8*	*53.5*		*12.8*		*9.9*		*20.3*		*7.3*		*14.85*	

Mason was forced into the starting lineup by Van Horn's injuries and eventual trade, but the shift didn't seem to suit him well. He's a fine defensive player on the perimeter, but as a 6′5″ small forward who gave up two or more inches to his opponent every night, he was sometimes overmatched. Unlike previous seasons, the Bucks had nobody on the roster who could bail him out of those match-ups, so his defensive rating suffered. Additionally, his Rebound Rate has declined precipitously the past two seasons for no apparent reason.

Offensively, Mason likes to isolate on the left wing from about 17 feet away and drive to the basket. He's very good going to the rim, as he has a quick first step and is an outstanding leaper who throws down one spectacular dunk a game. That helped him average a free-throw attempt for every two field-goal attempts the past two seasons, which has kept his TS% solid despite his lack of a three-point shot (he made just one in 2004–05).

The jumper is the one thing that prevents Mason from being a dynamite scorer. He shoots a line-drive shot with his hands way out in front of his body, so he isn't very accurate and needs a fair amount of clearance to get the shot off. That and the rebounding dip make him an unpalatable option as a starting small forward, but he should excel this season in a return to his sixth man role. Bobby Simmons can bang with the more physical forwards, and Mason can go back to letting his athleticism change games off the bench.

Zaza Pachulia　　　　center　　　　　　　　　　　**Age: 21**　**Height: 6-11**　**Weight: 240**
(91% C, 9% PF)　　　　　　　　　　　　　　　　　　　　　Most similar at age: Kwame Brown

Year		G	M/G	FG%	FT%	P/40	R/40	A/40	TS%		Ast		TO		Usg		Reb		PER	
2003-04	Orl	59	11.3	.389	.644	11.7	10.5	0.8	45.2	68	5.0	69	13.0	35	14.2	38	15.1	24	10.76	63
2004-05	Mil	74	18.9	.452	.746	13.1	10.8	1.7	52.6	33	8.2	21	12.4	20	14.8	29	15.8	25	14.32	30
2005-06	PRJ (26.1)			.449	.749	14.4	11.4	1.7	52.5		7.7		12.1		16.1		16.4		15.76	

Harris plucked Pachulia via the Bobcats when Orlando left him unprotected in the expansion draft. It was an astute but unheralded move. Pachulia showed sharp improvement in his second season and quickly is becoming one of the game's more skilled big men. Pachulia has soft hands and a great feel for the game for such a young player, frequently putting himself in position for easy lay-ups. He also sees the floor well and can handle the ball, which is why both his Assist and Turnover Ratios were above average.

Pachulia's big weakness is a lack of athleticism. He doesn't block shots—he had only 34 all last season, or about one for every 40 minutes—and he gets dunked on *a lot*. He'll have to learn how to move his feet into position to take charges, or otherwise he's going to be on more posters than Craig Ehlo. He also needs to get stronger so he's not so easily overpowered in the post.

Pachulia became a restricted free agent in the summer, providing an interesting dilemma for the Bucks. Based on his age and production, there seems to be little doubt that Pachulia would be worth a substantial investment. Plus, the Bucks played well with Pachulia on the court. He had the best net plus-minus on the team, and the Bucks went 19–15 when Pachulia played at least 20 minutes—compared to 11–37 the rest of the time.

But it seems unlikely that Pachulia would see 20 minutes in any game with the Bucks' addition of Bogut in the middle and the re-signing of Gadzuric. In addition, some have wondered if Pachulia is really as young as the media guide says. As a result, the Bucks let Pachulia sign with Atlanta in the offseason, where Pachulia will take over as the Hawks' starting center. Based on his projected stats, he's ready for the promotion.

Michael Redd　　　　shooting guard　　　　　　　**Age: 26**　**Height: 6-6**　**Weight: 215**
Defensive PER: 0.34 (92% SG, 8% SF)　　　　　　　　　　Most similar at age: Michael Finley

Year		G	M/G	FG%	FT%	P/40	R/40	A/40	TS%		Ast		TO		Usg		Reb		PER	
2002-03	Mil	82	28.2	.469	.805	21.4	6.4	2.0	59.0	6	9.4	55	6.0	2	20.8	21	9.4	7	21.05	6
2003-04	Mil	82	36.8	.440	.868	23.5	5.4	2.5	54.4	7	9.6	59	6.0	2	24.2	11	7.9	16	19.83	4
2004-05	Mil	75	38.0	.441	.854	24.2	4.4	2.4	53.6	24	9.0	63	7.0	4	25.6	8	6.4	37	18.30	8
2005-06	PRJ (40.0)			.448	.848	22.6	4.9	2.5	55.4		10.1		6.5		24.1		7.1		19.24	

Although Redd's PER has dipped for two straight seasons because he had take on a greater share of the Bucks' scoring load, he earned a maximum contract in the offseason that should keep him in Wisconsin for several more years.

Redd's focus on scoring diminished his performance in other areas last season. He normally is among the league leaders in TS% but it sank to 53.6 percent last season, as he had to force too many contested jumpers at the end of the shot clock. Redd also has shot only 35 percent on three-pointers the past two seasons, compared to 44 percent the two prior seasons. That's because a lot more of those three-pointers have been off the dribble or shot with a man in his face, but with two great passers in Ford and Bogut joining the lineup, Redd could get a lot more open looks. Finally, as with Mason, Redd's Rebound Rate took an unexpected plunge.

Although he's diligent, durable, and one of my favorite players (check the cover of the '03 edition), it's hard to make the case that Redd really is worth the maximum. He's not a good passer and his defense needs a lot of work, especially from the weak side. Furthermore, he's not in the top tier of shooting guards because he doesn't create shots off the dribble as easily as some of his peers. He's a fine shooter and his percentages should improve this season now that he has more help around him, but Milwaukee unquestionably overpaid to keep him. A quirk of the salary cap rules made it advantageous for Milwaukee to do so, but the fact it's a six-year deal could come back to bite them down the road.

Daniel Santiago   center   Age: 29   Height: 7-1   Weight: 260
(100% C)   Most similar at age: N/A

Year		G	M/G	FG%	FT%	P/40	R/40	A/40	TS%		Ast		TO		Usg		Reb		PER	
2003-04	Mil	54	13.1	.479	.678	12.3	7.5	1.4	53.6	23	9.3	31	12.4	28	13.2	47	10.9	72	11.18	58
2004-05	Mil	11	9.5	.333	.727	8.4	7.2	0.4	42.6		1.8		13.0		10.7		10.8		4.04	

A lumbering giant from Puerto Rico, Santiago's minutes diminished significantly with the arrival of Pachulia and he's likely to be searching for a new employer. Santiago has a soft touch around the basket but is so slow that he gathers more moss than rebounds and, like seemingly every Bucks big man, he blocks a shot about once every solstice. He might be worth a minimum contract as a third center, but that's the extent of his value.

Joe Smith   power forward   Age: 30   Height: 6-10   Weight: 225
Defensive PER: 0.23 (88% PF, 12% C)   Most similar at age: P. J. Brown

Year		G	M/G	FG%	FT%	P/40	R/40	A/40	TS%		Ast		TO		Usg		Reb		PER	
2002-03	Min	54	20.7	.460	.779	14.5	9.7	1.4	52.4	28	8.1	51	9.2	10	15.5	42	13.7	30	14.25	33
2003-04	Mil	76	29.7	.439	.859	14.7	11.4	1.4	51.0	40	8.0	59	8.4	2	16.0	41	16.6	10	16.57	20
2004-05	Mil	74	30.6	.514	.768	14.4	9.6	1.2	56.4	15	5.6	64	9.1	19	14.4	52	13.9	29	14.97	35
2005-06	PRJ (54.9)			.474	.796	14.5	10.3	1.3	53.0		6.8		9.5		15.7		15.0		15.28	

Smith was one of the keys to the Bucks' surprising play in 2003–04, but that season may have been over his head. His performance in 2004–05 was more consistent with his long-term averages, as he created fewer shots and was less of a factor on the glass.

Also, Smith had more trouble defensively than he experienced the year before. He loves to take charges and matches up well against long, slender players like Tim Duncan and Kevin Garnett. However, his lack of strength was a major problem because the Bucks' other frontcourt players had the same weakness. When paired with a muscular center like Brian Skinner it wasn't a big problem, but last year's Smith-Gadzuric combo was extremely vulnerable to strength mismatches.

Offensively, Smith's arsenal hasn't changed much. He shoots a jumper from either elbow with a long wind-up and can shoot a hook shot with either hand on the rare occasions he outmuscles somebody for post position. He's also a decent athlete who can finish, although those skills aren't as potent as they were when he was younger. With Smith under contract for two more seasons, it will be interesting to see if Bogut's arrival makes his strength shortcomings less of an issue.

Erick Strickland   shooting guard   Age: 32   Height: 6-3   Weight: 210
(78% SG, 17% PG, 5% SF)   Most similar at age: N/A

Year		G	M/G	FG%	FT%	P/40	R/40	A/40	TS%		Ast		TO		Usg		Reb		PER	
2002-03	Ind*	71	18.0	.429	.805	14.4	4.5	6.6	54.7	11	28.8	23	13.5	53	20.6	43	6.4	20	13.51	32
2003-04	Mil	43	13.3	.403	.863	16.2	5.0	6.3	52.9	20	24.8	8	14.9	62	22.4	19	7.2	25	13.96	25
2004-05	Mil	62	16.4	.375	.813	11.9	4.1	4.5	45.3	62	21.6	7	12.5	57	18.5	37	5.9	49	8.01	65
2005-06	PRJ (35.4)			.389	.808	12.7	4.1	5.3	48.2		23.9		14.0		19.0		5.9		9.81	

* Season rankings are as point guard

Often with an injury, it's not the replacement that causes the problem—it's the replacement's replacement. Last year, for instance, the Bucks were forced to start Desmond Mason at small forward instead of Keith Van Horn, but that didn't set them back too far. The bigger problem was Milwaukee being forced to play Strickland and Kendall Gill as Redd's backup because Mason could no longer fill that role.

Though still an energetic help defender, Strickland's offense was a huge disappointment, as he was both a wildly inaccurate shooter and entirely too turnover-prone. The projections say he should recover slightly this season, but it won't be in Milwaukee. With the Bucks' offseason additions, the free-agent Strickland will have to rediscover his jumper someplace else.

Maurice Williams			point guard										**Age: 23**	**Height: 6-1**	**Weight: 185**
Defensive PER: 0.04 (94% PG, 6% SG)														Most similar at age: Dee Brown	

Year		G	M/G	FG%	FT%	P/40	R/40	A/40	TS%		Ast		TO		Usg		Reb		PER	
2003-04	Uta*	57	13.6	.380	.786	14.7	3.7	3.9	43.3	61	16.7	31	11.2	38	22.6	18	5.8	46	9.36	55
2004-05	Mil	80	28.2	.438	.850	14.4	4.3	8.6	50.4	43	32.5	15	13.2	54	24.0	21	6.3	18	14.00	39
2005-06	PRJ (32.7)			.428	.844	15.6	4.3	7.7	49.6		29.0		12.0		24.7		6.4		14.40	

* Season rankings are as shooting guard

Williams is quick and has a great first step, qualities that enabled him to post solid numbers in his first year of regular point guard duty despite his scorer's instincts. Another inexpensive pickup by Harris—three years, $5.3 million—Williams got to the basket fairly easily and his talent for creating shots kept Milwaukee competitive after the James and Van Horn trades. He also surprised with his passing, nearly doubling his Assist Ratio from the previous season and finishing among the league leaders in assists.

Williams is a work in progress though. His quickness failed to produce many free throws, suggesting he needs to put more effort into drawing fouls. Plus, his jumper needs work, as he made only 32 three-pointers all season. Finally, the cost of all those drives was that Williams was turnover-prone, something he may be able to cut sharply as he gains more experience at the point.

Defensively, Williams needs work as well. He was beaten off the dribble with alarming frequency, and at 6′1″ he can be vulnerable to size mismatches against bigger guards. Regardless, the Bucks have to be encouraged that they found an inexpensive, developing point guard who can fill in adequately if T. J. Ford's spine problems return.

Andrew Bogut	center	**Age: 21**	**Height: 7-0**	**Weight: 245**

Bogut is an unbelievable passer for a big man, in the mold of Vlade Divac or Brad Miller. In the NCAA tournament he was able to dominate Utah's first two opponents without scoring by repeatedly finding cutters for lay-ups. He's also a top-notch rebounder despite average athleticism, and he has a varied offensive arsenal that includes 18-foot range on the jumper and an array of low-post moves. While Bogut isn't the shoe-in superstar that some other No. 1 overall picks have been, he should be a good player for a long time. The question is to what extent he'll make an impact at the defensive end, which is where the Bucks need the most help.

Ersan Ilyasova	small forward	**Age: 18**	**Height: 6-9**	**Weight: 220**

Ilyasova is originally from Uzbekistan but has played in Turkey for several years. He was thought of as a potential lottery pick until he hurt his ankle this past season. Ilyasova shoots extremely well for his size, reminiscent of Peja Stojakovic or Tim Thomas, but the ankle hadn't fully healed by draft day, which is why he dropped to the second round. Milwaukee probably will leave him in Turkey for another year or two and see what happens.

New Jersey Nets

Well that was a quick rebound. In less than a year, the New Jersey Nets have gone from the penthouse to the outhouse and back to the penthouse. At the end of it all they once again appear to be contenders for the Eastern Conference crown.

That didn't seem possible in the summer of 2004 when new owner Bruce Ratner initiated a fire sale that saw the Nets trade Kenyon Martin and Kerry Kittles, waive Lucious Harris, and fail to sign any free agent of note (unless you consider Ron Mercer and Eric Williams "of note"). Jason Kidd quickly demanded a trade and it looked like the Nets' mini-dynasty of three straight division titles was unraveling at warp speed.

But those moves had one goal—avoiding the luxury tax—and the Nets succeeded in doing so. With that out of the way, they worked on quickly rebuilding, and for general manager Rod Thorn it was his finest moment since acquiring Kidd four years earlier. New Jersey's first move was to sign Richard Jefferson to a contract extension, which at least assured the remaining players that the team wasn't going to turn into an East Coast version of the Clippers. The big enchilada came later—a blockbuster deal for Vince Carter that completely transformed New Jersey's season and probably its future too.

To get Carter, Thorn unloaded three players who were totally irrelevant to the Nets' plans—Eric Williams, Aaron Williams, and Alonzo Mourning—along with two of the three draft picks the Nets got from Denver in the Martin trade. The final tally from the two trades essentially was Martin for Carter and a first-round draft pick—a swap that is overwhelmingly in New Jersey's favor. (That pick, by the way, is an unprotected pick owned by the Clippers, so the Nets could have a very high first-round pick in June.)

Of course, the Nets didn't expect Carter to perform as well as he did. Carter had been blatantly mailing it in for Toronto, so some improvement was expected with the change of scenery. But he also had knee and Achilles problems and there were questions about whether he'd ever be willing to go to the basket with authority again. Additionally, the team's post-Carter enthusiasm quickly waned when Jefferson was lost for the season, and it appeared the Nets were doomed to the lottery.

Carter almost single-handedly changed that fate, putting on a nightly aerial show that reminded everyone why he had become so famous in the first place. Carter was devastating as a Net, averaging 27.5 points per game and shooting 42.5 percent on three-pointers. With a rejuvenated Vinsanity leading the way, New Jersey went 15–4 over its final 19 games to sneak into the East's final playoff spot—an accomplishment that seemed all but impossible when the season started.

Even with Carter's exploits, New Jersey's playoff run was as much luck as skill. New Jersey was the NBA's luckiest team according to the Expected Wins formula, winning 42 games when their point differential predicted 36. That difference allowed New Jersey to push past Cleveland to claim the final playoff spot.

The offense was what held the Nets back. Despite Carter's amazing second half and Kidd's presence at the point, the Nets were an incredibly bad offensive team. New Jersey finished 27th in the NBA in Offensive Efficiency and was dead last until Carter put the team on his back over the final 20 games.

New Jersey fared so badly for two simple reasons: It couldn't make shots, and it couldn't rebound the misses. The Nets shot 42.9 percent from the field, the second-worst mark in the league. Even the lowly Hawks, who had Antoine Walker on their team for half the season and a CBA roster for all of it, managed to shoot 44.1 percent. Second, the Nets were terrible on the offensive glass, rebounding only 25.5 percent of their missed shots—the league's third-worst figure.

The rebounding part is easy to understand—none of the Nets' big men leave opponents quaking in their boots. But some might be surprised to learn that the Nets had such a wayward stroke from the field. In addition to Kidd and Carter, they had Richard Jefferson for half a season and a decent scorer up front in Nenad Krstic. One would think that would be enough to create a passable offense.

Nets at a Glance

Record: 42–40, 3rd place in Atlantic Division

Offensive Efficiency: 98.3 (27th)

Defensive Efficiency: 100.4 (7th)

Pace Factor: 91.5 (20th)

Top-Rated Player: Vince Carter (PER 20.90, 14th overall)

Head Coach: Lawrence Frank. Again had team overachieving at defensive end.

Table 1. Nets True Shooting Percentage, 2004–05

Player	TS%
Eric Williams	57.0*
Vince Carter	55.7*
Nenad Krstic	54.7
League Average	**54.2**
Zoran Planinic	53.4
Jacque Vaughn	51.1
Travis Best	50.8
Jason Kidd	50.6
Jabari Smith	48.2
Clifford Robinson	47.1*
Jason Collins	47.1
Billy Thomas	47.9
Jabari Smith	46.8
Brian Scalabrine	46.8
Rodney Buford	43.7
Ron Mercer	42.2

Nets stats only

It would have been, too, except for one little problem: The other Nets were horrible. Carter and Krstic were a little above the league average in True Shooting Percentage, while Jefferson and Kidd were a little below. But the others? All except Eric Williams fell below the league average, and most were *way* below. In table 1 I've included the TS% of every Net who played at least 300 minutes in 2004–05. The picture is worth a thousand words.

So while the Nets had the nucleus of a good offensive team, the surrounding parts were severely lacking. Other than the "big four" of Kidd, Carter, Jefferson, and Krstic, no Net on the year-end roster had a PER higher than 13 or a TS% above the league average. Thus, the Nets were a dreadful offensive team overall even though they had one of the league's best offensive players.

This might sound like bad news, but actually it's *great* news. For New Jersey to improve is extremely easy—they just need to replace one or two of the awful players with good ones and they'll immediately be one of the better offensive teams in the league. It is much, much easier for a team like the Nets to improve than it is for one like, say, Memphis, who has a roster full of decent players but no great ones.

New Jersey worked on doing just that in the offseason. The Nets had a $5 million trade exception left over from the Kittles deal—which no longer looks like such a fire sale after he missed the season with back trouble—and originally used it to rope Portland's Shareef Abdur-Rahim in a sign-and-trade deal. Unfortunately, the Nets turned up some knee problems in Abdur-Rahim's physical and had to rescind the trade. Ultimately, the team settled for a deal for Philadelphia's Marc Jackson, a productive frontcourt player who should give them more scoring off the bench.

To fill out the backcourt, New Jersey used part of its midlevel exception on Cleveland's Jeff McInnis, who should be a major upgrade from Travis Best at backup point guard. In addition, New Jersey used its first-round pick on Texas A&M swingman Antoine Wright, who should give the Nets more scoring off the bench.

New Jersey has an additional weapon in its coach, Lawrence Frank. In a year and a half at the helm, he's already made an impression with his preparedness and ability to inspire the team defensively. He was particularly effective mixing in zone defenses during games to throw opponents off balance. New Jersey finished seventh in the league in Defensive Efficiency despite numerous injuries, no shot-blockers, and a paper-thin bench. Frank had Jacque Vaughn starting at shooting guard for a good portion of the year and managed to cover up the weakness on most nights. The most amazing stat was that the Nets were fourth in the NBA in defensive rebounding at 73.2 percent. This was accomplished with two frontcourt starters who seem allergic to rebounding and a 6′1″ shooting guard, speaking volumes about Frank's ability to get players in the right spots to succeed.

And succeed they will. Kidd was back to his old self after his return from offseason knee surgery and Jefferson will be back for a full season. Krstic is a softie but has real potential as a scorer and should make further progress in his second NBA season. Zoran Planinic, who played sparingly due to injury but showed great improvement as a scorer, also could play a key role. Add in a couple of offensive-minded free agents, a bench that can't possibly be worse than last year's group, and a healthy does of Vinsanity, and New Jersey should bounce right back to where they were two years ago. If it plays out that way, it will be the quickest recovery since Lazarus.

Travis Best — point guard
(60% PG, 40% SG)

Age: 33 Height: 5-11 Weight: 180
Most similar at age: David Wesley

Year		G	M/G	FG%	FT%	P/40	R/40	A/40	TS%		Ast		TO		Usg		Reb		PER	
2002-03	Mia	72	25.1	.396	.854	13.3	3.3	5.6	47.3	44	25.5	36	10.6	23	21.3	35	4.7	52	11.20	48
2003-04	Dal	61	12.5	.372	.870	9.0	3.6	5.9	44.5	56	33.2	15	9.8	16	16.0	62	4.9	46	10.10	59
2004-05	NJ	76	19.2	.420	.885	14.1	2.9	3.9	50.8	40	18.7	62	9.4	16	18.7	56	4.2	58	11.83	50
2005-06	PRJ (23.7)			.392	.842	11.5	3.3	4.3	47.2		22.8		10.5		17.3		4.5		10.13	

Best slightly improved upon a disappointing year in Dallas and looked like a scoring machine compared to the Nets' other alternatives off the bench. Although 5′ 11″, he was used often as a shooting guard in the same backcourt with Kidd, accounting for his poor Assist Ratio.

As a scorer, Best left a lot to be desired. He shot a poor percentage, didn't create a high volume of shots, and struggled from the three-point line (30.6 percent). His one saving grace was free-throw shooting, where he continues to be among the best in the league.

Best was on a one-year deal and the Nets don't appear to have a need for him in their revamped backcourt. Thus, he'll shop his passable numbers from New Jersey and hope to get a bite for the veteran's minimum.

Rodney Buford — shooting guard
(52% SG, 40% SF, 8% PF)

Age: 28 Height: 6-5 Weight: 195
Most similar at age: Calbert Cheaney

Year		G	M/G	FG%	FT%	P/40	R/40	A/40	TS%		Ast		TO		Usg		Reb		PER	
2003-04	Sac	22	6.4	.339	.500	11.6	4.3	2.0	35.0		10.1		5.7		18.4		6.3		6.18	
2004-05	NJ	64	20.5	.382	.822	13.5	5.8	1.9	43.7	63	9.1	62	5.8	3	18.1	39	8.2	14	9.42	57
2005-06	PRJ (26.9)			.392	.796	12.7	5.8	1.9	44.6		9.6		6.4		16.6		8.3		9.38	

The one Frank move that deserves second-guessing was the use of Buford as a key reserve for most of the season. Buford is the classic example of a poor jump shooter who nonetheless continues shooting from outside, resulting in a terrible shooting percentage and an even worse rate of free throws. The fact the Nets had two of the league's leading examples, with Ron Mercer being the other, was a major reason the offense stunk.

Nonetheless, Buford appeared to have delusions of grandeur regarding his offensive capabilities. His Brick Index of 2.91 was the fifth-worst in the NBA, so his lack of success was not an impediment to his willingness to launch. One half-expected him to start complaining that Vince Carter was getting more touches.

Buford was largely innocuous in other respects. His defense was okay, he didn't turn the ball over, and he helped out on the glass. If he were able to shoot in the low 40s and get to the line once in a while, those skills would make him a valuable bench player. Instead, his continued employment is highly unlikely.

Vince Carter — small forward
(53% SF, 43% SG, 4% PF)

Age: 28 Height: 6-6 Weight: 220
Most similar at age: Clyde Drexler

Year		G	M/G	FG%	FT%	P/40	R/40	A/40	TS%		Ast		TO		Usg		Reb		PER	
2002-03	Tor*	43	34.2	.467	.806	24.0	5.1	3.9	53.2	23	13.7	40	7.1	7	27.5	5	7.3	22	21.92	3
2003-04	Tor	73	38.1	.417	.806	23.6	5.0	5.0	50.1	37	15.7	21	10.1	22	30.8	2	7.2	46	19.93	5
2004-05	Tor-NJ	77	36.7	.452	.798	26.7	5.7	4.6	54.1	17	14.6	11	7.5	8	30.4	3	8.1	43	22.83	3
2005-06	PRJ (29.2)			.439	.819	24.5	5.4	4.5	52.6		14.6		8.5		29.2		7.7		20.35	

* Season rankings are as shooting guard

Carter's PER doesn't show it, but his year consisted of two seasons. The first act was in Toronto, where he was playing at about four percent of his full ability and averaged 15 points a game in 24 contests. Act II was the final 53 games in New Jersey, in which he was brilliant. Carter created shots in bunches, made most of them, and had a microscopic Turnover Ratio to boot. In little over half a season, he broke the team record for 30-point games.

(continued next page)

Vince Carter (continued)

In fact, most people don't realize this, but Carter was the single best player in the league over the season's final 20 games. His PER of 29.71 outranked everybody's, and his numbers look like something from a video game. He averaged 30.5 points per game, shot 50.6 percent from the field, and averaged only two turnovers per game. Included in that stretch was a 24-point first quarter against Boston and an *average* of 37 points in the season's final six games, which all were must-wins for the Nets to make the playoffs.

Carter also gave a much more serious effort at the defensive end, improved his rebounding significantly over his lackluster rate in Toronto, and proved to be a revelation with his skills as a passer. Best of all, the knee and Achilles problems that had sidelined Carter in Toronto never cropped up in New Jersey.

Nets fans still have worries about Carter because, as the Raptors learned, he can turn his switch off at a moment's notice. What he did in Toronto was worthy of all the scorn it received, as it was the most openly apathetic performance I've seen this side of Joe Barry Carroll. The Nets also have to worry about Carter's recent injury history and his playoff performance against Miami, when he settled for far too many jumpers.

But the Nets have a lot to be happy about. Carter gives them the explosive scorer they've lacked throughout the Kidd era, and the two of them with Jefferson should be an absolute terror on the fast break. Carter's rebirth in New Jersey was one of the best stories of 2004–05, and one hopes he can repeat the performance over a full season.

Jason Collins			center						**Age: 27**	**Height: 7-0**	**Weight: 255**	
Defensive PER: 2.64 (99% C, 1% PF)											Most similar at age: Mark Acres	
Year	**G**	**M/G**	**FG%**	**FT%**	**P/40**	**R/40**	**A/40**	**TS%**		**Ast**	**TO**	**Usg**	**Reb**	**PER**

Year	G	M/G	FG%	FT%	P/40	R/40	A/40	TS%		Ast		TO		Usg		Reb		PER	
2002-03 NJ	81	23.5	.414	.763	9.7	7.7	1.8	52.1	30	14.2	11	13.8	41	11.6	59	11.1	67	9.89	62
2003-04 NJ	78	28.5	.424	.739	8.3	7.2	2.8	49.7	54	21.4	2	13.6	44	11.8	58	10.3	73	10.03	67
2004-05 NJ	80	31.8	.412	.656	8.0	7.7	1.7	47.1	60	7.9	22	12.3	18	10.9	57	11.0	61	8.52	65
2005-06 PRJ (32.1)			*.412*	*.702*	*8.1*	*7.4*	*2.0*	*48.2*		*12.8*		*14.1*		*11.0*		*10.5*		*9.19*	

Collins is a poor leaper, can't block shots, doesn't rebound, and is practically worthless offensively. So why does he play? In a word: defense. Collins may not be a shot-blocking intimidator, but he takes as many charges as any player in the league and is constantly in position to help his teammates. He's also a tough, physical post defender who can push opponents a step further out and wall his man off from the boards so that another player can grab the rebound. As a result, he had the fifth-best Defensive PER in basketball.

However, those offensive deficiencies shouldn't be ignored. Collins may be more valuable than his stats show, but playing him for 30 minutes a night is seriously pushing it. Frank didn't have many options last season, but with the arrival of Abdur-Rahim and the continued development of Krstic, Frank should be able to ease Collins into a bench role more suited to his skill level.

Richard Jefferson			small forward						**Age: 25**	**Height: 6-7**	**Weight: 225**	
(78% SF, 21% PF, 1% SG)											Most similar at age: Corliss Williamson	

Year	G	M/G	FG%	FT%	P/40	R/40	A/40	TS%		Ast		TO		Usg		Reb		PER	
2002-03 NJ	80	36.0	.501	.743	17.3	7.1	2.8	56.3	8	13.8	34	10.7	28	18.7	26	10.2	14	16.56	15
2003-04 NJ	82	38.2	.498	.763	19.3	5.9	4.0	57.3	7	17.2	12	10.8	27	21.9	13	8.4	35	18.07	10
2004-05 NJ	33	41.1	.422	.844	21.6	7.1	3.9	53.7	23	14.0	15	13.9	56	25.8	5	10.1	14	16.53	11
2005-06 PRJ (59.2)			*.458*	*.799*	*19.0*	*6.5*	*3.5*	*55.2*		*14.7*		*11.3*		*22.7*		*9.2*		*16.62*	

Jefferson's numbers don't do him justice because he was playing out of position all season. Though technically a small forward while Eric Williams played shooting guard, Jefferson was taking on a much larger ballhandling role than he had in previous seasons and he was completely unsuited for it. That explains why his Turnover Ratio skyrocketed and his field-goal percentage dropped so much. Offensively, he was basically asked to do most of a shooting guard's job because Williams couldn't do it, and it stretched Jefferson's skill set to the limit. The other source of Jefferson's turnovers was spin moves to the basket—he had trouble resisting the urge to use his off arm as a barrier and picked up several offensive fouls as a result.

Carter's arrival absolved him of that duty, but Jefferson almost immediately suffered a ruptured ligament in his wrist and missed the rest of the season. This season Jefferson can return to his usual offensive role—streaking down the sidelines for fast-break dunks, taking bigger forwards off the dribble, and occasionally uncorking his improving jump shot.

In addition, Jefferson will have to be the Nets' primary wing defender because they'll be looking to keep Carter out of foul trouble. He already was one of the league's better defenders, and has the necessary athleticism and tenacity to raise it another notch. However, quicker guards give him trouble and may present match-up difficulties for New Jersey, as Miami's Dwyane Wade showed in the playoffs.

New Jersey signed Jefferson to a six-year, $76-million dollar extension prior to last season, which doesn't look so bad considering all the money teams have been throwing at second-tier stars in free agency the past two summers. As long as he comes back from the wrist injury and builds on the things he did in 2003–04, he'll provide a decent return on the investment.

Jason Kidd   **point guard**   **Age: 32**   **Height: 6-4**   **Weight: 210**
Defensive PER: 1.49 (100% PG)   Most similar at age: Gary Payton

Year		G	M/G	FG%	FT%	P/40	R/40	A/40	TS%		Ast		TO		Usg		Reb		PER	
2002-03	NJ	80	37.4	.414	.841	20.0	6.7	9.5	52.6	20	29.3	18	12.2	42	29.6	3	9.6	1	22.17	3
2003-04	NJ	67	36.6	.384	.827	16.9	7.0	10.1	48.5	42	32.5	16	11.3	31	29.0	3	10.0	1	19.67	6
2004-05	NJ	66	36.9	.398	.740	15.6	8.0	8.9	50.6	42	33.0	10	10.1	23	25.8	13	11.4	1	19.55	6
2005-06	PRJ (16.7)			.397	.785	15.6	7.1	9.1	50.7		33.2		11.0		26.0		10.2		19.43	

While Carter was The Man down the stretch, Kidd is equally indispensable to the Nets. New Jersey was 4–12 in his absence to star the season, and it was an ugly 4–12. The Nets averaged only 83.4 points per game while he was gone, nearly 10 less than they scored the rest of the season.

The Nets had to be heartened by Kidd's performance after coming back from knee surgery, because it was virtually a carbon copy of his 2003–04 campaign. Kidd led all guards in Rebound Rate and remained among the best defensive guards in the game, often defending opposing shooting guards while Travis Best or Jacque Vaughn guarded the point guard.

As always with Kidd, his jump shot remained a sore point. Kidd hit 36 percent on three-pointers, easily his best mark as a Net, but he hit just 39.8 percent overall and had a TS% below the norm for his position. But there's good news on this front. With Jefferson, Carter, Krstic, and Jackson around, Kidd should have to take on far less of a scoring load than he has the past few seasons and can focus on utilizing his best talent, passing, rather than his worst.

The Nets have Kidd under contract for five more years at the maximum so they'll need his knee to hold up. Luckily, big point guards have tended to age very well and Kidd's athleticism showed little slippage after he came back. Therefore, New Jersey should be able to get continued high-level production from the franchise's savior.

Nenad Krstic   **power forward**   **Age: 22**   **Height: 7-0**   **Weight: 240**
Defensive PER: 0.99 (70% PF, 30% C)   Most similar at age: Eddy Curry

Year		G	M/G	FG%	FT%	P/40	R/40	A/40	TS%		Ast		TO		Usg		Reb		PER	
2004-05	NJ	75	26.2	.493	.725	15.2	8.2	1.6	54.7	25	7.5	51	12.9	54	16.5	40	11.7	50	13.34	46
2005-06	PRJ (38.5)			.494	.741	16.4	8.5	1.7	55.2		7.7		12.6		17.5		12.1		14.64	

A former first-round pick of the Nets, Krstic stayed in Europe for two years and didn't debut until last season. Upon arrival he proved up to the challenge of playing in the NBA, taking over a starting spot early in the season and becoming the offense's third option by year-end. Krstic has a nice stroke from 17 feet and in, especially from either baseline, and has a growing array of post moves.

On the down side, he needs to get much stronger to hold his position in the post. That lack of muscle was a major reason his Rebound Rate was so poor. He also had a high Turnover Ratio, both because he's a poor ballhandler and because he set too many illegal screens. Defensively, the lack of strength prevents him from pushing players out in the post and was one reason the Nets had to play him at power forward instead of at center. He moves his feet fairly well and is a good screen-and-roll defender so the lack of strength didn't prevent him from posting a very solid Defensive PER—a rarity for a rookie. Still, he'll have to bulk up this season because the plan is for him to move to the middle full time. Plus, he needs to learn how to take a charge—he got called for numerous blocking fouls on badly acted flops.

Looking at the projections, it seems odd to compare Krstic to Eddy Curry, his most similar player, since one is skinny and the other is a wide load. The Similarity Scores see both as big men who score and shoot for a high percentage but don't rebound. Players of that ilk have made solid improvements in their early 20s and one might expect Krstic to do the same. If so, he'll go down as an impressive score for Thorn who took Krstic with the 24th overall pick in 2002.

Ron Mercer — small forward
(62% SF, 27% PF, 11% SG)   Age: 29   Height: 6-7   Weight: 215
Most similar at age: N/A

Year		G	M/G	FG%	FT%	P/40	R/40	A/40	TS%		Ast		TO		Usg		Reb		PER	
2002-03	Ind	72	23.1	.409	.802	13.4	3.7	2.7	43.9	53	14.0	38	6.8	3	18.3	37	5.2	50	9.32	48
2003-04	SA	39	13.2	.427	.765	15.1	3.8	1.7	44.6	56	8.3	62	9.8	21	19.5	35	5.4	52	9.25	56
2004-05	NJ	18	21.7	.411	.700	14.1	4.1	2.1	42.2		9.8		7.1		19.6		5.9		9.33	

Here's a simple guide to Ron Mercer: The math doesn't work. You can't shoot jumpers from a step inside the three-point line the entire game unless you're an unbelievable shooter, and Mercer doesn't fall in that class. His field-goal percentage doesn't seem that bad so coaches get lulled into thinking he's doing OK. However, because he never makes a three-pointer or takes a foul shot, his TS% is truly awful and he ends up killing the offense. The Nets learned their lesson and waived Mercer after the season as a luxury-tax amnesty cut.

If, for some reason, Mercer decided to stop his monogamous love affair with the 20-footer, he'd be a decent reserve. His size is an asset on defense, he handles the ball fairly well, and he's quick enough to get to the rim if it moves him to do so. Unfortunately, his shot selection prevents teams from benefiting from those other skills.

Zoran Planinic — shooting guard
(47% SG, 43% PG, 10% PF)   Age: 23   Height: 6-7   Weight: 200
Most similar at age: Rick Fox

Year		G	M/G	FG%	FT%	P/40	R/40	A/40	TS%		Ast		TO		Usg		Reb		PER	
2003-04	NJ	49	9.6	.411	.633	13.0	4.7	5.8	49.2		26.2		13.9		20.1		6.7		9.97	
2004-05	NJ	43	12.0	.448	.697	16.9	5.4	3.4	53.4	25	15.3	30	14.2	64	20.6	23	7.7	19	12.39	38
2005-06	PRJ (38.7)			.446	.703	17.6	5.5	3.6	53.4		15.6		13.5		21.3		7.9		13.07	

Planinic broke his left hand 15 games into the season and had trouble battling his way back into the lineup. That was an oversight by the Nets because he's a far better player than Rodney Buford or Ron Mercer. Planinic was drafted as a point guard and failed miserably as a rookie, but he's shown much more promise at the shooting guard spot.

Planinic's rate of 16.9 points per 40 minutes was a marked improvement from his rookie year, and he made a strong contribution on the boards too. At 6′7″ his best asset is an ability to post up against smaller guards, but he also has three-point range and some sneaky moves off the dribble. His jump shot doesn't have much rotation, though, which may explain his free-throw struggles.

To get major minutes in the Nets' improved backcourt, he'll have to improve his ballhandling and defense. Planinic makes too many turnovers and doesn't find the open man enough, which is one reason his point guard days are probably done. Defensively, he has fast hands but is a step slow and can be beaten off the dribble. He also had the highest foul rate among shooting guards at more than one per seven minutes. However, for a 23 year old who missed half the year, his 2004–05 campaign was an encouraging sign. If Planinic can take another step forward, the Nets will have found a valuable reserve.

Clifford Robinson — center
(62% C, 37% PF, 1% SF)   Age: 39   Height: 6-10   Weight: 240
Most similar at age: Sam Mitchell

Year		G	M/G	FG%	FT%	P/40	R/40	A/40	TS%		Ast		TO		Usg		Reb		PER	
2002-03	Det*	81	34.9	.398	.676	14.0	4.5	3.8	47.7	49	18.3	8	10.8	26	20.2	19	6.7	61	12.36	44
2003-04	GS*	82	34.7	.387	.711	13.6	4.5	3.8	47.3	55	18.5	9	11.8	37	19.1	25	6.5	66	10.78	56
2004-05	GS-NJ	71	23.8	.386	.639	12.6	5.0	2.5	47.1	59	11.7	7	9.0	4	16.3	20	7.1	70	10.35	52
2005-06	PRJ (5.3)			.364	.669	12.5	4.0	3.3	44.5		15.5		11.3		17.1		5.8		10.22	

* Season rankings are as power forward

The Nets picked up Robinson from Golden State at the trade deadline when they were short on frontcourt bodies, and he at least helped at the defensive end. Despite his advanced age, Robinson is an expert defender who uses his long arms and veteran tricks to compensate for his declining athleticism.

It's getting harder to live with that defense because the other numbers are so puny. Robinson is the worst rebounding big man in basketball and among the worst of all time. It's almost as if his hands repel the basketball when it comes off the rim. Not only was his Rebound Rate the worst among centers, finishing over 20 percent worse than his closest competition, but there were 27 *guards* who fared better than him.

Offensively, his only source of points is a jumper that gets flatter every year, and he hasn't hit the 40 percent mark in four years. He at least cut down his turnovers last season. Plus, with the Nets so desperate for scoring punch, having Cliffy fire away from 20 still was better than letting Buford or Collins pull the trigger. The Nets re-signed Robinson for this season, albeit in a more limited role, and his defense can provide a spark off the bench—as long as the Nets have other players to make up for his shooting and rebounding.

Brian Scalabrine			**power forward**							**Age: 27**	**Height: 6-9**	**Weight: 235**	
(75% PF, 22% SF, 3% C)												Most similar at age: Scott Padgett	
Year	**G**	**M/G**	**FG%**	**FT%**	**P/40**	**R/40**	**A/40**	**TS%**	**Ast**	**TO**	**Usg**	**Reb**	**PER**
2002-03 NJ*	59	12.3	.402	.833	9.9	7.8	2.5	48.7 47	16.6 15	16.6 57	13.5 49	11.1 8	8.87 52
2003-04 NJ	69	13.5	.394	.829	10.3	7.4	2.8	48.2 52	18.3 11	11.8 36	14.2 53	10.6 55	9.46 60
2004-05 NJ	54	21.6	.398	.768	11.6	8.4	3.0	46.8 66	14.4 8	12.8 52	16.5 41	11.9 47	11.01 60
2005-06 PRJ (42.9)			*.397*	*.770*	*10.6*	*8.0*	*2.6*	*47.7*	*15.0*	*13.3*	*14.6*	*11.2*	*10.44*

* Season rankings are as small forward

A jump-shooting forward with limited athleticism, Scalabrine was another Net whose minutes expanded far beyond his abilities in 2004–05. Scalabrine was a major part of the Nets' inaccuracy contingent, taking nearly a quarter of his shots from three-point range but making only 32 percent. For his career, he's a 39 percent shooter who barely averages 10 points per 40 minutes, so it's hard to get excited about his offense.

Defensively, Scalabrine fares a bit better. He has enough size to battle post players and is an active help defender who willingly takes charges. While his lack of quickness can be exposed in one-on-one matches and he blocks shots about once every lunar eclipse, Scalabrine's overall contribution is a positive one.

Scalabrine's main advantage is that he apparently has the best agent in the world. Believe it or not, Boston gave Scalabrine a five-year, $15 million deal after the season. I'm told that figure was in American dollars, not pesos. It's a lavish reward for a player whose limitations make him unsuited for use beyond 5-to-10 minutes a night, and I'm still researching to see if Isiah Thomas was secretly involved somehow.

Jabari Smith			**center**							**Age: 28**	**Height: 6-11**	**Weight: 240**	
(61% C, 39% PF)												Most similar at age: Stacey King	
Year	**G**	**M/G**	**FG%**	**FT%**	**P/40**	**R/40**	**A/40**	**TS%**	**Ast**	**TO**	**Usg**	**Reb**	**PER**
2003-04 Sac	31	5.5	.371	.600	15.1	7.3	2.6	40.6	11.4	7.2	21.1	10.9	9.10
2004-05 NJ	45	14.4	.419	.745	10.2	6.9	2.3	48.2 56	11.2 9	15.7 53	14.0 34	9.8 67	8.25 67
2005-06 PRJ (32.0)			*.422*	*.726*	*10.5*	*6.7*	*2.3*	*48.0*	*10.7*	*16.4*	*14.2*	*9.7*	*8.43*

Smith saw action because the Nets were desperately short of big men, and he showed why he hadn't been able to get off the end of the bench in his other NBA stops. Smith is a good passer for a big man, but if you were him you'd get rid of the ball too. His shooting percentages were terrible and his Rebound Rate was even worse. Moreover, he doesn't have the athleticism to be a major force at the defensive end. His size should enable him to stay in the league, but I'd be surprised if he played this many minutes again.

Billy Thomas			**shooting guard**							**Age: 30**	**Height: 6-4**	**Weight: 208**	
(65% SF, 34% SG, 1% PF)												Most similar at age: N/A	
Year	**G**	**M/G**	**FG%**	**FT%**	**P/40**	**R/40**	**A/40**	**TS%**	**Ast**	**TO**	**Usg**	**Reb**	**PER**
2004-05 NJ	25	14.2	.362	.778	10.3	4.0	1.9	47.0	9.1	7.3	13.5	5.9	8.18

Thomas debuted as a 29-year-old rookie when the Nets lost Jefferson, Mercer, and Planinic, but he failed in his main task of hitting jump shots. Advertised as a shooter, Thomas connected on only 30.4 percent of his three-point shots and 36.2 percent overall. Since he's small for an off guard and contributed little in other departments, Thomas will have a hard time adding a second year to his NBA career.

Jacque Vaughn   **point guard**   **Age: 30**   **Height: 6-1**   **Weight: 190**
(67% SG, 32% PG, 1% SF)

Most similar at age: Winston Garland

Year		G	M/G	FG%	FT%	P/40	R/40	A/40	TS%		Ast		TO		Usg		Reb		PER	
2002-03	Orl	80	21.1	.448	.776	11.2	2.8	5.5	50.8	32	29.2	19	12.2	43	16.9	56	4.0	60	10.51	51
2003-04	Atl	71	17.9	.386	.779	8.5	3.7	6.1	44.0	58	33.3	14	14.3	52	16.5	60	5.2	38	7.99	61
2004-05	NJ	71	19.9	.449	.835	10.6	3.0	3.8	51.1	37	18.2	63	11.0	37	15.1	67	4.3	55	8.83	65
2005-06	PRJ (31.0)			.427	.802	10.1	3.2	4.7	48.9		24.1		12.6		15.8		4.4		8.90	

The Nets signed Vaughn to a two-year deal before the season and were starting him down the stretch until he broke a bone in his foot. That says more about the Nets' desperation than it does about Vaughn's skill. Although he plays hard, pressures the ball, and is a positive influence in the locker room, his production is so unrelentingly mediocre that he's a stretch even as a backup.

Vaughn at least shot decent percentages last season, hitting 44.9 percent from the field and 33.3 percent on three-pointers. Of course, he did so mostly by restricting himself to only the most wide-open of shots. Consequently, the Nets were forced to play 4-on-5 offensively when he was on the court, as his Usage Rate was among the worst at his position.

Vaughn spent most of his time at shooting guard paired with Kidd in the backcourt, which accounted for the sudden drop in his Assist Ratio, but he's likely to return to a reserve point guard role this season. In fact, his role may shrivel to garbage time minutes since New Jersey added McInnis to be Kidd's primary backup at the point.

Antoine Wright   **shooting guard**   **Age: 21**   **Height: 6-7**   **Weight: 210**

The Nets drafted Wright to be an outside threat, but I'm dubious that he's the answer. Wright hit 45 percent on three-pointers at Texas A&M last season, but only 38 percent for his career. He's a poor free-throw shooter (65 percent career) and isn't an exceptional athlete. While his smooth ballhandling and knack for scoring should be assets for a bench that could greatly use a scorer, I wonder if New Jersey wouldn't have been better off going in a different direction with its first-round pick.

Mile Ilic   **center**   **Age: 21**   **Height: 7-1**   **Weight: 240**

The Nets' second-round pick is a similar case to that of Nenad Krstic a few years ago. He's a tall, thin Serbian who is offensively skilled but lacking in strength and soft on the glass. As with Krstic, the Nets will keep Ilic overseas for another year or two and see how he develops.

New York Knicks

Style over substance.

If I could describe the current Knicks with one phrase, that would be it. From the top of management to the last player on the bench, no team exudes more false bravado or incessant hype than this one.

It starts at the top. The Knicks hired Isiah Thomas in the middle of the 2003–04 season to become their general manager, a perfect example of the franchise's need to make a big short-term splash and worry about the long-term consequences later. Thomas was a big star as a player, talks smoothly, and looks good in a suit, so his arrival gave the Knicks' fans a reason to forget they were going nowhere fast.

Thomas's first moves as general manager reinforced that trend. He swung for the fences right away by trading for Phoenix's Stephon Marbury, but as with most Knicks deals there were long-term aspects to the deal that greatly hurt them. New York had to take on two enormous contracts (Marbury's and Penny Hardaway's) and then package all of its tradable assets into that trade, including two first-round draft picks.

Amazingly, everyone bought it. Commentators said Isiah had brought excitement back to the Garden, and fans wondered if Isiah's rebuilt Knicks would be able to challenge the Eastern Conference contenders. Having already overplayed his hand, Thomas kept throwing more chips on the table. He traded Keith Van Horn and Michael Doleac for Tim Thomas and Nazr Mohammed, a deal that was less disastrous than it first seemed but that nonetheless left the Knicks with a major hole at small forward last season.

In the offseason, Isiah went for the big splash again, signing a prominent "talent" in Jamal Crawford by trading all of New York's expiring contracts to Chicago. Crawford is certainly entertaining—he has a great crossover move, likes to throw it off the backboard to himself for dunks, and can get crazy hot from outside. But he also takes terrible shots, plays no defense, and hasn't improved in three years. In short, he's the perfect Knick. Two of the players Thomas gave up,

Dikembe Mutombo and Othella Harrington, arguably had better years than Crawford did.

Hence, when the season started, New York's inability to defend wasn't a big shock. Nor was it a surprise that Crawford kept taking bad shots, that the lack of draft picks starved the bench, or that a roster with 34 power forwards and one point guard proved difficult for the coaching staff to manage. And the Knicks were even worse than expected because Tim Thomas was awful and the defense underachieved even against the low standard that had been set for it.

From there, Isiah seemed resigned to take his medicine and start a real, honest-to-goodness rebuilding project. He traded Mohammed for one first-round draft pick and accepted Maurice Taylor's contract to get another first-rounder from Houston. After the season, he picked up yet another draft choice from the Suns when he traded Kurt Thomas for Quentin Richardson—the best trade of his tenure and one that made the Knicks lineup nearly 10 years younger.

But when free agency came around, Thomas's zeal for catching the big fish got the best of him. New York targeted three players for its midlevel exception: Antoine Walker, Kwame Brown, and Jerome James. If there are three more overrated players in the NBA, I'd like to know who they are. In true style-over-substance form, Thomas offered Washington Michael Sweetney in a sign-and-trade for Brown—Sweetney is both significantly better than Brown and seven months younger—and was only saved from disaster by the Wizards turning down the deal.

Ultimately, the Knicks ended up with the worst of the three players in James, handing $29 million to a 30-year-old player who has never stayed in shape and, though 7′1″, is among the worst rebounding centers in the game. Hands down, this was the worst free-agent signing of 2005, but it was classic New York. James had performed very well in a first-round playoff series, when everyone was watching. But that's a microscopic sample. What's more important is the previous four years, when he was reliably terrible. Thus, when the season starts, the Knicks are going to need some

Knicks at a Glance

Record: 33–49, tied for 4th place in Atlantic Division

Offensive Efficiency: 103.0 (16th)

Defensive Efficiency: 106.5 (26th)

Pace Factor: 92.9 (16th)

Top-Rated Player: Stephon Marbury (PER 21.93, 19th overall)

Head Coach: Larry Brown. Biggest task will be convincing these guys to play defense.

other smokescreen to draw attention away from the mess on the court.

Fortunately, they have it. New York hired Larry Brown to an extravagant five-year contract in the offseason. Why they think he'll stay for five years is beyond me, but that's beside the point. The bigger story is that the Knicks have another bauble to distract fans from the ongoing disaster.

Brown's savior credentials are better than that of the other talent Isiah brought in. Brown's track record of improvement everywhere he's coached is staggering, and in the short term he'll certainly make the Knicks better. He might even get them into the playoffs.

But he's the wrong guy for this team. If the Knicks are rebuilding and trying to develop their three first-round picks, Brown is the worst guy in the world for this job. His track record with rookies is terrible (does the name Darko ring a bell?) and he tends to favor veteran players. His logic is air-tight: He never stays long enough to see through a rebuilding project anyway, so it makes sense for him to get as many wins in the short term as he can. So the Knicks win 40 games this year instead of 35. It's not going to help them break into the East's upper crust unless the younger players develop, and that will never happen under Brown. Additionally, Brown's infamous impatience with personnel will prove disastrous if heeded, as the Sixers have learned in the years since Brown left.

What's so frustrating about the Knicks' myopia is that Isiah has a real eye for talent. No, seriously. His draft picks, both in his tenure with the Raptors and in his short time with the Knicks, have been outstanding. That includes his 2004 pick, Trevor Ariza, whom New York stole in the second round. Early returns in the summer league gave favorable reviews to his three choices in 2005 as well, especially point guard Nate Robinson.

But when a big-name player comes along, Thomas can't help himself. As a result, the Knicks are stuck in a continuing cycle of signing mediocre players to inflated contracts, and then trading those contracts near their expiration for a new wave of overrated millionaires.

For the 2004–05 Knicks, the biggest weakness was a lack of a defensive presence in the middle. Mohammed played well offensively and on the boards, but at 6'10" with limited leaping ability, he wasn't a threat to block and alter shots. The same goes for power forward Kurt Thomas and Michael Sweetney, who was pressed into service as the backup center at just 6'8". As a result, the Knicks rejected only 4.0 percent of opponent deliveries, the worst rate in the league. That deficiency directly impacted New York's allowing a 46.5 field-goal percentage to its opponents, the fourth-worst mark in the league. Outside of that area, the Knicks were a middling defensive team.

Table 1. Blocks per 100 field-goal attempts, 2004–05's worst

Team	Blocks/100 FGA	Cost (pts/gm)
New York	4.03	1.21
Milwaukee	4.33	1.07
Sacramento	4.55	0.97
Toronto	4.73	0.83
Philadelphia	4.85	0.74

As table 1 shows, the lack of blocks cost the Knicks about 1.2 points per game compared to the league average, if we assume each blocked shot is worth about 0.74 points to the defending team (from the PER formula).

New York again will be challenged at the defensive end this season. Ariza is the only regular who could be described as an above-average defender, although Richardson's penchant for taking charges should prove helpful. In the odd event he plays hard, James's size also could help the Knicks' post defense.

There's some room for optimism, too. For starters, New York might see some improvement at the offensive end. With Robinson and Richardson added to the backcourt, New York will no longer be so vulnerable every time Marbury checks out of the game. Last season New York played opponents nearly to a draw while Marbury was on the court but were outscored by a whopping 12.4 points per 48 minutes while he rested. Additionally, Tim Thomas is likely to bounce back from his off year, and with more minutes at his natural position, Michael Sweetney could give the Knicks their best post threat in years. Plus, first-round pick Channing Frye may also provide bursts of offense from the center spot and is a much-needed shot-blocker.

More importantly, the Knicks' salary cap situation is getting less awful than it's been in the past. The league's amnesty provision allowed New York to cut loose Jerome Williams, and guard Allan Houston is likely to retire. Dropping those two will save the team a small fortune—about $90 million once luxury taxes are included. Tim Thomas's and Penny Hardaway's bloated contracts expire after the season, while Rose and Taylor are free agents in 2007. At that point, New York could actually be under the salary cap if the Knicks can resist the urge to ramp up the treadmill again and deal Thomas and Hardaway for another overpaid faux star.

However, that strategy requires something that's been in short supply in New York—patience. Hiring Brown might provide a brief respite of hope, but his hiring is part and parcel of the larger trend of seeking quick fixes instead of permanent solutions. As long as the team remains transfixed by trades that provide immediate satisfaction but inflict long-term damage, the Knicks will never escape their seemingly endless cycle of 35-win seasons.

New York Knicks

Trevor Ariza   small forward   Age: 20   Height: 6-8   Weight: 200
(81% SF, 18% SG, 1% PF)   Most similar at age: Ricky Davis

Year		G	M/G	FG%	FT%	P/40	R/40	A/40	TS%		Ast		TO		Usg		Reb		PER	
2004-05	NY	80	17.3	.442	.695	13.5	7.0	2.5	50.3	47	11.7	35	11.7	43	16.7	44	10.0	19	13.24	37
2005-06	PRJ (8.1)			.469	.719	14.4	6.8	3.2	52.0		14.2		12.2		17.1		9.8		14.06	

An outstanding find in the second round of the draft, Ariza's athleticism made him difficult to contain in the open court and helped him earn above-average rebounding numbers despite a lack of muscle. Ariza also defended well and figures to only get better with time. He's long, can leap and has good quickness, so he could become a top-flight stopper down the road.

For now, he won't advance beyond his bench role until his jump shot improves. Ariza has a shaky outside shot and a limited game off the dribble, which kept both his scoring rate and his TS% below league norms. With his leaping ability, he should develop some post moves, although he'd have to build up his strength to go along with it. Nonetheless, he was only 19 years old last year and has already proven he belongs in the NBA. Isiah can be criticized for a great many things, but not this move.

Jackie Butler   power forward   Age: 20   Height: 6-10   Weight: 250
(100% PF)   Most similar at age: N/A

Year		G	M/G	FG%	FT%	P/40	R/40	A/40	TS%	Ast	TO	Usg	Reb	PER
2004-05	NY	3	1.7	1.000	1.000	80.0	0.0	0.0	102.5	0.0	17.0	41.9	0.0	90.84

Butler is an intriguing player whom the Knicks signed from the CBA near the end of the season. He turned pro straight out of high school but went undrafted, becoming a basketball nomad in the minors. However, his CBA stats suggest he was one of the best players in the league, if not the best, and he's still very young. If New York is smart it would bring him back for another look this season.

Jamal Crawford   shooting guard   Age: 25   Height: 6-5   Weight: 190
Defensive PER: 0.17 (87% SG, 12% PG, 1% SF)   Most similar at age: Brent Barry

Year		G	M/G	FG%	FT%	P/40	R/40	A/40	TS%		Ast		TO		Usg		Reb		PER	
2002-03	Chi*	80	24.9	.413	.806	17.2	3.7	6.7	49.6	40	25.1	38	10.1	20	24.3	15	5.1	41	15.33	22
2003-04	Chi	80	35.2	.386	.833	19.7	4.0	5.8	48.6	42	20.0	17	9.5	18	26.3	5	5.7	47	15.82	16
2004-05	NY	70	38.4	.398	.843	18.5	3.0	4.5	52.1	35	18.4	17	9.0	21	23.1	12	4.4	64	15.15	18
2005-06	PRJ (36.8)			.397	.834	17.9	3.4	5.2	51.3		20.7		9.3		23.3		4.9		14.99	

* Season rankings are as point guard

Crawford has shot below 40 percent from the floor for two straight seasons, and it's not hard to see why. He takes at least two horrible shots every game—I'm talking about awful, off-the-dribble, contested 20-foot heaves with 17 showing on the shot clock. I had always assumed this habit would go away as he got older, but it's proving quite stubborn.

Perhaps that explains why Crawford's game has shown zero development the past two seasons. His PER is stuck around 15, which makes him a questionable value at $8 million a year, and his defense is quite poor. Crawford has good quickness but lacks strength and doesn't show a great interest in staying close to his man, which is the main reason Chicago didn't mind letting him go. Between the shot selection and the defense, it will be very interesting to see how he coexists with Brown. Right now, Crawford could best be described as "playing the wrong way."

Additionally, Crawford appears to be falling in love with his jump shot. He took nearly half his shot attempts beyond the three-point line, which is far too many for a player with his quickness and finishing skills. But Crawford prefers to cross opponents over on the perimeter and go up for his jumper. It looks awesome when it goes in, but over time it's a lower-percentage play than getting to the basket.

That's not to say he lacks positives. Few guards create shots as easily as he does, and he's among the best ballhandling off guards in the game. He's also capable of playing the point, although his shoot-first mentality can get in the way. If he can just harness those skills and get a little less trigger-happy, the Knicks' investment in Crawford could reap more commensurate rewards.

Anfernee Hardaway — shooting guard
(63% SG, 37% SF) — Age: 34 — Height: 6-7 — Weight: 215
Most similar at age: Craig Ehlo

Year		G	M/G	FG%	FT%	P/40	R/40	A/40	TS%		Ast		TO		Usg		Reb		PER	
2002-03	Phx	58	30.7	.447	.794	13.8	5.8	5.3	49.9	37	23.6	10	14.6	55	20.1	25	8.2	11	13.00	34
2003-04	Phx-NY*	76	27.6	.411	.804	13.3	5.5	3.4	47.2	49	17.2	11	10.5	25	18.2	26	7.8	43	11.87	41
2004-05	NY	37	24.2	.423	.739	12.0	4.0	3.3	48.0	52	15.8	28	12.4	55	16.7	49	5.7	51	8.90	62
2005-06	PRJ (36.4)			.404	.780	12.4	5.1	3.6	46.5		16.7		13.3		17.6		7.2		10.00	

* Season rankings are as small forward

Hardaway has one year left on his contract and could become trade bait in the offseason. It would work for the Knicks as long as the contract they received in return expired in 2007, such as Thomas favorite Jalen Rose. If it's a longer-term deal then it's a tough sell for the Knicks.

In terms of his game, Penny ain't worth a dime. Hardaway no longer can create shots and the ones he's taking are much less accurate. He's also become turnover-prone in his old age and no longer contributes on the glass. While his smarts and long arms have made his slide less noticeable at the defensive end, it's hard to imagine a team desperate enough for back-court help to push Hardaway into a regular role.

Allan Houston — shooting guard
(83% SG, 17% SF) — Age: 34 — Height: 6-6 — Weight: 205
Most similar at age: Reggie Theus

Year		G	M/G	FG%	FT%	P/40	R/40	A/40	TS%		Ast		TO		Usg		Reb		PER	
2002-03	NY	82	37.9	.445	.919	23.7	3.0	2.8	56.3	10	10.8	51	8.7	13	24.7	9	4.4	54	17.67	12
2003-04	NY	50	36.0	.435	.913	20.5	2.7	2.2	53.9	11	9.4	61	9.6	19	22.1	20	3.8	63	14.69	22
2004-05	NY	20	26.6	.415	.837	17.8	1.7	3.2	52.9	28	14.6	34	7.3	9	20.6	24	2.5	66	12.48	35
2005-06	PRJ (34.8)			.418	.903	20.0	2.6	2.6	53.1		10.7		9.1		22.0		3.7		13.67	

Houston's knee continues to give him trouble and he was never healthy last season, even in the 20 games he played. He probably will have to retire, but was planning on giving it one more go in training camp. If he does hang up his sneakers ownership won't be upset—it would provide a $70 million bounty for the owners.

If he returns to the court, the question is whether Houston's knees will allow him to defend and create shots. If so, he could provide a major dollop of scoring off the bench and could squeeze Crawford and Richardson for minutes at shooting guard.

Jermaine Jackson — point guard
(85% SG, 8% SF, 7% PG) — Age: 29 — Height: 6-5 — Weight: 204
Most similar at age: N/A

Year		G	M/G	FG%	FT%	P/40	R/40	A/40	TS%		Ast		TO		Usg		Reb		PER	
2002-03	Atl	53	10.5	.364	.727	8.7	4.1	5.3	45.1	56	30.6	14	14.0	54	15.8	60	5.8	26	9.02	60
2003-04	Did not play																			
2004-05	NY	21	11.0	.515	.615	7.3	4.0	4.2	54.2		19.9		13.8		11.5		5.7		7.94	

Jackson is a CBA lifer who has periodically subsisted on 10-day contracts at the NBA level but has never scored or assisted enough to hang on to a job for long. That should continue to be the case.

Stephon Marbury — point guard
Defensive PER: 0.58 (100% PG) — Age: 28 — Height: 6-2 — Weight: 200
Most similar at age: Sherman Douglas

Year		G	M/G	FG%	FT%	P/40	R/40	A/40	TS%		Ast		TO		Usg		Reb		PER	
2002-03	Phx	81	40.0	.439	.803	22.3	3.2	8.1	52.0	23	24.7	39	9.9	19	30.3	1	4.6	53	20.06	8
2003-04	Phx-NY	81	40.2	.431	.817	20.1	3.2	8.8	51.9	16	28.2	28	9.8	15	29.0	4	4.7	53	20.35	4
2004-05	NY	82	40.0	.462	.834	21.7	3.0	8.1	57.5	7	27.3	30	9.5	17	28.1	6	4.4	53	21.93	3
2005-06	PRJ (39.8)			.441	.805	20.0	3.1	7.9	53.6		26.7		9.4		27.8		4.5		19.85	

Marbury has gotten a bad rap over the years for dominating the ball, not giving a full effort on defense, and alienating his teammates. While it's not entirely undeserved, you can say this about Marbury: Without him, the Knicks might have been worse than the Bobcats. He was the focal point of nearly every offensive play for New York, and despite that his percentages were all well above average for his position.

Marbury set career highs in field-goal percentage and free-throw percentage, a career *low* in turnovers, and made a massive improvement in TS%. Marbury isn't a natural outside shooter, but he was competent in that respect as well, hitting 35.4 percent. Obviously the new rules against hand checking helped him, as he has an amazing burst going to the rim with his right hand. Plus, as perhaps the strongest guard in the league, he can easily take contact and finish.

On Court vs. Off Court Point Differential Leaders, 2004–05

Player	Team	On court +/−	Off court +/−	Difference
Tim Duncan	SA	+15.1	−1.4	+16.6
Jason Kidd	NJ	+4.7	−11.3	+16.0
Manu Ginobili	SA	+14.7	−0.8	+15.5
Dirk Nowitzki	Dal	+9.3	−6.0	+15.3
Steve Nash	Phx	+12.4	−2.6	+15.0
Elton Brand	LAC	+2.9	−11.8	+14.7
Shawn Marion	Phx	+10.1	−4.4	+14.5
Tayshaun Prince	Det	+6.9	−6.0	+12.8
Stephon Marbury	NY	−0.4	−12.4	+12.0
Richard Hamilton	Det	+7.0	−5.0	+11.9

Marbury could stand to work harder on defense, especially in help situations, but the Knicks still were an astonishing 12 points per 48 minutes worse when he was off the court. Moreover, for somebody who gets such a bad rep it was notable that he didn't offer a peep of complaint about the state of his team. His silence was in marked contrast to the trade demands of a more heralded point guard across the river. Overall, it was unfortunate that his reputation kept Marbury off the All-Star team, because he was more deserving than several players who were there.

Malik Rose					**power forward**						**Age: 31**		**Height: 6-7**		**Weight: 245**
(74% PF, 17% SF, 9% C)													**Most similar at age: Duane Ferrell**		

Year		G	M/G	FG%	FT%	P/40	R/40	A/40	TS%		Ast		TO		Usg		Reb		PER	
2002-03	SA	55	33.4	.459	.791	17.0	10.5	2.6	53.8	21	11.7	27	16.1	58	19.8	20	15.2	18	16.06	21
2003-04	SA*	67	18.7	.428	.813	16.8	10.2	2.2	52.6	31	10.1	27	16.4	66	19.6	11	14.2	36	14.95	24
2004-05	SA-NY	76	19.4	.449	.737	14.5	9.2	1.6	51.1	46	7.6	47	14.9	62	16.9	39	13.2	35	12.06	54
2005-06	*PRJ (31.4)*			*.442*	*.740*	*15.0*	*9.4*	*1.8*	*51.2*		*8.9*		*14.9*		*18.1*		*13.4*		*13.09*	

* Season rankings are as center

The Knicks current roster has Maurice Taylor, Mike Sweetney, Malik Rose, and David Lee. That's four power forwards if you're scoring at home, and all of them have guaranteed deals through at least 2007. It would have been six if not for the Kurt Thomas trade and Jerome Williams's release. Obviously the Knicks need to unload more of this surplus, but the goal of getting under the salary cap sometime before the end of the millennium makes it more difficult. Rose and Taylor sport contracts that no other team will touch unless they can unload something even worse in return.

Rose's production slipped last season, which is understandable for a player dependent on his leaping ability as he enters his 30s. In his younger days he had used his hops and strength to become a competent frontcourt reserve despite standing just 6′7″, but it's increasingly difficult for him to keep up with the bigger players now that his athleticism is waning.

Rose could have some use for the Knicks, however, because he is strong enough to fill in at center and is a better defender than Michael Sweetney. Also, based on the projections he should bounce back a bit from his disappointing 2004–05 campaign. Considering Brown's preference for veteran players, I wouldn't be surprised to see Rose become a major part of the rotation.

Bruno Sundov   center   Age: 25   Height: 7-2   Weight: 260
(100% C)   Most similar at age: N/A

Year		G	M/G	FG%	FT%	P/40	R/40	A/40	TS%	Ast	TO	Usg	Reb	PER
2002-03	Bos	26	5.3	.250	.000	9.3	8.1	2.0	28.1	9.6	12.3	19.7	11.5	0.99
2003-04	NY	5	6.6	.400	.500	13.3	12.1	1.2	43.5	6.0	18.0	17.8	17.9	3.49
2004-05	NY	21	3.5	.297	1.000	13.7	7.1	1.1	33.0	4.4	13.1	23.0	10.2	0.96

The 7′2″ Croatian spent most of the year on the Knicks' bench, but he is unlikely to be in New York's plans with the additions of Frye and James. He's 25 but has never had a decent chance at playing time, and he hasn't done enough in his rare garbage time minutes to earn a more extended look. He can shoot the long ball, however, which may allow him to hook on somewhere.

Mike Sweetney   center   Age: 23   Height: 6-8   Weight: 270
(90% C, 10% PF)   Most similar at age: Gary Trent

Year		G	M/G	FG%	FT%	P/40	R/40	A/40	TS%		Ast		TO		Usg		Reb		PER	
2003-04	NY	42	11.8	.493	.724	14.5	12.7	1.1	54.4		6.6		15.1		15.4		18.1		17.12	
2004-05	NY	77	19.6	.531	.749	17.2	11.1	1.2	59.2	9	5.6	44	15.4	50	16.7	19	15.8	24	16.35	17
2005-06	*PRJ (24.5)*			*.519*	*.750*	*17.5*	*10.6*	*1.5*	*58.2*		*6.6*		*15.5*		*17.6*		*15.2*		*15.85*	

The Knicks appear to have no idea what they have in Sweetney. It's not surprising because he's caught in a logjam at power forward and didn't come with the excessive hype that greeted some of the other Knicks.

Nonetheless, Sweetney appears to be New York's second-best player after Marbury. He's a beast in the low post, with a wide frame that easily establishes position and a series of polished moves to finish things off. He especially likes to post up on the left block and spin back to the baseline for a jumper. Sweetney also has fantastic hands that allow him to catch difficult passes and snatch anything near him on the glass. His per-minute scoring and rebounding numbers from his first two seasons are excellent and he's only 23. And Isiah wanted to trade him for Kwame Brown?

Sweetney does have his weaknesses. He doesn't move well defensively and his pick-and-roll defense needs quite a bit of work, and he fouls too much. Plus, he's a bit short for his position, enabling opponents to shoot over him. He's especially prone to picking up offensive fouls setting screens, accounting for his high Turnover Ratio. Finally, he needs to improve his skills in passing out of double-teams, which are likely to be more common in the future.

One thing that may slow his development is his body type. Sweetney isn't in great shape and stands only 6′8″. Players of this ilk have tended to peak earlier than the long, slender types. Still, New York would be remiss in not handing him the starting power forward job, as he could easily average 16 and 10 while shooting over 50 percent.

Maurice Taylor   power forward   Age: 29   Height: 6-9   Weight: 255
(63% PF, 37% C)   Most similar at age: Marty Conlon

Year		G	M/G	FG%	FT%	P/40	R/40	A/40	TS%		Ast		TO		Usg		Reb		PER	
2002-03	Hou	67	20.6	.432	.725	16.3	6.9	1.9	47.2	52	8.7	46	13.1	46	20.7	15	10.0	54	11.43	50
2003-04	Hou	75	27.7	.480	.736	16.6	7.4	2.1	51.2	37	9.7	48	13.6	58	19.7	23	10.4	58	13.54	45
2004-05	Hou-NY	65	20.6	.455	.612	14.1	7.7	2.0	48.0	58	9.6	32	14.4	58	18.0	32	11.0	59	9.34	64
2005-06	*PRJ (50.0)*			*.455*	*.667*	*14.4*	*7.4*	*2.0*	*48.6*		*9.7*		*13.5*		*18.2*		*10.3*		*11.15*	

Houston donated Taylor to the Knicks in a midseason salary dump after the Rockets had become frustrated with Taylor's increasing offensive ineptitude. Taylor is a decent defender and can hit mid-range jump shots, which makes him look competent at first. But he provides nothing on the boards, settles for too many long jumpers, and rarely gets to the basket. As a result, his TS% is quite poor and he provides nothing to make up for it. Of the Knicks' four power forwards, Taylor ranks a clear fourth, so unless he makes some drastic improvements, he won't be leaving his seat much. He can defend, however, and that may endear him to Brown.

Kurt Thomas — power forward
Age: 33 Height: 6-9 Weight: 235
Defensive PER: 0.04 (81% PF, 18% C, 1% SF) Most similar at age: Brian Grant

Year		G	M/G	FG%	FT%	P/40	R/40	A/40	TS%		Ast		TO		Usg		Reb		PER	
2002-03	NY*	81	31.8	.483	.750	17.6	9.9	2.5	51.1	38	11.5	21	9.8	7	20.5	3	14.5	39	16.71	12
2003-04	NY	80	31.9	.473	.835	14.0	10.4	2.3	50.3	44	12.8	26	11.3	28	17.0	37	15.0	21	14.13	43
2004-05	NY	80	35.7	.471	.786	12.8	11.6	2.2	48.8	57	10.7	25	8.3	12	15.9	44	17.1	8	14.15	42
2005-06	PRJ (30.0)			.462	.781	12.5	10.9	2.2	48.2		11.1		10.1		15.5		15.8		13.29	

* Season rankings are as center

After the season, the Knicks traded Thomas to Phoenix for Quentin Richardson, and it will be interesting to see how he fits into the Suns' helter-skelter style. Thomas thrives in structured offensive environments, especially on screen-and-roll plays that allow him to get open jump shots. He is money from 18 feet, but that's the extent of his offensive game. Thomas no longer has a post game and rarely scores around the basket, averaging a pathetic one free throw attempt per game last season.

The rest of his value comes from defense and rebounding. Thomas destroyed his career high in rebounding last season by averaging 10.4 boards per game, helping to keep the Knicks respectable on the glass despite a lack of size. Additionally, he's a tough defender who can punch above his weight. His Defensive PER was poor last season, however, partly because he had to play center and partly because he's not getting any younger. Considering the Suns mainly picked him up for his toughness at the defensive end, they could be greatly disappointed.

Tim Thomas — small forward
Age: 28 Height: 6-10 Weight: 240
Defensive PER: -0.70 (91% SF, 8% PF, 1% SG) Most similar at age: George McCloud

Year		G	M/G	FG%	FT%	P/40	R/40	A/40	TS%		Ast		TO		Usg		Reb		PER	
2002-03	Mil	80	29.5	.443	.780	18.1	6.6	1.7	52.7	23	8.2	57	10.7	26	19.8	23	9.6	23	14.33	26
2003-04	Mil-NY	66	31.7	.446	.784	18.6	6.1	2.4	53.4	18	10.8	42	10.1	23	20.3	21	8.7	31	15.02	24
2004-05	NY	71	27.3	.439	.786	17.5	4.9	2.3	53.6	26	10.8	40	11.1	40	19.5	25	7.0	57	12.21	41
2005-06	PRJ (43.9)			.434	.767	16.7	5.6	2.1	53.1		10.5		10.8		18.9		7.9		12.64	

Thomas had an absolutely horrid start to the season—at one point he had the lowest PER of any starter in basketball. He rebounded in the second half, however, and posted numbers that weren't *too* far off his previous levels. When on his game Thomas is capable of dropping in 20 points thanks to his three-point stroke, as he hit over 40 percent for the second year in a row.

Thomas seems strangely disinterested, however. That can be seen both in his Rebound Rate, which is shameful for a 6′ 10″ forward with his talents, and in his Defensive PER. Thomas ranked among the worst defensive players in basketball last season, and it's tough to argue that the system was wronging him. New York allowed five points per 48 minutes more when Thomas was on the court, and his opponents torched him for a PER of 18.9. He's never had the greatest lateral movement, but this also was a function of effort. Unfortunately, the Knicks were rarely called to account for their many failures at the defensive end. That will change this year, and Thomas will lose minutes to Ariza unless the defense improves.

That scenario assumes he's still a Knick. Thomas has one year left on an absurd contract that could be used as trade bait by New York. As with Hardaway, the Knicks will need to make sure they don't take on too lengthy a deal in return, or they may never get under the cap. Ever.

Jerome Williams — power forward
Age: 32 Height: 6-9 Weight: 206
(59% PF, 40% SF, 1% C) Most similar at age: Ed Pinckney

Year		G	M/G	FG%	FT%	P/40	R/40	A/40	TS%		Ast		TO		Usg		Reb		PER	
2002-03	Tor	71	33.0	.499	.555	11.8	11.1	1.6	52.5	26	11.2	34	11.5	36	13.6	48	15.8	14	15.60	25
2003-04	Tor-Chi	68	24.1	.470	.684	10.3	11.6	1.8	52.2	28	13.1	25	13.4	55	12.2	60	16.6	11	14.77	35
2004-05	NY	79	15.3	.502	.669	11.9	9.3	1.4	56.3	16	6.5	55	15.3	65	12.6	64	13.3	33	13.20	47
2005-06	PRJ (25.6)			.477	.648	10.9	10.5	1.5	52.6		10.1		13.7		12.7		14.8		13.85	

(continued next page)

Jerome Williams *(continued)*

The Junkyard Dog became the Knicks' forgotten power forward as the season wore on, although he managed to get into 79 games. Williams shouldn't be dismissed so easily. He can be a valuable player at either forward spot, especially at the defensive end.

He remains among the quicker forwards and mixes that with good leaping ability and decent strength. That's made him a force on the boards, although his numbers tailed off considerably last season. Williams's physical skills also enabled him to defend a variety of players, with his defense getting better the less his man relies on strength. He had trouble with short, physical forwards like Corliss Williamson and Marcus Fizer but gave the quicker players headaches.

Williams was released by the Knicks using the luxury tax amnesty rule and announced his retirement almost immediately afterward. While he's still good enough to help a team, he's also battled foot and knee problems the past two years and can take solace in his being paid the final two years of his contract.

Channing Frye	center		Age: 22	Height: 6-11	Weight: 250

I want the Knicks to hire Ben Stein as the PA announcer this year, so he can intone, "Frye...Frye" every time this guy checks into the game. Frye's college rebound rate is a red flag—one every four minutes—but the other markers all point toward a strong pro career. Frye averaged two blocks and nearly a steal per game, hits his foul shots, and can finish strong around the basket. He also has great range on his jumper for a center, making him a natural pick-and-roll partner for Stephon Marbury.

Nate Robinson	point guard		Age: 21	Height: 5-9	Weight: 180

It's a shame for Robinson that he was traded to New York, because he would have been a perfect fit in Phoenix. Robinson is an Earl Boykins clone—an undersized guard who plays at warp speed and looks to score more than to pass. He's also a great athlete with a 43-inch vertical. However, he's not a great shooter and his size obviously will be an issue defensively. Nonetheless, as a 10-minute burst of energy off the bench, he should do wonders.

David Lee	power forward		Age: 22	Height: 6-10	Weight: 240

The final pick of the first round, Lee was miscast as a center at Florida, but should be able to showcase his versatility more as a pro. He's also a good rebounder and runs the floor well. Lee can score off the dribble but isn't much of a shooter, and his defense needs work. Overall, he seems like he'll be a solid reserve but his upside isn't great. In a rarity for a Knicks power forward, however, he at least isn't undersized.

f anyone out there knows what the Orlando Magic are doing, please raise your hand.

Orlando's 36–46 season may seem like another humdrum year of mediocrity, but in reality it was a mixture of the very good and the very bad. In the end, Orlando made some bird-brained front office moves that negated some incredibly positive stories on the court and put the Magic back into the lottery.

They didn't seem headed in that direction at the start of the season. Jon Weisbrod, in his first major act as the team's general manager, made two astute draft choices in high-schooler Dwight Howard and point guard Jameer Nelson. Taking Emeka Okafor instead of Howard would have been the safe route, but Weisbrod instead went for Howard's higher upside and deserves more credit than he's received for that move. It should benefit the Magic franchise for the next decade.

Unfortunately, he followed that stroke of brilliance with one idiotic move after another, starting with the trade of Tracy McGrady. Weisbrod essentially was baited into dealing his best player for pennies on the dollar even though McGrady still had a year left on his contract. The one positive from the deal was that it brought in three starters in Steve Francis, Cuttino Mobley, and Kelvin Cato, eliminating Orlando's depth problems with one stroke.

Weisbrod followed up that trade with an even worse deal, sending Drew Gooden, Steven Hunter, and second-round pick Anderson Varejao to Cleveland for Tony Battie. If you look carefully, you'll notice the three players he traded *all* are younger and substantially better than Battie, making it one of the worst three-for-one trades in league history.

In spite of it all, the Magic kicked off the year in fine form. Grant Hill, all but written off after losing four years to ankle injuries, suddenly came back fresh as a daisy and made the All-Star team. With Hill energizing the transition game and Francis playing some of the best basketball of his career, Orlando looked like a playoff team and Weisbrod looked like a genius.

The Magic were 18–14 in January and one of the league's most exciting teams. At the time, they led the NBA in Pace Factor with a run-and-gun attack inspired by assistant coach

---

Magic at a Glance

Record: 36–46, 3rd place in Southeast Division

Offensive Efficiency: 102.1 (21st)

Defensive Efficiency: 104.2 (18th)

Pace Factor: 97.1 (3rd)

Top-Rated Player: Grant Hill (PER 20.09, 27th overall)

Head Coach: Brian Hill. Let's hope the second time around has a happier ending.

Paul Westhead (he of Loyola Marymount fame), and rookies Howard and Nelson were coming on strong.

That's when Weisbrod acted again, in disastrous fashion. He decided the team needed more defense and sent Mobley to Sacramento for Doug Christie. This was a setback on multiple levels. First, the team's problem wasn't defense. Weisbrod was fooled by Orlando's fast pace into thinking the Magic were giving up too many points, but actually their Defensive Efficiency mark was right at the league average.

Second, apparently nobody pointed out to Weisbrod that Christie was damaged goods. The 34-year-old guard was dealing with ankle problems and not nearly the multidimensional force at either end that he had been in previous seasons. Christie had to have ankle surgery shortly after arriving, so what was already a bad trade turned out to be much worse (at this point in their respective careers, Mobley is a much better player).

But wait, there's more. Weisbrod made another questionable move late in the season when he fired coach Johnny Davis while the team was battling for a playoff spot. In Davis's place he hired assistant Chris Jent, who had been so far down the Magic's org chart that he sat behind the team's bench during games. Orlando was 31–33 at the time; they won five games the rest of the year. In fact, after the All-Star break the Magic were a miserable 8–22.

The shenanigans didn't stop once the season ended. Weisbrod conducted a coaching search but appeared to lose an internal power struggle, as his reputed pick, Flip Saunders, lost out on the job to former Magic coach Brian Hill. Weisbrod abruptly resigned, which probably wasn't such a bad thing for Orlando fans except for one thing: Orlando decided to appoint Dave Twardzik and Otis Smith as "co-GMs," an arrangement that hasn't been tried yet in the NBA. Twardzik's track record when he ran the show in Golden State from 1995 to 1997 makes Weisbrod look like Red Auerbach.

Now it's up to the Magic's tag-team partnership to undo the damage from Weisbrod's brief but tumultuous reign. Because of his moves, the Magic weren't be able to use their midlevel exception without going over the luxury tax line until, ironically, they invoked the tax amnesty rule to cut Christie over the summer. Orlando also seems interested in unloading Francis, who has undeniable talent but sometimes stifled the offense with his rampant overdribbling.

In the big picture, Magic fans shouldn't despair. Howard is the real deal, a stud power forward who had the best PER among rookies in his first year out of high school and became the youngest player in history to average a double-double. He eventually may be able to play center and all signs point to his being a nightly 20-10 guy within a couple of years. Nelson also played well as a rookie and it seems that, at worst, he'll be one of the best backup point guards in the league. And Hill, of course, shocked everyone both with his performance and durability.

One area in which the Magic need help is outside shooting. Orlando averaged fewer than four three-pointers a game last season to finish tied for 25th. Nearly a third of those came from two players—Mobley and Pat Garrity—who won't be factors this year (Garrity tore his ACL the last week of the season). Orlando was extremely vulnerable to zone defenses after the Mobley trade, which is one reason they slumped in the second half. That weakness goes hand-in-hand with their hole at shooting guard in the wake of the Mobley trade.

On paper, the Magic right now look like they would start Nelson and Francis together in the backcourt with Hill, Howard, and Cato on the front line. They also could start Hedo Turkoglu, who was one of the league's best sixth men before breaking his wrist late in the season, but that would require Hill to play shooting guard and expose both players defensively.

The Magic didn't help themselves with a couple of mystifying offseason moves either. First, they failed to make a hard sell to first-round draft pick Fran Vazquez, who decided to stay in Spain rather than come to Orlando. Second, the Magic's main free-agent acquisition was point guard Keyon Dooling, who is another poor-passing point guard on a team that already has two and doesn't answer the need for outside shooting.

As for the new coach, Brian Hill needs to get his team to play less one-on-one and share the ball more. Orlando had assists on only 52.2 percent of its made baskets, the second-lowest total in the league, and Grant Hill is the only starter whom one would consider a good passer. Orlando's low assist total is especially worrisome because they were a running team—normally teams that fast-break a lot have higher assist rates, because they have fewer half-court isolation plays.

Despite the lack of assists, Orlando also was prone to turnovers. The Magic committed miscues on 16.0 percent of their possessions, ranking 26th in the NBA. Francis was the main culprit with over four turnovers a game—he ranked third in the NBA—but Howard wasn't innocent either, making an assortment of rookie mistakes to lose the ball.

Because of the poor assist rate and high turnover totals, Orlando has made an intelligent decision to take Francis off the ball and make him a shooting guard. Considering the trend in the league towards smaller, quicker lineups, the Magic can get away with this. The question is whether Orlando can live with Nelson at the point or if they can find an upgrade on the free-agent market. Whatever they decide, they should keep running. Orlando was blazing upcourt after made baskets and catching teams off guard a year ago, and it helped disguise the team's shortcomings in the halfcourt. Additionally, they were very effective with a full-court trap after free-throws using Nelson, Howard, and Francis, and that should also stay in the playbook.

Up front the Magic are set, with Howard and Cato forming an imposing shot-blocking duo, but Vazquez's absence will hurt. He would have allowed Orlando to phase out Battie, who played 1,894 minutes last year despite an awful 8.52 PER. Mario Kasun, who performed adequately in limited minutes, is another option, and Orlando may seek help with its cap exceptions.

Overall, Orlando has a solid frontcourt anchored by one of the game's rising stars, two high scorers on the perimeter, and one of the game's best sixth men. If the new front office can avoid the mistakes of its predecessors and the Magic can get more precision and less dribbling in their halfcourt offense, they easily could find themselves in the playoffs.

Stacey Augmon				small forward										Age: 37		Height: 6-8	Weight: 213
(54% SF, 45% SG, 1% PF)														Most similar at age: Sam Mitchell			
Year		G	M/G	FG%	FT%	P/40	R/40	A/40	TS%		Ast		TO		Usg		Reb	PER
2002-03	NO*	70	12.3	.411	.750	9.8	5.5	3.2	47.4	44	20.7	15	12.0	45	14.4	51	8.0	12	9.27	50
2003-04	NO*	69	20.5	.412	.791	11.2	4.9	2.4	48.6	41	14.9	39	13.4	58	15.3	52	7.3	24	10.37	49
2004-05	Orl	55	12.1	.407	.740	11.6	6.0	2.2	48.0	55	10.3	46	11.6	42	14.3	53	8.8	33	9.78	55
2005-06	PRJ (14.7)			.392	.757	10.5	5.2	2.3	46.2		13.4		12.8		14.1		7.5	9.26

* Season rankings are as shooting guard

Augmon has long arms and is a capable defender, but his ineffective offense and antisocial behavior make him of questionable value. Besides, the Magic are well stocked at small forward with Hill and Turkoglu.

Augmon is signed for one more season, but the Magic might pay him to stay away after his boorish behavior in 2004–05, the lowlight of which was a one-game suspension for throwing a bottle of lotion at a reporter. Apparently, Augmon has had a media ban going for the past several years, although this was news to most of the media since no one wants to interview him anyway. In keeping with his jovial spirit, he also led the league in flagrant fouls.

Andre Barrett			point guard								Age: 23	Height: 5-10	Weight: 172
(100% PG)													Most similar at age: N/A
Year	G	M/G	FG%	FT%	P/40	R/40	A/40	TS%	Ast	TO	Usg	Reb	PER
2004-05 Hou-Orl	38	12.7	.363	.737	9.8	3.3	5.7	44.6	27.2	11.8	17.5	4.9	8.57

A poor man's Jameer Nelson, Barrett has the same problem with being undersized but doesn't have nearly the strength or offensive punch that Nelson provides. Barrett was the closest thing Orlando had to a pure point guard, but it's not as if he's John Stockton out there, and he probably sealed his fate by struggling to make shots. With another year of seasoning in the D-League he could come back and make a more credible run at a spot in a team's rotation.

Tony Battie			center								Age: 29	Height: 6-11	Weight: 240
Defensive PER: 1.23 (87% C, 13% PF)													Most similar at age: Jim Petersen
Year	G	M/G	FG%	FT%	P/40	R/40	A/40	TS%		Ast		TO		Usg		Reb		PER	
2002-03 Bos	67	25.1	.539	.746	11.6	10.3	1.2	57.8	6	9.5	33	9.3	5	11.7	58	14.6	37	15.24	26
2003-04 Bos-Cle	73	20.2	.443	.742	11.1	9.7	1.6	48.2	59	10.7	25	11.6	24	13.4	45	13.9	42	11.93	51
2004-05 Orl	81	23.4	.460	.723	8.3	9.5	0.9	49.8	49	4.2	52	15.6	52	9.4	67	13.4	47	8.52	64
2005-06 PRJ (41.7)			.459	.717	9.4	9.3	1.1	49.5		6.6		13.6		10.7		13.2		10.47	

Because Battie suffers from chronic knee problems, the wheels have come off for him in just two short seasons. Battie's performance has dropped noticeably in every statistical category as his leaping and quickness have suffered. He once was an explosive finisher around the basket but that part of his game has vanished, leaving him with a 12-foot jumper as his lone offensive weapon.

He still has some value at the defensive end, because he's a good help defender who plays hard and can be physical despite a thin build. The problem is that bigger centers like Shaq and Eddy Curry overwhelm him, and he's merely adequate as a shot-blocker. If the knees don't recover, Orlando should look at yanking Battie from the rotation in favor of Mario Kasun, especially since it's the last year of Battie's contract.

Kelvin Cato			center								Age: 31	Height: 6-11	Weight: 275
(99% C, 1% PF)													Most similar at age: Ervin Johnson
Year	G	M/G	FG%	FT%	P/40	R/40	A/40	TS%		Ast		TO		Usg		Reb		PER	
2002-03 Hou	73	17.2	.520	.532	10.6	13.7	0.6	53.5	23	5.2	67	14.5	49	11.4	61	19.7	3	15.46	20
2003-04 Hou	69	25.3	.447	.676	9.6	10.8	1.7	49.5	55	12.4	15	14.5	57	12.3	54	15.3	22	13.28	39
2004-05 Orl	62	24.6	.539	.783	11.3	10.9	1.0	60.0	5	5.0	48	13.8	37	10.6	60	16.0	23	14.91	27
2005-06 PRJ (32.1)			.491	.706	10.0	10.7	1.3	54.2		8.3		13.7		11.1		15.4		13.50	

After a slow start to his career, Cato has turned himself into a quality center, especially at the defensive end. Orlando allowed 6.4 points more per 48 minutes when Cato was off the court, even though his replacement, Tony Battie, was no defensive slouch himself. The reason is that Cato is one of the few centers who are big enough to fight the Shaqs and Yaos of the world in the post but nimble enough to step out and double-team the pick-and-roll. Cato also is a decent shot-blocker, although he's a bit slow off the ground, and an above-average rebounder.

Those defensive skills allow him to be a starting center despite a modest offensive repertoire. Cato gets most of his points on dunks and put-backs and otherwise mostly tries to stay out of the way, although he's developed a rapport with Francis on alleyoop plays. Because of his strict shot selection, Cato had the fifth-best TS% at his position last season. Surprisingly, he also shot 78 percent from the line.

(continued next page)

Kelvin Cato *(continued)*

Cato will be playing for his next contract in 2005–06 if the team can't agree with him on an extension. Since he's so important to the defense and the team is capped out, one might think an extension makes sense, but it would also deprive Orlando of a chance to get below the cap in the summer of 2007. For the Twardzik-Smith team, it's one of their first important decisions.

Doug Christie			shooting guard									**Age: 35**		**Height: 6-6**	**Weight: 205**
(80% SG, 13% PG, 7% SF)														Most similar at age: Dennis Johnson	

Year		G	M/G	FG%	FT%	P/40	R/40	A/40	TS%		Ast		TO		Usg		Reb		PER	
2002-03	Sac	81	39.3	.479	.810	11.0	5.0	5.5	59.0	5	32.6	2	12.5	49	14.9	49	6.8	32	14.99	22
2003-04	Sac	82	33.9	.461	.860	12.0	4.7	5.0	54.4	6	27.4	5	12.2	51	16.2	47	6.7	32	13.93	26
2004-05	Sac-Orl	52	29.3	.392	.897	9.0	4.6	5.2	47.1	57	24.9	2	15.5	66	15.3	56	6.8	33	9.92	51
2005-06	PRJ (24.7)			.416	.815	10.4	4.7	4.8	50.2		25.2		14.2		15.6		6.5		11.59	

Christie played in pain in 2004–05 and opted to go under the knife shortly after he was traded to the Magic. He won't be back, as the Magic waived him under the luxury tax amnesty rule over the summer. Dallas immediately scooped up Christie, inking him to a one-year deal to be a defensive specialist off the bench.

The question for Christie is how much of his poor performance was due to ankle problems and how much was the result of age? His production had been steadily declining for several years, but what was striking about 2004–05 were his steep drops in shooting percentages. His performance in the other categories was a reasonable facsimile of previous seasons—a high Assist Ratio, a decent Rebound Rate, and a high rate of steals. But the ankle may have affected his shooting more than other areas, as his percentage dropped by nearly 70 percentage points and his three-point mark fell even more.

If his shot recovers, Christie's defense and versatility should allow him to be a solid contributor off the bench, and he could provide Dallas with some inexpensive help. His days of starting are probably over, however.

Andrew DeClercq			center									**Age: 32**		**Height: 6-10**	**Weight: 255**
(100% C)														Most similar at age: N/A	

Year		G	M/G	FG%	FT%	P/40	R/40	A/40	TS%		Ast		TO		Usg		Reb		PER	
2002-03	Orl	77	17.2	.534	.644	11.0	10.2	1.6	56.2	13	11.3	24	18.2	69	11.9	57	14.6	33	11.30	52
2003-04	Orl	71	17.1	.477	.815	7.6	10.5	1.5	52.6	32	13.9	12	17.0	69	9.2	72	15.1	25	10.61	64
2004-05	Orl	8	6.1	.444	.333	7.3	8.2	0.0	43.6		0.0		8.8		8.3		12.0		5.43	

DeClercq lost his season to knee problems, which is unfortunate considering he was heading into free agency. He was a marginal frontcourt reserve to start with, and at 32 faces a tough road to get back into the playing rotation. However, he's expected back by the start of training camp and could help fill out Orlando's bench with his size and energy.

Steve Francis			point guard									**Age: 28**		**Height: 6-3**	**Weight:200**
Defensive PER: 0.99 (69% PG, 31% SG)														Most similar at age: Sam Cassell	

Year		G	M/G	FG%	FT%	P/40	R/40	A/40	TS%		Ast		TO		Usg		Reb		PER	
2002-03	Hou	81	41.0	.435	.800	20.5	6.0	6.1	54.1	14	21.1	56	12.6	45	26.9	6	8.7	3	20.58	6
2003-04	Hou	79	40.4	.403	.775	16.4	5.4	6.2	50.1	34	23.5	51	14.0	51	24.4	11	7.6	3	15.77	22
2004-05	Orl	78	38.2	.423	.823	22.3	6.0	7.3	52.1	30	22.2	55	12.9	53	29.0	4	8.5	4	18.88	9
2005-06	PRJ (41.1)			.413	.792	18.9	5.8	6.3	51.1		22.2		13.3		25.8		8.2		17.13	

Wanna guess who leads the NBA in technical fouls over the past three seasons? I'll give you a hint: It's not Rasheed Wallace. 'Sheed has been rung up 56 times, but Francis is the leader with 62. He doesn't have Wallace's histrionics, but he constantly gripes at the refs about calls when he drives to the basket. It's a problem because he'll often bark at the ref instead of running back on defense, permitting an open shot for the opponents at the other end.

Francis's feisty streak serves him well at the end of games, however, as he made five game-winning shots last season. Nobody doubts that he plays hard and he's certainly among the best scoring guards in basketball. However, his decision-making leaves a lot to be desired. Francis endlessly crosses the ball over at the top of the key, stalling the offense until he makes his move, and his shot selection is less than ideal. As a passer he has a lot of work to do too, with alleyoop plays being the lone exception. A favorite is the pass over the shoulder to a trailer in transition, which is brilliant if it works but it also leads to a lot of 4-on-1 breaks going the other way.

Although Orlando wants to move Francis to shooting guard to take advantage of his scoring skills and reduce his too-frequent turnovers, he'll need to learn how to score without taking 20 seconds off the shot clock in order to thrive there. Francis prefers shooting off the dribble and needs to improve at catching and shooting as he comes off a screen.

Wherever he plays he's a good defender and an outstanding rebounder for a guard, and there's no question he has All-Star talent. The Magic just wish he'd harness those abilities to produce All-Star results.

Pat Garrity   power forward   **Age: 29**   **Height: 6-9**   **Weight: 238**
(88% PF, 8% SF, 4% C)   Most similar at age: Walter McCarty

Year		G	M/G	FG%	FT%	P/40	R/40	A/40	TS%		Ast		TO		Usg		Reb		PER	
2002-03	Orl	81	31.9	.419	.830	13.4	4.7	1.9	55.1	16	12.3	25	7.8	4	14.1	45	6.8	60	11.16	53
2003-04	Orl	2	11.0	.333	—	3.6	0.0	1.8	33.3		25.0		0.0		7.2		0.0		0.51	
2004-05	Orl	71	13.5	.402	.879	13.6	5.2	1.3	50.5	49	6.0	59	7.9	8	14.5	51	7.6	68	9.06	65
2005-06	*PRJ (31.6)*			*.405*	*.850*	*13.1*	*5.0*	*1.6*	*51.9*		*9.4*		*8.0*		*14.2*		*7.3*		*9.86*	

Garrity came back from a knee injury that ruined his 2003–04 season but suffered the misfortune of another one at the end of the year. He tore his ACL in April but was hoping to return early in the season.

The Magic have kept Garrity in their rotation for years and even protected him in the expansion draft instead of promising center Zaza Pachulia. I've never understood why. Garrity is a deadly three-point shooter at 40.5 percent for his career, but he is so devoid of other talents that he's still overmatched at the NBA level. Defensively, Garrity lacks strength and quickness so he gets abused by opposing power forwards. He's also as bad a rebounding power forward as any in basketball. Offensively, the three-pointer is his only weapon—he has no off-the-dribble or post game to speak of, even when defended by a much shorter opponent. All of that adds up to a miniscule PER and a huge defensive liability. . . so why are they playing him again?

Grant Hill   small forward   **Age: 33**   **Height: 6-8**   **Weight: 225**
Defensive PER: 1.43 (65% SF, 32% SG, 3% PF)   Most similar at age: Bernard King

Year		G	M/G	FG%	FT%	P/40	R/40	A/40	TS%		Ast		TO		Usg		Reb		PER	
2002-03	Orl	29	29.1	.492	.819	20.0	9.8	5.8	56.8	5	21.2	4	14.6	54	24.1	8	14.0	2	20.78	5
2003-04	Orl		Out for the season																	
2004-05	Orl	67	34.9	.509	.821	22.5	5.4	3.8	56.5	7	14.2	13	10.4	31	23.6	8	7.6	48	20.09	5
2005-06	*PRJ (23.6)*			*.491*	*.818*	*20.8*	*5.9*	*4.0*	*55.0*		*15.4*		*11.7*		*22.8*		*8.2*		*18.69*	

Hill's return was amazing not just because he came back at all but because he played as if he hadn't missed a game. Despite four ankle surgeries and a life-threatening staph infection, Hill demonstrated that he hadn't lost a step, using his quickness and open-court talent to get numerous lay-ups. He also shot more consistently on mid-range jumpers than he had before the injury, and his defense was more than up to par as well.

The one area that seemed to have suffered was his leaping ability. While it improved as the year progressed, he didn't dunk nearly as often as he used to and his Rebound Rate declined sharply. He was once among the best rebounding forwards in basketball but he was below average last season. Should his leaping ability return in year two of the comeback, he'll be a nightly triple-double threat.

The hope now for Orlando is that Hill can stay in one piece for two more years. He's signed to a maximum contract through 2007 and Orlando's cap flexibility is extremely limited until it ends. As a result, Hill's continued health will be a prime determinant of whether Orlando can challenge for a playoff spot in the next two seasons.

Dwight Howard				**power forward**										**Age: 20**		**Height: 6-11**	**Weight: 240**

Defensive PER: 0.88 (88% PF, 12% C) — Most similar at age: Eddy Curry

Year	G	M/G	FG%	FT%	P/40	R/40	A/40	TS%		Ast		TO		Usg		Reb		PER	
2004-05 Orl	82	32.6	.520	.671	14.7	12.3	1.1	57.1	11	5.3	65	15.0	63	14.2	55	17.2	6	17.23	18
2005-06 PRJ (4.3)			*.545*	*.720*	*16.3*	*12.5*	*1.4*	*60.0*		*6.2*		*15.0*		*15.1*		*17.0*		*19.15*	

The irony of the NBA's newly-imposed 19-year-old age limit is that the Class of 2004 was easily the best batch of high schoolers ever to enter the league. Eight of the first 19 picks in the 2004 draft were high-schoolers and another (Andris Biedrins) was only 18. Three of those nine players—Howard, Al Jefferson, and Josh Smith—had a higher PER than any first-year high-schooler in history. All three guards—Shaun Livingston, Sebastian Telfair, and J. R. Smith—were good enough to start by the end of the year (albeit for rebuilding teams), and Biedrins's stats in limited minutes were impressive. If David Stern wanted to make the case that high schoolers aren't ready for the NBA, he chose the wrong year to make it.

Howard was easily the most impressive of the bunch. He had the highest PER among rookies and if voters looked beyond scoring averages, he would have won the Rookie of the Year award. Howard has great rebounding instincts reminiscent of a young Moses Malone and is an explosive finisher around the basket. He would have scored more often had the Magic run more plays for him, an oversight that Brian Hill should mend this season. Howard has a nice hook shot with his left hand and a rudimentary turnaround jumper, but the rest of his post game is still coming together. Right now he's a lot better on the right block. One thing that might prove troublesome as he develops is that he sometimes had trouble catching the ball in the post. That's one reason his Turnover Ratio was so high, and it's an area he'll need to improve in coming seasons.

Defensively, Howard is athletic enough to guard post players man-to-man and already is a super shot-blocker who returned nearly two shots a game to sender. However, the other areas need work. He's still learning how to help from the weak side and was often a step late to pick up penetrators. Also, he had trouble with some of the quicker power forwards who took him on the perimeter and forced him to move his feet.

Overall, he's an incredibly promising rookie who seems destined for stardom. Give Orlando credit for hitting a home run with its No. 1 pick.

Brandon Hunter				**power forward**							**Age: 25**		**Height: 6-7**	**Weight: 255**

(91% PF, 8% C, 1% SF) — Most similar at age: N/A

Year	G	M/G	FG%	FT%	P/40	R/40	A/40	TS%	Ast	TO	Usg	Reb	PER
2003-04 Bos	36	11.3	.457	.442	12.3	11.6	1.9	46.3	10.8	12.5	15.4	16.4	12.59
2004-05 Orl	31	7.2	.507	.538	17.0	12.3	0.5	52.7	2.6	19.1	17.2	18.1	12.05

Hunter is a poor man's Malik Rose who is extremely active on the glass and a high-percentage scorer around the basket. However, at just 6'7" he has some obstacles to overcome at the defensive end, especially since he lacks Rose's explosiveness. His numbers suggest he'd be a good fit as a team's fourth or fifth big man, but anything beyond that is probably a stretch.

Hunter didn't get many opportunities in Orlando last season and with Howard and others ahead of him at power forward, he would benefit from a change of scenery. He's a restricted free agent, but the Magic shouldn't put up much of a fight if he finds a more promising situation.

Mark Jones				**small forward**							**Age: 30**		**Height: 6-6**	**Weight: 215**

(65% SF, 35% SG) — Most similar at age: N/A

Year	G	M/G	FG%	FT%	P/40	R/40	A/40	TS%	Ast	TO	Usg	Reb	PER
2004-05 Orl	10	11.6	.290	.500	7.9	4.5	2.1	32.5	9.9	6.8	14.0	6.6	4.31

Perhaps the league's most anonymous player, Jones was signed late in the season when the Magic suffered several injuries and struggled mightily. As a swingman whose forte in the CBA was scoring, he'll need to shoot much better than last season's 29 percent to hold on to an NBA roster spot.

Mario Kasun — center
(100% C) Age: 25 Height: 7-1 Weight: 260
Most similar at age: N/A

Year		G	M/G	FG%	FT%	P/40	R/40	A/40	TS%	Ast	TO	Usg	Reb	PER
2004-05	Orl	45	7.9	.480	.558	13.3	14.4	0.9	50.5	4.3	17.2	14.4	21.1	11.81

Kasun is the new Cherokee Parks—a backup center who looks like a used coloring book. While not as heavily decorated as Parks, Kasun has colorful tattoos along his entire left arm.

On the court, he has a case for getting more minutes than he received in his first season in Orlando. His Rebound Rate of 21.1 would have ranked 3rd in the NBA had he played enough minutes, and he showed a decent ability to score around the basket as well. At 7'1", he obviously has the size to be a factor defensively, although he still needs to learn NBA positioning and his mobility could be better. Overall, he's a player for Magic fans to keep a close eye on this season, as he could make an impact off the bench.

Jameer Nelson — point guard
(97% PG, 3% SG) Age: 23 Height: 6-0 Weight: 190
Most similar at age: Terrell Brandon

Year		G	M/G	FG%	FT%	P/40	R/40	A/40	TS%		Ast		TO		Usg		Reb		PER	
2004-05	Orl	79	20.4	.455	.682	17.1	4.8	5.9	51.0	38	23.0	53	11.4	39	22.7	31	6.7	7	14.47	34
2005-06	PRJ (30.5)			.449	.706	17.9	4.7	5.8	51.0		22.5		10.6		23.2		6.6		15.23	

The Magic's first-round draft pick is probably more like 5'10" than his listed height, but apparently he was wearing heels the day he was measured. As a result, opponents were able to shoot right over him and he was an easy mark for guards looking to post up. He also has trouble getting beat on cuts off screens when his man is away from the ball—Mike Bibby murdered him on this when the Magic played Sacramento.

Fortunately, Nelson showed plenty of promise in his rookie season. Despite his stature he rebounds very well for his position, posting the seventh-best Rebound Rate among point guards. He also has a good first step that makes him a potent scoring threat. However, he needs to take some steps to improve his efficiency. For starters, he has to improve his three-point stroke since he made just 31 percent of his shots. Second, he needs to draw more fouls. With his penetration skills and strength, he should do better than a 6-to-1 ratio of field-goal attempts to free-throw attempts. Lastly, he has to improve as a passer—Orlando already has one point guard with dribble blindness, and that's more than enough.

While point guards often struggle mightily as rookies, Nelson was able to come in and play effectively, which is a strong sign that he'll quickly become a valuable contributor. That's not a bad payoff for the 20th overall pick in the draft, but Weisbrod hasn't received the credit he deserves for this selection.

Deshawn Stevenson — shooting guard
(69% SG, 26% SF, 5% PG) Age: 24 Height: 6-5 Weight: 210
Most similar at age: A. J. English

Year		G	M/G	FG%	FT%	P/40	R/40	A/40	TS%		Ast		TO		Usg		Reb		PER	
2002-03	Uta	61	12.5	.401	.691	14.7	4.5	2.1	44.4	51	9.9	54	12.2	47	19.9	28	6.8	31	8.15	55
2003-04	Uta-Orl	80	30.5	.432	.676	14.9	4.9	2.6	47.3	52	12.8	46	9.7	20	19.1	36	6.9	28	11.53	42
2004-05	Orl	55	19.8	.408	.554	15.8	3.7	2.5	45.6	61	11.6	55	9.6	24	19.7	30	5.5	55	9.26	59
2005-06	PRJ (61.7)			.421	.639	14.9	4.5	2.5	47.0		12.3		10.0		19.2		6.5		10.45	

I feel like Bill Murray in Groundhog Day when I sit down to write the comment for Stevenson each year, because the scouting report hasn't changed in the four years I've done the book. Stevenson still is a mid-range jump shooter and a decent athlete, but he isn't going to have much value unless he develops a three-point shot.

At least he was accurate from out there (37 percent) last season even though he didn't attempt it nearly enough. The result was that his TS% was again among the worst at his position. Despite good form on his shot, Stevenson also is a terrible foul shooter who hit just 55 percent last season, indicating that perhaps he's not devoting as much time to his craft as he ought to.

Stevenson brings some assets to the table that would make him a good bench player if his TS% wasn't so terrible. He's a good ballhandler who can play point guard in a pinch, and he finishes well in the open court. He's also an adequate defender who excels at chasing opponents around screens. And fortunately for him, he still has plenty of time to improve, because the Magic foolishly gave him a three-year, $8 million deal in the summer of 2004.

Hedo Turkoglu   small forward   **Age: 26**   **Height: 6-10**   **Weight: 220**
(89% SF, 9% PF, 1% SG, 1% C)   Most similar at age: Tim Thomas

Year		G	M/G	FG%	FT%	P/40	R/40	A/40	TS%		Ast		TO		Usg		Reb		PER	
2002-03	Sac	75	12.7	.422	.800	15.2	6.4	3.0	50.9	33	15.1	26	8.7	9	17.6	31	8.6	40	11.94	39
2003-04	SA	80	25.9	.406	.708	14.3	6.9	3.0	51.6	29	16.0	19	9.8	17	17.6	33	9.7	17	14.06	29
2004-05	Orl	67	26.1	.419	.836	21.4	5.3	3.5	53.2	29	13.3	22	10.3	30	23.5	9	7.5	53	16.04	14
2005-06	PRJ (45.1)			.425	.790	18.0	6.1	3.2	54.1		14.7		9.8		20.0		7.9		14.97	

Turkoglu is three inches taller than most NBA small forwards, but you'd never know it from looking at his stats. Despite his size, he was one of the worst rebounders at his position, ranking 53rd in Rebound Rate. He also has no post game and rarely blocks shots.

He's a very effective player, however. While it's odd to see a 6′10″ guy hanging out at the three-point line, Turkoglu is a career 38 percent marksman from long range. Additionally, he excels at putting the ball on the floor and then using his size to go over his defender for a short-range jumper. Turkoglu was much more aggressive with that move this season than he's been in the past and as a result he nearly doubled his free-throw attempts from the year before. And unlike most big guys, Turkoglu stays under control when he drives, with Assist and Turnover Ratios that are consistently above average for his position. His one quirk is a tendency to throw inaccurate passes a foot to the left or right of his target.

Overall, he was a good use of Orlando's midlevel exception and might have won the Sixth Man award had he stayed healthy. But the road to the starting lineup looks blocked by Grant Hill. Despite his size, Turkoglu isn't much of a post defender and would be overmatched at power forward, so he'll have to be content to spend half the game on the pine.

Fran Vazquez   power forward   **Age: 22**   **Height: 6-11**   **Weight: 230**
Translated 40-minute stats: 13.5 pts, 11.1 reb, 1.5 ast, .605 FG%, 14.07 PER

I'm a fan of Vazquez because it seems fairly obvious that he'll be able to contribute immediately. Vazquez is an energetic player who can rebound and block shots, but he also should be able to score more than advertised. He averaged 17.5 points per 40 minutes in Euroleague play and did it while shooting 69 percent from the floor, mainly because he's a strong finisher who also can hit a 15-footer. That translates to 13.5 points and 60 percent shooting in the NBA, which Orlando certainly would accept. Vazquez might need to get stronger to battle pro power forwards but we won't know for a while. He surprised the Magic by choosing to stay in Spain and may not be in a Magic uniform for a few years.

Travis Diener   point guard   **Age: 23**   **Height: 6-1**   **Weight: 175**

Orlando's second-rounder is certainly a good shooter, shooting 41 percent on three-pointers at Marquette. He also was surprisingly effective running the offense. The question is whether other point guards will eat Diener for lunch at the defensive end, because he's not very athletic and a bit small for the position at 6′1″.

Marcin Gortat   center   **Age: 21**   **Height: 7-0**   **Weight: 250**

The Polish big man was a late second-round pick and will stay overseas for the foreseeable future. He's regarded as a good athlete, but he didn't start playing hoops until a late age and still is very raw offensively.

Philadelphia 76ers

One step forward, one step back.

That's how it's gone for the 76ers the past few seasons, and the steps back could soon outnumber the steps forward. Since their glorious run to the Finals in 2000, the Sixers have a combined record of 167–161, and last year was emblematic of the previous three. Philadelphia had its usual high-scoring effort from Allen Iverson and showcased some exciting young talent in shot-blocking center Samuel Dalembert and high-flying rookie Andre Iguodala. But the 76ers also suffered from a weak bench, a misguided midseason trade, and a coaching strategy that mixed badly with the team's talent.

Philadelphia opened the season with new head coach Jim O'Brien, who had developed a strong reputation based on his solid performance in Boston. However, his playing style fit the Sixers' talent about as well as a pair of Daisy Dukes on a sumo wrestler. O'Brien had built much of his offensive attack in Boston around the three-point shot, but Philadelphia had almost no three-point shooters on the roster. That didn't stop the Sixers from finishing 10th in three-point attempts, even though they were only 20th in accuracy at 34.8 percent.

The Sixers wouldn't even have ranked 20th if not for O'Brien's lineup shift to favor three-point shooters, though they weren't always the most talented players. At small forward, for instance, he moved limited shooting specialist Kyle Korver into the starting lineup ahead of Glenn Robinson. He also found ample minutes for late-season pickup (and three-point shooter) Rodney Rogers down the stretch despite it being obvious to everyone else that the guy was finished.

O'Brien's offensive strategy became more bizarre when compared to his defensive approach. He preaches a strategy that fronts the post, sends lots of help, and protects the basket at all costs. What that allows is the three-pointer—the same play that is the centerpiece of his offense. You would think that if he thought threes were so important he would try a little harder to prevent them. Instead, Philly sent help defenders like crazy and led the NBA in three-pointers allowed.

Things really came to a head when the Sixers made a midseason trade for Chris Webber, creating perhaps the

76ers at a Glance

Record: 43–39, 2nd place in Atlantic Division

Offensive Efficiency: 100.8 (24th)

Defensive Efficiency: 101.5 (10th)

Pace Factor: 97.2 (2nd)

Top-Rated Player: Allen Iverson (PER 23.23, 9th overall)

Head Coach: Maurice Cheeks. Did decent job in Portland but inherits sticky situation.

worst fit between a player and system that I've ever seen. Offensively, Webber is a player who likes to orchestrate plays from the high post and look for teammates cutting off picks. Once he got to Philadelphia, he basically had to watch Iverson and stay out of the way. The result was his 20.82 PER in Sacramento plummeting to 13.14 in Philly.

And then there was the defense. O'Brien's system required Webber to front the post, step out against screen-and-rolls and race out to three-point shooters, which was inconceivable since the man was playing on one leg. He had virtually no chance of recovering out to three-point shooters in particular. That fact was made obvious when Toronto's Donyell Marshall made 12 of them in a game while matched up against Webber, tying an NBA record.

Yet the Sixers made it to the postseason, and their overall defensive numbers weren't terrible. All that trapping and rotating did have one big benefit for the Sixers—they forced more turnovers than any team in the league. Philadelphia's opponents gave up the ball on 16.7 percent of their possessions, compared to the league average of 14.8 (see table 1), and that advantage handed the Sixers an extra two points a game. In addition, Philly led the NBA in steals, feeding the break for a club that played the league's second fastest pace.

It's easy to see why the Sixers forced so many miscues. Iverson is a renowned ball hawk, Iguodala is great in the passing lanes, and Korver has quick hands and good anticipation. O'Brien's defensive style augmented these skills as well.

However, O'Brien had to make too great a sacrifice at the offensive end to play his chosen defenders. Useful scorers like Williamson and Thomas spent too much time on the end of the bench while lesser talents got their minutes. Robinson, meanwhile, spent the year on the injured list with a dubious injury after losing his starting job and was finally traded in February.

The Sixers ranked 24th in Offensive Efficiency despite what may have been the best season of Iverson's career. As usual, the diminutive guard led the league in scoring and created a shot almost any time he felt like it. Unusually, he also made a decent percentage of the shots he created. Iverson's

Table 1. Turnovers Forced per 100 Possessions—2004–05 Leaders

Team	TO/100 Possessions
Philadelphia	16.7
Memphis	16.6
New Jersey	16.4
Denver	16.3
Charlotte	16.0
League Average	**14.8**

ability to get to the basket put Philadelphia in the upper half of the league in free throw attempts despite having virtually no post game, and that was the one offensive area in which they were respectable.

This might lead some to conclude that the experiment of moving Iverson to the point was a success, but think again. The Sixers had the highest Turnover Rate in the league, turning it over on 16.7 percent of their possessions, and Iverson's Assist Ratio was near the bottom among point guards.

Worst of all, having the league's leading scorer also bring the ball up basically froze out everyone else. Iverson's Usage Rates are among the highest in history, and I'm not sure it's healthy for one player to have the ball so much unless he's named Jordan. Iverson used 35 percent of the Sixers' possessions while he was on the court, compared to 20 percent for a normal player, and somebody's touches had to go down to compensate. It wasn't a problem for a player like Korver, a stand-still three-point shooter who could feed off Iverson's penetration, but it left players who thrive off set plays out in the cold. The worst impact was on Webber whose Usage Rate dropped dramatically in Philadelphia. It didn't help that many times the Sixers were racing down the floor and already had a shot up before Webber could limp across halfcourt.

This year the Sixers will have to make a much better effort to mesh the skills of Webber and Iverson, and in O'Brien's place they have a new man trying to make it work. Like O'Brien, Maurice Cheeks is a Philadelphia guy, having played the point on the 76ers' championship team in 1983. Unlike O'Brien, Cheeks is seen as more of a player's coach. This was a problem with a rag-tag bunch like Portland, but with a veteran team like the Sixers it might not be such a bad thing.

Unfortunately, it's going to be difficult for the Sixers just to stay at the .500 level, because a series of poor contracts and bad trades has put them in a precarious position. The Sixers are going to be over the salary cap until at least 2008 because Webber and Iverson are making so much, which is one reason the Webber trade is looking like a fiasco. Philadelphia gave up Thomas, Skinner, and Williamson to get Web-

ber, and all three appear could have more value in 2005–06 than the man the Sixers acquired. Yet Webber is due close to $20 million a year for three more seasons.

Philadelphia won't have any new blood this year either. It had already traded its first-round pick and used all their available funds to re-sign their own free agents. Korver, Green, and Dalembert each got multiyear deals over the summer and the combined value of the contracts is north of $100 million. That pushes the Sixers right up against the luxury tax line and prevented them from adding players with their exceptions. In fact, the Sixers appeared likely to shed Aaron McKie using the Allan Houston rule in the collective bargaining agreement just so they could stay under the threshold. Dalembert is a decent starting center, but none of three is worth anything close to what Philadelphia paid. This continues a long-running trend of the Sixers overpaying their own players under King, and is the main reason they're in such dire straits cap-wise.

In another odd move, the Sixers essentially paid New Jersey to take productive big man Marc Jackson, giving their division rival $3 million and Jackson in return for "future considerations." Philadelphia needed to unload Jackson to avoid luxury tax and sign Steven Hunter—who is as good if not better—but it's still puzzling considering the simpler alternative of not paying so much to keep Korver. The bad contracts, weird trades and resulting lack of talent surrounding Iverson has focused attention on general manager Billy King, who enters 2005–06 with his fourth coach in the less than three years since Larry Brown left for Detroit. While the Iguodala pick in the draft could be a home run and Korver and Green, though overpaid, were nice second-round choices, King has swung and missed on his four biggest moves since Brown left. The Webber trade, re-signing an aging Derrick Coleman, extending Eric Snow, and trading Keith Van Horn for Robinson all set Philly back quite a bit; last summer's moves are likely to do the same.

Looking ahead, it's had to get too excited about the Sixers' chances. If Iverson plays as he did a year go and everyone stays healthy it's possible for the Sixers to make a playoff run, but that's about the best-case scenario. Webber can't possibly be as bad as a year ago and Dalembert and Iguodala figure to show some improvement, but the Sixers' starting lineup is hardly daunting. Additionally, contract woes have emaciated the bench, where Hunter is the lone reliable reserve. Plus, Webber's track record indicates he's more likely to play 50 or 60 games than the full 82. Add it all up and Cheeks may rue his homecoming. His first year in Philadelphia could be a long one, and the future isn't looking any brighter.

Matt Barnes — small forward
(78% SF, 14% SG, 8% PF)

Age: 25 Height: 6-7 Weight: 235
Most similar at age: George Lynch

Year		G	M/G	FG%	FT%	P/40	R/40	A/40	TS%		Ast		TO		Usg		Reb		PER	
2003-04	LAC	38	18.9	.457	.705	9.5	8.4	2.7	51.9	26	18.7	6	17.1	59	12.5	55	12.4	6	10.68	46
2004-05	Sac-Phi	43	16.7	.411	.603	9.2	7.4	3.2	46.5	58	15.2	8	16.2	63	13.6	59	10.7	10	8.88	59
2005-06	PRJ (33.7)			.431	.630	8.8	7.6	3.0	48.8		17.9		15.8		12.5		11.1		9.81	

Barnes didn't play a game after being included as a throw-in in the Webber trade, but he saw plenty of action in Sacramento. He's extremely active on the glass and has enough ballhandling skills to be used as a point forward, but his game is lacking in other areas. For example, Barnes is a poor outside shooter and doesn't own a great first step, so offensive rebounds are virtually his only source of points. He also makes too many turnovers and needs to get stronger to hold his own in the post. Barnes is a free agent and, as a native of Sacramento, may try again with the Kings this year.

Michael Bradley — power forward
(97% PF, 3% C)

Age: 26 Height: 6-10 Weight: 245
Most similar at age: N/A

Year		G	M/G	FG%	FT%	P/40	R/40	A/40	TS%		Ast		TO		Usg		Reb		PER	
2002-03	Tor	67	19.6	.481	.522	10.3	12.5	2.0	49.2	44	13.8	18	15.6	56	13.4	50	17.7	4	12.82	38
2003-04	Tor-Atl	16	6.2	.467	.500	6.1	9.3	0.4	47.2		4.2		29.3		7.8		13.1		4.11	
2004-05	Orl-Sac-Phi	18	6.6	.625	.375	11.1	9.4	1.7	60.0		8.0		13.3		11.0		13.2		11.74	

A human receipt, Bradley was thrown into the bag in two different trades to even out the salaries. When he got to play, he actually had one of his better seasons, shooting 62 percent in limited minutes and cutting his turnovers. He's running out of chances to get more consistent minutes, however, so one wonders if he might be better off playing in Europe for a year or two and getting more exposure and playing time.

Samuel Dalembert — center
(100% C)

Age: 24 Height: 6-11 Weight: 250
Most similar at age: Dale Davis

Year		G	M/G	FG%	FT%	P/40	R/40	A/40	TS%		Ast		TO		Usg		Reb		PER	
2002-03	Phi		Out for the season																	
2003-04	Phi	82	26.8	.541	.644	11.9	11.4	0.4	56.6	9	3.1	73	12.6	32	11.7	60	16.2	15	16.21	16
2004-05	Phi	72	24.8	.524	.601	13.2	12.1	0.8	54.3	28	3.7	59	16.5	60	13.2	42	17.0	18	14.37	29
2005-06	PRJ (38.4)			.516	.616	12.8	11.7	0.7	54.1		3.7		14.9		13.2		16.4		14.96	

Dalembert's season was a bit of a disappointment considering all the promise he had shown in 2003–04. He runs the court very well for a big man, has a nice turnaround jumper, and is a force on the offensive glass. Plus, he's one of the game's better rebounders and averaged a blocked shot every 15 minutes.

However, he more than undoes those blocked shots with his numerous goaltending violations. The NBA doesn't keep stats on this, but I would be shocked if he didn't lead the league by a wide margin. Now that he's been playing regularly for two years, he should have better judgment about which balls are on their way down, rather than simply swatting at anything he can reach. His other defensive areas could use improvement as well. Namely, he takes bad fouls and needs to get stronger to provide more resistance in the post.

Oddly, Dalembert's Turnover Ratio skyrocketed in 2004–05 for reasons that aren't entirely clear. The main culprits were his poor hands, which are a shame because he can elevate and finish over nearly anyone. As a whole, Dalembert's talent remains alluring. He took up the game at a late age and is still learning his craft, but at 24 he's young enough to improve considerably. Philadelphia overpaid to keep him, but this was the least objectionable of the Sixers' three free-agent signings, because the potential is certainly there.

Josh Davis   power forward   **Age: 25**   **Height: 6-8**   **Weight: 240**
(88% PF, 12% C)   Most similar at age: N/A

Year		G	M/G	FG%	FT%	P/40	R/40	A/40	TS%	Ast	TO	Usg	Reb	PER
2003-04	Atl	4	5.8	.400	1.000	8.7	8.7	0.0	46.0	0.0	26.9	10.5	12.3	2.07
2004-05	Phi	42	7.8	.378	.824	14.3	9.6	1.5	49.4	7.0	10.3	15.8	13.5	11.32

The CBA MVP in 2003–04, Davis got his shot at the big leagues in 2004–05 and was fortunate enough to play for a coach who valued three-point shooting over other skills—like running and dribbling, for instance. Davis is undersized for a power forward at 6′8″, and he doesn't have enough quickness to beat bigger players off the bounce. As a result, his pro destiny is probably limited to being an end-of-the-bench guy who can provide occasional outbursts of shooting when the match-ups are advantageous.

Willie Green   shooting guard   **Age: 24**   **Height: 6-4**   **Weight: 200**
(71% SG, 26% PG, 3% SF)   Most similar at age: Terry Dehere

Year		G	M/G	FG%	FT%	P/40	R/40	A/40	TS%		Ast		TO		Usg		Reb		PER	
2003-04	Phi	53	14.5	.401	.728	19.0	3.4	2.8	46.4	54	10.5	55	11.7	45	24.9	9	4.8	57	10.78	47
2004-05	Phi	57	18.7	.366	.776	16.4	5.0	3.8	45.7	60	15.3	29	11.5	45	21.7	18	7.0	26	9.54	54
2005-06	*PRJ (53.1)*			*.379*	*.739*	*16.0*	*4.6*	*3.5*	*46.4*		*14.9*		*11.4*		*21.3*		*6.4*		*10.00*	

While Green has a great first step and can create shots with ease, the shots he creates are the main problem. Green's TS% was among the worst at his position thanks to a 36.6 percent mark from the field, making it a dubious proposition for him to be so aggressive offensively. Also, he needs to work on his jumper, as he hit only 30 percent on three-pointers.

Defensively, Green is a bit of a tweener. He's small for a shooting guard and not quite quick enough for the point, so he needs to produce at the offensive end in order to have much value. In his first two seasons, he hasn't delivered.

Green was a restricted free agent, and the Sixers foolishly agreed to give him a five-year deal worth $17 million. The Sixers were waffling on signing the deal, however, because Green hurt his knee before he could ink the contract and will be out for most of the season. While I'd hate to see the Sixers weasel out of their agreement, the reality is that better players are available at the minimum salary. Besides, Philadelphia already has one guard dominating the ball, and Green is basically a lower-percentage, more turnover-prone version.

Andre Iguodala   shooting guard   **Age: 21**   **Height: 6-6**   **Weight: 207**
Defensive PER: 1.14 (75% SG, 25% SF)   Most similar at age: Paul Pierce

Year		G	M/G	FG%	FT%	P/40	R/40	A/40	TS%		Ast		TO		Usg		Reb		PER	
2004-05	Phi	82	32.8	.493	.743	11.0	6.9	3.7	58.0	7	17.5	20	13.6	62	13.3	64	9.7	3	13.49	31
2005-06	*PRJ (5.8)*			*.494*	*.798*	*12.5*	*7.0*	*3.9*	*58.8*		*17.2*		*13.0*		*14.6*		*9.9*		*14.78*	

A physical specimen with TNT in his knees, Iguodala might be the most athletic shooting guard in the league. It's inconceivable that the NBA didn't invite him to the dunk contest, as he had several of the best slams I saw all season. An early-season flying facial on Orlando's 6′11″ Kelvin Cato ranks at the top of my list.

Due to all the dunks, Iguodala was able to shoot a high percentage from the floor, and he drew enough fouls to have the seventh-best TS% at his position. However, he was rarely asked to contribute much at the offensive end. Iguodala isn't an instinctive offensive player, although he's a good passer, and also needs a lot of work on his jump shot. Those offensive limitations are the reason he averaged only 11 points per 40 minutes, an extremely poor total for a starting NBA off guard.

Fortunately, the Sixers can wait for his offense to come around because he's shown so much promise in other areas. Iguodala had one of the best Defensive PERs at his position and the Sixers used him as their stopper against top scorers. With his combination of strength, quickness, and leaping ability, it appears he could become an All-Defense caliber player. As an added plus, Iguodala had the fifth-best Rebound Rate among all backcourt players.

Looking ahead, what stands out about Iguodala is his uniqueness. No comparable player had a Similarity Score above 98, accounting for the low quality score in his projection. That's usually a good sign, since it indicates his skills are uncommon. He's an athletic freak who defends well, crashes the boards, and is only 21, so it's hard not to be excited about his promise.

Allen Iverson — point guard
Defensive PER: 1.21 (100% PG)
Age: 30 Height: 6-0 Weight: 165
Most similar at age: Isiah Thomas

Year		G	M/G	FG%	FT%	P/40	R/40	A/40	TS%		Ast		TO		Usg		Reb		PER	
2002-03	Phi*	82	42.5	.414	.774	26.0	3.9	5.2	50.0	34	15.1	31	9.5	21	32.1	2	5.8	44	21.12	5
2003-04	Phi*	48	42.5	.387	.745	24.8	3.5	6.4	47.8	49	17.4	24	11.2	40	34.5	1	4.9	55	19.22	5
2004-05	Phi	75	42.3	.424	.835	29.0	3.8	7.5	53.2	21	19.2	60	11.1	38	34.7	1	5.3	39	23.23	1
2005-06	*PRJ (5.8)*			*.404*	*.817*	*27.2*	*3.7*	*6.2*	*50.7*		*17.1*		*10.4*		*34.1*		*5.2*		*21.42*	

* Season rankings are as shooting guard

Iverson leading the league in scoring is no longer news, but doing it with a TS% above the league average is. In the past five seasons, including his MVP season in 2000–01, Iverson has never finished with a TS% better than the league mark. For him to create the volume of shots that he does while still making a relatively high percentage is an impressive accomplishment, and his PER overall rivaled that of his MVP year.

Helping him along were the new defensive rules, which gave players with superb quickness a tremendous advantage in getting to the basket. Because of that, Iverson set a career high in free-throw attempts per game—an unusual feat for a 29-year-old guard—and magnified the accomplishment with a career-high 83.5 percent from the line.

He could be even better if he'd stop shooting three-pointers. Iverson took 4.5 per game, a flabbergasting statistic. I mean, he's a 30 percent career shooter from out there, and over the past four years he's been even worse. Now that he's been playing for a decade, hasn't he figured out yet that he shouldn't be taking this shot? Iverson's TS% when he doesn't shoot a three is 54.7, which would have ranked 12th among all point guards. When he shoots a three, it's 46.7, which would put him in the bottom ten.

Defensively, Iverson has never been a great on-ball defender, but it's a different story on the weak side. He materializes from nowhere to dart into passing lanes and has averaged over two steals a game in every pro season. He normally converts those steals into lay-ups at the other end as well.

Iverson is signed for the max for four more seasons, and the Sixers have to be concerned about how he will hold up physically. He takes a beating on his drives to the hoop and virtually never comes out of the game, which was fine when he was 25 but might not work so well in his 30s. Additionally, Iverson is a Fluke Rule candidate whose numbers can be expected to slip somewhat this season. Small, quick guards like him have tended to burn out quickly but with $19 million a year committed to him, the Sixers will need Iverson to be an exception to the rule.

Marc Jackson — center
Defensive PER: 0.41 (87% C, 13% PF)
Age: 30 Height: 6-10 Weight: 253
Most similar at age: Vin Baker

Year		G	M/G	FG%	FT%	P/40	R/40	A/40	TS%		Ast		TO		Usg		Reb		PER	
2002-03	Min	77	13.5	.438	.765	16.2	8.7	1.4	50.8	37	7.2	55	11.6	17	17.9	16	12.3	57	13.35	40
2003-04	Phi*	22	27.2	.415	.790	13.8	8.4	1.2	49.8	45	7.2	61	9.7	9	16.0	42	11.9	48	13.19	47
2004-05	Phi	81	24.4	.465	.828	19.6	8.2	1.6	54.8	26	7.4	27	11.9	17	19.6	7	11.5	57	15.94	20
2005-06	*PRJ (40.5)*			*.447*	*.803*	*17.5*	*8.5*	*1.6*	*53.0*		*7.6*		*12.1*		*18.3*		*11.9*		*14.63*	

* Season rankings are as power forward

O'Brien quickly took a liking to Jackson and installed him as the starting center ahead of Dalembert for much of the season. Jackson is short for a center, however, and would have trouble jumping over this book. As a result, his Rebound Rates are poor and he blocked astonishingly few shots—less than one for every hundred minutes. He's also slow on defensive rotations and his lack of hops gives him problems finishing around the basket.

Where Jackson excels is at the offensive end, where he is unusually skilled for a player of his size. He loves to shoot jumpers from the top of the key and is very accurate from there. His wide frame allows him to establish excellent post position, which will be important for his new employers in New Jersey because he's their only player with much of a post game. Defensively, Jackson's strength helps him to muscle opposing centers, somewhat making up for his dearth of athleticism.

Jackson is signed for two more years at reasonable dollars, making his trade to New Jersey for scraps one of the offseason's biggest head-scratchers. Last season may be a high-water mark, as his shooting percentage was significantly higher than his career norms, but he'll give New Jersey a big boost regardless.

Kyle Korver small forward Age: 24 Height: 6-7 Weight: 210
Defensive PER: 0.92 (98% SF, 1% SG, 1% PF) Most similar at age: Jumaine Jones

Year		G	M/G	FG%	FT%	P/40	R/40	A/40	TS%		Ast		TO		Usg		Reb		PER	
2003-04	Phi	74	11.9	.352	.792	15.0	5.0	1.8	48.9	45	9.6	49	9.8	18	18.2	27	7.1	48	10.11	49
2004-05	Phi	82	32.5	.418	.854	14.1	5.7	2.7	58.8	2	13.0	25	9.7	27	14.7	51	8.0	46	12.84	39
2005-06	PRJ (29.4)			.393	.864	14.3	5.6	2.6	55.8		12.0		10.3		15.7		7.9		12.52	

Korver is an outstanding shooter and developed a great on-court rapport with Iverson, who would constantly look for him trailing the play when the Sixers were in transition. Korver shot 41 percent on three-pointers to help himself to the second-best TS% among small forwards, and since he didn't need the rock much he was a perfect complement to the ball-dominating Iverson.

Of course, that outside shot is pretty much his only skill. He rarely ever ventured inside the three-point line—74 percent of Korver's field-goal attempts were three-pointers—and when he did the results weren't pretty. Also, while Korver's Turnover Ratio doesn't seem bad at first glance, the number is very high once you consider Korver hardly ever had to dribble. He's a weak defender, too, although he partially makes up for his slow feet with fast hands and willingly takes charges.

Overall, it's hard for the Sixers to justify giving so many minutes to somebody so one-dimensional. Korver's PER was well below the league average and he's not providing much at the defensive end either. Unfortunately, the Sixers re-signed Korver to a five-year, $22 million deal. They could have obtained the same production for much less, so they have to hope that he'll continue improving. The projections say not to hold your breath.

Jamal Mashburn small forward Age: 33 Height: 6-8 Weight: 247

Year		G	M/G	FG%	FT%	P/40	R/40	A/40	TS%		Ast		TO		Usg		Reb		PER	
2002-03	NO	82	40.5	.422	.848	21.3	6.0	5.6	50.7	36	18.9	9	9.4	15	27.9	2	8.7	36	17.96	10
2003-04	NO	53	14.4	.392	.813	21.7	6.4	2.6	45.7	54	9.1	54	7.2	2	28.3	4	9.5	19	15.15	22
2004-05		Did not play																		

The Sixers own Mashburn's rights, but that's a mere technicality. His knee is shot and he'll never play again. Philadelphia's main reason for acquiring his rights is because Mashburn's contract won't count against the salary cap starting in March, relieving the Sixers of having to pay luxury tax.

Aaron McKie small forward Age: 33 Height: 6-5 Weight: 209
(52% SF, 48% SG) Most similar at age: Emanual Davis

Year		G	M/G	FG%	FT%	P/40	R/40	A/40	TS%		Ast		TO		Usg		Reb		PER	
2002-03	Phi	80	29.7	.429	.836	12.1	5.9	4.7	49.7	43	25.0	2	9.8	19	17.4	34	8.7	38	13.76	28
2003-04	Phi	75	28.1	.459	.757	13.1	4.8	3.7	55.0	10	21.1	2	11.1	32	16.6	39	6.8	53	13.95	30
2004-05	Phi	68	16.4	.430	.625	5.4	6.2	3.7	51.0	44	17.6	3	11.0	38	9.0	64	8.6	34	8.43	61
2005-06	PRJ (42.5)			.418	.713	9.4	5.3	3.9	50.2		20.6		11.4		13.6		7.5		10.90	

McKie has been a valuable contributor for the Sixers for a long time, but he might be at the end of the line. He was arguably the worst offensive player in basketball in 2004–05, with a pathetic rate of 5.4 points per 40 minutes that was easily the bottom among perimeter players. McKie has completely stopped going to the basket—he took only 16 free throws all season—which leaves him reliant on an awkward outside jumper to provide his increasingly rare baskets.

Conversely, McKie can get the job done defensively, as he is strong, smart, and can handle being matched up against bigger forwards. But for a player to provide such a pittance of offense, his defense can't just be adequate, it has to be exceptional. McKie falls far short on that count, so unless his scoring numbers double from a year ago, there's little room for him in an NBA rotation. The Sixers released McKie using the amnesty provision in the collective bargaining agreement, leaving him scrambling for employment.

Kevin Ollie   point guard   Age: 33   Height: 6-2   Weight: 105
(82% PG, 18% SG)   Most similar at age: N/A

Year		G	M/G	FG%	FT%	P/40	R/40	A/40	TS%		Ast		TO		Usg		Reb		PER	
2002-03	Mil-Sea	82	23.1	.451	.753	11.3	3.8	6.1	51.4	27	33.0	10	8.2	7	17.9	52	5.6	31	13.74	29
2003-04	Cle	82	17.1	.370	.835	9.7	4.9	6.7	51.0	27	36.0	8	12.5	40	16.8	59	6.9	8	12.15	45
2004-05	Phi	26	6.1	.355	.667	7.1	4.8	4.8	40.0		22.9		10.0		13.6		6.7		6.61	

The Sixers traded one bad contract for another when they sent Eric Snow to Cleveland for Ollie before the season. The bad news for Philly is that Snow can play a little, while Ollie can't play at all. The 33-year-old journeyman makes few mistakes, but he never had much athleticism to begin with and isn't improving in that category as he gets older. He could make some token appearances since the Sixers' bench is so weak, but basically the Sixers are sitting around waiting for this contract to expire in 2008.

Rodney Rogers   small forward   Age: 34   Height: 6-7   Weight: 255
(62% SF, 36% PF, 2% SG)   Most similar at age: George Lynch

Year		G	M/G	FG%	FT%	P/40	R/40	A/40	TS%		Ast		TO		Usg		Reb		PER	
2002-03	NJ*	68	19.2	.402	.756	14.7	8.1	3.3	48.3	48	15.4	14	13.1	47	19.2	24	11.5	47	11.63	49
2003-04	NJ*	69	20.4	.410	.765	15.3	8.7	3.9	49.2	47	17.5	12	12.5	46	20.6	19	12.4	41	14.17	42
2004-05	NO-Phi	58	23.6	.382	.743	13.0	7.2	2.5	46.2	59	12.0	32	13.2	53	17.6	43	10.1	17	8.90	58
2005-06	*PRJ (30.3)*			*.384*	*.754*	*13.5*	*7.7*	*3.1*	*46.5*		*13.8*		*14.5*		*18.3*		*10.9*		*10.31*	

* Season rankings are as power forward

Rogers was signed by New Orleans in the offseason but didn't exactly seem thrilled to be there. His PER at the time of his trade to the Sixers was nearly the worst in the league, and his defense may have been even worse than his offense.

Reunited with O'Brien who coached him in Boston, Rogers was more energetic but out of shape and woefully inaccurate, shooting 39 percent as a Sixer. It's a mystery why O'Brien cleared a spot in the rotation for Rogers considering how little he contributed at either end of the floor, especially when so many of those minutes came at the expense of the vastly more productive Marc Jackson. Fortunately, the Sixers weren't risking much by acquiring Rogers because his contract expired at the end of the season. As an overweight 34-year-old free agent coming off a bad year, he may find the market for his talents extremely limited.

John Salmons   shooting guard   Age: 26   Height: 6-7   Weight: 210
(65% SG, 34% PG, 1% SF)   Most similar at age: Eric Piatkowski

Year		G	M/G	FG%	FT%	P/40	R/40	A/40	TS%		Ast		TO		Usg		Reb		PER	
2002-03	Phi	64	7.8	.414	.743	10.5	4.7	3.7	50.2	32	22.7	14	14.0	53	14.9	48	6.9	29	9.52	45
2003-04	Phi	77	20.8	.387	.772	11.1	4.9	3.3	48.5	43	20.1	16	11.5	44	15.8	50	6.9	27	10.66	48
2004-05	Phi	58	17.1	.405	.729	9.5	4.9	4.6	51.1	46	21.9	5	12.9	59	14.0	59	6.8	32	9.69	53
2005-06	*PRJ (35.9)*			*.405*	*.735*	*10.2*	*5.0*	*3.8*	*50.2*		*20.8*		*12.0*		*14.5*		*7.0*		*10.64*	

Like a lot of Sixers, Salmons took more three-pointers last season, with nearly half his shot attempt coming from downtown. Unfortunately, he's not that good at them—he hit 34 percent, matching his career mark. Salmons otherwise was a wallflower on offense, averaging a meager 9.5 points per 40 minutes. He has the skills of a point guard despite standing 6'7", which accounts for his high Assist Ratio. Those skills don't include being able to shoot off the dribble, however, so it's hard to justify getting him many minutes.

Salmons is an above-average defender who can guard three positions because of his combination of size and quickness. That may keep him in Philadelphia's rotation again this season, but only because the Sixers are so lacking in options. It's also a contract year for Salmons, so it behooves him to pick up his scoring quickly.

Chris Webber (84% PF, 16% C)			power forward								Age: 32		Height: 6-10		Weight:245 Most similar at age: Tom Chambers			
Year	G	M/G	FG%	FT%	P/40	R/40	A/40	TS%		Ast		TO		Usg		Reb		PER
2002-03 Sac	82	33.8	.461	.607	23.5	10.7	5.6	48.5	47	16.8	11	9.9	16	29.5	1	14.4 22		20.90 6
2003-04 Sac	23	36.1	.413	.711	20.7	9.6	5.1	45.6	59	16.5	16	9.4	7	27.8	2	14.3 27		17.11 19
2004-05 Sac-Phi	67	35.4	.433	.794	22.0	10.3	5.4	47.2	65	16.9	6	9.7	23	28.9	2	14.5 24		18.60 14
2005-06 PRJ (19.1)			.431	.744	20.3	10.0	5.0	49.2		19.1		10.1		25.8		11.7		16.92

Considering that Webber was basically playing on one leg last season, what he accomplished was fairly remarkable. He averaged 22 points per 40 minutes, had one of the best Assist Ratios at his position, and remained effective on the glass despite his balky knee.

He was absolutely worthless on defense, however, and was especially exposed when he came to Philadelphia. Webber was easily beaten down the court by opposing big men and couldn't provide his guards with any help in the screen-and-roll. That was one reason his adjustment to Philly was so rocky. When he came to the Sixers he was asked to step out and trap the pick-and-roll, which had the same chance of happening as asking a monkey to read Shakespeare.

Webber hasn't fully adjusted his offensive game to the new realities of his limp either. He was far too aggressive in looking for his shot, since his game has mostly degenerated into shooting a semi-accurate mid-range jumper from the high post. He also can't finish at the rim anymore, which didn't stop him from trying. What he needs to do instead is take better advantage of his brilliance as a passer, especially now that he has a perfect recipient for his deliveries in Iverson. The Sixers need to adjust their offense to get Webber more involved, but Webber also needs to change his game and realize that he's no longer his team's top scoring threat.

Louis Williams	shooting guard	Age: 19 Height: 6-1 Weight: 175

A top-notch athlete who turned pro out of high school, Williams looks to be a poor man's Allen Iverson. Make that a destitute man. Like Iverson, Williams is a shooting guard who can score in bunches and easily create shots, but he would almost certainly have to play the point as a pro because of his small stature. And unlike Iverson, Williams has been extremely turnover-prone when he's played against other top high school talent, suggesting his ballhandling skills aren't up to snuff.

Toronto Raptors

It was another puzzling year north of the border. The Raptors continued their gentle glide toward the bottom of the standings with a slew of questionable personnel decisions, as well as the *de rigeur* backbiting and infighting.

This wasn't supposed to happen since the Raptors had replaced their management team after the last group committed the same sins. Nevertheless new coach Sam Mitchell spent most of his rookie season trying to stop the bleeding from assorted run-ins with his players, while new general manager Rob Babcock's mistakes included a horrendous draft pick and an even worse trade.

Let's run through the casualties before we try to sort out what's left of the mess. Things started heading downhill almost immediately for the Babcock regime when he used his first draft pick, No. 8 overall, on BYU stiff Rafael Araujo. Nobody predicted Araujo would be one of the top 15 picks and for good reason. He was overmatched from the beginning and isn't likely to get much better since he's already 24. It was a huge missed opportunity for the Raptors because the 2004 draft shaped up as one of the best in recent history. The player selected after Araujo, for instance, was Philadelphia's Andre Iguodala, who started immediately and is four years younger.

Meanwhile, Vince Carter was making it clear he wanted to be traded. He went through warm-ups with his headphones on (until the league told him to stop), half-heartedly launched fadeaway jump shots, and sleepwalked on defense, so much so that Mitchell was pulling him in fourth quarters. It may be the first time I've ever seen a player stop trying on *offense*.

Although something had to be done, the Raptors underestimated their leverage. With Carter signed for two and a half more seasons and other teams well aware of Carter's talents, Babcock could have waited him out. It wouldn't have been pleasant, but the rule of thumb in the NBA is that the trade offers start getting a lot more serious once the trade deadline rolls around.

Instead, two months before the deadline Babock sent Carter to New Jersey for three reserves and a pair of lottery-protected first-round draft picks. Freed from Toronto, Carter almost immediately blew up with the Nets, posting the league's highest PER over the season's final 20 games and carrying New Jersey to an unexpected playoff berth. Meanwhile, the Raptors floundered.

Moreover, Babcock handled another aspect of the deal quite badly. Alonzo Mourning was one of the players Toronto received but had no intention of playing for the Raptors. Babcock had all the leverage, because Mourning had three years left on his contract and Toronto could have suspended him without pay until he agreed to a buyout on heavily favorable terms. Instead, the Raptors bought out the remainder of his deal for roughly $10 million, which got them only minor savings and will take a chunk out of their cap for two more years. Essentially, they paid Mourning to go play for the Heat.

Babcock's personnel decisions took two more hits later in the year. First, after scathing criticism for not getting enough in the Carter trade, he got cold feet at the trade deadline and failed to deal Donyell Marshall. Marshall ended up leaving the Raptors as an unrestricted free agent after the season, giving Toronto nothing in return.

Then, Babcock again appeared to reach in the draft when he took Connecticut's Charlie Villanueva with the 7th overall pick. Villanueva isn't a stiff like Araujo, but most observers thought he would go several picks later. Further questions were raised when he passed up promising high-schooler Gerald Green to select Oklahoma State's Joey Graham with one of the picks from the Nets. Time will tell if those selections pay off, but most observers weren't optimistic.

Babcock's misdeeds were bad enough, but there also was a bad storm brewing in the Toronto locker room. To say Mitchell's first year was tumultuous would be an understatement, with point guard Rafer Alston being the eye of the storm. Alston got into multiple disputes with Mitchell, at one point threatening to quit the NBA and later walking out of a practice, which earned him a two-game suspension. The two reportedly had a halftime altercation after Alston was benched in the first half of a game, with Alston being led out of the arena by security. Additionally, Alston and forward Jalen Rose feuded most of the season, including one game where they refused to pass the ball to each other.

> ## Raptors at a Glance
>
> **Record:** 33–49, tied for 4th place in Atlantic Division
>
> **Offensive Efficiency:** 104.5 (10th)
>
> **Defensive Efficiency:** 105.9 (24th)
>
> **Pace Factor:** 94.7 (12th)
>
> **Top-Rated Player:** Donyell Marshall (PER 19.92, 28th overall)
>
> **Head Coach:** Sam Mitchell. Has tough-guy rep but needs to get better effort on D.

All of that would be hard enough to handle on a winning team, but with the Raptors mired in last place in the Atlantic Division for much of the season, it made the dysfunction that much more obvious. Perhaps that's why the team's defensive effort was so lame. Toronto ranked 24th in Defensive Efficiency, including the league's second-worst opponent field-goal percentage at 46.7 percent.

A big problem was the lack of quality interior players. Araujo was a bust, but remained in the starting lineup for much of the year, apparently at management's behest. When he departed games, the situation didn't improve much because of the Raptors' lack of size. Usually, rail thin Chris Bosh was pressed into service at center, paired with frail power forwards like Marshall and Matt Bonner. In addition, Rose and Alston were poor defenders, with Morris Peterson being the lone bright spot.

You can say this about the Raptors: At least they were entertaining. A year earlier under Kevin O'Neill, they were perhaps the most boring team in basketball. In 2004–05, they ran a lot more, thanks in part to Alston's arrival, and bombed away with zeal, finishing second in the league in three-point percentage. Rose, Peterson, Bonner, Marshall, and reserve Lamond Murray each hit 39 percent or better on three-pointers.

The Raptors excelled in another area that might surprise people—avoiding turnovers. Toronto turned it over on only 13.3 percent of its possessions, narrowly finishing behind Sacramento for the league lead. Because of the turnovers and the three-pointers, Toronto was able to have a good offense despite a below-average field-goal percentage.

However, all those Raptors jump shots came at a cost. With five players often hanging out on the perimeter, Toronto was easily the worst offensive rebounding team in the league, grabbing just 23.7 percent of opponent misses (see table 1). That fell well short of the league average of 28.7 percent, and on average it cost Toronto over two points per game.

That's one area where Villanueva may help. Unlike the other Raptors, he's at his best on the offensive glass and working around the basket. Unfortunately, he plays the same position as Bosh, a rising star who is clearly the centerpiece of the Raptors' rebuilding plan.

That plan is going to take a while even if everything goes smoothly. Raptors fans can take heart that the team played slightly better than its record last season—Toronto finished with 36 Expected Wins but won only 33 games. However, they built that record only because nearly every player had a career year.

If you look at every key Toronto player and compare what he had done in 2004–05 with his output the previous two seasons, you have to conclude that these guys were playing way over their heads—even though those heads were getting beaten to a pulp on many nights. Table 2 compares the 2004–05 PER of the key Raptors to their averages of the previous two seasons. Consider that only Bosh was in the developmental stage of his career.

Each one improved sharply in 2004–05, and each except Bosh is expected to decline sharply in 2005–06. The magnitude of this shouldn't be underestimated. If any one player saw his PER drop by a point or two, the team would hardly notice, but if seven key players do so at the same time, it's going to cost the team about 10 wins. So the Raptors, though they look at last year and may think they have 36-win talent, are really looking at a 26-win team heading into this season. Additionally, they'll be lucky to even replace Marshall's production with the 17.67 PER shown in the chart after the veteran forward signed with Cleveland. As of publication, the Raptors' only free-agent pickup was Spanish guard Jose Manuel Calderon, who will be an adequate backup point guard but won't come close to Marshall's impact.

There are a few positives to offset the bad news. Villanueva and Graham will inject some vitality and probably improve the defense quite a bit, and there's a distant possibility that Alvin Williams's chronic knee problems might abate enough to allow him to play. But the big picture still isn't pretty. Unless Bosh emerges as a superstar overnight, the Raptors are going to have a hard time staying out of last place in the Atlantic Division, much less making a playoff push. And as the final insult, when the Raptors look up at the top of the division, they'll see the bottoms of Vince Carter's sneakers.

Table 1. Worst Offensive Rebounding Teams, 2004–05

Team	ORB%	Cost per Game
Toronto	23.7	2.26
Philadelphia	25.4	1.47
New Jersey	25.5	1.37
Houston	26.3	0.99
Indiana	26.4	0.94
League Average	**28.7**	**0.00**

Table 2. Raptors' PER vs. Trend

Player	2002–03 and 2003–04 (Avg.)	2004–05	Change	Projected 2005–06	Change
Bosh	15.16	17.54	+2.38	18.98	1.44
Rose	13.70	16.56	+2.86	14.65	−1.91
Alston	14.02	16.46	+2.44	14.49	−1.97
Peterson	12.37	14.43	+2.06	12.95	−1.48
Bonner	—	14.64	—	13.35	−1.29
Marshall	18.69	19.92	+1.23	17.67	−2.25
Palacio	7.83	12.45	+4.62	10.15	−2.30
Murray	8.86	13.68	+4.82	12.21	−1.47
Average	**12.95**	**15.71**	**+2.92**	**14.31**	**−1.40**

Rafer Alston — point guard

Age: 29 Height: 6-2 Weight: 170

Defensive PER: 0.55 (100% PG)

Most similar at age: Mike James

Year		G	M/G	FG%	FT%	P/40	R/40	A/40	TS%		Ast		TO		Usg		Reb		PER	
2002-03	Tor	47	20.8	.415	.685	15.0	4.4	7.8	51.0	31	30.2	15	13.5	52	24.0	16	6.2	21	14.39	27
2003-04	Mia	82	31.5	.376	.769	13.0	3.5	5.8	50.9	29	28.1	30	9.7	14	19.6	43	4.9	42	13.65	30
2004-05	Tor	80	34.0	.414	.740	16.7	4.1	7.6	52.2	28	29.0	27	9.6	18	24.0	22	5.8	28	16.46	22
2005-06	PRJ (46.4)			.394	.724	14.8	3.9	6.6	50.9		27.9		10.2		22.2		5.5		14.49	

Babcock has been criticized for Alston's six-year, $24 million deal because of the ruckus Alston caused off the court, but on the court the Raptors got their money's worth. Alston was one of the keys to Toronto's offensive improvement, finishing above the league average for point guards in all three measures of creating offense—Usage Rate, Assist Ratio, and Turnover Ratio. The one thing that Alston could use is a floater when he drives the lane. Alston took nearly five three-pointers a game and hit 36 percent, but fared poorly inside the arc (45 percent), especially when he couldn't get all the way to the basket for a lay-up.

Defensively, Alston is like most of the Raptors. He didn't play particularly hard, and he didn't have that much skill to begin with. Alston has good quickness, which helped him average a steal and a half per game, but he lacks strength and should gamble less.

Despite their dissatisfaction with Alston's antics, the Raptors probably have to grin and bear it for at least another season since fixing the frontcourt is a higher priority. If he manages to behave and keeps up his numbers from last season, he could even draw some attention at the trade deadline.

Rafael Araujo — center

Age: 25 Height: 6-11 Weight: 280

(99% C, 1% PF)

Most similar at age: Eric Leckner

Year		G	M/G	FG%	FT%	P/40	R/40	A/40	TS%		Ast		TO		Usg		Reb		PER	
2004-05	Tor	59	12.6	.434	.782	10.6	10.0	0.9	49.2	55	4.1	54	19.5	68	12.4	48	14.1	37	6.87	69
2005-06	PRJ (23.6)			.433	.787	10.2	9.6	1.0	49.0		4.8		18.9		11.9		13.8		7.15	

One thing many fans, and indeed some teams, fail to understand is the importance of a player's age. For argument's sake, let's say the peak age for an NBA player is 26 and that a player under that age improves by about seven percent a year. This is a generalization, obviously, but follow along. If I draft a player who is 19 years old, he has seven years to improve before he reaches his peak. At the seven percent rate of improvement, he'll be 61 percent better by the time he's 26. But if I draft a player like Araujo who is 24, then he has only two years until his peak and will be only 15 percent better than when I drafted him.

In other words, if you're going to draft a 24-year-old rookie, you'd better be sure he's ready to be a major contributor immediately, because he's not going to get much better. The problem with the Raptors drafting Araujo wasn't because of his college performance—his numbers were as good as several other draftees. It's that he had already achieved most of his potential based on his age, so he would have had to be significantly *better*—40 percent better using this model—than the other collegians in order to achieve the same results as a pro.

But give Araujo credit for one thing: Unlike some of his teammates, he played very hard at both ends. Almost too hard, in fact, as he handed out several rough fouls. But that makes Araujo's rookie performance even harder to fathom. It wasn't a question of effort—he's just not very skilled. Araujo has zero athleticism and struggled to finish shots around the basket. It seemed like he was rushing his attempts, so perhaps he'll calm down and finish a few more of them this year. He'd have to do at least that just to be a competent second-stringer. The one surprise in his performance was his Rebound Rate. Araujo's rebounding numbers in college were outstanding and he has enough size to carve out a lot of space for himself even in the pros. Maybe those numbers will improve in his second season. In any case, it appears he was a wasted draft pick.

Matt Bonner — power forward

Age: 25 Height: 6-10 Weight: 240

(61% PF, 33% C, 6% SF)

Most similar at age: Victor Alexander

Year		G	M/G	FG%	FT%	P/40	R/40	A/40	TS%		Ast		TO		Usg		Reb		PER	
2004-05	Tor	82	18.9	.533	.789	15.2	7.3	1.2	59.6	3	5.9	61	6.9	4	14.1	57	10.4	63	14.64	38
2005-06	PRJ (23.8)			.507	.768	14.4	7.3	1.3	56.6		6.2		7.1		14.0		10.4		13.35	

Bonner was one of the NBA's biggest surprises in 2004–05. A second-round draft pick in 2003 who played in Italy for a year, he came back to North America and immediately proved he belonged. Bonner is a very unusual player because he's a big,

(continued next page)

Matt Bonner (continued)

wide-bodied guy who likes to hang out on the perimeter. Probably the most comparable player from recent history would be Matt Bullard, but Bullard wasn't getting minutes when he was Bonner's age so his name didn't come up in the Similarity Scores.

Bonner shot most of his jumpers from two-point range, which usually doesn't work out great numbers-wise, but his stroke was so consistent that he ended up with an outstanding 59.6 TS%. Because he rarely dribbled the ball, his Turnover Ratio also was excellent. Bullard's wide body and deadly jump shot made him a perfect pick-and-roll partner with Alston, and Toronto should take advantage of that more than they did last season.

Bonner's weaknesses start when the other team has the ball. He got absolutely destroyed on the boards and had trouble with almost every variety of defensive match-up. The Raptors often went to zone defenses to try to hide his shortcomings, especially when they used a frontcourt of Bonner, Marshall, and Bosh. That trio was deadly on offense, but the defensive cost was more than Toronto could bear on most nights.

Bonner is a restricted free agent, so it shouldn't be a problem for the Raptors to retain his rights. It might cost them a bit more than last season's minimum contract, but with Marshall gone, Bonner's role stands to increase significantly.

Chris Bosh			center						**Age: 21**		**Height: 6-10**	**Weight: 235**
Defensive PER: 0.90 (52% C, 48% PF)											Most similar at age: Joe Smith	

Year		G	M/G	FG%	FT%	P/40	R/40	A/40	TS%	Ast		TO		Usg		Reb		PER	
2003-04	Tor	75	33.5	.459	.701	13.7	8.9	1.2	51.3	39	7.6	52	10.5	14	15.8	21	12.8	54	15.16	23
2004-05	Tor	81	37.2	.471	.760	18.1	9.5	2.0	54.7	27	9.7	14	11.8	16	19.1	9	13.5	46	17.54	10
2005-06	*PRJ (33.5)*			*.477*	*.769*	*18.0*	*9.5*	*2.1*	*55.3*		*10.0*		*10.6*		*19.3*		*13.3*		*18.98*	

Another bizarre Raptors incident came in a 30-point loss to Memphis near the end of the season, when Mitchell left Bosh on the floor for 47 of the game's 48 minutes. Why Mitchell would have the franchise's future taking such an unnecessary beating is unfathomable, although he gave the predictable tough-guy response afterward.

"In tough times," Mitchell said, "you learn more by staying out there and getting embarrassed." As one Toronto columnist noted the next day, perhaps you learn that there are better franchises for which to play. Bosh will be a restricted free agent in two years, and needless punishments like that one aren't a great inducement for him to stick around.

Bosh's second season was a solid improvement from his first, as his numbers improved in nearly every category. Of note was his heightened ability to get to the line, as the southpaw was more willing to go to the basket to take contact, and showed a much-improved right hand. Bosh averaged better than a free throw for every two field-goal attempts, an outstanding rate that is normally the mark of a star talent. He made marked progress as a passer as well, with his Assist Ratio increasing 28 percent from the year prior. And of course, he was a much more aggressive scorer who increased his 40-minute rate by over four points.

The one thing the Raptors need to figure out is how to get him out of the middle. Bosh has a very slender frame with narrow shoulders and he's giving up 30 to 40 pounds to his opponent every night when he plays center. He should fill out some as he gets older, but he'll never be a widebody and there's some concern that all the banging will shorten his career. Regardless of position, Bosh needs to defend more energetically, although his shot-blocking skill is certainly a weapon.

Lest we forget, Bosh is only 21 and still learning on the job. While stardom appears in his future, expectations shouldn't be set too high for the coming season. Some want him to explode into a superstar right away, when in reality another step forward would be a very welcome development.

Donyell Marshall			power forward							**Age: 32**		**Height: 6-9**	**Weight: 230**
(82% PF, 17% SF, 1% C)												Most similar at age: Bill Laimbeer	

Year		G	M/G	FG%	FT%	P/40	R/40	A/40	TS%	Ast		TO		Usg		Reb		PER	
2002-03	Chi	78	30.5	.459	.756	17.5	11.8	2.3	51.3	36	10.6	37	10.5	24	19.6	21	16.2	9	18.44	11
2003-04	Chi-Tor	82	36.5	.461	.736	16.1	10.8	1.6	54.8	12	9.1	51	8.7	4	17.4	33	15.6	19	18.94	12
2004-05	Tor	65	25.3	.443	.791	18.2	10.4	2.0	59.1	4	9.4	35	5.6	2	17.4	34	14.7	23	19.92	9
2005-06	*PRJ (24.9)*			*.438*	*.760*	*15.4*	*10.2*	*1.8*	*54.4*		*9.6*		*7.9*		*16.6*		*14.4*		*17.67*	

Marshall has turned into an absolutely deadly shooter from the corners in recent seasons, which is how he's been able to increase his scoring rates and TS% in his early 30s. In a game against Philadelphia he tied an NBA record by hitting 12 three-pointers, nearly all of them coming from the corners. He's incredibly effective on side pick-and-roll plays, where he slides to the corner after setting the pick, because it's extremely hard for a help defender to rotate to him in time.

He was so good that is was troubling to see Araujo starting while Marshall spent half the game on the bench. Marshall had the highest PER on the team but played only 25 minutes per game, mainly because the Raptors wouldn't start him along-side Bosh. While the two hardly formed an imposing defensive combo, both are very good rebounders and can block shots. They wouldn't have been any worse than any other frontcourt combo the Raptors could have formed.

Considering he wasn't starting, here's my question: Why didn't he get any love for the Sixth Man award? While Marshall wasn't as sexy a pick as Ben Gordon, there's little doubt that he was a vastly more effective player. In addition to the high-percentage shooting and underappreciated rebounding, Marshall had one of the lowest Turnover Ratios in basketball. Although his defense isn't up to the level of many power forwards because he lacks strength and isn't a quick leaper, Marshall is still one of the 30 or so best forwards in basketball.

He's also now a Cavalier, after Cleveland beat out several teams for his services. His ability to stretch opposing defenses should be of great help to the shooting-starved Cavs, as will his ability to play both forward spots.

Lamond Murray				small forward									Age: 32		Height: 6-7		Weight: 235	
(84% SF, 9% PF, 7% SG)																Most similar at age: Chris Mills		
Year	G	M/G	FG%	FT%	P/40	R/40	A/40	TS%		Ast		TO		Usg		Reb		PER	
2002-03 Tor		Out for the season																
2003-04 Tor*	33	15.7	.353	.686	15.2	6.9	2.2	42.8	63	9.4	49	12.8	50	21.8	14	10.2	62	8.86	63
2004-05 Tor	62	14.8	.426	.763	16.1	7.1	2.0	53.7	21	9.7	52	12.1	47	17.6	35	10.1	16	13.68	33
2005-06 PRJ (38.7)			.394	.739	14.9	6.9	1.9	49.8		9.4		12.2		17.4		9.7		12.21	

* Season rankings are as power forward

Murray improved from his ghastly performance in 2003–04 and put up numbers more in line with his career norms. The problem is those numbers included the usual mail-in job on defense. Murray often gets caught snoozing on the weak side and is too stiff when guarding the ball, making him easy prey for opposing scorers.

Murray certainly can shoot the ball, however, and that kept him in the playing rotation for much of last season. He hit 44 percent on three-pointers and held his own on the boards. He also has enough elevation to hit mid-range jumpers with a hand in his face. Since the Raptors don't have much depth on the wings, Murray should again find some minutes, but he could end up being trade bait at the deadline because he's on the last year of his contract.

Milt Palacio				point guard									Age: 27		Height: 6-3		Weight: 210	
(75% PG, 25% SG)																Most similar at age: Bimbo Coles		
Year	G	M/G	FG%	FT%	P/40	R/40	A/40	TS%		Ast		TO		Usg		Reb		PER	
2002-03 Cle	80	24.7	.418	.747	8.0	4.8	5.2	46.6	52	31.7	13	16.0	59	14.3	64	6.7	18	8.24	61
2003-04 Tor	59	20.5	.349	.662	8.5	3.4	6.1	39.2	63	30.7	20	14.5	53	18.6	54	4.9	47	7.42	63
2004-05 Tor	80	19.2	.446	.742	12.2	3.5	7.3	50.7	41	33.1	9	12.3	49	19.8	52	4.9	47	12.45	46
2005-06 PRJ (32.6)			.414	.717	10.4	3.9	6.0	47.0		30.1		13.6		18.0		5.4		10.15	

Toronto's faster pace benefited Palacio as much as anybody. He's outstanding in transition but has no jump shot, so he struggles in halfcourt settings. With the faster pace, Palacio added nearly 100 percentage points to his field-goal percentage and improved his Assist and Turnover Ratios, making him a more credible option as a backup point guard.

In the open court, Palacio is especially tough when going to his right and has a habit of going right into the defender and getting himself to the line. He averaged .40 free-throw attempts per field-goal attempt, which is outstanding for a point guard, and that helped keep his TS% respectable despite his making only two three-pointers all season.

Also, Palacio was one of the Raptors' few quality defenders. He moves his feet well and at 6′3″ has good size for the position. However, he's an unrestricted free agent and will be playing the market after his relatively strong season in 2004–05.

Morris Peterson   shooting guard   **Age: 28**   **Height: 6-7**   **Weight: 215**
Defensive PER: 0.83 (64% SG, 34% SF, 2% PF)   Most similar at age: Sam Mack

Year		G	M/G	FG%	FT%	P/40	R/40	A/40	TS%		Ast		TO		Usg		Reb		PER	
2002-03	Tor*	82	36.0	.392	.789	15.6	4.9	2.6	48.8	46	12.6	41	8.5	8	19.4	24	7.0	51	12.63	34
2003-04	Tor	82	26.1	.405	.809	12.6	4.9	2.1	53.9	9	13.9	44	8.5	11	14.8	54	7.0	26	12.10	39
2004-05	Tor	82	30.6	.420	.832	16.4	5.4	2.7	54.3	21	12.8	44	7.7	10	18.0	40	7.7	18	14.43	25
2005-06	PRJ (59.0)			.408	.813	14.5	5.3	2.4	53.6		13.3		8.2		16.8		7.4		12.95	

* Season rankings are as small forward

The NBA doesn't keep official stats on this, but Peterson takes as many charges as any player in the league. It's one of the reasons he's been able to establish a niche as a defensive stopper on the wings. While he's hardly in the class of Bruce Bowen, Peterson certainly is in the upper tier of defenders at his position. He's also extremely durable—he hasn't missed a game in over three years and owns the league's longest current consecutive games streak at 278.

Offense is Peterson's undoing. He rushes too many long jumpers, especially early in the shot clock. That means that he tends to have low field-goal percentages even though he's a good shooter. He also performed terribly on the road. Peterson shot 46 percent and averaged 15 points per game at Air Canada Centre, but a meager 37 percent with 10 points on the road. The disparity was even worse in three-point percentage—his 46.3 percent at home dwarfed his 28.6 mark on the road.

Peterson moved into the starting lineup after the Carter trade and should be a fixture there this season. His defense makes him a worthwhile asset, but if he's going to be a quality starter, he needs to improve his shot selection and add more variety to his offensive game.

Jalen Rose   small forward   **Age: 32**   **Height: 6-8**   **Weight: 215**
Defensive PER: -0.23 (70% SF, 27% SG, 3% PF)   Most similar at age: Steve Smith

Year		G	M/G	FG%	FT%	P/40	R/40	A/40	TS%		Ast		TO		Usg		Reb		PER	
2002-03	Chi*	82	40.9	.406	.854	21.7	4.2	4.7	50.8	34	16.0	19	11.5	35	26.5	5	5.8	57	14.84	21
2003-04	Chi-Tor	66	37.9	.402	.810	16.4	4.3	5.3	48.5	44	20.7	15	13.1	56	24.2	10	6.1	42	12.57	36
2004-05	Tor	81	33.5	.455	.854	22.1	4.1	3.1	56.2	8	12.2	30	10.5	33	23.2	10	5.8	64	16.56	10
2005-06	PRJ (41.7)			.429	.850	19.8	4.2	3.9	53.0		15.3		11.6		23.4		5.8		14.65	

* Season rankings are as small forward

Rose had his best season in years and saved some of his best work for fourth quarters, earning the nickname "Captain Crunch" from Raptors fans. When Toronto needed a basket late in games, Mitchell usually diagrammed the plays for him. That makes sense looking at his stellar 22.1 points per 40 minutes and his TS%, which rocketed up to 56.2 percent last season.

Unfortunately for the Raptors, Rose in all likelihood will be coming back to earth this season. He's one of this season's Fluke Rule candidates (see the comment on Charlotte's Brevin Knight for the complete list), and as such can be expected to lose most of the gains from last season. He's extremely likely to revert to his past habit of scoring in the high teens per 40 minutes, with a mediocre TS%.

Those numbers would be easier to live with if Rose played much defense, but he's one of the worst defensive players in the league. Rose has the size to contest shots, but he doesn't move well laterally, isn't strong, and takes only marginal interest in the proceedings. He's being paid the maximum for two more seasons, however, so his spot in the lineup is secure as long as he isn't traded. That isn't likely, but not for lack of trying. The Raptors have been trying to unload Rose's contract almost since the day they acquired it, with little success.

It's intriguing to note, however, that Rose came off the bench for 16 games and played better than he did as a starter. While Rose raised a big stink about being a reserve, evidence suggests he could potentially be more useful as a scorer off the bench than he is in his current role as a starter.

Pape Sow   center   Age: 24   Height: 6-10   Weight: 250
(87% C, 13% PF)

Most similar at age: N/A

Year		G	M/G	FG%	FT%	P/40	R/40	A/40	TS%		Ast		TO		Usg		Reb		PER	
2004-05	Tor	27	9.4	.397	.593	9.7	8.9	0.3	44.4		1.5		12.2		11.6		13.7		7.63	

A second-round draft pick in 2004, Sow is an athletic big man with the potential to be a defensive force. Right now though he's more raw than a plate of sushi. Sow picked up the game at a late age and still hasn't mastered how to defend without fouling, averaging better than a foul every six minutes. He also hasn't figured out how to finish shots around the basket, and has no game whatsoever outside of five feet. Because he's so energetic and is still learning the Raptors will keep him around for another season, but considering he's already 24, this project needs to develop quickly.

Aaron Williams   center   Age: 34   Height: 6-9   Weight: 230
(77% C, 23% PF)

Most similar at age: N/A

Year		G	M/G	FG%	FT%	P/40	R/40	A/40	TS%		Ast		TO		Usg		Reb		PER	
2002-03	NJ	81	19.7	.453	.785	12.5	8.3	2.2	50.4	43	13.2	16	12.7	30	15.2	36	11.8	63	11.83	46
2003-04	NJ	72	18.6	.503	.677	13.4	8.8	2.4	54.9	15	14.0	11	15.3	61	15.7	22	12.5	58	13.20	40
2004-05	Tor	42	7.5	.460	.882	9.3	7.6	1.0	51.8		4.8		17.8		10.7		11.7		5.74	

The Raptors acquired Williams in the Vince Carter trade, but the last thing they needed was another power forward imitating a center. They had no place to play him, and Williams didn't exactly make a persuasive case for himself in his limited trials. Williams has one year left on his contract and the Raptors will probably look to package him in a trade to a team that's looking for cap relief. He's likely to have more value to Toronto in that scenario than he would on the court.

Alvin Williams   point guard   Age: 31   Height: 6-5   Weight: 195

Year		G	M/G	FG%	FT%	P/40	R/40	A/40	TS%		Ast		TO		Usg		Reb		PER	
2002-03	Tor	78	33.8	.438	.782	15.6	3.7	6.3	50.8	30	26.8	29	8.2	8	22.6	27	5.3	36	16.69	16
2003-04	Tor	56	30.9	.405	.776	11.4	3.5	5.2	46.3	53	26.8	39	9.3	11	18.8	52	5.0	41	11.34	53
2004-05	Tor		Out for the season																	

While Williams seems willing to try one more go-round on the court, he has chronic knee problems and may be forced to retire after having had three knee surgeries in the past 18 months. Unfortunately for Toronto, he signed a seven-year contract in 2001 with three years left on it. That means he's taking up a fair chunk of salary cap real estate while contributing nothing on the court. When healthy, Williams is a valuable performer because he defends well, can play both guard positions, and is a decent shooter. Therefore, the Raptors will be hoping he can pull a Kerry Kittles and make it back to the lineup.

Eric Williams   small forward   Age: 33   Height: 6-8   Weight: 220
(64% SG, 36% SF)

Most similar at age: Tony Campbell

Year		G	M/G	FG%	FT%	P/40	R/40	A/40	TS%		Ast		TO		Usg		Reb		PER	
2002-03	Bos	82	28.7	.442	.750	12.7	6.5	2.4	53.8	13	15.1	27	10.4	22	14.9	44	9.2	28	13.09	32
2003-04	Bos-Cle	71	26.6	.386	.760	15.1	6.1	2.5	49.3	42	12.9	34	9.5	13	18.2	28	8.6	33	12.42	38
2004-05	NJ-Tor	55	24.0	.430	.696	12.8	5.2	2.8	52.9	31	13.3	24	10.9	37	15.6	49	7.4	55	10.59	49
2005-06	*PRJ (30.8)*			*.402*	*.724*	*12.4*	*5.7*	*2.6*	*49.8*		*14.1*		*11.1*		*15.5*		*8.0*		*10.90*	

The third of Toronto's Williams contingent, Eric was traded at midseason for the second straight year, but this time he went from starting to the end of the bench. It was an odd turn of events for Williams because the Raptors were 10–8 with him as a starter, but he quickly faded out of the rotation as the year went on. The problem is that Williams replicates Peterson's role at the defensive end but isn't nearly the outside shooter that Peterson is. Also, Williams doesn't help out much on the glass, and since the Raptors were getting zilch from the center spot, they really needed the other four players to pitch in.

Williams has some skills, however, and if the Raptors don't trade him they should take better advantage of his ability to post up. Toronto had virtually no post offense in 2004–05, so utilizing William's talents could allow it to get more variety in the offensive attack. Certainly he's more valuable than Murray, so Mitchell should at least be able to find 10–15 minutes a night for Williams off the bench.

Loren Woods center **Age: 27** **Height: 7-1** **Weight: 260**
(100% C) Most similar at age: Vladimir Stepania

Year		G	M/G	FG%	FT%	P/40	R/40	A/40	TS%		Ast		TO		Usg		Reb		PER	
2002-03	Min	38	9.3	.382	.778	9.1	10.8	2.2	45.5		14.6		17.7		12.8		15.2		9.90	
2003-04	Mia	38	13.3	.458	.600	9.6	10.6	0.8	50.3	48	6.4	60	16.6	68	11.2	64	15.0	29	12.35	47
2004-05	Tor	45	15.8	.433	.576	9.9	12.4	1.0	46.3	63	4.5	50	15.2	46	12.1	51	18.9	7	11.30	45
2005-06	PRJ (32.9)			.444	.587	9.6	11.1	0.9	47.6		5.0		15.5		11.5		16.7		11.90	

Woods began the year as the starting center but was on the end of the bench by the time the season ended. At an athletic 7′1″, his talent for rebounding is undeniable, but the rest of his game has never come around. Woods has a very limited post game and his lack of strength and balance make it tough for him to finish shots around the basket despite his size. He also tends to fall asleep on defense and can't push bigger players out of the post, making him a mediocre defender despite his rebounding and shot-blocking abilities. Woods is under contract for this season at a very modest salary and could fill in as a backup center if his effort gets more consistent, but he has little to recommend him as a long-term solution.

Charlie Villanueva power forward **Age: 21** **Height: 6-11** **Weight: 240**

Before we completely condemn the Raptors for the Villanueva pick, let's discuss the positives. In college Villanueva averaged nearly a rebound every three minutes, even with another great rebounder on his own team, Josh Boone, stealing some away. He had a high rate of blocks, has a decent jump shot that seems to be improving, and he can really handle the ball for a 6′11″ guy. So why is everyone so down on him? The problem is that Villanueva seems to have inherited Derrick Coleman's head. Villanueva is a lazy defender and has a rep for having a bad attitude, and Toronto has enough players like that already.

Joey Graham small forward **Age: 23** **Height: 6-7** **Weight: 220**

Graham graded out as the best athlete in the draft, with incredible strength and good hops. I'm just wondering where that athleticism goes once the games start. Graham's rates of blocks, steals, and rebounds all were mediocre at best, and he averaged more turnovers than assists. He's a good defender and can hit the outside shot, but considering he's already 23, I'm not sure if he can be more than a reserve in the pros.

Roko Ukic point guard **Age: 21** **Height: 6-5** **Weight: 185**

A second-round pick by the Raptors, Ukic is 6′5″ but is a pure point guard. He's coming off a big year for KK Split in Croatia in which he averaged 18.5 points and nearly two steals a game. Unusually for a Euro, Ukic's weakness is a suspect jumper. He hit only 29.9 percent from the shorter European three-point distance last season, and 29.8 percent for his career in the Adriatic League. He also needs to add weight so he's not beaten up in the pros. Considering the work he needs to do, Ukic probably will stay overseas for another year or two.

Uros Slokar small forward **Age: 22** **Height: 6-10** **Weight: 238**
Translated 40-minute stats: 10.4 pts, 8.1 reb, 1.1 ast, .415 FG%, 10.31 PER

Slokar is a typical second-round pick: He's got decent size and is OK in some areas, but there's really nothing special here. Despite being slight of build, Slokar isn't afraid to stick his nose into the fray and gets his share of rebounds. He also has a decent jumper. If he can add 10 more pounds and extend the range to the three-point line, Toronto has a player, but for the time being Slokar should continue developing with his team in Italy.

Washington Wizards

It's always nice when you predict something and it actually comes true. In last year's book I projected Washington to post its highest win total in two decades, and they did just that. Washington's 45–37 mark was a 20-game improvement on the prior year, and they even won a round in the playoffs before flaming out against Miami in the second round.

The Wizards' improvement would have been much larger had they stayed healthy. Once again, their core group of three stars missed significant time with injuries. While the maladies weren't as chronic as in the Wizards' 25–57 debacle of the year before, Larry Hughes, Gilbert Arenas, and Antawn Jamison combined to miss 37 games. Additionally, several other key players spent significant time on the shelf. Jarvis Hayes was the key reserve on the wings before he missed the final 28 games with a knee injury, while it was a wasted year for the projected frontcourt of Etan Thomas and Kwame Brown. Thomas missed 35 games with an abdominal pull, while a sore foot cost Brown 40 contests. Both also struggled to get their timing back following the long layoffs and were markedly less effective than in 2003–04.

Overall, the Wizards lost 314 man-games to injury, narrowly missing New Orleans and Charlotte (315 apiece) for the league lead (although Indiana lost the most games when suspensions are included). Jamison hadn't missed a game in four years before joining the Wizards, but even he wasn't immune—a late-season battle with knee tendinitis sidelined him down the stretch. Washington's starting five of Arenas, Hughes, Jamison, Jared Jeffries, and Brendan Haywood played just 33 games together in the regular season. That Washington won 23 of them is a testament to how much talent is on the roster when everybody is healthy.

But if the Wizards were unlucky with respect to injuries, they certainly were fortunate in terms of wins and losses. Washington won 45 games despite giving up more points than it allowed. Based on its victory margin, the Wizards could have been expected to finish 40–42, which would have banished them to the lottery for another year. Washington made up the difference by getting unusually lucky in close

games. It led the league in wins by three points or less with 14, while losing only six of those contests. By going 14–6 in "50-50" games instead of a more normal 10–10, the Wizards posted a winning record despite a negative point differential.

Regardless of whether they had won 40 games or 45, it would have been an impressive improvement considering the Wizards won only 25 the year before. Two factors were the main difference: Jamison's arrival and the new hand-checking rules.

The more important factor was Jamison. Following the 2004 draft, Wizards general manager Ernie Grunfeld traded Jerry Stackhouse and Devin Harris, whom he had selected with the fifth overall pick, to Dallas for Jamison. Stackhouse was the incumbent starter at small forward but was playing out of position and had become hugely injury-prone, playing only 26 games the year before. Since Washington wasn't very deep (and still isn't), having a reliable starter was of paramount importance, and Jamison fit the bill. Furthermore, he was an upgrade in talent over Stackhouse. Jamison averaged 19.6 points per game and was slightly more active defensively than his predecessor (although this is like saying the Mojave desert is slightly wetter than the Sahara). More importantly, he played 68 games and stayed out there for 40 minutes in most of them, reducing the strain on the weak reserve unit.

The second major factor was the hand-checking rules. Arenas and Hughes are two of the quickest guards in the league, and they're exactly the kind of players who benefit greatly from the revised interpretation. With defenders unable to slow them down with a forearm on the way to the basket, both players repeatedly blazed to the rim and shattered their career highs in scoring. Arenas scored 25.5 points per game and made the All-Star team for the first time, while Hughes would have joined him had a broken wrist not kept him sidelined for the midseason soiree in Denver.

It wasn't just an increase in volume either. Both players improved their percentages significantly. The two guards each shot only 39 percent in 2003–04, which made it baffling that they shot so much. With the new rules, those numbers

> ## Wizards at a Glance
>
> **Record:** 45–37, 2nd place in Southeast Division
> **Offensive Efficiency:** 104.0 (11th)
> **Defensive Efficiency:** 104.2 (19th)
> **Pace Factor:** 95.8 (5th)
> **Top-Rated Player:** Larry Hughes (PER 21.63, 22nd overall)
> **Head Coach:** Eddie Jordan. One of the best in-game strategists but still has to improve the defense.

improved to 43 percent apiece. Plus, both saw massive spikes in free-throw attempts. Arenas and Hughes averaged .33 and .35 free throws per field goal attempt, respectively, in 2003–04. That shot up to .42 for both in 2004–05, a jump of nearly 20 percent apiece.

That trend echoed across Washington's other offensive stats. The Wizards were a horrible shooting team in 2003–04, ranking 27th in the league at 42.1 percent. Not surprisingly, they also ranked 27th in Offensive Efficiency. In 2004–05, the Wizards were still a pretty bad shooting team, finishing 23rd in field-goal percentage at .437. But because of the rules changes, Washington had a good offense despite the low-percentage shooting.

For a team to fare so well while shooting so poorly is a rarity, so let's take a closer look. Five factors determine the proficiency of an offense: field-goal percentage, three-pointers, offensive rebounding, turnovers, and free throws. Shooting percentage is easily the most important, followed by three-pointers. Every offense in the top dozen last season was well above average in at least one of those two categories . . . except the Wizards, who were bad at both.

In addition to the low field-goal percentage, Washington connected on only 34.6 percent of its three-pointers. They did manage to finish in the middle of the pack in total three-pointers, but Washington's overall shooting stats look more like a bottom 10 offense than a top 10 one.

Nevertheless, the Wizards were so good in the other three areas that they still managed to have a good offense. Let's start with turnovers. Washington led the league in 2003–04 with miscues on 17.6 percent of its possessions. The greatest sign of the growing maturity of the Hughes-Arenas backcourt is the extent to which they cut that number last season. Washington gave it away only 14.4 percent of the time in 2004–05, essentially earning the team three extra possessions a game.

Washington sparkled in the last two categories. The Wizards led the NBA in both free-throw attempts and offensive rebounds, two stats you'd normally associate with a behemoth front line like Miami's or Detroit's rather than a guard-oriented team like the Wizards. Yet sometimes truth is stranger than fiction, and here is an example. Because the guards constantly drove to the basket, rebounding lanes often opened up because the big men subsequently rotated to help.

Additionally, Washington's frontcourt was more than capable of taking advantage of the lanes, as athletic big men like Haywood, Jeffries, Jamison, and Etan Thomas eagerly cleaned up when Hughes or Arenas missed. (It must be said, however, that part of their motivation may have stemmed from the fact that this was the only way they would ever get the ball. Both guards could stand to share the wealth a little more when they head toward the rim.)

Even more shocking is all the free throws that resulted on those drives. Again, as a result of the new officiating standards, Arenas and Hughes could use their superior quickness to drive the lane at will, earning both players multiple attempts from the charity stripe. As an added bonus, many of the offensive boards by the big men also were converted into free-throw tries. All except Jamison averaged .4 free throws per field goal attempt or better.

Taken as a whole, those two enormous strengths allowed a team with poor outside shooting and horrible shot selection to emerge as one of the NBA's better offensive clubs, finishing 11th overall in Offensive Efficiency. Washington barely improved at all on defense, sliding up to 18th from 20th, but the offensive eruption was enough to nearly double its win total.

The bad news is that the Wizards will have some difficulty staying at that level. First, there's the so-called "Plexiglass Principle," which I introduced in the first edition of this book. The principle states that teams that improve by 15 or more games tend to lose some of those gains the following season. On average, such teams decline nearly four games in the standings, which would put Washington back to .500.

In addition, there's a major reason to think Washington might fare even worse: Hughes's departure as a free agent. A huge offer from Cleveland put the Wizards in a tight spot, because as good as Hughes was a year ago, it's questionable whether he's worth $60 million over five years. His departure left a crater-sized hole to fill in the backcourt, as Juan Dixon and Steve Blake also bolted as free agents and the Wizards weren't deep to begin with.

General manager Ernie Grunfeld found a replacement for Hughes and unloaded a problem child in one stroke when he completed a sign-and-trade deal that sent Kwame Brown and Laron Profit to the Lakers for Caron Butler and Chucky Atkins. Butler is a bit of a stretch as a shooting guard, but the Wizards were able to get a replacement without using their cap exceptions. That freed up money for Washington to sign the hyper-efficient Antonio Daniels, who can play both guard spots and will probably start, pushing Butler to small forward and Jamison to power forward. Atkins is an aging relic but should be able to handle the backup point guard spot, filling the void created by Blake's free agency. Brown, a former No. 1 overall pick, had finally worn out his welcome by staging a sick-out in the playoff series against Chicago. Grunfeld has to be laughing himself to sleep at night since he obtained two usable players in return.

Hughes's departure was a downer, but in the long term, this still should be one of the East's up-and-coming teams if the management doesn't screw it up. Every key player is on the good side of 30 and many are still improving rapidly. Arenas, for instance, is a mere pup at 23 yet is already among the best point guards in the game. Several secondary players also could show rapid improvement. Jarvis Hayes and Jeffries are both 24 and haven't lived up to their billing as first-round picks yet, but both showed enough last season to suggest they could turn the corner soon. Then there is Peter John Ramos, last year's second-round draft choice. The 7'3" Puerto Rican barely played, but he turns 20 this season and could help fill out the frontcourt. As an added plus, the cap situation is under control so the Wizards should be able to build on this base in coming seasons.

Fortunately, regardless of what Washington does it will have one of the game's better strategists at the helm. Eddie Jordan proved masterful at changing defenses to foul up opponents, helping to mask some of the weaknesses in a porous defense. That's his biggest challenge for the coming season. Young players often struggle to grasp defense, so it's not surprising that a roster with Washington's youth would

come around slowly in this department. But Jordan needs to demand more effort and less gambling, and he has to identify a defensive stopper. The two best ones right now are Jeffries and Hayes, but it is more a case of them looking good compared to their teammates than being exceptional defenders. Butler may be able to fill the void, too, although he didn't put too much effort into it as a Laker.

Overall, the Wizards should again be one of the league's better offensive teams, and one has to think the wave of injuries of the past two seasons will draw to a close sometime soon. They're a long way from challenging the Miamis and Detroits of the world, but with so much young talent and, for the first time in memory, a competent front office, the Wizards should remain playoff contenders for the foreseeable future even without Hughes. Fans have waited a quarter century for D.C. to have a quality team, but that wait is now over.

Gilbert Arenas					point guard							Age: 23		Height: 6-3		Weight: 191	
Defensive PER: 0.67 (88% PG, 12% SG)														Most similar at age: Steve Francis			
Year		G	M/G	FG%	FT%	P/40	R/40	A/40	TS%		Ast		TO		Usg		Reb	PER
2002-03	GS	82	35.0	.431	.791	20.9	5.4	7.2	54.0	15	23.5	51	13.2	50	26.8	7	7.2 10	18.53 9
2003-04	Was	55	37.6	.392	.748	20.9	4.9	5.3	51.2	23	17.7	61	14.5	55	26.5	5	6.9 10	15.88 21
2004-05	Was	80	40.9	.431	.814	24.9	4.6	5.0	56.5	8	16.7	65	9.8	20	27.3	8	6.5 16	21.29 4
2005-06	PRJ (33.4)			.423	.796	23.4	4.8	5.4	55.5		17.9		11.0		27.1		6.7	19.77

Arenas stayed injury free and enjoyed his best season as a pro, posting insane scoring numbers for a point guard while engineering a drastic reduction in turnovers. Obviously, the new rules against hand-checking were a huge help, as it made it virtually impossible for defenders to stay in front of him. Also, Arenas showed far better judgment on his forays to the basket, which helped slash the turnover total.

He still has a lot of work to do as a passer, however. Because Arenas is the top scorer and goes to the basket so much, he should be generating several easy baskets per game for Washington's big men. Instead, Arenas's Assist Ratio was very nearly the worst at the point guard position. For a player who otherwise is All-Star caliber in every respect, this is a glaring weakness. It's the one thing that keeps him from being the best point guard in the game.

It's easy to forget because he's only been in the league for four seasons, but Arenas still is very young and learning how to play the point. He's never going to be John Stockton, but one hopes that with another year of seasoning he can start using his penetration skills to find shots for his teammates as well as he finds shots for himself.

One quirk of Arenas is his penchant for waiting until the very last second before he goes to the basket in end-of-quarter situations. A good example was Game 5 against Chicago in the playoffs when Arenas caught the ball near midcourt with five seconds left and took a couple of dribbles near midcourt before going to the basket. He released the shot just before the buzzer and swished it through to give Washington the key victory.

I saw Arenas do the same thing in the regular season—he waits and waits until you're practically screaming "Go!" at the TV. In one game, he waited until three seconds were left before he started his move, and he still got all the way to the basket for a lay-up. Only a player as outrageously quick as Arenas can get away with this tactic, but its strategic value is obvious: Arenas is able to create a shot for himself despite the limited time, and the opponent has no time to respond. One wonders if opponents will change their strategy this season by sending several defenders at Arenas, which would force him to give up the ball and, in all likelihood, run out the clock.

| Steve Blake
(100% PG) | | point guard | | | | | | | | Age: 25 | Height: 6-3 | Weight: 172
Most similar at age: Bryce Drew |

Year		G	M/G	FG%	FT%	P/40	R/40	A/40	TS%		Ast		TO		Usg		Reb		PER	
2003-04	Was	75	18.5	.386	.821	12.8	3.4	6.0	50.9	30	27.0	37	16.5	61	19.3	45	4.7	51	10.92	57
2004-05	Was	44	14.7	.328	.805	11.8	4.4	4.3	46.8	58	20.3	59	12.5	53	17.2	66	6.2	23	8.36	68
2005-06	PRJ (34.2)			.375	.811	12.9	3.8	5.3	50.4		24.0		14.4		18.6		5.3		10.77	

Looks like a point guard, smells like a point guard . . . but is he really a point guard? Blake is the prototypical pure point guard in the eyes of most because he can handle the ball and looks to pass first, but there's one problem with that train of thought: Both his assist and turnover rates are terrible.

Perhaps that shouldn't surprise us since Blake constantly tries to set up plays from too far out on the court due to his inability to break down the defense off the dribble. Blake isn't a capable penetrator for two reasons. First, he doesn't have a great first step so it's hard for him to get past his man. Second, he's so scrawny that even when he gets a step he can't take a bump in traffic. Additionally, he's not a threat to score once he puts it on the floor, shooting a horrendous 27 percent from *inside* the arc last season.

Blake does have a few assets. He moves his feet well on defense and rebounds surprisingly well. Of course, that isn't going to matter if he doesn't start hitting shots and sharply reducing his turnovers. He's a free agent and supposedly has generated some interest, although I can't imagine why. Even in the best-case scenario, he's nothing more than a stopgap backup point guard.

| Damone Brown
(62% SF, 38% PF) | | small forward | | | | | | | | Age: 26 | Height: 6-8 | Weight: 202
Most similar at age: N/A |

Year		G	M/G	FG%	FT%	P/40	R/40	A/40	TS%	Ast	TO	Usg	Reb	PER
2002-03	Den	8	23.3	.300	.714	9.9	5.6	1.7	34.8	9.5	11.9	16.7	8.1	2.54
2003-04	NJ	3	5.7	.100	.500	7.1	11.8	0.0	13.8	0.0	8.4	26.6	16.7	-4.41
2004-05	Was	14	10.9	.371	.444	14.2	7.4	3.7	40.9	14.7	15.8	21.8	11.4	7.32

Signed as roster filler at the end of the year, Brown did nothing in his limited trial to suggest he can remain in the league on a permanent basis. Granted, he's managed to spend parts of three seasons in the league, but don't bet on him making it four.

| Kwame Brown
(80% PF, 19% C, 1% SF) | | power forward | | | | | | | | Age: 23 | Height: 6-11 | Weight: 248
Most similar at age: Donald Hodge |

Year		G	M/G	FG%	FT%	P/40	R/40	A/40	TS%		Ast		TO		Usg		Reb		PER	
2002-03	Was	80	22.2	.446	.668	13.4	9.6	1.3	49.6	48	7.6	46	14.4	45	16.1	26	14.2	40	13.65	38
2003-04	Was	74	30.2	.489	.683	14.4	9.8	2.0	54.7	16	11.3	21	14.2	51	15.6	25	13.8	43	15.74	20
2004-05	Was	42	21.6	.460	.574	12.9	9.1	1.7	49.7	54	8.2	20	16.8	64	15.2	30	12.8	54	10.34	57
2005-06	PRJ (42.3)			.476	.637	14.1	8.9	2.3	52.1		11.7		14.6		16.4		12.4		13.83	

2004–05 pretty much cemented Brown's status as one of the colossal busts in NBA draft history. The first overall pick in 2001 actually showed some promise the previous season when he had career highs across the board and looked poised to be the Wizards' starting power forward for the next decade or so.

Unfortunately, Brown had several setbacks this past season. He hurt his foot before the season and struggled to get his timing back upon returning. Making matters worse, his attitude soured when he failed to regain the starting job he owned a year earlier. Things degenerated to the point that the Wizards suspended Brown for the playoffs after he played hooky from a game early in the Chicago series.

Brown still has enviable physical skills, although he's not the kind of explosive force one might expect for somebody so highly touted. Still, his assets don't seem obviously inferior to those of Jermaine O'Neal. The problem is his poor work ethic and nonexistent motor. Brown has made precious little improvement in his low-post game and still falls asleep on defense several times a game, both signs that he's not devoting much energy to his craft. Additionally, his substandard rebounding is hard to explain. Brown had one of the worst Rebound Rates among power forwards last season, and his rate has declined each of the past two seasons.

The Wizards sent Brown to the Lakers in a sign-and-trade after the season, and that may be the best outcome for all parties. Brown clearly needs a fresh start, someplace where the home crowd won't boo him and the expectations of being a No.1 overall pick will be forgotten. It would be nice to see him in a smaller market with lower expectations, but his merely leaving Washington may be what he needs to finally get some production from his talents. All in all, the coming season may be the most important of his young career.

Juan Dixon																			
shooting guard										**Age: 27**		**Height: 6-3**		**Weight: 164**					
(66% SG, 33% PG, 1% SF)														Most similar at age: Vonteego Cummings					
Year		**G**	**M/G**	**FG%**	**FT%**	**P/40**	**R/40**	**A/40**	**TS%**		**Ast**		**TO**		**Usg**		**Reb**		**PER**	
2002-03	Was	42	15.4	.384	.804	16.7	4.5	2.5	46.4	47	10.7	53	11.3	38	22.0	17	6.6	35	10.97	39
2003-04	Was	71	20.8	.388	.799	18.0	4.0	3.7	47.6	51	14.6	41	11.1	35	23.0	14	5.6	49	13.48	29
2004-05	Was	63	16.7	.416	.897	19.2	4.5	4.2	51.8	38	16.6	24	10.2	31	23.0	13	6.3	39	15.23	15
2005-06 PRJ (50.6)				*.390*	*.849*	*17.6*	*4.0*	*4.2*	*48.6*		*16.4*		*11.0*		*22.9*		*5.6*		*13.59*	

Dixon had the best year of his career, and it would have been even better had he figured out the three-point line. He must have set the unofficial record for most shots taken with one foot hanging over the three-point line, with more 22-foot two-pointers than any player I can remember. Nearly every player who relies on outside shooting quickly develops a sixth sense for where the line is, but Dixon seems to be one of the rare few who doesn't have a map of the court hardwired into his brain.

Dixon needs that extra point whenever he can get it, because he's a career 30.8 percent shooter on three-pointers. He at least improved his TS% last season by upping that mark to 32.7 percent and shooting an impressive 89.7 percent from the line. Dixon also played much less selfishly than he had the previous season, and he improved his dribbling enough that the Wizards were able to use him as the backup point guard.

Dixon's best asset may be his defense. With the rule changes giving quicker players an advantage, he proved more valuable than ever because of his ability to keep quicker guards in front of him. Dixon is one of the lightest players in the league so he's dead meat against post players, but he was Washington's best perimeter defender last season.

His timing couldn't have been better. Prior to last season, the Wizards decided not to pick up Dixon's option for 2005–06, so he became an unrestricted free agent. Dixon parlayed that into a three-year deal with Portland, where he should be able to establish a niche on a team that is desperately short of shooting.

Jarvis Hayes																			
small forward										**Age: 24**		**Height: 6-7**		**Weight: 220**					
(74% SF, 23% SG, 2% PF)														Most similar at age: Ed O'Bannon					
Year		**G**	**M/G**	**FG%**	**FT%**	**P/40**	**R/40**	**A/40**	**TS%**		**Ast**		**TO**		**Usg**		**Reb**		**PER**	
2003-04	Was	70	29.2	.400	.786	13.2	5.2	2.1	45.6	55	11.1	39	11.5	37	16.8	38	7.2	45	9.40	52
2004-05	Was	54	28.9	.389	.839	14.2	5.8	2.3	47.5	56	11.0	38	8.4	15	17.3	38	8.2	37	11.07	45
2005-06 PRJ (51.1)				*.402*	*.833*	*14.0*	*5.5*	*2.4*	*48.3*		*12.0*		*9.5*		*17.1*		*7.7*		*11.15*	

Hayes might be the new Ron Mercer. He looks good when you watch him, but when you look at the numbers afterward you realize he probably did more harm than good. As with Mercer, Hayes's problem is that he's fallen in love with his jump shot. That works if you're a *great* shooter—somebody like Reggie Miller or Steve Kerr—but if you're just a *good* shooter, you need to find other ways to score too. Hayes constantly takes long jumpers off the dribble instead of going to the basket, which translates into a low shooting percentage and very few free throws. Add it all up, and he's a good shooter with a terrible True Shooting Percentage. So what's the point of having him on the floor?

Hayes is a capable defensive player, often playing the point at that end when the Wizards turned to trapping defenses. He's also fairly strong and holds his own in matchups against most small forwards. Still, he received unusually large dollops of playing time for somebody whose overall effectiveness was so minimal, and he might see his minutes sharply cut if he can't figure out a way to get himself some easy points between all the jump shots.

Brendan Haywood center **Age: 26** **Height: 7-0** **Weight: 268**
Defensive PER: 2.76 (100% C) Most similar at age: Kelvin Cato

Year		G	M/G	FG%	FT%	P/40	R/40	A/40	TS%		Ast		TO		Usg		Reb		PER	
2002-03	Was	81	23.8	.510	.633	10.4	8.4	0.6	56.1	12	5.4	65	12.0	23	10.7	64	12.4	55	13.54	39
2003-04	Was	77	19.3	.515	.585	14.5	10.4	1.2	54.7	17	7.0	54	13.0	36	14.7	35	14.6	32	17.24	9
2004-05	Was	68	27.4	.560	.609	13.7	10.0	1.2	58.8	11	5.8	42	13.8	41	13.2	47	14.0	42	16.52	16
2005-06	PRJ (36.8)			.522	.610	12.8	9.6	1.3	55.6		7.3		13.2		13.2		13.6		15.79	

Ernie Grunfeld signed Haywood to a five-year, $25 million extension before last season started, and right now that's looking like a whale of a deal for Washington. Jordan finally permitted Haywood to stay on the court for more than a few minutes at a time, and he responded with another strong campaign in the middle. Haywood has always been a high-percentage shooter but he took it another step forward last season, shooting 56.0 percent on a series of short hook shots and dunks. While the Wizards don't call many plays for him in the post, his footwork has improved considerably and Jordan might consider running more plays for him next season (if he can pry the ball away from Arenas and Jamison, that is). Haywood also has developed a more reliable way to get the ball—he's an excellent offensive rebounder who grabbed 12.2 percent of his teammates' misses.

Offensively, the next step is to work on his free-throw shooting. Haywood takes better than one free throw for every two field-goal attempts because most of his attempts are around the basket. If he improved to 70 percent or so from the line, it would add half a point per game to his average.

Also, Haywood is hugely important at the defensive end. He was Washington's best shot-blocker, averaging nearly two a game and altering many more. Plus, his size was a major asset in the middle—he's three inches taller than Ruffin or Thomas, the primary backups, so Washington deeply felt his absence when he checked out. Defensively, the Wizards gave up 9.9 points less per 48 minutes when Haywood played.

Another area for improvement is Haywood's work on the defensive glass. He sometimes takes himself out of position by going for blocks and doesn't have the lateral movement of some of the game's top-notch rebounders. Nonetheless, it's mystifying that such a good offensive rebounder can be so innocuous at the defensive end. Haywood's 15.8 percent defensive Rebound Rate barely exceeded his offensive rebounding output—for most players the rate nearly doubles. His inability to clean the glass resulted in the Wizards ranking among the league's worst teams overall on the defensive boards.

Larry Hughes shooting guard **Age: 26** **Height: 6-5** **Weight: 184**
Defensive PER: 1.36 (83% SG, 15% SF, 2% PG) Most similar at age: Ron Harper

Year		G	M/G	FG%	FT%	P/40	R/40	A/40	TS%		Ast		TO		Usg		Reb		PER	
2002-03	Was*	67	31.9	.467	.731	16.0	5.8	3.8	52.1	24	17.6	61	11.7	37	20.7	40	8.5	4	15.48	20
2003-04	Was	61	33.8	.397	.797	22.3	6.3	2.9	49.6	38	10.2	57	10.4	29	25.7	6	8.9	9	17.53	9
2004-05	Was	61	38.7	.430	.777	22.8	6.5	4.8	52.3	31	16.5	22	8.9	18	26.8	5	9.1	8	21.63	4
2004-05	PRJ (41.3)			.424	.769	21.4	6.4	4.1	51.5		14.7		9.9		25.3		8.9		18.91	

* Season rankings are as point guard

Hughes officially shed his "underrated" label last season to become a full-blown star to the tune of $60 million when Cleveland came calling in the offseason. Like Arenas, Hughes benefited greatly from the rules changes that favored quick players like him. He also cut his Turnover Ratio and was much more willing to share the ball, improving his Assist Ratio by over 60 percent. Combining those two factors enabled him to score at the same rate as he had the year before while costing the Wizards far fewer possessions in doing so. In addition, Hughes is an extremely effective rebounder from either guard spot.

Hughes can drive with either hand but prefers to pull up for the jumper when going left while he'll take it all the way to the rim from the right. He also has a slow-motion shot fake that he frequently uses to draw fouls—which he did in spades. In fact, it was the free throw that enabled him to be an effective scorer despite a poor shooting percentage and relatively few three-pointers. Hughes remains an erratic jump shooter but that didn't stop him from taking 3.4 three-pointers per game last season, hitting just 28.2 percent.

The three-point stats underline Hughes's greatest weakness—shot selection. Hughes frequently forced contested jumpers early in the shot clock, even though long-range shooting is his weakest area. It got so bad that Jordan had to bench him for most of the second half in a playoff game just so somebody else could touch the ball once in a while.

The other standout feature from Hughes's season was his defense. Out of the blue, Hughes had the league's highest steals average in 10 years and easily led the league. He was a big reason Washington was one of the league's best teams in forcing turnovers. However, that came at a price. Hughes often was beat on back-door cuts because he was trying to play the passing lanes and too often gave his man openings when he failed to get a steal. He was voted first-team All-Defense based on the steals, but that was an even bigger crock than Jamison's All-Star selection.

Although Cleveland may have overpaid, Hughes is a valuable player and should remain so for the next several seasons. Additionally, he and LeBron should be murder in transition and could even pair to form an oversized backcourt. The one concern for the Cavs is a worrying injury trend in recent seasons—Hughes has missed at least 15 games in three straight seasons.

Antawn Jamison   **power forward**   **Age: 29**   **Height: 6-9**   **Weight: 225**
Defensive PER: 0.60 (80% PF, 17% SF, 3% C)   Most similar at age: Ken Norman

Year		G	M/G	FG%	FT%	P/40	R/40	A/40	TS%		Ast		TO		Usg		Reb		PER	
2002-03	GS*	82	39.3	.470	.789	22.6	7.2	1.9	54.2	12	7.7	59	8.8	10	22.6	10	9.5	25	18.95	9
2003-04	Dal*	82	29.0	.535	.748	20.4	8.7	1.2	58.1	6	5.9	59	6.8	1	18.5	24	11.9	7	21.19	3
2004-05	Was	68	38.3	.437	.760	20.5	8.0	2.4	50.6	45	9.7	35	7.4	6	22.6	10	11.2	52	16.90	19
2005-06	*PRJ (43.3)*			*.453*	*.765*	*19.1*	*7.8*	*1.9*	*51.9*		*8.6*		*7.9*		*20.7*		*10.7*		*17.10*	

* Season rankings are as small forward

I talked in the introduction about the "New Guy" getting inordinate amounts of credit, and Jamison is another fine example. He was brought over from Dallas before the season and the Wizards won a lot more games this year, so people instinctively made the cause-and-effect connection that Jamison must be the reason. In a roundabout way you could argue he was—the Wizards went from awful to decent at his position—but that still wasn't any reason to put him on the All-Star team. Yet the same coaches who didn't consider him when he had a career year in Dallas in 2003–04 suddenly piled onto the Jamison bandwagon when he put up far inferior numbers as a Wizard last season. He essentially made the team ahead of Stephon Marbury, but it stretches the boundaries of reason to suggest that Jamison was a better player at any point last season.

Jamison's All-Star selection was especially baffling considering he still plays defense like his man is contagious. Jamison is especially deficient on the help side—much like Amtrak, he either arrives late or doesn't come at all. In late-game situations when the Wizards were on defense, Jordan would pull Jamison out and insert Ruffin in his place.

Despite those shortcomings, Jamison's scoring skills deserve acknowledgment. He has incredible hands and makes an amazing variety of short flips and runners around the basket. He's also a competent jump shooter who makes life miserable for bigger power forwards by running them around the perimeter. One thing he could add to the repertoire are some shot fakes to help him get to the line more, as Jamison was one of the few Wizards with a relatively low free-throw rate.

Jared Jeffries   **small forward**   **Age: 24**   **Height: 6-11**   **Weight: 230**
Defensive PER: 1.38 (76% SF, 23% PF, 1% C)   Most similar at age: J.R. Reid

Year		G	M/G	FG%	FT%	P/40	R/40	A/40	TS%		Ast		TO		Usg		Reb		PER	
2002-03	Was	20	14.6	.476	.552	10.9	8.0	2.2	52.1		14.2		18.6		14.0		11.8		11.09	
2003-04	Was*	82	23.3	.377	.614	9.7	8.9	1.9	42.6	64	12.5	29	14.4	60	13.7	56	12.4	42	8.68	64
2004-05	Was	77	26.1	.468	.584	10.4	7.5	3.0	51.3	42	14.3	13	14.7	58	13.6	57	10.5	11	11.16	44
2005-06	*PRJ (41.7)*			*.431*	*.585*	*10.3*	*7.7*	*2.9*	*47.8*		*14.7*		*14.9*		*13.9*		*10.8*		*10.61*	

* Season rankings are as power forward

Jeffries discovered a role in his third NBA season, taking over as the Wizards' perimeter defensive stopper. Because he's 6′11″ and has decent quickness, Jeffries proved a real headache for high-scoring small forwards. He also was among the Wizards' best help defenders, which is important on a team whose guards gamble so much.

The downside is that he's still a huge stretch as a starter because he's so ineffective on offense. Jeffries averaged only 10 points per 40 minutes and couldn't take advantage of all the easy opportunities that Hughes and Arenas gave him because he is such a terrible finisher. The Wizards can live with him scoring infrequently, but they need him to convert a higher percentage of his shots to justify his presence in the lineup. With the arrival of Butler and Daniels, Jeffries is likely to be pushed into a reserve role this year, and that usage is more consistent with his talents.

Anthony Peeler — shooting guard — Age: 36 Height: 6-4 Weight: 208
(77% SG, 18% SF, 4% PG)
Most similar at age: Steve Kerr

Year		G	M/G	FG%	FT%	P/40	R/40	A/40	TS%		Ast		TO		Usg		Reb		PER	
2002-03	Min	82	27.4	.415	.780	11.3	4.3	4.3	50.0	39	25.4	7	8.6	11	15.9	44	6.1	42	10.96	40
2003-04	Sac	75	18.5	.448	.836	12.4	4.4	3.5	57.5	2	21.0	14	13.5	59	14.5	55	6.5	34	11.79	41
2004-05	Was	40	13.2	.373	.889	11.6	4.9	4.3	48.4	49	20.5	10	11.5	44	16.5	46	6.9	28	10.23	47
2005-06	PRJ (30.5)			.404	.806	11.3	4.5	3.9	51.3		22.0		12.3		15.1		6.4		10.47	

Recruited for his three-point shooting, Peeler became unnecessary after Juan Dixon's emergence. Peeler led the NBA in three-point shooting in Sacramento at 48.2 percent, but it predictably declined to 38.5 percent—his career average—with the Wizards. That accounts for the main reason his PER dropped so much between the two seasons since Peeler remains a good ball-handler and rebounder for the position despite his advanced age. His role for the coming season isn't likely to change much, but he's good insurance if injuries hit key rotation players in the backcourt.

Laron Profit — small forward — Age: 28 Height: 6-4 Weight: 204
(65% SF, 26% SG, 7% PF, 2% PG)
Most similar at age: N/A

Year		G	M/G	FG%	FT%	P/40	R/40	A/40	TS%	Ast	TO	Usg	Reb	PER
2004-05	Was	42	10.2	.438	.640	12.7	7.1	3.5	48.9	16.5	13.3	16.8	10.0	11.45

Apparently worried that they didn't have enough undersized players from Maryland on the team, the Wizards added Profit to the roster in training camp and he hung on as an end-of-the-bench type all season. He was fairly effective in this role. Profit has decent quickness so he can handle his defensive responsibilities, and he rebounds very well for a perimeter player. He's a poor shooter, however, which limits the extent of his offensive contribution.

Last season was probably the high-water mark for Profit, but based on his performance he should be able to earn an NBA paycheck for another year or two. He was included as a throw-in to the Kwame Brown trade and may get some opportunities in a thin Laker backcourt.

Peter John Ramos — center — Age: 20 Height: 7-3 Weight: 275
(100% C)
Most similar at age: N/A

Year		G	M/G	FG%	FT%	P/40	R/40	A/40	TS%	Ast	TO	Usg	Reb	PER
2004-05	Was	6	3.3	.500	.500	22.0	8.0	0.0	50.6	0.0	21.6	23.1	12.4	7.94

The Puerto Rican project spent most of his first NBA season calmly taking in the proceedings from the end of the bench, so we know precious little about what he can deliver. Considering he's 7′3″ and showed some scoring aptitude in the Puerto Rican league, perhaps we'll see more of him this season.

Michael Ruffin — center — Age: 28 Height: 6-8 Weight: 246
(64% C, 36% PF)
Most similar at age: Bob Thornton

Year		G	M/G	FG%	FT%	P/40	R/40	A/40	TS%		Ast		TO		Usg		Reb		PER	
2003-04	Uta*	41	17.9	.325	.421	5.0	11.3	2.2	34.4	66	18.9	8	19.4	64	10.7	65	17.5	9	7.08	66
2004-05	Was	79	16.0	.414	.433	3.5	10.5	2.0	43.2	66	9.7	36	18.6	67	6.4	68	14.8	20	8.53	65
2004-05	PRJ (8.5)			.400	.396	4.0	9.9	2.4	40.4		13.1		19.7		7.5		14.5		7.98	

* Season rankings are as power forward

Ruffin is one of the most extreme players ever to take the floor in the NBA. Some players are poor scorers, but this guy is absolutely off the charts. Case in point: Ruffin's scoring rate of 3.5 points per 40 minutes is one of the worst in recent NBA history. It was so bad that the next worst player, Philadelphia's Aaron McKie, nearly doubled his output.

It's not just that Ruffin is a reluctant shooter either—he truly is a dreadful offensive player. He's had among the highest turnover rates in the league for two years running, and despite his infrequent shot attempts he manages to shoot a horrific percentage. This is extremely difficult to do. Most big men who rarely shoot get most of their attempts when opponents leave them wide open under the basket, thus enabling them to at least shoot a high percentage on their rare attempts. Ruffin somehow avoids getting those easy baskets, partly because he has bad hands and partly because he might be the worst finisher in basketball. Additionally, when he gets to the line he makes Shaquille O'Neal look like Reggie Miller.

Despite those weaknesses, Ruffin is marginally valuable because he's a good rebounder and plays solid defense. He also had a strong series against Chicago that may have upped his value in the free-agent market this summer. But let's be serious—Ruffin is so incredibly limited offensively that it's virtually impossible to pay him more than the minimum. Washington kept him in free agency, but thankfully they didn't pay much.

Etan Thomas (97% C, 3% PF)	center											Age: 27	Height: 6-9	Weight: 260 Most similar at age: Sean Rooks
Year		G	M/G	FG%	FT%	P/40	R/40	A/40	TS%		Ast	TO	Usg	Reb	PER
2002-03	Was*	38	13.5	.492	.638	14.2	12.9	0.2	55.0	10	1.5 61	16.4 59	14.4 43	19.0 2	15.82 24
2003-04	Was	79	24.1	.489	.647	14.8	11.1	1.4	53.8	22	8.1 44	13.5 43	15.6 24	15.6 18	16.39 14
2004-05	Was	47	20.8	.502	.528	13.6	10.0	0.8	52.1	38	3.9 58	12.9 33	14.2 36	14.1 40	12.92 39
2004-05	PRJ (40.5)			.486	.588	13.9	10.6	1.3	51.8		7.0	13.2	15.3	14.7	14.25

* Season rankings are as power forward

Thomas had a disappointing season on multiple levels. First, the injury bug that plagued his first three seasons came back, as he missed nearly half the season with an abdominal strain and re-injured it in the playoffs. Second, he wasn't nearly as effective as he had been the previous two seasons. Thomas saw less of the ball, was less active on the glass, and regressed significantly as a passer. The biggest change was in his Assist Ratio. Thomas had the worst rating in the league in 2002–03 before improving significantly in his first season under Jordan. All that went out the window last season, as his rate halved from the year before.

Overall, Thomas's declines were disappointing but hardly alarming. He still has the same basic subset of skills: He can hit a jump hook with either hand from the low post, is an effective offensive rebounder but less of a force on the defensive glass, and will block shots. Last season it just seemed his timing wasn't quite the same as he tried to come back from the injury. The Wizards should hope that was the problem since they have him under contract for five more years. Thomas has proven he can be one of the game's top backup centers if he can stay healthy, but he's only done that once in his five pro seasons.

Samaki Walker (56% PF, 40% C, 4% SF)	power forward											Age: 29	Height: 6-9	Weight: 260 Most similar at age: N/A
Year		G	M/G	FG%	FT%	P/40	R/40	A/40	TS%		Ast	TO	Usg	Reb	PER
2002-03	LAL	67	18.6	.420	.653	9.5	11.8	2.1	46.5	58	14.6 9	12.8 32	12.7 51	16.6 13	11.58 50
2003-04	Mia	33	12.7	.384	.659	10.0	10.7	0.6	44.4		4.3	10.8	12.7	15.1	10.39
2004-05	Was	14	9.6	.355	.667	7.2	5.4	1.2	37.1		5.7	18.1	11.3	8.3	2.97

Once again Walker found a situation where it seemed impossible for him to play his way out of the rotation, and somehow he found a way. Walker started slowly and ended up on the waiver wire when Ruffin took his job. He still has some promise as a rebounder off the bench, but in his last two stops he's shot 38 and 35 percent. Add in the fact that he's 29 and appears to be a serial underachiever, and not many teams are left that are willing to roll the dice—especially since he's already played for so many of them. Walker probably needs to earn a roster spot in training camp this year, and perhaps that will provide the kick in the pants he needs to get his career back on track.

Andray Blatche	power forward	Age: 19	Height: 6-11	Weight: 240

For the second straight year, Washington invested a second-round pick in a young-but-talented big man. Last year it was Peter John Ramos, this year it's Blatche. Blatche has a guard-in-a-center's-body mindset and seems to prefer playing on the perimeter to banging inside. If the Wizards can get him to develop a post game, they'll have a heck of a player.

Dallas Mavericks

For Mavericks fans, the news isn't nearly as bad as it sounds.

Dallas endured an uncomfortable year in 2004–05, as the team made a slew of personnel moves that mostly failed. It started with the decision not to match Phoenix's offer to free-agent guard Steve Nash, a move that blew up in the Mavs' faces spectacularly. Nash went on to have a career year and won the MVP award, while Dallas's offense wasn't its formerly magnificent self without its ringleader.

Then the Mavs turned around and used the money they didn't spend on Nash to acquire center Erick Dampier. Dampier was a Fluke Rule candidate in 2004–05 and he lived up to the Rule's prediction. His numbers bounced back to what he had done in 2002–03, leaving the Mavs overpaying for a slightly above-average center. To add insult to injury, Dampier proclaimed himself the league's second-best center (after Shaq) before the playoffs started, and then immediately was torched by Houston's Yao Ming in the first round.

Several other moves didn't work out. Dallas sent high-scoring forward Antawn Jamison to Washington in return for guards Devin Harris and Jerry Stackhouse. The jury is out on Harris, but Stackhouse was a downgrade from Jamison, the 2003–04 Sixth Man winner, and is less durable as well. Harris was announced as the team's starting point guard when the year began but quickly lost his position. In the long term, however, he could put this trade into the positive column for Dallas.

A pair of smaller-scale moves were disappointing. First, the Mavs sent disgruntled forward Danny Fortson to Seattle for center Calvin Booth. While Fortson was a pain in the butt, he could play. Booth can't and hardly left the Dallas bench. Then the Mavs pulled the trigger on a deal that sent guard Dan Dickau and a second-round pick to New Orleans for guard Darrell Armstrong. Armstrong was pretty much finished while Dickau became one of the league's most improved players.

Fortunately, two other deals worked out better, helping to salvage Dallas's season. First was the trade of Antoine Walker to Atlanta for Jason Terry and Alan Henderson, which accomplished two things. First, it got Walker off the team. He was a mismatch in Dallas from the get-go because a high-efficiency team like the Mavs didn't need a high-volume, low-efficiency gunner in its midst. Second, Terry saved the day when Harris proved unready and finished the year with a much higher PER than Walker. As an added bonus, Henderson proved more useful than expected off the bench.

But wait, there's more. Dallas made another strong move at the trade deadline by acquiring forward Keith Van Horn from Milwaukee while only giving up big man Calvin Booth. Van Horn's scoring provided a major boost off the bench, replacing the front-court production lost in the Jamison trade.

On balance, however, the off-season maneuvers set Dallas back substantially. As table 1 shows, Harris's position was the only spot where the Mavs made substantial improvement, and that was more because of the failures of Travis Best the previous season than anything Harris had done.

But here's the punchline: Even with their flubbed personnel moves, the Mavs won six more games than they had the previous season and nearly beat out champion San Antonio for the Southwest division crown.

The key was a radical improvement in Dallas's Defensive Efficiency. The Mavs had the best offensive team in history in 2003–04 but still won "just" 52 games because they ranked 26th in Defensive Efficiency. The 2004–05 Mavs were vastly improved defensively, ranking ninth overall. That improvement more than offset the points Dallas lost with the departures of Nash and Jamison.

Of particular note was the Mavs' ability to defend the three-point line. Dallas led the NBA in opponent three-point percentage at 33.0 percent, after ranking 25th a year earlier at 36.3 percent. Since their opponents tried over 16 trifectas a game, that difference alone saved the Mavs 1.45 points per game. Dallas's improvement against two-point shots was nearly as dramatic, improving from 28th to 7th, and that accounted for an even greater proportion of the Mavs'

Mavericks at a Glance

Record: 58–24, 2nd place in Southwest Division

Offensive Efficiency: 107.5 (5th)

Defensive Efficiency: 101.1 (9th)

Pace Factor: 94.9 (9th)

Top-Rated Player: Dirk Nowitzki (PER 26.18, 5th overall)

Head Coach: Avery Johnson. Emphasized defense and got results after he took over from Nelly.

Table 1. New Mavs vs. Old Mavs

2003–04	PER	2004–05	PER	Change
Nash	20.41	Terry	18.43	−1.98
Jamison	21.19	Stackhouse	15.90	−5.29
Walker	15.75	Dampier	15.21	−0.54
Best	10.10	Harris	14.70	+4.60
Najera	11.54	Henderson	12.40	+0.86
Fortson	16.00	Van Horn	15.66	−0.34
Delk	13.15	Armstrong	10.10	−3.05
Total	**15.45**		**14.63**	**−0.82**

improvement. Relative to the league, Dallas shaved its opponents' two-point output by 30 percentage points, saving 3.3 points per game.

Taken as a whole, the Mavs cut five points per game from their opponents' totals by making them miss more shots. Three people stand out as reasons why: (1) Dampier, (2) Josh Howard, and (3) Avery Johnson.

Dampier didn't impress statistically and he was hardly a dominant defender, but he gave the Mavs the bona fide center they had lacked. His presence also allowed Nowitzki to move to his natural power forward spot instead of getting killed in the middle, and meant the Mavs could spend most of the game in man-to-man instead of constantly tinkering with zones to hide their soft interior.

Howard took over a spot in the starting lineup and established himself as one of the league's best perimeter defenders in his second season, a category of player the Mavs hadn't possessed in the Nowitzki era. With Howard, Dallas could put somebody one-on-one against the league's top scorers without constantly double-teaming.

But the biggest factor may have been Johnson. He took over as head coach from Don Nelson late in the season, but had pinch-hit for Nelson on several occasions earlier in the year because of Nelson's health problems. While Nelly tended to focus on the offensive end, Johnson was much more adamant that Dallas commit to defense. His focus paid off. The Mavs went 25–6 in the 31 games Johnson was on the sideline, including 16–2 once he took the reigns for good. In those games, the Mavs held opponents to 42.7 percent shooting and gave up only 92.3 points per game—well below the season marks of 43.8 and 96.8, respectively.

Johnson will have to keep demanding that kind of attention at the defensive end, because the Mavs can't make their title hopes come to fruition just by scoring. Not that the Mavs will be starved for points. Their best player, Dirk Nowitzki, is one of the most efficient scorers in basketball. His combina-

tion of size and shooting skill is unmatched in NBA history, and if anything Dallas should get him the ball more this season.

Surrounding him are several other solid options. At the point, Terry is a high-percentage shooter who matched Nash in one category—they were the league's only two players to shoot 50 percent from the floor, 40 percent on three-pointers, and 80 percent from the line. On the wings are three athletic threats in Howard, Stackhouse, and Marquis Daniels. Though little-used, Daniels could be the best of the three, but he missed much of last season with ankle problems. Up front, Dampier doesn't offer much of a post game in the middle, but is a great offensive rebounder who can finish. Off the bench, Van Horn provided a shot in the arm with his deep shooting and also can fill in at small forward. Dallas occasionally played Van Horn and Nowitzki in the frontcourt together, and the combo proved unguardable for opposing big men. Finally, Harris should show improvement in his second season.

One name that doesn't figure in Dallas's plans is Michael Finley. The so-called "Allan Houston rule" in the new collective bargaining agreement allows teams to waive one player before the start of the season and avoid paying luxury tax on his contract. In the case of Finley, cutting him saved the Mavs about $50 million, and that's enough money that not even Mark Cuban can ignore it. Finley's departure left Daniels and Howard as the likely starters on the wings, a move that was overdue anyway. Dallas filled Finley's roster spot by signing Doug Christie to a low-risk deal in hopes he can provide a defensive presence off the bench.

Those luxury tax savings could encourage Cuban to spend somewhere else. Dallas needs a quality backup center, especially since Henderson's contract expired. The Mavs could turn to Pavel Podkolzin, their first-round pick in 2004, but the 7′5″ project showed little as a rookie. Shawn Bradley was another option, but he retired in the offseason. The Mavs signed Cavs bust DeSagana Diop to a three-year deal in the offseason, but he's unlikely to provide much help either.

If they can address that one shortcoming, Dallas has as good a case as anyone for being a championship team. The Mavs have fallen a bit under the radar the past two seasons, but considering they won 58 games, played much better at the end of the year, have an MVP candidate at forward, and perhaps the league's best bench, it's hard to fathom why. While San Antonio enters the season as the favorite to win the championship, Dallas will be lying in wait should the Spurs falter.

Tariq Abdul-Wahad — shooting guard — Age: 31 Height: 6-6 Weight: 235

Year		G	M/G	FG%	FT%	P/40	R/40	A/40	TS%	Ast	TO	Usg	Reb	PER
2002-03	Dal	14	14.6	.466	.500	11.2	7.8	4.1	47.0	23.7	7.9	16.2	10.8	12.61
2003-04	Dal	Did not play												
2004-05	Dal	Did not play												

Abdul-Wahad hasn't played in two years and probably won't play this year either because of chronic knee problems. Strangely, the Mavs haven't bought out his contract yet. He's still technically on the roster and his contract doesn't expire until 2007, but his only potential value is in evening out salaries in a trade.

Darrell Armstrong — point guard — Age: 37 Height: 6-1 Weight: 180
(78% PG, 22% SG)
Most similar at age: Derek Harper

Year		G	M/G	FG%	FT%	P/40	R/40	A/40	TS%		Ast		TO		Usg		Reb		PER	
2002-03	Orl	82	28.7	.409	.878	13.1	5.0	5.5	53.0	19	26.7	30	13.2	49	18.3	50	7.2	9	14.56	26
2003-04	NO	79	28.5	.395	.854	14.9	4.0	5.5	52.5	15	24.6	48	12.2	39	21.6	30	5.9	22	16.17	20
2004-05	NO-Dal	66	15.0	.321	.853	10.7	4.7	7.2	43.0	67	32.3	18	12.1	47	20.6	50	6.5	12	11.02	54
2005-06	PRJ (3.6)			.365	.872	11.7	4.2	6.2	48.4		29.3		13.0		19.3		6.0		13.42	

The Mavs picked up Armstrong just in time for him to start acting his age. Armstrong suddenly lost it in 2004–05, shooting a pathetic 32 percent from the floor but continuing to hoist three-pointers in spite of his wayward stroke. He shot 25 percent but took over a third of his shots behind the arc, continuing a terrible trend he started the year before in New Orleans.

Armstrong still can impact a game at the defensive end. He hustles like crazy and loves to pressure the ball, which reaped dividends in the Mavs' Game 7 win over Houston in the first round. He also rebounds well for his size and is a good free-throw shooter. Considering those attributes and the likelihood that his shooting should bounce back a little from last season's debacle, he should be able to find work this year as a backup point guard. It just won't be in Dallas, as the Mavs are set with Terry and Harris.

Shawn Bradley — center — Age: 33 Height: 7-6 Weight: 280
(100% C)
Most similar at age: Mark Eaton

Year		G	M/G	FG%	FT%	P/40	R/40	A/40	TS%		Ast		TO		Usg		Reb		PER	
2002-03	Dal	81	21.4	.536	.806	12.5	11.0	1.2	60.1	4	9.4	34	11.7	19	12.0	55	15.1	27	18.39	6
2003-04	Dal	66	11.7	.473	.837	11.3	9.0	1.0	52.3	33	8.1	45	6.9	1	11.8	59	12.2	61	15.68	21
2004-05	Dal	77	11.5	.452	.683	9.5	9.7	0.7	49.4	52	3.2	64	12.6	24	10.6	59	13.5	45	10.94	48
2005-06	PRJ (0.8)			.534	.718	10.0	9.7	1.1	57.7		7.8		13.4		10.4		14.0		14.35	

Bradley retired after the season due to a series of knee and hip problems that had radically diminished his effectiveness. Bradley retires as one of the best per-minute shot-blockers in league history, but unfortunately he was never able to live up to his selection as the No. 2 overall pick in 1993. His retirement could save the Mavs cap money if a doctor determines his injuries are career-ending (Bradley had three years left on his contract), but that would only matter if Dallas was under the cap, and that's never going to happen as long as Cuban is the owner.

Erick Dampier — center — Age: 30 Height: 6-11 Weight: 265
(100% C)
Most similar at age: Will Perdue

Year		G	M/G	FG%	FT%	P/40	R/40	A/40	TS%		Ast		TO		Usg		Reb		PER	
2002-03	GS	82	24.1	.496	.698	13.6	11.0	1.2	54.3	20	7.3	51	14.2	44	13.9	43	14.6	35	15.81	15
2003-04	GS	74	32.5	.535	.654	15.2	14.8	1.0	57.3	8	6.1	62	13.3	40	15.1	31	21.4	2	20.16	6
2004-05	Dal	59	27.3	.550	.605	13.5	12.5	1.3	58.0	15	6.0	39	16.4	59	13.5	40	17.4	14	15.21	26
2005-06	PRJ (26.8)			.517	.652	13.7	12.8	1.2	55.6		6.5		14.6		14.3		18.1		16.96	

A year ago I mentioned that Dampier was an example of a "Golden Fluke" because he had become the first person to have consecutive Fluke Rule seasons (see Brevin Knight comment in Charlotte chapter). I stand corrected. Dampier's birth date

(continued next page)

Erick Dampier (continued)

had been reported as a year earlier than it really was, so the league listed him as a 28-year-old in 2002–03 when he was really 27. Since the Fluke Rule applies only to players who are 28 or older, that makes a big difference.

But Dampier still was a Fluke Rule player in 2003–04, and his decline to his 2002–03 levels last season was entirely predictable. Dampier's amazing Rebound Rate looked particularly flukish and sank to a level more in line with his career norms. He's a fine rebounder though, and he generates offense by converting a high percentage of those boards into dunks and tip-ins. Oddly, Dampier is able to rebound well despite amazingly bad hands, and those hands are the cause of his high Turnover Ratio. He also tends to head straight for the boards and have his back turned to passes coming his way.

As a post player, Dampier isn't as much of a weapon. He can hit short hook shots near the basket and take advantage of glaring size disparities, but he has trouble with double-teams and doesn't spot the open man well.

Dampier's main impact comes on defense. While his effort level still comes and goes, he's the first player the Mavs have had in years who was both big enough to defend the post and athletic enough to block shots. The Mavs overpaid to get him, but he should continue to be an effective center for several more years.

Marquis Daniels			shooting guard										**Age: 24**	**Height: 6-6**	**Weight: 200**
(81% SG, 11% PG, 8% SF)														Most similar at age: Larry Hughes	
Year		G	M/G	FG%	FT%	P/40	R/40	A/40	TS%		Ast		TO		Usg		Reb		PER	
2003-04	Dal	56	18.5	.494	.769	18.4	5.6	4.5	53.6	14	19.2	19	7.3	5	21.5	26	7.7	21	20.10	3
2004-05	Dal	60	23.5	.437	.737	15.4	6.1	3.6	48.4	49	16.5	26	11.1	43	20.0	27	8.6	11	14.62	23
2005-06	PRJ (46.4)			.442	.751	15.7	5.9	3.8	49.3		17.4		10.0		20.1		8.2		15.56	

One of the top rookies of 2003–04, Daniels badly sprained his ankle prior to the start of the 2004–05 season and never got untracked. As often happens, he tried to play before the ankle was completely healed and probably did more harm than good, necessitating a stint on the injured list. Right as the ankle healed, he missed more time with an appendectomy before he finally returned late in the season.

Daniels plays like a smaller version of former Mav Cedric Ceballos. He's an instinctive scorer who can get points without having plays run for him because he moves without the ball and scores in transition. Daniels also excels at posting up, is a solid mid-range shooter, and unlike Ceballos handles the ball extremely well. Daniels can play the point in a pinch because of his dribbling skills and feel for the game, although shooting guard is his natural spot. As an added plus, he rebounds well.

Daniels has two weaknesses: outside shooting and defense. He shot 20 percent on three-pointers last season and the lack of range on his jumper makes it too easy for slower defenders to lay off him and play for the drive. Perhaps more important is his defense. Daniels has quickness and size but is very soft and doesn't show great intensity at that end of the floor. If he is to inherit Michael Finley's starting job, Daniels will need to greatly improve in that department.

Michael Finley			shooting guard										**Age: 32**	**Height: 6-7**	**Weight: 225**
Defensive PER: 0.67 (51% SG, 47% SF, 2% PF)														Most similar at age: Glen Rice	
Year		G	M/G	FG%	FT%	P/40	R/40	A/40	TS%		Ast		TO		Usg		Reb		PER	
2002-03	Dal	69	38.3	.425	.861	20.2	6.1	3.1	51.4	26	12.7	44	7.1	8	22.9	13	8.4	10	17.55	13
2003-04	Dal	72	38.6	.443	.850	19.3	4.7	3.1	53.9	10	13.8	45	5.4	1	20.7	31	6.4	39	17.81	8
2004-05	Dal	64	36.8	.427	.831	17.0	4.4	2.9	51.9	36	13.7	38	5.0	2	19.3	34	6.2	43	14.34	26
2005-06	PRJ (34.8)			.426	.823	17.0	4.7	2.7	51.8		13.0		5.8		19.3		6.4		14.95	

Finley's energy waned noticeably last season, and as a result he had his worst season as a Maverick. For an obvious example, look at his free-throw attempts. Finley never has had a great FTA rate, but last season it dropped precipitously to just one for every seven field-goal attempts. That's how he ended up with a mediocre TS% despite hitting 40 percent on three-pointers for a second straight season.

Finley's defense also dropped off a bit. For years he's been the Mavs' perimeter stopper, but last season he handed that role off to Josh Howard. While Finley remains athletic enough to be a decent defender, he's no longer in the upper tier at his position. Similarly, his Rebound Rate has fallen off the past two seasons after several years near the top of the shooting guard heap.

Finley's best skill at this point is his ability to avoid turnovers. He's not a great dribbler, but fortunately he knows it and sticks mostly to catch-and-shoot situations or taking a single bounce to his left for a mid-range jumper. Those skills should make him a valuable sixth man wherever he signs this summer. But it seems his days as an All-Star are well behind him.

Devin Harris (100% PG)			point guard							Age: 22	Height: 6-3	Weight: 185 Most similar at age: Baron Davis		
Year	G	M/G	FG%	FT%	P/40	R/40	A/40	TS%		Ast	TO	Usg	Reb	PER
2004-05 Dal	76	15.4	.429	.757	14.9	3.5	5.8	53.0	23	25.5 45	12.4 50	20.4 48	4.9 49	14.70 32
2005-06 PRJ (22.9)			.430	.759	16.6	3.6	5.9	53.6		24.6	11.7	21.7	5.0	16.40

Harris's rookie season wasn't nearly the failure that some made it out to be. Don Nelson jumped the gun by making Harris the starter in training camp when he wasn't ready for the job, but by the end of the year Harris was a quietly effective reserve. And as the projections show, he figures to improve substantially in his second season.

Harris's biggest weakness was a propensity for turnovers. His Turnover Ratio was well below average and his consecutive miscues in a playoff game against Houston got him yanked in favor of Darrell Armstrong. He also needs to improve his three-point shot. Harris had a reputation as an outside shooter in college but in his first year with the longer line hit only 33 percent from downtown. Improving on that mark is important because he has enough scorers around him to get a lot of open shots from the perimeter.

Otherwise, Harris has most of the tools. He has good quickness, is a very strong driver going to his right, and fares well in the open court. He needs to see the floor better though, because too many of those right-handed drives led to shots instead of passes.

Defensively, Harris fared better. He had the second-best rate of steals per minute in the league, and he has enough size to distract shooters. While he could probably gamble a bit less and certainly needs to hit the weights, he has all the makings of a high-quality defender down the road. In the short-term, he'll again be learning his craft as Terry's caddy, but he'll eventually justify Nelson's faith in using him as a starter.

Alan Henderson (71% PF, 18% C, 11% SF)			power forward							Age: 33	Height: 6-9	Weight: 240 Most similar at age: Cadillac Anderson		
Year	G	M/G	FG%	FT%	P/40	R/40	A/40	TS%		Ast	TO	Usg	Reb	PER
2002-03 Atl*	82	18.2	.468	.638	10.5	10.7	1.1	50.8	36	8.4 42	12.5 25	12.0 54	15.2 24	12.11 45
2003-04 Atl	6	11.3	.476	.667	14.1	12.4	1.2	50.8		7.0	10.5	15.5	17.5	18.25
2004-05 Dal	78	15.4	.527	.539	9.1	11.6	0.7	53.9	29	3.3 69	15.1 64	9.5 69	16.2 15	12.40 52
2005-06 PRJ (32.1)			.490	.565	8.7	10.7	0.8	51.0		4.9	15.7	9.8	15.1	11.29

* Season rankings are as center

Henderson was both surprisingly healthy and effective for the Mavs, filling a void at backup power forward until the Van Horn trade and also pitching in at center. Henderson no longer has the versatility that made him the league's Most Improved Player when he was a Hawk, but he still can hit the glass. His Rebound Rate was his strongest skill and directly impacted his high shooting percentage, as Henderson got most of his points on put-backs.

Otherwise, he was about as integral to the offense as Del Harris's clipboard. Henderson had the lowest Usage Rate among power forwards as he never tried to create his own shot. Even when getting rid of the ball, Henderson is a liability. He's a terrible passer who had the worst Assist Ratio at his position and nearly the worst Turnover Ratio too.

At least Henderson could defend. His willingness to bang partly made up for his physical limitations and probably will earn him another contract this season, though perhaps not in Dallas. Entering last season, that seemed like a long shot.

Josh Howard   **small forward**   **Age: 25**   **Height: 6-7**   **Weight: 210**
Defensive PER: 1.70 (84% SF, 14% PF, 2% SG)   Most similar at age: Lamond Murray

Year		G	M/G	FG%	FT%	P/40	R/40	A/40	TS%		Ast		TO		Usg		Reb		PER	
2003-04	Dal	67	23.7	.430	.703	14.5	9.3	2.4	48.5	47	12.8	35	8.9	11	17.3	36	12.7	4	15.72	18
2004-05	Dal	76	32.2	.475	.733	15.7	7.9	1.8	53.5	28	8.5	58	10.8	36	16.8	42	11.1	8	15.80	16
2005-06	PRJ (56.9)			.459	.720	14.8	8.4	2.0	51.8		10.1		10.4		16.7		11.6		15.43	

Howard showed little statistical improvement between his first and second season, as his increased shooting accuracy was offset by a decline in rebounds and a flurry of turnovers. What those statistics don't show, however, was Howard's emergence as a defensive stopper.

Howard became one of the team's key players because of his ability to defend the opponents' top perimeter scorer every night. He posted one of the best Defensive PERs in the league because he has quick feet and very long arms, and he was versatile enough to be the Mavs' primary defender on Steve Nash in the playoffs. He also helps out on the defensive end with his outstanding Rebound Rate, although it dropped from his rookie year.

Offensively, Howard is a jack-of-all-trades, master-of-none type. He has three-point range but is far too willing to fire away, hitting only 29.6 percent last season. He also needs to see the floor better when he drives and for a small forward he was whistled for a startling number of illegal screens.

Nonetheless, he might be the Mavs' second-best player, and he's a bargain too. Howard costs the Mavs barely $1 million a year for the next two seasons before he's eligible for an extension, making it easier for Mark Cuban to swallow some of the other big contracts dotting his roster.

Didier Ilunga-Mbenga   **center**   **Age: 25**   **Height: 7-0**   **Weight: 245**
(75% C, 25% PF)   Most similar at age: N/A

Year		G	M/G	FG%	FT%	P/40	R/40	A/40	TS%	Ast	TO	Usg	Reb	PER
2004-05	Dal	15	3.9	.429	.750	10.3	5.5	0.0	47.6	0.0	24.1	0.0	7.7	3.65

The big man from the Congo is a prime candidate to get some time in the D-League this season. The Mavs signed him because he shows great promise as a shot-blocker, but he has very little game experience and needs to play every night. With a longer look, the Mavs will have a better idea of what to do with him when his contract expires after the season.

Dirk Nowitzki   **power forward**   **Age: 27**   **Height: 7-0**   **Weight: 245**
Defensive PER: 1.28 (66% PF, 34% C)   Most similar at age: Rasheed Wallace

Year		G	M/G	FG%	FT%	P/40	R/40	A/40	TS%		Ast		TO		Usg		Reb		PER	
2002-03	Dal	80	39.0	.463	.881	25.8	10.1	3.1	58.1	3	11.3	33	7.2	3	25.5	5	14.0	24	25.58	2
2003-04	Dal*	77	37.9	.462	.877	23.1	9.2	2.8	56.1	10	11.3	22	7.3	3	23.2	3	12.7	56	22.52	2
2004-05	Dal	78	38.7	.459	.869	26.9	10.0	3.2	57.8	9	11.0	21	8.1	10	26.7	5	14.0	27	26.18	3
2005-06	PRJ (24.6)			.458	.845	23.9	9.6	2.9	56.5		11.2		7.5		24.7		13.2		23.52	

* Season rankings are as center

Despite the departure of his playmaking partner, Nowitzki raised his game a notch last season to become a legitimate MVP candidate. He's always been a great offensive player, but defensively Nowitzki might have been the most improved player in the league. Critiqued in the past for a lack of toughness, Nowitzki dramatically increased his effort level and was much more willing to bang inside. He also added a great strip move on players posting him up and edged his blocks up to a career-best 1.5 per game. Overall, his Defensive PER was in the upper ranks of his position, which seemed unthinkable three years ago.

Offensively, Nowitzki remains a great shooter—he hit a career-high 39 percent on three-pointers—but he's diversified his arsenal considerably. These days he gets many of his points on the right block, where he likes to shoot a fadeaway going to his left. The result is that he's getting to the line much more often. Nowitzki's free-throw attempts per game jumped from 5.5 in 2003–04 to 9.1 last season, accounting for his improved TS%.

One area for improvement is his approach against smaller players. Nowitzki murders players of his own size because they can't stay with him on the perimeter, but he has trouble wriggling free against shorter, quicker players whom he should dominate on the blocks. With another offseason of weightlifting and practice, perhaps he'll be able to overcome that one lingering weakness in his increasingly spectacular play. If he does, the MVP trophy could be his reward.

Pavel Podkolzin   center   Age: 20   Height: 7-5   Weight: 260
(100% C)

Most similar at age: NA

Year		G	M/G	FG%	FT%	P/40	R/40	A/40	TS%		Ast		TO		Usg		Reb		PER
2004-05	Dal	5	2.0	—	.500	4.0	8.0	0.0	56.8		0.0		69.4		6.1		11.2		-12.67

The Mavs' first-round pick in 2004, the Siberian giant hardly played last season. The 7'5" Podkolzin is a work in progress who may not be ready for years, if ever, but he will benefit as much as anyone in basketball from the D-League. A lack of game experience is the biggest thing holding him back right now.

Jerry Stackhouse   shooting guard   Age: 31   Height: 6-6   Weight: 218
(70% SG, 28% SF, 1% PG, 1% PF)

Most similar at age: Latrell Sprewell

Year		G	M/G	FG%	FT%	P/40	R/40	A/40	TS%		Ast		TO		Usg		Reb		PER	
2002-03	Was	70	39.3	.409	.878	22.0	3.8	4.6	52.8	24	16.3	28	10.0	26	27.2	7	5.6	48	18.68	9
2003-04	Was*	26	29.8	.399	.806	18.7	4.9	5.3	49.4	40	18.5	9	15.8	58	25.1	6	6.8	52	13.13	34
2004-05	Dal	56	28.9	.414	.849	20.6	4.5	3.1	52.5	32	12.4	49	10.3	33	23.2	11	6.3	40	15.90	14
2005-06	*PRJ (44.7)*			.403	.846	19.3	4.3	3.7	51.6		14.7		11.0		23.6		6.0		15.20	

* Season rankings are as small forward

Stackhouse missed his usual 26 games, this time with a groin injury, but when he played he was among the best sixth men in the league. Stackhouse is a low-percentage shooter whose shot has virtually no arc, but his overall TS% remains solid because he's so good at getting to the foul line. He has a great first step, especially going to his right, that earned him over five free throws a game last season. Despite his low arc, he's a great foul shooter too.

    Scoring is pretty much his sole contribution, however. Stackhouse is a middling defender who is more explosive than laterally quick, and he's not a player who creates shots for others or provides much help on the glass. That's why he'll probably continue in the reserve role for another season while the more versatile Daniels takes a starting spot. Stackhouse's ability to create shots is very useful when paired with the rest of the second unit or any time Nowitzki is off the floor. But with the starting unit, he's just taking shots away from players who shoot a higher percentage.

Jason Terry   point guard   Age: 28   Height: 6-2   Weight: 180
Defensive PER: 1.05 (90% PG, 10% SG)

Most similar at age: Kenny Smith

Year		G	M/G	FG%	FT%	P/40	R/40	A/40	TS%		Ast		TO		Usg		Reb		PER	
2002-03	Atl	81	38.0	.428	.887	18.1	3.6	7.8	54.9	8	28.3	24	11.8	38	25.4	11	5.2	40	18.29	11
2003-04	Atl	81	37.3	.417	.827	18.0	4.5	5.8	51.9	17	22.1	53	11.6	35	24.0	17	6.3	19	16.22	18
2004-05	Dal	80	30.0	.501	.844	16.5	3.1	7.1	60.6	3	30.8	24	10.5	30	21.2	40	4.4	54	18.43	12
2005-06	*PRJ (53.6)*			.450	.839	16.7	3.7	6.5	55.8		26.8		10.8		22.6		5.2		16.73	

Despite getting booted out of the starting lineup at the start of the season, Terry bounced back to post his best PER as a pro. Among guards, only Steve Nash had a better field-goal percentage, and Terry's 60.6 TS% was outstanding. Terry also hit 40 percent from the three-point line and his quickness was an asset on defense, where he played much harder than he had in Atlanta. In particular, he was much more willing to pressure the ball up court, which he rarely did as a Hawk.

    Terry has been criticized throughout his career for not being a "pure" point guard, but his Assist and Turnover Ratios were perfectly respectable last season. He also made a good backcourt partner with Daniels, because he could play off the ball and come off screens for his deadly jump shot while Daniels played the point. If Daniels becomes the starter this year, that arrangement could prove highly beneficial to Terry.

    No matter who he partners with, he'll have to put together a big year because he's heading into free agency. Terry has established that he can shoot and he's one of the fastest players in the league, but some teams still have lingering doubts about his abilities at the point. If he can remove those concerns with another strong season, he could see a windfall in the tens of millions of dollars.

Keith Van Horn			power forward								Age: 30		Height: 6-10 Weight: 240	
(64% PF, 35% SF, 1% C)													Most similar at age: Sam Perkins	

Year		G	M/G	FG%	FT%	P/40	R/40	A/40	TS%		Ast		TO		Usg		Reb		PER	
2002-03	Phi	74	31.6	.482	.804	20.1	9.0	1.6	55.6	11	7.2	54	11.5	37	20.5	17	13.2	34	17.29	16
2003-04	NY-Mil*	72	32.5	.454	.859	19.9	8.6	2.1	56.4	8	9.1	53	12.8	51	20.6	18	12.5	5	17.77	11
2004-05	Mil-Dal	62	24.2	.456	.815	18.5	7.8	2.0	55.0	22	9.5	33	10.3	28	19.4	22	10.9	60	15.66	29
2005-06	PRJ (41.4)			.447	.805	18.4	8.4	2.0	53.8		9.2		11.2		19.8		11.9		15.48	

* Season rankings are as small forward

Acquired in a midseason trade with Milwaukee, Van Horn took his hair gel and knee-high socks to Dallas and provided instant offense off the bench. He was especially lethal in combination with Nowitzki in the frontcourt, since few opponents had two big men who could stay with that duo on the perimeter. Van Horn is a quality outside shooter whose three-point shot has become more consistent as he's gotten more experience and is now among the best big men in the game from out there. He also can shoot a turnaround hook shot in the post, although he usually only goes to that move when he's playing against small forwards.

Van Horn can put the ball on the floor, mostly going to his right, but often gets the ball stripped on his way up for the shot because he doesn't protect it well. He's also a poor passer who doesn't notice double teams, and the disintegration in his Rebound Rate last season is cause for concern.

Furthermore, Van Horn is a defensive liability because he's a tweener. He's not quite quick enough to guard most small forwards but not strong enough to deal with many power forwards. Now that he's playing off the bench though, he rarely has to guard a quality scorer for long and can concentrate on his own impressive offensive arsenal. If the shots are falling, it could end up earning him the Sixth Man award, which would give him a nice send-off into free agency.

Denver Nuggets

Never let them tell you that a coach can't make a difference. It certainly made a world of difference in Denver last season, where the Nuggets muddled along under two coaches before George Karl rode in to save the day. Denver finished the year 32–8 after Karl took over, the best record of all-time by a team that changed coaches at midseason. Although they were knocked out in the first round by eventual champion San Antonio, that hardly diminished the luster of the Nuggets' spectacular second half.

Denver's management helped create the need for Karl in the previous offseason, when it left head coach Jeff Bzdelik dangling by a thread. He was coaching on a lame-duck contract and had an assistant, Michael Cooper, whom the Nuggets were obviously grooming as his replacement. Not surprisingly, Bzdelik's message didn't resonate with the players since they knew management didn't have his back.

Things started on a hollow note when shooting guard Voshon Lenard was lost for the season on opening night with a torn Achilles, and then quickly degenerated from there. The Nuggets had the league's most stagnant halfcourt offense in 2003–04, and the loss of Lenard's outside shooting only made it worse. Denver had made up for this weakness the previous season by running at every opportunity, but their pace slackened quite a bit at the start of 2004–05. That put more pressure on a halfcourt offensive "attack" that consisted of four guys standing around waiting for Carmelo Anthony to frontrim a jump shot. Thus, despite decent offensive talent, the Nuggets were among the worst offensive teams in the league at midseason.

At that point, Denver decided to pull the plug on Bzdelik, which they should have done in the summer. Instead, all the Nuggets got from the lame-duck maneuver was a waste of half a season. In Bzdelik's place they hired Cooper, but that proved an even bigger fiasco. Cooper's game management skills were so bad that he lost management's trust. In one close game he essentially forgot to put Andre Miller back in during the fourth quarter, and in another he called timeout almost immediately before a scheduled commercial break. Within three weeks he was gone.

> **Nuggets at a Glance**
>
> **Record:** 49–33, 2nd place in Northwest Division
> **Offensive Efficiency:** 103.5 (13th)
> **Defensive Efficiency:** 100.8 (8th)
> **Pace Factor:** 95.8 (4th)
> **Top-Rated Player:** Marcus Camby (PER 18.08, 50th overall)
> **Head Coach:** George Karl. Team played remarkably well for him, but youngsters needn't apply.

With the team having one foot in the grave, the Nuggets pulled the trigger again and called in Karl. His impact was immediate. The halfcourt offense came to life as the Nuggets used more motion and—here's an idea—ran actual plays instead of staring at each other figuring out what to do for 23 seconds. He also managed to push Denver to a much faster pace, taking advantage of the mile-high altitude and the Nuggets' outstanding team speed. Denver's fast-break points increased by nearly a third (see table 1), and with the help of that approach, the Nuggets went 19–1 at home after Karl took over. Overall, the Nuggets led the NBA in fast-break points and ran away with the lead once Karl took over.

Surprisingly, the Nuggets also shot much better on three-pointers under Karl. The other offensive improvements can be traced to his system, because the Nuggets had a higher assist rate and radically increased their fast-break scoring, but the three-pointers were mostly luck. Four players—Anthony, Earl Boykins, Greg Buckner, and DerMarr Johnson—greatly outperformed their career norms under Karl, and that helped propel the offense to an extra two points a night.

Denver's defensive improvement shouldn't be overlooked either. Knowing the coach would be around for a while, the Nuggets gave a much better accounting of themselves defensively. During Karl's reign, they were the league's fourth-best defense. The catalyst was Marcus Camby who came back from his usual midseason injury in time to energize Denver's renaissance with his shot-blocking and rebounding. But other Nuggets, especially Anthony and Andre Miller, defended much better after the coaching change.

Hiring a guy like Karl has its drawbacks, however. He's a veteran's coach who has a terrible track record with younger players, and his grumpiness has been known to cause rifts with his players after two or three seasons. In this case though, the Nuggets took a reasonable gamble. With three first-round picks traded to New Jersey in the Kenyon Martin trade, Denver won't have much young talent coming through the pipeline for a while. With most of the key players in their primes, this team has been built to win right now.

Table 1. Nuggets Before and After Karl

	Before	After
W–L	17–25	32–8
Offensive Efficiency	100.0	107.1
Defensive Efficiency	103.0	98.4
2-point FG%	46.5	49.3
3-point FG%	31.1	37.1
Assists/FG	.627	66.3
Fast-break pts/game	16.5	22.1

Karl's track record with young players is bad mainly because of his reluctance to play them at all. He did good work with Anthony, who was too good to just shove to the end of the bench, but the other youngsters suffered. Rodney White's playing time immediately ceased, while DerMarr Johnson mysteriously ended up on the bench for most of the San Antonio series in favor of inferior but older players like Buckner and Bryon Russell. On that note, the Nuggets had two late first-round picks this season but used one on forward Linas Kleiza, who may be stashed in Europe. The other, Julius Hodge, could provide plenty of help as a reserve on the wings if Karl deigns to use him.

The addition of Hodge may help, but Denver needs to upgrade at shooting guard because Johnson and Buckner are free agents and Lenard may not be back to his former self. The Nuggets were looking at several free agents with their midlevel exception but hadn't made any additions at publication time.

Considering their blazing finish, one might expect the Nuggets to roll to 55 or 60 wins and make a push to join the Western Conference elite. I'm not so sure. The Nuggets have some barriers to reaching the promised land that may prevent them from exceeding last season's win total. The biggest is Camby, who played 66 games and considered it one of his healthiest seasons. The Nuggets' frontcourt isn't terribly deep, with Nenê being the only decent backup, so if Camby misses 30 or 40 games with his usual assortment of injuries, it could set Denver back quite a bit. Last season, for instance, the Nuggets were 43–23 when Camby played and just 6–10 when he didn't. Four of the eight losses under Karl came with Camby on the sideline.

Second, Denver has another lame-duck situation to deal with, and this time it's in the front office. General manager Kiki Vandeweghe is on the last year of his contract and it's widely assumed that he won't be invited back. Vandeweghe successfully rebuilt the franchise in less than three years by trading Antonio McDyess for both Camby and Nenê, signing Andre Miller and Earl Boykins, drafting Anthony, and adding Kenyon Martin. Yet he's been criticized heavily for passing on Amare Stoudemire twice in the 2003 draft, once to take bust Nikoloz Tskitishvili, and he hasn't been able to address the Nuggets' problems at shooting guard.

Overall, one still has to be impressed with the job Vandeweghe has done, but apparently the Nuggets want somebody else in that chair. The worry is that Nuggets owner Stan Kroenke, who is tight with Karl, will give his coach far greater influence over personnel. This is a bad idea with a coach who is so veteran-oriented, because he'll make moves that aren't in the Nuggets' long-term interests.

A good example would be last year's trade of White and Tskitishvili to Golden State for Eduardo Najera and a future first-round pick, which was known to have Karl's support. On a strict talent level, there isn't too much to argue about. White and Najera are roughly equal as reserves, but Najera can play the frontcourt where Denver needed another body, and the pick might come in handy down the road.

The problem is that the contract implications were severe. Najera is due over $4 million this season while White and Tskitishvili became free agents. Once the cap rose in the offseason, it meant the Nuggets had made a major blunder. Had they not acquired Najera, they could have waived Lenard, traded one of their first-round picks, and been more than $10 million under the cap. That was enough money to sign one of the top free agents in a market chock full of shooting guards. Instead, Denver didn't have enough space to be relevant in the free-agent market and had to hunt for scraps with its midlevel exception. It's exactly the kind of short-sighted maneuver that prevents a team from achieving success in the long-term.

Regardless, Denver remains a deep and talented team. Anthony is a rising force as a scorer, Martin and Camby are defensive stalwarts in the paint, and Miller and Boykins excel at pushing the tempo. If they can fill the gap at shooting guard and Camby stays in one piece, the Nuggets could challenge the Western Conference elite. More likely, they'll fall a bit short of those exalted heights, but a 50-win season is well within reach, and that's nothing to scoff at.

Carmelo Anthony   small forward   Age: 21   Height: 6-8   Weight: 220
Defensive PER: 0.75 (85% SF, 11% PF, 3% SG, 1% C)   Most similar at age: Shareef Abdur-Rahim

Year		G	M/G	FG%	FT%	P/40	R/40	A/40	TS%		Ast		TO		Usg		Reb		PER	
2003-04	Den	82	36.5	.426	.777	23.0	6.7	3.0	50.9	34	10.5	45	11.4	34	25.8	5	9.0	25	17.53	12
2004-05	Den	75	34.8	.431	.796	23.9	6.5	3.0	52.6	35	10.2	48	11.8	44	26.1	4	9.6	26	16.68	9
2005-06	PRJ (21.5)			.434	.817	25.4	6.3	3.4	53.2		11.3		10.8		27.9		9.0		18.66	

Anthony's overall numbers were slightly down from his strong rookie season, but what they don't show is how much better he played after Karl took over. Anthony forced innumerable long jump shots at the start of the season, with his patented move being to catch the ball, stare at the ground for a second, then front-rim a jump shot. I can't imagine he made more than 15 percent of his shots when he tried this, yet he went to it about five times a game.

The biggest benefit of Karl's arrival was that he convinced Anthony to stop doing this and put the ball on the floor more. Anthony's first and second half stats tell the whole story—his three-point attempts were cut nearly in half, but he substantially increased his free-throw attempts and scored a whopping 5.7 extra points per 40 minutes.

Anthony Before and After All-Star Break

	Before	After
FG%	40.6	47.5
FGA/40 min	18.8	18.9
3-pt. att./40 min	2.9	1.6
FTA/40 min	7.5	11.1
Pts/40 min	21.9	27.6

Anthony still has areas to work on. He's not much of a passer and commits one palming violation a game trying to score off the dribble. He also needs to get tougher and more consistent on defense. Yet it's easy to forget how young he is and how much more he can develop in coming seasons. Already he's a fearsome scorer who can get his points inside or outside, and if he continues his second-half play for a full season, he could find himself on the All-Star team.

Earl Boykins   point guard   Age: 29   Height: 5-5   Weight: 133
Defensive PER: 1.40 (100% PG)   Most similar at age: Spud Webb

Year		G	M/G	FG%	FT%	P/40	R/40	A/40	TS%		Ast		TO		Usg		Reb		PER	
2002-03	GS	68	19.4	.429	.865	18.2	2.7	6.7	54.3	12	26.1	34	8.6	10	23.2	20	3.5	64	17.56	12
2003-04	Den	82	22.5	.419	.877	18.2	3.1	6.4	50.1	33	23.9	50	8.1	4	24.3	12	4.3	57	16.20	19
2004-05	Den	82	26.4	.413	.921	18.8	2.6	6.9	53.0	22	25.6	44	8.3	8	24.7	18	3.9	64	17.15	17
2005-06	PRJ (3.2)			.410	.907	17.6	2.8	6.4	51.2		24.9		8.4		23.9		4.0		15.79	

In spite of his Lilliputian size, Boykins is a devastating sixth man with outstanding quickness and one of the best mid-range games in basketball. Oddly for such a smaller player, he's not much of a passer—most of the offense he creates is for himself. He's also not a great deep shooter, with a 32.9 percent career mark on three-pointers.

His core competency is breaking down his man off the dribble and shooting a 15-footer. Boykins slithers past his defender at will and eventually works himself to a spot where, even at his size, he can get a good look at the basket. He does it while hardly turning the ball over. As an added plus, he's very effective at getting to the foul line and shot 92.1 percent from the stripe last season.

The Nuggets often played Boykins in a small backcourt with Andre Miller. Because Boykins isn't a great passer, he would be the one playing off the ball. He would curl off screens to get his shots, and was effective in that role. As if we needed more proof of his scoring capability, Boykins set an NBA record by scoring 15 points in an overtime period in a game against Seattle last season.

Defensively, the rules changes that put a premium on quickness helped Boykins quite a bit, as he posted one of the best Defensive PERs at his position. He is deceptively strong too, but he has problems with players dribbling up the court and shooting right over him. Overall, however, he's the best backup point guard in basketball.

Greg Buckner (91% SG, 8% SF, 1% PG)		shooting guard												**Age: 29**	**Height: 6-4**	**Weight: 210** Most similar at age: Blue Edwards
Year	G	M/G	FG%	FT%	P/40	R/40	A/40	TS%		Ast		TO		Usg		Reb	PER
2002-03 Phi*	75	20.2	.465	.802	11.9	5.7	2.5	51.9	30	16.2	18	10.5	23	14.5	46	8.4 41	11.62 43
2003-04 Phi	53	13.3	.377	.741	9.3	5.9	2.6	43.9	59	16.9	29	12.8	54	14.2	56	8.3 13	7.36 62
2004-05 Den	70	21.7	.528	.778	11.4	5.5	3.5	63.8	2	16.7	23	9.4	23	12.5	65	8.1 15	13.67 29
2005-06 PRJ (34.8)			.464	.768	10.9	5.1	3.3	55.4		17.0		10.2		13.6		7.4	11.32

* Season rankings are as small forward

Buckner shot unusually well last season in a year that missed qualifying for the Fluke Rule only by a technicality. I'm dubious that he can repeat those numbers. Buckner shot 52.8 percent when his career average is 47.4, and he shot 40.5 percent on three-pointers after barely clearing 27 the previous two seasons. Overall, he had the second-best TS% among shooting guards, and he'd never come anywhere close to that previously.

Buckner moves well without the ball and earns himself lay-ups that way, but otherwise he's not a skilled offensive player. He can't create shots off the dribble, he's too small to post up against anybody, and except for last year's barrage he's not much of an outside shooter.

He's stayed in the league because of his defense and rebounding. Buckner is tough, physical, and moves his feet well, making him a fairly reliable defensive player. Plus, his Rebound Rate has been consistently solid. He's a free agent and his shooting exploits should get him another contract, but buyer beware. Buckner's numbers are headed back to reality, which means he's only useful as a ninth or tenth man.

Marcus Camby Defensive PER: 1.83 (90% C, 10% PF)		center												**Age: 31**	**Height: 6-11**	**Weight: 235** Most similar at age: Jayson Williams
Year	G	M/G	FG%	FT%	P/40	R/40	A/40	TS%		Ast		TO		Usg		Reb	PER
2002-03 Den	29	21.2	.410	.660	14.4	13.5	3.1	44.4	66	14.6	10	8.4	3	19.8	7	19.7 4	17.63 9
2003-04 Den*	72	30.0	.477	.721	11.5	13.5	2.4	51.1	38	15.7	19	11.7	33	13.8	55	18.6 5	17.85 16
2004-05 Den	66	30.5	.465	.723	13.6	13.1	3.0	50.5	45	14.4	2	11.1	9	16.7	21	19.4 6	18.08 9
2005-06 PRJ (20.2)			.456	.705	11.5	12.3	2.9	49.3		16.0		11.0		14.4		17.6	16.37

* Season rankings are as power forward

Camby had one of his healthiest seasons ever and now has had the best two-year run in his career by missing "only" 26 games. The Nuggets will have their fingers crossed for three in a row, but the odds don't seem in their favor. Even last season, Camby missed games with a stunning variety of ailments: a strained left hamstring, a bruised tailbone, bronchitis, a back strain, a yeast infection, a sprained left ankle, a strained *right* hamstring, a sprained *right* ankle, a right hip contusion, and scurvy. OK, I made up two of those, but the rest all are true.

The Nuggets pumped Camby as a Defensive Player of the year candidate, but that was a stretch for two reasons. First, of course, are the aforementioned absences. Second, he didn't play that hard under Bzdelik. He often missed rotations and block-outs and didn't pick up his intensity until Karl took over. From that point he was brilliant, but it was only half a season. Camby averaged nearly four blocks a game after the All-Star break and dominated on the boards with 14.3 rebounds per 40 minutes in that same time period.

Offensively, Camby can finish around the rim but also loves to shoot jumpers from the foul line. He has increasingly relied on that in recent seasons and has forayed into the paint less frequently, resulting in a low rate of free throws and a correspondingly poor TS%. However, he's one of the best passing big men in basketball and is great at entering the ball on high-low plays. He also has a low Turnover Ratio, so his overall offensive game is fairly effective despite the low TS%.

Camby is 31 and had never played more than 63 games in a season before the past two campaigns. One can take that as a sign that he's healthier than ever, or as a sign that he's overdue, but one thing's for certain: His health will be the biggest determinant of Denver's success in 2005–06.

Francisco Elson   **center**   **Age: 29   Height: 7-0   Weight: 235**
(100% C)   Most similar at age: Andrew Lang

Year		G	M/G	FG%	FT%	P/40	R/40	A/40	TS%		Ast		TO		Usg		Reb		PER	
2003-04	Den	62	14.1	.472	.667	10.0	9.3	1.5	49.8	53	11.2	23	12.2	27	11.6	62	12.8	53	11.27	55
2004-05	Den	67	14.0	.468	.570	10.6	8.6	1.4	49.4	50	6.9	32	12.3	19	12.4	47	12.6	53	10.65	50
2005-06	PRJ (37.5)			.470	.603	10.3	8.6	1.6	49.4		8.9		12.4		12.0		12.4		11.12	

Elson was the Nuggets' fourth big man until the Najera trade but made little progress from his rookie season. He has good size but lacks strength, making him vulnerable to post-ups against bigger centers. Also, his rebounding has been a consistent disappointment. Elson has a rarely-seen jump hook shot with his right hand but otherwise stays out of the way offensively. With his development stalled and four big men ahead of him on the depth chart, his minutes this season will be infrequent... at least until Camby gets hurt.

Luis Flores   **point guard**   **Age: 24   Height: 6-2   Weight: 200**
(100% PG)   Most similar at age: N/A

Year		G	M/G	FG%	FT%	P/40	R/40	A/40	TS%	Ast	TO	Usg	Reb	PER
2004-05	GS-Den	16	4.8	.483	1.000	18.2	1.6	5.7	58.6	21.2	21.2	22.6	2.3	10.00

A throw-in to the Najera trade, Flores did little of note in his rookie campaign and will have a hard time getting minutes as the Nuggets' third point guard. That's particularly true since he's a score-first type who is still adjusting to the point. Flores is quick and does have a contract for this season, so he should make the team. He'll just have difficulty proving he's on it when the games start.

DerMarr Johnson   **shooting guard**   **Age: 25   Height: 6-9   Weight: 201**
(76% SG, 24% SF)   Most similar at age: Shane Battier

Year		G	M/G	FG%	FT%	P/40	R/40	A/40	TS%		Ast		TO		Usg		Reb		PER	
2003-04	NY	21	13.6	.371	.903	15.8	5.5	1.5	51.1		8.0		11.6		17.8		7.8		11.47	
2004-05	Den	71	17.4	.499	.792	16.3	4.9	2.4	60.5	5	11.6	54	11.7	48	16.2	52	7.2	22	13.97	28
2005-06	PRJ (32.2)			.472	.804	16.3	5.0	2.4	58.2		11.3		11.2		16.7		7.4		13.55	

Johnson had missed the majority of two seasons after a car accident but looked fully recovered as a Nugget last season. Johnson is extremely tall for a shooting guard and his height allows him to make an impact at the defensive end altering shots. It's tough to take advantage of his size at the offensive end, however, because he's rail thin and easily moved out of the post. Additionally, he's a poor ballhandler who struggles to create shots for himself.

Johnson does two things well: finishing in transition and shooting three-pointers. As such, he was particularly fortunate to end up in Denver. The Nuggets played the NBA's fourth-fastest pace and ran frequently, earning Johnson plenty of easy baskets, while his skill as a shooter assured his place in a lineup lacking that skill. Johnson hit 35.8 percent from outside the arc with his awkward-looking push shot, consistent with his career averages.

Johnson was on a one-year deal and is a free agent again, but he should generate much more demand after his solid season. He's still young and should be able to help a team looking for a solid perimeter defender who can hit open shots.

Voshon Lenard   **shooting guard**   **Age: 32   Height: 6-4   Weight: 205**
(98% SG, 2% SF)   Most similar at age: N/A

Year		G	M/G	FG%	FT%	P/40	R/40	A/40	TS%		Ast		TO		Usg		Reb		PER	
2002-03	Tor	63	30.6	.402	.804	18.6	4.4	3.0	50.2	33	12.6	45	9.0	16	22.5	15	6.3	40	14.39	27
2003-04	Den	73	30.6	.422	.791	18.6	3.6	2.7	51.2	26	11.9	51	8.0	9	20.7	29	5.0	54	13.49	28
2004-05	Den	3	18.0	.385	.625	21.5	4.4	4.4	49.1		16.0		5.3		26.1		6.6		15.02	

Lenard tore his Achilles tendon opening night but rehabbed the injury in time to be activated for the final two games. He's a reliable outside shooter on a team short of perimeter options, but the Nuggets face a tough decision with Lenard. If they

(continued next page)

Voshon Lenard (*continued*)

waive him they would dispense with a nearly $3 million obligation for the coming season. Since he's 32 and coming off a difficult injury, that might be the more prudent course. On the other hand, Denver has few options for replacing his outside stroke, so they might have to hang on and hope for a full recovery.

If he comes back, Lenard can help not only from the three-point line but also with his ability to post up against smaller guards. He's nothing special as a defender because he's short and has slow feet, so he'll have to keep the shots falling to stay in the lineup.

Kenyon Martin				power forward											Age: 28		Height: 6-9		Weight: 240	
Defensive PER: 0.99 (82% PF, 17% C, 1% SF)																		Most similar at age: George Lynch		
Year	G	M/G	FG%	FT%	P/40	R/40	A/40	TS%		Ast		TO		Usg		Reb		PER	
2002-03 NJ	77	34.1	.470	.653	19.5	9.7	2.8	51.1	35	11.3	32	11.8	40	22.7	9	13.9	25	16.86	18
2003-04 NJ	65	34.6	.488	.684	19.3	11.0	2.8	52.8	25	11.8	33	12.4	43	22.3	10	15.6	18	18.69	13
2004-05 Den	70	32.5	.490	.646	19.1	9.0	3.0	52.1	37	12.5	15	10.9	33	21.6	12	13.3	34	17.47	15
2005-06 PRJ (43.9)			*.481*	*.653*	*18.0*	*9.6*	*3.1*	*52.1*		*13.5*		*11.3*		*21.4*		*13.7*		*17.11*	

Martin was a mild disappointment after signing a big contract with the Nuggets in the offseason, as his Rebound Rate declined and he didn't create as many shots as he had in New Jersey. The 6′9″ jumping jack still is among the best defenders at his position thanks to his combination of hops and toughness, but one gets the lingering impression the Nuggets overpaid by giving up three first-round picks for the right to pay him $12 million a year.

Offensively, Martin's game hasn't changed much. He's outstanding in transition and very ordinary in the halfcourt, where he's an erratic jump shooter and can occasionally make short jump hook shots on the blocks. He did improve as a passer and cut down on his Turnover Ratio, probably because he didn't have to play as prominent an offensive role with the Nuggets.

Denver will be looking for more from him this season. He's 28 and entering the prime years for a big man, and with Denver running so much more under Karl, he figures to be one of the main beneficiaries. If he can get his 40-minute averages up to 20 and 10, Denver would feel much more confident that their investment in him was money well spent.

Andre Miller				point guard											Age: 29		Height: 6-2		Weight: 200	
Defensive PER: 0.83 (62% PG, 38% SG)																		Most similar at age: Eric Snow		
Year	G	M/G	FG%	FT%	P/40	R/40	A/40	TS%		Ast		TO		Usg		Reb		PER	
2002-03 LAC	80	36.4	.406	.795	14.9	4.3	7.4	49.5	39	29.1	20	11.2	31	23.3	19	6.0	24	15.12	25
2003-04 Den	82	34.6	.457	.832	17.1	5.2	7.1	54.1	8	27.3	36	11.7	37	23.0	22	7.0	6	18.81	9
2004-05 Den	82	34.8	.477	.838	15.6	4.7	8.0	54.1	14	31.3	21	12.1	44	22.8	30	7.0	5	16.57	20
2005-06 PRJ (35.4)			*.453*	*.832*	*14.6*	*4.6*	*7.1*	*52.7*		*29.4*		*12.7*		*21.8*		*6.6*		*15.47*	

Miller's numbers slipped in 2004–05, and given his stocky build there's some concern over how well he'll play as he gets into his 30s. He's a poor outside shooter (although he makes his foul shots), so he has nothing to fall back on if he loses a step.

For the moment, however, he's a very effective guard. Miller is great in transition and is the best alleyoop passer since Sherman Douglas. When he's paired with Boykins in the backcourt it's almost impossible to stop Denver from fast-breaking, and Miller frequently finishes them with high handoffs to Camby and Martin. In the halfcourt Miller doesn't see the floor quite as well, but he's a load for opposing point guards to stop in the post and has a variety of nifty pivot moves that he uses to free himself for short bank shots.

Miller isn't a great defender, but his numbers last season were passable and his ability to defend opposing shooting guards allowed Denver to pair him with Boykins. He's also an outstanding rebounder for a guard. Overall he figures to have a couple more strong seasons left in him, but the projections show that players with Miller's skill set don't fare well in their 30s.

Eduardo Najera   power forward   Age: 29   Height: 6-8   Weight: 235
(88% PF, 11% C, 1% SF)

Most similar at age: Cliff Levingston

Year		G	M/G	FG%	FT%	P/40	R/40	A/40	TS%		Ast		TO		Usg		Reb		PER	
2002-03	Dal	48	23.0	.558	.681	11.6	8.1	1.7	59.0	2	13.8	17	6.7	2	11.6	58	11.1	51	14.89	29
2003-04	Dal	58	12.4	.444	.652	9.8	8.7	1.4	48.3	51	10.6	40	12.3	41	11.7	62	11.9	49	11.54	54
2004-05	GS-Den	68	17.4	.450	.637	11.9	8.2	2.2	48.9	56	10.5	27	12.5	47	14.7	50	12.1	44	11.19	57
2005-06	*PRJ (57.7)*			*.458*	*.632*	*10.9*	*8.2*	*2.0*	*49.6*		*11.5*		*11.2*		*13.3*		*11.7*		*11.47*	

Denver acquired Najera in a midseason trade from Golden State and immediately plugged him into Elson's spot in the rotation. He's undersized for the power forward spot but very willing to throw his weight around and great at taking charges (more on this in the Nenê comment). Plus, on a running team like Denver, Najera's lack of height wasn't as big of a problem.

Najera shot 50.0 percent as a Nugget after hitting only 40.7 percent in Golden State, and his other numbers showed substantial improvement as well. Part of that was because he was shooting too many long jumpers in Golden State, but the other ingredient was the transition points he got as a Nugget. Unfortunately, he broke his hand the last week of the season and was a non-factor in the playoffs.

Najera should fill the same role this season, especially since veteran tough guys like him are among Karl's favorites. He'll have value if he keeps up his shooting percentage from the second half of the season, but it's more likely that the mark will drop closer to his career norms. If that's the case Denver again will be shopping for frontcourt help at midseason.

Nenê   center   Age: 23   Height: 6-11   Weight: 260
(51% C, 49% PF)

Most similar at age: Kwame Brown

Year		G	M/G	FG%	FT%	P/40	R/40	A/40	TS%		Ast		TO		Usg		Reb		PER	
2002-03	Den	80	28.1	.519	.578	14.9	8.7	2.6	54.5	17	13.6	14	16.5	61	17.4	21	12.7	51	15.52	19
2003-04	Den	77	32.5	.530	.682	14.5	8.0	2.7	57.8	5	14.8	9	16.1	64	15.6	23	11.1	71	14.80	25
2004-05	Den	55	23.9	.503	.660	16.0	9.9	2.6	55.1	22	12.2	5	14.3	43	17.6	15	14.6	34	15.61	22
2005-06	*PRJ (31.1)*			*.516*	*.634*	*15.0*	*8.5*	*3.3*	*55.8*		*16.2*		*15.3*		*17.3*		*12.1*		*15.20*	

Quick players usually are good leapers, and players who can't jump usually are slow. Nenê is a rare exception. He's extremely quick for a man of his size, reminiscent of Hakeem Olajuwon at times, and frequently steals the ball from guards when defending screen-and-roll plays. Unfortunately, he can't jump. That lack of leaping ability is the one limitation preventing him from becoming an upper-tier center.

Like a lot of players who don't leap well, Nenê tried to make up for it by taking charges. Despite coming off the bench, Nenê led the team in charges with 22. We know this because the Nuggets were the only NBA team to track charges in their media notes, which make for an interesting study.

I've included the charges drawn by every Nugget in the following chart. First, notice how rare they are. The team drew only 106 all season, or a little over one per game, and they were considered one of the better teams at this. Second, there's a huge disparity among players in how many they drew. Buckner played 1,522 minutes without drawing a single charge, while Najera drew 12 in 575 minutes. Najera's charge rate was more than double that of most his teammates and 50 times as much as Anthony's.

Nuggets Charges Taken, 2004–05

	Total	Charges per 100 Min.		Total	Charges per 100 Min.
Eduardo Najera	12	2.09	Kenyon Martin	6	0.26
Nenê	22	1.67	Earl Boykins	5	0.23
Francisco Elson	10	1.06	Wesley Person	1	0.22
Bryon Russell	10	0.97	DerMarr Johnson	1	0.08
Marcus Camby	18	0.89	Carmelo Anthony	1	0.04
Andre Miller	19	0.67	Greg Buckner	0	0.00
Nikoloz Tskitishvili	1	0.63			
			Team	**106**	**0.54**

(continued next page)

Nenê *(continued)*

What you'll notice about the Nuggets' leaders in charges is a common theme throughout the league—they're big men who can't block shots. Knowing that limitation, they opt to stay on the ground and try to force a turnover. Camby is the lone exception, which is a sign of his exceptional defensive skill, but Najera, Nenê, Elson, and Russell all fit the stereotype perfectly.

Offensively, Nenê runs the floor extremely well for a big man and took advantage of the Nuggets' transition offense to get many easy baskets. He has no jumper, however, and his post game is mostly limited to quick spin moves. He also fades away too much when he shoots inside, perhaps because of his poor leaping.

The Nuggets face their first important decision with Nenê as he's eligible for an extension before the season starts. Considering his youth and production, he's worth several million dollars a year, but his lack of elevation will be a roadblock to stardom.

Wesley Person (53% SF, 44% SG, 2% PF, 1% PG)					small forward						Age: 34		Height: 6-6		Weight: 205 Most similar at age: Dale Ellis	
Year	G	M/G	FG%	FT%	P/40	R/40	A/40	TS%		Ast		TO		Usg	Reb	PER
2002-03 Mem*	66	29.4	.456	.814	15.0	4.0	2.3	56.5	11	13.8	39	6.9	6	15.7 45	5.6 47	13.52 31
2003-04 Me-Po-At*	58	17.9	.401	.795	13.0	4.5	2.5	51.0	28	15.2	35	8.7	15	16.2 49	6.4 37	11.39 43
2004-05 Mia-Den	41	16.3	.473	.692	15.8	5.0	2.3	57.0	6	11.1	38	5.9	2	16.3 46	7.3 56	14.16 29
2005-06 PRJ (30.3)			*.414*	*.787*	*13.6*	*4.4*	*2.4*	*51.8*		*12.9*		*7.6*		*15.7*	*6.3*	*11.65*

* Season rankings are as shooting guard

After Miami cut Person at midseason, the Nuggets scooped him up and almost immediately inserted him into the rotation. Person rewarded Denver's confidence by shooting as well as he has in several years, hitting an amazing 48.5 percent on three-pointers as a Nugget and nearly scoring at the highest per-minute rate of his career.

Obviously, this can't be expected to continue, and it won't. Person's projected stats show that his two-month outburst was a brief windfall for Denver, but he's the same limited player he was in his previous stops. He's a poor defender and contributes little on the glass, so if his shooting isn't extraordinary, it's tough to justify his spot in the rotation. His hot shooting in Denver did have one benefit, however, as it probably earned him a contract for next season.

Mark Pope (61% PF, 39% C)					power forward				power forward Age: 33		Height: 6-10	Weight: 245 Most similar at age: N/A	
Year	G	M/G	FG%	FT%	P/40	R/40	A/40	TS%	Ast	TO	Usg	Reb	PER
2003-04 Den	4	5.0	.500	.000	4.0	6.0	0.0	41.0	0.0	55.1	6.6	8.3	-9.08
2004-05 Den	9	3.0	.333	—	5.9	11.9	1.5	33.3	7.1	12.5	10.6	16.6	9.98

Pope's career has defied all expectations. He can't play now, nor could he ever, but somehow he's still around. Since he seems to be a favorite of Karl's dating back to Milwaukee, he'll be waving a towel at the end of the bench again this year.

Bryon Russell (69% SF, 21% SG, 10% PF)					small forward						Age: 35		Height: 6-7		Weight: 225 Most similar at age: Rod Higgins	
Year	G	M/G	FG%	FT%	P/40	R/40	A/40	TS%		Ast		TO		Usg	Reb	PER
2002-03 Was	70	19.8	.353	.768	9.1	6.0	2.1	46.8	53	15.5	20	11.9	37	12.7 51	8.9 32	9.07 51
2003-04 LAL	72	13.1	.402	.769	12.2	6.2	3.0	53.0	19	18.7	7	9.7	15	14.7 49	9.1 23	11.63 42
2004-05 Den	70	14.7	.377	.792	12.0	6.7	2.8	53.7	24	13.4	21	8.9	15	14.0 55	9.9 20	11.79 44
2005-06 PRJ (24.4)			*.353*	*.740*	*10.8*	*6.3*	*2.5*	*48.3*		*14.3*		*10.4*		*13.6*	*9.2*	*9.97*

Brought in to babysit Carmelo Anthony, Russell earned time as Anthony's backup and didn't embarrass himself. Russell had a very hot November for the second year in a row, hitting 59 percent on three-pointers to beat out Rodney White for a spot in the rotation. Reality struck soon afterward, as he shot below 40 percent in every month the rest of the way. Once Person arrived, Russell's minutes faded faster than the Atkins diet, and he doesn't figure in Denver's plans for this season.

Nonetheless, his hot start probably earned him another one-year deal to come off somebody's bench. Fantasy players take note: He'll be a nice pick-up for the opening weeks, but remember that December 1 sell-by date.

| **Julius Hodge** | **shooting guard** | **Age:** | **Height: 6-7** | **Weight: 205** |

Five players from the ACC went in the lottery, but it was Hodge, the 20th overall pick, who was the conference's player of the year last season. While he lacks strength and can't shoot, he was an effective college player because he defends like crazy, rebounds extremely well for a guard, and handles the ball very well for a player of his size. He may be able to play point guard at times, although the Nuggets don't seem to need help in that area. Otherwise, his lack of a perimeter shot may prevent him from seeing extended action.

| **Linas Kleiza** | **small forward** | **Age: 20** | **Height: 6-8** | **Weight: 235** |

Kleiza can score and is young, but I'm not wild about the Nuggets using a first-round pick on him. Kleiza played inside at Missouri but will have to play the perimeter as a pro. Based on his miniscule blocks and steals totals he doesn't seem nearly athletic enough to pull it off. Additionally, he's not a great shooter (27 percent on threes, 73 percent on free throws) and can be turnover prone. Denver can park Kleiza in his native Lithuania for a year or two, but that's about the only benefit I can see from this pick.

| **Ricky Sanchez** | **small forward** | **Age: 19** | **Height: 6-11** | **Weight: 215** |

An unknown quantity who wasn't listed in the NBA's media guide for the draft, Sanchez committed to play for Memphis (the college) but turned pro instead and was snagged by Denver in the second round. At 6' 11" and just 215 pounds, he needs to spend a couple of years pumping iron and eating steak at every meal, but he has perimeter skills and is considered a very smooth scorer.

| **Axel Hervelle** | **power forward** | **Age: 22** | **Height: 6-9** | **Weight: 230** |
Translated 40-minute stats: 12.1 pts, 10.7 reb, 2.2 ast, .425 FG%, 10.74 PER

Denver drafted the Belgian in the second round because of his energy. Hervelle is like a European Ryan Bowen—a full-throttle player who hustles and gets lots of garbage baskets, although his Rebound Rate in Euroleague play wasn't that impressive. He isn't regarded as much of an offensive player, but he did make 14-of-31 three-pointers in the Euroleague last season, so perhaps he's improving.

Golden State Warriors

Not a bad save, eh?

Warriors general manager Chris Mullin stepped into his first year on the job and promptly started concocting bad ideas. He allowed Erick Dampier and Brian Cardinal to depart, gave fat contracts to Derek Fisher and Adonal Foyle, handed out generous contract extensions to Jason Richardson and Troy Murphy, and chose Mike Montgomery to come from the college ranks to coach his ill-chosen squad.

Nobody was surprised when the team quickly sunk to the bottom of the Pacific Division, and from there they became an afterthought the rest of the way. But a funny thing happened as well: The Warriors started getting better. Fisher and Foyle proved to be wasted money, but Richardson continued his development into one of the game's top shooting guards while Murphy finished sixth in the NBA in rebounding. Meanwhile, Montgomery didn't seem nearly as overmatched as some other recent college coaches and kept everybody on the same page.

Additionally, Mullin had an eye for talent. His first-round draft pick in 2004, Latvian teenager Andris Biedrins, showed he belonged in the league right away and could eventually be among the game's best centers. Mullin fleeced Phoenix by sending them a second-round pick for little-used forward Zarko Cabarkapa, who came to Golden State and began scoring in bunches. As a final move, Mullin dropped Eduardo Najera on the Nuggets, along with a first-round pick in 2007, to keep the Warriors out of the luxury tax.

And then there was the big trade. At the league deadline, Mullin orchestrated a deal that sent guard Speedy Claxton and center Dale Davis to New Orleans for guard Baron Davis. In terms of the talent exchanged, this one was a no-brainer. Mullin traded an aging big man he no longer needed and an oft-injured point guard for a far more talented (though still oft-injured) point guard.

The tricky part is Baron Davis's contract. He makes the league maximum and has three years left on his deal, so Golden State needs him to both stay healthy and play at a star level to justify sacrificing its cap flexibility for the foreseeable future. His recent history doesn't bode well, as Davis missed 83 games over the past three seasons and had a serious knee injury in college. He has a bad back and the knee still gives him trouble, so the Warriors will need some luck.

Fortunately for Golden State, Davis has youth on his side. That's the key variable in this deal that I think makes it worth the risk for the Warriors: Davis was only 25 when they pulled the trigger. If he was 31 with back and knee problems and I was paying him for three more years, I'd be worried. But a 25 year old? Chances were that he'd still play at a very high level when he was available, and considering that he didn't miss a game in his first three pro seasons, he could be more available than people thought over the next few years.

After the trade, Davis's impact was obvious. Golden State won more in its final 28 games with Davis than in the previous 54, going 14–5 when Davis played. That included a 12-game stretch when the Warriors went 11–1, which was the team's best mark over such a stretch in 30 years. Overall, Golden State went 18–10 after the trade, partly because several other players also returned from injury.

Let's take a closer look at Golden State's closing run, because that unit should pretty much stay the same this season. The Warriors were one of the league's most dreadful offensive teams for much of the season because Richardson was their only big-time scorer and other than Murphy, none of the interior players could score. The first part changed when Davis arrived, providing multiple sources of offense for the Warriors. The second switched at roughly the same time, as the Warriors traded Davis, Najera, and Clifford Robinson to open up minutes for Biedrins and Cabarkapa.

As a result, Golden State's offensive output exploded down the stretch (see table 1), increasing by more than 10 points a game after the trade. Relative to the man he replaced, Claxton, Davis's biggest impact was his ability to stretch the defense. Claxton shot only 19 percent on three-pointers, but Davis shot a more robust 34.1 percent and tried nearly eight a game. Yes, eight a game was pushing it as several of them were ill-advised, but the overall effect was positive. A

Warriors at a Glance

Record: 34–48, tied for 4th place in Pacific Division

Offensive Efficiency: 101.9 (22nd)

Defensive Efficiency: 104.0 (17th)

Pace Factor: 95.5 (7th)

Top-Rated Player: Baron Davis (PER 20.78, 25th overall)

Head Coach: Mike Montgomery. Handled college-to-pro transition better than most.

Table 1. Warriors Before and After Davis Trade

	Before	After
W–L	16–38	18–10
Pts.game	95.2	105.4
FG%	42.4	44.3
3-Pt%	33.6	37.0

result of the deal was that every Warrior perimeter player was a deadly outside shooter, opening up the real estate in the middle for drives to the rim and making the team far less susceptible to zones.

Nonetheless, one of Montgomery's challenges for this coming season is to reign in Davis's three-point mania. Davis has fallen in love with the shot and is particularly fond of shooting it off the dribble despite a questionable accuracy record. He is great shooting with his feet set, but he's a much more dangerous player going to the basket than firing long jumpers off the dribble. Hopefully his new coach can help him realize that.

Montgomery's other mission this year will be to develop the kids. Besides Fisher and Foyle, the key rotation players are 26 or younger. Rookie Ike Diogu could play a major role behind Murphy at power forward, and he makes eight. If Montgomery can get players like Cabarkapa, Biedrins, Mickael Pietrus, and Diogu to improve this season, Golden State's bench will be among the best in basketball.

Moreover, Montgomery deserves credit for coaxing a surprisingly strong defensive effort from his troops last season. Despite running a young team that was learning his system on the fly, Golden State finished 17th in Defensive Efficiency. That number would be even better if the Warriors could address their major deficiency: rebounding. While

Murphy was outstanding on the glass, he didn't have much competition from his own teammates. Golden State finished 27th in defensive rebounding percentage and 29th overall, setting back what was a solid defensive effort in other areas.

Fortunately, they seem well on their way. Much of Golden State's troubles stemmed from their heavy use of Clifford Robinson, who is an absolutely atrocious rebounder, and Najera didn't give them much either. But after the trade the Warriors were a much stronger rebounding team. Foyle replaced Robinson and contributed strongly, and Biedrins is a monster on the glass. Additionally, Diogu's college rebounding numbers suggest he'll be a big help too.

Add it all up and things are looking bright for Mullin's Warriors, even after his shaky start. Davis and Richardson lend star power to the backcourt, while up front Biedrins could be a breakout player this season. Murphy is very solid at power forward and Cabarkapa and Pietrus are young enough to get significantly better. If Pietrus's defensive skills can provide an upgrade at small forward, where Mike Dunleavy had an off year, the club could really take off.

The Warriors weren't expected to do much maneuvering in the offseason because Mullin already played his cards at the trade deadline. The team is already at the luxury tax limit and has few openings in its rotation anyway, so it's unlikely to use its cap exceptions. Luckily for Golden State, Mullin has a trade exception from the Clifford Robinson deal if the need arises.

He probably won't have to use it. With a young, exciting roster and a coach who is proving far more adept than expected, this should be one of the league's most improved teams in 2005–06. Golden State hasn't tasted the playoffs in over a decade, but it appears the league's longest drought will come to an end this year.

Andris Biedrins center **Age: 19 Height: 6-11 Weight: 240**
(95% C, 5% PF) Most similar at age: N/A

Year		G	M/G	FG%	FT%	P/40	R/40	A/40	TS%	Ast	TO	Usg	Reb	PER
2004-05	GS	30	12.8	.577	.475	11.4	12.3	1.3	57.0	6.0	10.0	11.3	17.7	14.69

I was very high on this guy coming out of the draft and nothing that happened last year changed my opinion. He's five months younger than Dwight Howard, yet his Rebound Rate and field-goal percentage indicate he can hang with the big boys. Plus, unlike a lot of Euros, Biedrins loves to play inside and has the physique to do it.

Perhaps the biggest surprise was his defensive competence. Biedrins is strong enough to defend post players and has the agility to provide plenty of help on the screen-and-roll. As he learns NBA defensive concepts, he figures to be a strong performer at both ends, with his rebounding providing an added boost. It will be interesting to see if he can wrest the starting center job away from Foyle this season, but even if he doesn't, keep an eye on this guy. In a few years he could be a star.

Zarko Cabarkapa — power forward — Age: 24 · Height: 6-11 · Weight: 225
(91% PF, 5% SF, 4% C) — Most similar at age: N/A

Year		G	M/G	FG%	FT%	P/40	R/40	A/40	TS%		Ast		TO		Usg		Reb		PER	
2003-04	Phx	49	11.6	.411	.660	14.2	6.9	2.8	46.1	58	12.7	27	17.2	63	19.0	26	10.2	63	8.37	65
2004-05	Phx-GS	40	11.9	.486	.815	20.0	8.6	2.1	57.9		9.6		11.5		19.8		12.4		16.88	

With Phoenix looking to drop salary, Cabarkapa was left on the Warriors' doorstep with a box of kittens and responded with a breakout performance. He had shown nothing in his rookie season in Phoenix but proved to be a versatile scorer as a Warrior. Cabarkapa has good hands, a soft touch, and unexpected three-point range. At his size, that made him an awfully tough match-up for opposing power forwards. He also can handle the ball, though he's a bit too fond of bringing it up himself, and is a smart scorer who knows how to use head fakes around the rim.

His biggest weakness is defense. Cabarkapa is both soft and extremely slow, so it's always a challenge for the Warriors to find a way to hide him at the defensive end. He may have to play more at small forward this season, but that presents just as much of a challenge due to his lack of foot speed. If he plays like he did last year, Cabarkapa's offense is too good to keep him on the bench all game, but his defensive liabilities will prevent him from seeing extended minutes.

Calbert Cheaney — small forward — Age: 34 · Height: 6-7 · Weight: 220
(62% SF, 36% SG, 2% PF) — Most similar at age: Stacey Augmon

Year		G	M/G	FG%	FT%	P/40	R/40	A/40	TS%		Ast		TO		Usg		Reb		PER	
2002-03	Uta*	81	29.0	.499	.580	11.9	4.8	2.8	51.4	29	17.1	23	11.3	40	15.3	47	7.3	20	9.80	43
2003-04	GS	79	26.1	.481	.610	11.7	5.0	2.6	49.3	41	16.3	18	10.2	24	15.1	46	7.3	44	10.55	47
2004-05	GS	55	17.3	.426	.649	10.5	5.2	2.7	44.4	61	12.8	27	9.2	18	14.7	50	7.5	52	7.76	63
2005-06	PRJ (26.1)			.450	.634	11.2	4.9	2.6	47.7		14.9		10.5		14.9		7.1		8.97	

* Season rankings are as shooting guard

Cheaney has been able to carve out a niche as a defensive specialist but is coming to the end of the line. He's been one of the league's most timid offensive players for years and his accuracy plummeted last season. Cheaney hit only 42.6 percent from the floor, and since he virtually never takes a three-pointer or gets to the foul line, that doomed him to a horrendous TS%. In addition, he's a poor rebounder, so unless he's an all-defense candidate, it's not worth keeping him on the court. Thanks to the development of young players like Pietrus and Cabarkapa, Cheaney will probably spend this season at the end of the Golden State bench.

Baron Davis — point guard — Age: 26 · Height: 6-3 · Weight: 223
(100% PG) — Most similar at age: Kenny Anderson

Year		G	M/G	FG%	FT%	P/40	R/40	A/40	TS%		Ast		TO		Usg		Reb		PER	
2002-03	NO	50	37.8	.416	.710	18.1	3.9	6.8	50.0	38	24.3	45	10.6	25	26.2	8	5.7	27	16.84	15
2003-04	NO	67	40.1	.395	.673	22.8	4.3	7.5	49.2	41	22.0	54	9.5	12	33.2	1	6.3	17	21.39	2
2004-05	NO-GS	46	34.4	.387	.761	22.4	4.4	9.2	51.5	35	26.8	33	9.7	19	32.0	2	6.4	16	20.78	5
2005-06	PRJ (24.1)			.393	.727	21.7	4.6	8.1	50.5		24.8		9.8		31.6		6.7		20.54	

Davis requested a trade before the season and got his wish once the Hornets got off to a miserable start. New Orleans's loss was Golden State's gain, as he energized the Warriors' offense with his ability to push the ball upcourt and create shots. Davis's combination of size and explosiveness make him a handful for opposing defenses, as he penetrates easily and can finish with dunks over taller players. He also has a soft shooting touch and is a clever post player against shorter defenders.

Now he needs to put all those skills into a more disciplined package. As I mentioned in the team comment, Davis needs to stop taking so many three-pointers and take better advantage of his physical gifts. Even when he doesn't shoot the three, he spends too much time crossing over at the top of the key rather than going toward the basket. He's also a mediocre passer who needs to see the court better.

Despite those knocks, he's an All-Star caliber guard who should be having his best seasons in the next few years. Davis is a rock-solid defender who can defend shooting guards because of his size and athleticism, and his ability to help on the boards should be beneficial too. If the Warriors can keep him on the court for 60 games or so, he should be their ticket to the playoffs. He also could be the team's first All-Star since Latrell Sprewell made it in 1996–97.

Mike Dunleavy　　small forward　　　　Age: 25　Height: 6-9　Weight: 230
Defensive PER: 1.16 (77% SF, 21% PF, 2% SG)　　　　Most similar at age: Hedo Turkoglu

Year	G	M/G	FG%	FT%	P/40	R/40	A/40	TS%		Ast		TO		Usg		Reb		PER	
2002-03 GS	82	15.9	.403	.780	14.3	6.6	3.2	50.5	38	16.2	17	13.2	44	17.5	33	8.7	35	12.52	35
2003-04 GS	75	31.2	.449	.741	15.0	7.6	3.8	54.7	11	18.9	5	12.3	45	18.4	25	10.9	10	15.04	23
2004-05 GS	79	32.5	.451	.779	16.5	6.8	3.2	53.9	20	15.1	10	10.0	28	18.7	31	9.8	24	14.52	26
2005-06 PRJ (68.5)			.438	.765	15.8	6.9	3.2	53.5		15.4		11.3		18.7		9.8		14.22	

Dunleavy hasn't quite lived up to his billing as the third overall pick in 2002. His lack of a first step has made it difficult for him to be a high-volume shot producer, while he isn't quite accurate enough to be a dead-eye perimeter ace either. His best skill is his versatility. Dunleavy handles the ball very well for his size and has great court vision, so he's one of the best passers at his position. Additionally, his lack of strength hasn't prevented him from contributing on the boards.

Dunleavy is at his best cutting off screens, as he moves well without the ball and the screener can give him the one-step advantage that he can't generate on his own. He also has steadily improved as a three-point shooter, hitting 38.8 percent last season, and really improved defensively. Dunleavy was overwhelmed in his first two seasons but his Defensive PER in 2004–05 was very respectable. At his height, he can contest shots from perimeter players and is less vulnerable in the post than one might expect. He'll never be a stopper, but with his height and willingness to help from the weak side, he's become better than expected.

His year was a slight disappointment though, because he regressed offensively from his sophomore season. Looking at Golden State's current starting five, his position and center are the two spots they could stand to upgrade the most. Since Dunleavy is due for an extension prior to the season, Mullin will have to think long and hard about whether he's the long-term answer at this spot.

Derek Fisher　　point guard　　　　Age: 31　Height: 6-1　Weight: 205
Defensive PER: 1.03 (59% PG, 41% SG)　　　　Most similar at age: Pooh Richardson

Year	G	M/G	FG%	FT%	P/40	R/40	A/40	TS%		Ast		TO		Usg		Reb		PER	
2002-03 LAL	82	34.5	.437	.800	12.2	3.4	4.2	52.0	26	24.4	42	7.7	3	16.1	59	4.8	51	11.87	41
2003-04 LAL	82	21.6	.352	.797	13.1	3.4	4.2	45.1	55	20.6	59	8.7	5	18.9	50	4.9	45	11.50	52
2004-05 GS	74	30.0	.393	.862	15.8	3.9	5.4	51.9	32	23.6	51	10.1	24	20.9	45	5.7	32	13.37	42
2005-06 PRJ (37.6)			.388	.800	12.9	3.6	4.8	48.7		23.9		9.6		18.3		5.0		11.49	

Fisher's contract was a hilarious waste of money, but he at least played better than he had the previous two seasons in L.A. Fisher got to showcase more of his offensive skills as a Warrior and was more than happy to pull the trigger on pull-up jumpers any time he had the ball in transition. He also rebounded from a poor shooting year by hitting 37.1 percent on three-pointers and a career-best 86.2 percent from the line.

Fisher's greatest value was on defense. He has toned it down a bit with the flopping but still draws lots of charges and is a strong help defender. Additionally, his strength allowed him to defend shooting guards, allowing Golden State to go frequently with a small backcourt of him and Claxton. That's no longer necessary with Davis around, but it could come in handy if Baron ends up back on the shelf at some point, a possibility that can't be ruled out.

Fisher has five years left on his $42 million deal and is going to be absolutely worthless by the end of it, but in the short term he gives Golden State a useful backup point guard whose experience could prove valuable during its playoff push.

Adonal Foyle　　center　　　　Age: 30　Height: 6-10　Weight: 270
(100% C)　　　　Most similar at age: Theo Ratliff

Year	G	M/G	FG%	FT%	P/40	R/40	A/40	TS%		Ast		TO		Usg		Reb		PER	
2002-03 GS	82	21.8	.536	.673	9.8	11.0	0.8	56.3	14	7.4	50	14.6	50	9.7	69	14.6	36	15.34	24
2003-04 GS	44	13.0	.454	.543	9.6	11.7	1.2	47.1	64	9.3	32	11.5	21	11.9	57	16.5	11	13.02	41
2004-05 GS	78	21.8	.502	.556	8.3	10.1	1.3	51.4	41	6.3	37	12.7	27	9.6	66	14.5	35	12.70	40
2005-06 PRJ (18.6)			.493	.578	8.6	10.2	1.3	51.2		7.5		13.0		10.0		14.4		13.20	

(continued next page)

Adonal Foyle *(continued)*

Here's a fun trivia question: Ask a friend to name the Warriors' all-time leading shot-blocker. He'll probably say Wilt Chamberlain or Nate Thurmond, but the NBA didn't keep track of blocks when those guys played, so the correct answer is Adonal Foyle.

A backup center being paid starter's money, Foyle did what he always does in 2004–05. He's a very solid defender who is extremely effective at blocking shots and does a decent job on the glass. He's also a fairly inept offensive player with almost no ability to create his own shot, although he has developed a decent eight-foot jumper from the baseline. Foyle at least manages to do a good job of staying out of the way by avoiding turnovers and not forcing shots, allowing the Warriors to live with his defensive contribution.

On paper Foyle is the Warriors' starting center entering the season, but that status is tenuous. Biedrins is breathing down his neck and the team also can go small and play Murphy at center. Even if Foyle remains the starter, he may not improve much on last year's 21.8 minutes per night.

Troy Murphy			power forward									Age: 25	Height: 6-11	Weight: 245			
Defensive PER: -0.04 (86% PF, 14% C)												Most similar at age: Lorenzen Wright					
Year		G	M/G	FG%	FT%	P/40	R/40	A/40	TS%		Ast		TO		Usg		Reb	PER
2002-03	GS	79	31.8	.451	.841	14.7	12.8	1.7	52.6	27	9.7	40	10.1	18	15.6	41	17.1 6	15.88 23
2003-04	GS*	28	21.8	.440	.750	18.3	11.3	1.3	50.1	51	6.0	63	10.2	13	20.4	6	16.0 16	16.75 13
2004-05	GS	70	33.9	.414	.730	18.1	12.7	1.6	49.5	53	7.5	50	8.4	14	20.1	19	18.3 4	16.84 22
2005-06	PRJ (36.5)			.422	.748	16.8	12.2	1.6	49.8		8.1		8.8		18.6		17.2	15.96

* Season rankings are as center

One of the best shooting big men in the game, Murphy was uncharacteristically inaccurate last year because of a broken thumb on his shooting hand. He suffered a brutal shooting stretch upon his return, shooting 32 percent in his first 10 games back to drag down his season totals. Murphy is deadly from middle ranges and moved out to the three-point line last season, hitting 39.9 percent from downtown. He should continue to focus on that shot, as it will make him a much more valuable player than the long two-pointers he had been hoisting previously.

Murphy gets the rest of his points on put-backs from offensive rebounds. Although he's not a leaper, he has a knack for tipping balls to himself and excels at muscling opponents out of the way for position. He has a limited post game, though, and has to learn how to make a lay-up with his right hand.

Also, Murphy struggled on defense, as his Defensive PER shows. He has slow feet, is a poor shot-blocker, and his post defense needs work. His inability to defend is a major reason Foyle is so important for Golden State, because Montgomery can hide Murphy on the opponent's weakest interior player. However, Murphy partly makes up for those deficiencies with his work on the boards.

Mullin rewarded Murphy with a six-year, $58 million extension before last season, and while Murphy probably won't justify that valuation, he's become a solid starter. Only by improving the defense and adding three-point range would he be worth the extravagant contract.

Mickael Pietrus			small forward									Age: 23	Height: 6-6	Weight: 215			
(63% SF, 33% SG, 3% PG)												Most similar at age: Todd Day					
Year		G	M/G	FG%	FT%	P/40	R/40	A/40	TS%		Ast		TO		Usg		Reb	PER
2003-04	GS*	53	14.1	.416	.693	14.9	6.4	1.4	52.8	21	8.2	63	12.1	50	16.4	46	9.0 8	12.84 33
2004-05	GS	67	20.0	.427	.698	19.0	5.6	2.4	53.9	19	10.7	41	12.0	46	20.5	21	8.1 42	14.16 31
2005-06	PRJ (55.3)			.413	.699	17.3	5.7	2.4	52.3		11.0		11.7		19.5		8.1	13.90

* Season rankings are as shooting guard

Pietrus is an intriguing player because of his ability to defend and shoot three-pointers, so it's puzzling that he didn't see more playing time. Offensively, he came on like gangbusters late in the season, shooting 6-for-6 on threes in a late-season win over Phoenix and posting two 25-point games in April. He's developed a knack for shooting the long ball coming off a curl, and although his overall percentage on threes was only 34.4 percent, he was making them at a much higher clip down the stretch.

Pietrus also has become much less passive offensively, as seen by the increase in his Usage Rate. He went to the rim more often and substantially improved his rate of free-throw attempts as a result. He's athletic enough to do damage on the drive, but needs to improve his off-the-dribble game and drop fewer passes. Additionally, his free-throw stroke needs work.

Long-term, Pietrus's best asset may be his defense. He's long, athletic, and can defend any of the perimeter positions, which should make him the team's stopper before long. Considering his offensive improvement, he's no longer a liability at either end of the floor, so he doesn't need to progress much further to claim a starting job.

| Jason Richardson | | | | | shooting guard | | | | | Age: 24 | Height: 6-6 | Weight: 225 |
| Defensive PER: 0.47 (79% SG, 18% SF, 3% PG) | | | | | | | | | | | | Most similar at age: Nick Anderson |

Year		G	M/G	FG%	FT%	P/40	R/40	A/40	TS%		Ast		TO		Usg		Reb		PER	
2002-03	GS	82	32.9	.410	.764	19.0	5.6	3.7	50.1	35	14.5	37	10.5	32	22.6	14	7.5	17	14.74	23
2003-04	GS	78	37.7	.438	.684	19.9	7.1	3.1	50.4	31	12.1	49	10.5	30	23.8	13	10.3	4	16.75	11
2004-05	GS	72	37.8	.446	.693	22.9	6.2	4.1	51.8	37	14.4	35	8.6	13	26.4	6	9.1	6	18.98	7
2005-06	PRJ (71.7)			.433	.708	20.6	6.4	3.5	51.2		13.3		9.5		24.2		9.0		17.00	

One of the game's most spectacular athletes, Richardson continues to steadily round out his game and is now among the better players at his position. In 2004–05 he became a much more potent scoring threat, introducing a nice pull-up bank shot from the right side and developing a post game that makes him a tough cover for small guards. He'll be even tougher once he learns how to read double-teams. Right now his instinct is to dribble away from the pressure rather than fire a quick pass, making it easier for the defense to regroup.

Richardson continues to take too many three-pointers but hit a somewhat respectable 33.8 percent last season. All that catching and shooting helps keep his turnovers down because he's a poor dribbler, but it also prevents him from using his athleticism to get to the free-throw line. Richardson also needs to improve his defense, as he again rated poorly. While he's strong and explosive, he isn't as nimble as some of his counterparts and needs to upgrade his effort level.

Despite these shortcomings, Mullin is looking wiser for giving Richardson a six-year, $70 million extension before the season, because he would have commanded similar dollars last summer on the free-agent market. At 24, Richardson is one of the best rebounders at his position and has blossomed into a first-rate scoring threat. His steady improvement bodes well for future seasons.

| Ansu Sesay | | | | | small forward | | | | | Age: 29 | Height: 6-9 | Weight: 225 |
| (70% PF, 30% SF) | | | | | | | | | | | | Most similar at age: N/A |

Year		G	M/G	FG%	FT%	P/40	R/40	A/40	TS%		Ast		TO		Usg		Reb		PER	
2002-03	Sea	45	10.0	.383	.571	8.4	6.5	2.1	40.4		14.0		15.2		13.6		9.6		6.09	
2003-04	Sea	57	10.2	.455	.696	13.7	6.3	1.3	50.4	36	7.9	55	9.6	14	15.4	45	8.8	27	12.98	36
2004-05	GS	16	8.0	.405	.542	15.3	11.9	3.8	46.6		16.5		11.0		20.5		17.1		14.73	

A little-used reserve forward whom the Warriors waived after the Davis trade, Sesay has played well in his limited opportunities over the past two seasons and deserves another chance to play his way into a team's rotation. His length is a defensive asset, and although he's not much of a shooter, he has managed to help in other areas.

| Nikoloz Tskitishvili | | | | | power forward | | | | | Age: 22 | Height: 7-0 | Weight: 245 |
| (69% PF, 31% C) | | | | | | | | | | | | Most similar at age: N/A |

Year		G	M/G	FG%	FT%	P/40	R/40	A/40	TS%		Ast		TO		Usg		Reb		PER	
2002-03	Den*	81	16.4	.293	.738	9.5	5.5	2.7	37.4	59	15.3	25	14.1	52	16.3	39	7.9	47	4.82	59
2003-04	Den	39	7.9	.328	.793	13.8	8.2	1.3	39.3		6.2		10.5		18.9		11.3		7.03	
2004-05	Den-GS	35	6.3	.297	.571	9.1	7.5	1.8	32.4		8.7		17.9		16.5		10.7		2.48	

* Season rankings are as small forward

A major bust with the fourth overall pick in 2002, Tskitishvili did virtually nothing in his limited playing chances for Denver and Golden State. His option wasn't picked up and he signed a free-agent deal to go to Minnesota over the summer. Considering he's only 22, he could be a prime example of the "second-draft" players I referenced in the Drew Gooden comment in the Cleveland section. He's lit it up in summer leagues the past two offseasons and remains seven feet tall, so it's a well-calculated risk by the T'wolves to see if he can contribute.

(continued next page)

Nikoloz Tskitishvili *(continued)*

Not that he's done much to hearten his fans so far. Tskitishvili was drafted as an outside shooting big man in the Dirk Nowitzki mold but has done nothing to justify that rep as a pro, hitting 29.3, 32.8, and 29.7 percent from the floor in his three pro seasons. Considering how skittish Tskitishvili's about going inside, he'll have to greatly upgrade his accuracy to keep a job in the pros.

Rodney White small forward   Age: 25 Height: 6-9 Weight: 230
(52% SF, 45% PF, 2% C, 1% SG)   Most similar at age: Tim Thomas

Year		G	M/G	FG%	FT%	P/40	R/40	A/40	TS%		Ast		TO		Usg		Reb		PER	
2002-03	Den*	72	21.7	.408	.784	16.6	5.5	3.1	46.9	45	12.5	46	16.1	56	22.2	16	7.9	14	9.73	44
2003-04	Den	72	13.7	.459	.750	21.9	6.7	2.4	52.7	22	9.2	51	12.0	41	23.5	10	9.3	21	16.34	14
2004-05	Den-GS	58	11.7	.419	.614	17.3	5.3	2.6	47.5	57	11.3	37	9.5	23	21.0	18	7.6	50	12.29	40
2005-06	PRJ (67.5)			.430	.716	18.1	5.9	2.4	49.3		10.2		12.0		21.5		8.3		12.92	

* Season rankings are as shooting guard

Golden State waived White after the season, but that may have been a mistake. He has scored in bunches every time he's been given the opportunity, and he has the size and shooting range to be an impact player off the bench. White has shot 37.9 and 40.0 percent on three-pointers the past two seasons and handles the ball well for a player of his size. While he could use a better mid-range game and needs to get to the rim more often, White's overall numbers suggest he could be a useful source of points. He'll come cheaply too, so keep an eye out for him in training camp.

Ike Diogu power forward   Age: 22 Height: 6-9 Weight: 250

Some were surprised that Diogu went No. 9 overall because of questions about his size. However, Diogu has freakishly long arms that allow him to score around the basket and block shots, and he's a polished offensive player who can score in the post or hit an outside jumper. On the down side, his rebound rate was nothing special and he was hugely turnover-prone at Arizona State. The Warriors will work him in for 10 minutes a night behind Murphy this year and see what Diogu can deliver.

Monta Ellis point guard   Age: 20 Height: 6-3 Weight: 175

A second-round pick by the Warriors, Ellis turned pro out of high school but will be 20 by the time the season starts. He's drawn comparisons to Sam Cassell and Chauncey Billups as a 6'3" point guard who looks to score first, but his athleticism is a question mark as is his ability to play the point. He would appear to be a prime candidate to go to the D-League, especially with the crowd Golden State has at point guard.

Chris Taft power forward   Age: 20 Height: 6-10 Weight: 250

Hailed as a potential top five pick before the season, Taft underachieved so badly that he ended up going in the second round. He's a prototypical back-to-the-basket scorer with a go-to move in his right-handed hook shot, and his size and athleticism are unquestioned. However, Taft alarmed scouts by looking comatose at times during the season. Even with the slothful moments, his rebound and block numbers were pretty good for a slow-paced Pitt team and he's quite young, so Taft could be a diamond in the rough.

Houston Rockets

Two years ago longtime Rockets general manager Carroll Dawson was making the last in a series of awful personnel moves that had doomed the team to irrelevance. Since then, he's come back strong.

Dawson's misdeeds at the end of the Rudy Tomjanovich era were particularly serious. He drafted Jason Collier and Bostjan Nachbar; gave long-terms deals to Moochie Norris, Maurice Taylor, and Shandon Anderson; and traded Richard Jefferson and Jason Collins for Eddie Griffin. Most teams would have sent Dawson up the creek, but Houston owner Leslie Alexander showed admirable patience.

Dawson has subsequently rewarded the Rockets with a string of slick moves, starting with his pursuit of Jeff Van Gundy in 2003. Van Gundy gave the team a strong hand after the inmates looked like they were running the asylum at the end of the Tomjanovich era. He also brought a passion for defense and a commitment to getting the ball to Chinese giant Yao Ming.

Dawson's master stroke came a year later in his theft of Tracy McGrady from the Magic. With his team capped out and little to offer, Dawson cobbled together a package of Steve Francis, Cuttino Mobley, and Kelvin Cato whom the Magic shockingly accepted. In one stroke, Dawson had the franchise heading back toward the upper tier of the Western Conference.

He followed that up with a few other solid moves, signing undervalued Bob Sura as a free agent and trading Eric Piatkowski and Adrian Griffin to Chicago for Dikembe Mutombo. However, things hit a snag at the start of the 2004–05 season. Because Dawson had traded the previous season's starting backcourt to get McGrady, Houston's offense was stuck in the mud. The backcourt of Charlie Ward and Jim Jackson hadn't beaten a defender off the dribble since the Nixon administration, and at power forward Juwan Howard and Maurice Taylor were battling to see who could do less to justify his large contract.

The power forwards were a problem all year, but Dawson's quick actions resuscitated the backcourt and saved the season. First, he sent Jackson to New Orleans for David Wesley, which gave the Rockets a strong perimeter defender and a reliable shooter to space the court. Then he sent backup point guard Tyronn Lue to Atlanta for Jon Barry, which upgraded the bench, and got a boost when Sura came back off the injured list. Dawson kept his hot hand at the trade deadline, when he picked up Mike James from Milwaukee for a song and paid a first-round pick as the ransom to dump Taylor's contract on the Knicks.

All told, those maneuvers made Houston one of the best teams in the league by the end of the season. After a 16–17 start, the Rockets finished with a 36–13 flourish. Houston went 31–11 when Yao, Wesley, Sura, and McGrady were in the starting lineup and pushed a strong Dallas team to seven games in the first round of the playoffs before bowing out.

While Dawson was making repairs to the backcourt, Van Gundy was proving his worth on the sidelines. Early in the season the Rockets were extremely slow and methodical, and after 22 games they were averaging a meager 86.9 points per game. McGrady, who almost always struggles in November, was barely averaging 20 points a game and making only 28 percent on three-pointers as he got used to an offense centered around Yao. With little help from the likes of Ward and Jackson, Houston was going nowhere fast.

A light-bulb moment for Van Gundy seemed to come when McGrady scored 13 points in the last 35 seconds of a dramatic comeback win over San Antonio. At that point, Van Gundy began loosening the reigns on the offense and McGrady started heating up. It still took Houston a little while to hit on all cylinders—they even lost twice in the same week to the Bobcats—but by New Year's Day the offense was clicking.

That made it easier for Houston to win games with defense, another Van Gundy trademark. His teams have finished in the top three in field-goal percentage defense in all seven of his full seasons coaching in the NBA. Houston finished second in that category, allowing opponents to shoot 42.3 percent, which doesn't seem possible looking at the

---

Rockets at a Glance

Record: 51–31, 3rd place in Southwest Division

Offensive Efficiency: 103.2 (15th)

Defensive Efficiency: 98.9 (4th)

Pace Factor: 90.9 (24th)

Top-Rated Player: Yao Ming (PER 23.22, 10th overall)

Head Coach: Jeff Van Gundy. Successfully changed gears at midseason to adjust to his talent.

roster. Houston started two fairly soft interior players in Yao and Howard, and several other Rockets (McGrady, Barry, Scott Padgett) are hardly all-defense candidates. But thanks to Van Gundy's detailed preparation and periodic prodding, Houston managed to be a top defensive team anyway.

One of the keys was Wesley. While he struggled on offense, he became the Rockets' perimeter stopper. Even at 6′2″, he's so strong that he could push opponents out of the post and keep them off balance on the perimeter. McGrady also gave a more consistent defensive effort than he had in previous seasons, while a rejuvenated Mutombo anchored the second unit.

The other thing Houston did extremely well was control the defensive boards, as table 1 shows. With huge centers in Yao and Mutombo, a great rebounder at the point in Sura, and lots of help from the other spots, the Rockets led the NBA in defensive rebounding percentage. Since their opponents were missing so many shots, the importance of this was magnified. By forcing misses and limiting second shots, Houston overcame a propensity to foul and an inability to force turnovers (they ranked 26th) to post the league's fourth-best mark in Defensive Efficiency.

By now you've probably noticed the Rockets players I've mentioned include an unusual number of older guys, and that's Houston's biggest liability entering next season. By draft day, Yao, McGrady, and reserve forward Scott Padgett were the only Rockets under 30. Several key players are going to be declining rapidly over the next two seasons. In the backcourt, James is 30, Sura is 32, Barry is 36, and Wesley and Ward are 35. Up front, Ryan Bowen is 30, Howard is 32, Vin Baker is 34, and Mutombo is 73. The Rockets will need to

rapidly replace this group if they're going to stay at the 50-win level.

Along the same vein, a mild concern is Van Gundy's weakness for 35-year-old ex-Knicks. Ward was this year's prime example, with his failure at the point taking half a season to repair, and Weatherspoon wasn't much better. This was after Van Gundy added Mark Jackson and Charles Oakley the previous season, neither of whom did squat. While the pool of players from his New York days is rapidly shrinking, it would be nice to see Van Gundy step out of his comfort zone in player acquisition.

Fortunately, Dawson kept dealing after the season. He tabbed guard Luther Head in the draft, who should provide some young legs in the backcourt and another shooter to open things up for Yao and McGrady. Dawson's second-round choice from a year ago, Greek point guard Vasilis Spanoulis, had a fantastic season in Europe and also could help soon.

Dawson's latest coup was the addition of forward Stromile Swift with the Rockets' midlevel exception. The athletic big man had been stuck behind Pau Gasol in Memphis and was periodically forced to play out of position at center. Now that he's been liberated, expect big things. Swift's projections call for 18.4 points per 40 minutes with a field-goal percentage in the high 40s, and he may be able to improve on that now that he'll be starting (most players put up better per-minute numbers when they start). At 26, he also answers Houston's need to get younger and provides cover if Howard can't make it back from a heart problem discovered at the end of last season. Van Gundy will rip out his few remaining hairs trying to get Swift focused at the defensive end, but in the long run this move should pay huge dividends for Houston.

With the McGrady-Swift-Yao core seemingly set for the future, Dawson now only needs to fill in around the edges to have a championship-caliber basketball team. He's not quite there yet. While last season's mid-stream repair job was impressive, the Rockets have too many age questions in the backcourt to rank with the league's prime contenders and playing in such a brutal division doesn't help. Van Gundy will make sure the Rockets defend like crazy, and that will get them to the playoffs, but they won't go much further unless Dawson can keep his hot streak going at least another year.

Table 1. Defensive Rebounding Percentage Leaders, 2004–05

Team	DRB%
Houston	74.5
Miami	74.1
San Antonio	73.6
New Jersey	73.2
Detroit	73.0
League Average	**71.3**

Vin Baker			power forward								Age: 34		Height: 6-11	Weight: 240	

(73% PF, 22% C, 5% SF) — Most similar at age: N/A

Year		G	M/G	FG%	FT%	P/40	R/40	A/40	TS%		Ast		TO		Usg		Reb		PER	
2002-03	Bos*	52	18.1	.478	.673	11.5	8.4	1.2	53.1	25	8.4	41	17.7	65	13.1	48	11.9	62	10.54	57
2003-04	Bos-NY	54	24.3	.481	.726	16.2	8.5	2.0	53.0	23	10.2	43	12.0	38	17.6	32	12.2	45	14.79	34
2004-05	NY-Hou	27	7.6	.310	.529	6.9	7.6	2.0	35.4		9.3		22.2		12.8		11.2		1.20	

* Season rankings are as center

The Rockets had to take back his salary in the Maurice Taylor trade but don't seem to have much use for Baker. While he can provide a bit of scoring in the post, his defensive inattention isn't likely to endear him to Van Gundy. Considering three power forwards are ahead of him on the depth chart, he faces long odds of getting any minutes.

Jon Barry			shooting guard								Age: 36		Height: 6-5	Weight: 210	

(71% SG, 27% SF, 2% PG) — Most similar at age: Danny Ainge

Year		G	M/G	FG%	FT%	P/40	R/40	A/40	TS%		Ast		TO		Usg		Reb		PER	
2002-03	Det	80	18.4	.450	.860	15.1	4.9	5.6	59.3	4	27.3	5	10.7	34	20.0	27	7.2	23	17.95	11
2003-04	Den	57	19.3	.404	.845	12.8	4.5	5.3	53.5	16	27.8	2	10.0	26	17.3	42	6.2	41	14.58	23
2004-05	Atl-Hou	69	21.8	.438	.873	12.1	4.2	4.4	57.0	11	21.1	8	10.6	36	16.0	53	6.2	44	13.37	32
2005-06	*PRJ (27.8)*			*.411*	*.852*	*12.1*	*4.4*	*4.9*	*53.9*		*23.7*		*11.7*		*16.4*		*6.2*		*12.98*	

Barry remains a productive force off the bench because of his high-efficiency play. While he's no longer adept at creating shots, he's such an accurate shooter and pinpoint passer that he makes an important offensive contribution. Barry nailed 45.1 percent of his three-point attempts as a Rocket by feeding off the attention given to McGrady and Yao, and his Assist Ratio again was among the best at his position.

Defensively, Barry hustles but his physical limitations make him a liability anyway. Additionally, he occasionally loses focus and spends more time arguing with the refs than guarding his man. But he's a clever player with good anticipation, and those skills allowed him to average nearly a steal a game even at 35. Barry re-signed with Houston over the summer and should again be a key reserve for the Rockets.

Ryan Bowen			power forward								Age: 30		Height: 6-9	Weight: 220	

(73% SF, 27% PF) — Most similar at age: Cliff Levingston

Year		G	M/G	FG%	FT%	P/40	R/40	A/40	TS%		Ast		TO		Usg		Reb		PER	
2002-03	Den*	62	16.1	.492	.659	8.9	6.3	2.2	51.9	31	17.3	13	13.8	48	11.4	55	9.2	29	12.80	33
2003-04	Den	52	7.5	.340	.833	4.7	8.9	1.8	39.5		21.9		7.3		7.7		12.3		9.99	
2004-05	Hou	66	9.2	.423	.667	7.4	5.0	1.2	46.2	67	5.7	63	4.8	1	9.5	68	7.4	69	7.65	69
2005-06	*PRJ (22.4)*			*.442*	*.642*	*7.7*	*5.7*	*1.7*	*47.5*		*10.4*		*8.3*		*10.1*		*8.3*		*9.27*	

* Season rankings are as small forward

A scrappy, energetic player whom the Rockets used to guard Dirk Nowitzki for much of the Dallas series, Bowen is at his best when used as a power forward against small lineups. That's why I listed his position there, even though he saw more time at small forward last season. Bowen can hit an open 15-footer but is extremely reluctant to create offense and seeks mainly to avoid turnovers. He has more value at the defensive end, where he is quick for his position and hustles like crazy. While Bowen can't handle strength match-ups, he defends well against tall, versatile types like Nowitzki.

The bad news is that Bowen's offense and rebounding are so bad that it's hard to live with his defense. Bowen had the second-lowest Usage Rate among power forwards, putting tremendous pressure on his teammates to create shots. Additionally, he fared poorly on his rare attempts and finished with an abysmal 46.2 TS%. Bowen re-signed with Houston over the summer, but will need to shoot better to get much action in an improved Rockets lineup.

Juwan Howard — power forward
(99% PF, 1% C)

Age: 32 Height: 6-9 Weight: 230
Most similar at age: Armon Gilliam

Year		G	M/G	FG%	FT%	P/40	R/40	A/40	TS%		Ast		TO		Usg		Reb		PER	
2002-03	Den	77	35.4	.450	.803	20.8	8.6	3.4	50.1	41	12.7	23	10.3	20	25.1	6	12.5	38	17.27	17
2003-04	Orl	81	35.5	.453	.809	19.1	7.9	2.2	51.3	36	9.4	50	10.6	19	21.4	16	11.2	52	15.58	29
2004-05	Hou	61	26.6	.451	.843	14.4	8.5	2.3	49.4	54	11.0	22	10.3	29	18.0	29	12.5	41	12.96	48
2005-06	PRJ (41.1)			.440	.789	15.9	7.9	2.3	49.4		10.3		11.1		19.2		11.3		13.64	

Included as an extra in the McGrady trade, Howard managed to disappoint his second team in two seasons. He lost his starting job to Maurice Taylor in training camp and got it back only because Taylor was playing even worse. Howard has become more dependent on his line-drive, double-clutching jump shot as he's gotten older, and last year his free-throw rate dropped tremendously. Since Yao was always in the post, Howard frequently played at the foul line and was dumping the ball into Yao. That helped Howard's Assist Ratio, but shooting jumpers from the foul line isn't really his game. Swift's skills should be much better suited.

Howard also had a bad case of the dropsies. Although his Turnover Ratio didn't change much, it seemed every time McGrady drove to the basket and passed to Howard, he would either drop the pass or fumble it enough that he had to stop and allow the defense to recover. Those missed connections cost him several easy baskets and helped explain the marked drop in his points per 40 minutes.

Defensively, the story was a little better. Howard isn't a terribly physical defender, but he has the size to force opponents away from the basket and gave a much more consistent effort than he had in Orlando. His athleticism is declining rapidly though, as he blocked only five shots all season—one fewer than Mike James.

Plus, Howard had some health issues. He went down with a sprained MCL in March and then was found to have a viral infection in his heart soon after. He is expected to be back for training camp, but his health concerns add another layer to the pie of disappointment he smashed in the Rockets' face.

Mike James — point guard
(98% PG, 2% SG)

Age: 30 Height: 6-2 Weight: 188
Most similar at age: David Wesley

Year		G	M/G	FG%	FT%	P/40	R/40	A/40	TS%		Ast		TO		Usg		Reb		PER	
2002-03	Mia	78	22.1	.373	.732	14.1	3.5	5.7	46.9	49	24.6	41	10.8	28	22.4	28	5.0	43	11.76	43
2003-04	Bos-Det	81	27.1	.414	.811	13.7	4.3	6.2	52.8	13	28.8	26	10.5	26	19.5	44	5.8	25	14.40	28
2004-05	Mil-Hou	74	25.1	.441	.752	18.7	4.5	5.7	53.4	18	22.2	56	9.0	10	24.2	19	6.6	10	16.52	21
2005-06	PRJ (54.7)			.423	.785	16.2	4.2	5.7	52.6		24.5		9.9		22.2		6.0		15.05	

James had the best season of his career while splitting time between Milwaukee and Houston. In both cities, it seemed strange that he didn't play more. As a Buck, James was in a strict time-share with Maurice Williams—the two would alternate quarters in most games. James was the better player at both ends of the court and should have been starting the whole time. Then, once he got to Houston, the Rockets could have moved Bob Sura to shooting guard, started James at the point, and brought David Wesley off the bench. Houston opted not to mess with the chemistry and brought James off the pine instead.

The Rockets should ponder that switch this season now that they have the time to implement it. While Wesley's defense would be missed, James is no slouch either, excelling at pressuring the ball up the court. Plus, he provides a much greater spark at the offensive end. James has a high-arcing shot that he releases from behind his head, making it extremely difficult to block and allowing him to hit it with defenders right in his face. He also kept a low Turnover Ratio, and while he's more of a shoot-first guard than a distributor, the presence of Sura and McGrady would make that less important. Finally, he helps out on the glass.

James isn't likely to equal last season's numbers, but he won't have to in order to have value for the Rockets. His combination of shooting and defense gave the team a shot in the arm once he arrived midway through last season and should do so again.

Tracy McGrady small forward Age: 26 Height: 6-8 Weight: 210
Defensive PER: 1.08 (69% SF, 29% SG, 2% PF) Most similar at age: Kobe Bryant

Year		G	M/G	FG%	FT%	P/40	R/40	A/40	TS%		Ast		TO		Usg		Reb		PER	
2002-03	Orl	75	39.4	.457	.793	32.6	6.6	5.6	56.4	7	15.0	28	7.1	1	34.5	1	9.5	26	30.25	1
2003-04	Orl	67	39.9	.417	.796	28.1	6.0	5.5	52.6	23	15.8	20	7.7	5	32.8	1	8.5	34	25.21	1
2004-05	Hou	78	40.8	.431	.774	25.2	6.1	5.6	52.6	34	17.5	5	7.9	10	31.2	2	8.3	37	22.95	2
2005-06	PRJ (21.2)			.426	.772	27.3	6.1	5.7	53.1		16.8		8.2		32.5		8.5		24.03	

If you're a fantasy player, one good strategy might be to avoid drafting McGrady and then try trade for him on December 1. McGrady got off to a horrid start for the second year in a row, shooting 40.7 percent in November and posting his worst month of the season in points, rebounds, assists, steals, field-goal percentage, and three-point percentage.

The rest of his year was better, but still a slight disappointment. McGrady shot too many three-pointers off the dribble and hit only 32.6 percent as a result. Since he was taking nearly six a game, it pretty much killed his TS%. He also took fewer shots than in the past, partly because he was deferring to Yao so much early in the season. McGrady seemed to be in a groove by the postseason, however, and torched Dallas in the playoffs. He averaged over 30 points and nearly seven assists for the series. Even in the 40-point blowout loss in Game 7, his final stat line was 27-7-7 in 36 minutes.

There's no doubt McGrady can keep that up for a full season, and perhaps he will now that he's had a year to acclimate to Houston's style. Few players are better at shooting mid-range jump shots off the dribble, and he's in a league of his own when it comes to creating shots without committing turnovers. If he can bounce back to the offensive heights he hit in his final two seasons in Orlando, Houston's odds of hanging with the big boys in the West improve significantly.

Yao Ming center Age: 25 Height: 7-6 Weight: 310
Defensive PER: 0.67 (100% C) Most similar at age: Gheorghe Muresan

Year		G	M/G	FG%	FT%	P/40	R/40	A/40	TS%		Ast		TO		Usg		Reb		PER	
2002-03	Hou	82	29.1	.498	.811	18.5	11.3	2.3	57.0	9	10.7	27	13.5	38	20.0	6	16.3	16	20.65	2
2003-04	Hou	82	32.8	.522	.809	21.3	10.9	1.8	58.6	4	7.9	47	13.2	37	21.5	4	15.4	21	21.88	3
2004-05	Hou	80	30.6	.552	.783	23.9	10.9	1.0	61.4	4	4.2	53	13.5	36	22.1	3	14.8	32	23.22	3
2005-06	PRJ (1.7)			.548	.750	23.6	12.2	1.7	60.7		7.2		12.9		23.1		16.9		24.05	

One of the strangest subplots of the season came when Houston struggled at the start of the year. Out of nowhere, a lot of "What is wrong with Yao Ming?" articles started popping up, as though it was clearly Yao's fault that Charlie Ward needed a walker to get across halfcourt. In truth, Yao already was well on his way to his best season as a pro and has shown slow but steady improvement in his three pro campaigns.

Yao is unusual because, despite his size, he doesn't overpower opponents with brute force the way Shaquille O'Neal does. Instead, Yao is a very good short-range shooter, and since nobody has a prayer of blocking his shot, he's a devastating scoring option. While Yao's 18.3 points per game average doesn't seem overly impressive, keep in mind that he averaged only 30 minutes a game. On a per-40-minute basis, he scored 23.9 points, and did it with one of the highest TS%s in the league. Yao is slowly learning how to play more physically as well, causing his free-throw rate to climb steadily.

The reason Yao averages so few minutes is tied to two factors. First, he frequently gets in foul trouble. Yao's foul rate actually increased quite a bit last season and he fouled out of eight games. The playoffs were even more extreme, as Yao completely dominated but couldn't stay on the court. He averaged over 21 points and shot 65 percent against Dallas but could play only 31 minutes a game.

Second, although Yao doesn't have great stamina, the Rockets have him running all over the place. On defense, they ask him to step out and trap screen-and-roll plays, then run back to the middle. On offense, he has to set a high screen for McGrady before he dives down the lane to a spot on the blocks. If he only had to run from block to block like Shaq, he might be able to stay on the court for much longer.

Despite the minutes limitations, Shaq is the only center more valuable than Yao (provided one doesn't consider Amare Stoudemire a center). The Rockets face a "decision" before the season starts on whether to give Yao an extension. It should take them about 0.3 seconds to offer him the max and keep him locked up in Houston for six more years.

Dikembe Mutombo center **Age: 39 Height: 7-2 Weight: 261**
(100% C) Most similar at age: Patrick Ewing

Year		G	M/G	FG%	FT%	P/40	R/40	A/40	TS%		Ast		TO		Usg		Reb		PER	
2002-03	NJ	24	21.4	.374	.727	10.7	11.9	1.5	44.5	64	9.1	38	16.3	59	14.3	41	17.0	11	11.24	54
2003-04	NY	65	23.0	.478	.681	9.7	11.7	0.7	52.3	34	5.9	65	12.7	33	10.5	67	16.7	10	14.35	30
2004-05	Hou	80	15.2	.498	.741	10.6	14.1	0.3	57.5	16	1.6	69	15.0	45	10.4	62	20.6	2	16.51	14
2005-06	PRJ (0.8)			.493	.685	11.0	14.0	0.5	55.1		3.4		13.4		11.1		19.5		16.64	

Mutombo's late-career surge continued in another city, as he dominated on the glass and sent back a shot every 11.7 minutes. With his combination of size and timing, Mutombo has always been able to change games at the defensive end. While he's no longer as mobile, his role in Houston was perfect for his skill set. He could come off the bench in brief spurts to give Yao a breather and bolster the defense, and he certainly did that. Houston gave up a staggering 10.6 points less per 48 minutes when Mutombo was on the court.

A bigger surprise was his rebounding. Mutombo had the second-best Rebound Rate among centers and did a lot of his damage at the offensive end, a place where the Rockets were very poor overall. He converted some of those into put-backs, accounting for most of his offense, but otherwise stayed out of the way and didn't try to force the issue. It was a welcome change from the previous two seasons.

Mutombo's age is an obvious concern, but he's not going to be any shorter next year and he played so well in 2004–05 that he'd be very valuable even if his productivity declines. The Rockets re-upped Mutombo in the offseason, and will use him to spell Yao once again.

Moochie Norris point guard **Age: 32 Height: 6-1 Weight: 185**
(71% PG, 29% SG) Most similar at age: N/A

Year		G	M/G	FG%	FT%	P/40	R/40	A/40	TS%		Ast		TO		Usg		Reb		PER	
2002-03	Hou	82	16.8	.406	.684	10.4	4.6	5.7	47.0	48	29.6	16	13.0	48	18.0	51	6.7	17	11.76	42
2003-04	NY	66	12.8	.369	.761	11.1	3.1	5.7	47.1	50	27.9	32	14.8	56	18.7	53	4.4	56	10.94	56
2004-05	NY-Hou	38	9.5	.321	.833	10.0	5.1	4.3	37.6		20.6		14.6		18.7		7.5		6.01	

Norris played sparingly for both the Knicks and Rockets and his skills have declined sharply in the past three seasons. Norris is a decent passer who can fill in at the point in a pinch, but he has few other skills and a big crowd lined up ahead of him for minutes. Besides, the Rockets already dumped him once. Fortunately for him, his contract is guaranteed for two more years, so he'll be a well-compensated spectator.

Scott Padgett power forward **Age: 29 Height: 6-9 Weight: 240**
(94% PF, 5% C, 1% SF) Most similar at age: Austin Croshere

Year		G	M/G	FG%	FT%	P/40	R/40	A/40	TS%		Ast		TO		Usg		Reb		PER	
2002-03	Uta	82	16.1	.402	.757	14.1	8.2	2.6	49.6	42	13.7	19	11.2	32	17.9	32	12.5	39	12.45	40
2003-04	Hou	58	9.4	.443	.750	14.7	10.2	1.7	55.2	10	10.2	44	9.7	10	15.9	43	14.7	24	15.71	28
2004-05	Hou	66	14.3	.421	.725	11.7	7.9	2.3	54.9	23	11.1	20	8.9	17	13.7	59	11.5	52	12.32	53
2005-06	PRJ (31.8)			.404	.736	12.3	8.0	2.3	51.4		11.5		10.2		15.0		11.8		11.37	

Padgett is a poor defensive player who has to make shots to keep his spot in the rotation. Last season he didn't enough make shots, and that ultimately cost him a regular role. While Padgett dropped in 39.7 percent of his three-point attempts, he generated so few attempts that it wasn't worth it to keep him on the court. Additionally, his Rebound Rate dropped off sharply and he will need to recover in that area.

Padgett has to score to compensate for his poor defense. He doesn't move well and his lack of strength makes him a liability against the West's high-scoring power forwards. With his contract guaranteed for one more season, Padgett will be the Rockets' insurance policy at power forward. The presence of Swift and Howard mean he'll have a hard time earning minutes, but he might be the best third-string power forward in the league*, for what that's worth. If he can create more shots and pick up the rebounding, a trade might land him a more regular assignment.

---
* Not including the Knicks

Rod Strickland   point guard   Age: 39   Height: 6-3   Weight: 185
(100% PG)   Most similar at age: N/A

Year		G	M/G	FG%	FT%	P/40	R/40	A/40	TS%		Ast		TO		Usg		Reb		PER	
2002-03	Min	47	20.3	.432	.738	13.4	4.0	9.0	49.2	41	34.9	9	12.3	44	23.4	18	5.6	30	15.38	21
2003-04	Orl-Tor	61	19.6	.425	.735	12.8	5.2	8.2	48.2	44	33.6	13	11.7	38	22.4	26	7.5	4	14.90	25
2004-05	Hou	16	12.3	.209	.900	5.7	5.5	8.0	29.5		37.9		15.6		19.2		8.1		4.51	

Houston brought Strickland in for a brief look when they were desperate for backup point guard help, but he was quickly found wanting. His dreadful 20.9 percent shooting tells most of the story, and one wonders if this was the final stop in Strickland's nomadic career.

Bob Sura   point guard   Age: 32   Height: 6-5   Weight: 200
Defensive PER: 0.34 (91% PG, 9% SG)   Most similar at age: Kelly Tripucka

Year		G	M/G	FG%	FT%	P/40	R/40	A/40	TS%		Ast		TO		Usg		Reb		PER	
2002-03	GS*	55	20.5	.412	.696	14.2	5.9	6.3	51.0	27	27.1	6	12.6	50	20.3	23	7.9	15	14.15	29
2003-04	Det-Atl*	80	20.8	.416	.757	14.3	7.8	5.6	50.9	29	25.2	7	11.4	41	20.7	30	11.1	2	16.23	13
2004-05	Hou	61	31.5	.427	.750	13.0	7.0	6.6	53.3	20	30.2	25	14.0	59	20.3	49	10.3	2	14.43	35
2005-06	*PRJ (32.7)*			*.414*	*.731*	*12.1*	*7.2*	*6.0*	*51.5*		*29.0*		*13.4*		*18.7*		*10.4*		*14.28*	

* Season rankings are as shooting guard

Sura's importance to the Rockets can be underlined in one stat. The Rockets went 42–16 when he started, and 9–15 when he didn't. When Sura was out at the beginning of the season, Houston had nobody who could push the pace and lacked a creative passer to set up shots. Sura also shot a surprising 35.5 percent on three-pointers, where he normally struggles, and his TS% was above the league norm as a result.

Sura played the point, but he might be better off at shooting guard with James at the point. While Sura can handle the ball, he was much less turnover prone when he played on the wings and he struggled to stay in front of quicker point guards defensively. He's not a pure shooter, but he has good size and strength and for a guard he's an unbelievable rebounder too. With James and Head around, it seems Houston can make the switch this year.

The other potential fly in the ointment is that Sura is 32 going on 100, and it's questionable how much longer he can stay in one piece. Both his back and knee provided constant trouble last season, and his aggressive style isn't doing him any favors in that regard. The Rockets aren't paying him much—$14 million over four years—so he's already been worth the investment, but he was Houston's third-best player last year and the Rockets can't afford for him to drop off much.

Charlie Ward   point guard   Age: 35   Height: 6-2   Weight: 190
(89% PG, 11% SG)   Most similar at age: N/A

Year		G	M/G	FG%	FT%	P/40	R/40	A/40	TS%		Ast		TO		Usg		Reb		PER	
2002-03	NY	66	22.2	.399	.774	12.9	4.8	8.3	54.0	17	36.5	7	11.3	33	21.2	36	7.1	12	15.90	18
2003-04	NY-SA	71	17.6	.410	.741	13.5	4.6	6.9	52.8	14	30.2	23	13.5	47	20.9	36	6.4	15	14.48	27
2004-05	Hou	14	25.7	.312	.846	8.3	4.3	4.8	45.3		22.8		12.5		15.0		6.3		8.65	

With Sura injured, Ward was the team's starting point guard to begin the year but was a complete flop. To be fair, injuries played a part. Ward underwent knee surgery after 14 games and is under contract again for this season. While he isn't expected to play much of a role, his ability to hit three-pointers and create steals might allow him to carve a niche if the knee is OK.

Clarence Weatherspoon power forward Age: 35 Height: 6-7 Weight: 270
(75% PF, 25% C) Most similar at age: Buck Williams

Year		G	M/G	FG%	FT%	P/40	R/40	A/40	TS%		Ast		TO		Usg		Reb		PER	
2002-03	NY	79	25.6	.449	.768	10.3	11.8	1.3	52.2	30	10.8	35	10.0	17	11.7	57	17.4	5	14.48	32
2003-04	NY-Hou	52	16.7	.493	.736	12.0	9.4	1.4	53.8	19	9.8	47	11.4	30	13.4	58	13.6	34	14.66	36
2004-05	Hou	40	13.1	.412	.829	9.4	9.3	1.3	47.5	62	6.2	56	9.3	21	11.8	66	13.6	31	8.91	66
2005-06	PRJ (28.5)			.437	.754	10.0	9.6	1.5	49.7		9.7		10.5		12.2		13.8		11.41	

Although Weatherspoon saw some minutes late in the season when Howard went down, he didn't do much with them. Because he's so short for his position, Weatherspoon gets his shot blocked as much as any player in basketball and has trouble finishing around the rim. He doesn't have a jumper either, so he's basically forced to play inside. While his muscle allows him to push out post players on the defensive end, they still can shoot right over him. His rebounding is nothing exceptional either. Overall, I'm puzzled why Scott Padgett didn't get the call ahead of Weatherspoon down the stretch, and don't expect to see that scenario repeated this year.

The Rockets waived Weatherspoon over the summer as their luxury tax amnesty cut, so Van Gundy won't have the chance to give him minutes this season. At his age as an undersized power forward, he'll have a tough time earning a roster spot this season, much less cracking a team's rotation.

David Wesley shooting guard Age: 35 Height: 6-1 Weight: 203
(80% SG, 18% PG, 2% SF) Most similar at age: Dana Barros

Year		G	M/G	FG%	FT%	P/40	R/40	A/40	TS%		Ast		TO		Usg		Reb		PER	
2002-03	NO	73	37.1	.433	.781	18.0	2.6	3.7	53.3	22	16.5	26	8.7	12	21.5	18	3.8	56	15.11	21
2003-04	NO	61	32.8	.389	.753	17.0	2.7	3.5	48.3	46	15.2	36	8.7	14	22.8	15	4.0	62	13.01	32
2004-05	NO-Hou	80	34.7	.398	.857	13.7	3.3	3.8	51.3	44	18.2	18	8.7	16	18.2	38	4.5	63	11.79	42
2005-06	PRJ (24.8)			.379	.788	13.8	2.9	3.6	48.4		17.2		9.1		18.9		4.1		11.39	

Even in his mid-30s, Wesley is a top-notch defensive player. He's shorter than every opponent he faces, but that doesn't impact him much because he's strong enough to push almost anybody out of the post. He has a tougher time when opponents come off screens firing, because they can shoot the ball right over him. Despite his age he moves well laterally, as he's never had a serious injury and thus is in better condition than most of his peers.

However, Wesley's game has really dropped off at the offensive end, and that may cost him a starting job this year. His field-goal percentage dipped under 40 percent for the second year in a row, and he created far fewer shots in Houston than he did as a Hornet. Wesley used to be able to get to the basket, but he rarely did last season even playing against bigger players as a shooting guard. His free throw rate has been in a downward spiral as a result. Based on the outcomes of similar players, the Rockets shouldn't be holding their breath for him to bounce back. He still has value because he'll hit open threes (38 percent as a Rocket) and defend, but Houston might be better off if he plays fewer minutes.

Luther Head point guard Age: 23 Height: 6-3 Weight: 185

Head improved dramatically in his senior year at Illinois, vaulting himself from a virtual unknown into the first round of the draft. Head is a good athlete, an active defender, and shoots well from the outside, so the mystery is what took him so long to put it all together. His challenge at the NBA level will be finding a position. He played shooting guard in college and the transition to the point is often a tough one, but he's at least an inch too short to play shooting guard full time.

Los Angeles Clippers

Remember those choose-your-own-adventure books, where the beginning would always be the same but the end would be different based on the choices the reader made?

The Clippers are kind of the opposite. The beginning is different from year to year, but it always ends the same—with another trip to the lottery. For fans of this team, the adventure has already been chosen.

L.A. at least put up a fight last season. It figured to be a playoff outsider when the season began, as they had lost out on the Kobe Bryant sweepstakes and hadn't come up with a Plan B. The bench was extremely thin and the absence of Kerry Kittles (who missed nearly the whole year with back trouble) only made things worse.

But lo and behold, the Clippers blasted Seattle by 30 on opening day, and a week later they beat Indiana on the road by 34. Bobby Simmons started raining jump shots from the corner and shutting down opposing scorers, on his way to the league's Most Improved Player award. With Elton Brand and Corey Maggette doing their usual damage and Marko Jaric off to a hot shooting start, the Clippers were in the unfamiliar position of playoff contenders. L.A. had its first five-game winning streak in nearly a decade (baby steps, people, baby steps) and stood at .500 as late as February 3 before fading down the stretch.

The Clippers blame that fade on a rash of injuries, and certainly they contributed. Kittles played only 11 games and was virtually worthless when he tried. Jaric missed almost half the season with a stress fracture in his foot, and backup point guard Shaun Livingston had two separate knee injuries that took him out for 52 games. Their absences forced L.A. to use Rick Brunson and rookie Lionel Chambers as the point guard combo for a major chunk of the season, which didn't boost their playoff push.

Equally damaging was L.A.'s slavish devotion to lottery pick Chris Kaman. The Clippers had begun the season with a small frontcourt of Brand and Chris Wilcox, and the duo worked well together. The Clippers were 14–11 in the 25

Clippers at a Glance

Record: 37–45, 3rd place in Pacific Division

Offensive Efficiency: 102.2 (20th)

Defensive Efficiency: 103.4 (14th)

Pace Factor: 91.4 (21st)

Top-Rated Player: Elton Brand (PER 22.54, 16th overall)

Head Coach: Mike Dunleavy. Coaxed a better defensive effort, but made some odd personnel choices.

games Wilcox started, including 11–8 in the season's first 19 games. But when Kaman came off the injured list, he was promptly handed Wilcox's job, for no apparent reason. While Wilcox withered on the bench and eventually fell out of the rotation, Kaman kept the job for most of the season. The Clippers went 21–29 in the 50 games Kaman started, which isn't surprising considering his inferior PER (see table 1; note that the gap was much greater when comparing Wilcox's stats as a starter).

Now one might think that because Wilcox is very light for a center at 6'10", 235, while Kaman is a more solidly built 7'0", 265, the PER difference between the two might be offset by a superior defensive performance. Nothing could be further from the truth. The Clippers gave up 2.4 points more per 48 minutes with Kaman on the court than with Wilcox. Even that understates matters because L.A. ran more when Wilcox played, increasing its Pace Factor. In spite of his size, Kaman is an atrocious defender. He narrowly missed qualifying for the Defensive PER ratings, but if he had his −0.06 Defensive PER easily would have been the worst among centers.

Wilcox wasn't the only option either. The Clippers had three centers who were better than Kaman, and none of them saw nearly as many minutes. Before the season, L.A. had picked up two very inexpensive big men in Zeljko Rebraca and Mikki Moore, and those two made the Clippers' frontcourt unusually deep. As table 1 shows, Rebraca and Wilcox had better seasons statistically than Kaman and produced better records as starters, while Rebraca, Wilcox, and Moore all had a much bigger defensive impact than Kaman. Yet all three played less.

In fact, the Clippers seemed to play their centers in inverse proportion to their effectiveness. Moore was nearly as big a liability as Kaman but saw more playing time than Wilcox, while Rebraca was the best of the bunch but barely played. Obviously this doesn't reflect terribly well on Clippers coach Mike Dunleavy, but one has to wonder if the blame is being directed in the right direction. The Clippers'

Table 1. Clippers Centers, 2004–05

Player	PER	Opp. Pts/48 When on Court	W–L As Starter	Minutes
Rebraca	14.02	104.3	1–1	928
Wilcox	13.52	106.9	14–11	1105
Kaman	13.14	109.3	21–29	1632
Moore	12.66	107.5	1–3	1178

approach with Kaman is terrifyingly similar to what they did with Michael Olowokandi, sticking a lottery center in the starting lineup in the hope that it would justify a pick that clearly wasn't working out. Perhaps it was a mandate from management.

Dunleavy had his positives. He is the Clippers' first credible coach since Larry Brown and in his second season he induced a significant defensive improvement. Simmons played a big part in that, posting the second-best Defensive PER in the league and giving the Clippers the stopper on the wings they had lacked the previous season. Other players, notably Corey Maggette, also turned in stronger efforts.

Where L.A. struggled was at the offensive end. The Clippers finished last in the NBA in three-pointers with 231, barely a quarter as many as the league-leading Suns hit. With Jaric and Kittles missing most of the year, Simmons was the only Clipper who could consistently hit an outside shot, and he was more of a mid-range guy than a mad bomber. Only four Clippers made more than one three-pointer—not one per game, one all year. The team leader, Jaric, was out for 32 games, while Maggette led the team in attempts but made only 30.4 percent. As a result, zone defenses gave L.A. huge problems, because nobody could make opponents pay for sagging into the paint (see table 2).

The Clippers also made too many turnovers. They ranked 23rd in the league with miscues on 15.9 percent of their possessions, perhaps because they were trying to jam the ball inside so often. As a result of the turnovers and lack of three-pointers, L.A. was 20th in Offensive Efficiency

Table 2. Fewest Three-Pointers per Game, 2004–05

Team	Three-Pointers
LA Clippers	2.82
Cleveland	3.66
Atlanta	3.71
Denver	3.90
Orlando	3.90
League Average	**5.60**

despite a solid field-goal percentage and above-average offensive rebounding.

The Clippers' weaknesses in three-point shooting and turnovers point to an obvious need in the backcourt. Help may be on the way. Livingston played very well in the final weeks of the season and, in just his second season removed from high school, seems ready to take over the offense.

Even better, the Clippers now have a real shooting guard, after spending last season with Maggette out of position. L.A. signed Cuttino Mobley from the Sacramento Kings, and he should dispense with the outside shooting problems. Mobley made 2.27 three-pointers per game last season, nearly as many as the entire Clippers team.

But as usual with the Clippers, there is plenty of bad news to offset the good. Let's start with Mobley. He's a 30-year-old middling talent who got a five-year deal worth $42 million. Unusually for the Clippers, they overpaid. Mobley will be 34 by the time the deal ends and it's extremely unlikely he'll still be a starting-caliber player by that point, but he'll be one of the highest-paid players on the team.

Additionally, the Clippers lost more than they gained. Simmons left as a free agent to sign a five-year, $47 million deal with Milwaukee. Those who pause to consider the irony will note that Simmons is both better and younger than Mobley, yet received a similar contract. Jaric also is gone, traded to Minnesota along with Chalmers for Sam Cassell and a first-round pick. One suspects the Clippers will use the veteran Cassell to mentor Livingston for half a season and then flip him at the trade deadline if, as one expects, they're out of playoff contention. It's not a bad deal for L.A. if they can squeeze a second first-round pick out of it, but in the short term Cassell's iffy health will further stress the bench.

The bench has thinned out already because Moore and Kittles are free agents, although the Clippers did manage to keep the underrated Rebraca with a multiyear deal. The draft won't provide much help either, as teenage first-round pick Yaroslav Korolev is at least a year away from contributing.

As long as Brand and Maggette stay healthy, the Clippers won't be awful, and that in itself is an improvement. But while we don't know how the script will begin for 2005–06, we already know how it will end. L.A. doesn't have nearly enough depth to withstand the usual bumps and bruises that accumulate over an NBA season, especially in the grueling Western Conference. Dunleavy will make the defense respectable, Livingston will provide cause for hope, and Brand might make the All-Star team, but the ending for this book hasn't changed.

Kenny Anderson   point guard

(100% PG)

Age: 35   Height: 6-1   Weight: 168

Most similar at age: Frank Johnson

Year		G	M/G	FG%	FT%	P/40	R/40	A/40	TS%		Ast		TO		Usg		Reb		PER	
2002-03	Sea-NO	61	18.6	.427	.789	13.1	4.7	7.0	45.7	55	29.1	22	11.0	30	22.7	26	6.8	16	13.53	31
2003-04	Ind	44	20.6	.441	.729	11.6	3.6	5.5	47.3	49	27.6	34	11.1	29	19.1	48	5.0	40	11.07	54
2004-05	Atl-LAC	43	17.3	.423	.730	10.9	4.7	5.5	46.7	59	26.4	35	13.3	55	18.1	58	6.6	9	10.03	58
2005-06	*PRJ (24.9)*			*.402*	*.712*	*10.9*	*4.0*	*5.4*	*43.8*		*25.5*		*12.4*		*18.4*		*5.6*		*10.39*	

Anderson made two stops last season and was waived at the end of both, leaving his career on thin ice for the coming season. His lack of a jump shot has become an increasing liability since he can no longer get in the paint, but he can run an offense. That skill and teams' constant needs for a backup point guard should get him a phone call at some point this season.

Elton Brand   power forward

Defensive PER: 1.37 (77% PF, 23% C)

Age: 26   Height: 6-8   Weight: 272

Most similar at age: Antonio McDyess

Year		G	M/G	FG%	FT%	P/40	R/40	A/40	TS%		Ast		TO		Usg		Reb		PER	
2002-03	LAC	62	39.6	.502	.685	18.7	11.5	2.6	54.3	18	11.4	31	11.7	38	20.5	16	15.8	13	21.71	3
2003-04	LAC	69	38.8	.493	.773	20.6	10.7	3.4	56.7	4	13.9	22	11.8	35	22.2	11	15.8	16	23.18	3
2004-05	LAC	81	37.0	.503	.752	21.6	10.3	2.8	55.4	21	11.2	19	9.9	26	23.6	9	15.3	19	22.54	7
2005-06	*PRJ (34.3)*			*.495*	*.762*	*19.7*	*10.4*	*2.8*	*55.5*		*12.0*		*10.3*		*21.8*		*15.3*		*21.39*	

The snubbing of Brand for the All-Star game has become such an annual ritual that it hardly seems like news anymore. Last season when Brand was predictably left off the Western Conference roster, the media focused much more on Chris Webber's alleged snub (yes, really) than the strange inattention Brand receives.

Brand is a difficult player for casual viewers to appreciate because he isn't great at one particular skill—he's just good at everything. He was above the league average for his position in every metric except three-point shooting, making him one of the league's best players overall.

Brand hurt his right hand during the course of the season but it may have been beneficial long-term. He started using his left much more often instead of going right all the time and ended up with a more diverse game around the basket. He struggles at times to score in the post against taller players, but his jump hook shot is a reliable weapon and he's very good at playing from the high post.

Defensively, Brand continues to be underrated. He blocked over two shots a game for the fourth straight season and has the size to battle opposing big men in the post. Additionally, he's a workhorse on the boards and his Defensive PER was very solid. It's no wonder that he's one of the few players the Clippers have paid good money in order to keep.

Rick Brunson   point guard

Defensive PER: 0.62 (89% PG, 11% SG)

Age: 33   Height: 6-4   Weight: 205

Most similar at age: Vinnie Del Negro

Year		G	M/G	FG%	FT%	P/40	R/40	A/40	TS%		Ast		TO		Usg		Reb		PER	
2002-03	Chi	17	11.5	.460	.833	12.2	3.9	7.3	54.3		33.2		15.7		19.3		5.4		13.42	
2003-04	Chi-Tor	40	10.3	.381	.871	11.5	3.6	8.0	49.7		35.1		14.1		20.1		5.1		13.05	
2004-05	LAC	80	24.3	.376	.770	9.0	3.8	8.4	46.0	62	40.2	3	12.4	51	19.4	53	5.7	31	11.66	51
2005-06	*PRJ (20.7)*			*.363*	*.747*	*8.4*	*3.9*	*7.5*	*44.4*		*36.9*		*13.4*		*18.1*		*5.7*		*10.76*	

A career nomad, Brunson emerged as a starter when Jaric and Livingston were hurt. At the age of 32, he managed to set career highs in nearly every category. Brunson makes a decent backup because he doesn't make too many mistakes, looks to distribute the ball and has enough size to contest shots.

As a starter, his weaknesses come to the fore. Brunson has trouble getting to the basket and is an iffy outside shooter, so his overall impact as a scorer is minimal. He also takes some bad gambles, especially when he attempts to stop fast breaks at halfcourt. Those shortcomings are the reason he's bounced around so much, and he'll be doing that again. Luckily, the playing time with the Clippers provided a billboard for his services and allowed him to hook on with Seattle in the offseason.

Lionel Chalmers		point guard								Age: 25	Height: 6-0	Weight: 180		
(90% PG, 10% SG)												Most similar at age: N/A		
Year	G	M/G	FG%	FT%	P/40	R/40	A/40	TS%		Ast	TO	Usg	Reb	PER
2004-05 LAC	36	12.0	.336	.625	10.3	2.9	4.7	40.9		22.4	11.4	18.3	4.2	6.39

The Clippers' second-round draft choice seemed completely overmatched in his limited minutes. Considering how old he already is, it's looking like a wasted pick. Chalmers is quick going to his left but has no outside shot and is short for the position. He has trouble finishing around the basket as well, resulting in a ghastly 33.6 shooting percentage. He's not much of a passer either. Chalmers was sent to Minnesota in the offseason as a throw-in to the Jaric trade, and it appears he'll have few opportunities to crack the rotation. At least three players are in line ahead of him for point guard minutes, so he'll require major improvement just to make the active roster.

Marko Jaric		point guard									Age: 27	Height: 6-7	Weight: 217				
(52% PG, 45% SG, 3% SF)													Most similar at age: Alvin Williams				
Year	G	M/G	FG%	FT%	P/40	R/40	A/40	TS%		Ast		TO		Usg		Reb		PER
2002-03 LAC*	66	20.9	.401	.752	14.2	4.6	5.6	49.8	38	24.5	9	13.1	52	20.8	22	6.4	37	14.36 28
2003-04 LAC	58	30.4	.388	.733	11.2	4.0	6.4	47.5	48	30.6	21	12.5	41	18.9	51	5.9	24	12.55 41
2004-05 LAC	50	33.1	.414	.720	11.9	3.9	7.3	50.0	46	33.9	7	11.0	35	20.4	47	5.8	30	13.93 40
2005-06 PRJ (32.5)			.408	.733	12.8	3.9	6.5	50.1		29.9		11.9		20.1		5.7		13.61

* Season rankings are as shooting guard

Jaric is huge for a point guard and would seem to be better off playing the shooting guard spot, but the Clippers' needs have forced him to play the point for the past two years. Jaric's best skill is his outstanding anticipation, which nets him over two steals per 40 minutes. He's especially good at picking off passes against odd-man breaks, making him a good last line of defense in transition.

Jaric shot the ball very well at the start of the season, especially going to his right, but faded as his foot problems worsened. He missed time twice during the season with stress fractures and his fragility seems to be worsening. In three seasons, he's missed 72 games.

When on the court Jaric is a good passer and a crafty shot-maker on drives to the basket. That has allowed him to play the point, but it takes him forever to get the ball up the floor against pressure defense and, at 6'7", it's a challenge for him to stay in front of quicker point guards. For all those reasons, he should look to move to the off guard spot. He has the opportunity now that he's a restricted free agent, because the Clippers historically have been reluctant to match other teams' offers. If he can stay healthy for 60 games and doesn't have to play the point, Jaric will be well worth a team's midlevel exception.

Chris Kaman		center									Age: 23	Height: 7-0	Weight: 265				
(100% C)													Most similar at age: Vitaly Potapenko				
Year	G	M/G	FG%	FT%	P/40	R/40	A/40	TS%		Ast		TO		Usg		Reb		PER
2003-04 LAC	82	22.5	.460	.697	10.8	10.0	1.8	50.2	50	11.5	19	21.0	74	13.6	43	14.8	31	9.57 69
2004-05 LAC	63	25.9	.497	.661	14.0	10.4	1.8	52.2	35	8.5	20	15.6	51	16.5	22	15.5	28	13.14 36
2005-06 PRJ (34.9)			.474	.688	13.2	10.0	2.2	50.9		11.4		16.8		16.4		14.5		11.78

I'm not a fan, but Kaman at least showed improvement from his dreadful rookie season. Kaman isn't nearly as good a ball-handler as he imagines but enjoys dribbling in the open court, which is one factor keeping his Turnover Ratio persistently high. He also gets stripped a lot on moves in the post, although he showed some added refinement this season. Kaman finished his shots more consistently around the basket, scored more often, and would have been a decent offensive player last season if not for the turnovers.

Defensively, he still needs a lot of work. Kaman provides no help against the screen-and-roll and his short arms prevent him from challenging shots the way you might expect from a seven-footer. I discussed in the team comment the Clippers' defensive problems with him in the game and won't repeat them here, but suffice it to say that L.A. could do better for a starting center.

Kaman faces a pivotal year in 2005–06. If he takes another step forward he can earn a contract extension from the Clippers and claim the starting center job for several more years. If he backtracks, as the projections expect, he may force L.A. to finally give up on his prospects of becoming a quality big man. If so, he can't say he didn't have his chance.

Kerry Kittles — shooting guard

Kerry Kittles (83% SG, 17% SF) — **shooting guard** — **Age: 31 Height: 6-5 Weight: 185** Most similar at age: N/A

Year		G	M/G	FG%	FT%	P/40	R/40	A/40	TS%		Ast		TO		Usg		Reb		PER	
2002-03	NJ	65	30.0	.467	.785	17.4	5.2	3.5	55.0	18	17.1	24	5.5	1	19.5	33	7.4	19	18.27	10
2003-04	NJ	82	34.7	.453	.787	15.1	4.6	2.9	52.6	23	15.6	33	7.2	4	17.8	40	6.6	33	14.72	21
2004-05	LAC	11	22.1	.384	.600	11.4	5.3	3.3	44.6		15.7		6.7		16.7		7.7		10.04	

It was a lost season for Kittles who had back trouble and barely played for the Clippers. It was bad timing too, because he's a free agent and would have been able to get another big contract had he stayed healthy. If he can bounce back from the injuries, Kittles's outside shot and ability to play the passing lanes make him a solid perimeter player, especially for a running team. Given his age, injury history, and recent decline in performance, nobody is going to pay too much to see if he can make it back to that level.

Shaun Livingston — point guard

Shaun Livingston (100% PG) — **point guard** — **Age: 20 Height: 6-7 Weight: 182** Most similar at age: Ricky Davis

Year		G	M/G	FG%	FT%	P/40	R/40	A/40	TS%		Ast		TO		Usg		Reb		PER	
2004-05	LAC	30	27.1	.414	.746	10.9	4.4	7.4	46.1	61	32.3	17	16.1	67	20.9	44	6.5	11	10.32	56
2005-06	PRJ (1.5)			.496	.761	12.6	4.4	7.9	52.1		34.3		14.5		20.6		6.6		13.15	

The Clippers selected Livingston with the fourth overall pick in the 2004 draft, and his first season was a mixed bag. On one hand, he showed outstanding talent as a passer, often making spectacular dishes that surprised teammates. At 6′7″ with piles of athleticism, he could be a special player down the road.

However, he's got a lot of work to do in the next couple of years. Livingston is an awful shooter with no jump shot whatsoever. He didn't make a three-pointer the entire season and struggled even on 15-footers. He's also missed 52 games with a dislocated kneecap and torn cartilage in his shoulder, raising questions about whether his thin frame can take the pounding at the NBA level. Defensively, he should be excellent in time with his size and quickness and is already a very solid rebounder. But he picked up a lot of touch fouls on the perimeter and his lack of muscle hampers his ability to fight through screens.

Livingston's overall numbers were poor, but he played much better last April. In 10 games, he shot 44.8 percent, averaged 7.4 assists per game, and sharply cut his glaringly high Turnover Ratio. That's encouraging, but realistically, he's at least a year away from being ready to start. With the Cassell acquisition, he won't have to.

Corey Maggette — shooting guard

Corey Maggette Defensive PER: 0.33 (57% SG, 42% SF, 1% PF) — **shooting guard** — **Age: 26 Height: 6-6 Weight: 225** Most similar at age: Jerry Stackhouse

Year		G	M/G	FG%	FT%	P/40	R/40	A/40	TS%		Ast		TO		Usg		Reb		PER	
2002-03	LAC*	64	31.3	.444	.802	21.4	6.4	2.5	56.4	6	10.1	53	12.0	39	22.3	12	8.9	33	17.31	12
2003-04	LAC*	73	36.0	.447	.848	22.9	6.5	3.4	58.6	4	13.0	32	12.1	43	23.7	8	9.7	16	20.02	4
2004-05	LAC	66	36.9	.431	.857	24.0	6.5	3.7	57.4	9	13.3	40	11.5	46	26.2	7	9.6	4	19.91	6
2005-06	PRJ (29.7)			.434	.849	22.6	6.2	3.7	57.6		14.1		11.4		25.2		9.1		19.20	

* Season rankings are as small forward

Maggette's defensive numbers were very poor in 2003–04 and on the surface they look similar for 2004–05. But Maggette spent much of the year playing the shooting guard spot instead of his natural small forward position, and that made him a bit of a liability. He actually expended much more effort at the defensive end than he did the previous season and, with Simmons gone, should put forth a passable effort at the small forward position this year.

Offensively, the Clippers have few complaints. Maggette is a foul-drawing machine with a lightning first step to the basket and enough strength to finish once he gets there. Among players with at least 500 field-goal attempts, his rate of free-throw attempts to field-goal attempts was exceeded only by Shaquille O'Neal, and unlike Shaq, Maggette hit 85.7 percent of his tries.

(continued next page)

Corey Maggette (continued)

The cost of all those forays to the basket is a high Turnover Ratio, but Maggette's isn't unduly high for a player who goes to the rim so much. Besides, all the free throws keep his TS% near the top at his position. The one thing the Clippers would like is if he'd rediscover his three-point stroke. Maggette hit only 30.4 percent last season after making 35.0 percent two years ago. If he can start hitting with more consistency, it will open up even more space for his drives. That, in turn, might boost his scoring average to the point that he'd nab his first All-Star berth.

Mikki Moore							power forward					Age: 30		Height: 7-0		Weight: 223
(90% PF, 6% SF, 4% C)														Most similar at age: Tim McCormick		
Year	G	M/G	FG%	FT%	P/40	R/40	A/40	TS%		Ast		TO		Usg	Reb	PER
2002-03 Atl	8	5.4	.385	.800	16.7	7.4	2.8	51.7		13.4		8.9		19.6	10.6	18.00
2003-04 Uta	32	12.4	.505	.857	13.1	8.5	1.9	56.8		12.2		14.2		14.7	13.1	13.29
2004-05 LAC	74	15.9	.502	.787	13.4	8.4	1.6	57.1	12	7.6	48	13.8	57	14.4 53	12.5 42	12.66 51
2005-06 PRJ (36.3)			*.483*	*.774*	*12.9*	*8.2*	*1.6*	*54.9*		*7.4*		*14.3*		*13.9*	*12.3*	*12.17*

I've been puzzled for years by teams' lack of interest in Moore, so it was pleasing to see him grab a role with Clippers. While he is nominally a center, Moore spent most of his time in L.A. backing up Elton Brand because the Clippers had so many pivot men. Moore is noticeably lacking in the muscle department and isn't much of a shot-blocker, but he makes up for it with quickness and smarts. He was nimble enough that the Clips used him at small forward on occasion in zone alignments, and with his wingspan he was able to cover a lot of ground.

Offensively, Moore is too frail to post up, but he moves well without the ball to get himself in position for dunks and short tries around the rim. He also has range out to about 12 feet on his jumper, and his good shot selection helped to keep his TS% high.

Altogether, he was a nice find by the Clippers and cost them peanuts. The second part might change this year since he's a free agent, but after years in the bushes Moore will finally have some well-deserved NBA job security.

Mamadou N'Diaye							center				Age: 30	Height: 7-0	Weight: 255
(100% C)												Most similar at age: N/A	
Year	G	M/G	FG%	FT%	P/40	R/40	A/40	TS%	Ast	TO	Usg	Reb	PER
2002-03 Tor	22	16.5	.448	.723	13.2	9.0	0.8	51.4	4.8	14.5	14.6	12.8	13.55
2003-04 Dal-Atl	28	13.1	.391	.746	10.7	12.2	0.0	51.6	0.0	15.9	10.9	17.3	12.91
2004-05 LAC	11	6.5	.400	.571	11.1	10.0	0.6	43.3	2.6	0.0	13.6	14.6	10.48

N'Diaye's numbers in his brief trials suggest he could be an OK backup center if given the chance, but those numbers don't show his defensive shortcomings. Although he's seven feet tall and has decent strength, N'Diaye needs to dial up the effort level considerably if he's ever going to be more than an end-of-the-roster guy. He's already 30, so time's-a-wasting.

Zeljko Rebraca							center					Age: 33		Height: 7-0		Weight: 265
(80% C, 20% PF)														Most similar at age: Mark West		
Year	G	M/G	FG%	FT%	P/40	R/40	A/40	TS%		Ast		TO		Usg	Reb	PER
2002-03 Det	30	16.3	.552	.792	16.2	7.5	0.7	59.6		4.4		14.2		15.9	11.2	14.05
2003-04 Det-Atl	24	11.4	.442	.767	13.3	8.5	0.9	50.4		5.3		15.0		15.2	12.0	10.49
2004-05 LAC	58	16.0	.568	.859	14.6	7.9	1.1	62.5	2	5.3	45	14.1	39	13.8 38	11.8 56	14.02 31
2005-06 PRJ (13.5)			*.518*	*.825*	*13.5*	*7.4*	*1.1*	*57.2*		*5.4*		*14.7*		*14.1*	*11.3*	*12.78*

Rebraca was a quality free-agent signing, costing the Clippers just $2.5 million and providing their most productive center. Rebraca is a skilled interior player who posted the second-best TS% among centers by hitting a variety of short hooks and feeds around the rim. He pulled this off while looking for his shot, resulting in nearly 15 points per 40 minutes. Defensively, he's not a great leaper but has good timing that allowed him to block shots at a decent rate. Plus, he has the heft to deny quality post position.

Rebraca does have his weaknesses. He was a foul magnet, getting whistled nearly once every seven minutes, and that prevented him from seeing extended minutes. He also has been very injury prone the past three seasons, including missing time with an irregular heartbeat. Finally, his lack of leaping ability makes him a liability on the boards. The positives outweigh the negatives though, so the Clippers chose well in bringing him back on a multiyear deal. If they've been paying any attention, Rebraca will have Kaman's starting job this year.

Quinton Ross (86% SG, 14% SF)		**shooting guard**								**Age: 24** **Height: 6-6** **Weight: 195** Most similar at age: Tariq Abdul-Wahad								
Year	G	M/G	FG%	FT%	P/40	R/40	A/40	TS%		Ast		TO		Usg		Reb		PER	
2004-05 LAC	78	21.3	.432	.673	9.6	5.1	2.6	47.1	56	12.5	47	9.2	22	13.5	62	7.6	20	8.86	63
2005-06 PRJ (38.0)			.426	.696	9.8	5.1	2.9	47.3		13.4		9.4		13.9		7.7		9.43	

Here's a bit of trivia: Along with Quinton Ross, the Clippers previously employed Quentin Richardson and Quintin Dailey—the only players with those names in NBA history.

An undrafted rookie, Ross ended up becoming a regular rotation player once Kittles was hurt and impressed with his defense. He has very quick feet and is a good leaper, and as such he has potential as a defensive stopper. He's very thin, however, so he can be overwhelmed in strength match-ups.

Ross's defense won't help him much if he doesn't improve his offense. He struggled to create shots and failed to make the ones he created. He's a terrible outside shooter who made only one three-pointer all season, and that's unacceptable from an NBA shooting guard. He'll somehow have to produce much more than the 9.6 points per 40 minutes he generated last season, or Ross will be limited to being an end-of-quarter defensive specialist.

Bobby Simmons Defensive PER: 2.68 (91% SF, 8% PF, 1% SG)		**small forward**								**Age: 25** **Height: 6-6** **Weight: 228** Most similar at age: Shandon Anderson								
Year	G	M/G	FG%	FT%	P/40	R/40	A/40	TS%		Ast		TO		Usg		Reb		PER	
2002-03 Was	35	10.8	.393	.914	12.7	8.2	2.1	47.1		12.9		5.1		16.4		12.1		13.03	
2003-04 LAC	56	24.6	.394	.834	12.7	7.6	2.8	48.8	46	15.6	22	11.8	40	16.3	42	11.2	9	12.61	37
2004-05 LAC	75	37.3	.466	.846	17.6	6.4	2.9	54.0	18	13.9	18	9.1	17	20.2	23	9.5	27	16.10	13
2005-06 PRJ (92.6)			.444	.852	16.2	6.8	2.9	52.8		14.5		9.7		19.4		10.1		15.20	

Simmons has always been able to defend and showed why this past season, posting the second-best Defensive PER in the league thanks to his combination of strength, quickness, and hustle. Simmons can defend three positions and should give his new team the Bucks the perimeter stopper they have been lacking for the past several years.

Offensively, Simmons took a major step forward by showcasing a much-improved jumper. Simmons became especially deadly from the corners but hit from all over, nailing 43.5 percent of his three-point attempts and adding nearly five points to his 40-minute scoring average. As opponents caught on to the threat, he started faking the shot and putting the ball on the floor to earn trips to the free-throw line. As an added plus, he's a good ballhandler—both his Assist and Turnover Ratios were well above average for his position.

Simmons was only 24 last season, so while the three-point percentage might drop a bit, the rest of his performance should hold up in Milwaukee next season. Considering his combination of defensive prowess and shooting accuracy, the Clippers will have a very difficult time replacing his contribution. As for the Bucks, $47 million for five years might seem a bit rich for Simmons, but with his defense he'll be worth the money as long as his PER stays above 15.

Chris Wilcox (82% C, 18% PF)		**center**								**Age: 23** **Height: 6-10** **Weight: 235** Most similar at age: Jason Caffey								
Year	G	M/G	FG%	FT%	P/40	R/40	A/40	TS%		Ast		TO		Usg		Reb		PER	
2002-03 LAC*	46	10.4	.521	.500	14.3	8.7	1.8	52.8		10.0		12.4		15.9		12.0		12.41	
2003-04 LAC*	65	20.6	.521	.700	16.7	9.1	1.5	55.7	8	8.1	58	12.6	47	17.1	35	13.5	37	15.32	31
2004-05 LAC	54	18.6	.514	.611	17.0	9.1	1.5	54.3	29	7.2	30	15.2	48	18.5	12	13.5	44	13.52	34
2005-06 PRJ (36.7)			.499	.661	15.8	8.8	1.6	53.4		8.5		13.8		17.5		13.1		13.97	

* Season rankings are as power forward

(continued next page)

Chris Wilcox *(continued)*

Wilcox put together a strong season off the bench in 2003–04 and seemed to be building on that when he began the 2004–05 season in the starting lineup. But despite solid shooting numbers, Wilcox lost his starting job and gradually faded out of the rotation as the year wore on.

This was a mystery to me. The 23-year-old lottery pick is a great finisher around the basket who consistently shoots a high percentage, and his ability to run the floor earned him lots of easy baskets. He's better at power forward than at center because he's a bit light and struggles defensively against bangers, but pairing him with Brand was a workable set-up. Also, Wilcox was much more effective as a starter, scoring 18 points per 40 minutes (compared to 14.9 as a sub) while shooting a higher percentage and making fewer turnovers.

In terms of weaknesses, Wilcox needs to get more consistent with his jumper and improve his free-throw shooting. He also misses an unusual number of dunks. Defensively, he has to get stronger and give a more consistent effort. However, if the Clippers give up on him he'll be another good example of the "second draft" players I talked about in the Drew Gooden comment in Cleveland's chapter. At some point, Wilcox's offensive skills will make him an NBA starter.

Yaroslav Korolev	**small forward**	**Age: 18**	**Height: 6-9**	**Weight: 215**

Korolev has been compared to Toni Kukoc in his ability to handle the ball and see the floor at his height. Scouts love him based on what he did in junior leagues as a teenager, but he has barely played against high-level competition, so it's hard to know what to expect from him as a pro. Regardless, the Clippers aren't expecting immediate dividends from this pick. The Russian teenager might be on the roster, but he's unlikely to play as much as Livingston did last year.

Daniel Ewing	**point guard**	**Age: 22**	**Height: 6-3**	**Weight: 185**

L.A.'s second-round draft pick, Ewing is a good athlete and defender but a question mark at the offensive end. Ewing looks to score much more than to pass, but at 6'3" will have to play point guard in the pros. Additionally, his shooting numbers are questionable across the board—he shot 43 percent, which is poor for a secondary scorer on a very strong Duke team. He also hit 75 percent from the line and 39 percent on threes for his career, neither of which send hearts racing. He'll have plenty of opportunities if the Clippers don't keep Jaric, but he looks like the second coming of Lionel Chalmers.

Los Angeles Lakers

Apparently, you can go home again. At least, that's what the Lakers are hoping. Embarrassed by a 34–48 debacle that saw them finish three games behind the Clippers (gasp!), L.A. set out to repair things by luring back Phil Jackson just one year after ousting him.

Jackson is probably very happy he wasn't around for the 2004–05 campaign. Despite having traded Shaquille O'Neal in the offseason, the Lakers went into the season thinking they could claim a playoff berth with a team built around Kobe Bryant and Lamar Odom and guided by new coach Rudy Tomjanovich. It started out well enough, as the Lakers were 28–24 in late February even though Bryant had missed 14 games. Then the wheels came off and L.A. went 6–24 over the final 30 games, playing virtually no defense while dropping out of the playoff race.

Since he's widely assumed to have played a role in pushing for the Shaq trade, a lot of the attention for the Lakers failures focused on Bryant. In particular, many thought Bryant was trying too hard to be the focal point of the offense and his unwillingness to share the ball was hurting the offense. But the offense wasn't L.A.'s problem. The Lakers were the league's seventh-best offensive team even though Bryant and Odom combined to miss 34 games between them.

L.A. had a poor field-goal percentage, but had a good offense anyway thanks to a barrage of three-pointers. The Lakers made nearly eight a game to finish fourth in the league in three-pointers. While the percentage wasn't anything to write home about—they hit right at the league average at 35.5 percent—the threes improved the Lakers' PSA to well above the league norm. Every key Laker except Chris Mihm and Brian Grant was a three-point threat, but the leader of the pack was point guard Chucky Atkins. Taking advantage of defenses collapsing against Bryant's drives, Atkins took over five attempts a game and hit 38.7 percent of his tries.

All that offense would have been enough to get the Lakers to the postseason if they had played even one iota of defense. Unfortunately they didn't. L.A. suffered from two big

problems. The first was serious, but not fatal—they couldn't force turnovers. The Lakers forced only 12.0 turnovers per 100 opponent possessions, the worst rate in basketball. As table 1 shows, L.A. was substantially worse even than the other bad teams in this category, finishing more than a turnover behind the rest of the laggards.

It's obvious why L.A. failed to force turnovers. With an aging Atkins at the point and stay-at-home types at the other spots, this team wasn't going to be pressuring the ball or jumping passing lanes. The Lakers were second to last in the NBA in steals, with only Caron Butler and Bryant getting more than one per game.

The lack of turnovers cost L.A. nearly three points a game, which is a big deal. But other teams—Miami for instance—managed to put together solid defensive seasons despite failing to force turnovers. L.A.'s real downfall at the defensive end was that they simply stopped trying.

Lakers at a Glance

Record: 34–48, tied for 4th place in Pacific Division

Offensive Efficiency: 104.9 (7th)

Defensive Efficiency: 108.0 (29th)

Pace Factor: 93.4 (14th)

Top-Rated Player: Kobe Bryant (PER 23.28, 8th overall)

Head Coach: Phil Jackson. He's back for another go, but don't expect title No. 10 any time soon.

The Lakers were competitive when Tomjanovich was in charge, but on February 2 he stepped down due to health problems. At that point, the Lakers appointed assistant Frank Hamblen as the interim coach for the rest of the season. They might as well have headed for the golf course right then because Hamblen openly admitted he wasn't interested in keeping the job and was hoping Phil Jackson would return the next season. If the coach doesn't want to be there, why should they?

The Lakers certainly played like they didn't want to be there. In the season's final 20 games, they were as bad a defensive team as I have ever seen, posting a Defensive Efficiency mark of 114.82. I don't know if I can put into words how bad that is, but consider that the average Defensive Efficiency in the NBA last season was 103.09. The very worst team, Atlanta, was at 108.39.

That means that in the final 20 games, the difference between the Lakers and the Hawks was greater than the difference between the Hawks and the league average. L.A. wasn't just worse than Atlanta—they were *twice as bad*. If the Lakers

Table 1. Fewest Opponent Turnovers per 100 Possessions, 2004–05

Team	Opp. TO/100 Poss.
L.A. Lakers	12.0
Minnesota	12.2
Miami	13.1
Phoenix	13.4
Milwaukee	13.6
League Average	**14.8**

had kept up that performance for a full season, they would have been the worst defensive team in history.

To be fair, L.A. was a bit unlucky at the defensive end. Their opponents hit 78.0 percent of their free-throw attempts, compared to the league average of 75.6. Since one can hardly claim L.A. played "bad defense" against free-throw shooters, one would expect this to revert to the norm next season. If so, it should improve the Lakers' defense by half a point a game even if they do nothing. But half a point is a pittance when you're more than six points behind the *next* worst team.

Obviously this was a question of effort since the Lakers didn't perform nearly as badly under Tomjanovich. They only waved the white flag when Hamblen started doing his please-don't-hire-me routine. The Lakers were the sixth-best defense in the NBA in Jackson's final season, and although some of the key players from that team are gone, he should be able to inspire a much more consistent effort than Hamblen did.

The key for Jackson, obviously, will be his relationship with Bryant. Trashing a former player in your book can be awkward when you come back to coach him the next season. Both parties seem prepared to bury the hatchet, but one wonders what will happen the first time Jackson thinks Kobe is shooting too much and wants him to run the triangle instead.

Jackson has several other players who need to show improvement if he's going to get the Lakers back to the playoffs. Odom never seemed comfortable last season and has to learn how to coexist with Bryant since both players like having the ball in their hands. In the middle, Chris Mihm had a strong season at the offensive end but the Zen Master needs to coax a stronger defensive performance from him.

His toughest challenge, however, will be Kwame Brown. The Lakers' main offseason maneuver was to trade Butler

and Atkins to Washington in a sign-and-trade deal for Brown, amounting to a calculated risk that they could turn around the former No. 1 overall pick's career. It's the classic "second draft" scenario that I discussed in the Drew Gooden comment in the Cleveland chapter. However, Jackson's specialty has been working with veterans, not developing youngsters, so the jury is out on whether he can get Brown squared away. And Brown isn't his only young big man. L.A. used a lottery pick on high-schooler Andrew Bynum, a soft-handed 7-footer who is likely to spend the entire season at the end of the bench.

In addition, L.A. struggled to get much done in the free agent market. The Lakers are targeting the summer of 2007 to make a big plunge and until then they're not adding any long-term contracts. That considerably reduced their attractiveness as a destination, so the Lakers seemed likely to get the scraps of the free-agent market at publication time. They'll need to dredge up a starting point guard and a backup at both guard spots.

At least general manager Mitch Kupchak now seems to have a plan. For too long in the Shaq era, he was on cruise control, because the team seemed capable of winning no matter how badly he mangled things. Now that his creativity has been challenged, he's getting a bit more clever. He wisely dumped Kareem Rush on Charlotte in return for a second-round pick and limited his risk in the Brown deal by guaranteeing only the first two years of the contract.

But the wounds of the past few seasons will take a long time to heal. With Brian Grant being waived to avoid paying luxury tax on his contract, Odom was all L.A. had to show for the Shaq trade. Signing Vlade Divac a year ago was a waste, as he is likely to retire from a back problem. None of Kupchak's recent draft picks have panned out either, although Brian Cook looks like he might change the score on that soon.

As a result, the Lakers are far too thin on talent for even the Zen Master to help much. With the team playing more for 2007–08 than the current season, hiring Jackson seemed as much a P.R. stunt as a commitment to righting the ship immediately. Jackson's arrival will help add some wins to the Lakers' column and may even get them to the .500 mark, but in a conference as loaded as the West is, expecting a return to the playoffs is asking too much of any coach—even this one.

Chucky Atkins				point guard									Age: 31	Height: 5-11	Weight: 160		

Defensive PER: -0.07 (100% PG)
Most similar at age: Damon Stoudamire

Year		G	M/G	FG%	FT%	P/40	R/40	A/40	TS%		Ast		TO		Usg		Reb		PER	
2002-03	Det	65	21.5	.361	.816	13.2	2.7	5.0	47.5	45	23.7	49	10.4	21	20.7	42	4.1	59	10.09	53
2003-04	Det-Bos	64	24.1	.397	.753	13.9	2.4	5.8	51.1	25	26.5	41	10.9	28	20.1	41	3.4	62	12.11	46
2004-05	LAL	82	35.4	.426	.803	15.4	2.7	4.9	55.8	9	23.5	52	10.0	22	19.4	54	4.1	61	13.39	41
2005-06	PRJ (31.2)			.397	.775	13.4	2.6	5.1	51.6		25.1		11.1		18.8		3.8		11.51	

Atkins was better than anyone could have expected offensively, leading the Lakers' three-point arsenal and having the most productive season of his career. Atkins took more than half his shots from behind the arc and hit 38.7 percent. Unlike a lot of bombers, he has some quickness and managed to get to the line a fair amount, resulting in one of the best TS%s among backcourt players. He's not a great passer and isn't going to break down defenses at the end of the shot clock, but he took advantage of the open shots Kobe and others provided.

Where Atkins broke down was at the defensive end. He's only 5'11" and doesn't have lightning quickness so even before the Lakers started giving up on defense, he was getting schooled. The one thing he did well was stopping 2-on-1 breaks, which is probably a good thing considering how many L.A. gave up, but he was all but useless in the halfcourt.

Atkins was traded to Washington in the Brown deal and will back up Gilbert Arenas. His perimeter shooting will come in handy with Washington and his defensive shortcomings won't be as big an issue if he's playing only 10 minutes a night off the bench. He never should have started in the first place, but he can be a solid reserve in that environment.

Tierre Brown				point guard									Age: 26	Height: 6-2	Weight: 189		

(87% PG, 13% SG)
Most similar at age: DeJuan Wheat

Year		G	M/G	FG%	FT%	P/40	R/40	A/40	TS%		Ast		TO		Usg		Reb		PER	
2002-03	Cle	14	11.9	.458	.786	15.6	7.2	9.3	49.9		30.9		17.4		25.8		10.1		17.55	
2003-04	NO	3	5.7	.500	.500	14.1	2.4	4.7	52.1		13.6		47.4		24.8		3.5		-9.95	
2004-05	LAL	76	14.0	.356	.787	12.5	3.5	5.8	43.7	66	25.4	46	12.1	45	21.0	41	5.2	41	9.43	61
2005-06	PRJ (35.7)			.364	.792	12.7	3.3	5.8	44.6		25.6		12.1		20.8		5.1		10.18	

The Lakers kept Brown as their backup backup point guard, and he spent the year showing why nobody else had thought to do so. Brown is very quick and doesn't have trouble penetrating defenses. What gives him great trouble, however, is completing the shot once he drives. Brown hit only 35.6 percent from the floor and he has to make shots since he doesn't see the floor well.

Brown is a free agent but the Lakers will be looking for a major upgrade at this position. His quickness should get him onto a roster next year, but he won't play this many minutes again unless he finds a jump shot.

Kobe Bryant				shooting guard									Age: 27	Height: 6-6	Weight: 220		

Defensive PER: 0.77 (95% SG, 3% SF, 2% PG)
Most similar at age: Paul Pierce

Year		G	M/G	FG%	FT%	P/40	R/40	A/40	TS%		Ast		TO		Usg		Reb		PER	
2002-03	LAL	82	41.5	.451	.843	28.9	6.6	5.7	55.0	17	16.0	30	9.6	23	32.5	1	9.3	8	26.15	1
2003-04	LAL	65	37.6	.438	.852	25.5	5.9	5.4	55.1	5	17.2	25	8.9	17	28.7	2	8.4	12	23.60	1
2004-05	LAL	66	40.7	.433	.816	27.1	5.8	5.9	56.3	12	17.4	21	11.8	51	31.2	1	8.7	9	23.28	1
2005-06	PRJ (29.4)			.433	.816	25.7	5.7	5.7	54.7		17.4		10.8		30.1		8.3		22.46	

Bryant is a new and interesting phenomenon in the world of sports—the athlete who tries to do and say everything right publicly, but comes across as an insincere phony as a result. He's never had an enemy, if you go by what he says in public. Yet everyone suspects his motives at every turn and it's all but assumed he was the driving force behind the ouster of Phil Jackson and Shaq in 2004.

Contrast Bryant with somebody like Allen Iverson or Charles Barkley, both of whom have said and done all kinds of nasty things, yet are immensely popular. What it comes down to is that the man on the street finds Barkley's and Iverson's reality a lot more believable than Bryant's. Bryant is far from the only example—Alex Rodriguez, for instance, would be one from the

(continued next page)

Kobe Bryant *(continued)*

baseball world. It's an ironic twist in an era when players try ever harder to cultivate their marketing image—if they try too hard, nobody believes them.

On the court, Bryant's 2004–05 campaign was remarkably similar to his final season with Shaq. His PER dipped only slightly, and his Rebound Rate, field-goal percentage, and Assist Ratio all were within a few percentage points of what he had done the year before. Bryant has become masterful at drawing fouls, specializing in swinging his arms through his opponents' arms while going up for a shot, and he again increased his free-throw rate last season.

The key difference was that Bryant had to create a lot more of the offense—hence the spike in his Usage Rate—and doing so sent his Turnover Ratio through the roof. Oddly, he nearly doubled his three-point attempts, even though he's a career 33 percent shooter and should be focusing on using his elusive dribbling skills to go to the basket more.

Now that he's reunited with Jackson, Bryant is at a crossroads in his career. Booting out Shaq and making it his own team didn't work last year, so he has to make nice with Phil and see if he can't regain the level of play he achieved two years ago. That may not be easy. While Bryant is only 27, he's had so much wear and tear in his 10-year career that his knees probably feel much older. If he can't coexist with Jackson, the Lakers may have to ponder the once unmentionable idea of trading Kobe.

Caron Butler			**small forward**									**Age: 25**	**Height: 6-7**	**Weight: 217**
Defensive PER: 0.26 (76% SF, 20% SG, 4% PF)													Most similar at age: Tariq Abdul-Wahad	
Year		G	M/G	FG%	FT%	P/40	R/40	A/40	TS%		Ast	TO	Usg	Reb	PER
2002-03	Mia	78	36.6	.416	.824	16.8	5.6	3.0	50.2	39	13.3 36	12.0 38	21.4 17	8.0 46	15.16 19
2003-04	Mia	68	29.8	.380	.756	12.3	6.4	2.5	44.0	57	13.6 28	9.8 20	17.4 35	9.1 24	10.72 45
2004-05	LAL	77	35.7	.445	.862	17.4	6.6	2.1	52.8	32	10.1 49	8.9 16	19.2 27	9.8 21	15.77 18
2005-06	PRJ (95.0)			.418	.820	15.3	6.3	2.4	50.0		11.9	9.8	18.7	9.2	14.04

The Lakers paid a heavy price by giving up Butler to get Kwame Brown. After a disappointing 2003–04, Butler came back strong with the Lakers and picked up steam during the year. Butler averaged 22.7 points over the season's final 10 games and had season bests in nearly every category in the month of April. His line-drive jump shot will never be a thing of beauty, but Butler began finding the net more consistently with it late in the season. He has a good first step and is an effective finisher in transition, so playing with the fast-paced Wizards should fit his style.

Defensively, Butler sometimes was overmatched in terms of quickness when asked to play shooting guard but otherwise did a solid job (for a half a season, that is—he mailed it in like all the other Lakers when Hamblen took over). With his quickness and strength he has the makings of a good defender and should become Washington's perimeter stopper this season. He also does a solid job on the boards and was one of the few Lakers who could play passing lanes to get steals.

Butler's strong finish provides hope that he can take another step forward next season. Even if he doesn't, Washington has a solid starter who should be a fixture in the lineup for several years. Considering the Wizards got him in return for a player they kicked off the team, they have to be pleased with the exchange.

Brian Cook			**power forward**									**Age: 25**	**Height: 6-9**	**Weight: 234**
(55% PF, 45% C)													Most similar at age: Pat Garrity	
Year		G	M/G	FG%	FT%	P/40	R/40	A/40	TS%		Ast	TO	Usg	Reb	PER
2003-04	LAL	35	12.6	.475	.750	14.0	9.1	1.8	50.5		10.5	8.9	15.8	13.5	14.04
2004-05	LAL	72	15.1	.417	.757	16.9	7.9	1.3	52.2	36	6.1 57	5.8 3	17.7 31	11.9 48	14.09 42
2005-06	PRJ (26.5)			.403	.762	16.3	7.5	1.2	51.3		6.0	6.1	17.3	11.3	13.84

Cook's PER makes it seem like he didn't improve, but he completely revamped his game in the offseason. To everyone's amazement, Cook started drilling three-pointers in preseason and never stopped, nailing 39.2 percent. He has a fast release too, making him a real threat on the perimeter and drawing opposing big men out of the paint.

The question for Cook is if he's relying on the three-pointer a bit too much. Nearly half his attempts were from beyond the arc and he averaged only one free throw attempt for every 12 field-goal tries, one of the worst rates in the league and a horrid ratio for an alleged post player. Cook has enough skill to do some damage in the paint, and if he can develop the inside portion of his game as well as the outside, the Lakers really will have an offensive force.

Los Angeles Lakers

Otherwise, he'll probably continue in his current role as a backup power forward for several years. His improvement as a shooter has been startling and the effort he obviously put in certainly is commendable, but one wonders if the focus on shooting isn't detracting from other facets of his game.

Vlade Divac — center
(100% C)   Age: 37   Height: 7-1   Weight: 260

Most similar at age: N/A

Year		G	M/G	FG%	FT%	P/40	R/40	A/40	TS%		Ast		TO		Usg		Reb		PER	
2002-03	Sac	80	28.2	.466	.713	13.3	9.6	4.6	51.9	32	23.0	1	12.8	31	17.4	20	12.9	49	15.64	18
2003-04	Sac	81	28.6	.470	.654	13.8	8.0	7.5	51.1	40	31.1	1	12.5	30	21.3	5	11.9	66	16.22	15
2004-05	LAL	15	8.7	.419	.667	10.5	9.8	5.8	46.9		27.4		20.2		18.4		14.7		10.35	

The Lakers' gamble on Divac in free agency didn't pan out, as a bad back limited him to only 15 games. It doesn't seem he'll feel any better this season, but fortunately the Lakers limited their risk. Divac's deal can be bought out for $2 million this year and the Lakers seem likely to take that route. As for Divac, he seems headed toward retirement. It's unfortunate to see one of the best passing big men ever drop off the map so suddenly, but this is what happens when 7-footers hit their late 30s.

Devean George — small forward
(65% SF, 34% SG, 1% PF)   Age: 28   Height: 6-8   Weight: 240

Most similar at age: N/A

Year		G	M/G	FG%	FT%	P/40	R/40	A/40	TS%		Ast		TO		Usg		Reb		PER	
2002-03	LAL	71	22.7	.390	.790	12.2	7.1	2.3	48.5	48	13.9	33	9.8	18	15.1	43	10.0	17	11.37	47
2003-04	LAL	82	23.8	.408	.760	12.4	6.8	2.3	49.2	44	13.8	27	10.8	29	15.1	47	9.7	15	11.53	43
2004-05	LAL	15	20.4	.356	.750	14.4	6.9	1.8	48.8		8.7		8.6		17.1		10.3		10.59	

George missed most of the season after having ankle surgery in July 2004, but he could play a big part in the Lakers' plans this season. His familiarity with the triangle offense and the departure of Caron Butler should give him a leg up in the race to be the Lakers' starting small forward, especially since he was the starter of record when Jackson last coached.

If he's going to keep the job though, he'll have to deliver more at the offensive end than he's done throughout his career. George is effective shooting three-pointers from the corner but struggles once he's asked to make a move. He's a career 39 percent shooter and his lack of a post game allows him to be defended by a smaller player. It's an important year for him because it's the last season of his current contract, so he'll need to show he's fully recovered from the ankle injury. Even then, he risks being banished to the bench if Jackson decides he'd rather play Odom at small forward and start Kwame Brown and Mihm on the front line.

Brian Grant — center
(94% C, 6% PF)   Age: 33   Height: 6-9   Weight: 254

Most similar at age: Buck Williams

Year		G	M/G	FG%	FT%	P/40	R/40	A/40	TS%		Ast		TO		Usg		Reb		PER	
2002-03	Mia	82	32.2	.509	.771	12.8	12.7	1.6	55.2	15	10.4	29	12.9	34	14.4	40	18.3	6	15.70	17
2003-04	Mia	76	30.3	.471	.782	11.5	9.1	1.2	50.2	49	8.5	40	10.1	12	13.5	44	12.9	52	12.07	50
2004-05	LAL	69	16.5	.493	.722	9.3	9.0	1.2	53.9	30	5.7	41	13.4	35	10.3	63	13.6	43	9.91	56
2005-06	*PRJ (35.5)*			*.463*	*.736*	*10.5*	*9.4*	*1.4*	*50.5*		*8.3*		*12.4*		*12.6*		*13.4*		*11.55*	

Grant is one of the league's hardest-working players, but his skills are rapidly deteriorating. Grant has no elevation left and can't score in the paint anymore, and even his 15-foot jump shot is drawing iron more than it used to. While he's effective at banging inside against bigger players, he no longer can outwork them for rebounds and doesn't have the mobility to help his teammates much defensively.

The Lakers waived Grant using the amnesty provision in the collective bargaining agreement. It saved them from paying a heap of luxury tax for two years, and the financial savings are pretty large compared to Grant's miniscule contributions these days. Fortunately for Grant, his attitude and toughness helped him catch on with Phoenix, who will hope Grant's performance bounces back enough for him to become a decent front-court reserve.

| **Jumaine Jones** | | | small forward | | | | | | **Age: 26** | | **Height: 6-8** | | **Weight: 218** |

Defensive PER: 0.60 (64% SF, 27% PF, 9% SG) — Most similar at age: Pat Garrity

Year		G	M/G	FG%	FT%	P/40	R/40	A/40	TS%		Ast		TO		Usg		Reb		PER	
2002-03	Cle	80	27.6	.434	.687	14.2	7.4	2.0	52.5	24	11.6	44	11.1	32	15.7	40	10.3	13	12.35	36
2003-04	Bos	42	8.9	.344	.609	10.0	7.3	1.5	43.8		10.1		13.7		13.1		10.3		7.62	
2004-05	LAL	76	24.1	.432	.733	12.6	8.7	1.4	55.6	12	6.8	63	7.7	9	13.1	60	13.1	1	13.07	38
2005-06	*PRJ (31.8)*			*.429*	*.726*	*13.0*	*8.0*	*1.6*	*55.0*		*8.2*		*8.8*		*13.7*		*11.8*		*13.13*	

Jones does two things. He shoots high-arcing three-pointers from the corner and he crashes the boards. You might think a 6′8″ forward who could rebound would play inside, but Jones took more than half his tries from beyond the arc and buried 39 percent. Almost all of them came from the corner, where he might as well have set up a chair and sunned himself while he waited for Kobe Bryant to drive and kick. Jones has no game off the dribble and is useless in the post, but he's milking his one offensive skill for all it's worth.

Defensively, Jones isn't very effective because he's too slow to play small forwards and a bit too short to stop power forwards. But the one thing he will do is rebound. While Jones is neither athletic nor strong, he has an amazing nose for the ball and posted the top Rebound Rate among small forwards last season. He's a good offensive rebounder too. When a shot goes up, he gets up from his chair in the corner and races in from the side, where opponents often don't notice him and fail to block out.

Jones is under contract for one more season and Butler's departure should open up some minutes for him off the bench. Phil Jackson hasn't historically been fond of this type of player, but with this roster he may not have much choice.

| **Stanislav Medvedenko** | | | power forward | | | | | | **Age: 26** | | **Height: 6-10** | | **Weight: 250** |

(63% C, 37% PF) — Most similar at age: N/A

Year		G	M/G	FG%	FT%	P/40	R/40	A/40	TS%		Ast		TO		Usg		Reb		PER	
2002-03	LAL	58	10.7	.434	.721	16.5	9.1	1.2	46.0	58	5.4	57	11.1	31	19.5	22	12.8	36	10.28	56
2003-04	LAL	68	21.2	.441	.767	15.6	9.5	1.6	47.9	53	8.1	57	8.4	1	18.0	29	13.5	35	13.55	44
2004-05	LAL	43	9.8	.455	.821	15.6	7.5	1.2	49.0		5.9		6.7		17.5		11.2		11.77	

Medvedenko came to the league with a lot of offensive potential, but he's never expanded his game beyond a fondness for taking 17-footers. That's kept his development stuck in neutral and explains his lack of minutes last season. Medvedenko is a poor defender and doesn't provide much help on the glass, so if he isn't scoring at a high rate he doesn't have much value. While he's shown bursts of being capable of expanding his game, he's never had success for a long period.

It's easy to see why. Medvedenko is part of the Ron Mercer family of players—they shoot lots of long two-point jump shots but rarely take threes and never get to the foul line. As such, it's virtually impossible for these players to have a high TS%. With no free throws or threes, he would need to hit over 50 percent from the floor to put up a respectable TS%, and that's a tall order when shooting long jump shots all game.

Medvedenko's familiarity with the Zen Master may earn him a few more minutes this season, but the Lakers' frontcourt is much deeper than it was two years ago and he'll be challenged to stay in the rotation for long.

| **Chris Mihm** | | | center | | | | | | **Age: 26** | | **Height: 7-0** | | **Weight: 265** |

Defensive PER: 0.75 (100% C) — Most similar at age: Mikki Moore

Year		G	M/G	FG%	FT%	P/40	R/40	A/40	TS%		Ast		TO		Usg		Reb		PER	
2002-03	Cle*	52	15.6	.404	.724	15.2	11.4	1.4	46.2	54	6.8	55	11.7	39	18.0	30	16.0	11	13.17	35
2003-04	Cle-Bos	76	17.5	.488	.663	14.5	12.4	0.6	53.1	27	3.7	72	15.9	63	14.8	34	17.6	7	14.62	27
2004-05	LAL	75	24.9	.507	.678	15.7	10.7	1.1	55.2	20	5.1	47	13.3	34	16.1	25	16.1	22	15.72	21
2005-06	*PRJ (45.3)*			*.490*	*.666*	*14.4*	*11.2*	*1.0*	*53.1*		*5.1*		*14.4*		*15.3*		*16.3*		*14.30*	

* Season rankings are as power forward

It took a while but Mihm has turned himself into a respectable center at both ends of the floor. He struggled to get his career untracked in Cleveland and an experiment with him at power forward probably did more harm than good. Now that he's entrenched in the middle he's blossomed into a quality center. Mihm has become a strong rebounder who can finish shots around the basket and will bust out the occasional jump hook from the post. While he's rarely the primary offensive option, he earned enough shots by moving to openings that his Usage Rate was above the league average at his position.

Defensively, Mihm averaged over two blocks per 40 minutes but needs to pick his spots better. Too often he went for a block he couldn't get and left the board exposed behind him. He's also on the light side for a center and could use a bit more strength. However, his Defensive PER was reasonable considering the Lakers' general apathy and should improve under Jackson.

Overall, the sign-and-trade of Gary Payton for Mihm and Jumaine Jones might be the best move of the Kupchak era. Admittedly, that's not saying much, but Mihm is giving L.A. solid production in the middle for less than $4 million a year, while other teams are paying stiffs twice that much in free agency.

Lamar Odom				power forward						Age: 26		Height: 6-10	Weight: 230	
Defensive PER: 1.01 (87% PF, 11% SF, 2% C)													Most similar at age: Billy Owens	
Year		G	M/G	FG%	FT%	P/40	R/40	A/40	TS%		Ast	TO	Usg	Reb	PER
2002-03	LAC*	49	34.3	.439	.777	17.0	7.8	4.2	51.9	28	17.7 11	13.9 50	21.6 14	10.7 10	14.56 23
2003-04	Mia	80	37.5	.430	.742	18.3	10.3	4.4	51.6	33	17.3 13	12.5 45	23.6 7	14.6 25	18.43 14
2004-05	LAL	64	36.3	.473	.695	16.8	11.3	4.1	53.9	28	18.2 4	12.3 45	20.6 16	16.9 9	17.26 17
2005-06	PRJ (35.3)			.455	.722	17.5	10.8	4.2	53.0		17.6	11.6	22.2	15.5	18.00

* Season rankings are as small forward

Odom didn't have the ball in his hands as much as he did in Miami. The cause is obvious—with Kobe Bryant hogging the ball so much, Odom's touches almost had to go down. That dropped his scoring and assist numbers, and the murmurs from L.A. were that Odom was struggling because of his pairing with Bryant. In reality, it wasn't so bad. Odom had the second-best season of his career and it would have been better if his free-throw shooting hadn't slumped so bad—a tough one to pin on Kobe.

Moreover, his lack of touches blinded some people to the other improvements in Odom's game. His development as a rebounder has been absolutely phenomenal, improving his Rebound Rate by 58 percent in only two seasons. Odom has worked on his body and become much stronger, and that's enabled him to become especially effective on the defensive glass. He was one of the ten best rebounding power forwards last season, and I don't think anybody could have foreseen that two years ago.

Additionally, he's become a very solid defender. Odom doesn't have the zip in his step to get lots of blocks or steals but he's learned how to use his size to contest shots. He also is quick enough to help out against the screen-and-roll and has added enough muscle to make post players earn their points.

So while some see his 2004–05 season as a disappointment, it was in many ways another step on his way to becoming an extremely well-rounded player. Odom may never be a 20-and-10 guy because he doesn't have the explosive quickness or deadly shot that most players of that type possess. But he's a pretty good second banana, and he's steadily getting better.

Sasha Vujacic				shooting guard						Age: 21		Height: 6-7	Weight: 193	
(79% SG, 18% PG, 3% SF)													Most similar at age: N/A	
Year		G	M/G	FG%	FT%	P/40	R/40	A/40	TS%		Ast	TO	Usg	Reb	PER
2004-05	LAL	35	11.5	.282	.947	10.0	6.2	5.1	40.3		24.1	7.8	18.0	9.2	8.85

The Lakers' first-round pick in 2004, Vujacic has a lot of work to do to establish a regular spot in the rotation. His 28.2 percent shooting speaks for itself, but he also is rail thin and badly needs to hit the weights. Vujacic handles the ball well for his size and could play point guard in spots, but it's not clear if he has the quickness to handle the job defensively. He's young enough to improve significantly and will have to in order to see minutes.

Luke Walton — power forward
(69% PF, 23% SF, 8% C)

Age: 25 Height: 6-8 Weight: 235
Most similar at age: Willie Anderson

Year		G	M/G	FG%	FT%	P/40	R/40	A/40	TS%		Ast		TO		Usg		Reb		PER	
2003-04	LAL	72	10.1	.425	.705	9.5	7.0	6.2	50.5	42	34.3	1	13.4	53	16.1	40	10.3	61	12.65	51
2004-05	LAL	61	12.6	.411	.708	10.3	7.4	4.8	49.2	55	23.1	2	16.5	67	16.3	42	11.1	56	11.33	56
2005-06	PRJ (33.5)			.414	.697	10.2	7.2	5.3	49.3		26.7		15.0		16.5		10.7		11.99	

Walton is an absolutely fantastic passer, but he's having trouble establishing a role because it's his only marketable skill. Being a great passer is one thing if you have a quick first step and can get to the basket because then the opportunities to set up teammates are constant. But in Walton's case, he's usually trying to feather a pass from the perimeter with a man in his face, and the result is that his Turnover Ratio nearly offsets his high rate of assists.

Walton's search for a position continues. He hit only 26 percent on three-pointers, so small forward is a tough sell, but he doesn't have much of a post game and is a very poor rebounder for a power forward. Similarly, he's a bit slow to guard small forwards and a bit small to battle in the paint. Jackson may find a role for Walton because of his passing skills, but George and Jones seem to be ahead of him on the depth chart and the power forward slot is just as crowded. The Lakers might be better off trading him for backcourt help.

Andrew Bynum — center

Age: 18 Height: 7-0 Weight: 300

If I had to bet on one player from the 2005 draft being a bust, it would be this guy. I say this without having seen him play. Simply put, the numbers are stacked against him. If you look at all the players who were (a) at least seven feet tall, (b) weighed at least 250 pounds, and (c) drafted between picks No. 4 and 15 in the NBA draft, you'll see their records border on tragic.

Bynum is the 20th such player in the past 20 years, and only one (Dikembe Mutombo) has made an All-Star team. In fact, only three others (Roy Tarpley, Bryant Reeves, and Chris Mihm) were any good for any length of time. The rest have been notorious busts—guys like Alex Radojevic, Yinka Dare, William Bedford, and DeSagana Diop. Bynum could be the one that beats the odds, I suppose, but if you look at the history of these picks, almost all fit the Lakers' profile—a team that was desperate for a center and reached for a player based on his alleged potential. History informs us that approach nearly always results in disaster.

Ronny Turiaf — power forward

Age: 22 Height: 6-10 Weight: 250

Turiaf has the requisite size and strength for the pros, but he isn't much of an athlete and struggles to finish shots around the basket. He plays with a lot of energy, however, which makes him a decent rebounder and shot-blocker. However, his career may be over before it begins. The Lakers' second-round pick was found to have an enlarged heart after the draft that required open-heart surgery and his basketball future is in doubt.

Von Wafer — shooting guard

Age: 20 Height: 6-5 Weight: 210

A second-round draft choice, Wafer has a good outside shot and the size and athleticism to be a decent pro shooting guard. However, he had attitude problems at Florida State and his college stats don't exactly portend greatness. Overall, he's the kind of guy who might benefit from some seasoning in the D-League, and that's exactly where he's headed.

Memphis Grizzlies

If you have a bad team with a couple of good players, it's easy to get better. Just replace the bad players with good ones and you have yourself a team.

But what do you do if everyone is just sort of OK? That's the dilemma facing Jerry West as he tries to get the Memphis Grizzlies to the next level. Memphis made the playoffs the past two seasons with a system predicated on winning with superior depth, and the formula has been successful in the regular season. The Grizzlies have yet to win a postseason game, however, as their starters have been overwhelmed by the superior front-line talent of other teams in the West.

After a bumpy start to the season, the playoffs were the last thing on Memphis's mind. The Grizzlies started the year 5–11 and the picture looked bleaker after head coach Hubie Brown abruptly resigned because of health problems. Brown had won the Coach of the Year award the previous season, so his departure came as a shock to everyone. Into the fire stepped Mike Fratello, who ironically had succeeded Brown 24 years earlier in Atlanta for three games.

Fratello set about doing what he does best—slowing down the pace and tightening the screws on defense. Under Brown, Memphis had played the 10th-fastest pace in the league, but last season they were the fourth slowest. The trapping, pressing style favored by Brown gave way to a more structured halfcourt defensive system under Fratello, which forced fewer turnovers but also gave up fewer easy shots.

The timing of the strategy shift was fortuitous because Memphis subsequently suffered a series of injuries. Its best player, Pau Gasol, missed 26 games with plantar fasciitis, while James Posey missed 27 with a variety of ailments and rarely looked 100 percent when he played. Those losses forced the Grizzlies to shorten their 10-man rotation, which was much more easily done with the halfcourt style Fratello implemented than in Brown's pressing system. Due to the injuries, everyone got an opportunity to play. Ten different players saw at least 1,200 minutes, and all but the wounded Posey had a PER above 13.

Fortunately, the Grizzlies were deep enough to survive the injuries. Memphis retained every key player from Brown's

50-win team in 2003–04 except for reserve forward Bo Outlaw. He was made expendable when the Grizzlies signed Brian Cardinal in the offseason. Besides Cardinal, the only new blood came from second-round draft picks Antonio Burks and Andre Emmett.

Once Fratello implemented his system, the Grizzlies began clicking, going 40–24 under the new boss. While Memphis didn't press as often, they again were outstanding at forcing turnovers. After leading the league in 2003–04, it tied for second in turnovers forced per possession last season. The Grizzlies created miscues on 16.6 percent of opponent possessions, nearly two percent more than the league average.

It was truly a team effort. The Grizzlies didn't have a single player with more than 100 steals, but nearly everybody was above average. The combined impact of having so many ball-hawking players was that the Grizzlies picked up steals in bunches. See table 1 for a count.

The major catalyst was the second unit. Cardinal and Bonzi Wells each averaged more than two steals per 40 minutes, which seems odd considering neither is terribly quick. Both have great anticipation, however, and that allowed them to pilfer the ball frequently. Fellow reserve Earl Watson wasn't far behind at 1.8 per 40 minutes, but only two starters—Jason Williams and Shane Battier—had high rates of picks.

Adding to the turnover toll was Memphis's love of taking charges. Battier and Cardinal particularly excel at this, but Posey, Watson and Lorenzen Wright also were more than willing to let a driving player run them over. The league didn't keep official stats on this, but if they did I'm sure Memphis led the league.

The other surprising aspect of Memphis's defense was the number of shots they blocked (also in table 1). Memphis sent back 7.7 percent of its opponents' attempts, a rate bested only by Portland and San Antonio. Again, it's hard to believe at first. As with the steals, no Grizzly had over 100 blocks, so it doesn't seem possible that their overall total could be so high. But every key Grizzly except Jason Williams

---

Grizzlies at a Glance

Record: 45–37, 4th place in Southwest Division

Offensive Efficiency: 102.5 (18th)

Defensive Efficiency: 99.9 (6th)

Pace Factor: 90.6 (27th)

Top-Rated Player: Pau Gasol (PER 22.57, 15th overall)

Head Coach: Mike Fratello. Turned team's season around while overcoming numerous player injuries.

Table 1. Memphis Grizzlies Steals and Blocks per 40 Minutes

Player	Stls/40	Blks/40
Brian Cardinal	2.46	0.53
Bonzi Wells	2.28	0.73
Earl Watson	1.84	0.42
Jason Williams	1.54	0.10
Shane Battier	1.45	1.22
James Posey	1.39	0.67
Stromile Swift	1.28	2.88
League average	**1.24**	**0.80**
Lorenzen Wright	1.01	1.21
Mike Miller	0.95	0.40
Pau Gasol	0.83	2.08

averaged at least 0.4 blocks per 40 minutes, and Stromile Swift had a stellar rate of 2.88 in limited minutes. Add it all up and they were a block party waiting to happen.

The blocks and steals helped make up for a major defensive shortcoming: rebounding. The Grizzlies have been pounded on the glass throughout the Gasol era and last year was no exception. Memphis grabbed only 69.9 percent of opponents' missed shots, ranking it 26th in the NBA. They weren't any better on the offensive glass and finished 28th overall in rebounding.

So Memphis's agenda for this season includes improving on the glass, upgrading the offense, and staying free of injuries. Then perhaps the Grizzlies can push into the upper echelons of the Western Conference. Memphis made a move to accomplish the first part by selecting Syracuse jumping jack Hakim Warrick in the first round. He's not the widebody that the Grizzlies need, but he should help out on the glass anyway.

That's a nice start, but Memphis's other moves indicate they may be going backwards rather than forwards. Of the four key bench players whose blocks and steals helped key the defense last season—Cardinal, Wells, Watson, and Swift—only Cardinal will be suiting up for Memphis this season. The Grizzlies painted themselves into a corner with respect to the luxury tax, and the only way out is to shed contracts. They spent the offseason shedding, as Swift and Watson left as free agents and Wells was dealt to Sacramento.

Wells had worn out his welcome anyway, earning a suspension for Memphis's final playoff game, and the trade brought back some value in Sacramento's Bobby Jackson. Jackson is getting up in years and hasn't been able to stay healthy the past three seasons, but if he stays in one piece he'll be a major upgrade over Jason Williams. He also can play off guard when Mike Miller checks out, filling in Wells's role.

The other players are replaceable too, though it remains to be seen how good the replacements will be. Watson's spot will go to Damon Stoudamire, whom the Grizzlies signed to a reasonable four-year, $17 million deal to take over at the point. He and Jackson should equal or exceed the production of the Williams and Watson combo that manned the point a year ago. Swift's position will go to Warrick, while seven-footer Jake Tsakalidis may provide some missing muscle in the paint.

Memphis shed two other key players in another puzzling deal when they sent Jason Williams, James Posey and Andre Emmett to the Heat in a five-team trade that returned only Miami's Eddie Jones and Utah's Raul Lopez. Lopez is expected to play in Spain this year, leaving Jones as the only gain from the trade. The deal appears to make no sense from either a talent or contract perspective, as Jones earns the maximum and is an inferior player compared to both Williams and Posey. Additionally, it does nothing to address Memphis's need for better rebounding.

However, in the big picture the offseason moves are likely to sacrifice Memphis's greatest attribute: its depth. Having Gasol for a full season will help, but even with him in the lineup Memphis's starting five is hardly an imposing group. Plus, with a now ordinary bench, the Grizzlies need the starters to do more than just break even.

The Grizzlies' failure to get over the hump points back to West. When Memphis hired The Logo, it was all but assumed that he would rebuild the team to seriously challenge for the title. Three years later, it's hard to see how he's moved things along. Four of the five starters were Grizzlies before West arrived, and three of his biggest additions, Wells, Posey and Watson, are already gone. Worst of all, the drafts under West have provided more misses than hits, most notably when the Griz had to cut 2003 first-rounder Troy Bell after just a year.

West has had his bright moments—signing Posey and Cardinal and drafting Burks in the second round—but the overall picture is pretty spotty. The Grizzlies' cap situation is a mess so they can't add any more players, and they had to dump so many contracts in the offseason that they undid most of the good of the previous two summers.

The net result is that Fratello is in a very tight spot. If he can overcome the free-agent defections and get this team back into the postseason, he'll have done an exceptional job. But that looks to be the high-water mark, presenting a long-term dilemma for the Grizzlies. Everyone except Gasol is just sort of OK, and that makes it hard for Memphis to move up the food chain. From a legend like Jerry West, we expect better.

Shane Battier — small forward

Age: 27 Height: 6-8 Weight: 220

Defensive PER: 2.16 (84% SF, 16% PF)

Most similar at age: Bryon Russell

Year		G	M/G	FG%	FT%	P/40	R/40	A/40	TS%		Ast		TO		Usg		Reb		PER	
2002-03	Mem	78	30.6	.483	.828	12.7	5.8	1.7	59.7	3	12.9	37	8.4	7	12.5	52	8.1	45	14.99	20
2003-04	Mem	79	24.6	.446	.732	13.7	6.2	2.1	54.4	13	13.1	31	7.3	3	14.9	48	8.8	29	15.36	20
2004-05	Mem	80	31.5	.442	.789	12.6	6.6	2.0	55.5	13	9.5	53	8.2	12	14.1	54	9.3	28	14.84	23
2005-06	*PRJ (37.1)*			*.438*	*.774*	*12.4*	*6.4*	*2.1*	*55.1*		*11.8*		*8.2*		*13.9*		*9.0*		*14.83*	

Battier is one of basketball's most underrated defensive players. He's fantastic from the help side, frequently racing over to take charges and often reaching in to poke balls away from drivers. Plus, while he's not an explosive leaper, he's big enough to block shots on occasion.

On the ball, Battier's size allows him to contest shots, but his lack of quickness makes him vulnerable off the dribble. This is especially obvious when he defends high-scoring shooting guards, as he sometimes was asked to do last season. However, he's one of the league's smartest players and knows how to disguise his physical limitations. Overall, his Defensive PER was among the best in basketball, and Battier was this defense's most pivotal player.

Offensively, he's a high efficiency, low volume player. Battier's favorite spot is the three-pointer from the left corner, and he hit 39 percent of his threes last season. He's not very smooth off the dribble, but at his size he can convert shots around the basket. Battier did a better job of getting to the line last season, partly thanks to some clever shot fakes, and that helped improve his TS%. However, he's become a bit too passive. Battier's Usage Rate is fairly low, and with the Grizzlies losing so much firepower in the offseason, they'll need him to step up and take a more active role.

Antonio Burks — point guard

Age: 25 Height: 6-1 Weight: 200

(90% PG, 9% SG, 1% SF)

Most similar at age: N/A

Year		G	M/G	FG%	FT%	P/40	R/40	A/40	TS%	Ast	TO	Usg	Reb	PER
2004-05	Mem	24	9.1	.467	.737	13.3	2.2	5.1	53.4	24.4	11.1	18.9	3.3	12.80

Burks played sparingly in his rookie season but did well enough to suggest he could handle a larger role. He's solidly built and has decent quickness so should Jackson's health problems return, Burks is an inexpensive replacement with a limited drop-off in quality. That's what the Grizzlies need so they can afford upgrades in other areas.

Brian Cardinal — power forward

Age: 28 Height: 6-8 Weight: 245

(92% PF, 8% C)

Most similar at age: Rodney Rogers

Year		G	M/G	FG%	FT%	P/40	R/40	A/40	TS%		Ast		TO		Usg		Reb		PER	
2002-03	Was	5	3.0	.250	1.000	10.7	13.3	2.7	41.0		14.5		14.5		17.1		19.7		13.84	
2003-04	GS	76	21.5	.472	.878	18.0	7.8	2.5	62.6	1	13.3	24	10.9	25	17.6	31	11.2	53	19.38	10
2004-05	Mem	58	24.7	.370	.873	14.6	6.3	3.2	51.0	47	15.2	7	11.7	38	18.8	24	8.9	65	13.97	43
2005-06	*PRJ (33.5)*			*.412*	*.852*	*15.4*	*6.7*	*2.9*	*56.0*		*14.8*		*11.6*		*17.8*		*9.5*		*15.76*	

So...which year is the fluke? Heading into his third season of regular minutes, that's the question regarding Cardinal. In 2003–04 with Golden State, he couldn't miss. Cardinal made 44.4 percent of his three-pointers and had the best TS% at his position. Last year he slumped badly, losing over 100 points on his field-goal percentage, slipping to 35.3 on three-pointers, and failing to get to the line as often as he did in Golden State.

While his shooting was a disappointment, Cardinal's defense was outstanding. As I pointed out in the team comment, he had an amazing rate of steals for somebody so slow. For that he can thank good anticipation and quick hands. Cardinal also takes charges and can be physical with opposing post players. However, his poor rebounding contributed to Memphis's woes on the glass, as his Rebound Rate of 8.9 is absolutely awful for a power forward.

The outlook for 2005–06 is that Cardinal's numbers should stabilize at a level somewhere between the past two seasons. Field-goal percentage tends to vary quite a bit from season to season, so the past two years were probably the two extremes of Cardinal's normal range of performance. If so, he'll be a more valuable player this season, and Memphis might consider using an alignment with him at power forward and Gasol at center more often. The rebounding would suffer, but the Grizzlies need the points.

Andre Emmett shooting guard Age: 23 Height: 6-5 Weight: 230
(85% PG, 15% SG) Most similar at age: N/A

Year		G	M/G	FG%	FT%	P/40	R/40	A/40	TS%		Ast		TO		Usg		Reb		PER	
2004-05	Mem	8	3.5	.333	.600	10.0	2.9	0.0	42.7		0.0		10.9		12.5		4.3		0.62	

A second-round pick in 2004, Emmett played only eight games and is a blank slate heading into this season. He was traded to Miami in the offseason and his odds of ending up in such a talented rotation seem a long shot. As a collegian, he showed an ability to score around the basket and rebound, but the jumper is iffy.

Pau Gasol power forward Age: 25 Height: 7-0 Weight: 240
(53% PF, 47% C) Most similar at age: Jermaine O'Neal

Year		G	M/G	FG%	FT%	P/40	R/40	A/40	TS%		Ast		TO		Usg		Reb		PER	
2002-03	Mem	82	35.9	.510	.736	21.1	9.8	3.1	57.0	6	12.7	24	11.8	41	22.2	11	13.7	27	20.66	7
2003-04	Mem	78	31.5	.482	.714	22.5	9.8	3.2	54.2	16	11.9	31	11.3	27	24.6	4	13.8	31	21.69	5
2004-05	Mem	56	32.0	.514	.768	22.3	9.2	3.0	58.2	7	12.0	17	12.1	42	23.8	8	12.9	38	22.57	6
2005-06	PRJ (33.3)			.503	.750	21.8	9.5	3.3	56.5		12.7		11.6		23.9		13.5		21.09	

Gasol had his best season in 2004–05, a fact that would be more obvious if his minutes weren't suppressed. Both Brown and Fratello kept him around 32 minutes per game, which is baffling considering he's easily the team's best player and stamina doesn't seem to be an issue. Even in the playoffs, Gasol played only 33 minutes a night, and he was dominating the Suns in the paint when he played.

Although Gasol lacks strength, he likes to play the post and is a very effective scorer on the blocks. He's at his best when he catches the ball on the move, depriving defenders of a chance to muscle him away from the hoop. He can score from a set position too, but it's easier for defenders to strong-arm him into a tough shot.

Gasol has a variety of short flips around the rim and is a good athlete, which enables him to post a high shooting percentage. Moreover, he draws plenty of fouls because he's always going toward the basket. He averaged better than a foul shot for every two field-goal attempts, but the cost is a high Turnover Ratio. Gasol gets stripped in the lane quite a bit and needs to protect the ball better. He also could use an up-and-under move and a better left hand, not to mention a few extra steaks with his tapas.

Defensively, Gasol's strength is an issue because of his inability to push people out of the post. He partly makes up for it with his shot-blocking ability, as only Swift had a higher rate of blocks. Gasol is less vulnerable at power forward than at center, but Memphis's lack of size forces him to play the middle often. Their best lineup this year might be with him in the middle and Cardinal at power forward, so one hopes Gasol can bulk up.

One also hopes Fratello will see the wisdom in keeping his best player on the court more. Gasol is an All-Star caliber player, but he has no chance of making the team unless he's allowed to be a more frequent participant. At this point, there's no good reason to deny him the extra minutes.

Ryan Humphrey power forward Age: 26 Height: 6-8 Weight: 235
(89% PF, 8% SF, 3% C) Most similar at age: N/A

Year		G	M/G	FG%	FT%	P/40	R/40	A/40	TS%	Ast	TO	Usg	Reb	PER
2002-03	Orl-Mem	48	9.3	.292	.590	8.4	8.9	1.0	33.9	6.4	13.4	13.7	12.7	4.04
2003-04	Mem	2	5.5	.250	—	7.3	10.9	3.6	25.0	14.3	28.6	20.3	15.5	-1.01
2004-05	Mem	35	9.1	.408	.486	12.9	11.0	0.8	42.8	3.6	15.5	17.3	15.5	10.16

Shockingly the Grizzlies kept Humphrey and cut Outlaw at the end of training camp. Humphrey turned out to be less awful than he'd been in his two previous seasons, but he didn't do anything to secure a long-term future in the league. Humphrey gives a good effort defensively and was effective from the help side. However, because he's an inch too short for a power forward and has no jumper, he's always going to struggle offensively. He's a free agent, but his minutes last season might have earned his career a stay of execution.

Dahntay Jones   shooting guard   Age: 25   Height: 6-6   Weight: 210
(97% SG, 2% SF, 1% PG)   Most similar at age: Mitchell Butler

Year		G	M/G	FG%	FT%	P/40	R/40	A/40	TS%		Ast		TO		Usg		Reb		PER	
2003-04	Mem	20	7.7	.283	.455	9.4	6.0	3.1	31.1		14.7		14.7		18.9		8.5		2.46	
2004-05	Mem	52	12.5	.437	.688	14.4	4.3	1.3	53.4	26	6.2	66	10.8	39	15.8	54	6.0	48	9.54	55
2005-06	PRJ (33.9)			.419	.681	14.0	4.5	1.4	51.2		6.6		11.3		15.9		6.5		9.29	

A first-round pick in 2003, Jones saw his first extended action last season and didn't exactly wow onlookers. He's a decent athlete who can score in transition and his 38.3 percent mark on three-pointers was a pleasant surprise, leading to a solid TS%. However, he's a terrible offensive player overall because he rarely creates his own shot and his teammates might as well be invisible.

Jones's defense is his strongest selling point, because he has good quickness and is big enough to bother shots at the shooting guard position. But if he doesn't figure out how to spot the open man and use his athleticism to create more shots, he'll have a limited role. The good news for Jones is that he'll get more chances this year because of Wells's departure.

Mike Miller   shooting guard   Age: 25   Height: 6-8   Weight: 218
Defensive PER: 0.92 (65% SG, 35% SF)   Most similar at age: Steve Smith

Year		G	M/G	FG%	FT%	P/40	R/40	A/40	TS%		Ast		TO		Usg		Reb		PER	
2002-03	Orl-Mem*	65	33.6	.434	.839	18.5	6.2	3.1	53.7	17	13.8	35	10.1	21	20.6	19	8.9	31	14.73	22
2003-04	Mem	65	27.2	.438	.723	16.3	4.9	5.2	53.2	18	22.8	9	10.5	31	21.1	28	6.9	29	14.86	20
2004-05	Mem	76	30.0	.505	.720	17.9	5.3	3.9	61.4	3	18.4	16	10.8	38	19.8	29	7.4	21	16.75	10
2005-06	PRJ (47.1)			.459	.746	17.0	5.4	3.8	56.4		17.8		9.9		20.2		7.5		15.04	

* Season rankings are as small forward

After three years of making virtually no progress, Miller stepped up his game in 2004–05 and became one of the best shooters in basketball. Miller has always had a beautiful stroke, but until last season his accuracy wasn't notable. That changed in a big way, with Miller hitting 43.3 percent of his three-pointers and shooting over 50 percent overall.

Miller is a strong right-handed driver, but he rarely does anything going to his left and doesn't take advantage of his size enough on offense. He averaged just under a free-throw attempt for every five field-goal attempts, a very poor ratio in light of the size advantage he has virtually every night. He did show signs of developing a post game last season and should work to develop that part of his offense in the offseason. Miller also is a good ballhandler who can play point guard in a pinch and sees the court well.

Defensively, Miller put together a stronger effort than he had in previous seasons. His size allows him to contest shots, but he's still vulnerable to the drive. Miller often defended the opposing small forward while Battier took the shooting guard, but that doesn't really help the Grizzlies much since Battier has most of the same limitations. One wonders if Miller would be better off as a small forward, but with Battier on the roster, it won't happen as a Grizzly.

James Posey   small forward   Age: 28   Height: 6-8   Weight: 215
(59% SF, 31% SG, 10% PF)   Most similar in '04-05: Bryon Russell

Year		G	M/G	FG%	FT%	P/40	R/40	A/40	TS%		Ast		TO		Usg		Reb		PER	
2002-03	Hou	83	30.3	.411	.833	14.2	6.8	2.9	51.9	26	15.5	22	12.1	40	17.6	32	9.8	20	13.58	29
2003-04	Mem	82	29.9	.478	.830	18.4	6.6	2.0	61.4	2	10.6	43	9.7	16	17.3	37	9.3	20	18.81	8
2004-05	Mem	50	27.6	.357	.865	11.7	6.3	2.5	50.0	48	12.1	31	12.3	49	15.4	48	8.9	30	10.48	50
2005-06	PRJ (36.1)			.411	.812	15.1	6.4	2.4	54.5		12.4		10.4		17.1		8.8		14.35	

Posey's 2003–04 season was a dream, but last year was a nightmare. Posey had foot problems in the preseason but tried to play through the pain, and the results were horrific. He shot only 35.7 percent, committed way too many turnovers, and wasn't nearly the defensive force that he was a year earlier. Posey's foot gave him less trouble later in the season so he was more active on defense, but his shooting slump lasted the entire season.

(continued next page)

James Posey *(continued)*

One presumes that he'll be able to rebound sharply in 2005–06, in which case the Heat will have themselves an upgrade on Eddie Jones at small forward. When he's on his game, Posey is a terror in transition and an incredibly effective ball thief. His athleticism also makes him a strong on-ball defender, especially since he's tough and takes charges. He probably won't shoot 38.6 percent on three-pointers again like he did in 2003–04, but the rest of his arsenal should bounce back.

Stromile Swift (66% PF, 34% C)			power forward							Age: 26	Height: 6-9	Weight: 225
											Most similar at age: Charles Smith	

Year		G	M/G	FG%	FT%	P/40	R/40	A/40	TS%		Ast		TO		Usg		Reb		PER	
2002-03	Mem*	67	22.1	.481	.722	17.5	10.4	1.2	54.2	19	6.1	61	13.4	37	17.9	15	14.6	34	18.02	7
2003-04	Mem*	77	19.8	.469	.725	19.0	9.9	1.0	53.0	28	4.7	70	10.8	15	19.5	12	14.0	40	19.22	7
2004-05	Mem	60	21.3	.449	.758	18.9	8.5	1.3	51.7	39	6.0	58	12.5	48	21.1	14	12.0	45	16.70	23
2005-06	PRJ (36.4)			.465	.755	18.4	9.3	1.2	53.1		5.8		11.0		19.8		13.0		18.04	

* Season rankings are as center

Swift revealed everything you want to know about him in one sequence in Game 4 of the playoffs against Phoenix. He made an audacious behind-the-back move on Phoenix's Shawn Marion that culminated in a dunk . . . and then earned a technical foul for doing a chin-up on the rim. Swift is a very talented offensive player who can soar in for dunks on the break and comfortably drain 15-footers in the set offense. But his mental errors can drive coaches batty and have prevented him from earning more playing time.

In Memphis his main obstacle to playing time has been Gasol, so Swift's move to Houston in free agency should enable him to double his minutes. That could translate into some big scoring numbers based on his per-minute averages. Look for Swift to figure prominently in the Most Improved Player voting next year (you didn't think they gave it to people who actually improved, did you?).

Swift occasionally played center last season, but at his size he's barely big enough for power forward, so that was a huge mistake. He was completely overpowered in the middle and only made up for it with his high shot-blocking rate. He also loses focus on defense at times, and that will undoubtedly test Jeff Van Gundy's patience.

Losing Swift without compensation was perhaps the biggest mistake of West's tenure in Memphis. He's known for years that Swift and Gasol play the same position, yet he never pulled the trigger on a trade that could have returned a true center or a steadier point guard. Swift was arguably the Grizzlies' second-best player, and Houston's contract offer wasn't extravagant. His loss will set the team back more than many realize.

Jake Tsakalidis (100% C)			center							Age: 26	Height: 7-2	Weight: 290
											Most similar at age: N/A	

Year		G	M/G	FG%	FT%	P/40	R/40	A/40	TS%		Ast		TO		Usg		Reb		PER	
2002-03	Phx	33	16.4	.452	.672	11.9	9.0	1.0	50.1	44	6.5	58	13.0	35	13.3	45	8.7	72	10.21	60
2003-04	Mem	40	13.3	.504	.590	12.8	9.6	1.4	53.2	25	9.0	37	11.5	22	13.7	41	13.7	45	12.47	46
2004-05	Mem	31	9.0	.500	.778	11.2	8.1	1.4	54.2		6.9		12.8		12.7		12.1		11.74	

Good thing they matched Cleveland's offer sheet, huh? Tsakalidis was a restricted free agent last summer and the Grizzlies stepped up to match a three-year, $8 million deal from the Cavs. Then they locked Tsakalidis in a freezer until June. The Georgian giant played sparingly despite the Grizzlies' glaring need at center, although he was modestly effective in his few chances.

Tsakalidis can hit short hook shots around the basket and get deep post position with his size. While he's not the most fleet of foot, his size presents an obstacle on defense and he's very effective when he plays against bigger centers. With Swift gone and Wright wanting out, Tsakalidis's role should increase substantially this season. Moreover, he fits the system much better now that Memphis is pressing less.

Earl Watson   point guard   Age: 26   Height: 6-1   Weight: 195
Defensive PER: 2.40 (97% PG, 3% SG)   Most similar at age: Anthony Carter

Year		G	M/G	FG%	FT%	P/40	R/40	A/40	TS%		Ast		TO		Usg		Reb		PER	
2002-03	Mem	79	17.3	.435	.721	12.7	4.8	6.6	50.5	31	30.3	3	11.9	43	19.6	30	6.7	33	14.60	26
2003-04	Mem	81	20.6	.371	.652	11.0	4.3	9.6	43.8	60	37.5	4	13.6	49	23.0	21	6.0	20	12.81	38
2004-05	Mem	80	22.6	.426	.659	13.6	3.6	7.9	50.0	45	31.5	20	14.6	62	23.4	24	5.1	45	13.04	43
2005-06	PRJ (38.1)			.409	.679	12.8	3.9	7.9	48.2		32.0		14.4		22.5		5.4		13.15	

Watson is the best defensive point guard in basketball, hands down. He gets no recognition in the All-Defense voting because he isn't a starter, but his effect on the Grizzlies last year was obvious. He moves his feet well, pressures the ball up the court, has fast hands, and is strong enough to rebuff bigger guards attempting to post him up. In fact, Memphis gave up 6.1 points less per 48 minutes when Watson was on the court. Some of that disparity was due to Watson replacing the inferior Jason Williams, but most was a reflection of Watson's skill.

Offensively, Watson isn't nearly as potent. He struggles from the perimeter, hitting 30.9 percent for his career and allowing defenders to sag off him. Watson is very quick and can get to the basket, but he's often out of control and thus has an excessive Turnover Ratio. On a positive note, he sees the court well and can find the open man, even though his Assist Ratio declined last season. Because of his quickness, he also can create shots at the end of the shot clock. He just needs to make more of them.

Watson is a free agent and his status was unclear at publication time, but it doesn't appear he'll be returning to Memphis. He may not be able to handle a full-time starting role unless his shooting improves, but one hopes that Watson soon will get recognition for his outstanding play at the defensive end.

Bonzi Wells   shooting guard   Age: 29   Height: 6-5   Weight: 210
(87% SG, 12% SF, 1% PG)   Most similar at age: Terry Teagle

Year		G	M/G	FG%	FT%	P/40	R/40	A/40	TS%		Ast		TO		Usg		Reb		PER	
2002-03	Por*	75	32.0	.441	.722	19.0	6.6	4.1	50.5	37	15.5	23	13.5	47	24.6	7	9.9	18	15.73	16
2003-04	Por-Mem	72	26.0	.427	.754	18.9	5.6	3.0	47.6	50	11.3	53	13.1	57	24.0	12	7.9	15	13.02	31
2004-05	Mem	69	21.6	.441	.750	19.4	6.2	2.1	51.5	42	9.2	61	10.3	34	22.4	15	8.7	10	15.93	13
2005-06	PRJ (38.3)			.434	.746	17.9	6.0	2.8	49.7		11.6		12.5		22.2		8.4		13.52	

* Season rankings are as small forward

Wells had a good season until the playoffs started. His ability to post up was a key for the second unit, as he was the only Grizzly other than Gasol who could score on the blocks. Wells averaged nearly 20 points per 40 minutes off the bench, mostly by shooting turnarounds in the post and high-arcing knuckleballs on the perimeter. He can't explode to the basket anymore and has a low free-throw rate as a result, but he's made up for it by becoming a passable perimeter shooter. A bigger mystery is the loss of his passing skills. Wells was a magician in his younger days but his Assist Ratio in Memphis was terrible last season.

Defensively, Wells didn't always defend well on the ball, but his anticipation for steals primed the Grizzlies' ability to force turnovers. Wells picked one every 18 minutes, and his rebounding ability was a nice bonus on a team that struggled on the glass. Unfortunately, Wells's surly attitude again has made him persona non grata. He feuded over minutes with Fratello and was asked to stay home from the Grizzlies' final playoff game.

Memphis ended up giving Wells away to Sacramento after the season, where he won't be complaining about playing time anymore. He'll see close to 40 minutes a night the way Rick Adelman rides his starters, and Sacramento's offensive system could revive his dormant passing skills. However, pairing him with Peja Stojakovic on the perimeter might leave the Kings very vulnerable on defense.

Jason Williams — point guard
Age: 30 Height: 6-1 Weight: 190
Defensive PER: 0.31 (100% PG)
Most similar at age: Johnny Dawkins

Year		G	M/G	FG%	FT%	P/40	R/40	A/40	TS%		Ast		TO		Usg		Reb		PER	
2002-03	Mem	76	31.7	.388	.840	15.3	3.5	10.5	50.1	37	36.8	6	9.8	18	26.2	9	5.0	45	17.12	14
2003-04	Mem	72	29.4	.407	.837	14.8	2.8	9.3	51.7	20	35.5	11	9.8	17	24.1	16	3.9	61	16.91	15
2004-05	Mem	71	27.5	.413	.792	14.7	2.5	8.2	52.2	29	32.8	13	10.7	32	23.8	23	3.5	66	15.48	26
2005-06	PRJ (33.5)			.407	.832	14.9	2.7	8.3	51.9		32.4		10.2		24.5		3.8		16.51	

For all the criticism he endures, Williams has become one of the game's better offensive point guards. Both his Assist Ratio and Turnover Ratio are very good for his position, and his TS% is always respectable despite terrible shot selection. Williams fancies himself a three-point shooter, taking more than half his tries from out there even though he's a career 31.5 percent marksman. It's maddening because Williams shot 50.6 percent on his two-pointers. One would expect that to give him ample motivation to venture inside the line more, but he doesn't.

Defense is another matter. Williams has good anticipation and gets his share of steals, but he provides very little help and often seems disinterested in the proceedings. As for rebounding, Williams only gets the board if it bounces out to halfcourt.

As a result of those shortcomings and his strained relationships with both Brown and Fratello, the Grizzlies weren't too upset to see Williams leave. But he's a valuable player nonetheless, and he should provide the Heat an immediate upgrade at the point. Moreover, if Stan Van Gundy can somehow convince Williams to play defense, the trade will end up a colossal steal for Miami.

Lorenzen Wright — center
Age: 30 Height: 6-11 Weight: 240
Defensive PER: 1.00 (99% C, 1% PF)
Most similar at age: P. J. Brown

Year		G	M/G	FG%	FT%	P/40	R/40	A/40	TS%		Ast		TO		Usg		Reb		PER	
2002-03	Mem	70	28.3	.454	.659	16.1	10.7	1.6	48.9	52	8.0	45	11.0	14	18.4	12	15.0	28	14.39	32
2003-04	Mem	65	25.8	.439	.733	14.6	10.6	1.7	47.4	60	9.0	36	9.7	10	17.4	16	15.0	28	14.00	35
2004-05	Mem	80	28.6	.469	.662	13.5	10.7	1.5	50.1	47	7.2	29	10.4	7	16.0	26	15.1	29	13.95	32
2005-06	PRJ (56.8)			.457	.686	14.1	10.6	1.8	48.9		8.7		10.9		17.0		15.0		13.80	

Wright defies logic, continuing to be a starting NBA center despite the fact that he is neither starter-quality nor a center. Offensively, Wright creates more shots than the average NBA big man because he can score inside or outside. However, he's not a high-percentage shooter from either spot. He likes to shoot 15-footers from the baseline but isn't terribly accurate, and he doesn't get to the line much for a big man. His other weapon is an ugly-looking, jump hook/fling that he shoots from the blocks, mostly into the front of the rim. Wright doesn't make turnovers, however, and can be effective from the high post dropping the ball down into Gasol.

Defensively, Wright rated fairly well despite being undersized. He's always had a knack for the boards and is one of the few Memphis big men who holds his own there. He also can block shots, but like Gasol he is outsized every night and has trouble defending physical post players.

Wright has a year remaining on a seven-year, $42 million deal but was enraged that the Grizzlies wouldn't extend it and demanded a trade over the summer. Considering Wright's age and the Grizzlies' cap situation, they should not extend Wright at any price. Long term they want a more traditional center in this spot, and the only other position for Wright currently belongs to Gasol. Obviously, Wright has made himself trade bait, and he could have a new home by the deadline.

Hakim Warrick — power forward
Age: 22 Height: 6-8 Weight: 218

An athlete in search of a position, Warrick is undersized for an NBA power forward but lacks the perimeter game to play on the perimeter. Nonetheless, he became a first-round pick because he's such a good leaper that Memphis figures he'll fit in somewhere. He could take over the off-the-bench energizer role that Outlaw filled two years ago, trapping all over on the press and getting easy baskets running the floor. In the halfcourt, however, he might be useless.

Lawrence Roberts — power forward
Age: 23 Height: 6-9 Weight: 240

The Grizzlies traded two future second-round picks and cash to Seattle in order to get Roberts, which seems a bit excessive for the 55th overall pick. Roberts is very strong, has a good post game, and is one of the best rebounders in the draft. Nevertheless, it's not clear how he'll fare at the defensive end, because he's neither long nor a good leaper and he's a bit slow-footed.

Minnesota Timberwolves

It was fun while it lasted.

Two years ago, the Minnesota Timberwolves decided to roll the dice that a pair of aging players could get the team to a championship before their bodies quit on them. The gamble nearly worked in 2003–04, as Sam Cassell and Latrell Sprewell teamed with Kevin Garnett to lead Minnesota to the West's best record before Minnesota fell to the Lakers in the Western Conference finals.

But in 2004–05, it was time pay the piper. Cassell had begun breaking down physically in the 2004 playoffs and struggled to stay healthy the entire season. Sprewell succumbed to age and indifference, losing much of his athletic burst while whining about not receiving a contract extension. Only another brilliant effort from Kevin Garnett saved the T'wolves from a losing season, but even Minnesota's meal ticket wasn't immune to the injury bug, battling a sore knee much of the season.

As a result, Minnesota missed the playoffs entirely, its first absence from the postseason in nine years. Coming on the heels of the franchise's best-ever season, it was a shock, and there were casualties. Long-time coach Flip Saunders got the ax midway through the season and team president Kevin McHale came downstairs to coach the team in the second half.

Removing Saunders didn't solve the real problem: The T'wolves were an old, slow team. Offensively, that manifested itself in a complete inability to get to the basket. With Cassell and backup Troy Hudson unable to penetrate defenses, nobody could break down the opponent off the dribble and create openings for other players. Sprewell's decline added to the problem. Once among the league's most athletic players, he had only two dunks the entire season and mostly shot long jumpers.

Besides those two, Minnesota's two best players were Garnett and Wally Szczerbiak. Garnett is brilliant, but he tends to be a jump shooter more than a slasher, while Szczerbiak rarely ventures into the paint. Consequently, the T'wolves were last in the NBA in free-throw attempts. Minnesota earned only .275 free throws for every field-goal attempt, compared to the league average of .324. The difference doesn't seem like much, but consider that Minnesota tried nearly 81 field goals a game. That means Minnesota was losing nearly four free throws per night, which is particularly painful when you consider they were the league's best free-throw shooting team at 79.6 percent.

Minnesota was near the bottom of the league in free-throw attempts even in the good ol' days of 2003–04, so it wasn't a new problem, just a more severe one. They had a good offense despite the lack of free throws because they shot the ball so well. Szczerbiak, Cassell, Garnett, and Fred Hoiberg all are deadly outside shooters, and those were the guys taking most of the shots. But Minnesota's offense wasn't nearly as deadly as the year before. The T'wolves were the league's fifth-best offense in 2004–05 but dropped to sixth last season (and more importantly, fell much closer to the league average), with the decline in free-throws being the main difference.

While the T'wolves' tired legs had a minor impact on the offense, the effect on the defense was enormous. Minnesota set NBA records for fewest steals and fewest turnovers forced, because nobody outside of Garnett could pressure the ball. Only three T'wolves stole the ball at a rate better than the league average, and two were reserves (Hoiberg and Anthony Carter). The other was Garnett, but the starters he played with were all well below the league average of 1.24 steals per 40 minutes. The best, Cassell, was at 0.95—more than 25 percent below the norm.

Technically, the T'wolves weren't the NBA's worst team at forcing turnovers, because the Lakers played a faster pace and actually forced fewer turnovers per possession. But Minnesota's record was hardly impressive. The T'wolves forced only 12.2 turnovers per 100 possessions, compared to the league average of 14.8, so that deficiency alone put them more than two points per game behind the competition (see table 1).

Further, while Minnesota's decline in free throws wasn't symbolic of a larger offensive decline, the paucity of steals and turnovers was a bigger factor. The T'wolves were the

Timberwolves at a Glance

Record: 44–38, 3rd place in Northwest Division

Offensive Efficiency: 104.9 (6th)

Defensive Efficiency: 103.7 (15th)

Pace Factor: 91.4 (22nd)

Top-Rated Player: Kevin Garnett (PER 28.35, 1st overall)

Head Coach: Dwane Casey. Long-time assistant gets his first shot in the big chair.

Table 1. Fewest Steals per 100 Possessions, 2004–05

Team	Stl/100 Poss.
Minnesota	6.15
L.A. Lakers	6.62
Miami	6.83
Milwaukee	6.89
Phoenix	7.05
League Average	**8.03**

league's sixth-best defense in 2003–04; just one year later, they were 15th. Minnesota actually was good in most other respects, as they had one of the lowest rates of fouls in the league, held opponents to a low field-goal percentage, and took care of the glass. But since they couldn't force turnovers, their opponents got too many chances to score. Eventually, some of the shots were bound to fall.

Minnesota had a plan for dealing with Cassell's and Sprewell's declines. They signed Troy Hudson to a six-year deal to be Cassell's heir at the point and brought in troubled big man Eddie Griffin to bolster the bench in a classic "second draft" scenario (see Drew Gooden comment in the Cleveland chapter). The problem was that Hudson was terrible, suffering from the after-effects of an ankle injury, while Griffin is a free agent and was unsigned at publication time.

Even worse, the T'wolves' have harmed their future prospects with a number of self-inflicted wounds. Five years ago Minnesota lost four first-round picks as a penalty for making an under-the-table deal with Joe Smith, and then added to their woes by using their two first-rounders in that time on Will Avery and Ndudi Ebi. When they've had money to spend, they've burned it on players like Michael Olowokandi, Trenton Hassell, and Smith rather than more carefully analyzing their opportunities.

That said, Minnesota missed out on the single most obvious way to improve their team by leaving Sprewell in the starting lineup all season. It seemed they were hoping the team would start clicking as it did a year earlier, but doing so the ignored better solutions. Most obviously, whither The Mayor? Hoiberg had the fourth-best PER on the T'wolves last year, behind Garnett, Cassell, and Szczerbiak. He finished second in the league in True Shooting Percentage and had the best plus/minus rating on the team. Both Saunders and McHale ignored this information, however, playing Hoiberg only 16.7 minutes per game while giving his minutes to underperforming players like Sprewell and Hassell.

Of course, Minnesota's struggles in 2004–05 beg the question: If they were an old team last year, what will they be like this year? The answers aren't promising. The only key T'wolves under 30 are Griffin, Hassell, Ebi, and first-round draft choice Rashad McCants. Griffin is a free agent and might not be back, and he's had a series of personal problems as well. Hassell is a limited defensive specialist who might have been over his head in 2003–04. Ebi turned pro out of high school and doesn't seem anywhere close to being ready. McCants could provide an answer at shooting guard, but he's a poor defender who won't help the team's biggest weakness.

Oh, and the rest of the team is a mess. Sprewell is out the door, while Hoiberg was found to have a heart problem in the offseason and will miss the beginning of the year at the very least. The T'wolves re-signed forward Mark Madsen—giving him a crazy five-year deal despite his horrendous 2004–05 season—but their only credible center is Olowokandi and there's only about one game in five where he seems to care. The T'wolves also are flirting with the luxury tax line and the cap situation is in shambles for several more years, with $40 million a year committed to just four players (Garnett, Szczerbiak, Hudson, and Hassell) through 2009.

Minnesota made two moves to bolster the backcourt. First, they traded Cassell and a conditional first-round pick to the Clippers for Marko Jaric, who is several years younger and a better defender. The move was tantamount to an admission that the T'wolves aren't serious contenders this season, but will help in the longer term. Minnesota also looked to get more athletic on the wings, signing Seattle wing Damien Wilkins to an offer sheet. The Sonics hadn't decided whether to match the offer at publication time.

In the big picture, T'wolves fans shouldn't be expecting Armageddon. Minnesota might not improve much, but it's not going to end up in last place either. They still have arguably the best player on the planet in Garnett, and the team would have been a top-four seed in the Eastern Conference. Jaric and Szczerbiak should space the floor with their shooting, and Hudson may bounce back with a much better season if his ankle is better.

But for a team with such a dominant player, it's a huge disappointment to see them wallowing around the .500 mark. The truth is that Minnesota has given Garnett so little help that not even his brilliance can prevent them from missing the playoffs. The gamble Minnesota took two years ago to bring in Cassell and Sprewell nearly succeeded, but the T'wolves will be feeling its toll for several more years.

Anthony Carter — point guard
(100% PG)

Age: 30 Height: 6-2 Weight: 195
Most similar at age: Haywoode Workman

Year		G	M/G	FG%	FT%	P/40	R/40	A/40	TS%		Ast		TO		Usg		Reb		PER	
2002-03	Mia	49	18.6	.356	.660	8.7	3.6	8.9	39.0	63	37.7	5	15.0	58	22.1	30	5.3	38	9.89	56
2003-04	SA	5	17.4	.297	—	10.1	5.1	5.5	29.7		19.7		19.7		24.6		7.2		0.21	
2004-05	Min	66	11.2	.407	.686	9.8	3.7	8.7	45.4	63	38.1	5	14.7	63	21.0	42	5.5	34	11.21	53
2005-06	*PRJ (25.7)*			*.399*	*.685*	*10.0*	*3.7*	*8.4*	*45.3*		*36.8*		*14.7*		*21.4*		*5.4*		*11.63*	

A defensive specialist with a history of knee problems, Carter's leg was feeling much better last season and he got into 66 games when Cassell and Hudson had health issues. Among guards, Carter might be the worst shooter in the league. In his six-year career, he's made only 12 three-point shots, and his career mark is 10.9 percent. No, that's not a typo. He doesn't fare much better from inside the arc and is an annual contender for the league's worst TS%.

Carter has wisely focused on passing at the offensive end, and his Assist Ratio usually ranks among the best in the game. Unfortunately, defenders know to play him for the pass and end up stealing many of his deliveries, so his Turnover Ratio is very high as well.

Carter was on a one-year deal but did enough defensively that Minnesota is likely to bring him back if they trade Cassell. If not, he'll catch on someplace as a backup point guard and hope that his knee holds up for another season.

Sam Cassell — point guard
(99% PG, 1% SG)

Age: 36 Height: 6-3 Weight: 185
Most similar at age: Gary Payton

Year		G	M/G	FG%	FT%	P/40	R/40	A/40	TS%		Ast		TO		Usg		Reb		PER	
2002-03	Mil	78	34.6	.470	.861	22.8	5.1	6.7	56.5	4	22.7	52	8.9	11	27.9	5	7.4	6	22.32	2
2003-04	Min	81	35.0	.488	.873	22.6	3.8	8.3	56.6	4	26.6	40	9.9	18	29.6	2	5.4	34	22.78	1
2004-05	Min	59	25.8	.464	.865	21.0	4.1	7.9	52.9	24	25.8	40	9.4	15	29.3	3	6.1	22	18.62	10
2005-06	*PRJ (8.0)*			*.462*	*.864*	*19.1*	*4.2*	*7.8*	*53.9*		*27.3*		*10.3*		*27.2*		*6.0*		*18.46*	

Cassell missed 23 games with injuries and was limited in several of the games he attempted to play. He was nursing a hamstring injury for most of the season and never quite got it 100 percent, which is why his minutes declined so much when he played.

Cassell remains an extremely clever operator offensively, but he couldn't operate at the same efficiency level he did in 2003–04. The sore legs took the oomph out of his long-range jumper, as shown by the sudden decline in three-point marksmanship. Cassell dropped from 39.8 percent to 26.2 percent, explaining the dive in his TS%. However, he was still deadly from mid-range. Cassell has a variety of herky-jerky hesitation moves that he uses to keep defenders off balance to clear space for his jump shot, especially going to his left. He's one of the game's smartest players too, throwing in enough head fakes and flat-out dives to get to the line a fair amount.

Defense has never been a strength of Cassell's and he was all but worthless last season, repeatedly getting beaten to the rim and offering little in the way of help for his teammates. As of now his offense is so impressive that it's worth keeping him in the starting lineup, but that could begin to change in the next year or two.

Cassell was traded to the Clippers after the season, but that may not be a permanent stop. The veteran would seem to be a better fit as a pickup for a contending team, and indeed that may happen soon enough. Look for Cassell to tutor Shaun Livingston for half a season and then, if the Clippers aren't in contention, to be shipped out at the trade deadline.

Ndudi Ebi — small forward
(100% SF)

Age: 21 Height: 6-11 Weight: 220
Most similar at age: N/A

Year		G	M/G	FG%	FT%	P/40	R/40	A/40	TS%	Ast	TO	Usg	Reb	PER
2003-04	Min	17	1.9	.429	.250	16.3	3.8	3.8	41.2	13.8	13.8	25.0	5.5	9.13
2004-05	Min	2	27.0	.524	.556	20.0	11.9	0.7	54.1	3.5	10.4	20.4	17.3	17.70

The T'wolves' first-round pick in 2003, Ebi played in only two games last season and doesn't seem to figure prominently in the T'wolves' plans for the coming season. However, it's worth mentioning that he played extremely well in the two games he saw action, averaging a point every two minutes and shooting 52.4 percent from the floor.

(continued next page)

Ndudi Ebi *(continued)*

At his height and weight Ebi's upside is as a poor man's version of Garnett—a long, slender mid-range jump shooter who can rebound. Until he adds more strength he has to play small forward, where Minnesota already has Szczerbiak. But he could figure into the rotation as a bench player if he can build on his brief bouts of productivity from last season.

Kevin Garnett					power forward							Age: 29		Height: 6-11		Weight: 220	
Defensive PER: 1.26 (62% PF, 38% C)														Most similar at age: David Robinson			
Year		G	M/G	FG%	FT%	P/40	R/40	A/40	TS%		Ast		TO		Usg		Reb		PER	
2002-03	Min*	82	40.5	.502	.751	22.7	13.3	6.0	55.3	11	20.4	6	9.4	16	27.1	4	18.8	1	26.38	2
2003-04	Min	82	39.4	.499	.791	24.6	14.1	5.1	54.7	13	16.8	15	8.7	3	28.7	1	20.0	1	29.43	1
2004-05	Min	82	38.0	.502	.811	23.3	14.2	6.0	56.7	13	20.4	3	9.7	24	28.0	3	20.9	2	28.35	1
2005-06	PRJ (5.4)			.506	.801	22.7	14.0	5.1	55.6		17.7		9.3		26.7		19.5		26.39	

* Season rankings are as small forward

Garnett had the league's best PER for a second-straight season and set an NBA record with his sixth straight 20-point, 10-rebound, five-assist season. The T'wolves' struggles cost him a second consecutive MVP trophy, and in fact he barely got a sniff in the voting. This was odd since he was not only the best player in the league, he also played about 600 more minutes than Shaquille O'Neal, Steve Nash, or Tim Duncan.

An interesting exercise is to look at how our perceptions of whether a team is "successful" color the award voting. For an example, look at the disparity in the MVP voting between LeBron James, Allen Iverson, and Kevin Garnett. Garnett's team went 44–38, Iverson's team was a game worse at 43–39, and James was one game below at 42–40.

Garnett's team won more games than the others, and Garnett was better individually too. As I mentioned, he had the highest PER in the league, and his Defensive PER was better than Iverson's or James's. He also played all 82 games, so there shouldn't have been any reason to vote James or Iverson ahead of Garnett.

Guess again. Iverson finished fifth in the voting, with a spot on 72 of the 127 ballots and two first-place votes. James came in sixth, named on 43 ballots. Garnett, meanwhile, came in 11th, with only 11 ballots (voters rank five names each).

What could possibly explain this difference? It could be a lot of things—certainly many people hold an inflated opinion of Iverson's value—but a lot had to do with the perception of the teams' seasons. Iverson's Sixers and James's Cavs finished right around where people expected, so voters felt free to give the two players credit for their accomplishments. But in Garnett's case, the T'wolves were thought of as a staggering disappointment. Before the season, many thought they would challenge for the Western Conference crown, and a few prognosticators thought they might win the title.

The T'wolves' failure to do this was not held against the people who made the predictions, but rather against Garnett. Hey, nobody likes to admit they were wrong. In this case, however, there were obvious reasons Minnesota couldn't repeat its 2003–04 success: Cassell and Sprewell weren't the same players. Unfortunately, a circumstance completely out of Garnett's control caused him to be left off nearly every MVP ballot, even though he probably should have won the award.

However, Garnett's season wasn't the tour de force that his 2003–04 campaign was. Defensively, his PER dropped because a sore knee prevented him from being as active. He still was one of the best defenders at his position but no longer a dominating force. Additionally, Minnesota's lack of quality big men often forced Garnett to play center, where his thin frame exposed him to nightly punishment. The effect can be seen in the decline in his blocks from 2.2 per game to 1.4.

Nevertheless, Garnett was awesome, finishing in the top three at his position in Usage Rate, Assist Ratio, and Rebound Rate. He boosted his rate of free throws to nearly 0.4 per field-goal attempt, a long-awaited increase that had been one of his few weak spots, and shot over 50 percent from the floor. With an offseason of rest, he should come back as good as ever next season. And now that the T'wolves are expected to be ordinary, he might even get back into the MVP discussion.

Eddie Griffin					power forward							Age: 23		Height: 6-10		Weight: 232	
(93% PF, 7% SF)														Most similar at age: Donyell Marshall			
Year		G	M/G	FG%	FT%	P/40	R/40	A/40	TS%		Ast		TO		Usg		Reb		PER	
2002-03	Hou	77	24.5	.400	.617	14.1	9.8	1.8	46.2	57	9.8	39	8.6	6	18.1	29	14.1	23	15.46	26
2003-04			Did not play																	
2004-05	Min	70	21.3	.387	.718	14.1	12.1	1.4	47.4	64	6.8	52	8.3	13	17.2	36	17.8	5	15.96	28
2005-06	PRJ (6.1)			.416	.729	15.7	11.7	1.7	50.3		8.1		8.4		18.4		17.3		17.37	

Griffin sat out in 2003–04 due to personal problems but resurfaced with the T'wolves and gave them a much-needed scorer off the bench. Griffin has an awkward outside shot that doesn't spin correctly and needs more arc, but he loves letting it fly from the three-point line. Although he's hit only 33 percent for his career, Griffin takes more than a third of his shots from out there.

Now for the bad news: The threes are actually a higher-probability proposition for him than going inside the line. Griffin is forced to shoot the long ball with at least a little arc, but from shorter distances he just slams line drives into the front of the rim. Because he lacks muscle, he can't post up inside, and he doesn't have a great knack for finishing around the rim. As a result, Griffin's TS% was 47.4, a brutal showing for a player who took so many shots.

Where Griffin had value was rebounding and shot-blocking. He used long arms and great timing to block over three shots per 40 minutes, helping the defense make up for its lack of widebodies. He also had among the best Rebound Rates at his position, again because of his long arms and quick hops.

One would think that Griffin could convert some more of those rebounds into points and stop hanging out at the three-point line so much. If he stays with the T'wolves, that should be one of Dwane Casey's biggest projects for the coming season. But he might have more value on another roster. Griffin plays the same position as Garnett, and there are spots where the T'wolves need help much more urgently.

Trenton Hassell				shooting guard						Age: 26		Height: 6-5		Weight: 200	
Defensive PER: 0.77 (78% SG, 22% SF)												Most similar at age: Calbert Cheaney			
Year	G	M/G	FG%	FT%	P/40	R/40	A/40	TS%		Ast		TO		Usg		Reb		PER	
2002-03 Chi	82	24.4	.367	.745	6.8	5.1	3.0	41.1	55	23.2	12	12.8	51	11.6	55	7.0	27	6.03	56
2003-04 Min	81	28.0	.465	.787	7.2	4.5	2.3	49.8	36	22.7	10	7.8	8	9.9	63	6.4	36	8.24	60
2004-05 Min	82	25.2	.474	.789	10.5	4.2	2.5	51.5	43	11.8	52	8.9	20	13.3	63	6.2	42	9.30	58
2005-06 PRJ (26.4)			.428	.770	9.1	4.5	2.6	48.1		16.9		9.6		12.5		6.4		8.70	

Hassell is only 6'5", but he's quick and a very good leaper. That makes him a standout defensive player, especially when he guards taller opponents. Hassell seems to be more effective when he plays small forward, as he did for much of 2003–04. In that role he can guard a taller opposing player and stay in front of him, and use his leaping ability to contest shots. That's what he did to Carmelo Anthony and Peja Stojakovic in the 2004 playoffs and it worked like a charm.

In 2004–05 Hassell seemed less effective for reasons that aren't entirely clear. He still was in people's faces, but the T'wolves weren't any more effective as a unit with Hassell on the court and his Defensive PER was fairly ordinary.

That's bad news for the T'wolves, because Hassell needs to be outstanding defensively to justify his spot in the rotation. Hassell can't shoot and rarely creates shots, forcing the T'wolves to play 4-on-5 offensively when he's in the game. The six-year, $24 million deal he signed before the season now looks extremely rich, but he can prove that 2004–05's defensive performance was a fluke. He has the skills to be an All-Defense caliber player, and the absence of Sprewell and Hoiberg should give him more opportunities to stymie small forwards.

Fred Hoiberg				shooting guard						Age: 33		Height: 6-5		Weight: 210	
(99% SG, 1% SF)												Most similar at age: Mario Elie			
Year	G	M/G	FG%	FT%	P/40	R/40	A/40	TS%		Ast		TO		Usg		Reb		PER	
2002-03 Chi	63	12.4	.389	.820	7.4	7.0	3.6	48.6	42	28.8	4	10.3	30	11.3	56	9.7	6	10.28	42
2003-04 Min*	79	22.8	.465	.845	11.8	5.9	2.4	61.1	3	18.6	8	7.5	4	12.5	56	8.4	36	13.61	32
2004-05 Min	76	16.7	.489	.873	13.7	5.7	2.7	66.4	1	12.7	45	4.6	1	13.5	61	8.4	12	16.77	9
2005-06 PRJ (21.3)			.448	.829	11.1	6.0	2.6	60.4		17.1		6.8		12.5		8.6		13.37	

* Season rankings are as small forward

Hoiberg was on pace to have the highest TS% in history until a late-season slump knocked him below 70 percent. He had an unbelievable year shooting the ball, making 48.3 percent of his three-pointers, and for good measure he posted the lowest Turnover Ratio at his position. His exalted level of efficiency meant Hoiberg could take relatively few shots and still be an extremely effective player, but apparently Minnesota had trouble doing the math. What else can explain Sprewell getting nearly twice as many minutes?

(continued next page)

Fred Hoiberg *(continued)*

Also, Hoiberg is a much better defender than people realize, with good upper body strength and a willingness to stick his nose in the fray. Plus, he's a very effective rebounder. Overall, he was one of the best values in the league at just $1.5 million. Unfortunately, Hoiberg was diagnosed with an aneurysm in his heart in the offseason and had to undergo surgery to have a pacemaker installed. The T'wolves were so confident he'd miss the entire season that they used him as their luxury tax amnesty cut.

Troy Hudson — point guard
(99% PG, 1% SG) — Age: 29 Height: 6-1 Weight: 175
Most similar at age: Nick Van Exel

Year		G	M/G	FG%	FT%	P/40	R/40	A/40	TS%		Ast		TO		Usg		Reb		PER	
2002-03	Min	79	32.9	.428	.900	17.3	2.8	7.0	53.1	18	26.7	31	10.8	27	23.9	17	4.0	61	15.16	24
2003-04	Min	29	17.3	.386	.818	17.3	2.8	5.6	49.2	40	21.5	57	10.4	25	24.3	13	4.1	60	12.43	42
2004-05	Min	79	21.9	.401	.778	16.0	2.4	6.5	49.1	51	25.7	42	10.3	26	24.2	20	3.6	65	12.01	49
2005-06	PRJ (41.5)			.398	.812	16.4	2.5	6.1	49.4		23.9		10.3		24.1		3.6		12.96	

The T'wolves insist that the ankle problem that sidelined Hudson in 2003–04 was the same reason he struggled in 2004–05. At this point, they might also consider the possibility that he's just not that good. Hudson's numbers the past two seasons have been extremely similar to those he posted in 2002–03, with one exception: He's not making shots.

Hudson's TS% has fallen south of 50 the past two seasons, but he continues to fire away. He's at his best coming off a screen-and-roll going to his right, but in the past he would explode all the way to the rim for a lay-up. Of late, he's been pulling up when he gets past the screen for a jumper that finds the rim more often than the net. It's maddening for Minnesota because he's doing it early in the shot clock, taking shots away from the T'wolves' many high-percentage marksmen.

Hudson has a six-year, $35 million deal that no other team will touch, so he'll get one more crack at regaining the effectiveness he showed in his first year in Minnesota. Since Cassell is likely to be traded, Hudson could even end up starting. In either case, he needs to tone it down with the long jumpers and get to the rim again.

Ervin Johnson — center
(100% C) — Age: 38 Height: 6-11 Weight: 255
Most similar at age: N/A

Year		G	M/G	FG%	FT%	P/40	R/40	A/40	TS%		Ast		TO		Usg		Reb		PER	
2002-03	Mil	69	17.0	.452	.682	5.2	10.1	0.8	49.2	50	11.3	23	16.0	57	6.5	71	14.7	32	9.47	65
2003-04	Min	66	14.6	.534	.607	5.3	9.6	1.0	55.1	13	14.2	10	17.7	70	6.3	74	13.7	47	8.58	71
2004-05	Min	46	8.9	.519	.640	7.1	11.0	0.6	56.2		2.8		20.2		7.6		16.1		8.15	

Johnson started for much of 2003–04, but at 38 he's worn out and barely played in 2004–05. He was on the last year of his contract and could pull the curtain on his 12-year NBA career at any time. More than his shot-blocking and rebounding, he'll be remembered for having the worst hands of any player in the past decade.

Mark Madsen — center
(95% C, 5% PF) — Age: 29 Height: 6-9 Weight: 245
Most similar at age: Terry Davis

Year		G	M/G	FG%	FT%	P/40	R/40	A/40	TS%		Ast		TO		Usg		Reb		PER	
2002-03	LAL*	54	14.5	.423	.590	8.9	8.1	1.9	45.8	56	14.9	15	10.6	25	11.9	55	11.5	49	9.32	60
2003-04	Min	72	17.3	.495	.483	8.3	8.7	0.9	50.6	44	8.5	42	14.2	53	9.7	71	12.4	60	9.41	70
2004-05	Min	41	14.7	.515	.500	5.8	8.5	1.2	52.6	32	5.7	42	19.1	67	7.4	69	12.4	54	6.76	70
2005-06	PRJ (31.3)			.462	.495	6.9	8.3	1.2	47.9		8.6		16.7		9.0		11.7		7.88	

* Season rankings are as power forward

Madsen missed the T'wolves' stretch run with a ruptured ligament in his wrist and wasn't terribly effective when he played, committing turnovers at a shocking rate and posting a Ruffin-esque 5.8 points per 40 minutes. Madsen has a reputation as a warrior in the paint, but his Rebound Rates have been consistently poor. Last season's mark of 12.4 was par for the course, suggesting his rep may be a bit overdone.

Amazingly, Minnesota gave him a five-year deal in the offseason, continuing a long pattern of the T'wolves greatly overpaying their own free agents. The one exception, of course, was Chauncey Billups, which may explain why Minnesota now is reluctant to lose anybody. Nonetheless, higher-quality players can be had for one-year deals at the veteran's minimum, so the T'wolves' determination to pay Madsen well into his 30s after such a horrible season is inexplicable. But it does go a long way toward explaining why they can't surround Garnett with quality players.

Michael Olowokandi   center   Age: 30   Height: 7-0   Weight: 270
(100% C)   Most similar at age: Andrew Lang

Year		G	M/G	FG%	FT%	P/40	R/40	A/40	TS%		Ast		TO		Usg		Reb		PER	
2002-03	LAC	36	38.0	.427	.657	12.9	9.6	1.4	45.7	61	7.5	49	15.6	54	16.3	23	13.2	47	10.46	59
2003-04	Min	43	21.5	.425	.590	12.0	10.6	1.0	44.6	70	6.2	61	13.9	46	15.5	29	15.0	26	11.14	60
2004-05	Min	62	19.6	.456	.667	12.1	10.7	1.0	48.0	58	4.5	51	14.2	40	14.6	31	15.7	26	10.34	53
2005-06	PRJ (29.1)			.448	.651	11.6	10.7	1.0	47.5		5.6		14.4		14.1		15.4		10.89	

Finally unmasked as a fraud, Olowokandi was eased into a bench role more in line with his talents last season and responded with the usual Kandi Man performance. He did reasonably well on the boards and blocked some shots, but he continued to be a low-percentage scorer who gets entirely too many plays called for him in the post.

Olowokandi at least has value as the team's lone source of quality size, which makes him somewhat useful in a 15-minutes a night role as a backup center. But first Minnesota has to identify somebody capable of being the starting center, and that's a difficult task considering how much cap space players like Olowokandi and Madsen take up.

Latrell Sprewell   small forward   Age: 35 Height: 6-5 Weight: 195
Defensive PER: 0.91 (59% SF, 41% SG)   Most similar at age: Byron Scott

Year		G	M/G	FG%	FT%	P/40	R/40	A/40	TS%		Ast		TO		Usg		Reb		PER	
2002-03	NY	74	38.6	.403	.794	17.0	4.0	4.6	49.7	44	19.2	8	10.0	20	22.6	9	5.9	55	14.29	27
2003-04	Min	82	37.8	.409	.814	17.7	4.0	3.7	49.3	43	15.5	23	8.6	9	22.6	12	5.7	56	14.63	26
2004-05	Min	80	30.6	.414	.830	16.7	4.1	2.9	48.9	51	13.3	23	9.4	21	21.1	16	6.1	63	12.10	42
2005-06	PRJ (34.8)			.394	.787	15.5	4.1	3.5	47.6		15.6		9.4		20.5		5.9		12.41	

Dumb and dumber: Before the season, the T'wolves offered Sprewell a three-year, $21 million extension. Sprewell refused.

Minnesota's offer represented a failure to distinguish between per-minute and per-game averages. Sprewell played nearly 40 minutes a game in 2003–04, so his scoring average was superficially impressive. Based on a 40-minute average, however, it wasn't anything special, and it was accompanied with a low TS%. As a result, any decline due to aging was likely to make him a marginal starter at best.

That's exactly what happened in 2004-05, as Sprewell lost most of the remaining spring in his step and became a jump shooter. The T'wolves kept track of dunks, and Sprewell's season total of two was the most shocking number—he used to get that in a quarter. In the chart, I've included each player's dunks along with his "dunk percentage," which is just dunks divided by field-goal attempts. As the chart shows, Sprewell had the team's lowest rate of dunks other than the point guards. Even Hoiberg more than tripled his rate, and other wings like Szczerbiak and Hassell dunked with far greater frequency. In fact, Ebi doubled Sprewell's dunk output in two games.

T'wolves Dunks, 2004–05

Player	Dunks	Dunk %	Player	Dunks	Dunk %
Kevin Garnett	86	6.3%	Mark Madsen	3	4.5%
Eddie Griffin	25	4.8%	Fred Hoiberg	2	0.7%
Trenton Hassell	23	4.8%	Latrell Sprewell	2	0.2%
Wally Szczerbiak	16	1.7%	Ervin Johnson	1	1.9%
John Thomas	11	13.2%	Sam Cassell	0	0.0%
Michael Olowokandi	8	2.3%	Anthony Carter	0	0.0%
Ndudi Ebi	4	19.0%	Troy Hudson	0	0.0%

(continued next page)

Latrell Sprewell *(continued)*

This is consistent with Sprewell's other numbers. His free throw rate declined sharply, tumbling to one attempt for every five field-goal tries, and the simultaneous dips in Usage Rate and TS% are a sure sign that he can't finish like he used to. Incredibly, 83 percent of Sprewell's shot attempts were jump shots, one of the highest rates in the league.

Defensively, Sprewell looked out of gas. His Defensive PER looks fairly solid, but cross-matches with Hassell account for some of that. He didn't play with nearly the same intensity or speed and played a big part in Minnesota's defensive decline last season.

Obviously, Sprewell should have taken Minnesota's offer last year, but now the market may have corrected too much in the opposite direction. Sprewell was getting few offers in free agency as of publication, but as long as he's on a short-term contract, he could provide some inexpensive help off the bench. Just don't expect many dunks.

Wally Szczerbiak				small forward										Age: 28		Height: 6-7	Weight: 235	
Defensive PER: 0.65 (78% SF, 20% PF, 2% SG)																Most similar at age: Sean Elliott		
Year		G	M/G	FG%	FT%	P/40	R/40	A/40	TS%		Ast		TO		Usg		Reb		PER
2002-03	Min*	52	35.3	.481	.867	19.9	5.3	3.0	56.7	8	13.2	43	8.5	10	20.9	20	7.4	18	17.27	14
2003-04	Min	28	22.2	.449	.828	18.3	5.7	2.1	53.9	16	10.1	48	8.6	10	19.9	22	8.0	39	15.26	21
2004-05	Min	81	31.6	.506	.855	19.6	4.7	3.0	59.5	1	13.9	17	9.6	24	20.5	20	7.0	58	17.11	8
2005-06	*PRJ (39.7)*			*.478*	*.837*	*18.2*	*4.9*	*2.8*	*56.6*		*13.5*		*9.4*		*19.9*		*7.1*		*15.55*

* Season rankings are as shooting guard

Szczerbiak quietly put together a very solid season for the T'wolves, avoiding injury for the first time in three years and finishing among the top 10 small forwards in PER. Szczerbiak nailed over 50 percent from the field and spiked it with an unusually high rate of free throws for a jump shooter, allowing him to lead all small forwards in TS%. Additionally, he showed quite a bit of improvement as a passer, as shown by his rising Assist Ratio.

Szczerbiak could be an even more potent weapon if he would shoot more three-pointers. For his career he shoots 40.4 percent from behind the arc, and he's particularly deadly from the corners. But Szczerbiak has always seemed much more comfortable shooting from 17 feet, and even last season he tried only two three-pointers a game. I suppose it's hard to complain considering his TS% last season, but a lot of that was due to a sharp uptick in free-throw attempts that may have been a one-year fluke. If that's the case, Szczerbiak is unnecessarily starving the best part of his game by not shooting threes.

Szczerbiak needs to put up big scoring numbers because he's a below-average defender. While he's strong and can keep opponents out of the post, he's a step slow and is easily beaten off the dribble. He also struggles to make plays from the help side. That creates a dilemma with the arrival of Rashad McCants, because McCants can't guard anybody either. One would think only one of the two can be on the court against most opponents, with Hassell or Jaric joining them.

Given those considerations, one wonders if now wouldn't be a good time for the T'wolves to trade Szczerbiak. He's coming off a good season and his value will never be higher, plus Minnesota would love to be rid of the cap-killing contract extension McHale gave him two years ago. If they could land a center or a point guard in return, it would be worth contemplating.

John Thomas				center										Age: 30		Height: 6-9	Weight: 265	
(87% C, 13% PF)																Most similar at age: Tony Massenburg		
Year		G	M/G	FG%	FT%	P/40	R/40	A/40	TS%		Ast		TO		Usg		Reb		PER
2004-05	Min	44	11.8	.488	.587	8.5	7.4	1.3	52.2	34	6.2	38	12.7	28	10.1	65	10.9	63	9.03	62
2005-06	*PRJ (35.8)*			*.474*	*.589*	*8.5*	*7.0*	*1.3*	*51.0*		*5.9*		*14.0*		*10.1*		*10.3*		*8.77*

A former first-round pick lifted from the scrap heap when the T'wolves ran short of big men, Thomas gave the T'wolves a physical presence inside. Though only 6′9″, he has huge biceps and could easily push opposing centers away from the basket. That helped in small doses, but Thomas also has severe limitations. Specifically he's a terrible rebounder and the only shot he can make is a dunk. Minnesota might invite him back if they need to fill out the roster, but if he's in the rotation it means something has gone horribly wrong.

| **Rashad McCants** | **shooting guard** | **Age: 21** | **Height: 6-4** | **Weight: 200** |

A top-notch shooter who hit over 40 percent on three-pointers in all three seasons at North Carolina, McCants has a scorer's instinct and seems to create his own shot with ease. Few scouts doubt his offensive talent, but his draft stock was hurt by questions about his defense and attitude. McCants is short for a pro shooting guard and showed little intensity at the defensive end, which could make it hard for the T'wolves to find minutes for him.

| **Bracey Wright** | **point guard** | **Age: 21** | **Height: 6-3** | **Weight: 210** |

In the second round, the T'wolves gambled that Wright could make the shift to point guard from a college shooting guard. Don't bet on it. Wright has too many markers working against him—his low rates of steals, blocks, and rebounds suggest he's not a great athlete, and he's not a great shooter either. Even if he can play the point, he might not be good enough to stick as a pro.

New Orleans Hornets

This is not looking good.

Basketball in New Orleans was a dubious enough proposition when they had a playoff team but in 2004–05, the Hornets were one of the worst teams in the league. Attendance dropped accordingly, raising new doubts about the city's NBA viability.

As for the basketball team, their season was over almost as soon as it began. The Hornets were competitive to start but lost several games by narrow margins to begin the year 0–7. Just as their luck began to turn, the Hornets were hammered by injuries to Baron Davis, Jamaal Magloire, and David West.

Management quickly threw in the towel and the Hornets spent the rest of the season building for the future. The injuries continued unabated all season, but they became irrelevant as the season wore on because by February the Hornets had traded most of their best players.

The first one out the door was backup point guard Darrell Armstrong, in one of the Hornets' best trades. New Orleans dealt him to Dallas for guard Dan Dickau, who was expected to be a salary-evening throwaway. Instead, Dickau started raining in jumpers from all over the court and took over the Hornets' starting point guard job. Unfortunately for New Orleans, Dickau became a free agent after the season and is almost certainly flying the coop.

Next up was long-time shooting guard David Wesley. Although his play had been slipping the past couple of years, the Hornets' moderate success had made the team complacent about replacing him. With the Hornets in last place and Wesley struggling more than ever offensively, they sprung into action. Wesley was sent to Houston for forwards Jim Jackson and Bostjan Nachbar. Jackson never showed up and eventually was offloaded to Phoenix for Maciej Lampe, Jackson Vroman, and Casey Jacobsen. The net result was four potentially helpful young players in return for Wesley.

The Hornets saved their biggest and most controversial deal for last. At the trade deadline, New Orleans sent point guard Baron Davis to the Warriors for Speedy Claxton and the expiring contract of Dale Davis. It was an unusual move

for a rebuilding team considering Baron Davis was only 25 and the Hornets' best player.

Granted, Davis had some strikes against him—he was making the max, he was injury-prone, and he had demanded a trade. But that doesn't make it a good trade. The player New Orleans acquired, Claxton, plays the same position and is just as injury-prone, but not nearly as good. More importantly, the Hornets failed to use the greatest asset generated by the trade: cap space. The deal gave New Orleans over $10 million in cap room, but the Hornets failed to pull the trigger on any major free agents in the offseason.

In fact, New Orleans wasn't reported to have made a single max-contract offer, nor did they show up on the radar for lesser amounts. Their only signing of note was European shooting ace Arvydas Macijauskas, who barely made a dent in their cap space. New Orleans used another small chunk of cap space to secure swingmen Rasual Butler and Kirk Snyder in a five-way trade, but left most of its free-agency bullets in the chamber.

Unfortunately, that suggests the trade was more about owner George Shinn's penny-pinching tendencies than a try at improving the basketball team. The fans in Louisiana are having a hard enough time getting excited about this team without Shinn starving it of talent. Making it twice as bad, they're getting fleeced as taxpayers by Shinn's agreement with the city, which is how the Hornets ended up in such a weak market in the first place.

Regardless of the motivation, the Davis trade removed any shred of doubt about the Hornets' future direction. With Davis gone, the Hornets' transition to the future was etched in stone and Byron Scott did his best to build for that future. First-round draft choice J. R. Smith was pushed into the starting lineup at midseason in his first year out of high school. While Smith seemed over his head on many nights, the accelerated learning undoubtedly helped his development and there's no denying he has some talent.

Smith wasn't the only one to see more burn. In addition to the aforementioned Dickau, players like Nachbar, Jacobsen, Vroman, and Lampe saw the court far more than they

> ## Hornets at a Glance
>
> **Record:** 18–64, 5th place in Southwest Division
> **Offensive Efficiency:** 95.95 (30th)
> **Defensive Efficiency:** 105.08 (23rd)
> **Pace Factor:** 90.02 (28th)
> **Top-Rated Player:** Chris Andersen (PER 18.54, 45th overall)
> **Head Coach:** Byron Scott. Had team playing hard in hopeless situation.

would have in other locales. All are in their early 20s and still developing, so it was noble of Scott to prioritize the team's future needs ahead of the win-loss record on his resume.

Additionally, Scott deserves a lot of credit for how hard his team played the entire season. Scott's best asset as a coach has always been his ability to motivate, and that rang true with this mismatched band. The Hornets were horrifically overmatched in talent on many nights, yet clawed their way to 18 wins mostly by hustling on defense. New Orleans's final rank of 23rd in Defensive Efficiency may not look impressive, but look at the lineup. New Orleans played most of the year with a leadfooted hobbit and a teenage rookie in the backcourt, two out-of-shape gunners at forward, and about three CBA guys in the rotation. Based on that lineup, 23rd seems pretty darn good. One could argue that despite winning only 18 games, Scott did one of his best coaching jobs in 2004–05.

Of course, Scott did have his shortcomings. For example, although he loves his Princeton offense, using a lot of the backdoor cuts on a team with no good passers seemed like a wasted effort. Overall New Orleans ranked dead last in the NBA in Offensive Efficiency, mainly because they couldn't get anything going to the basket. The Hornets were last in the NBA in free-throw attempts and the cause was clear: Nearly every possession terminated in a long jump shot, making it tough for the Hornets to draw fouls. The other effect of jumperitis was the low field-goal percentage. New Orleans's 41.5 percent mark was easily the league's worst, as was its 49.3 TS%.

Also, despite the addition of Dickau, the Hornets were an exceptionally bad three-point shooting team. The Hornets converted only 31.5 percent from downtown, ranking 29th in the NBA. It might surprise some to learn that the Hornets took more threes than average, with 20.1 percent of their shots being three-pointers compared to the league average of 19.6. The key culprit here was J. R. Smith, who took over a quarter of the team's three-point attempts on the season but made only 28.8 percent of his tries. The other leading practitioner of the ill-advised three was Davis. Now that Davis is no longer in the picture and Smith has a year of experience under his belt, the percentage should improve this year. That's particularly true given the addition of Macijauskas, a ridiculously accurate long-range shooter who should single-handedly remove that one weakness.

Other causes for optimism dot the roster. First-round draft choice Chris Paul should prove a worthy successor to Davis at the point, especially since Paul has superior shot selection. His addition moves Claxton to a reserve role, where he may be the best backup point guard in the league. Moreover, New Orleans's frontcourt is unusually talented for such a bad team. Discount free-agent signing Chris Andersen was a revelation and the team was able to re-sign him in the offseason for relatively modest dollars. He may be the starting center by opening day, because Magloire's request for a trade may be accommodated by the trade deadline. That won't be such an awful thing if it brings in a quality small forward, but Magloire is young and has a friendly contract, so New Orleans shouldn't be in any hurry.

The Hornets also are strong at power forward. Veteran P. J. Brown seems like an obvious trade candidate, but the Hornets like his locker-room presence and Louisiana roots enough that they haven't been shopping him. West has been completely forgotten about, but he had a strong rookie season two years ago and looks to be one of the game's best rebounding forwards.

Despite those positives, the Hornets have a long way to go before reaching respectability in the West. They still have gaping defensive holes at the wing positions and lack a go-to scorer, while they get a much greater home-court advantage from Bourbon Street than from the smattering of fans inside New Orleans Arena.

Look longer-term, however, and the picture gets a little brighter—at least, if you have faith that Shinn will eventually spend some money. The Hornets might have the best cap situation of any team in basketball. After this season, they'll lop $10 million off their payroll when the contracts of George Lynch, Claxton, and Casey Jacobsen expire. After 2006–07, the Hornets subtract another $10 million when the deals of Jamaal Magloire (if he stays) and P. J. Brown terminate. In any of the next three summers, this team should be able to bid for a max-level free agent if they're willing to commit the money.

For now, they'll be battling to avoid the worst record in the West. Scott again will have his troops playing hard, and young talents like Paul and Smith will provide occasional excitement. But even in the best-case scenario, the Hornets are at least a year away from serious playoff contention.

Chris Andersen   **center**   **Age: 27**   **Height: 6-10** **Weight: 220**
(100% C)   Most similar at age: Dale Davis

Year		G	M/G	FG%	FT%	P/40	R/40	A/40	TS%		Ast		TO		Usg		Reb		PER	
2002-03	Den	59	15.4	.400	.550	13.5	12.1	1.4	44.0	67	7.3	52	13.7	39	17.6	18	17.6	8	14.02	34
2003-04	Den*	72	14.3	.443	.589	9.4	11.6	1.4	48.6	48	10.5	41	14.4	61	11.3	63	16.0	15	14.48	40
2004-05	NO	67	21.3	.534	.689	14.3	11.5	2.0	58.1	14	9.5	15	11.1	11	15.5	28	17.2	16	18.54	7
2005-06	PRJ (50.4)			.481	.646	12.5	11.1	1.9	52.5		10.3		12.6		14.7		16.1		16.01	

* Season rankings are as power forward

Look past Andersen's annual embarrassments in the dunk contest and you'll see one of the game's most productive front-court players. Andersen is one of the best-leaping big men in the game, making him a force around the basket. He's at his best when fed for alleyoops in transition, where he can soar over opponents for dunks. His hops also give him an advantage slamming home offensive boards. Andersen's hops carry him on the defensive end as well, as he is one of the game's better rebounders and blocked a shot every 14 minutes.

Andersen rounded out his game by improving his other offensive skills. He stopped trying to handle the ball on the break, which had been a turnover waiting to happen when he was a Nugget. He developed a more reliable jumper from 12-to-15 feet, providing a reliable alternative to the dunk. And he added 100 points at the foul line, which is important because he averaged better than a free throw for every two field-goal attempts.

Andersen's biggest weakness is a lack of muscle. This was especially notable last year with him playing center, as he gives up 40 pounds to his opponent virtually every night. That makes him a liability in post defense and renders him less effective on the glass. Because of the lack of brawn, he can't establish effective post position offensively. Of course, if he returns to his natural power forward spot, the strength issue should be less of a factor.

In any case, Andersen was easily the Hornets' best player. Considering how well he played and how bad the rest of the Hornets were, it's puzzling that he played only 21 minutes a game. For much of the year, Scott started Rodney Rogers at power forward instead of Andersen, even though Rogers looked like he just got back from the Bellagio lunch buffet while Andersen was putting up monstrous numbers (for a Hornet) off the bench. It's an all-too-common example of a coach riding a familiar player (Rogers played for Scott in New Jersey) even when said player was obviously in need of replacement.

Andersen had played well in Denver too, but he has been virtually ignored on the free agent market. Andersen signed for the relative pittance of $1.5 million last season, and didn't command top dollars on the free agent market even after his big year. His is the latest example of teams looking at per-game averages instead of per-minute performance, and missing out on a talented player as a result.

P. J. Brown   **power forward**   **Age: 36**   **Height: 6-11** **Weight: 239**
Defensive PER: 0.16 (61% PF, 39% C)   Most similar at age: Horace Grant

Year		G	M/G	FG%	FT%	P/40	R/40	A/40	TS%		Ast		TO		Usg		Reb		PER	
2002-03	NO	78	33.4	.531	.836	12.8	10.7	2.3	59.2	1	15.5	13	10.3	21	13.7	47	15.6	15	17.68	15
2003-04	NO	80	34.4	.476	.854	12.1	10.0	2.3	52.7	26	14.8	21	9.6	8	14.9	47	14.8	23	16.33	22
2004-05	NO	82	34.4	.446	.864	12.6	10.5	2.5	51.2	43	12.0	16	8.8	16	15.8	45	15.7	17	15.54	31
2005-06	PRJ (32.7)			.453	.834	11.6	9.6	2.2	51.3		12.3		10.6		14.1		13.9		14.82	

The one exception to the Hornets' youth movement, the club feels Brown sets a good enough example for the young players that it's worth it to keep him around. Certainly few players would have bothered playing hurt for such an awful team, as Brown did last season. He played fairly well too, as his scoring and rebound rates were on par with his previous two seasons.

Defensively, Brown's skills have diminished more noticeably. He's still a tough, long-armed defender who can make life miserable for power forwards in the post, but Brown was overmatched when he attempted to play center. Unfortunately, Magloire's injury forced Brown into that role often, and his Defensive PER suffered as a result. Five years ago he probably could have handled the switch much better, but he's no longer an All-Defense caliber player.

However, at 36 he remains a quality power forward, as age is taking a remarkably light toll on his game from year to year. It's doubtful Brown will be a contributing player when the Hornets are ready to challenge for the playoffs again, but the possibility can't be completely ruled out.

Speedy Claxton — point guard
(100% PG)

Age: 27 Height: 5-11 Weight: 170
Most similar at age: Elliott Perry

Year		G	M/G	FG%	FT%	P/40	R/40	A/40	TS%		Ast		TO		Usg		Reb		PER	
2002-03	SA	23	14.1	.462	.684	14.7	4.8	6.4	50.9		26.8		12.5		22.0		6.9		15.84	
2003-04	GS	60	26.6	.427	.813	15.9	3.9	6.7	50.9	28	26.9	38	10.3	23	23.3	20	5.5	30	17.24	14
2004-05	GS-NO	62	30.1	.421	.736	15.3	3.9	8.0	49.3	50	30.8	23	9.8	20	24.1	15	5.9	27	15.85	23
2005-06	PRJ (28.6)			.428	.763	15.7	3.9	7.1	50.6		28.0		10.3		23.5		5.8		16.20	

Claxton is slated to be Chris Paul's understudy, and if that situation holds he'll be the best backup point guard in basketball. Claxton held down the starting job in Golden State for the better part of two seasons and generally did a good job of it. He is remarkably quick and gets into the lane with ease. He used to only look for his shot on the drive, but he's improved greatly as a passer the past two seasons and now is a respectable disher. He's also adept at drawing fouls on his drives, as his rate of 0.42 free throws per field-goal attempt is one of the best among point guards.

Claxton has one major offensive weakness—he can't shoot. He made only 18 percent from three-point range last season, and has been worse other years. Claxton is more reliable from 18 feet or so but tends to be the opponent's first choice when it has to leave somebody open. Moreover, the lack of three-pointers detracts from his TS%, which was well below average last season. Nonetheless, Claxton managed to create shots for himself and teammates while keeping the turnovers down.

Additionally, he's an excellent pressure defender and his height has proved less of a defensive liability than one might imagine. The biggest problem his size gives him is with durability. Claxton has missed 101 games the past three seasons and has never made it through a full season healthy. But for the 60 games or so that he's out there, Claxton will be a very solid floor general.

Dan Dickau — point guard
(99% PG, 1% SG)

Age: 27 Height: 6-0 Weight: 190
Most similar at age: Darrick Martin

Year		G	M/G	FG%	FT%	P/40	R/40	A/40	TS%		Ast		TO		Usg		Reb		PER	
2002-03	Atl	50	10.3	.412	.808	14.2	3.3	6.6	50.4	35	26.6	32	16.6	63	22.1	29	4.8	49	9.92	55
2003-04	Por	43	6.8	.378	.786	12.9	3.5	5.2	45.6		22.6		15.5		20.9		5.0		9.02	
2004-05	Dal-NO	71	29.4	.405	.833	17.0	3.4	6.6	51.8	34	25.7	43	10.8	33	24.8	17	5.2	43	14.85	31
2005-06	PRJ (48.6)			.407	.843	16.2	3.2	6.3	52.4		26.0		11.6		23.5		4.8		14.30	

Mr. Frodo was thrown into the Darrell Armstrong trade as an afterthought, but Dickau took his career off life support with a strong effort as a Hornet. He particularly shined from outside, showcasing the sweet jumper that made him a big star in college but had gone AWOL in the pros. Dickau finished at only 35 percent on three-pointers, but that's because he was forced to take so many at the end of the shot clock when the other Hornets couldn't create shots. When left open, his jumper was cash.

Dickau also fared well at running the point, using screens and the threat of his jumper to penetrate and create shots. He slashed his Turnover Ratio as well, perhaps because he was getting the first extended minutes of his career. However, he remains vulnerable to full-court pressure because he doesn't have the jets to blow by defenders and has trouble seeing over traps.

Despite his breakout season, Dickau has some major shortcomings. He's slow, small, and weak, the holy trinity of bad defense. That makes him an enormous defensive liability, particularly against big guards who like to post up. Additionally, it's virtually impossible to pressure the ball with him in the game because he's rarely in the same latitude as the dribbler.

Nonetheless, he should reap rich rewards from his performance in New Orleans. Dickau was still unsigned as of publication, but his ability to nail outside shots and run the point seemed likely to land him a permanent gig as a backup point guard.

Matt Freije — power forward
(87% PF, 13% SF)

Age: 24 Height: 6-10 Weight: 240
Most similar at age: N/A

Year		G	M/G	FG%	FT%	P/40	R/40	A/40	TS%	Ast	TO	Usg	Reb	PER
2004-05	NO	23	19.2	.291	.625	8.4	5.5	1.8	35.6	8.6	10.1	14.7	8.3	4.02

A second-round draft pick by the Heat in 2004, Freije was waived by Miami and picked up by New Orleans. He saw extensive action early in the season when the Hornets suffered numerous injuries in the frontcourt and even started 11 games.

(continued next page)

Matt Freije *(continued)*

Perhaps that wasn't the best thing for his career. Freije proved beyond any reasonable doubt that he didn't belong in the NBA, shooting 29.1 percent, rebounding like a guard, and offering limited resistance at the defensive end. That included a 26 percent mark in his alleged specialty, three-point shooting, and he offered little else. To say he can't get into the paint is an understatement: He played 23 games and took eight foul shots. Overall, it's hard to see Freije getting back into the pros without some major remedial work in the D-League.

Alex Garcia — shooting guard — Age: 25 Height: 6-3 Weight: 195
(99% SG, 1% SF) — Most similar at age: N/A

Year		G	M/G	FG%	FT%	P/40	R/40	A/40	TS%	Ast	TO	Usg	Reb	PER
2003-04	SA	2	6.5	.143	.500	9.2	0.0	0.0	19.0	0.0	11.3	25.6	0.0	-4.86
2004-05	NO	8	18.3	.346	.750	12.1	4.1	4.9	40.9	22.6	10.0	21.1	6.2	8.34

If it weren't for bad luck, this guy would have no luck at all. For the second year in a row Garcia earned a job out of training camp and then suffered a season-ending injury just a few games into the season. This time it was a torn ACL that did him in. With Claxton and Paul on the roster, his future is with another team. Wherever he ends up one hopes he can stay healthy long enough to establish a niche in the league.

Junior Harrington — point guard — Age: 25 Height: 6-4 Weight: 190
(53% PG, 43% SG, 4% SF) — Most similar at age: Walter Bond

Year		G	M/G	FG%	FT%	P/40	R/40	A/40	TS%		Ast		TO		Usg		Reb		PER	
2002-03	Den	81	24.3	.364	.652	8.5	5.0	5.6	40.7	62	29.3	17	16.4	61	17.1	54	7.3	8	6.55	63
2003-04			Did not play																	
2004-05	NO	29	19.0	.360	.829	11.9	4.6	4.5	42.1	66	20.9	9	13.8	63	20.3	26	6.9	31	7.63	66
2005-06	*PRJ (30.1)*			*.352*	*.701*	*9.8*	*4.6*	*4.8*	*41.0*		*24.3*		*14.5*		*17.5*		*6.7*		*7.23*	

Harrington was an abysmally bad offensive player in Denver in 2002–03, but New Orleans brought him back to the NBA last season anyway. Here's a shocker: He was terrible. Harrington has retained his special gift for line-driving 17-foot jumpers into the front of the rim, and unfortunately for the Hornets he was a much more aggressive shot-taker than he'd been in Denver.

Defensively, Harrington is a decent player. He's big for a point guard and moves his feet well, and those skills would be enough to get him work if he had even meager offensive skills. He doesn't though, and that's why the Hornets cut their losses and returned Harrington to oblivion at midseason.

Casey Jacobsen — shooting guard — Age: 23 Height: 6-6 Weight: 215
(62% SG, 36% SF, 1% PG, 1% PF) — Most similar at age: Keith Bogans

Year		G	M/G	FG%	FT%	P/40	R/40	A/40	TS%		Ast		TO		Usg		Reb		PER	
2002-03	Phx	72	15.9	.373	.686	12.9	2.9	2.6	49.3	41	14.6	35	11.0	35	16.1	43	4.1	55	9.22	51
2003-04	Phx	78	23.4	.417	.820	10.2	4.4	2.1	57.0	3	17.0	28	11.8	48	11.3	61	6.5	35	9.65	53
2004-05	Phx-NO	84	21.4	.404	.786	12.2	3.7	2.5	55.5	15	12.0	51	10.5	35	14.0	58	5.6	53	10.22	48
2005-06	*PRJ (32.0)*			*.392*	*.802*	*11.4*	*4.0*	*2.4*	*53.9*		*13.9*		*11.6*		*13.6*		*5.9*		*9.67*	

Acquired from Phoenix in the Jim Jackson trade, Jacobsen had the statistical oddity of appearing in 84 games in 2004–05 due to the schedule disparity between the Suns and Hornets. Jacobsen was one of the Hornets' true three-point threats, hitting 37 percent from downtown, but created shots so rarely that his offensive contribution was still meager.

While most reluctant shooters who specialize in three-pointers rarely get to the foul line, Jacobsen was an anomaly because he was there constantly. He averaged nearly a free throw for every two field-goal attempts, even though nearly half his shots were three-pointers. Jacobsen is a decent athlete and was able to get himself to the line by running the floor and utilizing left-handed drives to the basket.

Considering his high TS% the past two seasons, the mystery is why Jacobsen hasn't become more aggressive offensively. He can produce points at a high rate when he shoots, and he's athletic enough that there doesn't seem to be a major limitation on his shooting more often. But until he actually does, he's not going to have much value. Even as a backup shooting guard, he's a borderline performer. Heading into his free-agent year, it would be a good time for him to start gunning more often.

Maciej Lampe		center							**Age: 20**	**Height: 6-11**	**Weight: 275**	
(94% C, 6% PF)											Most similar at age: N/A	
Year	G	M/G	FG%	FT%	P/40	R/40	A/40	TS%	Ast	TO	Usg	Reb	PER
2003-04 NY-Phx	21	10.7	.489	.769	17.1	7.9	1.6	51.2	7.6	12.7	18.7	11.6	12.15
2004-05 Phx-NO	37	10.3	.371	.682	12.1	9.4	1.2	40.6	5.5	10.0	16.8	13.4	7.07

A plodding jump shooter who was traded twice before his 20th birthday, Lampe regressed significantly after showing promise as a rookie. The Hornets gave him plenty of chances after the trade, but Lampe's reluctance to do anything but shoot 17-foot jumpers from the top of the key is likely to hold him back. The lack of zip in his step also makes it tough for him to find acceptable defensive match-ups, although his size would be an asset were he to show an inclination to be physical. With West and Magloire returning from injury, Lampe is likely to see fewer chances this season.

George Lynch			small forward							**Age: 35**	**Height: 6-8**	**Weight: 235**		
(69% SF, 30% PF, 1% C)												Most similar at age: Rick Fox		
Year	G	M/G	FG%	FT%	P/40	R/40	A/40	TS%		Ast		TO		Usg		Reb		PER	
2002-03 NO*	81	18.5	.409	.554	9.7	9.4	2.8	46.4	55	19.0	7	9.5	12	13.9	46	13.7	29	12.87	37
2003-04 NO	78	21.8	.397	.667	8.8	7.3	2.7	47.2	50	20.2	3	11.1	31	13.2	54	10.8	11	10.12	48
2004-05 NO	44	21.2	.360	.739	7.0	7.5	3.8	41.2	63	18.0	2	16.6	64	13.6	57	11.2	7	7.83	62
2005-06 PRJ (29.2)			*.368*	*.628*	*8.6*	*7.6*	*3.0*	*43.2*		*17.2*		*13.0*		*13.9*		*10.9*		*9.81*	

* Season rankings are as power forward

The one-time defensive stalwart has been in rapid decline the past two seasons, and a foot injury last year didn't help matters. Lynch is a poor shooter but can't stop himself from winging three-pointers. As his athleticism has declined, he's grown more dependent on this "skill" for his offense. As a result, his TS% was an atrocious 41.2 percent. Additionally, he became immensely turnover-prone in 2004–05 for no apparent reason, offsetting his skill as a passer.

Defensively, Lynch is more advanced, but as with his offense he has lost considerable ground in recent seasons. The one thing he does reliably well is rebound, thanks to a muscular build and a healthy dose of toughness. The Hornets' acquisitions of Rasual Butler and Kirk Snyder make it unlikely that Lynch will keep his spot in the rotation. Considering he's also on the last year of his contract, this might be his final stop.

Jamaal Magloire			center							**Age: 27**	**Height: 6-11**	**Weight: 259**		
(100% C)												Most similar at age: Rony Seikaly		
Year	G	M/G	FG%	FT%	P/40	R/40	A/40	TS%		Ast		TO		Usg		Reb		PER	
2002-03 NO	82	29.8	.480	.717	13.8	11.9	1.4	54.1	21	8.6	40	15.4	53	15.2	35	17.2	10	15.41	21
2003-04 NO	82	33.9	.473	.751	16.1	12.2	1.2	55.1	12	6.6	58	15.4	62	17.6	15	18.0	4	17.11	10
2004-05 NO	23	30.6	.432	.602	15.4	11.7	1.7	48.0	57	7.9	23	16.0	55	19.4	8	17.5	13	12.80	38
2005-06 PRJ (47.2)			*.459*	*.689*	*14.6*	*11.3*	*1.3*	*51.9*		*7.3*		*15.1*		*17.2*		*16.4*		*14.74*	

As I mentioned in the Similarity Scores section, Magloire's 99.9 Similarity Score with Rony Seikaly at the same age was the best match of any player this season. However, Magloire's 2004–05 wasn't a good match for his own career, as his numbers declined sharply. Magloire had an abbreviated campaign thanks to an early-season broken finger, and by the time he returned the Hornets had long since been eliminated.

Magloire isn't as athletic as some other centers, but he has very long arms that make him extremely effective shooting hook shots from the low post. Unfortunately that shot failed to find the range last season, resulting in his field-goal percentage dip to 43.2 percent. Considering it was only a 23-game season for Magloire, I'd expect it to recover.

The bigger worry is where he'll be playing next year. Magloire has asked for a trade and the Hornets seem willing to accommodate him, but this looks to be a mistake considering he's signed for two more seasons at reasonable dollars. Wherever he ends up, Magloire provides an above-average starter at both ends of the floor, and he's entering the prime years for a big man.

Bostjan Nachbar small forward **Age: 25 Height: 6-9 Weight: 221**
(57% SF, 42% PF, 1% C) Most similar at age: Pat Garrity

Year		G	M/G	FG%	FT%	P/40	R/40	A/40	TS%		Ast		TO		Usg		Reb		PER	
2002-03	Hou	14	5.5	.355	.500	15.1	5.7	1.6	41.0		6.8		13.5		21.5		8.2		5.72	
2003-04	Hou	45	11.5	.356	.724	10.7	5.4	2.3	47.7	48	15.2	25	11.6	38	14.5	50	7.8	42	8.25	56
2004-05	Hou-NO	71	18.9	.393	.829	14.7	5.4	2.2	53.5	27	10.5	43	12.0	45	17.3	37	8.2	40	10.09	53
2005-06	PRJ (36.8)			.377	.812	13.2	5.5	2.2	51.2		11.5		11.9		16.0		8.1		9.58	

After two-and-a-half seasons spent at the end of Houston's bench, Nachbar got a reprieve with his trade to New Orleans. He didn't exactly make the Rockets rue the day they traded him, but Nachbar showed enough to at least get a new contract from the Hornets. His main stock in trade is as an outside shooter—nearly half his attempts were three-pointers and he hit 38 percent. Plus, he got out in transition enough to earn a fair number of free throws, although the Hornets would probably like to see him stop trying to go coast-to-coast with his defensive rebounds.

Defensively, Nachbar has good size for the position and decent feet on the perimeter, but he loses out in strength match-ups and doesn't have the quickness or leaping ability to make an impact from the help side. Overall he showed enough promise as a shooter to make up for his many deficiencies, and that's why he'll have the first crack at the backup small forward job this year.

Lee Nailon small forward **Age: 30 Height: 6-9 Weight: 238**
Defensive PER: 0.05 (77% SF, 20% PF, 3% SG) Most similar at age: Wayman Tisdale

Year		G	M/G	FG%	FT%	P/40	R/40	A/40	TS%		Ast		TO		Usg		Reb		PER	
2002-03	NY	38	10.7	.442	.824	20.7	6.9	2.6	49.4		9.6		11.8		24.6		10.1		14.28	
2003-04	Orl-Atl-Cle*	57	13.7	.450	.810	17.5	7.3	1.9	48.4	50	8.7	54	10.3	17	20.6	18	10.4	56	13.15	48
2004-05	NO	68	29.7	.478	.806	19.1	5.9	2.2	51.1	41	9.4	55	9.5	22	22.3	12	8.9	31	14.48	27
2005-06	PRJ (36.4)			.466	.778	17.1	6.4	2.0	50.1		9.2		10.2		20.5		9.5		13.10	

* Season rankings are as power forward

Same team, different city. The Hornets called in Nailon for another tour of duty after Matt Freije was found wanting, and Nailon delivered his now-familiar combination of instant offense and phantom defense. Nailon has a soft jumper from inside 15 feet and is great at using the glass, especially in pull-ups on transition. The result is that he's always been able to get his points, averaging over 19 per 40 minutes last season. He won't pass the ball much, but Nailon had a lot of value on an offense-starved team like the Hornets.

Defense is another matter. Nailon is too slow to play small forward and too weak to play power forward, and his lack of athleticism is a liability at either position. His Defensive PER was among the worst at his position, and on a subjective level the New Orleans forward combo of Nailon and Rogers had to be the worst defensive pairing in several years.

Nonetheless, those scoring numbers are nothing to sneeze at, and Nailon is certain to get a contract again for this season. His defensive inattention and shot-happy approach don't win him many fans among coaches, but rest assured that some team will be desperate enough for offense to give Nailon a call.

J. R. Smith shooting guard **Age: 20 Height: 6-6 Weight: 220**
Defensive PER: -0.77 (81% SG, 17% PG, 2% SF) Most similar at age: Ricky Davis

Year		G	M/G	FG%	FT%	P/40	R/40	A/40	TS%		Ast		TO		Usg		Reb		PER	
2004-05	NO	76	24.5	.394	.689	16.8	3.3	3.1	47.8	54	13.3	41	10.2	32	22.2	16	4.9	61	10.84	45
2005-06	PRJ (3.6)			.441	.715	18.8	3.4	3.2	51.6		13.9		10.0		22.8		5.4		12.87	

Smith's averages look impressive for a rookie coming to the NBA straight from high school, but on a per-minute basis his performance left a lot to be desired. Smith forced a slew of long jumpers, resulting in a 39.4 percent mark from the field. As noted in the team comment, his love affair with the three-pointer almost single-handedly killed New Orleans's percentage from beyond the arc. Smith needs to work on his ballhandling and develop an in-between game, which would help him take advantage of his athleticism and get to the line more often. That's not his only area for improvement. He was among the worst defenders in basketball and contributed nothing on the glass, both of which are surprising considering he has good size and can jump.

Smith was graded on a curve because of his youth, and certainly there's plenty to like. He reminds me a lot of a young Jason Richardson—he has a great vertical and can hit outside shots, but he has a long way to go to become a real basketball player. If he develops as well as Richardson has, the Hornets will have few complaints.

Jackson Vroman — center
(64% C, 35% PF, 1% SF)

Age: 24 Height: 6-10 Weight: 220
Most similar at age: Rony Seikaly

Year		G	M/G	FG%	FT%	P/40	R/40	A/40	TS%		Ast		TO		Usg		Reb		PER	
2004-05	Phx-NO	46	15.3	.412	.640	12.0	9.9	2.3	45.7	68	10.8	12	19.0	66	17.1	17	14.9	31	9.46	60
2005-06	PRJ (27.4)			.425	.670	12.6	9.6	2.5	47.2		11.9		17.9		17.0		14.5		10.99	

A throw-in to the Jim Jackson trade, Vroman was a second-round pick by Phoenix in 2004 but saw a fair amount of playing time after the trade. He's an undersized big man who tries to make up for his size with boundless energy, but he needs to bridle his enthusiasm for shooting. Vroman took far too many shots for a player with such limited offensive skills, resulting in a horrific TS% and one of the league's highest Turnover Ratios.

Should Vroman rein in his happy trigger finger, he has some potential as a power forward. He's athletic enough to get his share of points on the glass and runs the floor very well. Plus, his size isn't as much of an issue when he's not playing center. However, last year might have been his best shot at NBA minutes, because the Hornets' frontcourt will be much stronger this season.

David West — power forward
(59% PF, 39% SF, 2% SG)

Age: 25 Height: 6-9 Weight: 240
Most similar at age: Nazr Mohammed

Year		G	M/G	FG%	FT%	P/40	R/40	A/40	TS%		Ast		TO		Usg		Reb		PER	
2003-04	NO	71	13.1	.474	.713	11.7	12.8	2.6	51.9	31	16.2	17	12.9	51	15.3	45	18.8	3	16.51	21
2004-05	NO	30	18.4	.436	.680	13.5	9.3	1.7	47.9	59	7.9	44	14.6	60	17.2	35	14.1	26	11.10	59
2005-06	PRJ (69.8)			.457	.690	12.4	10.6	2.2	50.1		12.7		13.7		16.3		15.8		13.87	

Coming off a strong rookie season, West missed more than half of 2004–05 with a bone bruise on his knee and looked out of sorts when he returned. West seemed determined to take the most unreasonable shot possible, periodically drifting out to the perimeter to take a jumper off the dribble. That was out of character for him, and perhaps he won't press as much if he's in the lineup from the start.

West has very long arms for his height and was one of the league's best rebounders as a rookie, but he failed to deliver in that area last season. That mirrored an across-the-board decline in West's numbers, as his shooting percentage dipped and he made more turnovers. Because he was hanging around on the perimeter so much, West's offensive rebounding numbers dropped especially hard. That's a shame because it was the best part of his game as a rookie.

Based on the promise of his rookie season, West still should figure prominently in the Hornets' plans for this season. His ability to crash the boards and get easy put-backs should be especially valuable if the Hornets fire up as many bricks as they did a year ago.

Chris Paul — point guard
Age: 20 Height: 6-1 Weight: 195

The Hornets didn't really need a point guard, but Paul was too good to pass up with the fourth overall pick. All of his statistical markers say he'll be a stud in the pros: He picked nearly three steals a game, shot 47 percent on threes and 83 percent from the line, and had no problem getting to the basket or setting up teammates as a collegian. He should be a starter from day one, and chances are he'll be among the top contenders for the Rookie of the Year award. Just make sure to wear a cup if you're playing against him—his groin punch against N.C. State's Julius Hodge was one of the year's uglier moments.

Brandon Bass — power forward
Age: 20 Height: 6-7 Weight: 252

Bass was the SEC player of the year, so certainly there's some talent here, but he dropped to the second round because his size made teams wary. Bass is a decent athlete and can hit the open jumper, but he can't handle the ball well enough to play the perimeter and he's going to be giving up two inches every night at power forward. At least the LSU grad is staying close to home.

Phoenix Suns

Whoosh.

Phoenix's opponents never knew what hit them last season. Within seconds, the Suns were breezing downcourt and either popping a three-pointer or throwing down a slam dunk, often scoring in five seconds or less after an opponent's made basket.

Phoenix's blistering attack was the key to a shockingly successful season that saw the Suns post the NBA's best record before succumbing to San Antonio in the Western Conference finals. The Suns' 62 wins were the most in the NBA since the Lakers won 67 in 1999–2000, and their 33-game turnaround was the third-best in NBA history.

How did they go from lottery fodder to championship contender so quickly? That depends on whom you ask. Nearly everybody else settled on one answer last season: Steve Nash. The mop-topped Canadian point guard signed with the Suns as a free agent and was the eye of the Phoenix storm, constantly throwing the ball ahead to the Suns' hyper-athletic big men and driving the lane to kick the ball out for three-pointers. Nash's 11.5 assists per game were the most in the NBA in a decade.

Thanks to his exploits, Nash won the MVP award. But one could have made equally strong cases for Shawn Marion or Amare Stoudemire. Phoenix's high-flying big men converted Nash's passes into thunderous dunks. Their ability to routinely beat opposing frontcourt players down the court created most of the advantage situations that the Suns converted into lay-ups and three-pointers.

The threes came from the other two members of the Suns' starting five, Quentin Richardson and Joe Johnson. Richardson nearly led the NBA in three-pointers, while Johnson's 47.8 percentage was second only to Minnesota's Fred Hoiberg. Overall, the Suns shattered the NBA record for three-pointers in a season by averaging 9.7 per game, and they led the NBA in accuracy at 39.3 percent.

By now, you're probably thinking that this was an incredibly potent offense. You'd be correct. The Suns were one of the best offensive teams in history. We can't be sure where they rank because the NBA has only kept track of

> ## Suns at a Glance
>
> **Record:** 62–20, 1st place in Pacific Division
> **Offensive Efficiency:** 111.9 (1st)
> **Defensive Efficiency:** 103.8 (16th)
> **Pace Factor:** 98.3 (1st)
> **Top-Rated Player:** Amare Stoudemire (PER 26.69, 4th overall)
> **Head Coach:** Mike D'Antoni. Did what few coaches would dare: Let 'em run.

turnovers since 1973–74, but in the 32 seasons since then, the 2004–05 Suns are the second-best offense of all-time. We can tell by comparing their Offensive Efficiency to the league average, and seeing how other teams ranked against the league mark.

The Suns' Offensive Efficiency of 111.90 was nearly nine points higher than the league average of 103.09, while only one other team in history had even eclipsed eight. Table 1 shows the all-time leaders, and fans will quickly note that the top two teams on the chart had the same point guard. Nash had plenty of help in both stops and wasn't the primary weapon on either team, but the chart serves as confirmation of his incredible talent for creating high-percentage shots.

Offensively, the Suns excelled at everything except offensive rebounding. They turned the ball over on only 13.6 percent of their possessions, compared to the league mark of 14.8. They shot 47.7 percent from the floor, good for second in the league, and because of all the three-pointers, they led the league in TS% by a wide margin as table 2 shows. The Suns were at 57.0 percent compared to the league average of 52.1 percent, which meant every 20 Suns shots earned them an extra point on the competition.

The most amazing thing about the Suns' offense wasn't the individual brilliance of Nash or Stoudemire, but how all the pieces fit into the larger whole. The Suns were impossible to guard with the starting five on the floor because they had everything. Nash could break down defenses, start the break, and couldn't be left open to shoot. Johnson and Richardson were deadly three-point shooters who would make defenders pay for helping in the paint. Marion and Stoudemire were gazelles on the break who set up easy opportunities for the others. Marion also could shoot, meaning everybody on the perimeter had to be respected and leaving Stoudemire plenty of space to dominate in the post.

Fortunately for the Suns, that starting five stayed in one piece the entire season. The Sun's fantastic five missed only 13 games, allowing a team with virtually no bench to glide

Table 1. Greatest Offenses since 1973–74

Team	Year	Offensive Efficiency	League Average	Difference
Dallas Mavericks	2003–04	110.07	100.84	+9.23
Phoenix Suns	2004–05	111.90	103.09	+8.81
Denver Nuggets	1981–82	111.67	104.20	+7.47
Boston Celtics	1987–88	112.35	104.97	+7.38
Chicago Bulls	1991–92	112.34	105.01	+7.33

Table 2. Team TS% Leaders, 2004–05

Team	TS%
Phoenix	57.1
Miami	55.9
Boston	55.1
Seattle	54.6
Dallas	54.5
League Average	**52.9**

through the season unscathed. However, Phoenix's lack of depth came back to bite it in the playoffs when Joe Johnson's face-first landing in Dallas broke his orbital bone, limiting his contribution in the San Antonio series. Only two Suns bench players had a PER higher than 12, and several were much lower. Phoenix tried to fill in the cracks with veteran Jim Jackson, but he was overmatched as a starter and slowed the team down. The Suns also mistakenly traded Zarko Cabarkapa at midseason and then turned around and acquired Walter McCarty, who was brutal. Only backup center Steven Hunter provided a reliable contribution.

Phoenix papered over this weakness with a playing style that discouraged fouling. The Suns committed the fewest fouls in the league, which is doubly amazing when one considers they also played the league's fastest pace. Phoenix's defensive strategy was to avoid fouling at all costs, because that could produce foul trouble and force the Suns to rely on their shaky bench. As an added plus, the lack of whistles kept the game moving at the Suns' frenetic pace, quickly wearing out opponents. Looking at opponent free-throw attempts per field-goal attempt highlights the difference. As table 3 shows, Phoenix was well ahead of its peers.

Phoenix had led the league in this category in 2003–04 as well but widened its lead significantly last season. More importantly, the Suns managed to play competent defense even though they weren't fouling. Marion and Johnson both played very good on-ball defense, while Richardson took numerous charges and Hunter provided shot-blocking off the bench. The result was that the Suns finished 16th in Defensive Efficiency, a respectable showing for a team that was so undersized.

Table 3. Fewest Opponent Free-Throw Attempts per Field-Goal Attempt, 2004–05

Team	Opp. FTA/FGA
Phoenix Suns	.237
Portland Trail Blazers	.271
Detroit Pistons	.276
Minnesota Timberwolves	.277
Los Angeles Lakers	.279
League Average	**.324**

Seeing the Suns' runaway success in 2004–05 makes it seem like their success was preordained, but nothing could be more untrue. The Suns lineup looked completely mismatched when the season started, and Phoenix's use of a small starting five was thought of more as an "interesting experiment" than a trampoline to 60 wins.

Most coaches wouldn't have gone through with the experiment at all. This is why Phoenix's Mike D'Antoni so richly deserved the Coach of the Year award. He was willing to throw caution to the wind and try a lineup that he thought might work, putting his best five players on the floor and eschewing a true center. He realized his team needed to run to win with this lineup so he did without play calls, letting Nash freelance on nearly every possession. And since D'Antoni couldn't rely on his bench, he focused on minimizing fouls. The Suns double-teamed every opposing post threat to keep themselves out of foul trouble and lived with the results.

Stop and think to yourself about how many coaches would go through with this. In general, NBA coaches are control freaks, and few are laid-back enough to give up the reins for even a few seconds, much less a whole season. Other than Don Nelson, I'm hard-pressed to think of one other coach who would try something so bold as the Suns' lineup experiment, for fear of getting fired if it didn't work. D'Antoni was both brave and smart enough to realize it was Phoenix's only chance for success, and he rode it as far as he could.

Give the Suns credit too for realizing they could win with an unorthodox lineup. Team president Bryan Colangelo pursued Nash and Quentin Richardson as free agents in the summer of 2004, when other general managers might have focused on a center and ended up with a Calvin Booth situation.

Unfortunately, the loss to San Antonio in the playoffs got the Suns thinking about adding more size, so they will back as a much more conventional looking team in 2005–06. The Suns started by trading Richardson and a first-round pick to the Knicks for Kurt Thomas, a deal that seems tremendously one-sided for the Knicks. Thomas is 34 years old and under contract until 2009, while Richardson had virtually the same PER as Thomas in 2004–05 but is nearly eight years younger.

Phoenix added Thomas with the idea that he could play center and Stoudemire would return to power forward, but that seems odd. Thomas is an inch shorter and 10 pounds lighter than Stoudemire, so he'll be at even greater disadvantage than Stoudemire was. Finally, having Thomas starting and moving Stoudemire to power forward removes one of Phoenix's greatest advantages in the monumental quickness advantage that Stoudemire and Marion had on their opponents every night.

In addition, Phoenix seemed poised to lose the other half of its outstanding three-point shooting combo after the Hawks offered a ludicrous maximum contract to guard Joe Johnson. The Suns had a right to match the contract, but it would have been self-destructive. In one of the great bluffs in history, the Suns gave away Jake Voskuhl to Charlotte to make it appear like they were dumping salary to keep Johnson. That baited the Hawks into sweetening the pot by offering a sign-and-trade deal. Thus, while Phoenix may lose Johnson, it will get two first-round draft choices and a trade exception they can use during the season to fill his spot. If the deal is approved, that is—a messy situation with the Hawks' ownership was holding the trade up as of publication. Johnson isn't worth nearly that much money, so Atlanta's lunacy was a bad break for the Suns. Nonetheless,

they avoided worsening a bad situation by resisting the knee-jerk instinct to match Atlanta's offer.

For the moment, Johnson's job falls to Raja Bell. The Suns used their full midlevel exception to sign him in free agency, although outside shooting is not his forte. It's a bit puzzling why Phoenix went after him so hard when it seemed better options were on the table, but he'll at least provide a strong perimeter defender to replace Johnson. The Suns also erred in letting Hunter leave, signing a fading Brian Grant to replace him.

Taken as a whole, D'Antoni's grand experiment seems as if it will last only one season. Phoenix will start Nash, Bell, Marion, Stoudemire, and Thomas; bring Jackson, Grant, and Leandro Barbosa off the bench; and hope for the best. But in addition to strong years from the new guys, the Suns will need another dose of the magic dust that kept everyone healthy in 2004–05. Chances are it will blow away at some point this season, sending Phoenix down from the stratosphere and into the pack of teams chasing the Spurs. It was a great party while it lasted, but I fear it ended much too soon.

Leandro Barbosa (86% PG, 14% SG)		point guard									Age: 23	Height: 6-3	Weight: 188 Most similar at age: Latrell Sprewell				
Year	G	M/G	FG%	FT%	P/40	R/40	A/40	TS%		Ast		TO		Usg		Reb		PER
2003-04 Phx	70	21.4	.447	.770	14.7	3.3	4.4	55.3	6	21.1	58	15.3	59	18.2	55	4.8	49	12.70 39
2004-05 Phx	63	17.3	.475	.797	16.3	4.8	4.6	57.5	5	21.1	58	14.6	61	18.8	55	6.7	6	12.69 45
2005-06 PRJ (26.0)			.462	.803	16.8	4.3	4.6	56.9		20.5		13.7		19.7		6.2		14.03

Steve Nash should give Barbosa a share of his MVP trophy. Barbosa is lightning quick and has very long arms, but his inability to run the point when Nash was out of the game helped contribute to the Suns' poor record in Nash's absence. That, in turn, was a key factor in generating Nash's MVP buzz.

Barbosa's Assist and Turnover Ratios both were among the worst at his position, continuing the trend he established in his rookie year. He plays out of control and when he drives he almost always looks to score rather than to pass. He can score though. Barbosa has unusual form on his shot but is a good outside shooter, hitting 37 percent on three-pointers. In the paint he uses a variety of scoop shots to boost his field-goal percentage.

Barbosa's long arms and quickness would seem to make him a good defender, but he has yet to harness those skills and was average at best last season. However, he did manage to increase his Rebound Rate to among the best at his position.

Overall, Barbosa is quite young and his skills suggest he could become quite good. However, he needs to change positions. While 6' 3" is a bit small for a shooting guard, his long arms could allow him to make the switch, and it might stop the torrent of turnovers that are threatening to wash away his career.

Steven Hunter (100% C)		center									Age: 24	Height: 7-0	Weight: 240 Most similar at age: Theo Ratliff				
Year	G	M/G	FG%	FT%	P/40	R/40	A/40	TS%		Ast		TO		Usg		Reb		PER
2002-03 Orl	33	13.5	.544	.409	11.6	8.3	0.5	53.1		4.2		10.5		11.6		11.9		13.37
2003-04 Orl	59	13.4	.529	.333	9.5	8.6	0.6	50.4	47	5.3	68	12.8	34	10.4	68	12.5	59	11.16 59
2004-05 Phx	76	13.8	.614	.479	13.3	8.7	0.5	59.6	6	2.4	68	12.6	25	11.6	55	12.2	55	14.68 28
2005-06 PRJ (8.5)			.558	.417	13.6	8.8	0.8	53.6		4.2		11.3		13.5		12.4		14.36

Discarded by Orlando, Hunter surfaced in Phoenix and put together a strong season as a backup center. He was the Suns' best post defender and saw extended action against Tim Duncan in the conference finals. That's not saying much considering Phoenix's lack of size. Hunter's real skill is shot-blocking, as he sent back nearly a shot every 10 minutes. His length and timing could put him among the league leaders if he gets a starting job.

Offensively, Hunter has good footwork in the paint and runs the floor fairly well, so he gets his share of dunks and short flips around the basket. He can't create his own offense and he's a dreadful free-throw shooter, but he shot 61.4 percent last season by choosing his spots carefully.

Hunter signed a cap-friendly deal with the Sixers over the summer to be their backup center. He's not good enough to start because he doesn't rebound and has no post game, but as a second-teamer he's one of the league's better options. As a 24-year-old, shot-blocking seven-footer, it's a wonder more teams weren't beating down his door.

Jim Jackson			**small forward**							**Age: 35**		**Height: 6-6**		**Weight: 220**	
(90% SF, 6% SG, 4% PF)													Most similar at age: Mark Aguirre		
Year		G	M/G	FG%	FT%	P/40	R/40	A/40	TS%		Ast	TO	Usg	Reb	PER
2002-03	Sac*	53	19.5	.442	.855	14.9	8.0	3.6	50.1	36	17.2 22	11.7 42	18.4 36	10.7 3	12.41 36
2003-04	Hou	80	39.0	.424	.843	13.2	6.2	2.9	54.0	15	16.7 15	12.9 52	16.3 41	8.8 30	12.23 39
2004-05	Hou-Phx	64	31.1	.426	.931	13.5	5.4	3.7	55.3	15	17.5 4	12.7 51	16.4 47	7.6 49	10.93 47
2005-06	PRJ (29.5)			.407	.864	12.8	6.0	3.2	52.3		16.5	12.5	15.9	7.9	11.20

* Season rankings are as shooting guard

Jackson was traded from Houston to New Orleans but refused to report to the Hornets, eventually earning himself a second trade to Phoenix. He was moderately useful as a patch on the open sore that was Phoenix's bench, but once he had to start in the playoffs, his limitations became more obvious. Jackson creates very few shots and for a guy who only shoots threes from the corner, he's surprisingly turnover-prone. The three-ball is the one thing he has going for him offensively. He hit a scalding 46 percent as a Sun and is a 36.9 percent career shooter.

Jackson fares better at the defensive end, as he's one of the strongest players at his position and generally hustles. However, his leaping ability is toast, so his Rebound Rate has veered downward with age and he rarely alters shots. The Suns are fortunate to have him under contract for another season, because they have few other options off the pine. As long as he stays in that role, Jackson is a useful player.

Joe Johnson			**shooting guard**							**Age: 24**		**Height: 6-7**		**Weight: 230**	
Defensive PER: 0.99 (85% SG, 12% PG, 3% SF)													Most similar at age: Calbert Cheaney		
Year		G	M/G	FG%	FT%	P/40	R/40	A/40	TS%		Ast	TO	Usg	Reb	PER
2002-03	Phx*	82	27.5	.397	.774	14.2	4.7	3.7	47.2	51	18.0 10	9.2 13	19.3 25	7.7 48	11.61 44
2003-04	Phx	82	40.6	.430	.750	16.4	4.6	4.3	49.1	39	18.5 21	10.2 28	21.2 27	6.8 31	13.84 27
2004-05	Phx	82	39.5	.461	.750	17.3	5.2	3.6	55.6	14	17.1 22	8.7 17	18.7 36	7.0 27	15.18 17
2005-06	PRJ (56.3)			.440	.765	16.9	4.9	4.0	52.6		17.9	9.3	20.2	6.9	14.36

* Season rankings are as small forward

Johnson is a fine, durable player who has improved every year, plays solid defense, can handle multiple positions, and is a deadly shooter. That said, he might be the league's most overrated player. For somebody to offer a maximum contract for the next five years for Johnson's production is beyond ludicrous. For two teams to fight over who gets to do so . . . um, they know he's not that good, right?

This fact should become very obvious once the halo effect of the 2004–05 Suns goes away. The mirage that is Johnson's stardom was a combination of Phoenix's fast pace and Johnson's extremely high minutes. When people see that he averaged 17.1 points per game, had a 47.8 mark on three-pointers, and can play the point, they assume that Johnson is a star in the making. But Johnson's per-minute stats tell a different story. His 17.3 points per 40 minutes are nothing special, and despite all the threes his TS% was unexceptional because he gets to the line so rarely. None of Johnson's other numbers are strong selling points either, but Atlanta's $70 million act of desperation got him superstar money anyway.

Other than three-point shooting, defense is Johnson's best asset. His Defensive PER was very solid and his ability to guard the opponents' top perimeter threat every night was a key to the Suns' defense. He is big for his position and can defend any

(continued next page)

Joe Johnson *(continued)*

position other than center because he's so versatile. Johnson's other primary asset is durability. He hasn't missed a regular season game in over three years and rarely needs to come out of games, which is greatly helpful to a team like Phoenix that had no bench.

Those skills make him valuable and perhaps make him worth more than the midlevel exception. But contrary to popular belief, there is nothing in his track record to suggest he'll ever be a star-caliber player. As a result, the team that paid $70 million for him is getting a bologna sandwich when they thought they ordered filet mignon.

Shawn Marion				power forward									**Age: 27**	**Height: 6-7**	**Weight: 228**
Defensive PER: 1.23 (90% PF, 10% SF)														Most similar at age: Chris Morris	

Year		G	M/G	FG%	FT%	P/40	R/40	A/40	TS%	Ast		TO		Usg		Reb		PER	
2002-03	Phx*	81	41.6	.452	.851	20.3	9.2	2.3	53.8	16	10.1	51	8.0	5	21.7	13	13.0	3	21.32	3
2003-04	Phx*	79	40.7	.440	.851	18.6	9.2	2.7	51.3	31	11.7	37	8.5	8	20.8	16	13.5	3	19.92	6
2004-05	Phx	81	38.8	.476	.833	19.9	11.6	2.0	55.6	19	9.1	36	7.4	5	19.4	21	15.5	18	21.76	8
2005-06	PRJ (31.4)			.452	.829	18.4	10.0	2.3	53.9		10.9		8.3		19.7		13.7		19.68	

* Season rankings are as small forward

Marion had an off year in 2003–04 but bounced back strong last season, becoming just the second player in NBA history to finish in the top five in both steals and rebounding. The increase in his Rebound Rate was the most notable accomplishment. Marion already was among the best rebounding small forwards in the game but kicked it up another notch when he was asked to play inside last season, boosting his 40-minute rate by 2.4 rebounds.

Marion's underrated defensive talents also provided a big boost. Although he gave up pounds and inches every night, his long arms and quick leaping ability enabled him to post a Defensive PER well above the league average. Marion averaged two steals and 1.5 blocks per game, often diving into passing lanes to pick off errant throws. He wasn't the All-Defense talent that some claimed, but he was good.

Fortunately, Marion rarely had to guard big post players for long because he was such a match-up nightmare at the other end. With his ability to run the floor and hit three-pointers from the corner, bigger players couldn't keep up. Marion also is a strong driver going to his left, and while he's not a creative dribbler, he rarely turns the ball over. The result is a high-efficiency scorer who is able to get his points without having plays called for him.

It appears Marion will move back to his natural small forward spot this season, so he won't be able to run opposing big men ragged. But in the long term, it may be for the best. At his size the nightly pounding probably wasn't going to do any wonders for his career longevity, and with four years left on a max deal, the Suns need him to last a while.

Walter McCarty				power forward									**Age: 31**	**Height: 6-10**	**Weight: 230**
(88% PF, 11% SF, 1% C)														Most similar at age: Chuck Person	

Year		G	M/G	FG%	FT%	P/40	R/40	A/40	TS%	Ast		TO		Usg		Reb		PER	
2002-03	Bos*	82	23.8	.414	.622	10.2	5.9	2.2	54.0	14	16.7	14	10.6	24	12.3	53	8.4	42	10.81	48
2003-04	Bos	77	24.7	.388	.756	12.7	5.0	2.6	54.1	17	16.0	18	11.8	34	14.5	50	7.1	65	10.88	55
2004-05	Bos-Phx	72	12.6	.404	.517	11.5	6.1	1.6	52.5	34	7.8	45	11.2	35	12.6	65	8.6	66	8.08	68
2005-06	PRJ (24.0)			.399	.635	11.2	5.5	2.1	53.8		13.5		11.1		12.8		7.7		10.14	

* Season rankings are as small forward

The Suns acquired McCarty at midseason to help bolster their bench, but he looked much older than his 31 years. McCarty has no game left whatsoever beyond shooting threes from the corner. Although he's a 6′ 10″ power forward, McCarty took three quarters of his shots from beyond the arc last season. He made 35.5 percent, but because he hung out at the arc all game, he took just 29 free throws the entire season. McCarty also has degenerated into one of the game's worst big men on the glass with a pitiful 8.6 Rebound Rate.

McCarty used to make up for his shortcomings with defense and hustle, but those were in short supply last season. He has long arms and decent quickness, but he doesn't have the strength to defend the post and lacks the hops to block shots. As a result, he's really only useful as a corner man against zones. He's under contract for one more season, but don't expect the Suns to use him nearly as extensively as they did in 2004–05.

| Steve Nash | | | | | | | | | | | | | | | | | | point guard | | | | | | | | | | Age: 31 | Height: 6-3 | Weight: 195 |

Steve Nash   point guard   Age: 31   Height: 6-3   Weight: 195
Defensive PER: 0.96 (100% PG)   Most similar at age: Sam Cassell

Year		G	M/G	FG%	FT%	P/40	R/40	A/40	TS%		Ast		TO		Usg		Reb		PER	
2002-03	Dal	82	33.1	.465	.909	21.5	3.5	8.8	57.6	3	29.1	21	9.4	14	28.0	4	4.8	50	22.60	1
2003-04	Dal	78	33.5	.470	.916	17.3	3.6	10.5	59.0	3	37.1	6	11.3	32	25.3	8	4.9	48	20.41	3
2004-05	Phx	75	34.3	.502	.887	18.1	3.9	13.4	60.6	4	41.6	2	11.8	43	28.1	7	5.4	35	22.06	2
2005-06	PRJ (16.9)			.472	.890	16.9	3.8	11.0	58.3		37.5		11.5		25.9		5.2		19.79	

Nash had an unbelievable season, posting the league's second-best Assist Ratio, compiling a 60.6 TS%, and generally pushing the Suns to the top of the league's offensive charts. It takes a real nit-picker to point out that he was a bit turnover-prone and could have defended better, and there's no disputing that he's one of the premier offensive players in the game.

Nash's Assist Ratio is off the charts for a player who was also a high-caliber scoring threat, with his mastery of the pick-and-roll being especially lethal. He's a deadly shooter who was one of only two players to shoot over 50 percent from the field, 40 percent on three-points and 80 percent at the line. He also scores easily on the drive, as he can make running hook shots off the glass with either hand. He also likes to spin and shoot a turnaround over opposing guards in the paint. It wasn't a career year statistically except in assists—he had a higher PER in Dallas two years ago. Nonetheless, it was the fourth straight season he combined a blistering TS% with prolific shot-creating for himself and teammates, making him one of the game's most efficient players.

Here's the catch: He's not the MVP. I don't see how anyone could have watched the Suns last season and thought Nash was the league's most valuable player, because he wasn't even the best player on his own team. Unfortunately, it became accepted as gospel about three weeks into the season that Nash was an MVP candidate, largely because of the cult of the New Guy that I discussed in the introduction. While Nash and Stoudamire played brilliantly, the only way to defend a vote for Nash was to give him all the credit for everything Amare Stoudemire did too. Amazingly, enough voters took that leap of faith that Nash won the award. It was Nash's "making his teammates better," the masses decided, that allowed Stoudemire to improve so sharply.

Certainly, one can make a case that Stoudemire improved once Nash arrived. His scoring average jumped from 20.6 points to 26.0, and his field-goal percentage from 47.5 to 55.9. But here's my question: What about Stoudemire making Nash better? Nash never averaged anywhere close to 11.5 assists per game in the other eight years of his career, so it should be fairly obvious that Stoudemire's ability to finish what Nash started provided a crucial difference. Moreover, is it outlandish to suggest that Nash's career-highs in field-goal and three-point percentage owe more than a little to all the attention defenses were paying to Stoudemire?

One way to look at things is to break the PER down into its components. By doing so, we can see that not only was Stoudemire more valuable overall (his PER was 26.69 to Nash's 22.06), he was better even when the conversation focused just on offense. By taking out rebounds, blocks, steals and personal fouls, we can create an "Offensive PER" for every player in the league. The chart shows that Stoudemire, not Nash, was the best in basketball in this category, further supporting the idea that Stoudemire was the one whose accomplishments were more deserving of our praise.

As for the argument about Nash making his teammates better, the chart delivers that one a beating too. (A quick primer for those who didn't read the first edition of his book: The notion that a player can magically make a fellow player better is poppycock.) In second place last season was none other than Nash's former teammate Dirk Nowitzki, who seemingly should have fared much worse in Nash's absence.

Offensive PER Leaders, 2004–05

Player	Team	Offensive PER
Amare Stoudemire	Phx	19.93
Dirk Nowitzki	Dal	19.62
LeBron James	Cle	19.46
Steve Nash	Phx	19.46
Stephon Marbury	NY	19.30
Allen Iverson	Phi	19.10

(continued next page)

Steve Nash *(continued)*

Stoudemire's abundant skill was made clear in the conference finals when he went one-on-one against one of the game's premier defenders in Tim Duncan and ate his lunch. He scored over 30 points in every game despite Phoenix's defeat and finished with the league's best postseason PER. Yet because he wasn't the New Guy, he received almost no credit for Phoenix's accomplishments. Instead, his sudden improvement was taken as proof of the New Guy's impact, rather than the other way around.

Bo Outlaw					power forward							Age: 34		Height: 6-8		Weight: 220	
(86% PF, 10% SF, 4% C)															Most similar at age: N/A		
Year	G	M/G	FG%	FT%	P/40	R/40	A/40	TS%		Ast		TO		Usg		Reb	PER
2002-03 Phx	80	22.5	.550	.621	8.4	8.2	2.5	57.4	5	21.7	6	14.7	53	10.3	59	10.8 52	12.19 47
2003-04 Mem	82	19.6	.510	.526	9.5	8.5	2.2	52.2	29	17.2	14	13.2	52	11.7	61	12.1 46	13.13 49
2004-05 Phx	39	5.5	.353	.556	5.4	9.9	2.4	38.2		11.6		13.6		9.5		13.9	8.10

Outlaw signed with his former team after the Grizzlies cut him before the season, but he wasn't able to provide much of a spark off the bench. As an undersized power forward who relies on energy and athleticism to overcome his lack of size and inability to shoot, Outlaw could be nearing the end of the line. His rebounding numbers have become very ordinary and he doesn't get nearly as many garbage baskets as he used to, limiting his overall effectiveness. While he can be useful as a point man in traps, that's an extremely limited role, and it might not be enough to get him on a roster in 2005–06. If it does, it will be as much for what he contributes in the locker room as for what he does on the court.

Quentin Richardson					small forward							Age: 25		Height: 6-6		Weight: 230	
Defensive PER: 0.89 (68% SF, 32% SG)															Most similar at age: Todd Day		
Year	G	M/G	FG%	FT%	P/40	R/40	A/40	TS%		Ast		TO		Usg		Reb	PER
2002-03 LAC*	59	23.2	.372	.685	16.1	8.2	1.5	46.0	49	7.3	57	8.9	14	19.6	31	11.3 2	12.48 35
2003-04 LAC*	65	36.0	.398	.740	19.2	7.1	2.4	48.4	45	9.7	58	9.8	24	22.7	16	10.5 3	15.02 19
2004-05 Phx	79	35.9	.389	.739	16.6	6.7	2.2	52.2	36	10.6	42	7.4	6	17.6	34	9.0 29	13.59 35
2005-06 PRJ (36.6)			*.384*	*.715*	*16.5*	*7.1*	*2.4*	*49.8*		*10.8*		*8.6*		*19.1*		*9.8*	*13.81*

* Season rankings are as shooting guard

I included some stats on charges in the Denver section, which indicated that Nenê led the team with 22. I don't have full-season stats for the Suns, but according to the team Richardson drew eight in the month of March alone. That's an amazing transformation for a player who seemed allergic to defense for most of his tenure as a Clipper. It was one reason he was able to hold a starting job despite a season-long shooting slump.

Richardson needs to put that much effort into help defense because he has slow feet and is easily beaten off the dribble. However, the move to small forward helped limit his exposure to quicker players. Because he's very strong and can rebound, he was able to hold his own physically too.

Offensively, Richardson was almost exclusively a three-point shooter. He took eight attempts a game and made 35.8 percent, but he should vary his game more. Richardson took over 60 percent of his tries from beyond the arc but he doesn't need to. He has a great post game that the Suns didn't take advantage of, and that was one reason his numbers declined from what he achieved with the Clippers.

Richardson was traded to the Knicks after the season and will have to beat out Tim Thomas for the starting small forward spot. If he can't succeed, he'll still get major minutes off the bench alternating between the two wing spots, and his propensity for taking charges could soon make him a favorite of Larry Brown.

Paul Shirley			power forward						Age: 28	Height: 6-10	Weight: 230		
(100% PF)											Most similar at age: N/A		
Year	G	M/G	FG%	FT%	P/40	R/40	A/40	TS%	Ast	TO	Usg	Reb	PER
2002-03 Atl	2	2.5	.000	—	0.0	8.0	0.0	0.0	0.0	0.0	32.1	11.4	-28.41
2003-04 Chi	7	12.7	.435	.333	9.4	7.2	1.8	43.2	10.7	24.1	13.8	10.2	4.37
2004-05 Phx	9	3.3	.455	.500	16.0	2.7	4.0	47.0	17.9	6.0	20.3	3.8	9.73

Shirley was worthless on the court, but drew nationwide acclaim for a hilarious blog he began writing on NBA.com. Highlights include, "As I spend more and more time around basketball players, my brain power continues to diminish"; "Saying the Hawks are a bad basketball team is like saying that living in Beirut would be exciting—true, but not really the whole story"; and, my personal favorite, "Tom Gugliotta has the worst tattoo in the NBA. The barbed wire on the bicep is bad enough to put him in the running; the fact that it is the dreaded 'I thought I could get away with not having it complete the circumference of my arm' type puts him over the top. It is like wearing a tie that is not only ugly, but is a clip-on to boot."

His future as a writer seems to be much brighter than his future as a basketball player, however, as Shirley is 12th-man material at best. But hopefully he'll make a roster this year so he can keep entertaining us.

Amare Stoudemire			center						Age: 23	Height: 6-10	Weight: 245		
Defensive PER: 0.66 (84% C, 16% PF)											Most similar at age: Pau Gasol		
Year	G	M/G	FG%	FT%	P/40	R/40	A/40	TS%		Ast		TO		Usg		Reb		PER	
2002-03 Phx	82	31.3	.472	.661	17.2	11.2	1.2	53.0	26	6.0	63	14.4	48	18.3	13	15.9	17	16.14	14
2003-04 Phx*	55	36.8	.475	.713	22.4	9.8	1.5	53.6	20	5.9	66	13.5	57	22.9	8	14.4	26	19.77	8
2004-05 Phx	80	36.1	.559	.733	28.8	9.9	1.8	61.7	3	6.5	35	9.4	5	24.7	2	13.2	49	26.69	2
2005-06 PRJ (24.4)			.524	.726	25.9	10.2	1.9	58.2		7.1		11.0		24.1		14.0		23.51	

* Season rankings are as power forward

Stoudemire exploded onto the scene in 2004–05, taking his place as one of the game's superstars with a dominating offensive effort. Stoudemire's monstrous numbers in Usage Rate, Turnover Ratio, and TS% represent something of a holy trinity for scorers. First, he created a ton of shots, with his Usage Rate ranking second at his position. Second, he made almost all of them, shooting 55.9 percent from the floor and having the third-best TS% among centers. Finally, he accomplished the first two parts without turning the ball over, as only 9.4 percent of his possessions ended in miscues.

As I noted in the Nash comment, Stoudemire was the best offensive player in basketball last season—that's why he's the one we put on the cover. He has a blindingly quick first step going to his right and has added a mid-range jumper that defenders must respect. He's also amazing on the pick-and-roll with Nash, doing a great job of sealing his defender before rolling to the rim. Because he's such an explosive leaper, he can finish from anywhere inside 10 feet without needing to dribble.

Where Stoudemire needs work is on his defense. He wasn't as big as some of the other centers and could be hurt on the offensive glass. He also needs to focus on being a better help defender. Stoudemire didn't defend well against screen-and-roll plays either and was too easily faked off his feet. His overall Defensive PER was fairly poor but he has the ability to be one of the best defenders in the league. One hopes that with more muscle and experience he can make a better showing at that end. The expected move to power forward this year also should help.

The Suns and Stoudemire have an important item of business to take care of before the season, as Stoudemire is due for a contract extension. It should be a no-brainer for the Suns to offer him the max and make sure the rest of his promising career is spent in Phoenix.

Yuta Tabuse			point guard						Age: 25	Height: 5-9	Weight: 165		
(100% PG)											Most similar at age: N/A		
Year	G	M/G	FG%	FT%	P/40	R/40	A/40	TS%	Ast	TO	Usg	Reb	PER
2004-05 Phx	4	4.3	.167	1.000	16.5	9.4	7.1	45.1	25.5	8.5	24.7	13.2	15.59

Tabuse made the Suns team out of training camp and became the first Japanese player to play in the NBA, but he lasted only a few weeks before he was cut. Nonetheless, he is a big star in Japan, as I learned when I was there a year ago and repeatedly saw him in soft-drink commercials. Tabuse played well in his brief minutes but his size is a major impediment. He might be better off trying to get work in Europe and then getting a guaranteed deal to play in the U.S. a year or two down the road.

Jake Voskuhl   center   Age: 28   Height: 6-11 Weight: 255
(100% C)   Most similar at age: N/A

Year		G	M/G	FG%	FT%	P/40	R/40	A/40	TS%		Ast		TO		Usg		Reb		PER	
2002-03	Phx	65	14.6	.564	.667	10.5	9.5	1.5	60.4	2	12.4	18	16.6	62	10.8	63	13.4	46	11.81	48
2003-04	Phx	66	24.3	.507	.740	10.9	8.5	1.4	57.7	7	11.1	24	15.0	60	11.2	65	12.6	57	11.19	57
2004-05	Phx	38	9.5	.458	.684	8.9	10.2	1.9	52.8		9.0		17.7		10.5		14.4		8.64	

Voskuhl saw little action because the Suns decided to go with a smaller lineup, and he did little to change their minds. He's a high-percentage shooter around the basket but sets way too many illegal screens and gets hammered on the boards. Phoenix can accomplish that with Stoudemire and get a lot more offense in the bargain, so Voskuhl's skills had little value. Phoenix traded Voskuhl to Charlotte after the season in a salary dump, and he may have more chances to play with the Bobcats than in Phoenix's run-and-gun set-up.

Dijon Thompson   small forward   Age: 22   Height: 6-7   Weight: 210

A second-round draft pick, Thompson handles the ball well for his size and is a decent shooter. However, he has a reputation for coasting through games and it's questionable whether he has enough athleticism to make up for it at the pro level. He did show substantial improvement in his senior season, so perhaps the light bulb has begun to turn on.

Portland Trail Blazers

It's been quite a depressing few years for the Portland Trail Blazers. The one-time championship contenders slowly rotted over the past five seasons, with last season completing the tear-down job. Portland said goodbye to its final link to the glory days when Damon Stoudamire left as a free agent and then set about rebuilding around a new generation of Blazers.

Portland began the year with visions of playoff contention still dancing in its head. With a frontline featuring high-scoring forwards Zach Randolph and Shareef Abdur-Rahim alongside fly-swatting big man Theo Ratliff, the Blazers figured they could squeeze into the post-season if they stayed healthy and the guards made shots.

What happened instead was the usual Portland mess. Randolph and Abdur-Rahim both played the same position, but management was unable to find a trade for Abdur-Rahim that it found attractive. Thus, one of Portland's best talents was essentially wasted. Both Randolph and Abdur-Rahim also spent extended time on the injured list, missing 57 games between them. Ratliff signed a mammoth extension before the season and then promptly turned into a dog, averaging just 7.0 points per 40 minutes.

Darius Miles, the team's small forward of the future, earned a two-game suspension for hurling racial slurs at coach Maurice Cheeks, and Cheeks's reward for enduring this was getting fired weeks later. At shooting guard, both Derek Anderson and Nick Van Exel were limited by knee problems so the Blazers went much of the year with a dwarf backcourt of Sebastian Telfair and Stoudamire.

Portland had been a strong second-half team in previous seasons under Cheeks, but once Randolph was sidelined, the handwriting was on the wall. After Cheeks's dismissal the Blazers decided to build around the young guys. The veterans essentially took the year off at that point, with Van Exel, Anderson, and Ruben Patterson going on the shelf with dubious injuries, and interim coach Kevin Pritchard played youngsters like Telfair, Travis Outlaw, and Viktor Khryapa down the stretch. Portland went just 5–24 in its final 29 games after beginning the year at a more respectable 22–31.

Trail Blazers at a Glance

Record: 27–55, 4th place in Northwest Division

Offensive Efficiency: 100.1 (25th)

Defensive Efficiency: 104.5 (20th)

Pace Factor: 92.2 (19th)

Top-Rated Player: Shareef Abdur-Rahim (PER 18.72, 40th overall)

Head Coach: Nate McMillan. The former "Mr. Sonic" takes his show three hours down the road.

There were some bright spots despite the poor record. Defensively, Portland ranked only 20th in the league overall, but they did two things particularly well. First, they blocked shots. Portland sent back 8.0 percent of opponents' deliveries; only San Antonio blocked more. Ratliff and Joel Przybilla alone averaged nearly six blocks a game between them, while Miles averaged better than a block per game. Those three players accounted for the lion's share of Portland's rejection total, and it stands to decrease this season since Ratliff is likely to be a reserve. The second area in which Portland excelled was avoiding fouls. Portland's opponents got only .271 free-throw attempts for every field-goal attempt, with only Phoenix ranking above it.

Unfortunately, Portland failed in other areas. They gave up too many three-pointers, didn't force many turnovers, and were savagely beaten on the defensive boards (see table 1). Portland rebounded only 67.7 percent of opponents' misses, the worst rate in the league. Ratliff was an incredibly poor rebounder as a center, while the two midgets in the backcourt couldn't offer much help either. The price for Ratliff and Przybilla going after so many blocks was that the offensive boards often were exposed so Portland didn't gain much from their ventures.

Offensively, the Blazers were even worse, ranking 25th overall in Offensive Efficiency. Oddly, Portland's field-goal percentage was above the league average, as players like Randolph, Abdur-Rahim, and Miles had no problem converting shots around the basket. But two things helped set Portland back. First were the turnovers. Portland tied for the league's second-worst Turnover Ratio at 16.4 percent of its possessions, costing it nearly two points a game compared to the league average.

Second, relatively few of Portland's baskets were three-pointers. Here's an interesting paradox. The Blazers were above the league average in both two-point field-goal percentage and three-point percentage, but because they had such a low ratio of threes to twos, they were actually well *below* the league average in TS%. A low rate of free throws didn't help either.

Table 1. Worst Defensive Rebounding Teams, 2004–05

Team	DRB %
Portland	67.7
Phoenix	68.3
Sacramento	69.0
Golden State	69.7
Memphis	69.9
League Average	**71.3**

In short, things aren't looking terribly bright for Portland's immediate future. They struggled at both ends of the floor last season, and with Stoudamire and Abdur-Rahim gone in free agency, they've lost two of their three best players. The good news for Portland is that based on early returns, the young guys can play a little. Portland has put together a starting lineup of the future that figures to be competitive in short order:

- At point guard, Telfair showed plenty of rough edges in his first season out of high school but displayed two essential skills—the ability to penetrate at will and outstanding court vision.

- Shooting guard Travis Outlaw put up great numbers in limited minutes for a second straight season. At 21 years of age he should be ready to assume a much greater role this season and could be a breakout player.

- At small forward, the 24-year-old Miles has driven the Blazers crazy with his insubordination, but nobody doubts the talent is there. Late in the season, he scored 47 points *off the bench* in a game against Denver, signifying his monstrous athleticism.

- Randolph is already among the game's best power forwards, and presuming he can come back healthy from microfracture knee surgery, the 24-year-old brute should again be a nightly 20-10 threat.

- And at center, Joel Przybilla washed up in Portland with low expectations, but he was one of the league's most improved players and took Ratliff's job. At 26, he should hold the job for years.

That's not all. The Blazers have several more rising talents on the bench. Two 2004 first-round draft choices from Russia, Khryapa and Sergei Monia, look ready to become contributors. Monia in particular is an outstanding athlete and could become a key part of the rotation as early as this season. In 2005, the Blazers added to that haul with swingman Martell Webster who, like Outlaw, Telfair, and Miles, came to the NBA straight from high school. Webster has a sweet outside stroke and could be an important part of the second unit. Portland's other first-round pick, point guard Jarrett Jack, also could figure into the rotation. Finally, the Blazers took a dip into the free agent market to sign Washington guard Juan Dixon at very reasonable dollars. He'll provide some backcourt insurance if the rookies prove unready.

Stepping in to run things is Nate McMillan who took his act down I–5 after leading Seattle to the Northwest Division title in 2004–05. McMillan is a tough, no-nonsense coach whose demeanor should be a marked contrast to the mellow Cheeks, and his tough love is exactly what this roster needs. For one prominent example, Miles would have ended up on a stretcher had he tried with McMillan what he did with Cheeks. Expect the bellyaching about minutes and touches that plagued last year's team to be a thing of the past under McMillan's strong hand.

The bad news for McMillan is that the team's immediate prospects are severely limited by some bad contracts. General manager John Nash signed both Ratliff and Randolph to multiyear, cap-clogging extensions, with Ratliff's extension being particularly egregious. The Blazers gave him a three-year, $36 million deal before last season based on their enthusiasm over his late-season shot-blocking in 2003–04. Even then, however, they should have realized he was a limited player. Ratliff's PER for the season was only 14.43, and his 40-minute-averages of 10 points and nine rebounds were far short of star quality. That contract was at least double what Ratliff was worth, even before he tanked in 2004–05.

Thus, the Blazers won't be able to add much to their core through free agency. In fact, they did more subtracting than adding. Portland cut Nick Van Exel's non-guaranteed contract for the luxury tax savings, and then used the tax amnesty provision in the collective bargaining agreement to waive Derek Anderson. Despite those moves, the team won't be under the cap until at least 2007.

Thus, it's up to McMillan to try to turn these kids into winners. Nash has made some amazing missteps in his two years in Portland, but his eye for spotting young talent could help heal many of Portland's self-inflicted wounds. The Blazers won't contend for a playoff spot this year, but they'll be one of the league's most exciting young teams. If they make a deep postseason push in two or three years, don't say you weren't warned.

| **Shareef Abdur-Rahim** | | | **power forward** | | | | | | | | | | **Age: 29** | **Height: 6-9** | **Weight: 245** |

(64% PF, 24% SF, 12% C)

Most similar at age: Tom Gugliotta

Year		G	M/G	FG%	FT%	P/40	R/40	A/40	TS%		Ast		TO		Usg		Reb		PER	
2002-03	Atl	81	38.1	.478	.841	20.9	8.8	3.1	56.6	7	12.9	21	11.2	33	22.5	10	12.5	37	20.12	8
2003-04	Atl-Por	85	31.6	.475	.869	20.6	9.5	2.6	55.7	7	10.9	39	11.5	32	22.2	12	14.1	29	19.98	7
2004-05	Por	54	34.6	.503	.866	19.5	8.4	2.4	58.1	8	11.0	23	11.6	37	20.2	17	12.1	43	18.72	12
2005-06	*PRJ (52.1)*			*.479*	*.863*	*19.0*	*8.9*	*2.5*	*56.0*		*11.3*		*11.2*		*20.8*		*12.8*		*18.23*	

Though Abdur-Rahim missed 28 games to undergo elbow surgery and often had to play out of position, he put up his usual fine numbers. He's a polished scorer who can get points in a variety of ways. He has drifted outside more in recent years, hitting 38.5 percent of his three-pointers last season, but his line-drive jumper isn't always this consistent. That's when he turns to his moves in the post, featuring a right-handed jump hook shot, and his ability to score in transition. Abdur-Rahim also handles the ball well for his size, although he needs to protect it better around the basket.

Defensively, Abdur-Rahim is smaller than most power forwards and can be vulnerable to post-ups. Plus he doesn't offer much in the way of shot blocking. He partly makes up for it with quickness and can be very effective switching onto guards in pick-and-roll defense. He's also a solid if unspectacular rebounder.

The Blazers signed and traded Abdur-Rahim to New Jersey after the season, but the Nets rescinded the trade when they discovered a problem with Abdur-Rahim's knee. Sacramento quickly swooped in and signed him for the midlevel exception, making him one of the year's biggest free-agent bargains. He's not the flashiest of players and he's been stuck on bad teams his whole career, but he's one of the league's most productive power forwards.

| **Derek Anderson** | | | **shooting guard** | | | | | | | | | | **Age: 31** | **Height: 6-5** | **Weight: 195** |

(91% SG, 9% SF)

Most similar at age: John Starks

Year		G	M/G	FG%	FT%	P/40	R/40	A/40	TS%		Ast		TO		Usg		Reb		PER	
2002-03	Por	76	33.6	.427	.859	16.5	4.1	5.1	55.6	14	23.2	13	9.1	17	21.0	19	6.2	41	16.91	15
2003-04	Por	51	35.5	.376	.824	15.3	4.0	5.0	49.9	34	22.5	11	8.9	16	22.0	21	6.0	43	15.09	18
2004-05	Por	47	26.3	.389	.805	14.0	4.1	4.6	50.3	47	22.0	4	10.9	41	19.5	32	5.5	54	11.68	43
2005-06	*PRJ (53.8)*			*.393*	*.821*	*14.4*	*4.0*	*5.0*	*51.6*		*23.5*		*9.9*		*20.1*		*5.6*		*13.38*	

Injuries and inaccuracy are dragging down Anderson's career. Last season he hit under 40 percent from the field for the second year in a row, and this time he wasn't able to make up for it by getting to the line. Anderson's free-throw rate tanked last season, the result of a mounting injury toll. Anderson has been plagued by knee and back problems since he signed with Portland and has lost much of his explosiveness. He still can shoot, hitting 38.4 percent on three-pointers, but the versatility that used to characterize his game is gone.

Portland waived Anderson under the amnesty provision in the collective bargaining agreement, and he hadn't found a new employer as of publication. However, he could be an interesting gamble for a team using its $1.7 million exception. If the health problems abate, his ability to hit the outside shot and play quality defense should be an asset for a contending team.

| **Richie Frahm** | | | **shooting guard** | | | | | | | | | | **Age: 28** | **Height: 6-5** | **Weight: 210** |

(86% SG, 14% SF)

Most similar at age: N/A

Year		G	M/G	FG%	FT%	P/40	R/40	A/40	TS%	Ast	TO	Usg	Reb	PER
2003-04	Sea	54	8.6	.453	.885	15.7	4.8	2.1	60.8	13.2	3.9	15.1	6.7	15.83
2004-05	Por	43	11.6	.400	.840	13.1	4.9	2.4	54.3	11.5	7.2	15.1	6.5	12.46

A jump-shooting specialist who saw limited minutes, Frahm certainly can shoot the rock. He hit 38.8 percent on three-pointers last season, numbers that are especially impressive when one considers how poorly most players fare when their minutes come in small increments. In Frahm's case, there's a reason for the limited minutes: He couldn't guard a snail. Frahm struggled in nearly every defensive matchup but was especially poor when asked to guard smaller, quicker players. He's a free agent and wouldn't make a bad 12th man because of his ability to bust zones, but he won't see more action unless the defense improves.

Viktor Khryapa power forward Age: 23 Height: 6-9 Weight: 210
(54% PF, 44% SF, 2% C) Most similar at age: Terry Davis

Year		G	M/G	FG%	FT%	P/40	R/40	A/40	TS%		Ast		TO		Usg		Reb		PER	
2004-05	Por	32	16.3	.435	.548	10.3	8.3	1.9	47.4	63	9.1	37	16.5	66	13.8	58	11.0	58	8.90	67
2005-06	PRJ (38.0)			.449	.540	10.1	8.3	2.1	48.3		10.1		15.9		13.2		11.1		9.63	

A first-round pick in 2004, Khryapa missed most of the season with a broken foot but came back sooner than expected. Despite playing with screws in his foot, Khryapa showed himself to be a solid defender, especially at small forward, and showed a decent mid-range jumper. While Khryapa saw more of his minutes at power forward last season, it may not be his long-term spot because of a lack of muscle.

However, Khryapa was a pretty Khrappy offensive player last year. He'll have a hard time earning minutes ahead of his former CSKA Moscow teammate Sergei Monia at small forward unless he shows dramatic improvement. Khryapa showed some ability to finish at the basket, but he can't create his own shot and made far too many turnovers. He also needs to improve as a free-throw shooter and improve his shot selection.

Khryapa is young, and I'm sure he'll play better when he's had a summer of working out and conditioning. But his Euroleague stats suggested he would struggle mightily at the offensive end and he's done nothing to change that opinion. As a result, he may be the odd man out in Portland's forward rotation this year.

Darius Miles small forward Age: 24 Height: 6-9 Weight: 210
(64% SF, 35% PF, 1% SG) Most similar at age: Billy Owens

Year		G	M/G	FG%	FT%	P/40	R/40	A/40	TS%		Ast		TO		Usg		Reb		PER	
2002-03	Cle	67	30.0	.410	.594	12.3	7.2	3.5	43.5	57	16.5	16	16.7	58	18.2	28	10.1	15	9.65	50
2003-04	Cle-Por	79	26.3	.485	.642	16.6	6.9	3.1	51.4	30	14.3	26	11.5	36	20.5	19	10.3	14	16.02	17
2004-05	Por	63	27.0	.482	.600	19.0	7.0	3.0	51.1	42	12.0	33	14.6	60	23.2	11	10.2	13	15.46	20
2005-06	PRJ (54.9)			.466	.611	16.8	6.9	3.4	49.8		14.5		13.4		21.7		10.0		14.85	

If you ignore the boorish behavior and just look at the overall numbers, Miles didn't have a bad year. He had to take on a bigger scoring role and responded with 19.0 points per 40 minutes. He also started to develop a post game that he can use against shorter small forwards. Miles has always been an outstanding scorer in transition, but the past two seasons he's shot the ball more consistently in the halfcourt and is even throwing in the occasional three-pointer. Plus, he's a very solid rebounder for his position and a good ballhandler.

The downside is that despite his dribbling skill, Miles had a big spike in turnovers due to his expanded offensive role. Too many times he went to the basket without a clear idea of Plan B, which is why his future is as a supporting offensive player and not as the lead dog. Miles also needs to get more consistent at the defensive end. His size and quickness make him a tough player to score against when he's motivated, but he loafed on too many nights.

Perhaps McMillan can get him to play harder. If so, he'll have one of the game's better small forwards on his hands, because Miles's skills are undeniable. The ongoing question is whether he'll ever develop the maturity to go with them.

Travis Outlaw small forward Age: 21 Height: 6-9 Weight: 205
(65% SF, 21% SG, 14% PF) Most similar at age: Rashard Lewis

Year		G	M/G	FG%	FT%	P/40	R/40	A/40	TS%		Ast		TO		Usg		Reb		PER	
2003-04	Por	8	2.4	.429	.500	16.8	8.4	2.1	45.7		9.3		9.3		22.2		12.0		16.36	
2004-05	Por	59	13.4	.498	.653	16.1	6.1	1.8	53.2	30	8.4	59	10.4	32	17.7	33	8.2	41	15.45	21
2005-06	PRJ (13.5)			.496	.676	17.5	5.8	2.1	53.8		9.4		10.0		19.1		7.8		16.18	

Outlaw is a natural small forward but may have to play shooting guard this year unless Miles is traded. One thing is clear: He has to play somewhere. Outlaw is one of this season's most obvious breakout candidates (the rest of my starting five would be Stromile Swift, Chris Andersen, Zaza Pachulia, and Al Jefferson), having posted solid numbers as a reserve for two straight seasons. His jump shot has developed nicely the past two seasons and is now a reliable weapon from the middle ranges. Like many of the young Blazers, Outlaw is a terror in transition. However, he'll need to improve as a ballhandler to play on the perimeter.

Defensively, asking Outlaw to play shooting guard may be asking a bit much from a quickness perspective. However, he is a potentially awesome defender who has good size and he's an outstanding leaper. Outlaw needs to develop strength and improve on the boards, but he's only 21 years old. In time, his athleticism should win out.

Outlaw's development brings an interesting question to the fore for the Blazers. They already have Miles, Ruben Patterson, Monia, Khryapa, and Martell Webster on the roster. All of them either shooting guard or small forward. It seems Portland needs to do some housecleaning, but the question is who will draw the short stick and be traded. One thing is clear: It won't be this guy. Other than Webster, Outlaw is the youngest and most talented of the group.

Ruben Patterson				**small forward**												**Age: 30**	**Height: 6-6**	**Weight: 223**
Defensive PER: 1.17 (75% SF, 19% SG, 5% PF)																	Most similar at age: Duane Ferrell	
Year		**G**	**M/G**	**FG%**	**FT%**	**P/40**	**R/40**	**A/40**	**TS%**		**Ast**		**TO**		**Usg**		**Reb**	**PER**
2002-03	Por	78	21.2	.492	.627	15.7	6.4	2.4	53.0	18	12.2	42	14.1	53	18.5	27	9.6	24	14.52	24
2003-04	Por	73	22.6	.506	.553	12.3	6.5	3.4	53.0	20	19.2	4	14.5	56	16.5	40	9.3	22	14.54	27
2004-05	Por	70	28.0	.531	.599	16.5	5.6	2.8	55.8	9	13.4	19	14.2	59	18.8	29	8.0	45	15.78	17
2005-06	*PRJ (25.0)*			*.497*	*.587*	*14.1*	*6.0*	*2.7*	*52.6*		*14.5*		*13.5*		*17.6*		*8.5*	*14.29*

An energetic, up-tempo player, Patterson put together one of his best seasons in 2004–05. At the defensive end, he continues to be a stopper on the perimeter, with outstanding quickness and a bulldog mentality. His Defensive PER rated well despite the crumbling of his surrounding cast, and his toughness set a good example for the younger Blazers.

Offensively, Patterson's first step is outstanding, which allows him to be a decent scorer despite the complete lack of a jump shot. He hit 53.1 percent from the floor, mostly on driving lay-ups and fast breaks, and put up one of the best True Shooting Percentages at his position despite his usual terrible performance at the free-throw line. The only misgiving is his consistently high Turnover Ratio, the result of having to drive into crowds to get most of his points.

Patterson has had a checkered history, but he behaved himself much better last season and battled his way through 70 games with a sore knee. That performance may earn him what he really covets: a ticket out of town. Patterson is under contract for two more years and still is a very effective player, but with all the youth on the wings, he doesn't figure into Portland's plans. Teams will be much more likely to trade for him if he proves he's changed his stripes.

Joel Przybilla				**center**												**Age: 26**	**Height: 7-1**	**Weight: 245**
Defensive PER: 0.72 (100% C)																	Most similar at age: Duane Causwell	
Year		**G**	**M/G**	**FG%**	**FT%**	**P/40**	**R/40**	**A/40**	**TS%**		**Ast**		**TO**		**Usg**		**Reb**	**PER**
2002-03	Mil	32	17.0	.391	.500	3.5	10.6	0.9	42.4	69	13.7	13	21.7	72	5.5	72	15.6	21	7.98	69
2003-04	Mil-Atl	17	20.4	.360	.419	5.6	12.8	0.8	38.5		7.9		20.3		8.8		18.1	6.70
2004-05	Por	76	24.4	.598	.517	10.5	12.7	1.6	59.6	7	7.6	25	16.9	61	11.2	56	18.3	10	15.57	23
2005-06	*PRJ (15.7)*			*.572*	*.530*	*9.9*	*11.8*	*1.8*	*57.5*		*9.5*		*17.5*		*11.0*		*17.1*	*14.52*

This is crazy. A total of 123 voters cast ballots for the Most Improved Player award, but Przybilla, who was easily the league's most improved player, got only one of them. I say this every year, but if it's so hard for people to figure out that "most improved player" and "most increased playing time" don't mean the same thing, then perhaps they should just get rid of the award.

Przybilla's first four years in the NBA were largely a waste, as he ended up with more fouls than points in all four. You'd have a hard time believing the Przybilla who came to Portland was the same player. He reportedly lost 45 pounds in the off-season and went for quickness instead of bulk. He wasn't fat, but he perhaps was overdoing it on the protein shakes. Being lighter on his feet allowed him to go bonkers on the glass, posting a top-10 Rebound Rate among centers, and to send back a shot every 12 minutes.

His newfound nimbleness also helped at the offensive end, where he was a much stronger finisher around the basket. Przybilla shot 59.8 percent after shooting under 40 in three of his first four seasons. Perhaps most amazing was his hands. One wouldn't think losing weight would allow a player to catch the ball better, but for whatever reason Przybilla caught balls much more cleanly around the rim and was able to go up for dunks immediately.

Przybilla hit only 51.7 percent from the line, and even that was a career high, so obviously foul shooting isn't his forte. With all the whistles he draws around the basket, that's an area to focus on for improvement. Przybilla also is an atrocious

(continued next page)

Joel Przybilla *(continued)*
passer who frequently throws the ball away from the high post. At the defensive end, he goal-tended more shots than any player this side of Sam Dalembert and needs to improve his shot-blocking judgment.

But at $1.5 million a year, the Blazers will take it. Przybilla is a free agent after the season and will become much more expensive if he matches what he did last season. In the meantime, he gives the Blazers a very economical source of rebounds and blocked shots.

Zach Randolph			power forward											Age: 24		Height: 6-9		Weight: 253	
(79% PF, 21% C)																	Most similar at age: Antawn Jamison		
Year	G	M/G	FG%	FT%	P/40	R/40	A/40	TS%		Ast		TO		Usg		Reb		PER	
2002-03 Por	77	16.9	.513	.758	20.0	10.5	1.3	55.5	12	6.0	56	9.0	8	20.3	18	15.9	12	19.98	9
2003-04 Por	81	37.9	.485	.761	21.2	11.1	2.1	52.8	24	8.4	56	12.7	49	24.3	6	16.5	12	19.56	9
2004-05 Por	46	34.8	.448	.815	21.7	11.0	2.1	51.1	45	8.2	42	10.7	32	24.6	7	14.7	22	18.68	13
2005-06 PRJ (42.2)			.472	.775	21.1	10.6	2.1	52.7		8.5		10.9		24.3		15.0		19.04	

A widebody with a soft touch, Randolph is a load for opponents to handle in the post and a beast on the glass. His career is at a crossroads heading into this season. Randolph underwent microfracture knee surgery late in the season after the knee had bothered him all season, so he faces a challenge in resuming his former level of productivity.

In addition, two weaknesses continue to dog him. Offensively, he's gotten a reputation as a selfish player who won't pass out of double-teams. If that doesn't change his effectiveness as a post player will decline dramatically, because teams will be able to double him with impunity. Randolph will have to learn how to kick the ball quickly out of double-teams and re-post, earning him a better shot within seconds.

Defensively, Randolph has much to prove. He's slow of foot and not a great leaper, so he struggles to stay in front of quicker players. While he's a good rebounder, Randolph provides little in the way of shot-blocking and doesn't defend the post as well as one might expect from a player with his strength.

Despite those shortcomings, Randolph has plenty to offer. He's a nightly threat to get 20 and 10, and until last season he did it while shooting a high percentage. If McMillan can instill in him a spirit of sharing the ball on offense and stopping it on defense, Randolph could take his place as one of the game's top power forwards.

Theo Ratliff			center											Age: 32		Height: 6-10		Weight: 235	
(81% C, 19% PF)																	Most similar at age: Wayne Cooper		
Year	G	M/G	FG%	FT%	P/40	R/40	A/40	TS%		Ast		TO		Usg		Reb		PER	
2002-03 Atl	81	31.1	.464	.720	11.2	9.6	1.2	51.2	35	8.1	44	15.2	52	12.9	49	13.7	43	13.92	35
2003-04 Atl-Por	85	31.3	.485	.645	10.1	9.2	1.1	52.1	35	8.5	39	14.4	55	11.5	63	13.7	44	14.43	29
2004-05 Por	63	27.5	.447	.692	7.0	7.6	0.8	50.0	48	3.7	58	14.2	42	8.3	68	11.0	60	10.10	55
2005-06 PRJ (12.1)			.462	.667	8.5	8.3	1.0	50.6		7.0		15.2		10.2		12.0		11.30	

Ratliff is an amazing shot-blocker, returning a shot every 11 minutes, but the rest of his game has deteriorated badly. Ratliff's measly offensive output is especially poor when one considers the poor shooting percentage that accompanies it. Most players who rarely shoot limit themselves to dunks and lay-ups and thus shoot a high percentage, but Ratliff was in the mid-40s last season.

Ratliff was weak in most other areas too. His Assist and Turnover Ratios were below average for his position, and he provides little rebounding because he has no muscle. Ratliff's lack of strength was a major reason Portland got creamed on the defensive boards. He also wasn't able to push opposing centers out of the post, repeatedly giving up deep position. Sometimes he was able to recover in time to block the shot, but often the play ended in a lay-up or foul.

Unfortunately, the Blazers gave Ratliff a ridiculous three-year, $36 million extension before the season. They'll have to cross their fingers that Ratliff can return to his stellar play from the end of the 2003–04 season, because otherwise that money is headed straight down the Portland sewer system.

Ha Seung-Jin — center — Age: 20 — Height: 7-3 — Weight: 305
(100% C)   Most similar at age: N/A

Year		G	M/G	FG%	FT%	P/40	R/40	A/40	TS%		Ast		TO		Usg		Reb		PER	
2004-05	Por	19	5.5	.435	.545	10.0	6.9	0.8	46.7		3.7		28.7		13.1		9.3		2.21	

The first Korean to play in the NBA, Ha is a lumbering giant with little game experience and barely played for Portland. He'll probably spend this season in the D-League, after which time Portland will have a better evaluation of his skills.

Damon Stoudamire — point guard — Age: 32 — Height: 5-10 — Weight: 174
Defensive PER: 0.15 (75% PG, 25% SG)   Most similar at age: Michael Adams

Year		G	M/G	FG%	FT%	P/40	R/40	A/40	TS%		Ast		TO		Usg		Reb		PER	
2002-03	Por	59	22.3	.376	.791	12.4	4.7	6.2	46.0	54	27.9	25	11.2	32	20.9	37	7.1	11	12.12	39
2003-04	Por	82	38.0	.401	.876	14.1	4.0	6.4	50.8	31	28.4	27	10.2	20	22.0	29	5.9	23	14.83	26
2004-05	Por	81	34.1	.392	.915	18.5	4.5	6.6	51.0	39	24.4	49	8.7	9	25.9	12	6.5	14	16.66	20
2005-06	PRJ (22.1)			.388	.862	15.4	4.0	6.2	49.6		25.6		9.8		22.5		5.9		14.50	

Stoudamire has proved surprisingly resilient for a small guard, maintaining his productivity into his 30s and even handling a move to shooting guard with surprising flair. Stoudamire set a team record with a 54-point outburst against the Hornets and increased his scoring rate by 4.4 points per 40 minutes. He accomplished this with one of the lowest Turnover Ratios at his position, relying mostly on jump shots to carry him.

Stoudamire was a shaky outside shooter early in his career but has become much more consistent in his old age. He hit 36.9 percent on three-pointers and shot much more accurately off the dribble, especially going to his right. He's also grown fond of pulling up for three-pointers in transition, where taller players can't get in his face on the shot.

In addition, Stoudamire rebounded well despite his small stature. Unfortunately, because Portland had him playing at shooting guard for much of the season, he was a major defensive liability. He's not a great defender at the point either, but he'll put up a better Defensive PER next year when he moves back to the point. He signed a four-year deal with Memphis and will battle Bobby Jackson for the Grizzlies' starting job.

Sebastian Telfair — point guard — Age: 20 — Height: 6-0 — Weight: 165
(100% PG)   Most similar at age: Tony Parker

Year		G	M/G	FG%	FT%	P/40	R/40	A/40	TS%		Ast		TO		Usg		Reb		PER	
2004-05	Por	68	19.6	.393	.789	13.8	3.1	6.7	47.1	55	26.7	34	14.9	65	22.9	28	4.2	59	9.59	60
2005-06	PRJ (3.4)			.410	.788	15.9	3.3	6.4	47.7		24.0		13.7		24.7		4.5		10.41	

Telfair is the first point guard to jump straight from high school to the pros, and only had three comparable players as a result. Two of them, Tony Parker and Stephon Marbury, turned into stars. The other, Dajuan Wagner, was wracked by injuries.

Telfair certainly looks like he has the tools be a star point guard. He has a great first step and can get in the paint whenever he wants, even when opponents are playing five feet off him to stop the drive. Telfair also has outstanding court vision, though that didn't manifest itself in a high Assist Ratio as a rookie. Defensively, Telfair was good at pressuring the ball and should be able to hold his own once he learns the tricks of the trade.

Now for the bad news: Telfair has some major weaknesses that require work. The biggest is his shooting. Telfair hit 24.6 percent on three-pointers and 39.3 percent overall. Opponents routinely left him wide open from 15 feet because they were confident he would miss the shot. Because the jumper wasn't a threat, he was forced to drive into crowds in the paint, accounting for his very high Turnover Ratio.

If he gets a jumper, Telfair is going to be a heck of a point guard, but that's one of the hardest things to predict in a young player. Right now he's a very poor offensive player despite his dribbling talents, because defenses know what's coming. Telfair is an intriguing prospect regardless, but for stardom to be in the cards he has to learn how to shoot.

Nick Van Exel — shooting guard
(96% SG, 4% SF)

Age: 34   Height: 6-1   Weight: 190
Most similar at age: Tim Hardaway

Year		G	M/G	FG%	FT%	P/40	R/40	A/40	TS%		Ast		TO		Usg		Reb		PER	
2002-03	Dal	73	27.8	.412	.764	18.0	4.1	6.2	51.0	30	23.5	11	9.2	18	24.2	10	5.7	46	15.63	20
2003-04	GS*	39	32.2	.390	.707	15.6	3.3	6.6	46.9	52	25.5	46	9.7	13	24.2	14	4.7	52	13.02	37
2004-05	Por	53	30.6	.381	.784	14.5	4.0	5.6	49.4	48	24.9	1	10.1	30	21.3	20	5.7	50	12.47	36
2005-06	PRJ (28.2)			.384	.756	14.7	3.8	5.6	48.2		23.4		10.3		21.9		5.4		12.54	

* Season rankings are as point guard

For a guy with a bad knee and a height disadvantage, it was surprisingly hard for opponents to take advantage of Van Exel. He gave up at least three inches every night at shooting guard but handled it well. He has a good poke-away move he used when opponents posted him up, and as the season wore on teams seemed much more willing to go after Stoudamire. Van Exel played much harder on defense than he had the past few seasons, and since the team was going nowhere, he deserves credit for that.

Offensively, he can create shots but continues to be a low-percentage shooter. Van Exel is almost exclusively a jump shooter now and rarely gets to the foul line, so his 38.1 field-goal percentage didn't cut the mustard. He's a slick ballhandler though, and that should help him if he moves back to point guard this season.

Van Exel will be in a different uniform this year after the Blazers cut him over the summer. He'll be looking to sign with a contender for the veteran's minimum and provide some of his jump-shooting skill off the bench.

Martell Webster — shooting guard
Age: 19   Height: 6-7   Weight: 235

An outstanding shooter who has drawn comparisons to a young Glen Rice, Webster doesn't have the upside of some of the other high-schoolers but may be able to contribute immediately. Webster already has an NBA body at a rock-solid 235 pounds and has a good head on his broad shoulders, which the Blazers certainly could use. However, he seems a bit heavy for a shooting guard. Small forward might be a better position for his skills.

Jarrett Jack — point guard
Age: 22   Height: 6-3   Weight: 200

As an Atlanta resident, I saw plenty of Jack at Georgia Tech and generally liked what I saw. Jack reminds me a lot of Jamaal Tinsley: He's strong, defends well, and can take contact on the drive, but he struggles from the outside and can be turnover-prone. If he ends up being as good as Tinsley, the Blazers would be ecstatic. Even if he falls short, his defense should keep him in the league for several years.

Sacramento Kings

It's official: The window is shut.

Sacramento had one of the best teams in basketball in the past half decade, winning at least 50 games for five straight seasons and posting the league's best regular-season record in 2001–02. Unfortunately, they never quite put it together in the postseason to make a run at a title, and last season marked the official end of the Kings' status as contenders.

Sacramento traded longtime stalwarts Doug Christie and Chris Webber, and after the season sent popular sixth man Bobby Jackson to Memphis. With those moves, the Kings were left with just two players from their heyday, forward Peja Stojakovic and guard Mike Bibby.

One might think the end of the Sacramento dynasty is a sad occasion, but in reality the way the Kings' management has handled it is incredibly reassuring. Rather than let the team slowly crumble due to age, injuries, and cap issues, general manager Geoff Petrie has moved proactively to stem the pain. Much like Indiana's lightning-quick rebuild job in the post-Smits era, Sacramento is quietly positioning itself to make another run in a couple of years with the Bibby-Stojakovic-Brad Miller nucleus still in its prime.

Take a look at Sacramento's moves and you'll see why Petrie is one of the best in the business. Since the Kings got relatively close to a title two years ago, losing to Minnesota at the buzzer of Game 7, he figured he'd give things one more shot to start the season and see how they went. They went fairly well, all things considered, but the Kings weren't in it to do "fairly well." So Petrie decided to rebuild early rather than wait until it was too late.

The first casualty was Christie, with Petrie sending him out the door just as his value was about to decline precipitously. A 34-year-old guard with foot problems, Christie was an essential piece of the Kings for years but his future value looked to be minimal. Petrie exchanged him for Orlando guard Cuttino Mobley, who had one less year remaining on his contract and was a better player to boot. When Mobley departed as a free agent after the season, Sacramento was able to pocket the salary cap savings and sidestep a hefty luxury tax payment.

> ## Kings at a Glance
>
> **Record:** 50–32, 2nd place in Northwest Division
> **Offensive Efficiency:** 107.5 (4th)
> **Defensive Efficiency:** 105.1 (22nd)
> **Pace Factor:** 95.5 (8th)
> **Top-Rated Player:** Brad Miller (PER 20.71, 25th overall)
> **Head Coach:** Rick Adelman. Still one of the best, but his time may be running out.

Then came the big kahuna, the sure signal that the rebuilding had begun: Sacramento sent Webber to Philadelphia for Brian Skinner, Kenny Thomas, and Corliss Williamson. The trade was shocking not only because the Kings unloaded the centerpiece of the franchise, but also because of whom it returned. The Kings didn't get any star-caliber players, nor did they get any cap relief. Instead all they received were three middling frontcourt players.

That wasn't because it was a bad deal for the Kings—it was because Webber's market value had sunk that low. With a toxic contract and a bum knee, most teams were reluctant to take him on. C-Webb had put together a strong first half for the Kings, but that was partly because Rick Adelman's system managed to cover up Webber's burgeoning list of weaknesses. Webber confirmed this once he arrived in Philly, making Petrie look like a genius for unloading him just before the other shoe was about to drop.

On the court, Sacramento was its usual high-scoring self. With versatile big men like Webber and Miller, the Kings again were a brilliant ballhandling team. Sacramento led the NBA in assists and nearly had the fewest turnovers (they missed by two), a near-impossible combination that explains how the Kings could be so potent offensively. While Sacramento didn't have a single dominant scorer, the Kings had the league's fourth-best offense as a result of their skillful passing. Webber and Miller normally orchestrated things from the high post, but nearly every Sacramento player before and after the trades was a good ballhandler for his position. As a result, the Kings turned the ball over on only 13.2 percent of their possessions—the lowest ratio in the league as shown in table 1. Compared to the league average of 14.7, that meant Sacramento saved themselves roughly a point and a half per game simply by taking care of the ball.

The Kings' undoing came at the defensive end. Lacking both a shot-blocker and, with Christie's decline, a perimeter stopper, the Kings were a sieve. Sacramento ranked 22nd in Defensive Efficiency, making it hard for them to be a credible title contender, and they were lucky even to finish that high. Kings' opponents shot only 73.8 percent from the line, the

Table 1. Lowest Turnover Ratio, 2004–05

Team	TO/100 Possessions
Sacramento	13.2
Toronto	13.3
Dallas	13.5
Golden State	13.6
Phoenix	13.6
League Average	**14.7**

worst rate in the league, and that saved Sacramento nearly half a point per game.

The Kings' biggest weakness was interior defense, a fact that became obvious to the world when Seattle ne'er-do-well Jerome James dominated the Kings in the first round of the playoffs. Miller, though a brilliant offensive player, has always been a mediocre post defender and doesn't block shots. Pairing him with limping Webber, undersized Thomas, or overly soft Darius Songaila meant the Kings were seriously lacking in frontcourt defense.

Due to the frontcourt softness, the Kings were especially vulnerable on the offensive glass. Sacramento rebounded only 69.0 percent of opponent misses, a figure that ranked 28th out of the league's 30 teams. The Kings were especially poor after the Webber trade, since that was the one defensive area where he retained most of his pre-injury skill.

One thing that hurt Sacramento at both ends of the court, especially on defense, was its unusually thin bench. A few years ago the Kings were among the deepest teams in the league, but that changed radically as free agency and cap considerations created an exodus of talent. Moreover, the Kings lost sparkplug reserve Bobby Jackson only 25 games into the season, leaving them to make do with waiver wire pickup Eddie House and rookie Kevin Martin as the backcourt reserves. The situation was especially bad prior to the 1-for-3 Webber trade, as the expected bench help from free-agent pickup Greg Ostertag never materialized and lightweight Songaila became the only reliable reserve.

Fortunately, the Kings kept moving and shaking in the offseason to address some of those concerns. Petrie dealt injury-prone Jackson and free-agent failure Ostertag to

Memphis for guard Bonzi Wells (Ostertag subsequently was traded to Utah). Wells is a wing nut, but because Sacramento's clubhouse is relatively free of bad influences, he should be able to keep his composure. Besides, he's in a contract year, so the Kings only need him to behave for one season. Wells fills the gap created by Mobley's departure in free agency, and does so as a more potent scorer whose passing skills should fit in well in Sacramento.

Jackson's replacement is Jason Hart, whom the Kings lifted from Charlotte for a second-round pick. Hart has an economical contract and is a strong defender, so if his offense is even remotely as good as it was last season, the trade should be a steal. More backcourt help is on the way in the form of first-round draft pick Francisco Garcia, a long-armed wingman who should be able to contribute immediately. Last year's first-round pick, Kevin Martin, had a disappointing rookie year, but he could figure into the picture as well.

Up front, the Kings finally have enough bodies, but few of them are big enough. Miller is the key, with the Kings winning 32 of the 50 games he started a year ago. Since no other key player is taller than 6'9", the Kings desperately need him to stay healthy this year. However, the Kings deftly filled the power forward spot by inking Shareef Abdur-Rahim to a cap-friendly five-year, $30 million deal. Though still a bit small, he should be a major upgrade over Thomas. The three players from the Webber trade—Skinner, Thomas, and Williamson—round out the frontcourt. Additionally, the Kings have two restricted free agents in Songaila and Maurice Evans who could significantly improve the depth picture if they are retained or, more likely, signed and then traded.

With players like Bibby, Miller, and Stojakovic, the Kings will win their fair share of games again. But it's hard to envision them making the next climb up the mountain just yet. The Kings face serious luxury tax constraints for three more years and are winning too many games to find much help in the draft. While deft acquisitions like Abdur-Rahim, Wells, and Hart are helping to keep the Kings' heads above water, it doesn't seem they can remain among the Western Conference's elite much longer without continued retooling.

—◦—

Mike Bibby   point guard   **Age: 27**   **Height: 6-2**   **Weight: 190**

Defensive PER: 1.01 (100% PG)   Most similar at age: Jason Terry

Year		G	M/G	FG%	FT%	P/40	R/40	A/40	TS%		Ast		TO		Usg		Reb		PER	
2002-03	Sac	79	24.5	.470	.861	19.1	3.2	6.2	55.9	6	23.9	48	10.6	24	23.1	23	4.3	57	17.55	13
2003-04	Sac	82	36.4	.450	.815	20.2	3.7	6.0	56.4	5	22.7	52	9.0	8	23.9	19	5.3	36	19.16	7
2004-05	Sac	80	38.6	.443	.775	20.4	4.3	7.0	54.3	12	24.7	48	9.3	13	26.0	11	6.0	24	19.19	7
2005-06	PRJ (52.5)			.445	.796	18.7	3.8	6.3	54.8		23.0		10.1		23.5		6.4		17.69	

Sacramento Kings

Bibby continues to be one of the game's best guards, and if it weren't for Chauncey Billups, he'd have locked up "Best current player to never appear in an All-Star Game" status. Like most of the Kings, his game is built on efficiency. Even during a poor shooting year, Bibby's TS% ranked 12th among point guards, and as usual he did it while maintaining a very low Turnover Ratio.

Bibby is particularly adept at nailing jump shots. He shot 36 percent on three-pointers but was far more deadly from the middle ranges, especially when taking a quick dribble to his left. Bibby loves to do this by setting up a pick-and-roll play and then dribbling away from the screener, counting on a hedge by the opposing point guard to open up space on his left.

However, he failed to ignite in the postseason against Seattle. Bibby has a long history of outperforming in the postseason, but the Sonics forced him to shoot going to his right and he ended up making just 39 percent. That was a continuation of his late-season struggles which dovetailed with Miller's absence. Bibby only shot 41.7 percent in March and April while the big man was on the shelf because Miller wasn't feeding him for open jumpers.

Defensively, Bibby has really improved. He's small and can be bulldozed in the post by bigger guards, but he moves his feet well on the perimeter and combined with Mobley to give the Kings a competent defensive backcourt. He helped out the Kings' struggling frontcourt too, by posting a career best in Rebound Rate.

Bibby has slowly taken on a greater offensive load in his time in Sacramento and nearly took over the team's per-minute scoring lead last season. That could come to fruition this year, especially if Stojakovic's legs can't hold up, and if so this may be the year Bibby brings his All-Star drought to an end.

Erik Daniels			**small forward**						**Age: 23**	**Height: 6-8**	**Weight: 214**
(75% SF, 21% PF, 4% SG)										Most similar at age: N/A	

Year	G	M/G	FG%	FT%	P/40	R/40	A/40	TS%	Ast	TO	Usg	Reb	PER
2004-05 Sac	21	3.4	.333	—	7.2	10.0	2.2	36.1	10.6	21.4	13.0	14.4	4.57

An undrafted free agent, Daniels spent the year at the end of the Kings' bench and showed little in his few chances to play. He shot only 33 percent from the field and didn't manage a single free throw. His one saving grace was a high Rebound Rate, which may be enough to keep him around for another look this season.

Maurice Evans			**shooting guard**						**Age: 27**	**Height: 6-5**	**Weight: 220**
(97% SG, 3% SF)										Most similar at age: Gordan Giricek	

Year	G	M/G	FG%	FT%	P/40	R/40	A/40	TS%		Ast		TO		Usg		Reb		PER	
2004-05 Sac	65	19.0	.442	.756	13.5	6.5	1.5	51.1	45	7.0	65	7.0	5	14.7	57	9.4	5	12.15	40
2005-06 PRJ (41.6)			.416	.740	12.7	6.3	1.6	49.0		7.4		7.7		14.7		9.2		11.53	

Evans came over after spending two years in Europe and matched his projections nearly exactly by scoring at a moderate clip and provided a healthy dose of rebounding. Evans's Rebound Rate was among the top five at the shooting guard spot, and his athletic ability made him one of the Kings' better defenders too.

However, his offensive output leaves something to be desired. Evans didn't create shots and when he did they didn't often go in, as both his Usage Rate and TS% were below the norm for his position. He's a good finisher in transition but doesn't get to use those skills often in the halfcourt because he's not much of a dribbler. Thus, he settled for too many long jump shots and didn't get to the line enough. Additionally, Evans is a poor outside shooter, which allowed defenders to play him from the drive and keep him from his preferred real estate in the paint. On a positive note, he rarely turned the ball over.

Evans was a restricted free agent after the season and was unsigned as of publication time. With his ability to defend two positions and minimize turnovers, he should be a solid bench player somewhere, but his inability to create offense limits his usefulness to 15 minutes a night or less.

Eddie House			**point guard**						**Age: 27**	**Height: 6-1**	**Weight: 175**
(70% PG, 30% SG)										Most similar at age: Dee Brown	

Year	G	M/G	FG%	FT%	P/40	R/40	A/40	TS%		Ast		TO		Usg		Reb		PER	
2002-03 Mia*	55	18.6	.387	.861	16.0	3.9	3.4	44.7	57	14.7	64	7.8	4	22.8	25	5.7	28	12.08	40
2003-04 LAC	60	19.8	.359	.800	13.8	4.7	5.0	43.6	61	21.8	56	9.3	10	21.2	33	6.9	11	12.05	47
2004-05 Cha-Mil-Sac	68	13.1	.451	.852	17.8	3.7	4.3	52.5	27	18.9	61	6.9	4	21.3	39	5.4	37	15.74	24
2005-06 PRJ (36.5)			.417	.831	15.5	4.1	4.3	49.6		19.8		8.0		20.4		5.9		13.65	

* Season rankings are as shooting guard

(continued next page)

Eddie House *(continued)*

In one of the year's most bizarre roster moves, the Bobcats cut House despite his gangbusters start to the season. Milwaukee then gave him a try but let him go as well, leading House to finally find a home in Sacramento. With Jackson out, House stepped in as Bibby's backup and did a fine job. He's a shoot-first point guard, but that's less of a problem in Sacramento's system because the big men do so much of the passing.

Additionally, House's scoring ability was a welcome sight on a bench in need of more points. House has always been able to create shots, but he had been wildly inaccurate the previous two seasons. He stroked the ball much better in 2004–05, including a sizzling 45 percent on three-pointers, which helped him improve his TS% by nearly nine points. House also created very few turnovers, meshing well with the Kings' ball-protecting style.

The bad news is that House has two major failings. First, he can't get to the line. He usually shoots jumpers off the dribble rather than going to the rim, with the result being only 27 free-throw attempts all season. Second, he's a poor defender. Since he's undersized and not terribly quick, House became an immediate target for opposing offenses when he checked in. Despite those misgivings, his sharp shooting should land him another backup gig this season.

Bobby Jackson   point guard   Age: 32   Height: 6-1   Weight: 185
(50% PG, 50% SG)   Most similar at age: David Wesley

Year		G	M/G	FG%	FT%	P/40	R/40	A/40	TS%		Ast		TO		Usg		Reb		PER	
2002-03	Sac	69	20.8	.464	.846	21.4	5.2	4.3	56.1	5	16.8	62	9.8	16	23.1	21	7.0	14	18.37	10
2003-04	Sac	50	23.7	.444	.752	23.3	5.9	3.5	53.8	10	13.0	62	7.8	3	25.1	9	8.7	2	19.09	8
2004-05	Sac	25	21.4	.427	.862	22.5	6.3	4.4	53.7	17	16.1	65	7.6	5	25.4	14	9.2	3	17.97	16
2005-06	*PRJ (27.4)*			*.440*	*.802*	*21.2*	*5.8*	*3.9*	*54.2*		*15.8*		*9.5*		*22.6*		*8.1*		*16.60*	

Jackson has been the best backup point guard in basketball the entire time he's been in Sacramento . . . when he's played. Over the past three seasons his injury problems have grown more serious, with Jackson missing 102 games in that time.

When healthy, he's been brilliant. Jackson creates loads of shots, rarely turns the ball over, and is one of the best rebounding guards in basketball despite his lack of size. Last season he averaged a whopping 22.5 points per 40 minutes, the best average on the Kings, and did it with a TS% above the league average. Jackson can get to the basket with either hand or to pull up for jumpers against backpedaling defenders. The one thing he can't do is pass. Jackson has terrible court vision and will sometimes dribble the air out of the ball looking for his shot rather than give it up to a teammate.

Jackson is a quality defender as well. He often saw time at the shooting guard position and had enough quickness and strength to cover himself defensively. He'll rarely have to make that move this season as he was traded to the Grizzlies over the summer. Jackson figures to be spending most of his time at the point in Memphis, who could use a player with his scoring punch. However, the big question is whether Jackson can make it through the season in one piece. In recent years, the answer has been no.

Kevin Martin   shooting guard   Age: 22   Height: 6-7   Weight: 185
(72% SG, 28% SF)   Most similar at age: N/A

Year		G	M/G	FG%	FT%	P/40	R/40	A/40	TS%	Ast	TO	Usg	Reb	PER
2004-05	Sac	45	10.1	.385	.655	11.5	5.1	1.9	46.4	9.2	12.8	14.7	7.4	8.67

The Kings' first-round draft pick in 2004, Martin had a disappointing rookie campaign that saw him bounced from the rotation by the end of the season. Martin is quick and has a scorer's instincts, but he's not a three-point shooter and his off-the-dribble moves aren't very advanced. Martin's biggest weakness is a lack of strength. He's a beanpole who needs to hit the weights so he won't be posted up so easily by opposing guards. Adding strength also could benefit him at the offensive end since he could better use his height against opposing guards in post-ups. Overall, he'll need to vastly improve to earn a spot in an NBA rotation. With the Kings drafting Francisco Garcia and trading for Bonzi Wells and Jason Hart, Martin's minutes will be limited this year in any case.

Brad Miller			**center**							Age: 29		Height: 7-0		Weight: 261	
(95% C, 5% PF)												Most similar at age: Detlef Schrempf			
Year		G	M/G	FG%	FT%	P/40	R/40	A/40	TS%		Ast		TO	Usg	Reb	PER
2002-03	Ind	73	31.1	.493	.818	16.8	10.6	3.4	57.9	5	17.0	5	10.4 9	18.5 11	14.9 30	19.34 5
2003-04	Sac*	72	36.4	.510	.778	15.5	11.3	4.8	57.9	2	23.4	2	10.8 21	18.3 28	16.1 14	19.35 11
2004-05	Sac	56	37.3	.524	.812	16.8	10.0	4.2	59.6	8	20.0	1	7.9 1	18.4 13	13.9 41	20.71 4
2005-06	PRJ (31.1)			.505	.826	15.3	10.9	4.2	57.9		20.8		9.7	17.6	14.9	18.62

* Season rankings are as power forward

One of basketball's most underrated performers, Miller was having his best season before a broken leg derailed him in the final two months. He tried to come back for the playoffs but was completely overwhelmed at the defensive end, which is one reason Sacramento couldn't get out of the first round.

Miller is an absolutely phenomenal distributor for a big man. Look at those numbers in his chart—he was first among all centers in both Assist Ratio *and* Turnover Ratio. With his ability to see the court from the high post, Miller created oodles of shots for his teammates and plenty for himself as well. Miller's TS% has consistently been among the best at his position because he hits midrange jumpers, finishes well around the basket, and constantly gets to the foul line. Despite a serious lack of elevation, Miller is a major offensive threat because of his varied moves. Last season he was much more effective off the dribble than in previous years, repeatedly earning foul shots by faking a shot from the foul line and then driving left to the basket.

Miller is a weaker performer at the defensive end. He's a mediocre shot blocker due to his poor leaping and can be slow to the ball from the help side. While he has the requisite height for the center spot, strength match-ups can give him problems at times. Miller also gives up one easy a basket a game by complaining about no-calls instead of running back on defense. Additionally, his rebounding slipped last season.

Nonetheless, Miller is among the best centers in basketball. Other big men may be stronger or quicker, but none are as skilled. His combination of size, passing ability, and shooting touch is far less common than many people realize.

Cuttino Mobley			**shooting guard**							Age: 30		Height: 6-4		Weight: 215	
(80% SG, 20% SF)												Most similar at age: Rex Chapman			
Year		G	M/G	FG%	FT%	P/40	R/40	A/40	TS%		Ast		TO	Usg	Reb	PER
2002-03	Hou	73	41.7	.434	.858	16.8	4.0	2.7	53.7	19	13.3 42		10.6 33	19.6 32	5.7 45	14.72 24
2003-04	Hou	80	40.4	.426	.811	15.6	4.5	3.2	53.5	15	16.0 32		11.1 36	19.0 37	6.3 40	14.13 24
2004-05	Orl-Sac	66	36.2	.438	.820	19.0	3.8	3.1	55.5	17	14.0 37		9.9 27	20.4 25	5.4 56	14.98 19
2005-06	PRJ (74.5)			.428	.825	17.2	4.1	3.0	54.4		14.3		10.6	20.0	5.7	14.52

Mobley has been remarkably consistent at a moderate production level, scoring a bit more last season but otherwise posting a carbon copy of his previous two campaigns. Offensively, Mobley can be a handful because he has good quickness and is an excellent three-point shooter. Last season he drilled 44 percent from downtown and averaged a solid 19.0 points per 40 minutes. Mobley doesn't get to the basket often, but will post up against smaller guards and is a good jump shooter off the dribble. Overall he had one of the better TS%s at his position, making him a reliable source of points.

Where Mobley needs work is in the other aspects of his game. He's a mediocre ballhandler whose lack of elusiveness off the dribble is a major impediment to his getting to the basket more often. That makes him less able to take advantage of his quickness, and it's one reason his Usage Rate has never been terribly high. He also doesn't see the floor very well, so most of the shots he creates are for himself. And mysteriously, his Rebound Rate tanked last season. Defensively, Mobley struggles to defend in post situations against bigger guards because he's only 6′ 4″ and fairly wiry. He performs better in quickness match-ups, however, and his long arms can be an obstacle for jump shooters.

Mobley signed a five-year deal with the Clippers worth over $40 million, which is great news for him but not so great for his employers. While jump-shooting guards have tended to age better than their counterparts, Mobley will be 34 in the last season of the deal and isn't worth $8 million a year even now. His sweet touch will be an asset to the shooting-starved Clippers, but they badly overpaid for the privilege.

Greg Ostertag center **Age: 32 Height: 7-2 Weight: 280**
(100% C) Most similar at age: Alton Lister

Year		G	M/G	FG%	FT%	P/40	R/40	A/40	TS%		Ast		TO		Usg		Reb		PER	
2002-03	Uta	81	23.8	.518	.510	9.1	10.4	1.1	53.1	24	9.6	32	18.2	68	10.6	65	15.8	18	11.50	51
2003-04	Uta	78	27.6	.476	.579	9.8	10.7	2.3	50.6	45	16.5	5	13.3	42	13.1	48	16.7	9	14.33	32
2004-05	Sac	56	9.9	.440	.342	6.3	12.0	2.7	43.2	70	12.7	4	14.8	44	10.2	64	17.3	15	9.91	57
2005-06	PRJ (18.4)			.476	.500	8.4	10.5	2.2	49.5		14.9		15.2		11.7		15.7		11.85	

A free-agent pickup by the Kings who was supposed to be the backup center, Ostertag was a tremendous disappointment and was out of the rotation once the Kings acquired Skinner in the Webber trade. It's now clear that Ostertag's 2003–04 season was a fluke, and that he should be evaluated based on the years before and after. In those seasons, he brought two strong skills to the table—a strong talent for rebounding and an underrated ability to find the open man.

However, the rest of his game was terribly weak. Ostertag's Usage Rate is ghastly because he has trouble catching passes cleanly and going up quickly for a shot. Hence, even when he's left open he's sometimes unable to convert it into two points. Additionally, his shooting percentages are sinking faster than Atlantis. Last season Ostertag suffered a complete meltdown at the free-throw line, shooting a horrific 34.2 percent. That's bad news for a player who depends on free throws for much of his scoring, and it was a major reason Ostertag's TS% was the worst at his position.

Ostertag was traded back to Utah after the season, and his rebounding and physical defense still can be an asset in spurts. The projections suspect that he will bounce back from last season and play more like the player he was in 2002–03, in which case he'll be a useful asset off the bench for Jerry Sloan.

Brian Skinner center **Age: 29 Height: 6-9 Weight: 265**
(95% C, 5% PF) Most similar at age: Kurt Thomas

Year		G	M/G	FG%	FT%	P/40	R/40	A/40	TS%		Ast		TO		Usg		Reb		PER	
2002-03	Phi	77	17.9	.550	.602	13.3	10.6	0.5	57.4	7	3.9	72	12.8	33	12.7	50	15.5	23	15.36	23
2003-04	Mil	56	28.2	.497	.572	14.9	10.4	1.2	51.3	38	7.0	55	11.1	19	16.2	20	15.2	23	14.35	31
2004-05	Phi-Sac	49	19.2	.507	.357	9.9	11.9	1.8	49.4	51	8.7	19	12.5	23	12.1	50	17.2	17	13.72	33
2005-06	PRJ (51.7)			.506	.511	12.2	10.9	1.4	51.7		7.4		12.4		13.7		15.6		13.94	

Skinner was a good example of the danger of small sample sizes. At the time of the trade, Skinner had an awful PER in Philadelphia and was banished to the end of the Sixers' bench. But by looking at Skinner's career numbers rather than the paltry minutes he'd received in Philly, one could see that he'd give the Kings a serviceable player. Skinner's previous two campaigns had been very solid, and by year-end he had posted similar numbers in 2004–05.

Defensively, Skinner is badly undersized for a center but makes up for it with strength. He has enough muscle to battle opposing big men and push them away from the basket, making him a good counter off the bench when opponents are wearing out Miller. Additionally, he's a good rebounder despite his small stature, using his strength to chisel out space under the boards. Skinner also blocked over two shots per 40 minutes, which is prolific by Kings' standards.

Offensively, Skinner has been a high field-goal percentage shooter throughout his career, but free throws were a different story. Apparently Ostertag was contagious, because Skinner suffered the same free-throw malaise that afflicted his teammate. Skinner's embarrassing 35.7 percent mark was a major reason his TS% slumped. In fact, had he shot a more normal 60 percent, his PER would have been over a point higher.

Skinner seemed to have trouble adjusting to playing the high post in Sacramento but adjusted as the year went on and was finding open men by the end of the year. He's not a threat to score from out there, but he does have a nice right-handed jump hook that he can get off against shorter centers. He needs to move without the ball better though, as he tends to just stand there rather than rolling to the basket after he sets a screen.

Those weaknesses prevent him from being a starting-caliber center, but as Miller's understudy he's a nice weapon to turn to off the bench. Philadelphia made a mistake by giving up on him so quickly last season, but their pain is the Kings' gain.

Darius Songaila (82% PF, 18% C)					power forward											Age: 27	Height: 6-9	Weight: 248 Most similar at age: Gerard King
Year	G	M/G	FG%	FT%	P/40	R/40	A/40	TS%		Ast		TO		Usg		Reb		PER	
2003-04 Sac	73	13.4	.487	.807	13.8	9.2	2.0	54.1	18	11.9	32	10.7	20	14.9	48	13.7	32	14.60	37
2004-05 Sac	81	20.6	.527	.847	14.6	8.3	2.7	56.6	14	13.0	13	9.7	25	15.8	46	11.5	51	14.93	36
2005-06 PRJ (46.2)			.501	.831	14.4	8.3	2.6	54.9		12.5		10.4		15.9		11.8		14.45	

Songaila is the prototypical Sacramento King—a good-shooting European who handles the ball but doesn't rebound or play defense. Songaila doesn't have great elevation but shoots a high percentage by hitting jumpers from the free-throw line and moving without the ball for lay-ups. Because he has no post game whatsoever and isn't a threat off the dribble, his Usage Rate is below average despite his shooting touch.

Songaila's major shortcoming is at the defensive end. He is neither terribly strong nor quick and so he can be steamrolled by the West's many star power forwards. He lacks the hops to block or challenge shots, and his rebounding slumped last season after a strong rookie campaign. Adelman often tempted fate last season by playing Songaila and Webber together in the frontcourt, a combo that proved to be grossly overmatched on defense.

Songaila became a restricted free agent after the season and his status wasn't settled by publication time. With Abdur-Rahim, Thomas, and Williamson ahead of him at power forward and Stojakovic also able to play there at times, it doesn't appear the Kings have a major role for Songaila anyway. Looking for a sign-and-trade might be their best option.

Peja Stojakovic Defensive PER: 0.70 (97% SF, 3% PF)					small forward											Age: 28	Height: 6-10	Weight: 229 Most similar at age: Glen Rice
Year	G	M/G	FG%	FT%	P/40	R/40	A/40	TS%		Ast		TO		Usg		Reb		PER	
2002-03 Sac	82	31.3	.481	.875	22.5	6.5	2.3	60.0	2	10.1	52	7.3	2	20.6	18	8.7	37	19.64	6
2003-04 Sac	81	40.3	.480	.927	24.1	6.2	2.1	62.4	1	9.1	52	8.1	6	21.4	15	8.8	28	21.72	2
2004-05 Sac	66	38.4	.444	.920	21.0	4.5	2.2	58.4	3	10.0	50	7.4	7	20.2	24	6.3	61	17.29	7
2005-06 PRJ (28.1)			.449	.904	21.5	5.5	2.3	58.1		11.0		8.1		19.4		7.1		16.74	

Stojakovic followed up the best season of his career with one of the worst, dropping off in every important area and losing 16 games to hamstring problems. Stojakovic is perhaps the sweetest shooting forward in basketball, drilling 40.2 percent of his three-pointers and hitting over 92 percent from the line for a second straight season. His TS% again ranked in the top three at his position, although it dropped from 2003–04's lofty heights because Stojakovic shot much worse on two-point shots. He hit 51.1 percent from inside the arc in 2003–04 but 47.6 percent last year.

Unlike a lot of jump shooters, Stojakovic creates a decent amount of shots. He didn't create as many in 2004–05 as he had in previous seasons, accounting for the sharp decline in his 40-minute scoring rate. Also, he moves well without the ball to free himself for jumpers and gets a couple of lay-ups a game on back cuts. Occasionally, he will cut along the baseline when the ballhandler was just over halfcourt and surprise defenders by getting a pass for a lay-up. He and Doug Christie clicked especially well on this play.

Of course, Stojakovic has to score at a high rate because he's a mediocre player in other respects. He doesn't see the court well and generates few shots for his teammates. He's a middling defender who has the size to challenge shots but offers below-average lateral movement and help defense. Additionally, his rebounding slumped badly in 2004–05 and was among the worst at his position, which is shameful for a 6′ 10″ small forward.

The overall package remains enticing, especially when one considers Stojakovic's history playing with and without Webber. Over the past few seasons, he has been far more effective with Webber off the court, and the Kings need to hope that trend continues now that Webber is gone. The Kings badly need Stojakovic to recover to his 2003–04 levels if they hope to challenge Phoenix for the Pacific Division crown.

Kenny Thomas — power forward
(89% PF, 7% C, 4% SF) Age: 28 Height: 6-7 Weight: 245
Most similar at age: Jerome Kersey

Year		G	M/G	FG%	FT%	P/40	R/40	A/40	TS%		Ast		TO		Usg		Reb		PER	
2002-03	Hou-Phi	66	30.0	.465	.746	13.5	10.7	2.3	51.7	34	12.8	22	13.3	48	16.2	37	15.6	17	14.94	28
2003-04	Phi	74	36.5	.469	.752	14.9	11.1	1.6	52.7	27	9.0	52	13.9	59	17.1	36	16.4	13	15.94	25
2004-05	Phi-Sac	73	29.7	.470	.762	16.8	9.9	2.8	51.5	41	13.1	12	11.3	36	19.2	20	13.8	30	15.18	33
2005-06	PRJ (65.0)			.477	.750	15.2	10.2	2.4	53.0		12.5		12.6		17.7		14.5		15.59	

The best of the three players Sacramento acquired in the Webber trade, Thomas was a good fit for the Kings' system since he loves to play from the elbows. That's where Sacramento's big men usually catch the ball to initiate the offense, and Thomas is a threat to score from there with either the shot or the drive. As an added bonus, playing further out reduces Thomas's pronounced tendency to pick up three-second violations.

As far as "big men" go, Thomas is pretty small. He's only 6′7″, but makes up for his lack of height with a combination of strength, toughness, and versatility. He is able to score in the post despite giving up inches, and likes to use a rocker step move from the elbow that allows him to out-maneuver opposing big men. He's also a decent mid-range shooter, even though his shot is a bit flat.

Defensively, Thomas is strong enough to be a decent post defender and do a solid job on the boards, and quick enough to switch on pick-and-rolls and do a decent job staying in front of smaller players. However, Thomas's size exacerbates a problem up and down the roster. Thomas, Skinner, and Williamson all are at least two inches shorter than average for their position, and Miller and Abdur-Rahim aren't behemoths either. That's the reason the Kings were so easily bullied in the paint, and figures to be a problem again in the coming season.

Overall, Thomas is a solid player, but he's better suited to a bench role. Abdur-Rahim's arrival assures that's exactly where he's headed, at least if the Kings don't trade him first.

Corliss Williamson — small forward
(84% PF, 16% SF) Age: 32 Height: 6-7 Weight: 245
Most similar at age: Juwan Howard

Year		G	M/G	FG%	FT%	P/40	R/40	A/40	TS%		Ast		TO		Usg		Reb		PER	
2002-03	Det	82	25.1	.453	.790	19.2	6.9	2.0	51.5	32	8.8	55	10.6	25	22.5	11	10.3	12	15.71	17
2003-04	Det	79	19.9	.505	.731	19.1	6.5	1.4	54.6	12	6.6	58	13.2	54	20.4	20	8.8	26	14.38	28
2004-05	Phi-Sac	72	21.2	.467	.799	19.4	6.8	2.0	53.6	25	9.1	57	10.1	29	20.2	22	9.8	22	14.59	25
2005-06	PRJ (40.0)			.458	.766	17.5	6.3	1.8	51.9		8.4		11.1		19.7		8.8		13.48	

Williamson played the majority of his Sacramento minutes at small forward last season, which is why I listed him at that spot even though he saw more time at power forward overall. At either forward spot, Williamson is a strong scorer to bring in off the bench. He averaged over 19 points per 40 minutes for a fourth straight season thanks to a variety of post moves and drives from the high post. While he gets a huge number of his shots rejected because he's short for a post player, Williamson converts such a high percentage of the ones that slip through that he's one of the league's most productive sixth men.

However, Williamson can't start because he's a poor outside shooter and a defensive liability. The lack of shooting makes it tough to spot him minutes at small forward unless he's paired with a big man who can shoot, such as Songaila last season. Defensively, he's a step slow at small forward and his lack of height makes him an easy target at power forward. While Williamson is strong enough to root opponents out of prime real estate, he can do almost nothing once his opponent catches the ball.

Of the contracts the Kings picked up in the Webber trade, Williamson's is the most tradable, so it will be interesting to see whether the Kings can convert him into a more usable asset. On another club, Williamson's ability to score off the bench would be coveted, but Sacramento already has plenty of scorers and really needs some big men who can defend. At some point this year, a swap would seem to be in the offing.

Francisco Garcia — shooting guard
Age: 24 Height: 6-7 Weight: 190

Garcia was the oldest player picked in this year's draft, so his college numbers should be taken with a grain of salt. However, unlike recent "old men" who were busts—think Dan Dickau and Rafael Araujo—Garcia has a number of items in his favor. He handles the ball well for his size, is a decent shooter, and is an active defender with long arms. That's about as well as the Kings could hope to do with the 23rd pick.

San Antonio Spurs

Watch a nationally televised NBA game during the course of the season and you're likely to see one of three teams: The Lakers, the Cavaliers, or the Heat. Fast forward to June, and you're likely to see the Spurs.

Despite the team's inability to click with Madison Avenue, San Antonio is unquestionably the league's premier franchise. After winning its third crown in seven years while the Lakers spontaneously combusted, that title is no longer in doubt. In fact, San Antonio has the best winning percentage in major sports over the past eight seasons. And while the league might have been disappointed to see a one-horse town like San Antonio in the Finals, they'd better get used to it. With incredible depth, great coaching, and a superstar centerpiece, the Spurs could add several more crowns to their stockpile before the end of the Tim Duncan era.

The Spurs won 59 games and scraped by Detroit in seven games in the Finals, so most fans think of them as a decent but hardly dominant champion. In actuality, the Spurs were a much stronger team than people realize. San Antonio's victory margin of +7.8 points per game would normally produce 66 wins, not 59, and even that number is only as low as it is because Duncan missed 16 games with an ankle injury. Furthermore, San Antonio eviscerated a murderer's row of Western Conference playoff opponents before reaching the Finals. They won four of five against a Denver team that had lost only three games since the All-Star break, took care of a 52-win Seattle team in six, and then railroaded a 62-win Phoenix team in five. Not since the 1995–96 Rockets has a champion had to battle such a difficult postseason slate.

Once again, the defense led the way. San Antonio was No. 1 in Defensive Efficiency for the fourth time in five years and by a wide margin. The Spurs' mark of 95.8 points allowed per 100 possessions was nearly two points better than second-place Chicago and seven ahead of the league average. Table 1 shows that it was, in fact, the fourth-best defensive performance since the NBA began tracking turnovers in 1973–74—and it still fell short of what they had done a year earlier. The chart shows the top defenses of the past three decades by comparing their Defensive Efficiency against that season's league average. The Spurs now own three of the top five spots.

Spurs at a Glance

Record: 59–23, 1st place in Southwest Division

Offensive Efficiency: 104.9 (8th)

Defensive Efficiency: 95.8 (1st)

Pace Factor: 91.1 (23rd)

Top-Rated Player: Tim Duncan (PER 27.13, 2nd overall)

Head Coach: Gregg Popovich. His message shows no signs of growing stale.

Of course, stifling opponents is nothing new for the Spurs. In every one of the eight full seasons Popovich and Duncan have been together, San Antonio has finished in the top three in field-goal percentage defense. Last season they were second only to Chicago, with one of the keys being their shot-blocking. San Antonio blocked a higher proportion of opponents' shots than any team in basketball, rejecting 8.5 percent (see table 2). Duncan and Rasho Nesterovic provided most of the blocks, although Nazr Mohammed took over Rasho's role late in the year.

San Antonio's defensive strategy tied in beautifully with its skills. Knowing they had the two shot-blockers behind them, the Spurs could crowd opponents on the perimeter and force them to drive the ball to the basket. They did just that, as only 13.9 percent of their opponents' field-goal attempts came on three-pointers, another league-leading total. To put this in perspective, the league average was 19.6, so San Antonio shaved nearly a third off the league average. As table 3 shows, San Antonio was ahead of the competition by leaps and bounds.

Denying the three and blocking shots were the keys to San Antonio's defensive success, but this team was good at everything. Led by the quick hands of Manu Ginobili, San Antonio forced 15.8 turnovers per 100 opponent possessions, the fifth-best rate in the league. With Tim Duncan controlling the glass, San Antonio rebounded 73.6 percent of its opponents' misses for the NBA's third-best performance. The Spurs achieved all this without fouling, allowing a below-average rate of free throws per field-goal attempt.

Sum it all up and you have one of the best defensive performances in history, which provided the catalyst for a championship. Not that the offense was too shabby. Ginobili's development as a scoring option propelled the Spurs to their best offensive output in several years. Moreover, it allowed the Spurs to further diversify an attack that once consisted mainly of post plays for Tim Duncan. Now with both Ginobili and Tony Parker able to run high pick-and-rolls, the Spurs have three strong weapons.

Pulling the strings was Gregg Popovich, who has enjoyed an unusually long run of success for an NBA coach by striking

Table 1. All-Time Defensive Efficiency Leaders

Team	Year	Defensive Efficiency	League Average	Difference
San Antonio	2003–04	92.31	100.84	−8.53
New York	1992–93	96.77	105.07	−8.20
New York	1993–94	95.85	103.72	−7.83
San Antonio	2004–05	95.80	103.09	−7.29
San Antonio	1998–99	92.81	99.97	−7.16

Table 2. Blocked Shot Percentage, 2004–05 Leaders

Team	Blocks/ 100 FGA
San Antonio	8.5
Portland	8.0
Memphis	7.7
Detroit	7.7
Denver	7.4
League Average	**6.1**

Table 3. Fewest Three-Point Attempts Allowed, 2004–05

	Opp. Threes per 100 FGA
San Antonio	13.9
Indiana	17.1
Cleveland	17.4
Golden State	18.1
Toronto	18.2
League Average	**19.6**

the right balance between buddy and dictator. Few coaches command more respect from their players, and even after nine seasons he's able to demand intense defense with no complaints. With little fanfare, he's had the longest run of continued success with the same team this side of Jerry Sloan.

The defense is Popovich's trademark, but he also has a very unusual substitution strategy. Most coaches take the starters out once each half. In the first half, for instance, they will rest their starters either at the end of the first quarter or the beginning of the second, and then get them back into the game early to midway through the second quarter. Popovich did it differently, resting many of his starters twice each half. He didn't do it with everybody—Parker came out only once, and usually Duncan did too. But the other players rapidly shuttled in and out of the lineup.

For instance, Ginobili would come out at the seven-minute mark of the first quarter, come back later in the quarter when Duncan checked out, check back out in the middle of the second quarter, then return to finish the half. Bruce Bowen and Nazr Mohammed followed similar patterns. Popovich continued this approach in the playoffs, when most coaches are playing their starters 40 or 45 minutes a night. Even in Game 7 of the Finals, Ginobili played just 35 minutes.

The other aspect of Popovich's success that's so amazing is that he's also the team president. Few people have ever filled both jobs effectively, even those with star-studded resumes. Pat Riley, for instance, was a flop as a coach/president because he kept making short-term deals that sabotaged the team's longer-term interests. Yet Popovich's administration

has been remarkably long-sighted. They've studiously avoided bad contracts, drafted overseas players like Ginobili years before they were ready to play in the States, and haven't succumbed to making midseason panic trades. In fact, when they dealt Malik Rose and a first-round pick to the Knicks for Nazr Mohammed at the trade deadline last year, it was San Antonio's first midseason trade since Popovich took over.

Other than winning the lottery for Duncan, San Antonio's draft strategy of finding obscure foreign players has played the biggest part in its success. Parker and Beno Udrih were late first-round picks, while Ginobili was a late second-rounder. The Spurs own the rights to a stable of foreign players, many of whom are very young. Luis Scola, perhaps the best player in Europe, was a late second-round pick and could be a Spur in another year or two. San Antonio also owns the rights to big men Robertas Javtokas (Lithuania), Viktor Sanikidze (Georgia), Sergei Karaulov (Russia), and Ian Mahinmi (France), making them a virtual basketball U.N. All of them are developing overseas on somebody else's dime.

Their ability to find players isn't limited to the draft. In recent years the Spurs picked players like Stephen Jackson, Devin Brown, and Malik Rose off the scrap heap. That nose for inexpensive talent is why the Spurs are champions and the Timberwolves were in the lottery. Both have great power forwards, but San Antonio has found so much other talent that the Spurs are 20–18 in Duncan's career when he *doesn't* play—roughly matching how Minnesota fared with Garnett in the lineup for 82 games last season.

For this season, San Antonio's big find is Argentine big man Fabricio Oberto, who projects to give them a decent offensive big man off the bench to pair with Robert Horry. Oberto used up much of San Antonio's midlevel exception, so the Spurs' other moves will be low-level free agents signing for the minimum.

The Spurs don't need much help though. Parker and Udrih are a dynamic point guard combo, and both are quite young and getting better. Ginobili has established himself as one of the league's most entertaining and dynamic players, while Brent Barry should bounce back from a disappointing year shooting. Bruce Bowen is among the very best defensive players in the game, and Mohammed, Nesterovic, Oberto, and Horry make a nice frontcourt even in Duncan's absence.

With Popovich demanding excellence and the Spurs consistently delivering it, they're a tough team to bet against. From top to bottom, this may be the best-run organization in sports. As a result, the NBA better get used to promoting Tim and Manu and Tony along with Kobe, Shaq, and LeBron. Whether they like it or not, the Spurs are going to be on the tube again this June and probably for several Junes after that.

Brent Barry (96% SG, 4% SF)			shooting guard											Age: 34	Height: 6-7	Weight: 210 Most similar at age: Jon Barry
Year	G	M/G	FG%	FT%	P/40	R/40	A/40	TS%		Ast		TO		Usg		Reb	PER
2002-03 Sea	75	33.1	.458	.795	12.5	4.9	6.2	59.7	3	32.7	1	12.0	44	18.0	39	7.1 25	15.86 19
2003-04 Sea*	59	30.6	.504	.827	14.1	4.5	7.6	66.8	1	35.8	9	14.5	54	19.1	47	6.7 13	18.28 11
2004-05 SA	81	21.5	.423	.837	13.8	4.4	4.1	58.0	8	19.5	14	8.4	12	16.9	46	6.4 38	14.01 27
2005-06 PRJ (25.0)			.440	.819	12.9	4.5	5.5	59.0		26.8		11.0		17.3		6.6	14.96

* Season rankings are as point guard

It was an off year for him, but Barry provided outside shooting that the Spurs needed. His TS% was among the best in history in his final season in Seattle but sank to less exalted levels with the Spurs. Barry hit 35.7 percent of his three-pointers, the first time in six years he was below 40 percent, and his overall shooting mark slipped to 42.3 percent. Barry's phenomenal Assist Ratio also sank to more normal levels, as he wasn't asked to create as much offense as he had in Seattle. On a positive note, his Turnover Ratio dropped substantially since he rarely had to dribble.

Barry is a liability on defense, but he's a smart player who mastered how to send opponents toward help defenders. A good example came in the Finals, when Detroit had trouble exploiting a mismatch with Barry guarding Tayshaun Prince, because Barry would front Prince. That forced Detroit to throw a pass that led Prince directly into Tim Duncan, and the Pistons were reluctant to try that.

The smarts and good height for his position have enabled Barry to cope with a lack of strength and declining lateral quickness. As long as he can hold his own at the defensive end, Barry should give San Antonio plenty of value over the final three years of his contract, because he is likely to have a much better year shooting the ball.

Bruce Bowen Defensive PER: 1.74 (91% SF, 7% PF,2% SG)			small forward											Age: 34	Height: 6-7	Weight: 200 Most similar at age: Tyrone Corbin
Year	G	M/G	FG%	FT%	P/40	R/40	A/40	TS%		Ast		TO		Usg		Reb	PER
2002-03 SA*	72	34.0	.466	.404	9.1	3.7	1.8	56.3	12	16.1	29	10.2	29	10.3	57	5.4 49	9.07 52
2003-04 SA*	82	32.0	.420	.579	8.6	3.9	1.7	51.2	27	15.0	37	11.9	49	10.7	62	5.4 51	8.17 61
2004-05 SA	82	32.0	.420	.634	10.3	4.3	1.9	52.1	37	9.1	56	6.9	3	12.3	62	6.3 59	9.53 56
2005-06 PRJ (26.4)			.412	.588	9.3	4.0	1.9	51.2		12.0		9.9		11.4		5.6	8.49

* Season rankings are as shooting guard

One of the game's top defenders, Bowen nearly won the Defensive Player of the Year trophy last season and is an annual member of the All-Defense team. Bowen is at his best against players who like to score off the dribble, as his quick feet, long arms, and dogged determination present a frustrating combination. Bowen isn't as effective against post players, but he's quick enough to defend point guards. In San Antonio's two key wins in the Finals in Games 5 and 7, Bowen's defensive stops on Detroit point guard Chauncey Billups provided the difference. Bowen also is a good help defender and can distract opponents when he plays at the top of a zone.

His play has earned Bowen a reputation as a cheap player, with both Ray Allen and Vince Carter calling him out during the season. Bowen has a tendency to step under players as they go up for a jump shot, causing them to land awkwardly, and that's what drew Carter's ire. But when one considers he's been playing for nearly a decade and has guarded the opposing team's best scorer for most of it, Bowen has gotten into relatively few kerfuffles.

Offensively, the only thing Bowen can do is hit three-pointers from the corner. Fortunately, he knows this, and that's what keeps his Turnover Ratio so low. Bowen shot 40.3 percent on threes but is an absolutely terrible shooter off the dribble and has trouble finishing around the basket. He's also a poor foul shooter and a surprisingly bad rebounder.

That's why Bowen's PER is poor. Nevertheless, his skills as a defensive stopper are valuable to the Spurs. Yet one wonders if San Antonio wouldn't be better with Ginobili playing the stopper role, as he did at times in the playoffs, and Barry starting alongside him. We won't find out anytime soon, because the Spurs hardly need to shuffle the deck right now.

Devin Brown shooting guard Age: 27 Height: 6-5 Weight: 220
(59% SG, 39% SF, 2% PF) Most similar at age: Bryant Stith

Year		G	M/G	FG%	FT%	P/40	R/40	A/40	TS%		Ast		TO		Usg		Reb		PER	
2002-03	SA	12	4.6	.500	1.000	21.8	12.7	3.6	55.1		11.2		28.0		26.7		18.4		13.70	
2003-04	SA*	58	10.8	.434	.811	14.9	8.3	2.1	51.2	32	11.0	41	12.7	50	17.7	32	11.7	8	13.10	35
2004-05	SA	67	18.5	.423	.792	16.0	5.7	3.0	53.0	27	14.2	36	8.7	15	19.0	35	8.3	13	14.57	24
2005-06	PRJ (89.2)			.416	.796	15.4	6.0	2.7	51.9		13.2		9.9		18.5		8.6		13.92	

* Season rankings are as small forward

Brown and Bryant Stith had one of the highest similarity Scores at 99.7. Both were chunky 6′5″ guys who rebound well for their size, scored inside or out, but shot a low percentage. Brown hasn't played a lot of minutes, but he's been an underrated sub in his three years in San Antonio because he defends well, plays two positions, and can hit an open shot.

One would think that would create free-agent demand for him, but it doesn't appear to be in the cards. Brown had back trouble toward the end of last season and a lot of teams shied away from him because of it. He hadn't signed with anyone at publication time, but I would expect him to re-sign with San Antonio by the time camp opens. If that's the case and the back is OK, he'll continue to provide one of the league's best deep reserves, as well as one of the least expensive.

Tim Duncan power forward Age: 29 Height: 6-11 Weight: 260
Defensive PER: 3.08 (52% PF, 48% C) Most similar at age: Patrick Ewing

Year		G	M/G	FG%	FT%	P/40	R/40	A/40	TS%		Ast		TO		Usg		Reb		PER	
2002-03	SA	80	33.9	.513	.710	23.7	13.1	4.0	56.4	8	14.1	16	11.1	30	26.3	4	19.0	3	26.94	1
2003-04	SA	69	36.6	.501	.599	24.4	13.6	3.4	53.4	21	11.6	35	10.0	12	27.5	3	19.0	2	27.03	2
2004-05	SA	66	33.4	.496	.670	24.4	13.3	3.3	54.0	27	11.6	18	8.2	11	27.2	4	19.4	3	27.13	2
2005-06	PRJ (13.1)			.500	.660	23.4	13.2	3.3	53.7		11.7		9.5		26.0		18.3		25.12	

As I mentioned in the Ben Wallace comment, I can understand how Wallace won the Defensive Player of the Year award because he played substantially more minutes than Duncan did. What I don't get is all the other years. The coaches have voted Duncan first-team All-Defense six of the eight seasons he's been in the league, but the writers have this giant blind spot toward him when it comes to Defensive Player of the Year voting. Last season, for instance, Duncan got only six votes for the award and finished fourth in the voting. Marcus Camby, who played fewer minutes and was less effective when he played, got 19. Huh?

The past two years Duncan has been the linchpin of two of the best defensive teams in history, and yet he has never won the Defensive Player of the Year trophy. He wasn't even the highest-finishing Spur, as his teammate Bowen beat him in the voting for two straight seasons. I realize Duncan isn't as spectacular as some other players and doesn't come flying in from left field to swat shots into the 12th row, but is that really our criteria? If the writers are covering teams for 82 games they should be able to see beyond this. The guy is a one-man roadblock.

What people fail to understand about Duncan is how hard it is to combine dominant shot-blocking with dominant rebounding. Most players who block shots do so in part by leaving the defensive boards exposed. If a player leaves his man to go for a block and jumps as high as he can to get it, his man has an open path to the basket. Thus, if the player fails to block the shot, his man can easily get an offensive rebound and score. Duncan almost never gets out of position like this. He blocks some shots without jumping at all and on others he uses his long arms and timing to deflect the shot with just a quick hop. As a result, he never leaves the offensive boards exposed even as he's blocking shots at a prodigious rate. Last season Duncan blocked 3.1 shots per 40 minutes while posting the third-best Rebound Rate at his position, both of which were better rates than Wallace's.

Duncan had the league's best Defensive PER by far, and his numbers the year before were just as dominant. Over the past two seasons, the Spurs gave up 7.3 points more per 48 minutes when Duncan left the court. The same numbers for Bowen, Wallace, and Artest are 3.0, 3.3, and 4.6 respectively. No disrespect to those three, but Duncan is clearly the best defensive player in the game. Maybe some day the writers will notice.

Offensively, he's no slouch either. His trademark bank shot from the left block is the centerpiece of a diverse post game. Duncan has markedly cut his Turnover Ratio the past two seasons, but he needs to develop more moves going to his left and it would be nice if he'd learn how to shoot a lefty lay-up. Otherwise, the only noteworthy accomplishment is Duncan's incredible consistency. His past three seasons are virtual carbon copies, and it seems he can keep producing them ad infinitum.

San Antonio Spurs

Manu Ginobili — shooting guard · Age: 28 Height: 6-6 Weight: 205
Defensive PER: 2.71 (59% SG, 39% SF, 2% PF) · Most similar at age: Eddie Jones

Year		G	M/G	FG%	FT%	P/40	R/40	A/40	TS%		Ast		TO		Usg		Reb		PER	
2002-03	SA	59	28.4	.438	.737	14.7	4.5	3.9	55.6	13	19.4	17	14.1	54	18.2	38	6.5	36	14.68	25
2003-04	SA	77	29.4	.418	.802	17.5	6.1	5.2	53.6	13	21.2	13	11.7	47	22.7	17	8.5	11	18.48	6
2004-05	SA	74	29.6	.471	.803	21.6	6.0	5.3	60.9	4	20.1	12	12.0	53	24.6	10	8.8	8	22.32	3
2005-06	PRJ (32.3)			.447	.794	19.4	6.1	5.1	58.1		20.6		12.2		23.4		8.6		19.93	

Ginobili is one of the league's most daring offensive players, which has quickly earned him a following among fans. He will throw passes to guys who don't even know they're open, specializing in cross-court bounce passes. He's perfected a play with Tony Parker where Parker throws it to him just over crosscourt and then cuts down the lane like he's about to set a pick. If Parker's defender turns his back, which happened about once a game, Ginobili would fire a laser beam on the bounce for a Parker lay-up. Ginobili has the same approach off the dribble, going behind his back frequently and changing directions at knee-breaking angles on drives to the basket.

His daredevil style makes him turnover-prone, but it's also made him incredibly difficult to stop—even though defenders know he goes left every time. With the rules against hand-checking giving an advantage to quicker players, Ginobili had free rein to go to the basket and took advantage. His free-throw rate ballooned more than 50 percent even though his field-goal attempts were basically unchanged. As a result, his TS% shot up to the top four at his position and his 40-minute scoring average increased by over four points. Ginobili also has become a steady outside shooter, hitting 37.6 percent, and few guards are better rebounders.

As an added plus, Ginobili is an outstanding defensive player. He has incredibly quick hands and during the Finals he arguably did a better job on Richard Hamilton than Bruce Bowen did. The Spurs don't employ him as a defensive stopper, but he could easily fill the role if needed.

When Ginobili signed a six-year, $52 million deal to stay with the Spurs a year ago, some worried that San Antonio had overpaid. Now it appears that Manu is the one who got the short end. With the rules shifting to suit his audacious style, he's become one of the best guards in basketball.

Dion Glover — shooting guard · Age: 27 Height: 6-5 Weight: 225
(58% SG, 42% SF) · Most similar at age: N/A

Year		G	M/G	FG%	FT%	P/40	R/40	A/40	TS%		Ast		TO		Usg		Reb		PER	
2002-03	Atl	76	24.9	.427	.784	15.6	6.0	3.0	51.2	28	14.6	36	11.2	36	19.0	35	8.5	9	13.56	30
2003-04	Atl-Tor	69	23.8	.390	.769	15.1	6.5	3.2	47.1	53	14.6	40	11.5	43	20.0	34	9.3	7	12.14	38
2004-05	SA	7	9.7	.364	.800	14.7	6.5	2.4	47.3		11.2		6.2		18.7		9.0		13.96	

Glover spent much of the year playing in Turkey, and if the Euroleague gave out a "Most Disappointing Player" award, he would have won it hands down. He became the first player to do worse in the Euroleague than in his previous season in the NBA since I began tracking those who made the jump. The Spurs picked him up on a 10-day contract late in the season and Glover fared a bit better offensively, but his defensive inattention fit poorly with Popovich's demanding style. He'll be scavenging for another contract this season, but he has the talent to help a team off the bench. Of course, he'll have to pick up the defense before suitors get serious.

Robert Horry — power forward · Age: 35 Height: 6-10 Weight: 240
(90% PF, 10% C) · Most similar at age: Lionel Simmons

Year		G	M/G	FG%	FT%	P/40	R/40	A/40	TS%		Ast		TO		Usg		Reb		PER	
2002-03	LAL	80	29.3	.387	.769	8.9	8.8	4.0	48.8	45	26.5	3	12.7	45	13.5	49	12.3	40	12.38	43
2003-04	SA	81	15.9	.405	.645	12.2	8.4	3.1	49.6	46	18.3	10	10.0	13	16.2	39	11.8	50	14.50	39
2004-05	SA	75	18.6	.419	.789	12.9	7.7	2.3	53.3	31	10.9	24	12.1	41	15.4	48	11.2	54	14.89	37
2005-06	PRJ (32.3)			.400	.729	11.1	8.1	2.9	51.4		17.5		12.3		14.5		11.2		13.14	

(continued next page)

Robert Horry (*continued*)

A small chorus of people think Horry's playoff heroics are overblown since his career playoff stats (11.7 points per 40 minutes, 43.2 FG%) are almost exactly the same as his regular season stats (11.6, 43.1) Don't believe them. Here's the thing about the playoffs: Nearly everybody's stats go down because of the increase in competition, with the average drop being seven percent. Somebody who can maintain his averages or increase them slightly isn't just treading water—he is significantly dialing up his play. Seen in that light, Horry's playoff numbers are easier to square with his many memorable shots. That said, he's a pretty ordinary player most of the time. He's just happened to be on teams with dominant big men for virtually his entire career, and to his credit he's taken advantage of his chances to take big shots.

Horry hit 37.0 percent on three-pointers and rediscovered his stroke at the free-throw line. Hence, his TS% was decent despite a low field-goal percentage. Horry also defended well at the power forward spot, especially when he didn't have to deal with wide-bodied post players and surprisingly blocked over two shots per 40 minutes.

Horry isn't as effective on offense, at least until June rolls around. He has no post game and can't create his own offense. He's also a poor rebounder, and since he's no spring chicken, one has to worry about how long he can keep producing at this level. But after what he did last spring, the Spurs aren't in any hurry to unload him. Horry re-signed with San Antonio as a free agent and will again serve as the Spurs' top frontcourt reserve.

Linton Johnson — small forward — Age: 25 — Height: 6-8 — Weight: 225
(53% SF, 40% PF, 7% SG) — Most similar at age: N/A

Year		G	M/G	FG%	FT%	P/40	R/40	A/40	TS%		Ast		TO		Usg		Reb		PER	
2003-04	Chi	41	18.0	.355	.595	9.4	9.9	1.5	39.4	59	9.5	50	13.1	53	13.7	52	14.2	1	9.60	51
2004-05	SA	2	7.5	.000	—	0.0	8.0	0.0	0.0		0.0		33.3		6.4		11.2		-3.45	

The Spurs brought Johnson in on a one-year contract but he spent nearly the entire season nursing an ankle injury. He's an athletic forward who rebounds very well but is severely limited offensively. San Antonio may try to sign him again this season and see if he can become a defensive stopper, but the Spurs' roster already is looking crowded.

Sean Marks — center — Age: 30 — Height: 7-0 — Weight: 245
(58% C, 42% PF) — Most similar at age: N/A

Year		G	M/G	FG%	FT%	P/40	R/40	A/40	TS%	Ast	TO	Usg	Reb	PER
2002-03	Mia	23	9.7	.373	.667	9.7	6.3	0.5	41.2	3.6	16.9	13.6	9.1	3.71
2003-04	SA	Did not play												
2004-05	SA	23	10.6	.338	.786	12.5	9.2	1.3	41.2	6.2	12.2	17.6	12.8	8.63

Why is Marks in the league? At first I thought it was a ploy by the Spurs to have every continent represented on their roster, but really, does New Zealand count as anything? Marks can hit a mid-range jumper, but the Kiwi from Cal is severely lacking in the muscle department and has never played well in his many NBA stops.

Tony Massenburg — center — Age: 38 — Height: 6-9 — Weight: 250
(61% C, 39% PF) — Most similar at age: Kevin Willis

Year		G	M/G	FG%	FT%	P/40	R/40	A/40	TS%		Ast		TO		Usg		Reb		PER	
2002-03	Uta	58	13.7	.448	.774	13.8	7.9	0.9	50.8	39	5.1	68	14.9	51	15.6	34	11.9	61	9.19	66
2003-04	Sac	59	13.4	.475	.683	12.7	9.5	1.5	50.9	42	9.0	35	14.0	49	14.3	37	14.2	37	9.64	68
2004-05	SA	61	11.5	.407	.762	11.2	9.3	0.8	46.7	61	3.8	57	15.2	47	13.9	37	13.0	51	8.44	66
2005-06	*PRJ (10.6)*			*.411*	*.734*	*11.1*	*8.3*	*1.0*	*45.8*		*6.0*		*15.4*		*13.2*		*11.8*		*8.20*	

During the first decade of his career, Massenburg played on more bad teams than perhaps any player in history. So it's only fair that he got a championship ring in what might have been his last season. Massenburg is incredibly strong and can handle playing much bigger centers in the post. But his lack of height and leaping ability inhibits his rebounding, and he can't make shots. That hasn't stopped him from trying, which is another problem—he might be better off taking fewer shots and shooting a higher percentage instead of trying to score every time he catches the ball in the post. He's a hard-working player so he could land on the end of a bench again this season, but at 38 with a shiny, new ring, it might be a nice time to bow out.

Nazr Mohammed (98% C, 2% PF)			center					Age: 28	Height: 6-10	Weight: 250 Most similar at age: LaSalle Thompson			
Year	G	M/G	FG%	FT%	P/40	R/40	A/40	TS%	Ast	TO	Usg	Reb	PER
2002-03 Atl	35	12.8	.421	.634	14.3	11.5	0.5	45.2	2.9	12.0	17.1	16.4	12.31
2003-04 Atl-NY	80	20.1	.521	.592	14.7	11.8	0.9	54.2 18	5.3 67	14.2 50	15.2 30	16.8 8	16.15 17
2004-05 NY-SA	77	25.1	.480	.674	15.1	12.1	0.7	52.1 37	3.4 62	12.8 29	16.1 23	17.7 12	16.42 16
2005-06 PRJ (45.9)			.497	.625	14.5	12.0	0.9	52.7	4.5	12.8	15.5	17.1	16.61

Just a guess, but I'd say he's the best player ever whose first name ended in "zr." The "Spuzrs" acquired Mohammed from the Knicks at midseason after he had delivered a surprisingly potent offensive attack for New York. He wasn't quite as effective offensively in San Antonio, probably because he was over his head to begin with, but he gave San Antonio the rebounding and shot-making that Nesterovic couldn't.

Mohammed is a smart player who has a nose for the ball on the glass, resulting in one of the best Rebound Rates among centers. He's an outstanding help defender too. Mohammed doesn't block as many shots as Duncan or Rasho—although he blocked shots at an uncharacteristically high rate in his 23 games as a Spurs—but he can use his body to root out post players and will take charges.

Offensively, Mohammed has an ugly hitch in his jump shot and shoots mostly line drives, but he has become reasonably accurate with it from inside 12 feet. That and the offensive rebounds allow him to subsist as an offensive player despite having a limited post game and terrible hands. Overall, he's an upgrade from Nesterovic, and the Spurs probably wouldn't have won the title without him.

Rasho Nesterovic (100% C)			center					Age: 29	Height: 7-0	Weight: 270 Most similar at age: Andrew Lang			
Year	G	M/G	FG%	FT%	P/40	R/40	A/40	TS%	Ast	TO	Usg	Reb	PER
2002-03 Min	77	30.4	.525	.642	14.7	8.6	2.0	53.6 28	11.2 25	9.7 6	16.1 27	12.2 58	14.74 29
2003-04 SA	82	28.7	.469	.474	12.1	10.8	1.9	47.3 61	11.7 18	11.0 17	15.5 28	15.0 27	15.27 22
2004-05 SA	70	25.5	.460	.467	9.2	10.3	1.6	46.3 64	7.6 26	12.4 21	12.3 49	15.0 30	12.00 43
2005-06 PRJ (30.6)			.476	.515	11.0	9.9	1.8	48.6	9.3	11.5	13.9	14.2	13.43

Nesterovic went to the bench late in the season when the Spurs could no longer live with his lack of offensive production. Nesterovic is a good defensive player who has wide shoulders and excellent timing on blocks, making him an imposing obstacle in the middle. He also does a decent job on the boards.

Offensively, he's become increasingly useless. Nesterovic's 46.0 percent shooting doesn't look so bad until you realize he took 30 foul shots the entire season, a pathetic total for an alleged center. He probably wasn't anxious to shoot more, as he shot under 50 percent for a second straight season with his awkward, one-handed free-throw routine. Nesterovic is decent at playing the high-low game with Duncan and can hit a jump shot from the foul line if left open, but his overall contribution is minimal.

For those reasons, he'll shift to a reserve role this season. The arrival of Oberto means Nesterovic may be headed for a string of DNPs unless somebody gets injured, which isn't what the Spurs were hoping for when they gave him $42 million two years ago. The Spurs are shopping him to anyone who will listen, but chances are they'll be stuck with this contract for a while.

Tony Parker point guard **Age: 23 Height: 6-2 Weight: 180**
Defensive PER: 1.71 (98% PG, 2% SG) Most similar at age: B. J. Armstrong

Year		G	M/G	FG%	FT%	P/40	R/40	A/40	TS%		Ast		TO		Usg		Reb		PER	
2002-03	SA	67	39.1	.464	.755	18.3	3.1	6.2	54.2	16	24.0	47	11.0	29	24.3	14	4.5	54	16.46	17
2003-04	SA	75	34.4	.447	.702	17.1	3.7	6.4	51.6	21	24.8	47	10.8	27	24.1	15	5.1	39	15.60	23
2004-05	SA	80	34.2	.482	.650	19.5	4.4	7.2	52.8	25	25.0	47	10.9	34	27.3	9	6.4	17	17.97	15
2005-06	PRJ (27.1)			.449	.752	18.5	3.1	5.7	53.4		22.0		10.0		24.2		4.4		16.22	

Parker signed a six-year, $66 million extension before last season that seems a lot less overvalued after his strong 2004–05 campaign. Parker boosted his 40-minute scoring rate to 19.5 points per 40 minutes and became a much heavier participant in the offense, boosting his Usage Rate to the 9th-best among point guards. Parker still has a long way to go as a shooter, converting only 27.6 percent on three-pointers, but he's so quick that he has no trouble getting into the paint for shots. When he drives, Parker has one of the best floaters in basketball and his release is so quick that big men rarely get a piece of it.

Defensively, Parker has become much better. He has quick feet and has developed his upper body to the point that he's no longer easy pickings for opposing guards in the post. Overall, his Defensive PER was among the best at his position, a marked improvement from where he was just two years ago. He also made progress as a rebounder.

Parker continues to struggle with game-to-game consistency and his turnovers tend to come in bunches, which sours some people on his overall contribution. The Spurs would like to see him drive and dish more often and improve the jumper, but they'll gladly take six more years of this.

Glenn Robinson small forward **Age: 32 Height: 6-7 Weight: 240**
(77% SF, 21% PF, 2% SG) Most similar at age: N/A

Year		G	M/G	FG%	FT%	P/40	R/40	A/40	TS%		Ast		TO		Usg		Reb		PER	
2002-03	Atl	69	37.6	.432	.876	22.2	7.1	3.2	51.9	29	11.2	47	13.5	46	25.8	6	10.0	16	16.73	13
2003-04	Phi	42	31.9	.448	.832	20.9	5.7	1.7	51.8	27	6.8	57	12.7	49	23.5	9	8.0	40	15.00	25
2004-05	SA	9	17.4	.442	.870	22.9	6.1	2.0	51.7		7.8		6.9		25.4		8.5		17.10	

The Big Dog signed with San Antonio late in the year after he spent most of it on Philadelphia's injured list under dubious circumstances. Robinson lost his starting job to Kyle Korver before the season and then wasn't seen again, only resurfacing when he was traded to New Orleans and waived by the Hornets. At that point the Spurs picked him up for some scoring off the bench, but he struggled with his shot during the playoffs.

Robinson is a free agent and will attract interest from contending teams looking to get a scorer with their cap exception. Although he's unlikely to return to the Spurs, his time in San Antonio should help. He played as hard on defense as he has his entire career and had a good 40-minute scoring rate, which had to pique other teams' interest.

Beno Udrih point guard **Age: 23 Height: 6-3 Weight: 205**
(100% PG) Most similar at age: Luke Ridnour

Year		G	M/G	FG%	FT%	P/40	R/40	A/40	TS%		Ast		TO		Usg		Reb		PER	
2004-05	SA	80	14.4	.444	.753	16.4	2.9	5.2	54.9	11	22.9	54	11.7	42	21.5	37	4.2	57	14.24	37
2005-06	PRJ (37.1)			.431	.772	17.2	3.0	4.9	53.0		21.0		10.6		22.3		4.3		14.48	

San Antonio's first-round pick in 2004 stepped into the rotation immediately and played much better than expected, at least until Detroit's pressure defense turned him into a crazed turnover machine in the Finals. Udrih is a scorer more than a passer, even more so than Parker in that regard. He's a good outside shooter who hit 40.9 percent of his three-pointers and his size and quick release allow him to hit shots while defended. The lefty doesn't have the extra gear to get to the basket, however, and rarely breaks down defenses off the dribble.

Udrih was solid if unspectacular at the defensive end, but considering his size he was a surprisingly poor rebounder. For his sophomore campaign, he'll have to hone his point-guard skills and improve his penetration ability. He's a good backup right now, but if he's ever going to be a starter, he has to be more than a shooting specialist.

Mike Wilks (52% SG, 48% PG)			point guard								Age: 26		Height: 5-11	Weight: 180 Most similar at age: N/A	
Year		G	M/G	FG%	FT%	P/40	R/40	A/40	TS%		Ast		TO	Usg	Reb	PER
2002-03	Atl-Min	46	15.0	.338	.787	8.5	4.1	5.3	43.6	59	31.9	12	9.7 15	15.6 61	5.9 25	9.25 58
2003-04	Hou	26	5.6	.472	.833	13.8	4.4	4.7	60.6		26.0		10.7	17.2	6.4	14.36
2004-05	SA	48	5.8	.416	.750	11.7	3.6	4.8	48.2		22.7		10.7	18.0	5.0	11.01

A steady third-string point guard who rarely shoots but turns it over even less, Wilks is classic end-of-the-bench material and might be back in the same role this year. Although he's undersized, Wilks's ability to pressure the ball upcourt is an additional asset, and he can hit an open jump shot.

Ian Mahinmi	power forward	Age: 19 Height: 6-10 Weight: 230

The Spurs are known for finding sleepers late in the draft, but this one is a stretch even by their standards. Mahinmi is a backup in the French League, which is considerably weaker than the ones in Italy or Spain, and while his athleticism drew strong reviews, his rates of rebounds and blocks aren't exceptional. The Spurs will leave him in France for a couple more years and hope they have a Ginobili or Scola by the end of it.

Seattle SuperSonics

B elievers in the contract-year theory won't find a better laboratory than the 2004–05 Seattle Sonics. With seven key players, the coach, and the general manager all on the last year of their contracts, Seattle faced the prospect of nearly every important person in the franchise scattering to the four corners of the globe after the season.

One might think that lack of continuity might not be conducive to a winning environment. That's especially true when one considers the Sonics had won only 37 games the year before and had done little in the offseason to suggest they'd be an improved team.

But improved they were. The Sonics stunned the league by racing out to a 17–3 start en route to 52 wins and the Northwest Division championship. They even took eventual champ San Antonio to six tough games in the playoffs before falling short in the second round.

Many aspects of Seattle's season were amazing, and we'll get to all of them in a minute. The most impressive was the Sonics' ability to win with a lame-duck coach. It's accepted as a truism in the profession that a coach with less than a year left on his contract is a dead man walking and thus can't command his players' respect. Seattle seemed to be the perfect example of this before the season, as the Sonics wouldn't extend head coach Nate McMillan's deal and it seemed his fourth year would be his final one at the helm of the Sonics.

It turns out the latter was true, but not before McMillan won the division and nearly took Coach of the Year honors for his performance. After the year the tables were turned, and it was McMillan who dumped the Sonics rather than the other way around. He accepted a substantial offer from Portland while Seattle settled on long-time assistant Bob Weiss to take over.

McMillan achieved his success with relatively few tweaks to the previous season's formula. He inserted Luke Ridnour as his starting point guard in place of the departed Brent Barry and welcomed second-year forward Nick Collison to the lineup after he'd missed his entire first year with a shoulder injury. As a whole the Sonics were largely the same team that took the floor in 2003–04. They could shoot the lights out but were soft defensively and lacked a superstar.

The one major difference was that the Sonics were much more physical in 2004–05. The addition of Danny Fortson in a trade with Dallas, the return of Collison, and the use of Reggie Evans as the starting power forward combined to make the Sonics much tougher than a year before. The rest of the Sonics weren't any meaner, but the foursome of Fortson, Collison, Evans, and James fouled like mad and rebounded in bunches. Fortson had the league's highest foul rate by a mile, and with James and Collison he gave the Sonics three of the league's top six foulers (see table 1). Oddly, the Sonics didn't have an unusual rate of fouls overall. They just had four players in charge of enforcement to allow the others to roam the perimeter.

Similarly, the Sonics were beasts on the boards. Evans had the league's highest Rebound Rate while Fortson ranked fifth. Collison was well above average as well. Those three were especially effective on the offensive boards, adding another layer to the Sonics' already efficient offense. Seattle was the league's second-best offensive rebounding team in 2004–05, grabbing 32.4 percent of its missed shots. This strength complemented the Sonics' two other offensive skills—shooting threes and avoiding turnovers—because the two factors combined to create a lot of missed shots.

Because of those physical players, the Sonics slowed things down considerably from the year before. Though often misunderstood as a running team, Seattle played one of the league's slowest paces in 2004–05. That's very unusual for a high-caliber offensive team. Most great offensive teams have above-average Pace Factors because they can generate open shots so quickly, but Seattle's unique combination of three-point shooting and offensive rebounding made it much more potent in the halfcourt.

In fact, Seattle's field-goal percentage was below the league-average. It was the other things—the numerous three-pointers and offensive rebounds, the ability to avoid turnovers, and the high rate of free throws for a jump-shooting team—that made the Sonics such a devastating offensive team. The Sonics were a rarity as a result—they won 52

SuperSonics at a Glance

Record: 52–30, 1st place in Northwest Division

Offensive Efficiency: 108.1 (3rd)

Defensive Efficiency: 106.1 (25th)

Pace Factor: 90.8 (25th)

Top-Rated Player: Ray Allen (PER 20.90, 24th overall)

Head Coach: Bob Weiss. Long-time assistant takes over after Nate McMillan bolted for Portland.

Table 1. Fouls per 40 Minutes Leaders (Minimum 500 Minutes)

Player	Team	PF/40 Min
Danny Fortson	Sea	10.1
Rafael Araujo	Tor	8.5
Jerome James	Sea	8.4
Curtis Borchardt	Uta	7.5
Al Jefferson	Bos	7.4
Nick Collison	Sea	7.3

games despite shooting a lower field-goal percentage than their opponents.

That brings us to the Sonics' weakness. Despite the improved toughness and rebounding, this was a bad defensive team. Seattle ranked 25th in Defensive Efficiency, with poor help defense being its undoing. The Sonics allowed the lowest rate of assisted baskets in the league, implying that they were getting beat off the dribble and the help defense was arriving too late to stop the shot attempt. Only 51.6 percent of Sonics' opponents' baskets were assisted, compared to the league average of 59.2 (see table 2). Extrapolating, one could say that the Sonics allowed about three baskets a game when they should have forced an extra pass instead. Seattle wasn't good at any aspect of defense except rebounding, but the high opponent field-goal percentage that resulted from unchallenged drives to the basket was what really killed them.

Nevertheless, it was a magical year for the Sonics. Their offense was so good that they could be well below average defensively and still cruise into the second round of the playoffs. That leads us to the obvious question: How many games would they win if this same crew came back and played some defense?

Unfortunately, we're unlikely to know the answer since free agency scattered so many Sonics far and wide. The franchise cornerstone, Allen, re-signed for a five-year, $80 million deal, but other losses were nearly important. Chief among them was guard Antonio Daniels, who fled for Washington. He was among the league's best sixth men last season, posting an 18.08 PER in 2,022 minutes off the bench, and replacing him with one of nearly the same quality will be extremely difficult. The Sonics signed Clipper castaway Rick

Table 2. Lowest Opponents' Assisted Baskets Rate, 2004–05

Team	Opp. Ast/FG
Seattle	.516
Orlando	.522
Dallas	.526
Washington	.527
Atlanta	.549
League Average	.592

Brunson to fill the backup point guard spot, but he won't provide half the offense Daniels did.

Radmanovic, Murray, and Evans also were unsigned as of publication time, though it appeared either Radmanovic or Evans would stick around to hold down the power forward spot. James also left after the Knicks made him a ridiculous contract offer, but based on his PER, replacing him with Collison will actually improve the team quite a bit. A more important loss might be reserve forward Damien Wilkins, who seemed primed to step into a more prominent role but had signed an offer sheet with Minnesota at publication time.

The draft probably won't provide immediate help either. The Sonics went all-French with their selections, taking big man Johan Petro and swingman Mickaël Gelabale. Petro figures to take over James's role as the resident project-center-who-occasionally-plays-hard, while Gelabale's best-case scenario is that he could fill Wilkins's role off the bench.

Additionally, financial constraints continue to limit the Sonics' ability to bring in talent. Seattle has perhaps the worst arena deal in the NBA. Not only is Key Arena more outdated than a Rubik's cube, the Sonics control relatively little of the revenue passing through. That makes it fairly difficult for the club to turn a profit unless the payroll is kept low and ancillary expenses on things like coaches and general managers are minimized. Thus, Seattle couldn't match Portland's offer for McMillan and happily settled for the low-cost Weiss as his successor. General manager Sund re-signed, but only after a protracted negotiation. The Sonics still are under the cap for the coming season but haven't been vigorously pursuing other free agents due to their financial constraints.

This at least has forced them to be more creative. Much like the Oakland A's were forced into their "Moneyball" strategy by a limited budget, the Sonics have been one of the league's foremost teams in using statistical analysis to try to further their chances. As I mentioned in the introduction, they employed a full-time analyst last season, and awareness of the power of this approach goes all the way up to team president Wally Walker. The only way they're going to stay on top of the Northwest Division is by implementing these tactics the way Billy Beane did in baseball—identifying inexpensive free agents, finding pockets of talent that the market is undervaluing, and taking calculated risks on the development of young players.

For now, however, those limitations seem serious enough to threaten Seattle's return to the postseason. The Plexiglass Principle says teams that improve sharply in one season tend to lose some of those gains a year later. In Seattle's case it's a hard theory to argue against. Between the free-agent departures, the club's limited ability to replace those players, and the likelihood that Allen will decline as he gets into his 30s, this year's Sonics look more like a .500 team than a division champ.

Ray Allen shooting guard Age: 30 Height: 6-5 Weight: 205
Defensive PER: 0.69 (75% SG, 25% SF) Most similar at age: Mitch Richmond

Year		G	M/G	FG%	FT%	P/40	R/40	A/40	TS%		Ast		TO		Usg		Reb		PER	
2002-03	Mil-Sea	76	37.9	.439	.916	23.8	5.3	4.6	56.5	9	16.3	27	9.7	24	27.1	8	7.8	16	21.34	4
2003-04	Sea	56	38.4	.440	.904	24.0	5.3	5.0	56.6	4	17.2	26	10.0	25	27.1	4	7.8	17	21.74	2
2004-05	Sea	78	39.3	.428	.883	24.3	4.5	3.8	55.5	16	13.5	39	8.0	11	27.2	4	6.9	29	20.90	5
2005-06	PRJ (39.9)			.427	.881	22.2	4.7	4.2	55.6		15.6		8.9		25.9		7.1		19.62	

One of 2004–05's most durable myths was the idea that Ray Allen was having a career year. Allen got off to a scorching start, hitting 45.3 percent on three-pointers in November, and so did the Sonics. As a result, people connected the dots and said Allen's big year was propelling Seattle forward. That became less true as the year went on, but people kept on saying it. Allen's final numbers were perfectly consistent with his previous two seasons, and in fact his PER was slightly worse. But because Seattle was a surprise team and commentators were searching for a player who was the difference, they settled on Allen.

The more interesting question for the Sonics is what Allen's future holds. They just gave him a five-year, $80 million deal, which means they'll need him to perform at a high level until age 34. Guards don't tend to age as well as big people, so this is something of a risk on the Sonics' part, especially since Allen isn't a superstar to begin with. Nonetheless, jump-shooting guards tend to last better than players who rely on quickness, and Allen's shot is as pure as any in the game. He may not be worth $16 million a year in 2009–10, but he should retain some of his value. Did the Sonics overpay? Probably. Was it as bad as the deal Jerome James signed with the Knicks? Not even close.

As far as 2004–05, Allen's year was so typical that there's not a lot to discuss. His field-goal percentage dipped slightly and took his TS% down with it, but overall he provides the same deadly combination of shooting touch and shot-creating skill. He's especially tough shooting jumpers while dribbling to his left because his release is so quick. Allen also has a unique ability to jump off the wrong foot, fake like he's laying the ball up with his right hand, then pull the ball across his shoulders and lay it in with the left.

Defensively, Allen's not so hot. His Defensive PER wasn't as poor as some of his teammates', but his lateral movement is only average and he doesn't have the strength to keep big guards off the blocks. Overall he's a solid second-tier star, but he'll have to stay at that level for five more years for Seattle's $80 million investment to make sense.

Mateen Cleaves point guard Age: 28 Height: 6-2 Weight: 205
(100% PG) Most similar at age: N/A

Year		G	M/G	FG%	FT%	P/40	R/40	A/40	TS%	Ast	TO	Usg	Reb	PER
2002-03	Sac	7	3.1	.261	.750	11.6	5.8	7.3	32.3	20.5	28.7	27.3	7.8	-3.90
2003-04	Cle	4	23.0	.304	.500	6.5	3.0	8.3	31.4	39.7	10.4	19.2	4.3	6.78
2004-05	Sea	14	4.6	.357	.750	8.0	3.7	4.3	41.2	20.5	8.1	14.8	5.4	9.06

Cleaves hung on as a third-string point guard for most of the year but his pro career has failed to gain traction. A chronic inability to shoot has rendered Cleaves a poor man's Rick Brunson, casting his eye about for a 10-day contract wherever he might find one.

Nick Collison power forward Age: 25 Height: 6-9 Weight: 255
(51% PF, 49% C) Most similar at age: Marlon Maxey

Year		G	M/G	FG%	FT%	P/40	R/40	A/40	TS%		Ast		TO		Usg		Reb		PER	
2003-04	Sea	Out for the season																		
2004-05	Sea	82	16.9	.540	.703	13.4	10.8	0.9	57.3	10	4.4	67	12.4	46	13.6	60	16.6	13	15.10	34
2005-06	PRJ (38.0)			.519	.715	13.3	10.6	1.0	55.7		4.5		12.8		14.0		16.4		14.91	

The Sonics should make Collison their starting power forward this season even if Evans and Radmanovic stay. His performance in his first pro action was impressive, as his long arms and quick hops made him a very strong rebounder and one of the Sonics' better frontcourt defenders as well. The one exception was when he had to play center, where at 6'9" he was a bit small for the position and also provided little in the way of shot-blocking.

Offensively, Collison was a high-percentage scorer whose TS% was among the best at his position, but he needs to be more involved in the offense. Collison rarely shot unless he was wide open under the basket and almost never initiated his own offense. He has a decent mid-range jump shot but rarely uncorked it last season so he should look for it more. Additionally, he needs to find the open man better, as his Assist Ratio was awful.

According to the projections, Collison's field-goal percentage might be due for a fall. Few players can shoot as high as 54.0 percent year after year. If that's the case, Collison will need to make up for it by expanding his offensive game and creating more shots. Since last year was effectively his rookie year, he should be able to take another step forward. If so, he'll give the Sonics a solid starter at a position that was a weak spot a year ago.

Antonio Daniels								point guard						Age: 30		Height: 6-4	Weight: 205
Defensive PER: 1.05 (66% PG, 34% SG)																Most similar at age: Eric Snow	
Year	G	M/G	FG%	FT%	P/40	R/40	A/40	TS%		Ast		TO		Usg		Reb		PER	
2002-03 Por*	67	13.0	.452	.855	11.5	3.3	3.9	57.2	7	25.3	8	9.5	20	14.7	50	5.0	52	13.32	33
2003-04 Sea	71	21.3	.470	.842	15.1	3.8	7.9	59.6	2	35.6	10	7.3	2	21.0	34	5.5	29	19.66	5
2004-05 Sea	75	27.0	.438	.816	16.7	3.3	6.1	55.7	10	27.0	31	6.8	3	22.2	32	5.1	44	18.08	13
2005-06 PRJ (31.0)			.444	.826	15.1	3.5	6.3	57.0		29.6		7.5		21.0		5.3		17.45	

* Season rankings are as shooting guard

Daniels played brilliantly off the bench for a second straight season, combining two skills that are rarely seen in tandem. Daniels has one of the lowest Turnover Ratios in the game, with a microscopic 6.8 mark last season. Most players who make few turnovers do so by hanging out on the perimeter, but not Daniels. Despite the paucity of mistakes, he got to the line with amazing frequency. Daniels averaged nearly a free throw for every two field-goal attempts, an astronomic rate for a point guard. That led to a very strong TS% despite his struggles from outside. Daniels made only 29.7 percent of his three-point attempts, which was the only reason his TS% sank from the year before.

Daniels fared well in other areas too. He created shots at a decent clip and the only reason his Assist Ratio dropped was because he spent more time at shooting guard last season. Defensively, he was the Sonics' best point guard and his Defensive PER was above the league average. Overall, there's little to complain about.

That's why his departure for Washington will hurt the Sonics so much. Conversely, Daniels should help the Wizards immensely. His ability to avoid turnovers should pay dividends on such a turnover-prone team, and he should allow Gilbert Arenas to play off the ball more. He'd be a contender for the Sixth Man award too, except for one thing—he's played so well that he'll probably be starting this year.

Reggie Evans								power forward						Age: 25		Height: 6-8	Weight: 245
Defensive PER: 0.85 (77% PF, 23% C)																Most similar at age: Etan Thomas	
Year	G	M/G	FG%	FT%	P/40	R/40	A/40	TS%		Ast		TO		Usg		Reb		PER	
2002-03 Sea	67	20.4	.471	.519	6.2	13.0	1.0	51.0	33	11.6	30	17.7	60	7.8	61	19.2	1	10.42	55
2003-04 Sea	75	17.1	.406	.561	6.8	12.7	1.0	47.1	56	10.1	45	19.8	66	8.9	66	17.8	8	9.89	59
2004-05 Sea	79	23.9	.476	.534	8.2	15.6	1.2	51.2	44	5.9	62	19.3	69	10.2	67	23.9	1	12.94	49
2005-06 PRJ (2.3)			.453	.564	8.2	13.7	2.7	49.3		16.6		16.2		10.5		19.6		12.34	

Evans is a rare player because he's so extreme in so many categories, the most prominent being rebounding. He had the best Rebound Rate in all of basketball last season, thanks to a wide body and a single-minded focus on the glass. Evans didn't even bother looking to create shots unless he got a rebound or he was wide open under the basket. Instead he goes straight to the weak side under the rim and looks for a carom. Even when he gets a board, Evans has trouble converting. He's short for a power forward and not a great leaper, so he frequently gets his deliveries sent back. He did develop a better left hand last season though, and that helped him on several occasions.

Evans was extreme in other areas too. He had a monstrously high Turnover Ratio because he set so many illegal screens, detracting from his contribution on the boards. His Usage Rate also is very low, although it actually improved from the past two seasons because he got more offensive rebounds to feed himself some easy points.

Defensively, Evans's strength and determination make him effective against post players, but his lack of height allows opponents to shoot over him. He's also not as effective against perimeter-oriented players because quickness isn't his forte.

Evans attracted several suitors as a restricted free agent who started for a playoff team, but was unsigned at publication time. If he stays, the Sonics would be better off starting Collison anyway. Evans's rebounding and defense were important, but in the big picture his inability to score detracted from the offense. Besides, last year's output might have been slightly over his head. He's a useful reserve, but he only started as a last resort.

Danny Fortson (99% C, 1% PF)			center							Age: 29	Height: 6-8	Weight: 260 Most similar at age: Tyrone Hill		
Year	G	M/G	FG%	FT%	P/40	R/40	A/40	TS%		Ast	TO	Usg	Reb	PER
2002-03 GS	17	13.1	.370	.655	10.6	13.1	2.2	44.2		12.8	16.0	14.4	17.4	9.82
2003-04 Dal	56	11.1	.511	.815	13.9	16.0	0.6	60.5	1	4.0 71	16.4 67	12.4 51	21.9 1	16.00 19
2004-05 Sea	62	16.9	.522	.880	17.7	13.3	0.3	68.2	1	1.5 70	20.8 70	14.8 30	20.3 3	16.91 12

After barely playing for two years, Fortson came over from Dallas and became one of the key players on Seattle's devastating second unit. He also engendered one of the league's great sound effects—a train whistle that Key Arena played when Fortson made a big play. Only Detroit's Big Ben chime for Ben Wallace is better.

Fortson has no projections for 2004–05 because no player was similar enough. Every other player in the league had at least one comparable player with a Similarity Score of 95.0 or greater. Fortson's best was just 92.9. It shows how out of the ordinary his 2004–05 season was. Let's start with the positives. Fortson is an incredible rebounder who ranked fifth in the league in Rebound Rate and had been No. 1 two of the previous three seasons. Like Reggie Evans, Fortson pulls down so many boards because he is incredibly strong and has a nose for the ball. Unlike Evans, he also has a soft touch around the basket and can finish plays when others set him up. He hit his free throws too, enabling Fortson to post the highest TS% in basketball at 68.2.

On the negative side, Fortson is one of the worst ballhandlers in basketball history, finishing last in the entire league in both Assist Ratio *and* Turnover Ratio. Additionally, as I mentioned in the team introduction, Fortson had the highest foul rate in the league last year. In fact, he ran away from the competition and made it virtually impossible to play him extended minutes. Fortson had the best PER among Sonics frontcourt players but averaged only 16.9 minutes per game because he was so often in foul trouble. When a player, on average, picks up six fouls every 24 minutes, it sets an upper limit on how long he can play. Many times he didn't even last that long—on four occasions he fouled out in 13 minutes or less, including one where it took him just six.

Since Fortson's basic defensive strategy was to mug everybody he saw, I thought the Sonics could have used him more strategically. McMillan tended to bring him in at the end of the first quarter, which is a horrible time to bring in a player like Fortson because the other team was usually in the bonus by then. Thus, all of the non-shooting fouls Fortson committed— many of which were pushing fouls going for offensive rebounds—produced two shots at the other end. If instead McMillan had used Fortson to start quarters, the impact of his fouls would have been less damaging. Yes, Seattle's opponents would get into the bonus quicker, but most of the fouls after that point would be shooting fouls anyway. Using Fortson to end quarters was like giving away free points.

Fouls weren't the only thing holding Fortson's minutes down. He also can be very prickly in the locker room and already has worn out his welcome in Golden State and Dallas. Nonetheless, his toughness and physical play was a key reason the Sonics put together such a strong season. With Seattle's frontcourt free-agent departures, he should play as prominent a role as the fouls will allow this year.

Jerome James (100% C)			center							Age: 30	Height: 7-1	Weight: 272 Most similar at age: Melvin Turpin		
Year	G	M/G	FG%	FT%	P/40	R/40	A/40	TS%		Ast	TO	Usg	Reb	PER
2002-03 Sea	51	15.0	.478	.587	14.4	11.3	1.4	50.6	40	7.2 56	20.0 70	17.5 19	16.6 14	13.07 41
2003-04 Sea	65	15.2	.498	.660	13.1	9.3	1.3	53.5	24	7.7 51	19.7 72	14.6 36	13.0 50	11.30 54
2004-05 Sea	80	16.7	.509	.723	11.8	7.2	0.6	53.3	31	2.7 67	18.4 64	12.9 45	11.0 59	9.83 58
2005-06 PRJ (9.1)			*.488*	*.690*	*11.9*	*7.8*	*0.8*	*51.7*		*4.5*	*19.4*	*13.1*	*11.5*	*10.32*

It's amazing that a player can be pushing 30 and still have GMs gushing over his potential. James played well for one week against a team with two 6′7″ power forwards and a center who came back too soon from a broken leg. For those five games against Sacramento, and about three others during the course of the year, James played hard and looked like a legitimate starting NBA center. His reward was a five-year, $30 million contract. What a country.

In the other games, James was a total stiff. James is enormous and can score in the post with a right-handed hook shot from the left block, but only against single coverage. Once a double-team appears he's immediately rendered clueless and rarely finds the open man. Additionally, James has visions of being a point guard and dribbles far too often for a player of his size. That's why his Turnover Ratio remains stubbornly high. James was a good rebounder three years ago, but he's not doing much of that lately either. His Rebound Rate was well below average for his position and dropped sharply for the second year in a row.

When James is motivated he can be a real factor on defense, because he can root players out of the post and he blocked a shot every 12 minutes last season. But like Fortson, it's difficult to keep him on the court for long because he fouls at such a high rate. That's another in a long litany of reasons the Knicks wasted $30 million on James. They want him to be the starting center, but he has no chance of being able to average more than 25 minutes a game because of the fouls. Of course, that's irrelevant since he shouldn't be starting anyway. He's a useful backup center if his play doesn't slip too much further, because he can score in the post and is an OK defender. But considering the money New York paid, this was the worst free-agent signing of the summer.

Ibrahim Kutluay			small forward						Age: 31	Height: 6-6	Weight: 200	
(75% SF, 17% SG, 8% PG)											Most similar at age: N/A	
Year	G	M/G	FG%	FT%	P/40	R/40	A/40	TS%	Ast	TO	Usg	Reb	PER
2004-05 Sea	5	2.4	.000	—	0.0	3.3	0.0	0.0	0.0	66.7	5.7	4.9	-13.13

Speaking of idiotic signings ... Kutluay had two good games against the United States in the Olympic tune-ups that attracted Seattle's attention. The Sonics ignored the mountain of evidence compiled in Euroleague play that Kutluay would be overmatched at the NBA level and subsequently signed him to a two-year contract. Lo and behold, he was overmatched at the NBA level. By midseason, Kutluay was back in Turkey and the Sonics were left icing their wounds.

Rashard Lewis			small forward						Age: 26	Height: 6-10	Weight: 215	
Defensive PER: 1.27 (85% SF, 11% PF, 4% SG)											Most similar at age: Keith Van Horn	
Year	G	M/G	FG%	FT%	P/40	R/40	A/40	TS%		Ast		TO		Usg		Reb		PER	
2002-03 Sea	77	39.5	.452	.820	18.3	6.6	1.7	53.7	15	8.4	56	9.1	12	20.1	21	9.7	21	16.70	14
2003-04 Sea	80	36.6	.435	.763	19.4	7.1	2.4	52.7	21	10.6	44	8.1	7	21.4	14	10.4	13	17.45	13
2004-05 Sea	71	38.0	.462	.777	21.6	5.8	1.4	57.1	5	6.3	64	8.2	13	21.5	15	8.8	32	19.45	6
2005-06 PRJ (45.4)			.453	.790	20.1	6.6	1.9	55.3		8.3		8.3		21.2		9.8		18.37	

Lewis had a career year in 2004–05, earning his first All-Star appearance on the basis of improvements at both ends of the floor. Offensively, Lewis shot as frequently as he had in past seasons but was much more accurate. He nailed 40.1 percent on three-pointers and 46.2 percent overall, both of which were career highs. Additionally, he took more threes than ever, averaging over six attempts per game. Consequently, his TS% jumped from an ordinary 52.7 to an outstanding 57.1.

Lewis is a tough player for opponents to cover due to his size. At 6′ 10″, he can post up small forwards on the left block and turn toward the baseline for a smooth jump shot. But against bigger players, Lewis can run them ragged on the perimeter and beat them with his trademark three-pointer from the left corner. The one missing link in Lewis's game is an ability to score off the dribble. Lewis is a limited ballhandler who at most will take one dribble to either side before pulling up for a jumper.

Lewis also was an improved defender in 2004–05. He's always had the ability because of his height for a small forward, but the effort improved considerably in 2004–05, resulting in a very solid Defensive PER. Lewis isn't a great leaper but set a career high by averaging nearly a block per game. Overall, it was an extremely solid season for the Sonics' second banana, and Lewis should be able to take another step forward in his development since he's only 26.

Ronald Murray			shooting guard						Age: 26	Height: 6-4	Weight: 210	
(82% SG, 10% PG, 8% SF)											Most similar at age: Juan Dixon	
Year	G	M/G	FG%	FT%	P/40	R/40	A/40	TS%		Ast		TO		Usg		Reb		PER	
2002-03 Mil-Sea	14	4.4	.355	.625	17.4	2.6	3.2	39.1		10.5		16.8		27.6		3.8		6.54	
2003-04 Sea	82	24.7	.425	.715	20.0	4.0	4.1	49.7	37	14.9	38	10.9	33	25.1	7	5.9	44	15.34	17
2004-05 Sea	49	18.0	.361	.738	15.6	4.4	2.9	43.3	65	12.5	48	11.0	42	22.4	14	6.5	36	9.78	52
2005-06 PRJ (58.0)			.403	.708	17.4	4.2	3.8	47.5		15.0		10.7		23.1		6.2		13.14	

(continued next page)

Ronald Murray *(continued)*

Murray took a major step backward after his surprise season of 2003–04, as he seemed to react poorly to the limited minutes he saw in the Sonics' revamped backcourt rotation. Murray's quickness off the dribble makes him adept at creating shots, but last season he repeatedly forced shots and struggled to a 36.1 percent mark from the floor.

Murray needs to deliver at the offensive end because he's a poor defender. He's an inch or two short for a shooting guard and doesn't have any other strengths to offset it. Besides the fact that he's a bit slow for the point, it's impossible to play Murray at the point on offense because of his shoot-first mentality.

Murray became a restricted free agent after the season but was unsigned as of publication time. With Daniels gone, one would expect the Sonics to match reasonable offers for Murray, but they'll let the market set a price before they match it.

Vitaly Potapenko		center								**Age: 30**	**Height: 6-10**	**Weight: 285**
(95% C, 5% PF)												Most similar at age: N/A
Year		**G**	**M/G**	**FG%**	**FT%**	**P/40**	**R/40**	**A/40**	**TS%**		**Ast**	**TO**	**Usg**	**Reb**	**PER**
2002-03	Sea	26	15.5	.441	.759	10.3	8.8	0.4	49.2		3.0	18.6	12.1	13.0	8.20
2003-04	Sea	65	21.8	.489	.641	12.9	8.2	1.5	51.1	41	9.1 34	13.3 41	14.9 33	12.0 63	11.22 56
2004-05	Sea	33	10.2	.517	.871	14.0	9.3	1.1	58.1		5.1	9.9	13.9	13.6	14.45

The Ukraine Train played very well for the Sonics in limited minutes, hitting 51.7 percent from the field and improving his Rebound Rate from the previous year's disappointing level. Potapenko has some rudimentary skills in the paint and can hit a jumper from the foul line, but his best skill is his willingness to throw his body around. That makes him a good fit in the Sonics' foul-first-ask-questions-later frontcourt system, and with James gone (and possibly Radmanovic and Evans), Potapenko could earn a much larger role. He won't match last year's numbers, but something along the lines of his 2003–04 season is very possible and would be an improvement on Jerome James.

Vladimir Radmanovic		power forward								**Age: 25**	**Height: 6-10**	**Weight: 227**
Defensive PER: 0.47 (74% PF, 23% SF, 3% C)												Most similar at age: Jumaine Jones
Year		**G**	**M/G**	**FG%**	**FT%**	**P/40**	**R/40**	**A/40**	**TS%**		**Ast**	**TO**	**Usg**	**Reb**	**PER**
2002-03	Sea	72	26.5	.410	.706	15.2	6.8	2.0	50.8	38	10.7 36	11.0 28	18.2 28	10.0 55	12.99 36
2003-04	Sea	77	30.2	.425	.748	15.9	7.0	2.4	53.3	22	12.7 28	9.7 11	18.0 30	10.3 60	15.06 32
2004-05	Sea	63	29.4	.409	.786	16.0	6.2	1.9	53.3	32	8.9 38	9.3 20	17.9 30	9.5 64	13.68 44
2005-06	*PRJ (36.8)*			*.401*	*.759*	*14.9*	*6.5*	*2.0*	*52.0*		*10.4*	*10.1*	*17.3*	*9.7*	*13.66*

I love agents, because they can say anything without any fear of being called on it. Take Radmanovic, for instance. Here's what his agent had to say about his client last year. "It was unconscionable that he didn't start one game last year. You had a kid average 29.5 minutes. If you get his minutes up to 35, his production would be 17 [points] and eight [rebounds]."

OK, quick math lesson here, folks. You can see in the chart that Radmanovic doesn't average 17 and eight when he gets *40* minutes, much less 35. In fact, he's never come close his entire career and isn't projected to get any closer this year. It wasn't unconscionable that Radmanovic didn't start. He just wasn't that good.

Despite the Sonics' success, 2004–05 was a major step back for Radmanovic. He posted career lows in shooting percentage and Rebound Rate, and sported perhaps the worst hair in the NBA in the last decade with his mini-braids in the first round of the playoffs.

Radmanovic is an excellent shooter who can frustrate opposing big men by launching away from outside—last season he hit 38.9 percent from downtown. The trouble is that he hasn't expanded his game beyond that skill. Radmanovic has no game off the dribble and hasn't developed a strong shot-fake move to complement his sweet shooting. Additionally, he gets steamrolled at the power forward spot by opposing big men and his inability to rebound sets back the frontcourt.

Radmanovic does have good anticipation in the passing lanes, however, and moves his feet fairly well. The obvious solution would be to move him to small forward, but that's problematic because Lewis plays the same position. As a result, the Sonics' best option may be to trade Radmanovic someplace where he can play his natural position. Vlad's agent is all wrong that the big problem is with Seattle's unwillingness to play him. The problem is that they can't play him at the one position he's best suited to play.

Luke Ridnour — point guard
Defensive PER: 0.39 (99% PG, 1% SG)

Age: 24 Height: 6-2 Weight: 17
Most similar at age: Vonteego Cummings

Year		G	M/G	FG%	FT%	P/40	R/40	A/40	TS%		Ast		TO		Usg		Reb		PER	
2003-04	Sea	69	16.1	.414	.823	13.7	3.9	5.9	49.6	37	26.0	43	12.7	43	20.6	38	5.4	35	13.12	34
2004-05	Sea	82	31.4	.405	.883	12.8	3.2	7.5	50.4	44	33.3	8	10.3	25	21.6	35	4.9	50	14.58	33
2005-06	PRJ (69.9)			.404	.885	13.0	3.3	7.1	50.9		32.2		10.4		21.3		4.9		14.86	

Ridnour was handed the starting point guard job to begin the season and kept it all year, which was strange because Daniels obviously was much better. Ridnour made improvements from his rookie year, however. He had one of the best Assist Ratios in the game and repeatedly found Allen and Lewis open for three-pointers. Like Daniels, he was able to create shots without turning the ball over much, although his rates weren't as impressive as Daniels's.

In addition, Ridnour shot the ball well from outside, hitting 37.6 percent on three-pointers and 88.3 percent from the line. The problem was that he didn't shoot nearly as well on two-pointers, and those accounted for three-quarters of his shots. As a result, Ridnour ended up at 40.5 percent overall and his TS% was an unimpressive 50.4. Ridnour needs to get better at finishing shots on his drives to the rim, perhaps by learning to hit floaters rather than going all the way to the basket and allowing the defense to catch up.

Defensively, Ridnour was better than he'd been as a rookie. But when compared to the NBA standard rather than his own previous performance, he still was poor. Ridnour has quick hands but lacks strength and had trouble keeping dribblers in front of him. Those shortcomings led to a poor Defensive PER.

Seattle could live with Ridnour's infrequent scoring and defensive struggles last season because they could bring Daniels into the game. Now that Daniels is gone, the Sonics desperately need Ridnour to step up at both ends. He'll be playing 35 to 40 minutes a night, but unless he steps up he'll be the lineup's weakest link.

Robert Swift — center
(100% C)

Age: 20 Height: 7-0 Weight: 245
Most similar at age: N/A

Year		G	M/G	FG%	FT%	P/40	R/40	A/40	TS%	Ast	TO	Usg	Reb	PER
2004-05	Sea	16	4.5	.455	.556	8.3	2.8	1.1	50.1	5.3	19.1	10.4	4.1	4.95

The Sonics' first-round draft pick in 2004 spent the entire season watching the proceedings. Swift could play a much bigger role this season now that James is gone, but since he came to the NBA straight from high school he's an unknown quantity at this point.

Damien Wilkins — small forward
(76% SF, 22% PF, 2% SG)

Age: 25 Height: 6-6 Weight: 225
Most similar at age: Todd Day

Year		G	M/G	FG%	FT%	P/40	R/40	A/40	TS%		Ast		TO		Usg		Reb		PER	
2004-05	Sea	29	17.9	.435	.618	14.1	5.1	2.0	50.0	49	9.5	54	7.1	5	16.9	40	7.4	54	13.36	36
2005-06	PRJ (42.6)			.434	.602	13.9	5.2	2.2	50.0		10.2		7.4		16.8		7.6		14.04	

Wilkins got his first chance at the pros and made the most of it, posting solid numbers off the bench and earning a starting job late in the season when Lewis was injured. Wilkins wasn't particularly remarkable in any area save one: He didn't turn the ball over. By sporting one of the lowest Turnover Ratios at his position, Wilkins could make it easier for the Sonics to live with his shaky shooting. Wilkins is a decent athlete and can create shots if he has to, but his 27.1 mark on three-pointers and 61.8 from the line indicate that his stroke could use some work. He also rebounded very poorly for a small forward, probably because he's an inch or two undersized for the position.

Like seemingly every Sonic, Wilkins became a restricted free agent after the season and signed an offer sheet with Minnesota as of publication time. His ability to provide a solid backup for Lewis is only relevant if Radmanovic leaves, so Seattle's financial constraints probably will prompt them to choose one or the other.

Johan Petro   center   **Age: 19**   **Height: 7-1**   **Weight: 250**
Translated 40-minute stats: 11.2 pts, 10.0 reb, 1.4 ast, .410 FG%, 10.29 PER

Along with Robert Swift, the Sonics now have two teenage centers to develop, but neither is likely to contribute this season. Petro has a prototype NBA body and showed flashes of his athleticism in Euroleague play—he averaged over three steals per 40 minutes. However, his rebound numbers were disappointing and his offensive game is rudimentary.

Mickaël Gelabale   small forward   **Age: 22**   **Height: 6-7**   **Weight: 210**
Translated 40-minute stats: 10.5 pts, 8.5 reb, 2.3 ast, .531 FG%, 12.09 PER

With Gelabale, Petro, and 2002 pick Paccelis Morlende, the Sonics now own the rights to three French players. All three may stay in France for the 2005–06 season, but Gelabale is the most likely to help right away. He plays tough defense and rebounds well for a small forward. Plus, although he's not much of a scorer, opponents will need to respect his jump shot.

Utah Jazz

Call it a case of foul play.

After coming up with two big free-agent signings in Carlos Boozer and Mehmet Okur, the Utah Jazz thought they would be able to challenge the Western Conference elite. Instead, the Jazz suffered through a 26–56 nightmare punctuated by a ridiculous rate of fouls and several major injuries. Boozer missed the season's final 31 games, star forward Andrei Kirilenko missed 41, and Okur frustrated Jerry Sloan all season with his loafing.

Most people look at the Jazz's disappointing season and see it as a failure on the part of Boozer and Okur to deliver. While there is an element of truth to that, focusing on those two completely misses the point. The Jazz's season turned into a train wreck for two reasons: First, they couldn't find a decent point guard, and second, they couldn't stop fouling.

Point guard was the first and most obvious thing to go wrong. The Jazz signed Carlos Arroyo to a four-year, $16 million deal in the offseason, but he ended up in Sloan's doghouse from the get-go. The demanding coach was frustrated both with Arroyo's defensive inattention and, perhaps worse, an inexplicable offensive decline from a player who had been one of Utah's best the year before. Arroyo and Sloan weren't on speaking terms by midseason, and the Jazz ended up trading Arroyo to Detroit for a future first-round draft pick.

That left Utah scrambling all season, sifting through the grab-bag of leftovers that included CBA veteran Keith McLeod, Phoenix castoff Howard Eisley, and oft-injured Raul Lopez. The position was a huge liability the entire season and magnified Utah's lack of outside shooting. Utah was 29th in the NBA in three-pointers and 28th in accuracy, hitting just 32.8 percent of its three-pointers. The center, Okur, often was the best shooter on the court.

The point guards also killed Utah in terms of turnovers, as it had the league's third-highest Turnover Ratio. Part of that was offensive fouls generated by Utah's Mortal Kombat style of play (more on that in minute), but much was a result of the guards' inability to set the table for other players. As a result, players like Boozer, Okur, and Kirilenko often had to create their own offense at the end of the shot clock.

> ## Jazz at a Glance
>
> **Record:** 26–56, 5th place in Northwest Division
> **Offensive Efficiency:** 101.1 (23rd)
> **Defensive Efficiency:** 107.0 (28th)
> **Pace Factor:** 90.8 (26th)
> **Top-Rated Player:** Andrei Kirilenko (PER 24.45, 7th overall)
> **Head Coach:** Jerry Sloan. Competitive as ever, but his system was uniquely unsuited to new defensive rules.

Not surprisingly then, the Jazz finished only 23rd in Offensive Efficiency. Utah was above the league average in field-goal percentage and well above it in free-throw attempts, yet the Jazz's TS% was substandard due to the lack of a three-point threat. Throw in the turnovers, and it was a fairly inefficient offense.

Looking ahead, one positive for Utah was that three players who won't be playing major roles in 2005–06 accounted for a huge portion of the offensive struggles. Keith McLeod, Kris Humphries, and Kirk Snyder seemed deadlocked in a season-long war to see who could take the most inappropriate shot. Each took a relatively large number of shots despite a TS% in the bottom five of their position. While each individual's impact wasn't large, the cumulative effect was significant.

An even greater contributor to the 2004–05 disaster was the defense. Utah ranked a mere 28th in Defensive Efficiency despite the presence of the league's leading shot-blocker in Kirilenko. At first glance, the Jazz's performance seems adequate. Utah's opponent field-goal percentage was above the league average, but not by an extravagant amount. Additionally, the Jazz were a good defensive rebounding team and forced an above-average number of turnovers.

Unfortunately, they fouled with such alarming frequency that it was virtually impossible for them to be a good defensive team. This is nothing new for Utah, as they had shown a similar propensity for fouling in 2003–04. The Jazz committed a foul on 14.7 percent of opponent possessions, compared to the league average of 11.5 percent. The difference between Utah and the No. 2 team was greater than the difference between No. 2 and the league average.

Amazingly, they fouled even more in 2004–05, and led the league in fouls by a wide margin despite playing one of the league's slowest paces. Utah fouled on 15.7 percent of opponent possessions, compared to the league rate of 12.2. I said a year ago that the Jazz's foul stats look like they were playing in a different league than everyone else. In 2004–05, it looked like they were playing a different sport. The difference between Utah and the No. 2 team was greater than the

Table 1. Jazz Foul Rates, 2004–05

	Total Fouls	Opp. FTA/FGA	% of Opp. Poss. With FTA
Jazz	2189	.445	15.7
Next Closest	2028	.375	13.7
League Average	1856	.324	12.2

difference between No. 2 and No. 20. The result was that Utah gave up .445 free-throw attempts per field-goal attempt (see table 1); the league average was .324. With such a disadvantage in the free-throw column, Utah's defense had no chance.

Why does Utah foul so much? Considering much of the personnel changed between the two seasons, the obvious answer is Sloan. It's long been established that the Jazz play bumper cars on offense, running opponents into a series of screens with a uniquely physical style. That approach carries over to the defensive end as well. Sloan's teams will never run around a screen when it can be run over instead and take the mantra of "no lay-ups" to extremes. The troubles at point guard only fed the hacking frenzy, as the Jazz had trouble stopping penetration and often had to foul in desperation. Similar weaknesses emerged on the wings, as Gordan Giricek and Matt Harpring were far too slow to competently defend the perimeter.

Another factor that hurt Utah was the revised rules on hand-checking. Utah's physical style was poorly adapted to the new landscape, adding a slew of touch fouls to Utah's already mountainous total. Additionally, Sloan was unusually slow to adjust to the change in officiating, as there was no perceptible change in style despite the poor results.

For Sloan, the past two years have been polar opposites. 2003–04 brought out all his best qualities: His toughness, resilience, and ability to motivate his players. As a result, he nearly led a band of underdogs to the playoffs and finished second in the Coach of the Year voting. Conversely, 2004–05 brought out all the worst. Not only did it expose the shortcomings in his defensive strategy, it also showcased his other glaring weakness: rash personnel decisions.

Sloan has largely escaped scorn for his bizarre personnel moves, but that's an oversight on the part of the media. From Quincy Lewis to DeShawn Stevenson to Michael Ruffin, Sloan has given starting jobs to as many awful players as any coach in history. Last year's showcase was Alex Radojevic, who started six games for Utah last season. It's not a stretch to say he's the worst player to start multiple games in an NBA season in the past 25 years. Radojevic finished with a PER of –1.82—in other words, he would have been more valuable busking at halfcourt.

Meanwhile, the Jazz had a perfectly capable starting center sitting on the bench. Sloan was upset with Okur's periodic sluggishness but completely overreacted by yanking him from the lineup. Okur became the first Jazz center in 26 years to score over 1,000 points in a season, yet it took Sloan 67 games to get the Turkish big man into the starting lineup.

It wasn't a banner year for the front office either. The Jazz's recent drafts can politely be described as "underperforming," which is one reason the team has been in a steady freefall. Some of that has been bad luck—the Jazz couldn't have known that Raul Lopez would blow out both knees. But a lot has been bad talent evaluation. Utah's two first-round picks in 2004, Humphries and Snyder, looked completely overmatched, and other first-rounders have been similarly unproductive. Since taking Kirilenko in 1999, Utah's drafts under general manager Kevin O'Connor have yielded Stevenson, Curtis Borchardt, Aleksandar Pavlovic, Lopez, Humphries, and Snyder.

After the season, the Jazz traded three of those players—Borchardt, Lopez, and Snyder—to Memphis as a side deal in the five-team, Antoine Walker megatrade, getting Greg Ostertag in return. The fact that they would trade three first-rounders for a backup center is proof of the Jazz's struggles on draft day. O'Connor made another questionable move this year, taking Illinois's Deron Williams with the third overall pick even though most analysts had Wake Forest's Chris Paul rated higher. Utah expects Williams to take over the starting point guard job immediately, but his shooting could be a question mark.

Williams is one of the few changes to the roster. Shooting guard Raja Bell left as a free agent and the Jazz were scrambling to add a perimeter player as of publication. There's a sense in Utah that they'll still be OK. The Jazz figure if Boozer and Kirilenko stay healthy, they'll be able to make a run at a playoff spot. That might be overstating things considerably. The Jazz were 10–12 even when Boozer and Kirilenko were on the court together, so their return is hardly a panacea. Additionally, Utah's bench shapes up as a huge weakness at the perimeter spots.

The real change needs to happen on the sidelines, where Sloan has to be flexible enough to change his game plan. With an offseason to ponder what went wrong in 2004–05, he'll hopefully conclude that the league won't let teams win anymore with smashmouth basketball and give the defense a softer touch. Otherwise, the Jazz are destined to strike a sour note regardless of the health of their star players' health.

Raja Bell — shooting guard
(97% SG, 3% SF)

Age: 29   Height: 6-5   Weight: 210
Most similar at age: Blue Edwards

Year		G	M/G	FG%	FT%	P/40	R/40	A/40	TS%		Ast		TO		Usg		Reb		PER	
2002-03	Dal*	75	15.6	.441	.676	7.8	4.9	1.9	50.9	35	17.5	12	13.2	45	10.0	58	6.8	52	7.92	53
2003-04	Uta	82	24.6	.409	.786	18.1	4.8	2.1	50.0	32	9.5	60	9.8	23	21.8	25	7.4	23	12.69	34
2004-05	Uta	63	28.4	.454	.747	17.3	4.5	2.0	52.7	30	9.7	58	8.7	18	19.5	31	7.0	28	12.14	41
2005-06	PRJ (46.3)			.427	.764	16.0	4.6	2.1	51.0		11.0		9.7		19.2		7.0		11.43	

* Season rankings are as small forward

Lest you think everyone from the Virgin Islands is as laid-back as Tim Duncan, let me introduce you to Mr. Bell. This native of St. Croix had 10 technical fouls and two flagrants last year, and that was an off year for him. The year before he had 15 T's and six flagrants.

Bell was the Jazz's leading three-point shooter last season but hit fewer than one a game. He was accurate, however, nailing 40 percent. That would come as a shock to those who saw him just a few years ago. Bell's jumper has improved tremendously in that time despite a relatively flat trajectory. That should give his new employers in Phoenix hope that he can fill the shooting void left by Quentin Richardson's departure.

Bell also is a feisty defender who was Utah's perimeter stopper. He was the only Jazz perimeter player who could reliably keep his man in front of him, allowing him to take over a starting job at shooting guard early in the season. Plus, he's a fairly athletic finisher, though we saw little evidence of that last year in the Jazz's halfcourt offense. On the down side, he shoots way too many mid-range jumpers and is a poor passer.

While Bell's defensive and athletic skills make him a helpful player, Phoenix seriously overpaid for his services with a five-year, $24 million deal. Bell will be well-compensated until he's 33, but considering he hasn't been that good even in his prime, his jumper will have to keep improving for Phoenix to have any hope of getting its money worth.

Carlos Boozer — power forward
(89% PF, 11% C)

Age: 24   Height: 6-9   Weight: 258
Most similar at age: Billy Owens

Year		G	M/G	FG%	FT%	P/40	R/40	A/40	TS%		Ast		TO		Usg		Reb		PER	
2002-03	Cle	81	25.3	.536	.771	15.8	11.9	2.1	57.7	4	11.6	29	11.3	35	15.9	39	16.6	7	17.92	13
2003-04	Cle	75	34.6	.523	.768	17.9	13.2	2.3	56.7	5	11.3	37	10.2	14	18.6	27	18.1	7	20.77	6
2004-05	Uta	51	34.7	.521	.698	20.5	10.3	3.3	56.0	17	13.2	11	12.5	49	23.2	10	16.0	16	19.18	11
2005-06	PRJ (37.4)			.518	.730	19.3	10.8	2.8	56.1		12.1		11.2		21.7		15.5		19.80	

Ain't karma a bummer? Boozer's reward for backstabbing Cleveland was disappointment in Athens, an off year on a bad team, a public calling-out from Jerry Sloan at midseason, and a season-ending injury.

In between Boozer struggled to adjust to a more prominent offensive role. The Jazz used him much as they used Karl Malone in the past, throwing to Boozer in the post and then running a series of cuts away from the ball. That helped Boozer's Assist Ratio quite a bit, but he never seemed comfortable as a scorer. Boozer's game in Cleveland was as a high-percentage finisher who thrived away from the ball, getting many of his points on put-backs and dishes from teammates. His post repertoire is fairly limited, with a turnaround over his right shoulder being a primary weapon. He's much better from the high post, where he loves to drive left. In fact, opponents should just play him as though he's left-handed.

Offensively, Boozer shot 52.1 percent and averaged over 20 points per 40 minutes. Nonetheless, his season was a letdown for a couple of reasons. First, he failed to build on the promise of his dynamite first two seasons in the league and his Rebound Rate withered considerably. Additionally, Boozer's defense was a huge disappointment. He is neither tall nor terribly athletic for his position, so he struggles to challenge shots by opposing post players and blocked less than half a shot per game. Moreover, he often seemed to be going at half speed, especially in transition defense.

For 2005–06, he'll need to remedy those weaknesses. The good news for the Jazz is that Boozer is quite young and he put up some good numbers last year. With a more sustained defensive effort and better health, he can give the Jazz their money's worth on his fat contract.

Curtis Borchardt center   **Age: 25** **Height: 7-0** **Weight: 240**
(100% C)   Most similar at age: Eric Leckner

Year		G	M/G	FG%	FT%	P/40	R/40	A/40	TS%		Ast		TO		Usg		Reb		PER	
2002-03	Uta		Out for the season																	
2003-04	Uta	16	16.1	.393	.778	9.0	8.4	2.3	45.4		15.5		18.6		13.7		12.0		7.90	
2004-05	Uta	67	12.8	.430	.732	9.3	10.4	2.3	49.2	54	10.9	11	17.1	62	12.9	44	16.2	21	9.27	61
2005-06	PRJ (33.2)			.432	.732	9.4	10.0	2.5	49.1		11.8		16.4		13.0		15.6		9.82	

The injury-prone big man finally stayed healthy in 2004–05, but the news was more bad than good. At least when he was injured, Jazz fans could think, "Well, maybe this Borchardt guy can play if he gets healthy." Now they know, unequivocally, that he can't.

Borchardt was an unusually poor finisher around the basket for a player of his size. He has bad hands, but not the way most players do. Borchardt catches the ball cleanly, but often loses the grip when he goes up for a shot, helping to account for a high Turnover Ratio. Plus, because of Borchardt's ponderous speed he struggled at the defensive end. Overall, he looks like a bust, but he has one year left on his contract to prove us wrong. Borchardt was traded to Boston after the season, and he's likely to spend all year at the end of the bench given the Celtics' crowded frontcourt.

Jarron Collins center   **Age: 27** **Height: 6-11** **Weight: 255**
(99% C, 1% PF)   Most similar at age: Jake Voskuhl

Year		G	M/G	FG%	FT%	P/40	R/40	A/40	TS%		Ast		TO		Usg		Reb		PER	
2002-03	Uta	22	19.1	.442	.710	11.4	5.7	1.3	53.0		9.6		13.0		12.9		8.6		8.20	
2003-04	Uta	81	21.4	.498	.718	11.1	7.3	1.8	58.7	3	13.6	13	14.0	47	12.3	55	11.3	70	11.11	62
2004-05	Uta	50	19.2	.414	.697	8.9	6.8	2.5	50.9	43	12.1	6	11.2	12	12.0	53	10.6	64	7.92	68
2005-06	PRJ (16.8)			.455	.714	9.6	6.8	2.2	54.4		13.4		13.1		11.9		10.5		9.46	

Collins is an inch shorter than his twin brother in New Jersey, but his characteristics as a player are nearly identical. He rarely scores and is a terrible rebounder for his size, but he makes his living at the defensive end. Collins is a solid defender who specializes in taking charges, although he's not quite on a par with his brother in this realm.

Unlike his brother, this Collins hasn't lucked into a starting job yet. With Okur, Boozer, and a re-acquired Ostertag in line ahead of him for minutes, his luck doesn't figure to change any time soon, but that may be for the best. In a limited role, Collins's abysmal offensive output isn't quite so glaring, and his defense provides a lift on a team short of defenders.

Howard Eisley point guard   **Age: 33** **Height: 6-2** **Weight: 185**
(86% PG, 14% SG)   Most similar at age: Terry Porter

Year		G	M/G	FG%	FT%	P/40	R/40	A/40	TS%		Ast		TO		Usg		Reb		PER	
2002-03	NY	82	27.3	.417	.848	13.3	3.3	7.9	55.2	7	35.0	8	11.8	39	20.9	39	4.9	47	14.04	28
2003-04	NY-Phx	67	21.8	.368	.854	12.6	3.5	7.5	46.9	51	31.7	18	11.4	34	21.6	31	5.2	37	12.29	43
2004-05	Uta	74	19.3	.398	.795	11.6	2.5	7.0	47.0	57	31.2	22	13.8	58	20.9	43	3.9	63	9.23	63
2005-06	PRJ (34.5)			.378	.810	11.2	2.9	6.9	47.2		31.4		13.3		19.5		4.3		10.40	

The Jazz picked up Eisley after Phoenix released him in preseason, but his second tour of duty in Utah wasn't as successful as his first. Eisley not only shot below 40 percent, he did almost nothing to supplement that poor percentage. He hit only 26 percent of his three-pointers, rarely got to the line, and his monstrously high Turnover Ratio more than offset a decent Assist Ratio. Also, Eisley defended poorly, as he no longer has the quick feet needed to keep opposing point guards out of the middle, and he was one of basketball's worst rebounders.

Needless to say, his career is in jeopardy heading into this season. Eisley is 33 years old and lacks a guaranteed contract for this season. While backup point guards almost always manage to hang on somewhere, Eisley's employment this season may be only in 10-day increments.

Gordan Giricek (87% SG, 13% SF)		shooting guard							**Age: 28**	**Height: 6-5**	**Weight: 210** Most similar at age: Allan Houston		
Year		G	M/G	FG%	FT%	P/40	R/40	A/40	TS%	Ast	TO	Usg	Reb	PER
2002-03	Mem-Orl	76	28.3	.436	.820	17.4	4.4	2.6	52.9 25	11.8 48	12.4 48	19.5 34	6.3 38	12.05 37
2003-04	Orl-Uta	73	28.0	.436	.854	16.2	4.4	2.4	52.1 25	12.0 50	10.1 27	18.7 39	6.9 30	13.21 30
2004-05	Uta	81	20.5	.448	.810	17.2	4.4	3.3	51.6 40	14.9 32	9.8 25	21.3 19	6.8 34	12.84 34
2005-06	PRJ (75.6)			.440	.805	16.5	4.4	2.8	52.1	13.3	10.3	19.7	6.7	12.52

Utah signed Giricek to a long-term deal in free agency, but he was ill-suited to provide the perimeter threat the offense so desperately needed. Giricek is a decent shooter, but is much more comfortable from middle ranges than shooting the long ball. Giricek shot 36.2 percent on three-pointers but attempted only one per game because his instinct is to shoot off the dribble going to his right. Unfortunately, he rarely goes all the way to the paint so he doesn't draw fouls, and that keeps his TS% low.

Giricek didn't fare much better at the defensive end either. He's a better athlete than he's given credit for but his lateral movement is a shortcoming and he needs more muscle. As a result of those two factors, Giricek quickly lost his starting job to Bell.

With Bell departing and the Jazz lacking an obvious solution at shooting guard, Giricek once again begins the season with the shooting guard job as his to lose. Realistically, he'd be a much better option as a bench player, and he'd fit in more easily on a club that wasn't counting on him to stretch the defense. Instead, he'll probably lose his job by midseason again.

Ben Handlogten (78% C, 22% PF)		center							**Age: 32**	**Height: 6-10**	**Weight: 240** Most similar at age: N/A		
Year		G	M/G	FG%	FT%	P/40	R/40	A/40	TS%	Ast	TO	Usg	Reb	PER
2003-04	Uta	17	10.1	.532	.667	15.8	12.8	1.4	57.7	8.0	13.4	16.5	18.4	17.17
2004-05	Uta	21	14.1	.518	.529	12.8	8.8	1.8	52.5	8.3	14.8	15.1	12.4	10.19

An overachieving, undersized center, Handlogten played sparingly the past two seasons for the Jazz and might play less with the addition of Ostertag. Handlogten's best asset is his consistently high field-goal percentage, which is a result of careful shot selection. He also rebounded extremely well two seasons ago but dropped off significantly in that area last year. His lack of size hurts him at the defensive end at the center spot, and he has to play there because he's too slow to stay in front of most power forwards. If Handlogten rebounds the way he did in 2003–04, he's a very useful reserve. Otherwise, he's 12th man material. For this year, my money would be on the latter.

Matt Harpring Defensive PER: -1.02 (93% SF, 7% PF)		small forward							**Age: 29**	**Height: 6-7**	**Weight: 231** Most similar at age: Larry Johnson		
Year		G	M/G	FG%	FT%	P/40	R/40	A/40	TS%	Ast	TO	Usg	Reb	PER
2002-03	Uta	78	32.8	.511	.792	21.4	8.0	2.1	58.8 4	9.1 54	11.0 31	21.6 15	12.2 4	19.29 8
2003-04	Uta	31	36.6	.471	.688	17.7	8.7	2.2	52.4 24	10.4 46	10.7 26	20.7 17	13.5 2	16.15 15
2004-05	Uta	78	33.1	.489	.778	16.9	7.4	2.2	54.9 16	10.5 44	10.5 34	18.8 30	11.5 5	15.53 19
2005-06	PRJ (74.6)			.473	.761	16.4	7.6	2.1	53.4	10.4	10.8	18.8	11.6	15.06

Harpring has battled knee problems the past two seasons and that's been killing him on defense. He was never a speedster, but his inability to stay in front of quick forwards reached epic proportions last season as Harpring posted the worst Defensive PER in basketball. Harpring is probably better off at power forward, even though he's a couple of inches short. His strength and physical play are a better fit there, and he can hold his own against power forwards under the boards.

That also might help him out at the offensive end, since he's not a great outside shooter anyway. Harpring is fantastic at moving without the ball and draws lots of fouls by making hard cuts to the basket for lay-ups. He's also pretty good shooting from the middle ranges, although he's not a three-point shooter and has a fairly long wind-up. That's most of his repertoire. Harpring isn't going to create shots off the dribble and his post game is surprisingly poor for such a physical player.

Unfortunately, moving to power forward isn't an option with Boozer on the team. It would make sense for the Jazz to trade either Harpring or Boozer to get more help for the backcourt, clearing out more minutes for whomever is left. Otherwise, Harpring will see relatively few minutes as a backup forward, and many of them will come in tandem with Boozer, who makes a poor partner for him.

Kris Humphries — power forward
(68% PF, 31% SF, 1% C)

Age: 20 Height: 6-9 Weight: 235
Most similar at age: Kwame Brown

Year		G	M/G	FG%	FT%	P/40	R/40	A/40	TS%		Ast		TO		Usg		Reb		PER	
2004-05	Uta	67	13.0	.404	.436	12.7	9.0	2.0	41.9	69	9.4	34	12.2	43	18.4	26	14.0	28	9.40	63
2005-06	PRJ (10.3)			.427	.442	13.8	8.7	2.4	44.3		10.6		12.8		19.0		13.6		10.48	

Utah's first-round draft pick in 2004, Humphries was a complete flop as a rookie. He was billed as a high-scoring forward but instead posted the worst TS% among all small forwards. Humphries was incredibly ambitious, constantly seeking to score when he caught the ball in the high post but mostly floating off-the-dribble jumpers that barely grazed the rim. He managed to draw fouls at a high rate, but even that worked out badly since Humphries is an atrocious foul shooter—he made only 43.6 percent last season. If he had shot the league average, his TS% would have increased nearly five percent. While that's still terrible, it wouldn't have been the hideous, "please stop shooting" disaster that unfolded last season.

Humphries also struggled defensively. He's a tweener who isn't quick enough to play small forward and has to work on building the strength to play power forward. Humphries's biggest shortcoming was in help defense, a responsibility he often abdicated. He at least held his own on the boards.

Humphries was only 19 last season, so it's far too early to write him off. He has a quick first step and is able to create shots, so perhaps this year he won't be so anxious to force the action. If he can do that and improve the free-throw shooting, the Jazz may have themselves a worthy backup for Boozer. But the early returns are hugely disappointing.

Andrei Kirilenko — power forward
(59% PF, 41% SF)

Age: 24 Height: 6-9 Weight: 225
Most similar at age: Stromile Swift

Year		G	M/G	FG%	FT%	P/40	R/40	A/40	TS%		Ast		TO		Usg		Reb		PER	
2002-03	Uta*	80	27.7	.491	.800	17.4	7.6	2.5	59.8	1	12.8	40	12.6	43	18.2	29	11.5	6	21.17	4
2003-04	Uta	78	37.1	.443	.790	17.7	8.7	3.4	55.9	6	15.2	20	13.4	54	21.0	17	13.5	36	22.71	4
2004-05	Uta	41	32.9	.493	.784	19.0	7.6	3.9	59.9	2	17.5	5	11.9	40	21.2	13	11.7	49	24.45	4
2005-06	PRJ (7.9)			.471	.797	18.3	8.0	3.9	58.2		17.3		12.8		21.3		12.4		22.19	

* Season rankings are as small forward

Kirilenko is one of the game's most unique and underrated players, and it was his early-season knee injury that sent Utah's season into a tailspin. Kirilenko hasn't captured the fancy of legions of fans because he isn't a high-volume scorer nor a great outside shooter. He's just incredibly effective at taking advantage of his chances. Kirilenko's height and incredibly long arms allow him to finish in traffic and dunk over taller players. He's also fast, enabling him to get baskets in transition, and moves well without the ball to put himself in position for easy shots.

In addition, Kirilenko continues to hone his passing skills. His Assist Ratio wasn't anything special two years ago but last season was among the top five at his position. He needs more arc on his jumper and could use some post moves, but those are the only nits to pick about his game.

Defensively, Kirilenko is devastating, with incredibly long arms that he uses to contest shots. Kirilenko used those arms to lead the league in blocked shots, continuing an odd trend. For the past six seasons, the league leader in blocked shots has been 6'10" or shorter. This era of short shot-blockers like Kirilenko and Ben Wallace is an anomaly. The leader has been 6'11" or taller in each of the preceding 25 seasons.

Less well-known is Kirilenko's ability to pilfer dribblers. He nearly led the team in steals despite playing only 41 games. Overall, Utah gave up 8.3 more points per 48 minutes when he was off the court. Essentially, the Jazz were OK defensively as long as Kirilenko played but became the worst in the league as soon as he checked out.

Kirilenko lacks the strength of most power forwards, but he can play small forward alongside Boozer and shred opponents with his versatility. Alternatively, he can partner with Harpring in the frontcourt, where each covers the other's weaknesses. Harpring's muscle can protect Kirilenko from strength match-ups, while Kirilenko's quickness can save Harpring from guarding speedy small forwards. Regardless of how the Jazz line up, Kirilenko will be the centerpiece. His low-volume, high-percentage offense makes him unusual for an NBA superstar, but make no mistake: This is one of the ten best players in the league.

Randy Livingston — point guard
(62% PG, 38% SG)

Age: 30   Height: 6-4   Weight: 209

Most similar at age: N/A

Year		G	M/G	FG%	FT%	P/40	R/40	A/40	TS%		Ast		TO		Usg		Reb		PER	
2002-03	NO	2	6.0	.500	1.000	20.0	0.0	3.3	61.5		17.0		0.0		19.9		0.0		19.64	
2003-04	LAC	4	12.0	.200	.667	6.7	5.8	3.3	31.6		19.4		19.4		14.8		8.6		1.67	
2004-05	Uta	17	13.4	.423	.882	11.3	2.1	7.9	53.8		37.8		11.8		19.7		3.0		13.28	

Livingston's career just won't die. 2004–05 marked the third straight year he was picked up at the end of the season by a team in search of point guard help, as Utah grabbed him when Lopez went on the shelf. Livingston has had several knee injuries and can't outrun my cursor, but he's a smart player who doesn't turn the ball over, and coaches like that from their backup point guards. Utah might have been his last stop, but we've thought that before. Check back in March when the injuries start piling up; chances are that Livingston's phone will ring once again.

Raul Lopez — point guard
(100% PG)

Age: 25   Height: 6-0   Weight: 175

Most similar at age: Negele Knight

Year		G	M/G	FG%	FT%	P/40	R/40	A/40	TS%		Ast		TO		Usg		Reb		PER	
2003-04	Uta	82	19.7	.432	.856	14.1	3.8	7.5	50.4	32	29.1	25	16.6	62	23.9	18	5.9	21	12.01	48
2004-05	Uta	31	16.7	.422	.818	12.4	3.0	9.5	53.8	15	38.5	4	14.7	64	22.8	29	4.3	56	12.77	44
2005-06	*PRJ (32.7)*			*.418*	*.838*	*13.3*	*3.4*	*7.9*	*50.7*		*31.9*		*14.4*		*23.2*		*5.0*		*12.52*	

Lopez's once-promising career has been ruined by a series of knee injuries. He held down the backup point guard job last year until the knee trouble struck again and fared OK at the offensive end. His Turnover Ratio was way too high, but he was able to set up teammates and was one of Utah's few three-point threats, hitting 44 percent. Lopez has an unusually high dribble, helping account for the turnovers, but he runs the break well and operates pretty well on the pick-and-roll.

Defensively, it's another story. Lopez looked like he was back in his native Spain...at a bullfight. Because of the knee injuries, he couldn't stay in front of a turtle. His defensive shortcomings were the reason he failed to earn a starting job despite Utah's utter lack of offensive skill at the point.

Lopez was traded to the Grizzlies after the season, but that's a mere formality. He's heading back to Spain to play this season, where his lack of quickness should be less of a liability. It's a shame the knee injuries extinguished his potential so quickly.

Keith McLeod — point guard
(100% PG)

Age: 26   Height: 6-2   Weight: 188

Most similar at age: Vonteego Cummings

Year		G	M/G	FG%	FT%	P/40	R/40	A/40	TS%		Ast		TO		Usg		Reb		PER	
2003-04	Min	33	11.8	.329	.767	9.0	3.5	6.0	43.6		31.2		15.4		17.5		5.1		8.04	
2004-05	Uta	53	26.1	.350	.767	12.0	3.3	6.8	44.0	65	29.2	26	12.3	48	22.0	34	5.1	46	10.34	55
2005-06	*PRJ (37.8)*			*.360*	*.772*	*12.4*	*3.2*	*6.5*	*45.2*		*28.2*		*12.4*		*21.4*		*4.9*		*10.96*	

McLeod did nothing to earn the Jazz point guard job but was handed it anyway when the other candidates disqualified themselves. McLeod wasn't quite the defensive sieve that Arroyo and Lopez were, nor quite the offensive disaster that Eisley was, so Jerry Sloan settled on him.

McLeod played well offensively early in the season but quickly fell off the pace as the year progressed. He shot only 35 percent on the season, which is pretty awful when one considers he rarely shot three-pointers. McLeod preferred to take 15-footers off the dribble, which had the predictable result of killing his TS%: McLeod's ugly 44.0 mark was among basketball's worst.

McLeod isn't a great defender either, but he handles the ball well enough that he could be a decent backup point guard if he made a shot once in a while. Another team will probably take that chance this season, but there's almost no chance of him being a starter again.

Mehmet Okur   center
Defensive PER: 0.38 (69% C, 31% PF)

Age: 26   Height: 6-11   Weight: 249
Most similar at age: Vin Baker

Year		G	M/G	FG%	FT%	P/40	R/40	A/40	TS%		Ast		TO		Usg		Reb		PER	
2002-03	Det	72	19.0	.426	.733	14.5	9.8	2.1	51.4	34	11.5	22	10.7	12	17.6	17	14.5	38	14.75	28
2003-04	Det	71	22.3	.463	.775	17.2	10.6	1.7	53.8	21	8.6	38	12.6	31	19.1	13	14.4	34	18.34	8
2004-05	Uta	82	28.1	.468	.850	18.3	10.7	2.9	56.9	17	13.5	3	11.4	14	20.3	6	16.6	20	18.95	6
2005-06	PRJ (46.5)			.463	.813	16.6	10.6	2.4	55.6		12.0		11.4		18.9		15.8		17.90	

Statistically, Okur had the best season of his career. He thrived offensively in Utah's motion offense, getting numerous catches near the basket to set up free-throws or turnaround jumpers in the paint. He especially likes to shoot the turnaround from the left block after faking toward the baseline. As a result of the easy shots, he scored at a very high rate for a center and did so with a good TS% as well. Okur also shoots well from outside and is extremely effective both passing and shooting from the high post. As an added plus, he's a strong rebounder.

Unfortunately, Jerry Sloan never took a shine to him. The major reason was defense. Okur tended to casually jog back on defense and wasn't a good fit for the physical defensive tactics that Sloan prefers. He's not a shot-blocker nor is he terribly strong, so even when he played hard his defensive contribution was fairly limited. An additional black mark was the awful mullet he sported for much of the season.

Nonetheless, Sloan made a huge mistake by starting players like Radojevic and Collins while leaving Okur on the pine for much of the season. Okur was one of the Jazz's most effective offensive players, and his rebounding alone gave him some value at the defensive end. Giving him more minutes this year could add a few easy wins to Utah's ledger.

Alex Radojevic   center
(100% C)

Age: 29   Height: 7-3   Weight: 250
Most similar at age: N/A

Year		G	M/G	FG%	FT%	P/40	R/40	A/40	TS%	Ast	TO	Usg	Reb	PER
2004-05	Uta	12	10.7	.316	.700	5.9	8.8	1.9	40.6	8.9	33.8	11.0	12.4	-1.82

Seriously, why was this guy in the NBA? Anyone? I'm speechless.

Kirk Snyder   small forward
(52% SF, 47% SG, 1% PF)

Age: 22   Height: 6-6   Weight: 225
Most similar at age: Corey Benjamin

Year		G	M/G	FG%	FT%	P/40	R/40	A/40	TS%		Ast		TO		Usg		Reb		PER	
2004-05	Uta	68	13.3	.372	.667	14.9	5.3	1.6	45.6	60	7.6	61	12.5	50	19.3	26	8.3	36	8.48	60
2005-06	PRJ (28.8)			.386	.661	15.5	5.6	1.8	47.1		8.4		12.4		19.5		8.8		9.52	

Snyder was Utah's other 2004 draft disappointment, and his shot selection was arguably even worse than Humphries's. Snyder was billed as a smooth ballhandler coming out of college, but showed little interest in passing and was turnover-prone offensively. He kept firing away all season though, posting an above-average Usage Rate despite a deplorable 45.6 TS%.

Snyder didn't fare better on defense, especially when he guarded post players. Snyder was repeatedly burned on the blocks by bigger forwards and might have to play shooting guard to survive. Of course, his ballhandling numbers were bad even for a small forward, so that may be just as much of a stretch for him.

Snyder compounded matters by acting like an idiot. After a dunk against Houston he began taunting the Rockets' bench; Sloan went old school on him and suspended him. Later in the year Snyder got into a fight with Dallas's Jerry Stackhouse in a hallway after a game. Adding injury to insult, reports indicated he got his butt kicked.

Overall, his year was a complete failure. The Jazz were more than happy to include Snyder in the five-way trade for Ostertag, sending him to New Orleans. Snyder's contract is guaranteed for two more seasons, but he will need to shape up quickly if he wants his career to last a second beyond that. Both on and off the court, he has plenty to learn.

| **Deron Williams** | **point guard** | | **Age: 21** | **Height: 6-3** | **Weight: 210** |

Scouts are in love with Williams, but I have my suspicions. He shot 43 percent from the field and 67 percent from the line, neither of which augur stardom. Additionally, for a college point guard to average fewer than one steal per game suggests insufficient athleticism. Finally, he lost weight right before the draft and looked impressive in workouts, but I'm suspicious as to whether he can keep the pounds off. He certainly can pass and is an OK outside shooter, but I think they might have been better off taking Chris Paul.

| **C. J. Miles** | **shooting guard** | | **Age: 18** | **Height: 6-6** | **Weight: 207** |

A second-round pick, Miles turned pro out of high school and won't pay dividends for a couple of years, if ever. Scouts regard him as adequate in several areas but not particularly impressive in any single one, so Utah will send him to the D-League and see what Miles can produce.

| **Robert Whaley** | **center** | | **Age: 23** | **Height: 6-10** | **Weight: 260** |

An impressive banger despite his short stature for a center, Whaley has more baggage than O'Hare Airport and will be an interesting fit with Sloan in Utah. He had been a junior college All-American but lasted only half a season at Cincinnati before being dismissed for academic and attitude problems. His resume also includes multiple run-ins with the law and substance abuse issues. Other than that, I'm sure he's a great guy.

Shooting Guards

PER	Player	Team
23.28	Bryant, Kobe	LAL
23.17	Wade, Dwyane	Mia
22.32	Ginobili, Manu	SA
21.63	Hughes, Larry	Was
20.90	Allen, Ray	Sea
19.91	Maggette, Corey	LAC
18.98	Richardson, Jason	GS
18.30	Redd, Michael	Mil
16.77	Hoiberg, Fred	Min
16.75	Miller, Mike	Mem
16.59	Miller, Reggie	Ind
15.96	Hamilton, Richard	Det
15.93	Wells, Bonzi	Mem
15.90	Stackhouse, Jerry	Dal
15.23	Dixon, Juan	Was
15.20	Childress, Josh	Atl
15.18	Johnson, Joe	Phx
15.15	Crawford, Jamal	NY
14.98	Mobley, Cuttino	Orl-Sac
14.97	Davis, Ricky	Bos
14.80	Gordon, Ben	Chi
14.68	Allen, Tony	Bos
14.62	Daniels, Marquis	Dal
14.57	Brown, Devin	SA
14.43	Peterson, Morris	Tor
14.34	Finley, Michael	Dal
14.01	Barry, Brent	SA
13.97	Johnson, DerMarr	Den
13.67	Buckner, Greg	Den
13.62	Smith, Steve	Cha-Mia
13.49	Iguodala, Andre	Phi
13.37	Barry, Jon	Atl-Hou
13.28	Jones, Fred	Ind
12.84	Giricek, Gordan	Uta
12.48	Houston, Allan	NY
12.47	Van Exel, Nick	Por
12.43	Piatkowski, Eric	Chi
12.39	Planinic, Zoran	NJ
12.27	West, Delonte	Bos
12.15	Evans, Maurice	Sac

Small Forwards

PER	Player	Team
25.75	James, LeBron	Cle
22.95	McGrady, Tracy	Hou
22.83	Carter, Vince	Tor-NJ
21.82	Pierce, Paul	Bos
20.09	Hill, Grant	Orl
19.45	Lewis, Rashard	Sea
17.29	Stojakovic, Peja	Sac
17.11	Szczerbiak, Wally	Min
16.68	Anthony, Carmelo	Den
16.56	Rose, Jalen	Tor
16.53	Jefferson, Richard	NJ
16.23	Prince, Tayshaun	Det
16.10	Simmons, Bobby	LAC
16.04	Turkoglu, Hedo	Orl
15.87	Jackson, Stephen	Ind
15.80	Howard, Josh	Dal
15.78	Patterson, Ruben	Por
15.77	Butler, Caron	LAL
15.53	Harpring, Matt	Uta
15.46	Miles, Darius	Por
15.45	Outlaw, Travis	Por
15.43	Smith, Josh	Atl
14.84	Battier, Shane	Mem
14.72	Mason, Desmond	Mil
14.59	Williamson, Corliss	Phi-Sac
14.52	Dunleavy, Mike	GS
14.48	Nailon, Lee	NO
14.32	Harrington, Al	Atl
14.16	Person, Wesley	Mia-Den
14.16	Deng, Luol	Chi
14.16	Pietrus, Mickael	GS
14.07	Wallace, Gerald	Cha
13.68	Murray, Lamond	Tor
13.59	Jones, Eddie	Mia
13.59	Richardson, Quentin	Phx
13.36	Wilkins, Damien	Sea
13.24	Ariza, Trevor	NY
13.07	Jones, Jumaine	LAL
12.84	Korver, Kyle	Phi
12.29	White, Rodney	Den-GS

Point Guards

PER	Player	Team
23.23	Iverson, Allen	Phi
22.06	Nash, Steve	Phx
21.93	Marbury, Stephon	NY
21.29	Arenas, Gilbert	Was
20.78	Davis, Baron	NO-GS
19.55	Kidd, Jason	NJ
19.19	Bibby, Mike	Sac
19.05	Billups, Chauncey	Det
18.88	Francis, Steve	Orl
18.62	Cassell, Sam	Min
18.57	Tinsley, Jamaal	Ind
18.43	Terry, Jason	Dal
18.08	Daniels, Antonio	Sea
18.06	Knight, Brevin	Cha
17.97	Parker, Tony	SA
17.97	Jackson, Bobby	Sac
17.15	Boykins, Earl	Den
16.87	Hart, Jason	Cha
16.66	Stoudamire, Damon	Por
16.57	Miller, Andre	Den
16.52	James, Mike	Mil-Hou
16.46	Alston, Rafer	Tor
15.85	Claxton, Speedy	GS-NO
15.84	House, Eddie	C-M-S
15.57	Jones, Damon	Mia
15.48	Williams, Jason	Mem
15.23	Hinrich, Kirk	Chi
15.18	Payton, Gary	Bos
15.11	Goldwire, Anthony	Det-Mil
15.07	Delk, Tony	Atl
14.85	Dickau, Dan	Dal-NO
14.70	Harris, Devin	Dal
14.58	Ridnour, Luke	Sea
14.47	Nelson, Jameer	Orl
14.43	Sura, Bob	Hou
14.25	Johnson, Anthony	Ind
14.24	Udrih, Beno	SA
14.13	Lue, Tyronn	Hou-Atl
14.00	Williams, Maurice	Mil
13.93	Jaric, Marko	LAC

(continued next page)

PER by Position *(continued)*

Shooting Guards

PER	Player	Team
12.14	Bell, Raja	Uta
11.79	Wesley, David	NO-Hou
11.68	Anderson, Derek	Por
10.90	Welsch, Jiri	Bos-Cle
10.84	Smith, J. R.	NO
10.31	Bogans, Keith	Cha
10.23	Peeler, Anthony	Was
10.22	Jacobsen, Casey	Phx-NO
10.02	Rush, Kareem	LAL-Cha
9.97	Diaw, Boris	Atl
9.92	Christie, Doug	Sac-Orl
9.78	Murray, Ronald	Sea
9.69	Salmons, John	Phi
9.54	Green, Willie	Phi
9.54	Jones, Dahntay	Mem
9.52	Hunter, Lindsey	Det
9.42	Buford, Rodney	NJ
9.30	Hassell, Trenton	Min
9.26	Stevenson, DeShawn	Orl
9.00	Harris, Lucious	Cle
8.93	Pavlovic, Aleksandar	Cle
8.90	Hardaway, Anfernee	NY
8.86	Ross, Quinton	LAC
8.56	Newble, Ira	Cle
8.01	Strickland, Erick	Mil
7.63	Harrington, Junior	NO

Small Forwards

PER	Player	Team
12.21	Thomas, Tim	NY
12.10	Sprewell, Latrell	Min
11.80	Kapono, Jason	Cha
11.79	Russell, Bryon	Den
11.16	Jeffries, Jared	Was
11.07	Hayes, Jarvis	Was
10.93	Jackson, Jim	Hou-Phx
10.68	Griffin, Adrian	Chi
10.59	Williams, Eric	Tor
10.48	Posey, James	Mem
10.43	Jones, James	Ind
10.31	Butler, Rasual	Mia
10.09	Nachbar, Bostjan	Hou-NO
9.96	Nocioni, Andres	Chi
9.78	Augmon, Stacey	Orl
9.53	Bowen, Bruce	SA
8.93	Anderson, Shandon	NY-Mia
8.90	Rogers, Rodney	NO-Phi
8.88	Barnes, Matt	Sac
8.48	Snyder, Kirk	Uta
8.43	McKie, Aaron	Phi
7.83	Lynch, George	NO
7.76	Cheaney, Calbert	GS
5.10	Smith, Theron	Cha

Point Guards

PER	Player	Team
13.39	Atkins, Chucky	LAL
13.37	Fisher, Derek	GS
13.04	Watson, Earl	Mem
12.77	Lopez, Raul	Uta
12.69	Barbosa, Leandro	Phx
12.45	Palacio, Milt	Tor
12.36	McInnis, Jeff	Cle
12.27	Banks, Marcus	Bos
12.01	Hudson, Troy	Min
11.83	Best, Travis	NJ
11.66	Brunson, Rick	LAC
11.22	Arroyo, Carlos	Uta-Det
11.21	Carter, Anthony	Min
11.02	Armstrong, Darrell	NO-Dal
10.34	McLeod, Keith	Uta
10.32	Livingston, Shaun	LAC
10.04	Dooling, Keyon	Mia
10.03	Anderson, Kenny	Atl-LAC
9.80	Duhon, Chris	Chi
9.59	Telfair, Sebastian	Por
9.43	Brown, Tierre	LAL
9.41	Gill, Eddie	Ind
9.23	Eisley, Howard	Uta
8.95	Snow, Eric	Cle
8.83	Vaughn, Jacque	NJ
8.75	Ivey, Royal	Atl
8.36	Blake, Steve	Was

Power Forwards

PER	Player	Team
28.35	Garnett, Kevin	Min
27.13	Duncan, Tim	SA
26.18	Nowitzki, Dirk	Dal
24.45	Kirilenko, Andrei	Uta
22.85	O'Neal, Jermaine	Ind
22.57	Gasol, Pau	Mem
22.54	Brand, Elton	LAC
21.76	Marion, Shawn	Phx
19.92	Marshall, Donyell	Tor
19.77	Gooden, Drew	Cle
19.18	Boozer, Carlos	Uta
18.72	Abdur-Rahim, Shareef	Por
18.68	Randolph, Zach	Por
18.60	Webber, Chris	Sac-Phi
17.47	Martin, Kenyon	Den
17.34	LaFrentz, Raef	Bos
17.26	Odom, Lamar	LAL
17.23	Howard, Dwight	Orl
17.20	McDyess, Antonio	Det

Centers

PER	Player	Team
26.95	O'Neal, Shaquille	Mia
26.69	Stoudemire, Amare	Phx
23.22	Ming, Yao	Hou
20.71	Miller, Brad	Sac
19.55	Ilgauskas, Zydrunas	Cle
18.95	Okur, Mehmet	Uta
18.54	Andersen, Chris	NO
18.11	Gadzuric, Dan	Mil
18.08	Camby, Marcus	Den
17.54	Bosh, Chris	Tor
17.52	Wallace, Ben	Det
16.91	Fortson, Danny	Sea
16.52	Haywood, Brendan	Was
16.51	Mutombo, Dikembe	Hou
16.50	Chandler, Tyson	Chi
16.42	Mohammed, Nazr	NY-SA
16.35	Sweetney, Mike	NY
16.22	Curry, Eddy	Chi
16.17	Brezec, Primoz	Cha

Power Forwards

PER	Player	Team
16.95	Varejao, Anderson	Cle
16.90	Jamison, Antawn	Was
16.84	Murphy, Troy	GS
16.70	Swift, Stromile	Mem
16.59	Jefferson, Al	Bos
16.39	Wallace, Rasheed	Det
16.35	Okafor, Emeka	Cha
16.30	Laettner, Christian	Mia
15.96	Griffin, Eddie	Min
15.66	Van Horn, Keith	Mil-Dal
15.55	Haslem, Udonis	Mia
15.54	Brown, P. J.	NO
15.41	Walker, Antoine	Atl-Bos
15.18	Thomas, Kenny	Phi-Sac
15.10	Collison, Nick	Sea
14.97	Smith, Joe	Mil
14.93	Songaila, Darius	Sac
14.89	Horry, Robert	SA
14.64	Bonner, Matt	Tor
14.46	Harrington, Othella	Chi
14.23	Allen, Malik	Mia-Cha
14.15	Thomas, Kurt	NY
14.09	Cook, Brian	LAL
13.97	Cardinal, Brian	Mem
13.68	Radmanovic, Vladimir	Sea
13.52	Croshere, Austin	Ind
13.34	Krstic, Nenad	NJ
13.20	Williams, Jerome	NY
12.96	Howard, Juwan	Hou
12.94	Evans, Reggie	Sea
12.76	Kukoc, Toni	Mil
12.66	Moore, Mikki	LAC
12.40	Henderson, Alan	Dal
12.32	Padgett, Scott	Hou
12.06	Rose, Malik	SA-NY
11.54	Fizer, Marcus	Mil
11.33	Walton, Luke	LAL
11.19	Najera, Eduardo	GS-Den
11.12	Davis, Antonio	Chi
11.10	West, David	NO
11.01	Scalabrine, Brian	NJ
10.34	Brown, Kwame	Was
9.81	Gugliotta, Tom	Bos-Atl
9.40	Humphries, Kris	Uta
9.34	Taylor, Maurice	Hou-NY
9.06	Garrity, Pat	Orl
8.91	Weatherspoon, Clarence	Hou
8.90	Khryapa, Viktor	Por
8.08	McCarty, Walter	Bos-Phx
7.65	Bowen, Ryan	Hou

Centers

PER	Player	Team
15.94	Jackson, Marc	Phi
15.72	Mihm, Chris	LAL
15.61	Nenê	Den
15.57	Przybilla, Joel	Por
15.38	Foster, Jeff	Ind
15.33	Mourning, Alonzo	NJ-Mia
15.21	Dampier, Erick	Dal
14.91	Cato, Kelvin	Orl
14.68	Hunter, Steven	Phx
14.37	Dalembert, Samuel	Phi
14.32	Pachulia, Zaza	Mil
14.02	Rebraca, Zeljko	LAC
13.95	Wright, Lorenzen	Mem
13.72	Skinner, Brian	Phi-Sac
13.52	Wilcox, Chris	LAC
13.32	Davis, Dale	GS-Ind
13.14	Kaman, Chris	LAC
12.92	Thomas, Etan	Was
12.80	Magloire, Jamaal	NO
12.77	Harrison, David	Ind
12.70	Foyle, Adonal	GS
12.66	Drobnjak, Predrag	Atl
12.52	Blount, Mark	Bos
12.00	Nesterovic, Rasho	SA
11.96	Traylor, Robert	Cle
11.30	Woods, Loren	Tor
11.12	Pollard, Scot	Ind
11.11	Perkins, Kendrick	Bos
10.94	Bradley, Shawn	Dal
10.88	Collier, Jason	Atl
10.65	Elson, Francisco	Den
10.45	Ely, Melvin	Cha
10.35	Robinson, Clifford	GS-NJ
10.34	Olowokandi, Michael	Min
10.34	Ekezie, Obina	Atl
10.10	Ratliff, Theo	Por
9.91	Grant, Brian	LAL
9.91	Ostertag, Greg	Sac
9.83	James, Jerome	Sea
9.68	Doleac, Michael	Mia
9.46	Vroman, Jackson	Phx-NO
9.27	Borchardt, Curtis	Uta
9.03	Thomas, John	Min
8.53	Ruffin, Michael	Was
8.52	Battie, Tony	Orl
8.52	Collins, Jason	NJ
8.44	Massenburg, Tony	SA
8.25	Smith, Jabari	NJ
7.92	Collins, Jarron	Uta
6.87	Araujo, Rafael	Tor
6.76	Madsen, Mark	Min

Appendix II
TS% by Position

Shooting Guards

TS%	Player	Team
66.4	Hoiberg, Fred	Min
63.8	Buckner, Greg	Den
61.4	Miller, Mike	Mem
60.9	Ginobili, Manu	SA
60.5	Johnson, DerMarr	Den
58.2	Miller, Reggie	Ind
58.0	Iguodala, Andre	Phi
58.0	Barry, Brent	SA
57.4	Maggette, Corey	LAC
57.3	Piatkowski, Eric	Chi
57.0	Barry, Jon	Atl-Hou
56.3	Bryant, Kobe	LAL
56.1	Wade, Dwyane	Mia
55.6	Johnson, Joe	Phx
55.5	Jacobsen, Casey	Phx-NO
55.5	Allen, Ray	Sea
55.5	Mobley, Cuttino	Orl-Sac
55.4	Smith, Steve	Cha-Mia
55.1	Jones, Fred	Ind
54.7	Davis, Ricky	Bos
54.3	Peterson, Morris	Tor
54.3	Childress, Josh	Atl
54.2	Allen, Tony	Bos
53.6	Redd, Michael	Mil
53.4	Planinic, Zoran	NJ
53.4	Jones, Dahntay	Mem
53.0	Brown, Devin	SA
52.9	Houston, Allan	NY
52.8	Hamilton, Richard	Det
52.7	Bell, Raja	Uta
52.6	Gordon, Ben	Chi
52.5	Stackhouse, Jerry	Dal
52.4	West, Delonte	Bos
52.3	Hughes, Larry	Was
52.1	Crawford, Jamal	NY
51.9	Finley, Michael	Dal
51.8	Richardson, Jason	GS
51.8	Dixon, Juan	Was
51.8	Welsch, Jiri	Bos-Cle
51.6	Giricek, Gordan	Uta
51.6	Pavlovic, Aleksandar	Cle

Small Forwards

TS%	Player	Team
59.5	Szczerbiak, Wally	Min
58.8	Korver, Kyle	Phi
58.4	Stojakovic, Peja	Sac
58.3	Pierce, Paul	Bos
57.1	Lewis, Rashard	Sea
57.0	Person, Wesley	Mia-Den
56.5	Hill, Grant	Orl
56.2	Rose, Jalen	Tor
55.8	Patterson, Ruben	Por
55.6	Prince, Tayshaun	Det
55.6	Jones, Eddie	Mia
55.6	Jones, Jumaine	LAL
55.5	Battier, Shane	Mem
55.4	James, LeBron	Cle
55.3	Jackson, Jim	Hou-Phx
54.9	Harpring, Matt	Uta
54.1	Carter, Vince	Tor-NJ
54.0	Simmons, Bobby	LAC
53.9	Pietrus, Mickael	GS
53.9	Dunleavy, Mike	GS
53.7	Murray, Lamond	Tor
53.7	Jones, James	Ind
53.7	Jefferson, Richard	NJ
53.7	Russell, Bryon	Den
53.6	Williamson, Corliss	Phi-Sac
53.6	Thomas, Tim	NY
53.5	Nachbar, Bostjan	Hou-NO
53.5	Howard, Josh	Dal
53.2	Turkoglu, Hedo	Orl
53.2	Outlaw, Travis	Por
52.9	Williams, Eric	Tor
52.8	Butler, Caron	LAL
52.6	Mason, Desmond	Mil
52.6	McGrady, Tracy	Hou
52.6	Anthony, Carmelo	Den
52.2	Richardson, Quentin	Phx
52.1	Bowen, Bruce	SA
51.8	Anderson, Shandon	NY-Mia
51.8	Jackson, Stephen	Ind
51.3	Jeffries, Jared	Was
51.1	Nailon, Lee	NO

Point Guards

TS%	Player	Team
62.5	Jones, Damon	Mia
60.9	Billups, Chauncey	Det
60.6	Terry, Jason	Dal
60.6	Nash, Steve	Phx
57.5	Barbosa, Leandro	Phx
57.5	Goldwire, Anthony	Det-Mil
57.5	Marbury, Stephon	NY
56.5	Arenas, Gilbert	Was
55.8	Atkins, Chucky	LAL
55.7	Daniels, Antonio	Sea
54.9	Udrih, Beno	SA
54.3	Bibby, Mike	Sac
54.2	Lue, Tyronn	Hou-Atl
54.1	Miller, Andre	Den
53.8	Lopez, Raul	Uta
53.7	Payton, Gary	Bos
53.7	Jackson, Bobby	Sac
53.4	James, Mike	Mil-Hou
53.4	Hart, Jason	Cha
53.3	Sura, Bob	Hou
53.2	Iverson, Allen	Phi
53.0	Boykins, Earl	Den
53.0	Harris, Devin	Dal
52.9	Cassell, Sam	Min
52.8	Parker, Tony	SA
52.6	Johnson, Anthony	Ind
52.5	House, Eddie	C-M-S
52.2	Alston, Rafer	Tor
52.2	Williams, Jason	Mem
52.1	Francis, Steve	Orl
52.0	Banks, Marcus	Bos
51.9	Fisher, Derek	GS
51.8	Tinsley, Jamaal	Ind
51.8	Dickau, Dan	Dal-NO
51.5	Davis, Baron	NO-GS
51.2	Delk, Tony	Atl
51.1	Vaughn, Jacque	NJ
51.0	Nelson, Jameer	Orl
51.0	Stoudamire, Damon	Por
50.8	Best, Travis	NJ
50.7	Palacio, Milt	Tor

Shooting Guards

TS%	Player	Team
51.5	Wells, Bonzi	Mem
51.5	Hassell, Trenton	Min
51.3	Wesley, David	Hou
51.1	Evans, Maurice	Sac
51.1	Salmons, John	Phi
50.3	Anderson, Derek	Por
49.4	Van Exel, Nick	Por
48.4	Daniels, Marquis	Dal
48.4	Peeler, Anthony	Was
48.2	Newble, Ira	Cle
48.0	Hardaway, Anfernee	NY
47.9	Diaw, Boris	Atl
47.8	Smith, J. R.	NO
47.5	Harris, Lucious	Cle
47.1	Ross, Quinton	LAC
47.1	Christie, Doug	Sac-Orl
47.1	Rush, Kareem	LAL-Cha
46.5	Bogans, Keith	Cha
45.7	Green, Willie	Phi
45.6	Stevenson, DeShawn	Orl
45.3	Strickland, Erick	Mil
43.7	Buford, Rodney	NJ
43.5	Hunter, Lindsey	Det
43.3	Murray, Ronald	Sea
42.1	Harrington, Junior	NO

Small Forwards

TS%	Player	Team
51.1	Miles, Darius	Por
51.0	Wallace, Gerald	Cha
51.0	McKie, Aaron	Phi
50.8	Harrington, Al	Atl
50.6	Smith, Josh	Atl
50.3	Ariza, Trevor	NY
50.0	Posey, James	Mem
50.0	Wilkins, Damien	Sea
49.6	Deng, Luol	Chi
48.9	Sprewell, Latrell	Min
48.8	Butler, Rasual	Mia
48.6	Kapono, Jason	Cha
48.4	Nocioni, Andres	Chi
48.0	Augmon, Stacey	Orl
47.5	Hayes, Jarvis	Was
47.5	White, Rodney	Den-GS
46.5	Barnes, Matt	Sac
46.2	Rogers, Rodney	NO-Phi
45.6	Snyder, Kirk	Uta
44.4	Cheaney, Calbert	GS
41.9	Griffin, Adrian	Chi
41.2	Lynch, George	NO
36.7	Smith, Theron	Cha

Point Guards

TS%	Player	Team
50.6	Kidd, Jason	NJ
50.4	Williams, Maurice	Mil
50.4	Ridnour, Luke	Sea
50.0	Watson, Earl	Mem
50.0	Jaric, Marko	LAC
49.5	Hinrich, Kirk	Chi
49.5	McInnis, Jeff	Cle
49.5	Knight, Brevin	Cha
49.3	Claxton, Speedy	GS-NO
49.1	Hudson, Troy	Min
48.6	Dooling, Keyon	Mia
48.4	Gill, Eddie	Ind
48.4	Ivey, Royal	Atl
47.1	Telfair, Sebastian	Por
47.1	Duhon, Chris	Chi
47.0	Eisley, Howard	Uta
46.8	Blake, Steve	Was
46.7	Anderson, Kenny	Atl-LAC
46.6	Arroyo, Carlos	Uta-Det
46.1	Livingston, Shaun	LAC
46.0	Brunson, Rick	LAC
45.4	Carter, Anthony	Min
44.5	Snow, Eric	Cle
44.0	McLeod, Keith	Uta
43.7	Brown, Tierre	LAL
43.0	Armstrong, Darrell	NO-Dal

Power Forwards

TS%	Player	Team
61.9	Laettner, Christian	Mia
59.9	Kirilenko, Andrei	Uta
59.6	Bonner, Matt	Tor
59.1	Marshall, Donyell	Tor
58.8	Haslem, Udonis	Mia
58.7	LaFrentz, Raef	Bos
58.2	Gasol, Pau	Mem
58.1	Abdur-Rahim, Shareef	Por
57.8	Nowitzki, Dirk	Dal
57.3	Collison, Nick	Sea
57.1	Howard, Dwight	Orl
57.1	Moore, Mikki	LAC
56.7	Garnett, Kevin	Min
56.6	Songaila, Darius	Sac
56.4	Smith, Joe	Mil
56.3	Williams, Jerome	NY
56.0	Boozer, Carlos	Uta
55.9	Harrington, Othella	Chi
55.6	Marion, Shawn	Phx
55.4	Jefferson, Al	Bos

Centers

TS%	Player	Team
68.2	Fortson, Danny	Sea
62.5	Rebraca, Zeljko	LAC
61.7	Stoudemire, Amare	Phx
61.4	Ming, Yao	Hou
60.0	Cato, Kelvin	Orl
59.6	Hunter, Steven	Phx
59.6	Przybilla, Joel	Por
59.6	Miller, Brad	Sac
59.2	Sweetney, Mike	NY
58.9	Harrison, David	Ind
58.8	Haywood, Brendan	Was
58.3	O'Neal, Shaquille	Mia
58.3	Curry, Eddy	Chi
58.1	Andersen, Chris	NO
58.0	Dampier, Erick	Dal
57.5	Mutombo, Dikembe	Hou
56.9	Okur, Mehmet	Uta
56.5	Chandler, Tyson	Chi
55.9	Blount, Mark	Bos
55.2	Mihm, Chris	LAL

(continued next page)

TS% by Position *(continued)*

Power Forwards			Centers		
TS%	Player	Team	TS%	Player	Team
55.4	Brand, Elton	LAC	55.1	Foster, Jeff	Ind
55.0	Van Horn, Keith	Mil-Dal	55.1	Nenê	Den
54.9	Padgett, Scott	Hou	55.1	Gadzuric, Dan	Mil
54.8	Gooden, Drew	Cle	55.0	Brezec, Primoz	Cha
54.7	Krstic, Nenad	NJ	55.0	Ilgauskas, Zydrunas	Cle
54.2	McDyess, Antonio	Det	54.8	Jackson, Marc	Phi
54.0	Duncan, Tim	SA	54.7	Bosh, Chris	Tor
53.9	Odom, Lamar	LAL	54.3	Dalembert, Samuel	Phi
53.9	Henderson, Alan	Dal	54.3	Wilcox, Chris	LAC
53.4	Varejao, Anderson	Cle	53.9	Grant, Brian	LAL
53.3	Horry, Robert	SA	53.3	James, Jerome	Sea
53.3	Radmanovic, Vladimir	Sea	52.6	Madsen, Mark	Min
53.1	Croshere, Austin	Ind	52.6	Pachulia, Zaza	Mil
52.5	McCarty, Walter	Bos-Phx	52.2	Thomas, John	Min
52.3	Kukoc, Toni	Mil	52.2	Kaman, Chris	LAC
52.2	Cook, Brian	LAL	52.1	Thomas, Etan	Was
52.1	Martin, Kenyon	Den	52.1	Mohammed, Nazr	NY-SA
52.0	O'Neal, Jermaine	Ind	51.6	Ekezie, Obina	Atl
51.7	Swift, Stromile	Mem	51.5	Perkins, Kendrick	Bos
51.6	Davis, Antonio	Chi	51.5	Mourning, Alonzo	NJ-Mia
51.5	Thomas, Kenny	Phi-Sac	51.4	Foyle, Adonal	GS
51.2	Allen, Malik	Mia-Cha	51.2	Davis, Dale	GS-Ind
51.2	Brown, P. J.	NO	50.9	Collins, Jarron	Uta
51.2	Evans, Reggie	Sea	50.6	Pollard, Scot	Ind
51.1	Randolph, Zach	Por	50.5	Camby, Marcus	Den
51.1	Rose, Malik	SA-NY	50.1	Drobnjak, Predrag	Atl
51.0	Cardinal, Brian	Mem	50.1	Wright, Lorenzen	Mem
50.6	Jamison, Antawn	Was	50.0	Ratliff, Theo	Por
50.5	Garrity, Pat	Orl	49.8	Battie, Tony	Orl
49.9	Wallace, Rasheed	Det	49.4	Elson, Francisco	Den
49.8	Fizer, Marcus	Mil	49.4	Skinner, Brian	Phi-Sac
49.7	Brown, Kwame	Was	49.4	Bradley, Shawn	Dal
49.5	Murphy, Troy	GS	49.4	Collier, Jason	Atl
49.4	Howard, Juwan	Hou	49.2	Borchardt, Curtis	Uta
49.2	Walton, Luke	LAL	49.2	Araujo, Rafael	Tor
48.9	Najera, Eduardo	GS-Den	48.2	Smith, Jabari	NJ
48.8	Thomas, Kurt	NY	48.0	Magloire, Jamaal	NO
48.0	Taylor, Maurice	Hou-NY	48.0	Olowokandi, Michael	Min
47.9	West, David	NO	47.1	Robinson, Clifford	GS-NJ
47.9	Okafor, Emeka	Cha	47.1	Collins, Jason	NJ
47.8	Walker, Antoine	Atl-Bos	46.7	Massenburg, Tony	SA
47.5	Weatherspoon, Clarence	Hou	46.5	Ely, Melvin	Cha
47.4	Khryapa, Viktor	Por	46.3	Woods, Loren	Tor
47.4	Griffin, Eddie	Min	46.3	Nesterovic, Rasho	SA
47.2	Webber, Chris	Sac-Phi	46.1	Traylor, Robert	Cle
46.8	Scalabrine, Brian	NJ	46.0	Doleac, Michael	Mia
46.2	Bowen, Ryan	Hou	45.9	Wallace, Ben	Det
46.0	Gugliotta, Tom	Bos-Atl	45.7	Vroman, Jackson	Phx-NO
41.9	Humphries, Kris	Uta	43.2	Ruffin, Michael	Was
			43.2	Ostertag, Greg	Sac

Appendix III
Assist Ratio by Position

Shooting Guards			**Small Forwards**			**Point Guards**		
AST	Player	Team	AST	Player	Team	AST	Player	Team
24.9	Van Exel, Nick	Por	20.6	James, LeBron	Cle	41.9	Knight, Brevin	Cha
24.9	Christie, Doug	Sac-Orl	18.0	Lynch, George	NO	41.6	Nash, Steve	Phx
23.6	Diaw, Boris	Atl	17.6	McKie, Aaron	Phi	40.2	Brunson, Rick	LAC
22.0	Anderson, Derek	Por	17.5	Jackson, Jim	Hou-Phx	38.5	Lopez, Raul	Uta
21.9	Salmons, John	Phi	17.5	McGrady, Tracy	Hou	38.1	Carter, Anthony	Min
21.7	Hunter, Lindsey	Det	16.6	Pierce, Paul	Bos	34.8	Duhon, Chris	Chi
21.6	Strickland, Erick	Mil	15.5	Prince, Tayshaun	Det	33.9	Jaric, Marko	LAC
21.1	Barry, Jon	Atl-Hou	15.2	Barnes, Matt	Sac	33.3	Ridnour, Luke	Sea
20.9	Harrington, Junior	NO	15.1	Griffin, Adrian	Chi	33.1	Palacio, Milt	Tor
20.8	Wade, Dwyane	Mia	15.1	Dunleavy, Mike	GS	33.0	Kidd, Jason	NJ
20.5	Peeler, Anthony	Was	14.6	Carter, Vince	Tor-NJ	32.9	Johnson, Anthony	Ind
20.1	Ginobili, Manu	SA	14.3	Jeffries, Jared	Was	32.8	Payton, Gary	Bos
19.9	West, Delonte	Bos	14.2	Hill, Grant	Orl	32.8	Williams, Jason	Mem
19.5	Barry, Brent	SA	14.2	Jones, Eddie	Mia	32.8	Snow, Eric	Cle
19.2	Hamilton, Richard	Det	14.0	Jefferson, Richard	NJ	32.5	Williams, Maurice	Mil
18.4	Miller, Mike	Mem	13.9	Deng, Luol	Chi	32.5	Hart, Jason	Cha
18.4	Crawford, Jamal	NY	13.9	Szczerbiak, Wally	Min	32.3	Livingston, Shaun	LAC
18.2	Wesley, David	Hou	13.9	Simmons, Bobby	LAC	32.3	Armstrong, Darrell	NO-Dal
18.0	Smith, Steve	Cha-Mia	13.4	Patterson, Ruben	Por	31.8	Arroyo, Carlos	Uta-Det
17.5	Iguodala, Andre	Phi	13.4	Harrington, Al	Atl	31.5	Watson, Earl	Mem
17.4	Bryant, Kobe	LAL	13.4	Russell, Bryon	Den	31.3	Miller, Andre	Den
17.1	Johnson, Joe	Phx	13.3	Turkoglu, Hedo	Orl	31.2	Eisley, Howard	Uta
16.7	Buckner, Greg	Den	13.3	Sprewell, Latrell	Min	30.8	Claxton, Speedy	GS-NO
16.6	Dixon, Juan	Was	13.3	Williams, Eric	Tor	30.8	Terry, Jason	Dal
16.5	Hughes, Larry	Was	13.0	Korver, Kyle	Phi	30.2	Sura, Bob	Hou
16.5	Daniels, Marquis	Dal	12.8	Mason, Desmond	Mil	29.2	McLeod, Keith	Uta
16.5	Jones, Fred	Ind	12.8	Cheaney, Calbert	GS	29.0	Alston, Rafer	Tor
15.8	Hardaway, Anfernee	NY	12.3	Nocioni, Andres	Chi	27.9	Lue, Tyronn	Hou-Atl
15.3	Green, Willie	Phi	12.2	Wallace, Gerald	Cha	27.7	Goldwire, Anthony	Det-Mil
15.3	Planinic, Zoran	NJ	12.2	Rose, Jalen	Tor	27.3	Marbury, Stephon	NY
14.9	Davis, Ricky	Bos	12.1	Posey, James	Mem	27.0	Daniels, Antonio	Sea
14.9	Giricek, Gordan	Uta	12.0	Rogers, Rodney	NO-Phi	26.9	Billups, Chauncey	Det
14.9	Welsch, Jiri	Bos-Cle	12.0	Miles, Darius	Por	26.8	Davis, Baron	NO-GS
14.6	Houston, Allan	NY	11.8	Smith, Josh	Atl	26.7	Telfair, Sebastian	Por
14.4	Richardson, Jason	GS	11.7	Ariza, Trevor	NY	26.4	Anderson, Kenny	Atl-LAC
14.2	Brown, Devin	SA	11.4	Anderson, Shandon	NY-Mia	26.2	McInnis, Jeff	Cle
14.0	Mobley, Cuttino	Orl-Sac	11.3	White, Rodney	Den-GS	26.2	Hinrich, Kirk	Chi
13.7	Finley, Michael	Dal	11.1	Person, Wesley	Mia-Den	26.1	Tinsley, Jamaal	Ind
13.5	Allen, Ray	Sea	11.0	Hayes, Jarvis	Was	25.9	Jones, Damon	Mia
13.3	Maggette, Corey	LAC	10.8	Thomas, Tim	NY	25.8	Cassell, Sam	Min

(continued next page)

Assist Ratio by Position *(continued)*

Shooting Guards

AST	Player	Team
13.3	Smith, J. R.	NO
13.2	Miller, Reggie	Ind
13.2	Bogans, Keith	Cha
12.8	Peterson, Morris	Tor
12.7	Hoiberg, Fred	Min
12.5	Rush, Kareem	LAL-Cha
12.5	Ross, Quinton	LAC
12.5	Murray, Ronald	Sea
12.4	Stackhouse, Jerry	Dal
12.1	Childress, Josh	Atl
12.0	Jacobsen, Casey	Phx-NO
11.8	Hassell, Trenton	Min
11.6	Piatkowski, Eric	Chi
11.6	Johnson, DerMarr	Den
11.6	Stevenson, DeShawn	Orl
10.8	Pavlovic, Aleksandar	Cle
10.8	Gordon, Ben	Chi
9.7	Bell, Raja	Uta
9.7	Allen, Tony	Bos
9.5	Newble, Ira	Cle
9.2	Wells, Bonzi	Mem
9.1	Buford, Rodney	NJ
9.0	Redd, Michael	Mil
8.3	Harris, Lucious	Cle
7.0	Evans, Maurice	Sac
6.2	Jones, Dahntay	Mem

Small Forwards

AST	Player	Team
10.7	Pietrus, Mickael	GS
10.6	Richardson, Quentin	Phx
10.5	Nachbar, Bostjan	Hou-NO
10.5	Harpring, Matt	Uta
10.5	Smith, Theron	Cha
10.3	Augmon, Stacey	Orl
10.2	Jackson, Stephen	Ind
10.2	Anthony, Carmelo	Den
10.1	Butler, Caron	LAL
10.0	Stojakovic, Peja	Sac
9.8	Butler, Rasual	Mia
9.7	Murray, Lamond	Tor
9.5	Battier, Shane	Mem
9.5	Wilkins, Damien	Sea
9.4	Nailon, Lee	NO
9.1	Bowen, Bruce	SA
9.1	Williamson, Corliss	Phi-Sac
8.5	Howard, Josh	Dal
8.4	Outlaw, Travis	Por
8.2	Jones, James	Ind
7.6	Snyder, Kirk	Uta
7.5	Kapono, Jason	Cha
6.8	Jones, Jumaine	LAL
6.3	Lewis, Rashard	Sea

Point Guards

AST	Player	Team
25.8	Banks, Marcus	Bos
25.7	Hudson, Troy	Min
25.7	Dickau, Dan	Dal-NO
25.6	Boykins, Earl	Den
25.5	Harris, Devin	Dal
25.4	Brown, Tierre	LAL
25.0	Parker, Tony	SA
24.7	Bibby, Mike	Sac
24.4	Stoudamire, Damon	Por
24.3	Ivey, Royal	Atl
23.6	Fisher, Derek	GS
23.5	Atkins, Chucky	LAL
23.0	Nelson, Jameer	Orl
22.9	Udrih, Beno	SA
22.2	Francis, Steve	Orl
22.2	James, Mike	Mil-Hou
21.2	Dooling, Keyon	Mia
21.1	Barbosa, Leandro	Phx
20.3	Blake, Steve	Was
19.2	Iverson, Allen	Phi
18.9	House, Eddie	C-M-S
18.7	Best, Travis	NJ
18.2	Vaughn, Jacque	NJ
16.7	Arenas, Gilbert	Was
16.1	Jackson, Bobby	Sac
15.5	Gill, Eddie	Ind
12.9	Delk, Tony	Atl

Power Forwards

AST	Player	Team
27.7	Kukoc, Toni	Mil
23.1	Walton, Luke	LAL
20.4	Garnett, Kevin	Min
18.2	Odom, Lamar	LAL
17.5	Kirilenko, Andrei	Uta
16.9	Webber, Chris	Sac-Phi
15.2	Cardinal, Brian	Mem
14.4	Scalabrine, Brian	NJ
13.5	Fizer, Marcus	Mil
13.4	Gugliotta, Tom	Bos-Atl
13.2	Boozer, Carlos	Uta
13.1	Thomas, Kenny	Phi-Sac
13.0	Songaila, Darius	Sac
12.9	Walker, Antoine	Atl-Bos
12.5	Martin, Kenyon	Den
12.0	Brown, P. J.	NO
12.0	Gasol, Pau	Mem
11.6	Duncan, Tim	SA
11.2	Brand, Elton	LAC

Centers

AST	Player	Team
20.0	Miller, Brad	Sac
14.4	Camby, Marcus	Den
13.5	Okur, Mehmet	Uta
12.7	Ostertag, Greg	Sac
12.2	Nenê	Den
12.1	Collins, Jarron	Uta
11.7	Robinson, Clifford	GS-NJ
11.5	Blount, Mark	Bos
11.2	Smith, Jabari	NJ
10.9	O'Neal, Shaquille	Mia
10.9	Borchardt, Curtis	Uta
10.8	Vroman, Jackson	Phx-NO
9.7	Ruffin, Michael	Was
9.7	Bosh, Chris	Tor
9.5	Andersen, Chris	NO
8.8	Ely, Melvin	Cha
8.8	Wallace, Ben	Det
8.8	Traylor, Robert	Cle
8.7	Skinner, Brian	Phi-Sac

Power Forwards

AST	Player	Team
11.1	Padgett, Scott	Hou
11.0	Nowitzki, Dirk	Dal
11.0	Howard, Juwan	Hou
11.0	Abdur-Rahim, Shareef	Por
10.9	Horry, Robert	SA
10.7	Thomas, Kurt	NY
10.6	Laettner, Christian	Mia
10.5	Najera, Eduardo	GS-Den
10.2	Croshere, Austin	Ind
10.0	Wallace, Rasheed	Det
9.7	Gooden, Drew	Cle
9.7	Jamison, Antawn	Was
9.6	Taylor, Maurice	Hou-NY
9.5	Van Horn, Keith	Mil-Dal
9.4	Humphries, Kris	Uta
9.4	Marshall, Donyell	Tor
9.1	Marion, Shawn	Phx
9.1	Khryapa, Viktor	Por
8.9	Radmanovic, Vladimir	Sea
8.5	LaFrentz, Raef	Bos
8.4	Harrington, Othella	Chi
8.3	Davis, Antonio	Chi
8.2	Randolph, Zach	Por
8.2	Brown, Kwame	Was
7.9	West, David	NO
7.8	McCarty, Walter	Bos-Phx
7.7	Haslem, Udonis	Mia
7.6	Rose, Malik	SA-NY
7.6	Moore, Mikki	LAC
7.5	McDyess, Antonio	Det
7.5	Murphy, Troy	GS
7.5	Krstic, Nenad	NJ
6.8	Griffin, Eddie	Min
6.6	O'Neal, Jermaine	Ind
6.6	Allen, Malik	Mia-Cha
6.5	Williams, Jerome	NY
6.2	Weatherspoon, Clarence	Hou
6.1	Cook, Brian	LAL
6.0	Swift, Stromile	Mem
6.0	Garrity, Pat	Orl
6.0	Varejao, Anderson	Cle
5.9	Bonner, Matt	Tor
5.9	Evans, Reggie	Sea
5.7	Bowen, Ryan	Hou
5.6	Smith, Joe	Mil
5.3	Howard, Dwight	Orl
4.7	Okafor, Emeka	Cha
4.4	Collison, Nick	Sea
4.4	Jefferson, Al	Bos
3.3	Henderson, Alan	Dal

Centers

AST	Player	Team
8.5	Kaman, Chris	LAC
8.2	Pachulia, Zaza	Mil
7.9	Collins, Jason	NJ
7.9	Magloire, Jamaal	NO
7.6	Doleac, Michael	Mia
7.6	Przybilla, Joel	Por
7.6	Nesterovic, Rasho	SA
7.4	Jackson, Marc	Phi
7.3	Perkins, Kendrick	Bos
7.2	Wright, Lorenzen	Mem
7.2	Wilcox, Chris	LAC
7.2	Brezec, Primoz	Cha
6.9	Elson, Francisco	Den
6.9	Davis, Dale	GS-Ind
6.7	Ilgauskas, Zydrunas	Cle
6.5	Stoudemire, Amare	Phx
6.5	Drobnjak, Predrag	Atl
6.3	Foyle, Adonal	GS
6.2	Thomas, John	Min
6.0	Dampier, Erick	Dal
5.8	Haywood, Brendan	Was
5.7	Grant, Brian	LAL
5.7	Madsen, Mark	Min
5.7	Chandler, Tyson	Chi
5.6	Sweetney, Mike	NY
5.3	Rebraca, Zeljko	LAC
5.1	Foster, Jeff	Ind
5.1	Mihm, Chris	LAL
5.0	Cato, Kelvin	Orl
4.9	Mourning, Alonzo	NJ-Mia
4.5	Woods, Loren	Tor
4.5	Olowokandi, Michael	Min
4.2	Battie, Tony	Orl
4.2	Ming, Yao	Hou
4.1	Araujo, Rafael	Tor
4.0	Pollard, Scot	Ind
3.9	Thomas, Etan	Was
3.8	Massenburg, Tony	SA
3.7	Ratliff, Theo	Por
3.7	Dalembert, Samuel	Phi
3.6	Collier, Jason	Atl
3.5	Curry, Eddy	Chi
3.4	Mohammed, Nazr	NY-SA
3.3	Harrison, David	Ind
3.2	Bradley, Shawn	Dal
3.2	Gadzuric, Dan	Mil
2.9	Ekezie, Obinna	Atl
2.7	James, Jerome	Sea
2.4	Hunter, Steven	Phx
1.6	Mutombo, Dikembe	Hou
1.5	Fortson, Danny	Sea

Appendix IV
Turnover Ratio by Position

Shooting Guards			Small Forwards			Point Guards		
TO	**Player**	**Team**	**TO**	**Player**	**Team**	**TO**	**Player**	**Team**
4.6	Hoiberg, Fred	Min	5.6	Kapono, Jason	Cha	6.2	Goldwire, Anthony	Det-Mil
5.0	Finley, Michael	Dal	5.9	Person, Wesley	Mia-Den	6.7	Delk, Tony	Atl
5.8	Buford, Rodney	NJ	6.9	Bowen, Bruce	SA	6.8	Daniels, Antonio	Sea
7.0	Redd, Michael	Mil	7.0	Butler, Rasual	Mia	6.9	House, Eddie	Cha-Mil-Sac
7.0	Evans, Maurice	Sac	7.1	Wilkins, Damien	Sea	7.6	Jackson, Bobby	Sac
7.1	Smith, Steve	Cha-Mia	7.4	Richardson, Quentin	Phx	7.8	McInnis, Jeff	Cle
7.1	Harris, Lucious	Cle	7.4	Stojakovic, Peja	Sac	8.1	Jones, Damon	Mia
7.3	Miller, Reggie	Ind	7.5	Carter, Vince	Tor-NJ	8.3	Boykins, Earl	Den
7.3	Houston, Allan	NY	7.7	Jones, Jumaine	LAL	8.7	Stoudamire, Damon	Por
7.7	Peterson, Morris	Tor	7.9	McGrady, Tracy	Hou	9.0	James, Mike	Mil-Hou
8.0	Allen, Ray	Sea	8.1	Jones, Eddie	Mia	9.0	Hart, Jason	Cha
8.4	Barry, Brent	SA	8.2	Battier, Shane	Mem	9.1	Lue, Tyronn	Hou-Atl
8.6	Richardson, Jason	GS	8.2	Lewis, Rashard	Sea	9.3	Bibby, Mike	Sac
8.7	Rush, Kareem	LAL-Cha	8.4	Hayes, Jarvis	Was	9.3	Hinrich, Kirk	Chi
8.7	Brown, Devin	SA	8.9	Russell, Bryon	Den	9.4	Cassell, Sam	Min
8.7	Wesley, David	Hou	8.9	Butler, Caron	LAL	9.4	Best, Travis	NJ
8.7	Johnson, Joe	Phx	9.1	Simmons, Bobby	LAC	9.5	Marbury, Stephon	NY
8.7	Bell, Raja	Uta	9.2	Cheaney, Calbert	GS	9.6	Alston, Rafer	Tor
8.9	Hughes, Larry	Was	9.2	Prince, Tayshaun	Det	9.7	Davis, Baron	NO-GS
8.9	Hassell, Trenton	Min	9.3	James, LeBron	Cle	9.8	Claxton, Speedy	GS-NO
9.0	Crawford, Jamal	NY	9.4	Sprewell, Latrell	Min	9.8	Arenas, Gilbert	Was
9.2	Ross, Quinton	LAC	9.5	Nailon, Lee	NO	10.0	Atkins, Chucky	LAL
9.4	Buckner, Greg	Den	9.5	White, Rodney	Den-GS	10.1	Kidd, Jason	NJ
9.6	Stevenson, DeShawn	Orl	9.6	Szczerbiak, Wally	Min	10.1	Fisher, Derek	GS
9.8	Giricek, Gordan	Uta	9.7	Jones, James	Ind	10.3	Ridnour, Luke	Sea
9.8	West, Delonte	Bos	9.7	Mason, Desmond	Mil	10.3	Hudson, Troy	Min
9.9	Mobley, Cuttino	Orl-Sac	9.7	Korver, Kyle	Phi	10.3	Payton, Gary	Bos
10.0	Piatkowski, Eric	Chi	10.0	Dunleavy, Mike	GS	10.4	Knight, Brevin	Cha
10.1	Newble, Ira	Cle	10.1	Williamson, Corliss	Phi-Sac	10.4	Billups, Chauncey	Det
10.1	Van Exel, Nick	Por	10.3	Turkoglu, Hedo	Orl	10.5	Terry, Jason	Dal
10.2	Dixon, Juan	Was	10.4	Hill, Grant	Orl	10.6	Johnson, Anthony	Ind
10.2	Smith, J. R.	NO	10.4	Outlaw, Travis	Por	10.7	Williams, Jason	Mem
10.3	Stackhouse, Jerry	Dal	10.5	Rose, Jalen	Tor	10.8	Dickau, Dan	Dal-NO
10.3	Wells, Bonzi	Mem	10.5	Harpring, Matt	Uta	10.9	Parker, Tony	SA
10.5	Jacobsen, Casey	Phx-NO	10.6	Jackson, Stephen	Ind	11.0	Jaric, Marko	LAC
10.6	Barry, Jon	Atl-Hou	10.8	Howard, Josh	Dal	11.0	Dooling, Keyon	Mia
10.6	Childress, Josh	Atl	10.9	Williams, Eric	Tor	11.0	Vaughn, Jacque	NJ
10.8	Miller, Mike	Mem	11.0	McKie, Aaron	Phi	11.1	Iverson, Allen	Phi
10.8	Jones, Dahntay	Mem	11.0	Pierce, Paul	Bos	11.4	Nelson, Jameer	Orl
10.9	Jones, Fred	Ind	11.1	Thomas, Tim	NY	11.5	Duhon, Chris	Chi
10.9	Anderson, Derek	Por	11.4	Griffin, Adrian	Chi	11.6	Snow, Eric	Cle

Shooting Guards

TO	Player	Team
11.0	Murray, Ronald	Sea
11.1	Daniels, Marquis	Dal
11.2	Hamilton, Richard	Det
11.5	Green, Willie	Phi
11.5	Maggette, Corey	LAC
11.5	Peeler, Anthony	Was
11.7	Johnson, DerMarr	Den
11.7	Pavlovic, Aleksandar	Cle
11.7	Welsch, Jiri	Bos-Cle
11.8	Bryant, Kobe	LAL
11.9	Bogans, Keith	Cha
12.0	Ginobili, Manu	SA
12.2	Gordon, Ben	Chi
12.4	Hardaway, Anfernee	NY
12.5	Davis, Ricky	Bos
12.5	Strickland, Erick	Mil
12.9	Wade, Dwyane	Mia
12.9	Salmons, John	Phi
12.9	Hunter, Lindsey	Det
12.9	Allen, Tony	Bos
13.6	Iguodala, Andre	Phi
13.8	Harrington, Junior	NO
14.2	Planinic, Zoran	NJ
15.4	Diaw, Boris	Atl
15.5	Christie, Doug	Sac-Orl

Small Forwards

TO	Player	Team
11.6	Augmon, Stacey	Orl
11.7	Ariza, Trevor	NY
11.8	Anthony, Carmelo	Den
12.0	Nachbar, Bostjan	Hou-NO
12.0	Pietrus, Mickael	GS
12.1	Murray, Lamond	Tor
12.2	Deng, Luol	Chi
12.3	Posey, James	Mem
12.5	Snyder, Kirk	Uta
12.7	Jackson, Jim	Hou-Phx
13.1	Harrington, Al	Atl
13.2	Rogers, Rodney	NO-Phi
13.6	Smith, Theron	Cha
13.7	Anderson, Shandon	NY-Mia
13.9	Jefferson, Richard	NJ
13.9	Smith, Josh	Atl
14.1	Nocioni, Andres	Chi
14.2	Patterson, Ruben	Por
14.6	Miles, Darius	Por
14.7	Jeffries, Jared	Was
15.0	Wallace, Gerald	Cha
16.2	Barnes, Matt	Sac
16.6	Lynch, George	NO

Point Guards

TO	Player	Team
11.7	Udrih, Beno	SA
11.8	Nash, Steve	Phx
12.1	Miller, Andre	Den
12.1	Brown, Tierre	LAL
12.1	Arroyo, Carlos	Uta-Det
12.1	Armstrong, Darrell	NO-Dal
12.3	McLeod, Keith	Uta
12.3	Palacio, Milt	Tor
12.4	Harris, Devin	Dal
12.4	Brunson, Rick	LAC
12.5	Blake, Steve	Was
12.9	Francis, Steve	Orl
13.2	Williams, Maurice	Mil
13.3	Anderson, Kenny	Atl-LAC
13.4	Banks, Marcus	Bos
13.6	Tinsley, Jamaal	Ind
13.8	Eisley, Howard	Uta
14.0	Sura, Bob	Hou
14.3	Gill, Eddie	Ind
14.6	Barbosa, Leandro	Phx
14.6	Watson, Earl	Mem
14.7	Carter, Anthony	Min
14.7	Lopez, Raul	Uta
14.9	Telfair, Sebastian	Por
14.9	Ivey, Royal	Atl
16.1	Livingston, Shaun	LAC

Power Forwards

TO	Player	Team
4.8	Bowen, Ryan	Hou
5.6	Marshall, Donyell	Tor
5.8	Cook, Brian	LAL
6.9	Bonner, Matt	Tor
7.4	Marion, Shawn	Phx
7.4	Jamison, Antawn	Was
7.6	LaFrentz, Raef	Bos
7.9	Garrity, Pat	Orl
8.0	Allen, Malik	Mia-Cha
8.1	Nowitzki, Dirk	Dal
8.2	Duncan, Tim	SA
8.3	Thomas, Kurt	NY
8.3	Griffin, Eddie	Min
8.4	Murphy, Troy	GS
8.6	Varejao, Anderson	Cle
8.8	Brown, P. J.	NO
8.9	Padgett, Scott	Hou
9.0	Wallace, Rasheed	Det
9.1	Smith, Joe	Mil
9.3	Radmanovic, Vladimir	Sea

Centers

TO	Player	Team
7.9	Miller, Brad	Sac
8.3	Wallace, Ben	Det
8.3	Doleac, Michael	Mia
9.0	Robinson, Clifford	GS-NJ
9.4	Stoudemire, Amare	Phx
10.1	Brezec, Primoz	Cha
10.4	Wright, Lorenzen	Mem
10.8	Drobnjak, Predrag	Atl
11.1	Camby, Marcus	Den
11.1	O'Neal, Shaquille	Mia
11.1	Andersen, Chris	NO
11.2	Collins, Jarron	Uta
11.4	Foster, Jeff	Ind
11.4	Okur, Mehmet	Uta
11.7	Davis, Dale	GS-Ind
11.8	Bosh, Chris	Tor
11.9	Jackson, Marc	Phi
12.3	Collins, Jason	NJ
12.3	Elson, Francisco	Den
12.4	Pachulia, Zaza	Mil

(continued next page)

Turnover Ratio by Position *(continued)*

Power Forwards				Centers		
TO	Player	Team		TO	Player	Team
9.3	Weatherspoon, Clarence	Hou		12.4	Nesterovic, Rasho	SA
9.3	Okafor, Emeka	Cha		12.5	Gadzuric, Dan	Mil
9.7	Webber, Chris	Sac-Phi		12.5	Skinner, Brian	Phi-Sac
9.7	Garnett, Kevin	Min		12.6	Bradley, Shawn	Dal
9.7	Songaila, Darius	Sac		12.6	Hunter, Steven	Phx
9.9	Brand, Elton	LAC		12.6	Traylor, Robert	Cle
9.9	Gooden, Drew	Cle		12.7	Foyle, Adonal	GS
10.3	Van Horn, Keith	Mil-Dal		12.7	Thomas, John	Min
10.3	Howard, Juwan	Hou		12.8	Mohammed, Nazr	NY-SA
10.4	Laettner, Christian	Mia		12.8	Ilgauskas, Zydrunas	Cle
10.6	O'Neal, Jermaine	Ind		12.9	Thomas, Etan	Was
10.7	Randolph, Zach	Por		12.9	Collier, Jason	Atl
10.9	Martin, Kenyon	Den		13.0	Pollard, Scot	Ind
11.0	McDyess, Antonio	Det		13.3	Mihm, Chris	LAL
11.2	McCarty, Walter	Bos-Phx		13.4	Grant, Brian	LAL
11.3	Thomas, Kenny	Phi-Sac		13.5	Ming, Yao	Hou
11.6	Abdur-Rahim, Shareef	Por		13.8	Cato, Kelvin	Orl
11.7	Cardinal, Brian	Mem		13.8	Haywood, Brendan	Was
11.8	Haslem, Udonis	Mia		14.1	Rebraca, Zeljko	LAC
11.9	Kirilenko, Andrei	Uta		14.2	Olowokandi, Michael	Min
12.1	Horry, Robert	SA		14.2	Ely, Melvin	Cha
12.1	Gasol, Pau	Mem		14.2	Ratliff, Theo	Por
12.2	Humphries, Kris	Uta		14.3	Nenê	Den
12.3	Walker, Antoine	Atl-Bos		14.8	Ostertag, Greg	Sac
12.3	Odom, Lamar	LAL		15.0	Mutombo, Dikembe	Hou
12.4	Collison, Nick	Sea		15.2	Woods, Loren	Tor
12.5	Najera, Eduardo	GS-Den		15.2	Massenburg, Tony	SA
12.5	Swift, Stromile	Mem		15.2	Wilcox, Chris	LAC
12.5	Boozer, Carlos	Uta		15.3	Curry, Eddy	Chi
12.6	Kukoc, Toni	Mil		15.4	Sweetney, Mike	NY
12.7	Jefferson, Al	Bos		15.6	Kaman, Chris	LAC
12.8	Scalabrine, Brian	NJ		15.6	Battie, Tony	Orl
12.8	Croshere, Austin	Ind		15.7	Smith, Jabari	NJ
12.9	Krstic, Nenad	NJ		15.7	Chandler, Tyson	Chi
13.1	Harrington, Othella	Chi		16.0	Magloire, Jamaal	NO
13.6	Fizer, Marcus	Mil		16.1	Ekezie, Obina	Atl
13.8	Moore, Mikki	LAC		16.2	Blount, Mark	Bos
14.4	Taylor, Maurice	Hou-NY		16.3	Mourning, Alonzo	NJ-Mia
14.5	Davis, Antonio	Chi		16.4	Dampier, Erick	Dal
14.6	West, David	NO		16.5	Dalembert, Samuel	Phi
14.8	Gugliotta, Tom	Bos-Atl		16.9	Przybilla, Joel	Por
14.9	Rose, Malik	SA-NY		17.1	Borchardt, Curtis	Uta
15.0	Howard, Dwight	Orl		18.3	Harrison, David	Ind
15.1	Henderson, Alan	Dal		18.4	James, Jerome	Sea
15.3	Williams, Jerome	NY		18.6	Ruffin, Michael	Was
16.5	Khryapa, Viktor	Por		19.0	Vroman, Jackson	Phx-NO
16.5	Walton, Luke	LAL		19.1	Madsen, Mark	Min
16.8	Brown, Kwame	Was		19.5	Araujo, Rafael	Tor
19.3	Evans, Reggie	Sea		20.6	Perkins, Kendrick	Bos
				20.8	Fortson, Danny	Sea

Shooting Guards			Small Forwards			Point Guards		
Usg	Player	Team	Usg	Player	Team	Usg	Player	Team
31.2	Bryant, Kobe	LAL	31.3	James, LeBron	Cle	34.7	Iverson, Allen	Phi
30.8	Wade, Dwyane	Mia	31.2	McGrady, Tracy	Hou	32.0	Davis, Baron	NO-GS
27.5	Gordon, Ben	Chi	30.4	Carter, Vince	Tor-NJ	29.3	Cassell, Sam	Min
27.2	Allen, Ray	Sea	26.1	Anthony, Carmelo	Den	29.0	Francis, Steve	Orl
26.8	Hughes, Larry	Was	25.8	Jefferson, Richard	NJ	28.7	Tinsley, Jamaal	Ind
26.4	Richardson, Jason	GS	25.6	Pierce, Paul	Bos	28.1	Marbury, Stephon	NY
26.2	Maggette, Corey	LAC	24.9	Jackson, Stephen	Ind	28.1	Nash, Steve	Phx
25.6	Redd, Michael	Mil	23.6	Hill, Grant	Orl	27.3	Arenas, Gilbert	Was
25.5	Hamilton, Richard	Det	23.5	Turkoglu, Hedo	Orl	27.3	Parker, Tony	SA
24.6	Ginobili, Manu	SA	23.2	Rose, Jalen	Tor	26.6	Knight, Brevin	Cha
23.2	Stackhouse, Jerry	Dal	23.2	Miles, Darius	Por	26.0	Bibby, Mike	Sac
23.1	Crawford, Jamal	NY	22.3	Nailon, Lee	NO	25.9	Stoudamire, Damon	Por
23.0	Dixon, Juan	Was	22.1	Harrington, Al	Atl	25.8	Kidd, Jason	NJ
22.4	Murray, Ronald	Sea	21.8	Mason, Desmond	Mil	25.4	Jackson, Bobby	Sac
22.4	Wells, Bonzi	Mem	21.5	Lewis, Rashard	Sea	24.8	Hinrich, Kirk	Chi
22.2	Smith, J. R.	NO	21.1	Sprewell, Latrell	Min	24.8	Dickau, Dan	Dal-NO
21.9	Davis, Ricky	Bos	21.1	Deng, Luol	Chi	24.7	Boykins, Earl	Den
21.7	Green, Willie	Phi	21.0	White, Rodney	Den-GS	24.2	Hudson, Troy	Min
21.3	Giricek, Gordan	Uta	20.7	Kapono, Jason	Cha	24.2	James, Mike	Mil-Hou
21.3	Van Exel, Nick	Por	20.5	Szczerbiak, Wally	Min	24.1	Claxton, Speedy	GS-NO
20.8	Rush, Kareem	LAL-Cha	20.5	Pietrus, Mickael	GS	24.0	Williams, Maurice	Mil
20.8	Bogans, Keith	Cha	20.2	Simmons, Bobby	LAC	24.0	Alston, Rafer	Tor
20.6	Planinic, Zoran	NJ	20.2	Stojakovic, Peja	Sac	23.8	Williams, Jason	Mem
20.6	Houston, Allan	NY	20.2	Williamson, Corliss	Phi-Sac	23.4	Watson, Earl	Mem
20.4	Mobley, Cuttino	Orl-Sac	19.5	Thomas, Tim	NY	23.3	Billups, Chauncey	Det
20.3	Harrington, Junior	NO	19.3	Snyder, Kirk	Uta	23.1	Arroyo, Carlos	Uta-Det
20.0	Daniels, Marquis	Dal	19.2	Butler, Caron	LAL	23.0	Delk, Tony	Atl
20.0	Miller, Reggie	Ind	18.9	Prince, Tayshaun	Det	22.9	Telfair, Sebastian	Por
19.8	Miller, Mike	Mem	18.8	Patterson, Ruben	Por	22.8	Lopez, Raul	Uta
19.7	Stevenson, DeShawn	Orl	18.8	Harpring, Matt	Uta	22.8	Miller, Andre	Den
19.5	Bell, Raja	Uta	18.7	Dunleavy, Mike	GS	22.7	Nelson, Jameer	Orl
19.5	Anderson, Derek	Por	18.0	Nocioni, Andres	Chi	22.2	Daniels, Antonio	Sea
19.3	Finley, Michael	Dal	17.7	Outlaw, Travis	Por	22.2	Hart, Jason	Cha
19.2	Smith, Steve	Cha-Mia	17.6	Richardson, Quentin	Phx	22.0	McLeod, Keith	Uta
19.0	Brown, Devin	SA	17.6	Murray, Lamond	Tor	21.7	Lue, Tyronn	Hou-Atl
18.7	Johnson, Joe	Phx	17.6	Rogers, Rodney	NO-Phi	21.6	Ridnour, Luke	Sea
18.5	Strickland, Erick	Mil	17.5	Wallace, Gerald	Cha	21.6	McInnis, Jeff	Cle
18.2	Wesley, David	Hou	17.3	Hayes, Jarvis	Was	21.5	Udrih, Beno	SA
18.1	Buford, Rodney	NJ	17.3	Nachbar, Bostjan	Hou-NO	21.4	House, Eddie	C-M-S
18.0	Peterson, Morris	Tor	17.1	Smith, Josh	Atl	21.2	Terry, Jason	Dal

(continued next page)

Usage Rate by Position *(continued)*

Shooting Guards

Usg	Player	Team
17.9	Jones, Fred	Ind
17.5	West, Delonte	Bos
17.5	Hunter, Lindsey	Det
17.3	Pavlovic, Aleksandar	Cle
17.0	Welsch, Jiri	Bos-Cle
16.9	Barry, Brent	SA
16.8	Allen, Tony	Bos
16.8	Diaw, Boris	Atl
16.7	Hardaway, Anfernee	NY
16.5	Peeler, Anthony	Was
16.3	Piatkowski, Eric	Chi
16.2	Johnson, DerMarr	Den
16.0	Barry, Jon	Atl-Hou
15.8	Jones, Dahntay	Mem
15.6	Childress, Josh	Atl
15.3	Christie, Doug	Sac-Orl
14.7	Evans, Maurice	Sac
14.0	Salmons, John	Phi
14.0	Jacobsen, Casey	Phx-NO
13.9	Harris, Lucious	Cle
13.5	Hoiberg, Fred	Min
13.5	Ross, Quinton	LAC
13.3	Hassell, Trenton	Min
13.3	Iguodala, Andre	Phi
12.5	Buckner, Greg	Den
12.5	Newble, Ira	Cle

Small Forwards

Usg	Player	Team
16.9	Wilkins, Damien	Sea
16.9	Butler, Rasual	Mia
16.8	Howard, Josh	Dal
16.7	Ariza, Trevor	NY
16.4	Jackson, Jim	Hou-Phx
16.4	Jones, Eddie	Mia
16.3	Person, Wesley	Mia-Den
15.6	Williams, Eric	Tor
15.4	Posey, James	Mem
14.7	Cheaney, Calbert	GS
14.7	Korver, Kyle	Phi
14.3	Griffin, Adrian	Chi
14.3	Augmon, Stacey	Orl
14.1	Battier, Shane	Mem
14.0	Russell, Bryon	Den
13.9	Smith, Theron	Cha
13.6	Lynch, George	NO
13.6	Jeffries, Jared	Was
13.6	Barnes, Matt	Sac
13.1	Jones, Jumaine	LAL
13.1	Jones, James	Ind
12.3	Bowen, Bruce	SA
11.4	Anderson, Shandon	NY-Mia
9.0	McKie, Aaron	Phi

Point Guards

Usg	Player	Team
21.0	Brown, Tierre	LAL
21.0	Carter, Anthony	Min
20.9	Eisley, Howard	Uta
20.9	Livingston, Shaun	LAC
20.9	Fisher, Derek	GS
20.6	Armstrong, Darrell	NO-Dal
20.5	Payton, Gary	Bos
20.4	Jaric, Marko	LAC
20.4	Harris, Devin	Dal
20.3	Sura, Bob	Hou
20.0	Johnson, Anthony	Ind
19.8	Palacio, Milt	Tor
19.4	Brunson, Rick	LAC
19.4	Atkins, Chucky	LAL
18.8	Barbosa, Leandro	Phx
18.7	Best, Travis	NJ
18.6	Dooling, Keyon	Mia
18.4	Banks, Marcus	Bos
18.1	Anderson, Kenny	Atl-LAC
17.9	Jones, Damon	Mia
17.4	Goldwire, Anthony	Det-Mil
17.3	Duhon, Chris	Chi
17.2	Ivey, Royal	Atl
17.2	Blake, Steve	Was
15.5	Gill, Eddie	Ind
15.5	Snow, Eric	Cle
15.1	Vaughn, Jacque	NJ

Power Forwards

Usg	Player	Team
31.4	O'Neal, Jermaine	Ind
28.9	Webber, Chris	Sac-Phi
28.0	Garnett, Kevin	Min
27.2	Duncan, Tim	SA
26.7	Nowitzki, Dirk	Dal
25.3	Walker, Antoine	Atl-Bos
24.6	Randolph, Zach	Por
23.8	Gasol, Pau	Mem
23.6	Brand, Elton	LAC
23.2	Boozer, Carlos	Uta
22.6	Jamison, Antawn	Was
21.6	Martin, Kenyon	Den
21.2	Kirilenko, Andrei	Uta
21.1	Swift, Stromile	Mem
20.7	Wallace, Rasheed	Det
20.6	Odom, Lamar	LAL
20.2	Abdur-Rahim, Shareef	Por
20.1	Gooden, Drew	Cle
20.1	Murphy, Troy	GS

Centers

Usg	Player	Team
27.4	O'Neal, Shaquille	Mia
24.7	Stoudemire, Amare	Phx
22.1	Ming, Yao	Hou
21.1	Ilgauskas, Zydrunas	Cle
20.8	Curry, Eddy	Chi
20.3	Okur, Mehmet	Uta
19.6	Jackson, Marc	Phi
19.4	Magloire, Jamaal	NO
19.1	Bosh, Chris	Tor
18.9	Collier, Jason	Atl
18.6	Drobnjak, Predrag	Atl
18.5	Wilcox, Chris	LAC
18.4	Miller, Brad	Sac
18.0	Mourning, Alonzo	NJ-Mia
17.6	Nenê	Den
17.5	Ely, Melvin	Cha
17.1	Vroman, Jackson	Phx-NO
16.8	Brezec, Primoz	Cha
16.7	Sweetney, Mike	NY

Power Forwards

Usg	Player	Team
19.4	Van Horn, Keith	Mil-Dal
19.4	Marion, Shawn	Phx
19.2	Thomas, Kenny	Phi-Sac
19.1	Okafor, Emeka	Cha
18.8	Cardinal, Brian	Mem
18.7	Fizer, Marcus	Mil
18.4	Humphries, Kris	Uta
18.2	McDyess, Antonio	Det
18.1	Harrington, Othella	Chi
18.0	Howard, Juwan	Hou
18.0	Taylor, Maurice	Hou-NY
17.9	Radmanovic, Vladimir	Sea
17.7	Cook, Brian	LAL
17.6	Jefferson, Al	Bos
17.4	Marshall, Donyell	Tor
17.2	West, David	NO
17.2	Griffin, Eddie	Min
16.9	Rose, Malik	SA-NY
16.9	Croshere, Austin	Ind
16.9	Kukoc, Toni	Mil
16.5	Krstic, Nenad	NJ
16.5	Scalabrine, Brian	NJ
16.4	Allen, Malik	Mia-Cha
16.3	Walton, Luke	LAL
15.9	Thomas, Kurt	NY
15.8	Brown, P. J.	NO
15.8	Songaila, Darius	Sac
15.6	LaFrentz, Raef	Bos
15.4	Horry, Robert	SA
15.2	Brown, Kwame	Was
14.7	Najera, Eduardo	GS-Den
14.5	Garrity, Pat	Orl
14.4	Smith, Joe	Mil
14.4	Moore, Mikki	LAC
14.2	Gugliotta, Tom	Bos-Atl
14.2	Howard, Dwight	Orl
14.2	Laettner, Christian	Mia
14.1	Bonner, Matt	Tor
13.8	Khryapa, Viktor	Por
13.7	Padgett, Scott	Hou
13.6	Collison, Nick	Sea
13.3	Varejao, Anderson	Cle
13.3	Haslem, Udonis	Mia
12.8	Davis, Antonio	Chi
12.6	McCarty, Walter	Bos-Phx
12.6	Williams, Jerome	NY
11.8	Weatherspoon, Clarence	Hou
10.2	Evans, Reggie	Sea
9.5	Bowen, Ryan	Hou
9.5	Henderson, Alan	Dal

Centers

Usg	Player	Team
16.7	Camby, Marcus	Den
16.5	Kaman, Chris	LAC
16.3	Robinson, Clifford	GS-NJ
16.1	Traylor, Robert	Cle
16.1	Mohammed, Nazr	NY-SA
16.1	Mihm, Chris	LAL
16.0	Wright, Lorenzen	Mem
16.0	Blount, Mark	Bos
15.5	Andersen, Chris	NO
14.8	Pachulia, Zaza	Mil
14.8	Fortson, Danny	Sea
14.6	Olowokandi, Michael	Min
14.6	Wallace, Ben	Det
14.2	Thomas, Etan	Was
14.0	Smith, Jabari	NJ
14.0	Doleac, Michael	Mia
14.0	Harrison, David	Ind
13.9	Massenburg, Tony	SA
13.8	Rebraca, Zeljko	LAC
13.5	Ekezie, Obinna	Atl
13.5	Dampier, Erick	Dal
13.3	Gadzuric, Dan	Mil
13.2	Dalembert, Samuel	Phi
13.2	Haywood, Brendan	Was
12.9	Borchardt, Curtis	Uta
12.9	James, Jerome	Sea
12.8	Perkins, Kendrick	Bos
12.4	Elson, Francisco	Den
12.4	Araujo, Rafael	Tor
12.3	Nesterovic, Rasho	SA
12.1	Woods, Loren	Tor
12.1	Chandler, Tyson	Chi
12.1	Skinner, Brian	Phi-Sac
12.0	Collins, Jarron	Uta
11.7	Foster, Jeff	Ind
11.6	Hunter, Steven	Phx
11.2	Przybilla, Joel	Por
10.9	Collins, Jason	NJ
10.6	Bradley, Shawn	Dal
10.6	Cato, Kelvin	Orl
10.5	Davis, Dale	GS-Ind
10.5	Pollard, Scot	Ind
10.4	Mutombo, Dikembe	Hou
10.3	Grant, Brian	LAL
10.2	Ostertag, Greg	Sac
10.1	Thomas, John	Min
9.6	Foyle, Adonal	GS
9.4	Battie, Tony	Orl
8.3	Ratliff, Theo	Por
7.4	Madsen, Mark	Min
6.4	Ruffin, Michael	Was

Appendix VI
Rebound Rate by Position

Shooting Guards				Small Forwards				Point Guards		
Reb	Player	Team		Reb	Player	Team		Reb	Player	Team
11.3	Childress, Josh	Atl		13.1	Jones, Jumaine	LAL		11.4	Kidd, Jason	NJ
9.8	Allen, Tony	Bos		12.7	Smith, Theron	Cha		10.3	Sura, Bob	Hou
9.7	Iguodala, Andre	Phi		12.5	Smith, Josh	Atl		9.2	Jackson, Bobby	Sac
9.6	Maggette, Corey	LAC		12.2	Griffin, Adrian	Chi		8.5	Francis, Steve	Orl
9.4	Evans, Maurice	Sac		11.5	Harpring, Matt	Uta		7.0	Miller, Andre	Den
9.1	Richardson, Jason	GS		11.4	Nocioni, Andres	Chi		6.7	Barbosa, Leandro	Phx
9.1	Hughes, Larry	Was		11.2	Lynch, George	NO		6.7	Nelson, Jameer	Orl
8.8	Ginobili, Manu	SA		11.1	Howard, Josh	Dal		6.7	Tinsley, Jamaal	Ind
8.7	Bryant, Kobe	LAL		10.8	Deng, Luol	Chi		6.6	Anderson, Kenny	Atl-LAC
8.7	Wells, Bonzi	Mem		10.7	Barnes, Matt	Sac		6.6	James, Mike	Mil-Hou
8.6	Daniels, Marquis	Dal		10.5	Jeffries, Jared	Was		6.5	Livingston, Shaun	LAC
8.4	Hoiberg, Fred	Min		10.2	Pierce, Paul	Bos		6.5	Armstrong, Darrell	NO-Dal
8.3	Brown, Devin	SA		10.2	Miles, Darius	Por		6.5	Arenas, Gilbert	Was
8.2	Buford, Rodney	NJ		10.1	Jefferson, Richard	NJ		6.5	Stoudamire, Damon	Por
8.1	Buckner, Greg	Den		10.1	Harrington, Al	Atl		6.4	Goldwire, Anthony	Det-Mil
8.0	Wade, Dwyane	Mia		10.1	Murray, Lamond	Tor		6.4	Davis, Baron	NO-GS
7.9	Diaw, Boris	Atl		10.1	Rogers, Rodney	NO-Phi		6.4	Parker, Tony	SA
7.7	Peterson, Morris	Tor		10.1	Wallace, Gerald	Cha		6.3	Williams, Maurice	Mil
7.7	Planinic, Zoran	NJ		10.0	Ariza, Trevor	NY		6.2	Blake, Steve	Was
7.6	Ross, Quinton	LAC		9.9	Russell, Bryon	Den		6.2	Banks, Marcus	Bos
7.4	Miller, Mike	Mem		9.8	Butler, Caron	LAL		6.1	Hinrich, Kirk	Chi
7.2	Johnson, DerMarr	Den		9.8	Williamson, Corliss	Phi-Sac		6.1	Cassell, Sam	Min
7.2	West, Delonte	Bos		9.8	Anderson, Shandon	NY-Mia		6.0	Hart, Jason	Cha
7.1	Welsch, Jiri	Bos-Cle		9.8	Dunleavy, Mike	GS		6.0	Bibby, Mike	Sac
7.1	Bogans, Keith	Cha		9.7	James, LeBron	Cle		6.0	Johnson, Anthony	Ind
7.0	Green, Willie	Phi		9.6	Anthony, Carmelo	Den		6.0	Gill, Eddie	Ind
7.0	Johnson, Joe	Phx		9.5	Simmons, Bobby	LAC		5.9	Claxton, Speedy	GS-NO
7.0	Bell, Raja	Uta		9.3	Battier, Shane	Mem		5.8	Alston, Rafer	Tor
6.9	Allen, Ray	Sea		9.0	Richardson, Quentin	Phx		5.8	Ivey, Royal	Atl
6.9	Peeler, Anthony	Was		8.9	Posey, James	Mem		5.8	Jaric, Marko	LAC
6.9	Harrington, Junior	NO		8.9	Nailon, Lee	NO		5.7	Brunson, Rick	LAC
6.8	Salmons, John	Phi		8.8	Lewis, Rashard	Sea		5.7	Fisher, Derek	GS
6.8	Christie, Doug	Sac-Orl		8.8	Augmon, Stacey	Orl		5.5	Duhon, Chris	Chi
6.8	Giricek, Gordan	Uta		8.6	McKie, Aaron	Phi		5.5	Carter, Anthony	Min
6.7	Newble, Ira	Cle		8.6	Jones, Eddie	Mia		5.4	Nash, Steve	Phx
6.5	Murray, Ronald	Sea		8.3	Snyder, Kirk	Uta		5.4	Delk, Tony	Atl
6.4	Redd, Michael	Mil		8.3	McGrady, Tracy	Hou		5.4	House, Eddie	C-M-S
6.4	Barry, Brent	SA		8.2	Prince, Tayshaun	Det		5.4	Jones, Damon	Mia
6.3	Dixon, Juan	Was		8.2	Hayes, Jarvis	Was		5.3	Iverson, Allen	Phi
6.3	Stackhouse, Jerry	Dal		8.2	Nachbar, Bostjan	Hou-NO		5.3	Billups, Chauncey	Det
6.2	Jones, Fred	Ind		8.2	Outlaw, Travis	Por		5.2	Brown, Tierre	LAL

Shooting Guards

Reb	Player	Team
6.2	Hassell, Trenton	Min
6.2	Finley, Michael	Dal
6.2	Barry, Jon	Atl-Hou
6.0	Hunter, Lindsey	Det
6.0	Gordon, Ben	Chi
6.0	Harris, Lucious	Cle
6.0	Jones, Dahntay	Mem
5.9	Strickland, Erick	Mil
5.7	Van Exel, Nick	Por
5.7	Hardaway, Anfernee	NY
5.6	Hamilton, Richard	Det
5.6	Jacobsen, Casey	Phx-NO
5.5	Anderson, Derek	Por
5.5	Stevenson, DeShawn	Orl
5.4	Mobley, Cuttino	Orl-Sac
5.3	Piatkowski, Eric	Chi
5.2	Smith, Steve	Cha-Mia
5.2	Davis, Ricky	Bos
5.1	Rush, Kareem	LAL-Cha
4.9	Smith, J. R.	NO
4.6	Pavlovic, Aleksandar	Cle
4.5	Wesley, David	Hou
4.4	Crawford, Jamal	NY
4.3	Miller, Reggie	Ind
2.5	Houston, Allan	NY

Small Forwards

Reb	Player	Team
8.1	Pietrus, Mickael	GS
8.1	Carter, Vince	Tor-NJ
8.1	Jackson, Stephen	Ind
8.0	Patterson, Ruben	Por
8.0	Korver, Kyle	Phi
7.6	Jones, James	Ind
7.6	Hill, Grant	Orl
7.6	Jackson, Jim	Hou-Phx
7.6	White, Rodney	Den-GS
7.5	Butler, Rasual	Mia
7.5	Cheaney, Calbert	GS
7.5	Turkoglu, Hedo	Orl
7.4	Wilkins, Damien	Sea
7.4	Williams, Eric	Tor
7.3	Person, Wesley	Mia-Den
7.0	Thomas, Tim	NY
7.0	Szczerbiak, Wally	Min
6.3	Bowen, Bruce	SA
6.3	Mason, Desmond	Mil
6.3	Stojakovic, Peja	Sac
6.2	Kapono, Jason	Cha
6.1	Sprewell, Latrell	Min
5.8	Rose, Jalen	Tor

Point Guards

Reb	Player	Team
5.2	Payton, Gary	Bos
5.2	Dickau, Dan	Dal-NO
5.1	Daniels, Antonio	Sea
5.1	Watson, Earl	Mem
5.1	McLeod, Keith	Uta
4.9	Palacio, Milt	Tor
4.9	Knight, Brevin	Cha
4.9	Harris, Devin	Dal
4.9	Ridnour, Luke	Sea
4.7	Snow, Eric	Cle
4.6	Dooling, Keyon	Mia
4.4	Marbury, Stephon	NY
4.4	Terry, Jason	Dal
4.3	Vaughn, Jacque	NJ
4.3	Lopez, Raul	Uta
4.2	Udrih, Beno	SA
4.2	Best, Travis	NJ
4.2	Telfair, Sebastian	Por
4.2	Lue, Tyronn	Hou-Atl
4.1	Atkins, Chucky	LAL
4.0	Arroyo, Carlos	Uta-Det
3.9	Eisley, Howard	Uta
3.9	Boykins, Earl	Den
3.6	Hudson, Troy	Min
3.5	Williams, Jason	Mem
3.3	McInnis, Jeff	Cle

Power Forwards

Reb	Player	Team
23.9	Evans, Reggie	Sea
20.9	Garnett, Kevin	Min
19.4	Duncan, Tim	SA
18.3	Murphy, Troy	GS
17.8	Griffin, Eddie	Min
17.2	Howard, Dwight	Orl
17.1	Okafor, Emeka	Cha
17.1	Thomas, Kurt	NY
16.9	Odom, Lamar	LAL
16.7	Gooden, Drew	Cle
16.7	Varejao, Anderson	Cle
16.6	Jefferson, Al	Bos
16.6	Collison, Nick	Sea
16.3	Haslem, Udonis	Mia
16.2	Henderson, Alan	Dal
16.0	Boozer, Carlos	Uta
15.7	Brown, P. J.	NO
15.5	Marion, Shawn	Phx
15.3	Brand, Elton	LAC
15.0	McDyess, Antonio	Det

Centers

Reb	Player	Team
22.1	Gadzuric, Dan	Mil
20.6	Mutombo, Dikembe	Hou
20.3	Fortson, Danny	Sea
20.1	Foster, Jeff	Ind
19.9	Chandler, Tyson	Chi
19.4	Camby, Marcus	Den
18.9	Woods, Loren	Tor
18.9	Wallace, Ben	Det
18.3	O'Neal, Shaquille	Mia
18.3	Przybilla, Joel	Por
18.0	Perkins, Kendrick	Bos
17.7	Mohammed, Nazr	NY-SA
17.5	Magloire, Jamaal	NO
17.4	Dampier, Erick	Dal
17.3	Ostertag, Greg	Sac
17.2	Andersen, Chris	NO
17.2	Skinner, Brian	Phi-Sac
17.0	Dalembert, Samuel	Phi
16.9	Mourning, Alonzo	NJ-Mia
16.6	Okur, Mehmet	Uta

(continued next page)

Rebound Rate by Position *(continued)*

Power Forwards			Centers		
Reb	Player	Team	Reb	Player	Team
14.8	O'Neal, Jermaine	Ind	16.2	Borchardt, Curtis	Uta
14.7	Randolph, Zach	Por	16.1	Mihm, Chris	LAL
14.7	Marshall, Donyell	Tor	16.0	Cato, Kelvin	Orl
14.5	Webber, Chris	Sac-Phi	15.8	Sweetney, Mike	NY
14.1	LaFrentz, Raef	Bos	15.8	Pachulia, Zaza	Mil
14.1	West, David	NO	15.7	Olowokandi, Michael	Min
14.0	Nowitzki, Dirk	Dal	15.6	Davis, Dale	GS-Ind
14.0	Humphries, Kris	Uta	15.5	Kaman, Chris	LAC
13.9	Smith, Joe	Mil	15.1	Wright, Lorenzen	Mem
13.8	Thomas, Kenny	Phi-Sac	15.0	Nesterovic, Rasho	SA
13.6	Weatherspoon, Clarence	Hou	14.9	Vroman, Jackson	Phx-NO
13.4	Wallace, Rasheed	Det	14.8	Ming, Yao	Hou
13.3	Williams, Jerome	NY	14.8	Ruffin, Michael	Was
13.3	Martin, Kenyon	Den	14.6	Nenê	Den
13.2	Rose, Malik	SA-NY	14.5	Foyle, Adonal	GS
13.2	Walker, Antoine	Atl-Bos	14.4	Ilgauskas, Zydrunas	Cle
13.0	Davis, Antonio	Chi	14.1	Araujo, Rafael	Tor
12.9	Gasol, Pau	Mem	14.1	Thomas, Etan	Was
12.8	Harrington, Othella	Chi	14.0	Traylor, Robert	Cle
12.8	Brown, Kwame	Was	14.0	Haywood, Brendan	Was
12.5	Howard, Juwan	Hou	13.9	Miller, Brad	Sac
12.5	Moore, Mikki	LAC	13.7	Ekezie, Obina	Atl
12.1	Abdur-Rahim, Shareef	Por	13.6	Grant, Brian	LAL
12.1	Najera, Eduardo	GS-Den	13.5	Wilcox, Chris	LAC
12.0	Swift, Stromile	Mem	13.5	Bradley, Shawn	Dal
12.0	Croshere, Austin	Ind	13.5	Bosh, Chris	Tor
11.9	Scalabrine, Brian	NJ	13.4	Battie, Tony	Orl
11.9	Cook, Brian	LAL	13.2	Doleac, Michael	Mia
11.7	Kirilenko, Andrei	Uta	13.2	Stoudemire, Amare	Phx
11.7	Krstic, Nenad	NJ	13.0	Brezec, Primoz	Cha
11.5	Songaila, Darius	Sac	13.0	Massenburg, Tony	SA
11.5	Padgett, Scott	Hou	12.9	Pollard, Scot	Ind
11.3	Fizer, Marcus	Mil	12.6	Elson, Francisco	Den
11.2	Horry, Robert	SA	12.4	Madsen, Mark	Min
11.2	Jamison, Antawn	Was	12.2	Hunter, Steven	Phx
11.1	Walton, Luke	LAL	11.8	Rebraca, Zeljko	LAC
11.1	Gugliotta, Tom	Bos-Atl	11.5	Jackson, Marc	Phi
11.0	Khryapa, Viktor	Por	11.1	Ely, Melvin	Cha
11.0	Taylor, Maurice	Hou-NY	11.0	James, Jerome	Sea
10.9	Van Horn, Keith	Mil-Dal	11.0	Ratliff, Theo	Por
10.7	Allen, Malik	Mia-Cha	11.0	Collins, Jason	NJ
10.6	Laettner, Christian	Mia	10.9	Collier, Jason	Atl
10.4	Bonner, Matt	Tor	10.9	Thomas, John	Min
9.5	Radmanovic, Vladimir	Sea	10.6	Collins, Jarron	Uta
8.9	Cardinal, Brian	Mem	10.4	Blount, Mark	Bos
8.6	McCarty, Walter	Bos-Phx	10.4	Curry, Eddy	Chi
8.5	Kukoc, Toni	Mil	9.8	Smith, Jabari	NJ
7.6	Garrity, Pat	Orl	9.6	Harrison, David	Ind
7.4	Bowen, Ryan	Hou	9.3	Drobnjak, Predrag	Atl
			7.1	Robinson, Clifford	GS-NJ

About the Author

As an NBA writer for ESPN.com's Insider and the *New York Sun,* John Hollinger employs an analytical approach to pro basketball to reveal how we can use the numbers behind the game to understand what's happening on and off the court. Hollinger authored the 2004–05 *Pro Basketball Forecast* and the 2002–03 and 2003–04 *Pro Basketball Prospectus,* and has appeared on numerous radio stations. Since 1996 he also has shared insights on the game from his site, Alleyoop.com. Hollinger lives with his wife Judy in Atlanta, where he hopes to witness a playoff game sometime before the end of the century.